Semantic Web Services

Rudi Studer · Stephan Grimm ·
Andreas Abecker (Eds.)

Semantic Web Services

Concepts, Technologies, and Applications

With 102 Figures

Editors

Rudi Studer
Universität Karlsruhe
Inst. Angewandte Informatik und
Formale Beschreibungsverfahren
76128 Karlsruhe
Germany
studer@aifb.uni-karlsruhe.de

Andreas Abecker
Forschungszentrum Informatik (FZI)
Haid-und-Neu-Str. 10-14
76131 Karlsruhe
Germany
abecker@fzi.de

Stephan Grimm
Forschungszentrum Informatik (FZI)
Haid-und-Neu-Str. 10-14
76131 Karlsruhe
Germany
grimm@fzi.de

ISBN 978-3-642-08987-9 e-ISBN 978-3-540-70894-0

ACM Classification: H.4, D.2, I.2, J.1

Springer is a part of Springer Science+Business Media
springer.com

Cover design: KünkelLopka, Heidelberg

Contents

Introduction

Rudi Studer, Stephan Grimm and Andreas Abecker

FZI Research Center for Information Technologies, University of Karlsruhe, Germany
{studer,grimm,abecker}@fzi.de

Motivation for the Topic of this Book

Web Service (WS) technology and the idea of a Service-Oriented Architecture (SOA) for web-based, modular implementation of complex, distributed software systems seem to become a tremendous success [17, 9]. In just a few years, the service-oriented approach not only gained considerable interest in Computer Science research, but was also taken up with a unique unanimity by all big international players in the IT industry, such as IBM, Microsoft, Hewlett Packard, and SAP.

Distributed software systems conquer more and more fields of daily life,[1] and the software itself becomes more and more powerful. On the other hand, such software systems also become increasingly complex, and the software bridges more and more between formerly separated, *heterogeneous* areas.[2] Hence, the matter of how to structure modular systems and how to achieve interoperability between heterogeneous parts becomes a key to success. The effective and efficient realisation of such modular, interoperable, large-scale software systems is facilitated by Web Services and SOA because they provide a *standardised* architecture for modular systems, for creating new functionality from existing building blocks, and for enabling communication between heterogeneous elements.

In contrast to the former, technologically well-founded, approaches that addressed (at least partially) similar goals, such as CORBA or Multi-Agent Systems, the current approach seems to have some striking advantages:

- It is simple, based on simple, open protocols.
- These protocols does not require or require only a limited amount of additional software.

[1] See, for instance, the ever growing importance of embedded software systems in the automotive area, or the thrilling new opportunities opened up by Ubiquitous Computing and RFID technology

[2] Consider, e.g., cross-platform implementations, cross-department workflows, cross-organisational application integration, or even cross-national eGovernment processes

- It is a conservative extension of accepted Internet standards which proved to work, also platform independently.
- It allows easy encapsulation of existing code and applications.

Maybe even more important for the success of SOA than purely technological issues is the fact that times have changed to some extent:

- Standardisation of some levels of software communication is commonly accepted through the success of the Internet.
- Supporting business processes and understanding business logic becomes more important than mastering low-level computer functionality.
- Interoperability in a networked world is going to be considered a bigger competitive advantage than binding customers through proprietary software and protocols.

All such considerations led to an atmosphere which facilitates the widespread industrial take-up of ideas like SOA and Web Services. Nevertheless, it would be an illusion to think that we have already found the golden bullet for solving all problems of interoperability in heterogeneous systems, as required for Enterprise Application Integration or Business-to-Business solutions. Essentially, Web Service standards provide a communication medium for distributed systems, but they cannot yet ensure that the communicating parties "speak the same language"–which is necessary for smooth, fully automated system interoperation.

For illustrating the deficiencies of existing SOA solutions, let us use the following analogy. If two parties want to communicate, they might want to send a letter by mail. Hence they need paper and pen for writing, they need stamps, postal offices, etc. which provide a transport infrastructure. They also need some addressing schemes and coding standards, such as ZIP codes. All this can be considered as given in the SOA approach with its lower levels for message transport, etc. For really communicating, our two parties also need to know the grammar and the lexicon of the English language. Even this might be considered as given in SOA technology, e.g. through the Web Service Description language.

However, such standards for structure, syntax, and vocabulary of Web Service functionality do not yet offer the semantics and the pragmatics of the used vocabulary. Software systems cannot know that the words bank and credit institute may be used in many cases as synonyms; that a flower shop in particular sells roses, tulips, and cloves because they are flowers; that flower shops *may* offer seedlings of salad or vegetables, but not always do – if a certain shop does not, a market-garden is the more appropriate address; that flower shops sometimes also sell greeting cards because they go often along with a bouquet of flowers; or that a market-garden may also produce the flowers for the flower shop, and thus might offer cheaper prices, but less floristic services. Coming back to our analogy, we can say that by writing a letter, *real* communication between the two parties is only achievable if they both share a common understanding of how language refers to concepts prevalent in the real world, and if both know which constraints and which background knowledge is typically associated with these concepts.

All such common-sense reasoning as well as general or business-specific background knowledge are typically not available in a computer system. Hence it is still often the case that also in today's most developed service-oriented software scenarios, there is much manual, human intervention required in order to interpret the semantics of informal descriptions of service functionality, or in order to harmonise incompatible data schemata or communication protocols.

Semantic Web Technology

This is the moment where Semantic Web (SW; see [1]) technology comes into play. Its aim is exactly to harmonise semantical discrepancies in software systems by providing machine-interpretable semantics, and to "understand" ambiguous descriptions – thus achieving a new quality of intelligent and automated information processing in the web [6, 28].

This is done on the basis of semantically rich meta data for webpages, for web-accessible data or multimedia resources, etc. This meta data is expressed in powerful, logic-based, representation languages (which are in part already standardised by the World Wide Web Consortium W3C) that refer to the controlled vocabulary of shared and quasi standardised domain knowledge models, so-called ontologies [10, 29]. The ultimate goal of such an approach–based upon formal, expressive languages and shared, controlled vocabularies–is to make semantics machine-processable to a much bigger extent than it is today.

Semantic Web Services

Semantic Web Services (SWS) employ such Semantic Web technology in the Web Services area: service functionality, Web Service inputs and outputs, their preconditions and effects, etc., all are expressed in knowledge representation languages, referring to shared ontological vocabularies [20, 30, 3, 16]. In this way, a higher degree of automation and more precise results can be achieved:

- When searching for a service providing a specific functionality, ontologies and associated thesauri can provide synonyms of words, the taxonomic structure of service capabilities, relationships between service capabilities, etc.
- When trying to harmonise different data formats for two services which have to exchange messages, ontologies can provide elaborated conceptual data models for message descriptions which facilitate automated translation.
- When mediating different communication protocols of services to work together, highly expressive Semantic Web languages can provide well-founded means to describe interaction patterns in communication protocols.
- When trying to compose complex business processes from given partial processes implemented by a number of Web Services, automated planning algorithms from Artificial Intelligence can be employed, provided the semantics of the input services is formally defined.

About this Book

This book aims to be a self-contained compendium of material for newcomers in the field, starting with the basics, and also coming to a level of technical depth which is sufficient to start one's own concrete technical work in the area. We aim at providing the necessary theoretical and practical knowledge for understanding the essential ideas and the current status of Semantic Web Services research. The reader should be familiar with Computer Science basics and fundamental terminology; prior knowledge in Semantic Web technology or Artificial Intelligence is useful, but not required. The book mainly addresses advanced Computer Science students or researchers, as well as practitioners with a good theoretical background, interested in the future of computing. It provides a snapshot of ongoing research in the SWS area and might be used as a supplementary textbook for Semantic Web, Artificial Intelligence, Web Services, or Middleware lectures. It shall also serve as an introductory and survey volume for IT professionals who prepare the step from Web Service programming to Semantic Web Services or who want to assess the potential of this new technology.

In order to achieve these goals, we followed some principles guiding the preparation of this book:

- The book aims at a *complete coverage of the topic and its background.* Therefore, we included in Parts I and II of the book introductory chapters on Web Services and SOA, as well as on the most important Semantic Web fundamentals, in order to provide all necessary prior knowledge for the SWS topic.
- The aim of a comprehensive discussion of Semantic Web Services also led to the goal of finding a *balance between theoretical foundations and practical or practice-oriented topics.* This led to the decision of discussing in Part III of the book the overall SWS life cycle and technology foundations in a principled survey manner, whereas Part IV contains concrete application examples and implementation issues.
- We tried to have all chapters reasonably *self-contained*, such that they could be taken (by a reader familiar with the required background) as stand-alone papers, also including their own list of references. Definitely, the several parts of the book can be read stand-alone.
- Although we had this aim of providing relatively self-contained chapters, we also tried to ensure a maximum level of *consistency between chapters*, meaning that we avoided redundancies and tried to ensure a consistent use of terminology and overall idea of SWS – which is mainly based on Chap. 6.
- The book is not committed to a specific knowledge representation or service description approach (such as OWL-S or WSMO), but tries to give a fair and comprehensive account of today's existing solutions.

It should be noted that the SWS topic is still pretty young; by far not all technical discussions are completed yet nor is any technical basis finally standardised. Consequently, this early stage of SWS research is also reflected in the content of the various chapters and their level of overall integration.

Structure of the Book

The structure of this book, divided into parts and chapters, is as follows.

Part I briefly presents the basics of current, non-semantic Web Services and SOA technology:

- Chapter 1 motivates the basic idea of Web Services and SOA.
- Chapter 2 introduces the Web Service technology stack and technical fundamentals of SOA, and thoroughly discusses the most important standards, protocols, and basic technologies underlying the approach (such as SOAP, WSDL, and UDDI).

Part II introduces major ideas and some basic technology of the Semantic Web:

- Chapter 3 introduces the basic ideas of knowledge representation and processing, in particular with respect to ontologies as a key feature of the Semantic Web.
- Chapter 4 gives a pragmatic introduction to ontology engineering.
- Chapter 5 explains the overall Semantic Web idea with ontology-based meta data, and meta data annotation of Web resources as its core concepts.

Part III presents the major principles and technological components of the SWS approach:

- Chapter 6 sketches the overall vision and idea of SWS and introduces the basic notions used in the subsequent chapters.
- Chapter 7 shows the principles and the major, widespread approaches for SWS description by ontology-based meta data.
- Chapter 8 illustrates the usage of such semantic description for precise discovery and selection of Web Services.
- Chapter 9 discusses several ways of how to compose complex Web Services from simpler ones.
- Chapter 10 identifies various kinds of heterogeneity prevalent in SWS scenarios and shows ways to overcome them with semantic mediation technologies.

Part IV illustrates implementation and application aspects of Semantic Web Services:

- Chapter 11 gives an impression of contemporary, implemented SWS technology by discussing basic tool categories for Semantic Web Services and showing many example implementations.
- Chapter 12 uses elements of the SWS technology as introduced in the former parts of the book for adding a new functionality to existing legacy systems in the area of Electronic Government. Concretely, an approach is shown which supports tracking of changes in an evolving world down to the affected service implementations.
- Chapter 13 describes some more application examples in the domain of Electronic Government. Here, the focus is on interoperability of different software systems.

- Finally, Chap. 14 shows two applications of SWS technology in the eHealth area. Again, interoperability is a major aim, and also the easier use of new mobile technologies is addressed.

Practical Relevance of the SWS Topic

At the time of editing this book, Semantic Web Services were a highly active research and development topic. Initiatives such as OWL-S, WSMO, IRS-III, or METEOR-S have gained a high level of visibility and produced valuable research results. Issues such as intelligent service discovery or fully automated service composition were subject to widespread ongoing research in many labs. Standardisation efforts such as OWL-S, WSMO, WSDL-S or SWSF (all submitted to W3C and partially discussed in OASIS and OMG) have found their way into relevant standardisation processes. Big IT companies like Hewlett Packard, SAP, and IBM have taken up the topic in their research agendas and belong to the major drivers in the field. Semantic Web Service approaches are investigated as a base technology for supporting other relevant Web Service issues such as policy modelling or quality of service [15, 32]. Other approaches to distributed computing, such as Peer-to-Peer or Grid computing, settle upon Web Services as an underlying technology and can thus also be "lifted" to Semantic Peer-to-Peer or Semantic Grid computing [14, 23].

However, regarding real-world practical applications, Semantic Web Services are still looking for their "killer applications". In this book, we included case studies from the healthcare and the government area. Both are perfect application domains for SWS[3]; however, in eBusiness, it is not yet clear which scenarios definitely need SWS functionality – although company-internal application integration (EAI) and cross-organisational business processes in Business-to-Business (B2B) relationships were a main driver for the development of SWS technology. There is a number of published applications, mostly in the prototype status:

- Logistics – In [25], logistics supply chains are generated on-the-fly, while changing availability of transportation alternatives may require real-time reconfiguration of service networks.

---

[3] eHealth and eGovernment seem to be fruitful for a number of reasons: both are characterised by a huge number of parties, the software of which should seamlessly interoperate (e.g. all doctor's surgeries with all hospitals and all health insurance companies); interoperability is a critical issue since both domains face a strong pressure for significant cost reductions; moreover, legal regulations enforce a better software process interoperability in some fields of eGovernment; traditionally, both domains are to some extent resistant against some market mechanisms which reduce interoperability problems in some eBusiness scenarios (e.g. when a big Original Equipment Manufacturer presses its suppliers or vendors to use a specific software that is compliant with its own systems, or when a certain de-facto standard arises for any economic reason which does not apply to public authorities); last but not the least, in spite of their huge heterogeneity, both areas have some tradition in standardisation and are thus prepared for the use of ontologies etc.

- Tourism – In [12, 7, 33], travel Web Services are composed for a virtual travel agency in an automated way, in order to loosen the currently centralised structures of the travel business.
- Collaborative work – Reference [11] presents a simple demonstrator for the ad hoc composition of virtual teams, exploiting semantic descriptions for matchmaking of appropriate collaborators and for facilitating interoperability of involved software applications.
- Finance – Reference [5] demonstrates automatic selection and composition of account monitoring and message delivery Web Services in an eBanking scenario where a user is automatically notified if he/she is financially overcommitted.
- Telecommunication – Reference [8] explains how British Telecom aims at an easier integration of new business partners into their BT Wholesale's B2B Gateway through SWS technology.
- Bioinformatics – Reference [24] employs SWS methods and models for a semantic workflow tool which configures and manages complex workflows for processing information about protein sequences in genes. Similar approaches are also under work in other bioinformatics labs. Reference [18] compares several architectural alternatives for semantics-based bioinformatics software, and draws some general conclusions about the potential for applying SWS technology in bioinformatics. We suspect that a similar application potential exists also in other eScience domains with complex information processing tasks.
- Business Intelligence (BI) – similarly to the above-mentioned bioinformatics example, [27] uses the IRS-III Semantic Web Service framework for integrating heterogeneous applications and for reusing code of existing BI software. Such a usage of SWS technology, namely easier web-based construction of software workbenches from existing code, seems to be possible and useful in many other domains too.
- Geographic Information Systems (GIS) – Recently, more and more spatial-related data becomes publicly available and opens up new opportunities for space-oriented information services which combine different information streams at runtime, within a given context. To this end, the integration of manifold heterogeneous data at different layers of abstraction is important. For instance, [31] describes an emergency management system based on a Semantic Web GIS, with SWS as the technological basis for achieving data interoperability and for interfacing different software services.

The examples above illustrate potential SWS use cases and show under which conditions the provided functionality can be used beneficially. It seems decent to think that large-scale SOA installations with thousands of available services and high expectations with respect to process automation cannot be realised at all *without* models of formalised semantics and powerful inferences acting upon them. However, the lack of widespread industrial take-up of SWS technology shows that practitioners are not yet fully convinced. Nevertheless, independent from possible future SWS usage scenarios in eBusiness or eScience, we suspect a remarkable success of SWSs in two further areas: Semantics-Based Software Engineering and Pervasive Computing.

Semantics-Based Software Engineering

Let us call our first vision *Semantics-Based Software Engineering* (SBSE, cp. [21, 22]). Imagine a software engineering scenario within a company that often builds large-scale software solutions from many components (modules, packages, classes, etc.) with different functionality, many of them being slight variations of others. In such a situation, the semantic description of components could facilitate the manual discovery of reusable components by employing well-known techniques from ontology-based information retrieval, thus increasing significantly the programmers' productivity. Components could be linked with supporting documentation, FAQs, example usages, etc. Usage constraints and interdependencies with other components would be modelled formally to enable automated consistency checks. Moreover, the semantic description of general, as well as domain-specific usage policies would facilitate automated policy enforcement for checking the consistency of system configurations, or for tracing the effects of policy changes. While the "general" SWS scenario strives for full automation, the SBSE vision keeps the human in the loop: software development tasks are supported, facilitated, and controlled by the system, thus leading to an approach which is much more realistic in the short term.

Pervasive Computing and Ubiquitous Intelligence

Another scenario, much more ambitious than the aforementioned, is the idea of *Ambient, Ubiquitous Intelligence, or Pervasive Computing*, where human–computer interaction is supported by networked physical devices which act as sensors or as actuators and are embedded in our clothes or in our everyday working and living environments, tools, or electrical appliances. For instance, the MyCampus project at Carnegie Mellon University [26] describes ubiquitous, context-aware, personalised information services in three sample domains: at a University campus, in a museum, and in a smart office environment. Reference [4] presents context-aware, policy-based, and personalised computing services in a smart meeting room. All such scenarios imply the seamless ad hoc interoperability of a variety of software components, which requires a high degree of automation in composition and mediation. Moreover, the implementation of intelligent system behaviour can benefit from the higher level of abstraction provided by declarative modelling of policies, context, behaviour, etc.

Acknowledgments

The work presented in this book is the result of cooperation in many inspired and committed teams, which could not have taken place without the generous financial support by many public and private institutions and organisations. At this place, we want to thank all these co-financing partners which made ambitious IT research possible and which helped to shape the future of our working environments.

Let us mention with special emphasis the European Commission (EC) which co-funded two ground-breaking research projects laying the foundations for a widespread adoption of SWS approaches in Europe:

1. SWWS (Semantic Web Enabled Web Services, funded by the EC under grant FP5-IST-2001-37134) was probably the first endeavour to join forces of several European research institutions and commercial players to come to a common, eBusiness-driven vision of Semantic Web Service technology as a basis for Enterprise Application Integration and Business-to-Business Interoperation.
2. DIP (Data, Information and Process Integration with Semantic Web Services, funded by the EC under grant FP6-IST-507483) continued the SWWS efforts and came up with the Web Service Modelling Ontology (WSMO), an ontology-based, comprehensive SWS framework.

Many of the chapters benefit from the work done in these two projects. Let us also mention especially the European OntoGov project (Ontology-enabled eGov Service Configuration, funded by the EC under grant FP6-IST-507237) which substantially supported the editors' work. OntoGov employed semantics-based service modelling methods for change management as part of service management in Electronic Government.

For the US authors, we have to mention DARPA which considerably supported the success of SWS research through its DAML programme.

Other projects which supported some of our chapter authors, include the following:

- ARTEMIS (A Semantic Web Service-Based P2P Infrastructure for the Interoperability of Medical Information Systems, funded by the EC under grant FP6-IST-002103)
- ASG (Adaptive Service Grid, funded by the EC under grant FP6-IST-004617)
- COCOON (Building Knowledge Driven and Dynamically Adaptive Networked Communities within Healthcare Systems, funded by the EC under grant FP6 IST-507126)
- CollaBaWü (Collaborative, Component-Based Business Application Software Development within the Financial Service Provider Domain in Baden-Wüerttemberg, funded by the German Federal State of Baden-Württemberg)
- DERI-Lion (funded by Science Foundation Ireland)
- Esperonto (Application Service Provision of Semantic Annotation, Aggregation, Indexing and Routing of Textual, Multimedia, and Multilingual Web Content, funded by the EC under grant FP5-IST-2001-34373)
- FIT (Fostering Self-Adaptive e-Government Service Improvement Using Semantic Technologies, funded by the EC under grant FP6-IST-027090)
- InfraWebs (Intelligent Framework for Generating Open (Adaptable) Development Platforms for Web-Service Enabled Applications Using Semantic Web Technologies, Distributed Decision Support Units and Multi-Agent Systems, funded by the EC under grant FP6-IST-511723)

- Knowledge Web (Network of Excellence, funded by the EC under grant FP6-507482)
- Monadic Media (funded under the ITEA scheme by the government of Italy)
- RW2 (Reasoning With Semantic Web Services, funded by the Austrian government in the FIT-IT programme)
- SEKT (Semantically Enabled Knowledge Technologies, funded by the EC under grant FP6-IST-506826)
- TSC (Triple-Space Computing, funded by the Austrian government in the FIT-IT programme).

References

1. T. Berners-Lee, J. Hendler, and O. Lassila. The Semantic Web. *Scientific American*, 284, May 2001.
2. C. Bussler, J. Davies, D. Fensel, and R. Studer, editors. *The Semantic Web: Research and Applications, First European Semantic Web Symposium, ESWS 2004*, volume 3053 of *LNCS*. Springer-Verlag, 2004.
3. L. Cabral, J. Domingue, E. Motta, T.R. Payne, and F. Hakimpour. Approaches to Semantic Web Services: an Overview and Comparisons. In *[2]*, pages 225–239, 2004.
4. H. Chen, T. Finin, A. Joshi, L. Kagal, F. Perich, and D. Chakraborty. Intelligent Agents Meet the Semantic Web in Smart Spaces. *IEEE Internet Computing*, 8, November/December 2004.
5. J.M. López Cobo, S. Losada, Ó. Corcho, V.R. Benjamins, M. Niño, and J. Contreras. SWS for Financial Overdrawn Alerting. In McIlraith et al. [19], pages 782–796.
6. J. Davies, R. Studer, and P. Warren, editors. *Semantic Web Technologies – Trends and Research in Ontology-based Systems*. John Wiley & Sons, 2006.
7. J. Domingue, S. Galizia, and L. Cabral. The Choreography Model for IRS-III. In *Hawaii International Conference on System Sciences (HICSS 2006)*, 2006.
8. A. Duke, M. Richardson, S. Watkins, and M. Roberts. Towards B2B Integration in Telecommunications with Semantic Web Services. In Gómez-Pérez and Euzenat [13], pages 710–724.
9. T. Erl, editor. *Service-Oriented Architecture: Concepts, Technology, and Design*. Prentice Hall PTR, 2005.
10. D. Fensel. *Ontologies: A Silver Bullet for Knowledge Management and Electronic Commerce*. Springer-Verlag, 2001.
11. M. Flügge and K.-U. Schmidt. Using Semantic Web Services for ad hoc Collaboration in Virtual Teams. In *Berliner XML Tage*, pages 187–198, 2004.
12. M. Flügge and D. Tourtchaninova. Ontology-derived Activity Components for Composing Travel Web Services. In *Berliner XML Tage*, pages 133–150, 2004.
13. A. Gómez-Pérez and J. Euzenat, editors. *The Semantic Web: Research and Applications, Second European Semantic Web Conference, ESWC 2005*, volume 3532 of *LNCS*. Springer-Verlag, 2005.
14. P. Haase, S. Agarwal, and Y. Sure. Service-Oriented Semantic Peer-to-Peer Systems. In C. Bussler et al., editor, *Workshop Web Information Systems Engineering*, volume 3307 of *LNCS*, pages 46–57. Springer-Verlag, 2004.
15. J. Miller, J. Arnold, J. Cardoso, A. Sheth, and K. Kochut. Quality of Service for Workflows and Web Service Processes. *Journal of Web Semantics*, July/August, 2004.

16. A.P. Sheth, J.A. Miller, Z. Wu, K. Verma, and K. Gomadam. The METEOR-S Approach for Configuring and Executing Dynamic Web Processes. Technical report, June 2005.
17. D. Krafzig, K. Banke, and D. Slama, editors. *Enterprise SOA: Service Oriented Architecture Best Practices*. Prentice Hall PTR, 2004.
18. P.W. Lord, S. Bechhofer, M. D. Wilkinson, G. Schiltz, D. Gessler, D. Hull, C.A. Goble, and L. Stein. Applying Semantic Web Services to Bioinformatics: Experiences Gained, Lessons Learnt. In McIlraith et al. [19], pages 350–364.
19. S. A. McIlraith, D. Plexousakis, and F. van Harmelen, editors. *The Semantic Web - ISWC 2004: Third International Semantic Web Conference*, volume 3298 of *LNCS*. Springer-Verlag, 2004.
20. S.A. McIlraith, T. Cao Son, and H. Zeng. Semantic Web Services. *IEEE Intelligent Systems*, 16(2):46–53, 2001.
21. D. Oberle. *Semantic Management of Middleware.* Springer-Verlag, February 2006.
22. D. Oberle, S. Lamparter, S. Grimm, D. Vrandecic, S. Staab, and A. Gangemi. Towards Ontologies for Formalizing Modularization and Communication in Large Software Systems. *Journal of Applied Ontology*, 2006.
23. A. Polleres, I. Toma, and D. Fensel. Modeling Services for the Semantic Grid. In C. Goble, C. Kesselman, and Y. Sure, editors, *Semantic Grid: The Convergence of Technologies*, number 05271 in Dagstuhl Seminar Proceedings. Internationales Begegnungs- und Forschungszentrum fuer Informatik (IBFI), Schloss Dagstuhl, Germany, 2005.
24. S. Potter and J.S. Aitken. A Semantic Service Environment: A Case Study in Bioinformatics. In Gómez-Pérez and Euzenat [13], pages 694–709.
25. C. Preist, J. Esplugas Cuadrado, S. Battle, S. Grimm, and S.K. Williams. Automated Business-to-Business Integration of a Logistics Supply Chain Using Semantic Web Services Technology. In Y. Gil, E. Motta, V.R. Benjamins, and M.A. Musen, editors, *International Semantic Web Conference*, volume 3729 of *LNCS*, pages 987–1001. Springer-Verlag, 2005.
26. N. Sadeh, F. Gandon, and O. Buyng Kwon. Ambient Intelligence: The MyCampus Experience. In T. Vasilakos and W. Pedrycz, editors, *Ambient Intelligence and Pervasive Computing*. ArTech House, 2006.
27. D. Sell, L. Cabral, E. Motta, J. Domingue, and F. Hakimpour. A Semantic Web based Architecture for Analytical Tools. In *7th International IEEE Conference on E Commerce Technology (IEEE CEC 2005)*, 2005.
28. S. Staab and H. Stuckenschmidt, editors. *Semantic Web and Peer-to-Peer.* Springer-Verlag, November 2005.
29. S. Staab and R. Studer. *Handbook on Ontologies.* International Handbooks on Information Systems. Springer-Verlag, 2004.
30. K. Sycara, M. Paolucci, A. Ankolekar, and N. Srinivasan. Automated Discovery, Interaction and Composition of Semantic Web Services. *Journal of Web Semantics*, 1(1):27–46, September 2003.
31. V. Tanasescu, A. Gugliotta, J. Domingue, L. Gutiérrez Villarías, R. Davies, M. Rowlatt, and M. Richardson. A Semantic Web GIS based Emergency Management System. In *Workshop on Semantic Web for eGovernment Held in conjunction with ESWC 2006*, 2006.
32. J.M. Bradshaw, R. Jeffers, M. Johnson, A. Tate, J. Dalton, A. Uszok, and S. Aitken. KAoS Policy Management for Semantic Web Services. *IEEE Intelligent Systems*, 19, July/August 2004.
33. M. Zaremba, M. Moran, and T. Haselwanter. Applying Semantic Web Services to Virtual Travel Agency Case Study, Poster Presentation. In Y. Sure and J. Domingue, editors, *ESWC*, volume 4011 of *LNCS*, pages 782–796. Springer-Verlag, 2004.

Part I

Web Services Technology

1

Towards Service-Oriented Architectures

Stefan Fischer and Christian Werner

Institute for Telematics, University of Lübeck
{fischer,werner}@itm.uni-luebeck.de

Summary. This chapter is meant as a motivation of why and how Web Services have evolved. Starting from the increasing need for integration of IT solutions, we argue that Web Services have something to offer, especially for the important fields of Business-to-Business (B2B) and Enterprise Application Integration (EAI). However, this is only the beginning of a new road, leading to the radically new software technology of Service-Oriented Architectures (SOA).

1.1 Integration: The New Challenge

This book is about Semantic Web Services, and before we can talk about the new and fascinating "semantics" part, it will be helpful to consider the foundations, namely to look at the Web Service technology itself. Web Services themselves are a relatively new phenomenon and have been under development for only slightly more than five years. During this time, they have gained a lot of attention and have also already gone through their hype phase. Meanwhile, they are accepted as one of the most important technologies when talking about *application integration*. In this context, they have been brought together with many other buzzwords that have been coming up in recent years.

1.1.1 The Need for Integration

First, Web Services have been considered as a new kind of *middleware*, taking their place between application and network. Here, they are in competition with other similar approaches such as CORBA, Java RMI, OSF DCE, etc. One can very well argue that Web Services have an excellent chance to become the dominating middleware, due to their extensive support of Internet technologies – one of the most important and relatively rarely mentioned being the use of URIs/URLs as addressing scheme – and the massive support by IT industry, resulting, for instance, in an excellent tool chain support throughout the software life cycle.

Second, Web Services have been chosen as one of the base technologies in *grid computing*, another major recent buzzword. A computing or storage grid works just like a water or electrical grid – just press a button and the grid delivers as much water or power as you need. In IT terms, you just plug in your terminal and get as much storage capacity or computing power as you need. The resources will be provided by the grid, which consists of some cooperation software and lots of more or less powerful computers. As a user, you do not see the computers, you just see the grid (or the plug) and its services. And grid services are provided as Web Services, so that is where they come into the game. Whenever your grid application makes use of one of the grid's services, it calls a Web Service.

Third and final example, Web Services are the basic component in most *SOA* approaches. SOA means *Service-Oriented Architecture*, and it is the latest hype in enterprise application software architecture design. SOA will most likely become one of the most important technologies within the next few years. Due to its importance, we will come back to it at the end of this chapter.

All these technologies are related to integration. Why is integration obviously so important that it triggers the development of so many new buzzwords, hypes, and serious new technologies?

This has to do with the famous real-world phenomenon of *globalisation*. Today, goods and services are traded and provided worldwide. Companies are no longer restricted to their home base, but often produce their products in different countries. There, they cooperate with other companies they might not have heard of a few weeks before. Or they might even buy other companies which fit into their portfolio or provide a certain service that the buying company urgently needs.

In order to survive in a globalised world, the IT infrastructure of such companies needs to be adjusted to the new requirements. This basically means two things. First, integration has to take place on an internal level. It will be necessary that applications in different domains can work together, based on the same stock of data. This is not as simple as it might sound: just consider as an example the merger of Daimler and Chrysler and the need to integrate these two completely different IT worlds. Second, integration has to take place on an external level. Applications of different business partners have to cooperate, e.g. in a selling–buying process. This is a major challenge based on heterogeneous technologies, but a major success factor for a globally operating company.

How can integration be achieved? Let us first have a look at an obvious candidate – the Internet and especially the World Wide Web.

1.1.2 B2C: Great New World?

One could well argue that the Web offers everything you need in order to conduct business. In fact, probably millions of web-based applications are in use today, so a lot of business is going on already. Looking closely at these applications, one will realise that they all have one very specific property: they are *interactive* applications, which means that there is a always a human on one end of the line (*human–machine interaction*). Take, e.g., all the well-known ticket-booking applications for flights, railway travel, etc. They are very well suited for interaction between a user and the application, providing a usually very nice and stylish user interface. Most of them are the so-called *business-to-consumer (B2C)* applications, i.e. individuals use them to conduct all kinds of businesses on the web.

However, when we talk about globalisation and integration, we usually mean something else: it is the companies that need to cooperate. Usually, we then talk about B2B applications. So, can we use the same technologies to organise this cooperation, i.e. to implement B2B applications?

The answer is clearly no, and the reason for this is the already mentioned interactivity of B2C applications. B2B applications are inherently *non-interactive*; instead, nearly every transaction is expected to be executed automatically. Only then, such applications really make sense, because of the gain of speed and efficiency. What therefore is needed is not human–machine, but *machine–machine interaction*. Why does it not make sense to use the existing interface of web applications for B2B applications?

B2C applications use a standardised page description language to create these interfaces the name of which is *HTML*. HTML does a great job: it is simple, flexible, robust and very expressive, especially with its partner *Cascading Style Sheets (CSS)*, but it does just that: it describes page layouts. This is great for user interfaces, but it is not good for automatised interactions between applications. Applications need to exchange clean data, just describing the objects of the application domain which need to be exchanged. Let us look at an example.

When you book a flight on the Lufthansa or British Airways website, you will typically be presented a list of available flights. For a human user, it is absolutely no problem to understand the content of the page, since it has been nicely rendered by the web browser. The web browser got, from the Lufthansa web server, something like

```
<tr><td>FRA</td><td>SFR</td><td>10:00</td><td>12:00</td></tr>
```

The browser need not understand the application-specific semantics of this code, it just needs to understand the meaning of *tags* such as `<tr>` – in this case indicating a new line in the table displaying all flights. For an automated application-specific processing (i.e. not simply layout oriented), however, this is not sufficient, since there is absolutely no information available on what the application domain of this code is. We as humans can tell that most likely this describes a flight from Frankfurt to San Francisco which leaves at 10 in the morning and arrives at noon, but the "dumb" computer can not.

To summarise, HTML is not enough for B2B applications. If we want to make use of applications which are available on the Internet today in B2B contexts, we need to provide different interfaces.

1.1.3 B2B and EAI: Today's Solutions

Before we see how the new integration solution works, let us have a look at some earlier approaches that have been developed in order to create interoperable applications in the business world. We already called the interaction between companies B2B. There was (and still is) a second big movement that covered the integration question on an inter-company level. It is called *Enterprise Application Integration (EAI)*, but in essence, from a technical point of view, it is the same as B2B.

The name of these solutions has already been mentioned: middleware. The purpose of middleware is usually twofold. First, it is meant to abstract away from the details and the complexity of network programming which includes bit-wise encoding of messages and their transfer to specific destinations. Second, it provides a uniform way of describing interfaces of objects relevant in a certain application. Based on these interfaces, services provided by one object can be used by other objects using the interface's description.

First solutions such as Sun's Remote Procedure Call (RPC) were simple and straight-forward, but today's dominant technologies such as the Common Object Request Broker Architecture (CORBA) developed by the OMG or Sun's Enterprise Java Beans provide a full-featured framework for creating powerful distributed applications. And even more important, this framework can be very well used to integrate existing applications by providing them with a new wrap-around interface which can then be used by other applications.

This sounds good, but it did not really work out. Mainly, three types of reasons can be given:

1. Complexity
   Most of today's middleware approaches employ complex communication protocols which make it rather difficult to implement them. Consequently, there are typically rather few implementations to choose from. In addition, they are often incompatible, as has been reported for a number of CORBA implementations. This is critical for any kind of integration approaches for applications created by different companies.
2. Lack of standardisation
   Whenever a new middleware was invented, most of the important underlying technologies were invented too. This includes, for instance, all the communication protocols between application components, all the pre-defined services (such as name service or trader service), and also basic features such as the scheme for addressing objects of the system. It is obviously hard to convince others who have been using a certain scheme all the time to use a new (just invented) one when nobody else is doing that.
3. Political reasons
   Information technology's short history has already shown that technologies invented by one company are rarely adopted by their competitors. A typical example is the programming language Java which has been developed by Sun while, in turn, Microsoft released a competing language realising similar concepts. Another example is middleware: Microsofts DCOM has never been accepted or supported by Sun, and Suns Java 2 Enterprise Edition (J2EE, which includes Enterprise Java Beans) has never been supported by Microsoft.

   A typical example is the programming language Java which has been developed by Sun and never been liked by Microsoft. So they invented their own Java but gave it a different name. The same is true for middleware: Microsoft's

DCOM has never been accepted or supported by Sun, and Sun's Java 2 Enterprise Edition (J2EE, which includes Enterprise Java Beans) has never been supported by Microsoft.

As a result, instead of integration, we got many IT islands in the 1990s, and there was no simple way to let them cooperate. Shortly before the year 2000, however, the pressure by IT industry's customers became big enough to make it think about a solution to these problems. In the next section, we will see how Web Services addresses them. The next chapter will then give a more technical, in-depth introduction into the most important components of Web Services.

1.2 Web Services as a New Solution

As one may have guessed by now, the Web Service technology tackles the major problems that come with other technologies, as mentioned above. And this is certainly by design and not by accident. Here is what one of the standard documents says what a Web Service is: "A Web Service is a software system designed to support interoperable machine-to-machine interaction over a network. It has an interface described in a machine-processable format (specifically WSDL). Other systems interact with the Web Service in a manner prescribed by its description using SOAP messages, typically conveyed using HTTP with an XML serialisation in conjunction with other Web-related standards" [W3C Web Services Architecture].[1]

From this definition, two of the three main questions are already answered: Web Services use standardised and open web technology wherever possible, from URIs as the basic addressing scheme over XML as the basic description language to the use of Internet protocols for message transport. The next few paragraphs describe why these are advantages.

1.2.1 URI as Addressing Scheme

The concept of Universal Resource Identifiers and their more practicable subset, the Uniform Resource Locator, was developed for the World Wide Web. It is used to uniquely identify any single resource on the web, especially documents and applications. The concept is very well introduced and well under stood. In addition, there is massive infrastructure available that supports all kinds of operations on URIs, namely their mapping on more concrete addresses as used by computers to find the resource identified by a URI. The most important part of this infrastructure is the *Domain Name System (DNS)* which maps host names to IP addresses. Another important role is played by the web server which maps the rest of the URL to a local path in the file system.

Why is this so important? Obviously, this infrastructure can simply be used for Web Services. When a service user calls a specific Web Service, the URI of this service is known. Then, the features of DNS and the existing web servers can easily be used to find this service. There is absolutely no need to develop something like a new name service: everything is already there.

[1] `http://www.w3.org/TR/ws-arch/`

1.2.2 XML as the New Lingua Franca

XML as such is just another data description language, and this is exactly what is needed: a simple and standardised language that can be used to describe data structures. It is not that such languages have not existed before: just think of ASN.1, the data description language coming from the OSI world. As with many things, XML came just at the right point in time, and it provided a number of features that quickly made it popular with a huge community:

- XML is simple. It is very easy to define a data structure in XML, due to its intuitive hierarchical structure.
- XML is ASCII. Every XML data structure is human-readable. This might result in performance problems, but it brings a lot of advantages, for instance when debugging a service.
- XML is self-describing. An XML data structure contains both a description of its structure and the content itself.
- It has been standardised by the World Wide Web Consortium (W3C), which is the most important standardisation body in the context of World Wide Web protocols and languages.

In Web Services, everything is based on XML. As can be seen from the above definition, it is not only the definition of data structures, but all message exchanges and also the service descriptions are based on this new universal data description language.

1.2.3 Exchanging XML Messages

In order for two distributed application components to communicate with each other, they need to exchange messages. As we already know, the messages are described in XML, but how does the exchange protocol look like? How are messages encoded? How are they finally transported over the network?

Many people say that these are the core questions when designing a middleware, so one can argue well that the solutions in this field belong to the core of Web Service technology. The protocol that is used to encode XML messages is called *Simple Object Access Protocol (SOAP)*, or, more correctly as of today, the *XML Protocol (XMLP)*. And it is really simple: it just defines a general pattern of how XML Web Service messages have to look like, it defines a few so-called *message exchange pattern* that can be used by Web Service partners, and it defines how XML type information can be encoded in such messages. It also gives some hints how such messages can be transported over the Internet: just use one of the existing application-level protocols such as the web protocol HTTP or the email protocol SMTP.

Why is it good to use such existing protocols? Obviously again, these are well-established technologies, and there is a mass of products available which can simply be used. Most importantly, one can use web or email servers in order to receive Web Service calls and forward them to their appropriate end points. Such servers are available everywhere, and every system administrator knows how to configure and administrate them. So, we have the same advantage as with DNS: the infrastructure is there and just waits to be used. And protocols such as HTTP and SMTP have been verified over and over again: they simply work, and interoperability questions simply do not arise anymore today.

1.2.4 Creating Services Based on XML Messages

How, after all, does a service user know how a message has to look like in order to use a provided service? Here, we have to mention the second most important Web Service technology, the *Web Service Description Language (WSDL)*. WSDL is defined in XML, and it is used to define how Web Service interfaces look like. This basically means that it describes how incoming and outgoing messages look like and where such services are available (in terms of a URI). Once such a definition exists and gets published, a service user can read it and then knows how to call a Web Service. Since everything is again in XML, the messages to be transferred can be immediately deduced from the service description. And on the service side, it is easy to decode incoming service messages: just use one of the many existing XML parsers and read the message into your service program. All in all, creating a Web Service usually only means copying an already existing object into a certain location – and that is it.

1.2.5 And Politics?

What is not obvious from the above definition is the political question. Why are Web Services much better accepted and supported within the IT industry than any other middleware technology?

One may well argue that Web Services have been invented by Microsoft. The above-mentioned SOAP has been brought up by Microsoft. And right from the beginning, Microsoft was interested in making this an open standard, which had so far not exactly been one of Microsoft's core strategies. As a result, other companies such as IBM and Hewlett-Packard and later on Sun Microsystems jumped onto the bandwaggon. With this support, Web Services on the one hand get a lot of publicity and on the other hundreds of developers started to create languages, protocols and, most importantly, tools. Today, from all middleware and integration technologies, Web Services get the best tool support along the life cycle. It has been the core or it has been fully integrated into today's most relevant enterprise application architectures, namely Microsoft's .Net and Sun's J2EE. Meanwhile, we see applications being created that consist of both .Net and J2EE (and other) components, so it obviously works. Still, a few things are missing.

1.2.6 What is Missing?

Since their creation in the late 1990s, Web Services have gained a lot of momentum. Many people are sure that this is the new integration technology. However, there are still a few things to do in order to make it real and have the Web Service technology universally accepted. From the authors' point of view, there are at least the following three points to mention:

1. Well-established directory services
   Directory services are needed in order to find available Web Services. Web Service providers publish their services in such a directory, and Web Service users look for services that best fit their needs. In the best case, applications know what they need and then automatically check directories for corresponding services (we will later in this book see how semantics help in this respect). Surely, this need has been openly visible from early on, and with the specification of *Universal Description, Discovery, and Integration (UDDI)*, there is a solution available. However, UDDI in its use as a global Web Service directory today does not have the best image. This is due to the fact that basically everybody is allowed to publish new service entries. Sounding good at first hand, this quickly results in lots of dummy entries and dangling pointers to no longer existing services. As a result, the quality of the global UDDI directory is not good, so that UDDI is not often used for serious applications (though on an enterprise-level, the UDDI technology is widely adopted, since here, the entries can be controlled). In order to create a really useful global service directory, some kind of quality management needs to be put into effect.
2. Security
   In Web Service technology's early days, security never has been a big issue, due to the need to first make Web Services really work. The typical way of talking about it was "Great, Web Services work over firewalls". This is true, because Web Services are typically transported using the HTTP protocol, and the HTTP port is usually open on a firewall, but certainly is a bad argument – which administrator likes the thought that all kinds of active codes can be transported into his systems? Today, many solutions around Web Service security exist, including something like SOAP proxies in order to allow security checks on incoming Web Service calls, XML encryption which allows confidential calls of Web Services, and XML signature for Web Service message authentication. Actually, there are so many security standards available right now that it is already too much. For making Web Services really happen, a small set of security standards has to be identified that needs to be supported by all serious Web Service users and providers. A first step has been done by the so-called WS-Security standard that provides such a basic set of services. It is now necessary to promote this approach more actively.
3. Interoperability
   It certainly sounds strange that interoperability is one of the major problems with Web Services, when we just said that Web Services are all about integration. It is true, there is a number of open standards which are easy to implement and ubiquitously available. The bad thing is there are already too many of these standards. We mentioned this above for the field of security, but this is also already true for the basic standards such as SOAP/XMLP, WSDL, or UDDI; in other words those technologies that need to be present in order to make Web Services run at all. Basically, there are two problems. First, some companies might tweak the standard just a little bit in order to make them work better with their own tools. Second, there are different versions of these basic standards. Unfor-

tunately, they are usually not interoperable. The newest WSDL standard, for instance, uses keywords which have not been available in earlier standards, and discards others. As a result, a WSDL 1.1 interpreter will not be able to decode a WSDL 2.0 description, making it impossible for the user to call this specific service.

There is already a solution for this problem, provided by the organisation *WS-Interoperability (WS-I)*. WS-I defines the so-called *profiles* which contain a set of standards. Whenever a company declares that its services are compatible with a certain WS-I profile, it guarantees that all the relevant standards are implemented in a standard-conforming way. As of today, WS-I has published the Basic Interoperability Profile. Companies which are really interested in global and automatised interaction with other companies will have to make their services compatible to these profiles.

And after all, this book is about Semantic Web Services. In the last section of this chapter, we will look, as promised, at the new idea of service-oriented architectures and explain how a formally described semantics may play a major role in making them real.

1.3 The Future: SOA

Web Services are a basic building block in the creation of SOA. These SOAs are expected to be the future architecture of enterprise applications. As can be told from the name, the idea is that future applications will be built upon services. This is, however, not the whole picture; service-oriented computing has already been the concept of CORBA and similar approaches. SOA go a step further and propose a completely new way of creating applications. In the SOA vision, they will no longer be programmed, but instead *composed* of loosely coupled components which will be imported from servers from all over the world. Required services will be dynamically – potentially during run time – searched and called when needed. Such an architecture is well suited to map the dynamic environment that enterprises are confronted with in today's globalised world. If, for instance, two companies form a new strategic alliance or just create a new customer–supplier relationship in the real world, the vision says that in the IT world this will simply mean abandoning a few services and selecting a few new ones.

The question certainly is, how realistic this vision is today. Above, we have already discussed a few obstacles such as unused security features, lack of interoperability, or missing high-quality directory services. However, even when all these are available, would you, as the Chief Information Officer, lay the fate of your company in the hands of some obscure services that you probably do not really know anything about?

The probably much more realistic scenario is an implementation of SOAs within the boundaries of an enterprise, i.e. as a new approach towards EAI. Here, the company has full control over all services and service offers and can thus make sure that all applications that the company relies on will really be operational.

Since the rest of this book is on semantics and Web Services, we consider it useful to provide a first hint at how these two big trends in Web Services – SOA and semantics – fit together.

We have mentioned several times now that Web Services is on integration, automatisation, and machine–machine interaction. In order to fully automate the communication between application components, the search for new Web Services also needs to go into this direction. In a perfect SOA world, an application component in need for a specific service describes this need in its problem domain and sends it to a directory service. This service will "understand" the need of the component and look for matching services. From the list of found matches, the component selects one service and automatically binds it to the running application.

Today, this is not possible, because a formal description of the functionality of a service is not available. This book shows what needs to be done in order to make the vision real.

2

Architecture and Standardisation of Web Services

Christian Werner and Stefan Fischer

Institute for Telematics, University of Lübeck
{werner, fischer}@itm.uni-luebeck.de

Summary. Since Web Services are complex artefacts that rely on sophisticated protocols and data formats, it is important to have effective strategies for dealing with this complexity. As a basic concept, the Web Service technologies are structured in a stack model. It is crucial for every Web Service developer to have this model in mind and to have a clear understanding how the single items work together. In this chapter, we will first give an overview of the Web Service technology stack. Then, we will step through this model and discuss the different core technologies in detail. This includes different variants of Web Service transport bindings, SOAP, WSDL and UDDI.

2.1 Web Services Technology Stack

The *W3C Web Service Architecture Working Group* has developed a model that describes how Web Services are generally structured, called the Web Service Technology Stack. However, in order not to limit the scope of Web Service technology, this model has been purposely designed on a very abstract level, i.e. without specifying technologies used for the implementation. Other W3C working groups are providing such technology specific bindings.

The current version of the *Web Service Architecture Document* has been released on 11 February 2004 and is publicly available at `http://www.w3.org/TR/2004/NOTE-ws-arch-20040211/`. Figure 2.1 depicts the basic structure of the Web Service technology stack.

The "Communications" block, which some authors also call "Wire Stack", is the basis for all other layers. It comprises generic transport mechanisms that can be used to send messages over the Internet. In terms of classical network architecture these technologies are located on the "Application Layer" (or "Layer 7") of the ISO/OSI Protocol Reference Model. Typical examples would be HTTP, SMTP, FTP, etc. All these protocols can be used with Web Services and each protocol does provide specific benefits and drawbacks. The Web Service Technology Stack does not determine which transport mechanism should be used, since the optimal choice may heavily depend on the specific use case. We will have a detailed look on this topic in the following section.

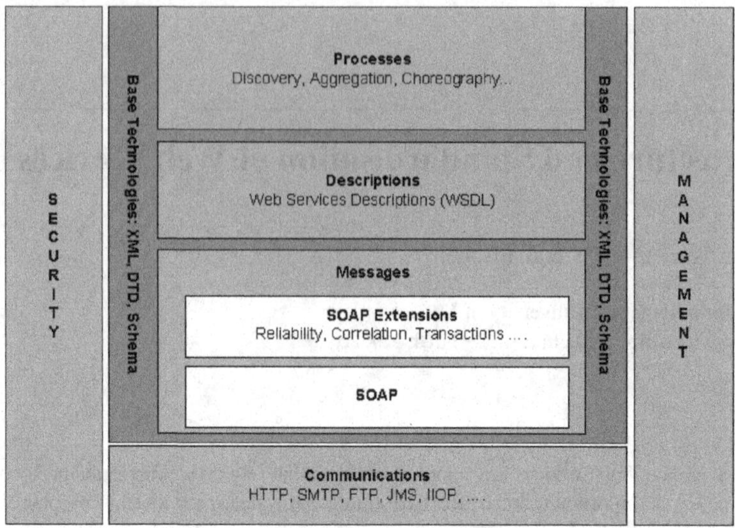

Fig. 2.1. The web service technology stack (*taken from the W3C web service architecture document*)

The core technology of Web Services is located on the next higher layer. The "Messages" block provides basic functionalities for encapsulating network messages in a neutral way that is independent from a certain programming language or operating systems. The goal here is to find message representation that can be syntactically understood by humans as well as computers. Unfortunately, this does not mean that the meaning of a message can be understood by everybody. Technologies for semantic interoperability will be focussed in the following parts of this book. The key technology for achieving syntactical interoperability in the Web Service world is XML. In Fig. 2.1 this is indicated by the dark box around *Messages*, *Descriptions* and *Processes*.

The *Simple Object Access Protocol (SOAP)* is an XML language itself. It provides a composable framework for packaging and exchanging XML messages. In particular, it provides a platform- and application- independent message format. Furthermore, a number of extensions have been developed for SOAP. With these it is possible to provide additional protocol features, such as reliable message transport or support for transactions.

The layer above is named *Descriptions*. Here we find technologies that are used for describing Web Services in a formal way. Such a description is crucial because a Web Service consumer needs exact access parameters before the service can be used. This includes data about the service location as well as a specification of supported data types and operations. The most widely used solution here is the *Web Service Description Language (WSDL)*. It is important to note that WSDL does cover only the technical but not the semantical description of a service. So with WSDL it is possible to express that "This service has an operation `echo` which takes a string as parameter and returns another string." A human can guess from the operation's name that the two strings will be identical, but machines do need an additional semantic service description in order to discover services that provide suitable operations for a given problem.

The very top layer comprises *Processes*. One of the most important processes in the field of Web Services here is the discovery of a service. Web Services can be distributed all over the world and they might be used from all over the world too. How can we locate a Web Service that fits the user's needs? The most popular solution here is *Universal Description, Discovery and Integration (UDDI)*. This worldwide service registry can be visualised as a huge phone book. A service provider can publish a Web Service in this registry and if somebody is looking for a specific Web Service he or she can query the UDDI registry by specifying certain search criteria. Although there are mechanisms in UDDI for realising things like data replication, it is basically a centralised approach and therefore UDDI contradicts the concept of service distribution in some way. Anyhow, distributed service registries are harder to maintain and no solution for practical usage have been developed yet. A more active approach for building up service registries is called *Web Service Inspection (WS-Inspection)*. Here the service directory looks actively for new services and registers them.

Besides service discovery, there are more *Processes* that are important in a Web Service world. For instance, it is possible to combine a number of services in order to complete a certain task. Here we are talking about Web Service aggregation or Web Service composition.

In addition to the concepts and tasks that are located on the different layers in the Web Service Technology Stack, there are some issues that are relevant to all layers. The most important one here certainly is *Security*, shown as a column on the very right side of Fig. 2.1. In April 2002, Microsoft and IBM introduced the *Web Service Security (WS-Security)* specification. It provides a comprehensive security framework that is based on two other W3C standards as core components, namely *XML Encryption* and *XML Signature*.

A second area that is relevant to all layers of the Web Service technology stack is *Management*, shown in the very right side of Fig. 2.1. Since the Web Service technology primarily targets the domain of business applications, where the availability and reliability of a service might be crucial, it is very important that there are capable measures for monitoring and controlling the state of a Web Service. If we think of "pay per use" scenarios, it is also desirable that the service provides a certain *Quality of Service (QoS)*, e.g. by sending back query results within a given time interval. IBM addresses this issue in a framework called *Web Service Level Agreement (WSLA)*, which has been introduced in 2003. We will not discuss Web Service management here in detail, because it is still a very active area in research and therefore out of scope for this chapter.

In the remainder of this chapter, we will discuss the different layers of the Web Service Technology Stack, from bottom to top, more in detail.

2.2 Web Services Transport

A very important feature of the Web Service technology is that virtually any transport mechanism can be used for transporting the network messages (usually we are talking about SOAP messages here). In the Web Service world, such a transport mechanism is called a *binding*. In contrast to other middleware approaches like CORBA or Java RMI which have fixed transport mechanisms in form of proprietary protocols, the idea here is to rely on existing standards. Another benefit is that the application domain of Web Services is not limited by the binding. We have the freedom to choose a binding that meets the demands of a certain application domain best.

Anyhow, the used binding affects the way in which messaging takes place in an important aspect. The SOAP specification defines the concept of message exchange patterns (MEPs). A MEP is a template that defines how messages are exchanged between SOAP nodes. We will see an example on this in the later part of this section.

2.2.1 HTTP

The most popular binding by far is SOAP-over-HTTP because HTTP is ubiquitously available and its build-in addressing and error-handling functionalities are fully covering SOAP's needs. SOAP-over-HTTP is the only binding that is available as a W3C recommendation. The recommended version to use with SOAP is HTTP/1.1. Even though the HTTP binding is not mandatory, virtually all modern SOAP implementations do provide a HTTP binding.

The HTTP binding provides two MEPS: the Request–Response MEP and the Response MEP. Both can be easily illustrated with an example depicting two SOAP nodes exchanging messages.

The Request–Response MEP is based on the HTTP-POST command. Node A uses a HTTP client and sends out a POST request that carries a SOAP document to node B, which is running a HTTP server. Node B processes this request and sends out a HTTP response, carrying the answer to that request in the form of another SOAP document. In contrast to that, the Response MEP is based on HTTP-GET. Node A sends out a GET request, where the request information is directly encoded in the HTTP request URL. Node B sends back a SOAP document in the HTTP response. So, here SOAP is only used in the response, but not in the request.

With the Request–Response MEP HTTP is perfectly suitable for realising *Remote Procedure Calls (RPC)* over SOAP. Unfortunately, the use of HTTP has also a number of disadvantages. HTTP is a client–server protocol and has not been designed for transferring messages between SOAP nodes in a peer-to-peer manner. Asynchronous messaging, where SOAP nodes can communicate independently from a fixed request–response cycle, is not supported. However, more and more Web Service applications, especially in the field of grid computing, do require peer-to-peer messaging.

2.2.2 Email

In July 2002, the W3C released a note about SOAP-over-email. In contrast to HTTP, which is a synchronous request/response protocol, SOAP-over-email supports asynchronous messaging. As shown in Listing 2.1 the XML Web Service message is placed inside the body of an email message, which is sent to its receiver using common mail transport protocols. Of course, unlike a normal email, this message will not be interpreted by a human reader but by the receiving SOAP engine.

By specifying more than one receiver in the mail header (e.g. by using the `To:` field) it is possible with this binding to realise a point-to-multipoint MEP, which is clearly an advantage over HTTP.

It is important to note that the SOAP-over-email specification is not limited to a certain mail transport protocol. Anyhow, most implementations are currently supporting only SOAP transport over SMTP although using POP3 or IMAP might be an interesting alternative in certain scenarios.

2.2.3 Message Queuing Systems

Another approach for sending Web Services messages asynchronously is the use of message queueing systems like *Microsoft Message Queuing* or *Java Message Service (JMS)*. Both are based on TCP, providing a reliable store-and-forward communication mechanism. Such systems are queueing all messages on a separate queuing server in order to temporally decouple the processes of sending and receiving them. This particularly means that one can send messages even if the receiving party is currently busy or not connected to the network (Fig. 2.2).

At a first sight, this approach seems to be pretty close to the email transport – message queues in the form of mailboxes and temporal decoupling of sending and receiving are used here as well. However, in fact, message queuing systems are very complex and powerful systems that are widely used in the field of large-scale enterprise applications. In addition to just queuing messages, they are closely cooperating

```
From: soap-engine@service-consumer.example.com To:
soap-engine@doNothing-company.example.com Subject: RPC Request
Date: Thu, 29 Nov 2004 16:24:03 EST Message-Id:
<EE492E16A090090276D208424960C0C@service-consumer.example.com>


<?xml version="1.0" encoding="UTF-8"?>
  <soapenv:Envelope xmlns:soapenv="http://schemas.xmlsoap.org/soap/envelope/"
                    xmlns:xsd="http://www.w3.org/2001/XMLSchema"
                    xmlns:xsi="http://www.w3.org/2001/XMLSchema-instance">
 <soapenv:Body>
  <ns1:doNothing
          soapenv:encodingStyle="http://schemas.xmlsoap.org/soap/encoding/"
          xmlns:ns1="http://services.doNothing-company.example.com/service1"/>
 </soapenv:Body>
</soapenv:Envelope>
```

Listing 2.1. Using eMails for transporting XML network messages

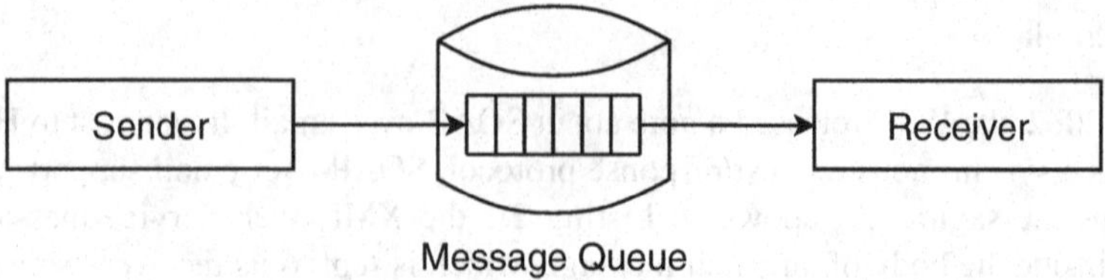

Fig. 2.2. Point-to-point communication over a message queue

with the database management systems providing sophisticated mechanisms for managing data persistency, processing transactions and data locking.

Like SOAP-over-email, such systems do also support application layer multicast, realising a point-to-multipoint MEP. Furthermore, as illustrated in Fig. 2.3, message queues can be used to implement a publisher/subscriber communication model. Here a sender does not directly address the receiver but sends the message to a message queue that is associated with a certain topic. The queuing server finally delivers this message to all system that have previously subscribed to that queue.

2.2.4 Direct Messaging over TCP and UDP Sockets

The concept of reusing standardised application protocols like SMTP or HTTP for Web Service message transport has two major drawbacks. First, these protocols usually provide features that are not necessarily useful in conjunction with Web Services, because they have been originally designed for use in a different context. Second, full-scale application protocols are causing a significant amount of overhead to the communication.

Microsoft has been the first company that put much effort into the development of alternative, more light-weight bindings. The basic idea here is to remove application layer protocols like HTTP or SMTP completely from the Web Service technology stack and send the messages directly over TCP or UDP sockets. Unfortunately, these

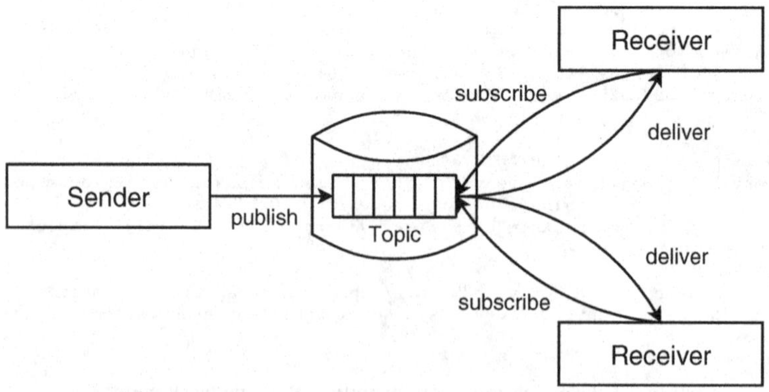

Fig. 2.3. Publisher/subscriber communication over a message queue

protocols are lacking suitable mechanisms for addressing Web Service. With these protocols it is only possible to address different applications on an Internet host using TCP or UDP port numbers. However, it is usually desired that more than one Web Service can be implemented within a single application (which is usually an application server). Therefore, a more fine-grained addressing scheme is needed. This missing feature has to be implemented in the messaging layer of the Web Service Technology Stack, which makes the concept of using TCP or UDP sockets more complicated again.

An implementation of SOAP-over-TCP is included in the Web Service Enhancements (WSE) 2.0 package. The basic idea here is to remove the application layer protocol completely and to put the required addressing information directly into the SOAP header using WS-Addressing, which is a standardised extension for SOAP. The WSE 2.0 provide two versions of TCP-based messaging: synchronous and asynchronous. With synchronous TCP the request and response messages are exchanged over a common TCP connection realising a Request–Response MEP. In the asynchronous mode, the TCP connection is closed after a single message has been sent, realising one-way messaging. Asynchronous TCP messaging increases flexibility but leads to more protocol overhead at the same time.

SOAP-over-UDP has been specified by Microsoft, BEA, Lexmark and Ricoh in September 2004. Currently, there is only an experimental implementation of an SOAP-over-UDP binding. It supports one-way messaging over unicast, multicast and broadcast, providing the greatest flexibility of all currently available bindings. It is notable that in contrast to the multicast features of email and message queuing systems, the UDP multicast uses IP multicast, which significantly increases efficiency.

As a major drawback of this binding, the size of a SOAP message is limited to about 64 KBy in order to fit into a single UDP datagram. Unlike TCP, UDP does not provide any congestion or flow control mechanisms. Furthermore, it is an unreliable transport protocol, i.e. messages might get lost.

2.3 SOAP: XML Messages

As already mentioned in the beginning of this chapter, SOAP can be seen as a core component of the Web Service Technology Stack. It has been designed as a lightweight protocol for exchanging structured information in distributed environments. SOAP is, and that is the most important advantage over competing technologies like Java RMI or CORBA, absolutely independent from a certain operating system, a programming language or special runtime components.

Extensibility has been a major design goal. SOAP itself does not provide any features for realising secure messaging, message routing or reliability, but instead it implements a sophisticated extension model which allows to incorporate even very special demands.

The most recent version of SOAP is 1.2, which was standardised by the W3C in June 2003. The specification is split up into two major parts: *SOAP Version 1.2 Part 1: Messaging Framework* and *SOAP Version 1.2 Part 2: Adjuncts*. The first part describes on an abstract level the structure of the *SOAP Envelope* and how SOAP can be bound to an underlaying transport mechanism. The second part is more concrete. It defines a data model and a set of data types that can be used for realising *Remote Procedure Calls (RPC)*. Furthermore, the SOAP-over-HTTP binding is specified, defining how SOAP messages can be transported using the HTTP GET and POST commands.

2.3.1 SOAP Message Format

The structure of a SOAP message is illustrated in Fig. 2.4. The root element of a SOAP message is *Envelope*. It encloses one or two child elements: an optional *Header* and a *Body*.

If the header is present, it carries information that do not directly belong to the payload of the message. For example, the header may provide authentication information by putting username and password into a separate block. Another header block could carry a transaction ID, indicating that this message belongs to a set of messages that are part of an ongoing transaction.

The *Body* element is mandatory. It contains the actual payload of a SOAP message. The SOAP specification does not define intentionally any constraints about the data in the message body, one can include all kinds of XML data here. The used data format is application specific.

Of course, this high degree of freedom imposes the risk of ambiguity. How can we ensure that all Web Service applications in the world use unambiguous data formats? SOAP addresses this issue by the intensive use of XML namespaces. As

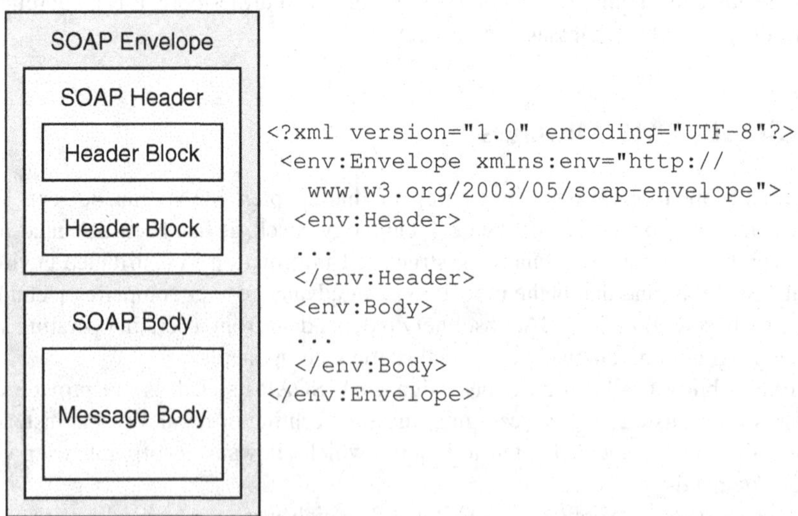

Fig. 2.4. Structure of a SOAP message, schematic view (*left*) and XML representation (*right*)

shown in Fig. 2.4, all elements belonging to the SOAP envelope are carrying a common namespace prefix. The SOAP specification defines a set of namespaces that are exclusively reserved for the SOAP protocol itself. SOAP extensions and application data should be separated by using different namespaces.

In addition to that, namespaces are also used for versioning. Each version of the SOAP protocol uses a unique namespace. A receiver can detect the used protocol version by evaluating the namespace URIs. An example for this is also visible in Fig. 2.4. Here the used namespace URI for envelope elements is `http://www.w3.org/2003/05/soap-envelope`, which indicates SOAP Version 1.2. With SOAP Version 1.1 the namespace URI would be `http://schemas.xmlsoap.org/soap/envelope`.

2.3.2 Communication Patterns

In addition to a common message format the SOAP specification defines a model for describing how the communication takes place. As already introduced in Sect. 2.2 such a description is called a *Message Exchange Pattern (MEP)*. It describes the interactions between the communication parties. As already mentioned in the previous section, not all bindings are supporting all possible MEPs. Or – in other words – the available MEPs are part of the used binding.

In Part 1 of the SOAP specification, we can find a formal characterisation what a MEP is and how a new one can be defined. In Part 2, two MEPs for the HTTP binding are provided: A Response-MEP and a Request–Response MEP. The first one is used in conjunction with the HTTP GET command and the second one with HTTP POST.

A typical example using the Response-MEP is illustrated in Listing 2.2. A reservation terminal queries the reservation data from the central computer system of a car rental company by sending the corresponding `reservationID`. The

```
Request: GET /info?reservationID=384DA3F  HTTP/1.1 Host:
sunshinecars.example.org Accept: text/html;q=0.5,
application/soap+xml

Response: HTTP/1.1 200 OK Content-Type: application/soap+xml;
charset="utf-8" Content-Length: nnnn <?xml version='1.0' ?>
<env:Envelope xmlns:env="http://www.w3.org/2003/05/soap-envelope">
 <env:Body>
  <res:reservationInfo
    xmlns:res="http://sunshinecars.example.org/reservation">
    <res:vehicle>Standard SUV</res:vehicle>
    <res:customer>
        <res:name>John Smith</res:name>
        <res:ID>1674927356</res:ID>
    </res:customer>
    <res:pickup>2005-09-12T12:00:00:00.000Z</res:pickup>
    <res:dropoff>2005-09-19T12:00:00:00.000Z</res:dropoff>
    <res:rate>69,00 USD per day</res:rate>
  </res:reservationInfo>
 </env:Body>
</env:Envelope>
```

Listing 2.2. Using SOAP with HTTP GET

`reservationID` is directly encoded as a parameter in the HTTP GET request (printed in bold letters). The Web Service sends its response back to the requesting system using SOAP. The application payload is included in the SOAP body element. As shown in this example, it is advisable to use a separate namespace for application-specific data.

The Response-MEP of the HTTP-Binding is suitable for all scenarios where we have only barely structured information in the request message, because all request parameters must be encoded in a sequence of values. With the Request-Response MEP we can use SOAP for the request as well.

Figure 2.3 shows the same example when using the Request-Response MEP. It is obvious that the protocol overhead for the Request is significantly higher than with the Response MEP. On the other hand, we can include hierarchically structured data in the request when using SOAP.

A general drawback of using application specific XML data within the SOAP body is that the application developer has to take care of an adequate mapping between the data types of the programming language and their representation in XML. In the following section we will present a more convenient way.

```
Request: POST /info HTTP/1.1 Host: sunshinecars.example.org
Content-Type: application/soap+xml; charset="utf-8" Content-Length:
nnnn

<?xml version='1.0' ?> <env:Envelope
xmlns:env="http://www.w3.org/2003/05/soap-envelope">
 <env:Body>
  <res:reservationRequest
    xmlns:res="http://sunshinecars.example.org/reservation">
    <res:reservationID>384DA3F</res:reservationID>
  </res:reservationRequest>
 </env:Body>
</env:Envelope>

Response: HTTP/1.1 200 OK Content-Type: application/soap+xml;
charset="utf-8" Content-Length: nnnn

<?xml version='1.0' ?> <env:Envelope
xmlns:env="http://www.w3.org/2003/05/soap-envelope">
 <env:Body>
  <res:reservationInfo
    xmlns:res="http://sunshinecars.example.org/reservation">
    <res:vehicle>Standard SUV</res:vehicle>
    <res:customer>
        <res:name>John Smith</res:name>
        <res:ID>1674927356</res:ID>
    </res:customer>
    <res:pickup>2005-09-12T12:00:00:00.000Z</res:pickup>
    <res:dropoff>2005-09-19T12:00:00:00.000Z</res:dropoff>
    <res:rate>69,00 USD per day</res:rate>
  </res:reservationInfo>
 </env:Body>
</env:Envelope>
```

Listing 2.3. Using SOAP with HTTP POST

2.3.3 RPC and SOAP Data Encoding

The most widely used MEP is the Request-Response MEP. As already mentioned, it is perfectly suitable for realising Remote Procedure Calls (RPCs).

However, two very important features are missing so far for realising RPCs with SOAP: first a common model that describes how RPCs are expressed in XML and second a common approach for encoding language-specific data types in XML. Both issues are addressed in the SOAP specification Part 2.

In Listing 2.4 we can see how both things are working and how they can be combined.

```
Request: <?xml version="1.0" encoding="UTF-8"?> <soapenv:Envelope
  xmlns:soapenv="http://www.w3.org/2003/05/soap-envelope"
 xmlns:soapenc="http://www.w3.org/2003/05/soap-encoding"
  xmlns:xsd="http://www.w3.org/2001/XMLSchema"
  xmlns:xsi="http://www.w3.org/2001/XMLSchema-instance"
  xmlns:res="http://sunshinecars.example.org/reservation">
   <soapenv:Body>
     <res:getReservationInfo soapenv:encodingStyle=
        "http://www.w3.org/2003/05/soap-encoding">
       <in0 xsi:type="soapenc:string">dab37a3e4f</in0>
     </res:getReservationInfo>
  </soapenv:Body>
</soapenv:Envelope>

Response: <?xml version="1.0" encoding="UTF-8"?> <soapenv:Envelope
 xmlns:soapenv="http://www.w3.org/2003/05/soap-envelope"
 xmlns:soapenc="http://www.w3.org/2003/05/soap-encoding"
 xmlns:rpc="http://www.w3.org/2003/05/soap-rpc"
 xmlns:xsd="http://www.w3.org/2001/XMLSchema"
 xmlns:xsi="http://www.w3.org/2001/XMLSchema-instance"
 xmlns:res="http://sunshinecars.example.org/reservation">
  <soapenv:Body>
    <res:getReservationInfoResponse soapenv:encodingStyle=
      "http://www.w3.org/2003/05/soap-encoding">
     <rpc:result>getReservationInfoReturn</rpc:result>
      <getReservationInfoReturn id="id0"
        xsi:type="res:ReservationInfo">
        <customerInfo id="id1" xsi:type="res:CustomerInfo">
          <ID   xsi:type="soapenc:string">27463782</ID>
          <name xsi:type="soapenc:string">John Smith</name>
        </customerInfo>
        <dropoff xsi:type="soapenc:date">
            2005-09-12T12:00:00.000Z</dropoff>
        <pickup  xsi:type="soapenc:date">
            2005-09-19T12:00:00.000Z</pickup>
        <rate    xsi:type="soapenc:string">
            69,00 USD per day</rate>
        <vehicle
         xsi:type="soapenc:string">Standard SUV</vehicle>
      </getReservationInfoReturn>
    </res:getReservationInfoResponse>
  </soapenv:Body>
</soapenv:Envelope>
```

Listing 2.4. SOAP messages of the RPC call `ReservationInfo getReservationInfo (String reservationID)`

There are two requirements defined in the SOAP specification about RPC-style messaging:

1. The body of the request message contains only one element.
2. This element must have the same name as the RPC operation and carries all input parameters.

Both requirements are clearly visible in the example.

The response message is required to satisfy the following three basic rules, which are also clearly depicted in the example shown in Fig. 2.4:

1. The SOAP body must contain a single element. There are no restrictions about its name.
2. For each return parameter there is a child element with the name of that parameter.
3. If the return type is not null, there must be an additional child element with a namespace of `http://www.w3.org/2003/05/soap-rpc` and the name `result`. It contains the name of the element that shall be interpreted as the return value of this RPC operation. If it is null, such an element must not exist.

Although we find some further details in the SOAP specification, e.g. about error handling, these five rules are sufficient for understanding the basics of RPC-style SOAP messaging. As already mentioned, we will now have a look at our example focussing the predefined SOAP data encoding schema.

The use of SOAP encoding is indicated by using the namespace `http://www.w3.org/2003/05/soap-encoding`. In our example, the according namespace prefix is `soapenc`. As we can see in the request as well as in the response message, all simple input and output parameters are of a type with that prefix. Complex types are indicated to be constructed using the SOAP encoding schema by using the attribute `soapenv:encodingStyle` with `http://www.w3.org/2003/05/soap-encoding` as value. Thus, the receiving SOAP engine knows that it may interpret these XML constructs and pass them as native data types in the used programming language to the application instead of passing the XML data directly. In Java for instance, such constructs are typically mapped to Java Bean types.

Although SOAP Encoding and RPC-Style messaging may be used independently from each other, it is very common to combine both features. They make SOAP messaging very comfortable for the programmer. With both features enabled the SOAP engine can automatically handle serialisation and deserialisation of most data types and can also map Web Service operations to simple function or method calls.

2.4 WSDL: Web Service Description

Another crucial building block for Web Services as a universal middleware technology is a powerful and well-structured *Interface Definition Language (IDL)*. The basic task of an IDL is to provide an exact and machine readable definition of service interfaces. A service consumer interprets the IDL description of a service provider in order to generate service calls that are compatible with the according service interfaces.

There are existing IDL approaches for JAVA-RMI and CORBA but these are not adequate for Web Services, because they are inconsistent with the ideas of being extensible, XML-based just to name a few.

Therefore the *Web Service Description Language (WSDL)* has been developed. The most recent version is WSDL 2.0 which has been published by the W3C in August 2005 as a working draft. Equally to the SOAP specification, the WSDL specification is split up into two major parts: *WSDL Version 2.0 Part 1: Core Language* and *WSDL Version 2.0 Part 2: Adjuncts*. The fist part specifies the structure of the WSDL documents on an abstract level, i.e. independently from a specific messaging protocol or transport mechanism. The second part specifies primarily the use of WSDL together with SOAP and HTTP.

As shown in Listing 2.5 a WSDL 2.0 document is typically structured in five main sections: *documentation*, *types*, *interface*, *binding* and *service*. In the following we will explain each section in detail and point out the interrelations between them.

```
<?xml version="1.0" encoding="utf-8" ?> <description
     xmlns="http://www.w3.org/2005/08/wsdl"...>

  <documentation>
  ...
  </documentation>

  <types>
    <xs:schema>
        <xs:element name="someElementName" .../>
    ...
    </xs:schema>
  </types>

  <interface>
    <operation name="someOpName" ...>
        <input element="someElementName" ...>
        ...
        <output ...>
        ...
    </operation>
    ...
  </interface>

  <binding name="someBindingName"...>
      <operation ref="someOpName" .../>
  ...
  </binding>

  <service>
      <endpoint binding="someBindingName" ...>
  ...
  </service>
</description>
```

Listing 2.5. Typical structure of a WSDL service description

The *documentation* section contains additional textual information on how to use the described service for humans. Its content is meant as an endorsement to the other sections of this WSDL description, which are mainly meant to be interpreted by machines. This endorsement is very important because WSDL can provide only a *partial* description of the service. It can express how the messages should look like that go in and out of a service operation. However, it cannot express application level semantics like. "First call operation X, then call operation Y with the result of X as the first input parameter".

Of course this documentation endorsement is far away from covering the needs of all Web Service applications. The problem is that a human is needed to interpret this documentation section. For automated service composition, more advanced approaches are necessary, which will be covered in Part III of this book.

In the *types* section all data types that will be used in the input and output messages of our service operations are declared. This is typically done using XML Schema. Unlike other XML grammar description languages (e.g. DTDs) XML Schema provides a very sophisticated type system which can be directly used for specifying basic data types like integers, strings and dates as well as compound data types. Furthermore, extensions and restrictions of existing data types can be described.

The *interface* section basically is the core component of a WSDL description. Here each service operation is listed and its inputs and outputs are specified by referencing the according data type definitions which were specified in the types section. Up to this point the service description is abstract, i.e. independent from a certain messaging format or transport mechanism.

In the *binding* section we are mapping our abstract service operations to concrete ones. We specify the used messaging format (e.g. SOAP 1.2) and the protocol used for message transport (e.g. HTTP 1.1). The according service operation, declared in the interface section are referenced using the *ref* attribute.

In the *service* section we finally define service *endpoints*. An endpoint references a previously defined binding and provides all necessary technical information for accessing its service operations. This is typically done by providing the URL of the Web Service.

2.4.1 Example

Listing 2.6 shows a complete WSDL 2.0 example describing the reservation Web Service from Subsect. 2.3.2 using the Request–Response MEP. Again we can see the main sections of a WSDL description: *types*, *interface*, *binding* and *service*. We have omitted the optional *documentation* in this example.

In the *types* section we see a XML Schema definition of the data type we will use with our Web Service. We need to specify a message format for the request as well as for the response message (see also Listing 2.3 for details).

In the *interface* section we specify all service operations that our Web Service provides. In WSDL 2.0, each operation is mapped to predefined message exchange

```
<?xml version="1.0" encoding="utf-8" ?> <description
  xmlns="http://www.w3.org/2005/08/wsdl"
  targetNamespace= "http://sunshinecars.example.org/reservation"
  xmlns:tns= "http://sunshinecars.example.org/wsdl/reservation"
  xmlns:res= "http://sunshinecars.example.org/reservation"
  xmlns:wsoap= "http://www.w3.org/2005/08/wsdl/soap">
  <|types|><xs:schema
    xmlns:xs="http://www.w3.org/2001/XMLSchema"
    targetNamespace="http://sunshinecars.example.org/reservation"
    xmlns="http://sunshinecars.example.org/reservation">
    <xs:element name="reservationRequest">
      <xs:compleyType><xs:sequence>
        <xs:element name="reservationID" type="xs:string"/>
      </xs:sequence></xs:complexType>
    </xs:element>
    <xs:element name="reservationInfo">
      <xs:complexType><xs:sequence>
        <xs:element name="vehicle" type="xs:string"/>
        <xs:element name="customer" type="customerType"/>
        <xs:element name="pickup" type="xs:date"/>
        <xs:element name="dropoff" type="xs:date"/>
        <xs:element name="rate" type="xs:string"/>
      </xs:sequence></xs:compleType>
    </xs:element>
    <xs:complexType name="customerType"><xs:sequence>
      <xs:element name="name" type="xs:string/>
␣␣␣␣␣␣<xs:element␣name="ID"␣type="xs:string/>
    </xs:sequence></xs:complexType>
  </xs:schema></types>
  <|interface| name="reservationInterface">
    <operation name="reservationInfoOperation"
      |pattern="http://www.w3.org/2005/08/wsdl/in-out"|>
      <input messageLabel="In"
        element="res:reservationRequest"/>
      <output messageLabel="Out"
        element="res:reservationInfo"/>
    </operation>
  </interface>
  <|binding| name="reservationSOAPBinding"
    interface="tns:reservationInterface"
    type="http://www.w3.org/2005/08/wsdl/soap"
    wsoap:protocol=
    "http://www.w3.org/2003/05/soap/bindings/HTTP">
    <operation ref="tns:reservationInfoOperation" wsoap:mep=
      "http://www.w3.org/2003/05/soap/mep/request-response"/>
  </binding>
  <|service| name="reservationService"
    interface="tns:reservationInterface">
    <endpoint name="reservationEndpoint"
      binding="tns:reservationSOAPBinding"
      address=
    "http://sunshinecars.example.org:8080/reservation.cgi"/>
  </service>
</description>
```

Listing 2.6. Example WSDL document describing the reservation web service

patterns which are specified in the WSDL standard. Note that these MEPs are different from the SOAP MEPs discussed in the previous sections. In our example the service operation takes an incoming message and answers with an outgoing one.

Therefore we reference the appropriate WSDL message exchange pattern by using the URI `http://www.w3.org/2005/08/wsdl/in-out`.

The *binding* section binds the interface with all its service operations to a concrete messaging format and a message transport protocol. As shown in the example, this is done by specifying the appropriate URIs. For each operation we can define binding specific parameters. In Listing 2.6 we can see a specification for the messaging MEP using the URI `"http://www.w3.org/2003/05/soap/mep/request-response"`. Note that this MEP is specific for the used messaging format while the one specified in the *interface* section is more abstract. Of course both specifications must be compatible with each other.

Finally we can use the *service* section to describe the so-called service endpoint for our interface. In our example the specified address is a HTTP URL. Again, the endpoint format must match with the parameters of the *binding* section. With a SOAP-over-email binding the endpoint would be an email address.

2.5 UDDI: Web Service Discovery

UDDI, which is an acronym for *Universal Description, Discovery and Integration*, is a platform independent, electronic technology for general purpose business registries. Anyhow, the Web Service technology has been a key factor for designing UDDI in its current form and therefore UDDI can be seen as a directory service for Web Services. As well as SOAP and WSDL, it is a core component of the Web Service Technology Stack. The first version of UDDI has been introduced by Microsoft, IBM and Ariba in the year 2000. Today UDDI is available in version 3.0 and has been ratified as an OASIS standard in February 2005. The UDDI working group at OASIS has currently more than 20 companies as members. Most recent information about the latest UDDI developments are available from the UDDI website.[1]

The UDDI v3.0 standard is divided into four groups of documents: A *Feature List* which describes the changes to version 2, the *Technical Specification* describing the architecture of UDDI in detail, a set of XML Schema documents describing the used *data structures* in UDDI and finally a set of WSDL documents, describing a common *API* for working with UDDI.

In the most basic setup, UDDI is a fully centralised approach for realising a directory service, i.e. if a business wants to add an entry to the UDDI repository it contacts the UDDI operator and adds its data manually either by using a web browser or by using the UDDI Web Service interface. The data is stored locally on the computer system of this operator. Other businesses can then query this data from there.

Of course there can be more than one registry operator and it is probably unwanted that all registries are providing different information sets. Therefore, UDDI provides mechanisms for replicating the data between several UDDI nodes. These nodes form an *UDDI Operator Cloud*.

[1] `http://www.uddi.org/`

2.5.1 Components and Data Structures

A UDDI registry can be seen as a composition of three components, analogously to the different types of phone books: *White Pages*, *Yellow Pages* and *Green Pages*.

The *White Pages* contain the basic information about a business, like mailing address, phone or fax numbers, etc.

The *Yellow Pages* are very similar to the *White Pages*. The difference is that all entries are grouped according to an industrial categorisation here. So the *Yellow Pages* are the right place if one is not looking for a certain company but a certain *type* of business.

In the *Green Pages* we find technical information about the services provided by a business.

For each component the UDDI specification provides well-defined data structures (in form of XML Schema documents) which all UDDI nodes must be able to process. The following components are declared as the core of the UDDI information model in the UDDI Specification document.

As shown in Fig. 2.5 there are four core data types:

1. The `<businessEntity>` element is the top-level data structure that holds all information about a business and its services. While the enclosed `<businessService>` structures contain detailed information about the services, other child elements describe more general properties of a business, such as phone and fax numbers, mailing address, etc.
2. In `<businessService>` elements we find a non-technical description of business services. It can contain a service name and a descriptive text. Furthermore, it can contain a set of *service categories* (a so-called *categoryBag*) that characterise this service, e.g. with respect to a certain geographic region,

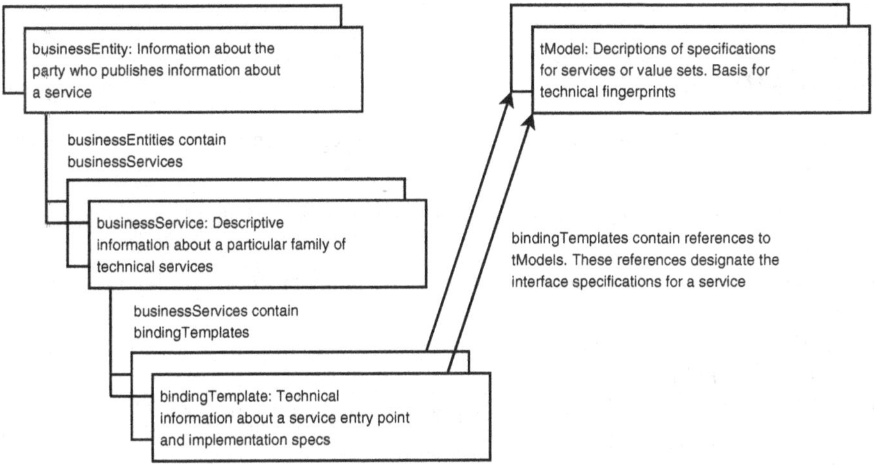

Fig. 2.5. Core UDDI data types (*Taken from the UDDI v3.0 specification*)

industry or product. There is also the possibility of including a digital signature for this service description. Finally, there is at least one references to a `<bindingTemplate>`.

3. A `<bindingTemplate>` provides a technical description of a business service. It specifies an access point, which can be used to invoke the service. There are no technical restrictions how the specification of an access point must look like. It is basically a string which represents a technical interface. This could be an URL, an email address or even a telephone number. A `<bindingTemplate>` can also contain its own *categoryBag*, but unlike the *categoryBag* of a `<businessService>` element we find *technical* categories in there. For instance, it could contain the categories "production", "stable", "testing" or "unstable". A `<bindingTemplate>` may also provide several natural language descriptions of the technical details of this service. Furthermore, it contains at least one `<tModel>` element.
4. The `<tModel>` structure is probably the most important one in UDDI. Here we can specify wire protocols, interchange formats and interchange sequencing rules for the business service. It is the basis for providing a "technical fingerprint" of a service which can be used to identify suitable services for service compositions with respect to their technical compatibility. Of course, it is very important to express this data in an unambiguous and commonly understandable language. The UDDI specification does not prescribe a common format but refers to the following suitable examples: *RosettaNet Partner Interface Processes specification*, *Open Applications Group Integration Specification* and various *Electronic Document Interchange (EDI)* efforts.

All UDDI data structure instances have unique identifiers, which can be used as a query key when using the UDDI APIs. In UDDI 2.0 this identifier is 128 bit long and is written as a hexadecimal number. An example could look like this:
`uddi:3DF43C1F-83A1-BB39-007E-F487BA25CC04`.

2.5.2 API Overview

For the communication between clients and UDDI registry nodes, UDDI specifies a rich set of APIs:

- *UDDI Inquiry* is used for querying business entities and their service descriptions.
- *UDDI Publication* refers to registering and updating business entities and service descriptions.
- *UDDI Security* realises authentication and access control (typically used together with UDDI Publication).
- *UDDI Custody Transfer* is used for transferring the custody for a UDDI record from one node to another.
- *UDDI Subscription* allows clients to register for notification messages if certain UDDI records are changed.

- *UDDI Replication* is used for replicating UDDI records between the nodes within a *UDDI operator cloud.*
- *UDDI Subscription Listener* must be implemented by all clients that use the *UDDI Subscription* API, which defines this as a mandatory interface.
- *UDDI Value Set* must be implemented by an UDDI client in order to allow a UDDI node to perform certain checks on data before it is written into the registry.

In the following two subsections, we take a closer look on the two most important UDDI APIs: to query a UDDI registry and to add new entries.

2.5.3 Using UDDI Inquiry

The UDDI Inquiry API provides two different sets of operations for querying an UDDI registry: the `find_xxx` and the `get_xxx` operations.

The first is used primarily for reducing the size of the search space. Thus, the `find_xxx` operations are primarily useful if only very few things are known about the wanted service. The result of such an API call contains a list of entries. Their data type depends on the type of the query. In a second step a client can retrieve more specific properties of these entries using the `get_xxx` operations. The `find_xxx` operations follow a "drill-down" pattern while the `get_xxx` operation follow a "browse" pattern.

There are different variants of the `find_xxx` and `get_xxx` operations available for all UDDI core data structures:

- With `find_business` and `get_businessDetail` a client can retrieve information about one or more `<businessEntity>` elements.
- With `find_service` and `get_serviceDetail` a client can retrieve information about one or more `<businessService>` elements.
- With `find_binding` and `get_bindingDetail` a client can retrieve information about one or more `<bindingTemplate>` elements.
- With `find_tModel` and `get_tModelDetail` a client can retrieve information about one or more `<tModel>` elements.

A typical API call could look like this (the SOAP and HTTP data is not shown in this example):

```
<uddi:find_tModel generic="3.0"
  xmlns:uddi="urn.uddi-org:api_v3">
  <uddi:name>Sunshine</uddi:name>
</uddi:find_tModel>
```

The UDDI specification does not prescribe any fixed algorithms for processing search requests. Current UDDI implementations are mainly based on string matching. However, a typical response message to this call might look like this:

```
<uddi:tModelList generic="3.0" operator="IBM"
    xmlns:uddi="urn.uddi-org:api_v3">
  <uddi:tModelInfos>
    <uddi:tModelInfo
        tModelKey="uddi:3DF43C1F-83A1-BB39-007E-F487BA25CC04"/>
      <uddi:name>Sunshine Cars Inc. reservation service</uddi:name>
```

```
    </uddi:tModelInfo>
    <uddi:tModelInfo
        tModelKey="uddi:2342D4B5-8AA0-FE04-83DB-FFBB023CABC5"/>
      <uddi:name>Sunshine Inn Motel electronic check-in</uddi:name>
    </uddi:tModelInfo>
    <uddi:tModelInfo
        tModelKey="uddi:BB54CF23-F52B-40A4-B8FA-0038B35A9FD3"/>
      <uddi:name>Sunshine Fruits Import Corp. price list service</uddi:name>
    </uddi:tModelInfo>
  <uddi:tModelInfos>
</uddi:tModelList>
```

The client could now retrieve additional information about the three business services in the result set by calling the `get_tModelDetail` operation with the according UDDI identifiers as parameters.

Furthermore, this API provides the `find_relatedBusiness` operation which allows to locate `<businessEntity>` entries which are somehow related to a known one. This UDDI feature is not implemented using automated reasoning about the registry data. Both publishers of the related `<businessEntity>` must manually specify this relation. Note that the *isRelatedTo* relation in UDDI is always symmetric (*isRelatedTo(X,Y)* $\rightarrow$ *isRelatedTo(Y,X)*). We will show how this is technically implemented in the end of the following subsection.

2.5.4 Using UDDI Publication

Equally to querying a UDDI registry, the UDDI specification defines an API for inserting and deleting registry entries, called *UDDI Publication*. UDDI Publication is very similar to UDDI Inquiry and its usage is straightforward. For inserting or deleting an entry the appropriate service operations are named `save_xxx` and `delete_xxx`, where `xxx` must be substituted by `binding`, `business`, `service` or `tModel`.

Unlike *UDDI Inquiry*, which provides a service that should be generally accessible for everyone, the access to *UDDI Publication* needs to be restricted in most cases. It is typically undesired that everybody is able to modify all registry entries.

Although the details of access control are not part of the UDDI specification and thus must be constituted by the registry operators, the UDDI specification does provide basic measures for implementing various types of access control policies. Most of these measures are managed by the *UDDI Security* API and will not be discussed here in detail. Basically a publisher is usually required to authenticate before getting write access to a UDDI registry. The registry will issue a so-called `authToken` which can be thought of as some kind of session ID. This token must be included in the `<authInfo>` Element in all operation calls which require write access.

In UDDI 2.0 the UDDI Publication API provides additional operations for managing the so-called *publisherAssertions* which are the technical basis for processing `find_relatedBusiness` calls. Again, the *isRelatedTo* relation in UDDI is always symmetric. Since two businesses are involved here, the control over this registry entry is slit-up: A `publisherAssertion` issued by business A has basically the meaning "X is related to Y". In order to become visible in the registry, this relation must be acknowledged by business B. B must issue the corresponding publisherAssertion counterpart "Y is related to X". In this way both parties control half of the relationship.

An example illustrates the use of the add_publisherAssertion operation:

```
<add_publisherAssertions xmlns="urn:uddi-org:api_v3" >
   <authInfo>FFFFF</authInfo>
   <publisherAssertion>
       <fromKey>uuid:957A2C6B-EE22-470D-DBC7-104243335CD3</fromKey>
       <toKey>uddi:4BF4A41B-A3AC-BB39-D18A-B683BA311B02</toKey>
       <keyedReference
          tModelKey="uddi:uddi.org:relationships"
          keyName="Holding Company"
          keyValue="parent-child" />
   </publisherAssertion>
</add_publisherAssertions>
```

The contents of the elements <fromKey> and <toKey> are referencing the two <businessEntity> entries which are related to each other. The value in the <authInfo> element must be a valid authToken that authorises the sender of this add_publisherAssertion to be in charge of controlling the <businessEntity> referenced in the <fromKey> element. The content of the <keyedReference> element specifies what kind of relation is described by this publisherAssertion. Also here the used vocabulary is not specified in the UDDI standard and thus may be implementation specific.

In order to have visible effects on the registry, a second, inverse publisherAssertion must be issued by somebody who controls the <businessEntity> entry referenced in the <toKey> element.

Besides add_publisherAssertion the Publication API also provides functionalities for deleting, monitoring and updating publisherAssertions. They are called delete_publisherAssertion, get_assertionStatusReport, get_publisherAssertions and set_publisherAssertions.

2.6 The Web Service Role Model: How Things Are Working Together

In the previous section we have discussed various technologies for implementing Web Services. With these building blocks it is possible to model even very complex usage scenarios. The *W3C Web Services Architecture Working Group* has released a document describing typical Web Service Architectures in more than 30 different usage scenarios.[2]

However, despite this complexity, there is a quite regular pattern in all Web Service application scenarios, which is commonly called the "Web Service Role Model" or the "SOA Triangle". It is illustrated in Fig. 2.6. Each participating software component can take on the role of a *service provider*, a *service requester* or a *registry agency*.

[2] http://www.w3.org/TR/ws-arch-scenarios/

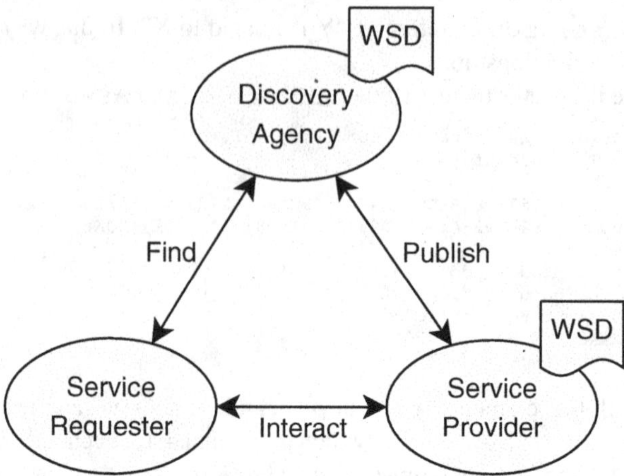

Fig. 2.6. The Web Service Role Model: relationships between service requester, service provider and discovery agency

The *service provider* describes the service it provides with a *Web Service Description (WSD)* document. This is necessary because a service requester needs this service description in order to interact with the provided service correctly. Today WSDL is the only language which is commonly used for describing service interface. However, the *W3C Web Services Architecture Working Group* does not prescribe a certain data format and therefore WSD documents might be written in any suitable language. Alternative approaches like OWL-S and WSMO, which might become relevant for practical use in near future, will be discussed in Chap. 7.

There are several ways for the service requester to get this WSD document. It is easiest to get it directly from the service provider, but unfortunately this is not always possible. The service requester and the service provider might not even know each other at this point.

Therefore, we need the third role: the *registry agency*. The service provider can use the registry agency in order to make its service description publicly available. After publishing the service description a service requester can query the registry agency and if it finds a suitable service it can directly access the WSD document. Finally, the service requester can interact with the service provider.

The technologies for implementing the registry and accessing other service components are usually UDDI and SOAP. However, no mandatory technology is specified by the *W3C Web Services Architecture Working Group*. Generally it is also possible to use any suitable data format for these tasks.

At a first glance the Web Service Role Model looks quite simple but in fact there are several obstacles. First of all the WSD document is, as already described in the section about WSDL, usually only a partial service description with focus on the *technical* parameters of the service. Therefore, the service consumer must usually interpret this description in order to get a full understanding of the service and how it is used.

In the following example, we want to check a customer's credit card limit with a creditCardCheck Web Service. All we know is the customer's name. The service provides three service operations with the following operation signatures:

1. `String getCreditCardNo(String CustomerID)`
2. `Boolean checkCreditLimit(String CreditCardNumer)`
3. `String getCustomerIDbyName(String Name)`

By looking at the operation names a human programmer can figure out quite easily that it is usually required to call operation number 3 first. Then we can call operation number 1 in order to get a valid credit card number and with this we can finally call `checkCreditLimit`. However, if we think of a scenario with a computer selecting a prior unknown service, it is quite hard to make a failsafe decision in what sequence these operations must be called in order to complete a certain task.

Therefore, it is usually required to have more expressive service description if we want to select or combine prior unknown services at runtime. This description should not be limited to the technical service parameters but must also include the service semantics. This problem will be discussed Part III of this book.

Another very basic problem may occur when searching for suitable Web Services in a registry agency. As already stated in Sect. 2.5, UDDI does not define a standard vocabulary for describing Web Services and therefore it is very hard to implement automated service discovery with today's repositories. This problem field will be addressed in the Chap. 7 and 8.

All in all, the technologies described in this chapter are generally ready for use. SOAP, WSDL and UDDI are providing similar functionalities as competing older technologies like Java-RMI or CORBA but are much more flexible in use. However, as stated in Chap. 1, some visions of the Web Service research community have not become reality so far. This is especially true for things like automated service composition and the mappings between business processes and Web Service operations. So there is still a big gap between the idea of fully automated B2B processes and what Web Service technology can do today. Therefore, research in this field is still very active. The combination of Semantic Web technology and Web Services is considered a promising approach for bridging this gap.

References

1. M. Birbeck, J. Diamond, J. Duckett, O.G. Gudmundsson, P. Kobak, E. Lenz, S. Livingstone, D. Marcus, S. Mohr, N. Ozu, J. Pinnock, K. Visco, A. Watt, K. Williams, and Z. Zaev. *Professional XML*. Wrox Press, 2001.
2. K. Cagle, J. Duckett, O. Griffin, S. Mohr, F. Norton, N. Ozu, I. Stokes-Ress, J. Tennison, and K. Williams. *Professional XML schemas*. Wrox Press, 2001.
3. T. Erl. *Service-Oriented Architecture: : A Field Guide to Integrating XML and Web Services*. Prentice Hall PTR, 2004.
4. I.T. Foster. The Anatomy of the Grid: Enabling Scalable Virtual Organizations. In *Euro-Par '01: Proceedings of the 7th International Euro-Par Conference Manchester on Parallel Processing*, pages 1–4, London, UK, 2001. Springer-Verlag.

5. C. Germain-Renaud and D. Monnier-Ragaigne. Grid Result Checking. In *CF '05: Proceedings of the 2nd Conference on Computing Frontiers*, pages 87–96, New York, USA, 2005. ACM Press.
6. M. Girardot and N. Sundaresan. Millau: An Encoding Format for Effcient Representation and Exchange of XML Over the Web. In *9th International World Wide Web Conference*, pages 747–765, Amsterdam, Netherlands, May 2000.
7. W. Hoschek. The Web Service Discovery Architecture. In *Proceedings of the ACM/IEEE Conference on Supercomputing*, pages 1–15. IEEE Computer Society Press, 2002.
8. W. Iverson. *Real World Web Services*. O'Reilly, 1. edition, 2005.
9. E. O'Tuathail and M.T. Rose. RFC 3288: Using the Simple Object Access Protocol (SOAP) in Blocks Extensible Exchange Protocol (BEEP), June 2002.
10. A. Tanenbaum. *Computer Networks*. Prentice Hall PTR, 2002.
11. M. Tian, T. Voigt, T. Naumowicz, H. Ritter, and J. Schiller. Performance Considerations for Mobile Web Services. In *IEEE Communication Society Workshop on Applications and Services in Wireless Networks*, July 2003.
12. C. Werner, C. Buschmann, and S. Fischer. WSDL-Driven SOAP Compression. *International Journal on Web Service Research*, 2(1):18–35, 2005.
13. C. Werner, C. Buschmann, T. Jäcker, and S. Fischer. Enhanced Transport Bindings for Efficient SOAP Messaging. In *IEEE International Conference on Web Services*, pages 193–200. IEEE Computer Society, July 2005.

Part II

Semantic Web Technology

3

Knowledge Representation and Ontologies

Logic, Ontologies and Semantic Web Languages

Stephan Grimm[1], Pascal Hitzler[2] and Andreas Abecker[1]

[1] FZI Research Center for Information Technologies, University of Karlsruhe, Germany
{grimm, abecker}@fzi.de
[2] Institute AIFB, University of Karlsruhe, Germany,
hitzler@aifb.uni-karlsruhe.de

Summary. In Artificial Intelligence, knowledge representation studies the formalisation of knowledge and its processing within machines. Techniques of automated reasoning allow a computer system to draw conclusions from knowledge represented in a machine-interpretable form. Recently, ontologies have evolved in computer science as computational artefacts to provide computer systems with a conceptual yet computational model of a particular domain of interest. In this way, computer systems can base decisions on reasoning about domain knowledge, similar to humans. This chapter gives an overview on basic knowledge representation aspects and on ontologies as used within computer systems. After introducing ontologies in terms of their appearance, usage and classification, it addresses concrete ontology languages that are particularly important in the context of the Semantic Web. The most recent and predominant ontology languages and formalisms are presented in relation to each other and a selection of them is discussed in more detail.

3.1 Knowledge Representation

As a branch of symbolic Artificial Intelligence, *knowledge representation* and *reasoning* aim at designing computer systems that reason about a machine-interpretable representation of the world, similar to human reasoning. *Knowledge-based systems* have a computational model of some domain of interest in which symbols serve as surrogates for real-world domain artefacts, such as physical objects, events, relationships, etc. [45]. The *domain of interest* can cover any part of the real world or any hypothetical system about which one desires to represent knowledge for computational purposes.

A knowledge-based system maintains a *knowledge base* which stores the symbols of the computational model in form of statements about the domain, and it performs *reasoning* by manipulating these symbols. Applications can base their decisions on domain-relevant questions posed to a knowledge base.

3.1.1 A Motivating Scenario

To illustrate principles of knowledge representation in this chapter, we introduce an example scenario taken from a B2B travelling use case. In this scenario, companies frequently book business trips for their employees, sending them to international meetings and conference events. Such a scenario is a relevant use case for Semantic Web Services, since companies desire to automate the online booking process, while they still want to benefit from the high competition among various travel agencies and no-frills airlines that sell tickets via the Internet. Automation is achieved by computational agents deciding about whether an online offer of some travel agency fits a request for a business trip or not, based on the knowledge they have about the offer and the request. Knowledge represented in this domain of "business trips" is about flights, trains, booking, companies and their employees, cities that are source or destination for a trip, etc.

Knowledge-based systems use a computational representation of such knowledge in form of statements about the domain of interest. Examples of such statements in the business trips domain are "companies book trips for their employees", "flights and train rides are special kinds of trips" or "employees are persons employed at some company". This knowledge can be used to answer questions about the domain of interest. From the given statements, and by means of automated deduction, a knowledge-based system can, e.g., derive that "a person on a flight booked by a company is an employee" or "the company that booked a flight for a person is the person's employer".

In this way, a knowledge-based computational agent can reason about business trips, similar to the way a human would. It could, e.g., tell apart offers for business trips from offers for vacations, or decide whether the destination city for a requested flight is close to the geographical region specified in an offer, or conclude that a participant of a business flight is an employee of the company that booked the flight.

3.1.2 Forms of Representing Knowledge

If we look at current Semantic Web technologies and use cases, knowledge representation appears in different forms, the most prevalent of which are based on semantic networks, rules and logic. Semantic network structures can be found in RDF graph representations [30] or Topic Maps [41], whereas a formalisation of business knowledge often comes in form of rules with some "if-then" reading, e.g., in business rules or logic programming formalisms. Logic is used to realise a precise semantic interpretation for both of the other forms. By providing formal semantics for knowledge representation languages, logic-based formalisms lay the basis for automated deduction. We will investigate these three forms of knowledge representation in the following.

Semantic Networks

Originally, semantic networks stem from the "existential graphs" introduced by Charles Peirce in 1896 to express logical sentences as graphical node-and-link diagrams [43]. Later on, similar notations have been introduced, such as conceptual graphs [45], all differing slightly in syntax and semantics. Despite these differences, all the semantic network formalisms concentrate on expressing the taxonomic structure of categories of objects and the relations between them. We use a general notion of a semantic network, abstracting from the different concrete notations proposed.

A *semantic network* is a graph whose nodes represent concepts and whose arcs represent relations between these concepts. They provide a structural representation of statements about a domain of interest. In the business trips domain, typical concepts would be "Company", "Employee" or "Flight", while typical relations would be "books", "isEmployedAt" or "participatesIn". Figure. 3.1 shows an example of a semantic network for the business trips domain.

Semantic networks provide a means to abstract from natural language, representing the knowledge that is captured in text in a form more suitable for computation. The knowledge expressed in the network from Fig. 3.1 coincides with the content of the following natural language text.

> *Employees of companies are persons, while both persons and companies are legal entities. Companies book trips for their employees. These trips can be flights or train rides which start and end in cities of Europe or the USA. Companies themselves have locations which can be cities.*
> *The company UbiqBiz books the flight FL4711 from London to New York for Mister X.*

Typically, concepts are chosen to represent the meaning of nouns in such a text, while relations are mapped to verb phrases. The fragment [Company] $\xrightarrow{\textit{books}}$ [Trip] is

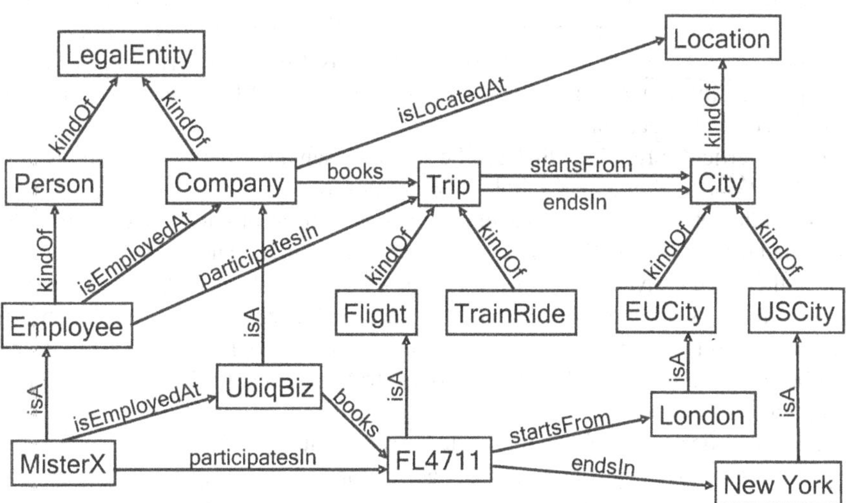

Fig. 3.1. A semantic network for business trips

read as "companies book trips", expressed as a binary relation between two concepts. However, this is not mandatory; the relation $\xrightarrow{books}$ could also be "lifted" to a concept Booking with relations $\xrightarrow{hasActor}$, $\xrightarrow{hasParticipant}$ and $\xrightarrow{hasObject}$ pointing to Company, Employee and Trip, respectively. In this way, its ternary character would be expressed more accurately than in the original network where the information about an employee's involvement in booking is implicit.

In principle, the concepts and relations in a semantic network are generic and could stand for anything relevant in the domain of interest. However, some particular relations for some standard knowledge representation and reasoning cases have evolved.

The semantic network in Fig. 3.1 illustrates the distinction between general concepts, like Employee, and individual concepts, like MisterX. While the latter represent concrete individuals or objects in the domain of interest, the former serve as classes to group together such individuals that have certain properties in common, as e.g. all employees. The particular relation which links individuals to their classes is that of *instantiation*, denoted by $\xrightarrow{isA}$. Thus, MisterX is called an instance of the concept employee. The lower part of the network is concerned with knowledge about individuals, reflecting a particular situation of the employee MisterX participating in a certain flight, while the upper part is concerned with knowledge about general concepts, reflecting various possible situations.

The most prominent type of relation in semantic networks, however, is that of *subsumption*, which we denote by $\xrightarrow{kindOf}$. A subsumption link connects two general concepts and expresses specialisation or generalisation, respectively. In the network in Fig. 3.1, a flight is said to be a special kind of trip, i.e. Trip subsumes Flight. This means that any flight is also a trip; however, there might be other trips which are not flights, such as train rides. Subsumption is associated with the notion of inheritance in that a specialised concept inherits all the properties from its more general parent concepts. For example, from the network one can read that a company can be located in a European city, since $\xrightarrow{locatedAt}$ points from Company to Location while EUCity is a kind of City which is itself a kind of Location. The concept EUCity inherits the property of being a potential location for a company from the concept Location.

Other particular relations that can be found in semantic network notations are, e.g., $\xrightarrow{partOf}$ to denote part-whole relationships, etc.

Semantic networks are closely related to another form of knowledge representation called frame systems. In fact, frame systems and semantic networks can be identical in their expressiveness but use different representation metaphors [43]. While the semantic network metaphor is that of a graph with concept nodes linked by relation arcs, the frame metaphor draws concepts as boxes, i.e. frames, and relations as slots inside frames that can be filled by other frames. Thus, in the frame metaphor the graph turns into nested boxes.

The semantic network form of knowledge representation is especially suitable for capturing the taxonomic structure of categories for domain objects and for expressing general statements about the domain of interest. Inheritance and other relations between such categories can be represented in and derived from subsumption hierarchies. On the other hand, the representation of concrete individuals or even data values, like numbers or strings, does not fit well the idea of semantic networks.

Rules

Another natural form of expressing knowledge in some domain of interest are *rules* that reflect the notion of consequence. Rules come in the form of IF-THEN constructs and allow to express various kinds of complex statements. Rules can be found in logic programming systems, like the language Prolog [31], deductive databases [34] or business rules systems.

The following is an example of rules expressing knowledge in the business trips domain, specified in their intuitive if-then reading.

(1) IF *something is a flight* THEN *it is also a trip*
(2) IF *some person participates in a trip booked by some company*
THEN *this person is an employee of this company*
(3) FACT *the person MisterX participates in a flight booked by the company UbiqBiz*
(4) IF *a trip's source and destination cities are close to each other*
THEN *the trip is by train*

The IF part is also called the body of a rule, while the THEN part is also called its head. Typically, rule-based knowledge representation systems operate on facts, which are often formalised as a special kind of rule with an empty body. They start from a given set of facts, like rule (3) above, and then apply rules in order to derive new facts, thus "drawing conclusions".

However, the intuitive reading with natural language phrases is not suitable for computation, and therefore such phrases are formalised to predicates and variables over objects of the domain of interest. A formalisation of the above rules in the typical style of rule languages looks as follows.

(1) `Trip`$(?t)$ $:-$ `Flight`$(?t)$
(2) `Employee`$(?p) \wedge$ `isEmployedAt`$(?p, ?c)$ $:-$
`Trip`$(?t) \wedge$ `books`$(?c, ?t) \wedge$ `Company`$(?c) \wedge$
`participatesIn`$(?p, ?t) \wedge$ `Person`$(?p)$
(3) `Person(MisterX)` $\wedge$ `participatesIn(MisterX,FL4711)` $\wedge$
`Flight(FL4711)` $\wedge$ `books(UbiqBiz,FL4711)` $\wedge$ `Company(UbiqBiz)` $:-$
(4) `TrainRide`$(?t)$ $:-$
`Trip`$(?t) \wedge$ `startsFrom`$(?t, ?s) \wedge$ `endsIn`$(?t, ?d) \wedge$ `close`$(?s, ?d)$

In most logic programming systems, a rule is read as an inverse implication, starting with the head followed by the body, which is indicated by the symbol $:-$ that resembles a backward arrow. In this formalisation, the intuitive notions from the text, that were concepts and relations in the semantic network case, became predicates linked through variables and constants that identify objects in the domain of interest. Variables start with the symbol ? and take as their values the constants that occur in facts such as (3).

Rule (1) captures inheritance – or subsumption – between trips and flights by stating that "everything that is a flight is also a trip". Rule (2) draws conclusions about the status of employment for participants of business flights. From the facts (3), these two rules are able to derive the implicit fact that "MisterX is an employee of UbiqBiz".

While the rules (1) and (2) express general domain knowledge, rule (4) can be interpreted as part of some company's travelling policy, stating that trips between close cities shall be conducted by train. In business rules, e.g., rule-based formalisms are used with the motivation to capture complex business knowledge in companies like pricing models or delivery policies.

Rule-based knowledge representation systems are especially suitable for reasoning about concrete instance data, i.e. simple facts of the form `Employee(MisterX)`. Complex sets of rules can efficiently derive implicit facts from explicitly given ones. They are problematic if more complex and general statements about the domain shall be derived which do not fit a rule's head.

Logic

Both forms, semantic networks as well as rules, have been formalised using logic to give them a precise semantics. Without such a precise formalisation they are vague and ambiguous, and thus problematic for computational purposes. From just the graphical representation of the semantic network in Fig. 3.1, e.g., it is not clear whether companies can only book flights for their own employees or for employees of partner companies as well. Neither is it clear from the fragment $\boxed{\text{Company}} \xrightarrow{books} \boxed{\text{Trip}}$ whether every company books trips or just some company. Also for rules, despite their much more formal appearance, the exact meaning remains unclear when, e.g., forms of negation are introduced that allow for potential conflicts between rules. Depending on the choice of procedural evaluation or flavour of formal semantics, different derivation results are being produced.

The most prominent and fundamental logical formalism classically used for knowledge representation is the "first-order predicate calculus", or *first-order logic* for short, and we choose this formalism to present logic as a form of knowledge representation here. First-order logic allows one to describe the domain of interest as consisting of objects, i.e. things that have individual identity, and to construct logical formulas around these objects formed by predicates, functions, variables and logical connectives [43]. We assume that the reader is familiar with the notation of first-order logic from formalisations of various mathematical disciplines.

Similar to semantic networks, most statements in natural language can be expressed in terms of logical sentences about objects of the domain of interest with an appropriate choice of predicate and function symbols. Concepts are mapped to unary, relations to binary predicates. We illustrate the use of logic for knowledge representation by axiomatising parts of the semantic network from Fig. 3.1 more precisely.

Subsumption, e.g., can be directly expressed by a logical implication, which is illustrated in the translation of the following fragment.

$$\boxed{\text{Employee}} \xrightarrow{kindOf} \boxed{\text{Person}} \qquad \forall x : (Employee(x) \rightarrow Person(x))$$

Due to the universal quantifier, the variable x in the logical formula ranges over all domain objects and its reading is "everything that is an employee is also a person".

Other parts of the network can be further restricted using logical formulas, as shown in the following example.

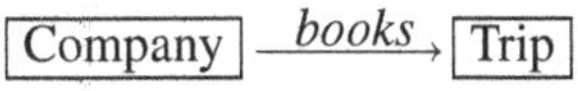

$$\boxed{\text{Company}} \xrightarrow{books} \boxed{\text{Trip}} \qquad \begin{array}{l} \forall x, y : (books(x,y) \rightarrow Company(x) \wedge Trip(y)) \\ \forall x : \exists y : (Trip(x) \rightarrow Company(y) \wedge books(y,x)) \end{array}$$

The graphical representation of the network fragment leaves some details open, while the logical formulas capture the booking relation between companies and trips more precisely. The first formula states that domain and range of the booking relation are companies and trips, respectively, while the second formula makes sure that for every trip there does actually exist a company that booked it.

In particular, more complex restrictions that range over larger fragments of a network graph can be formulated in logic, where the intuitive graphical notation lacks expressivity. As an example, consider the relations between companies, trips and employees in the following fragment.

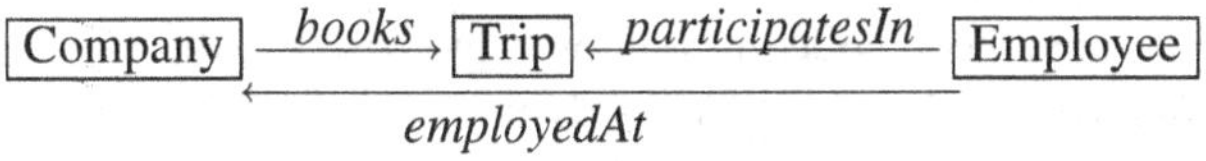

$$\boxed{\text{Company}} \xrightarrow{books} \boxed{\text{Trip}} \xleftarrow{participatesIn} \boxed{\text{Employee}}$$
$$\text{Company} \xleftarrow[employedAt]{} \text{Employee}$$

$$\forall x : \exists y : (Trip(x) \rightarrow Employee(y) \wedge participatesIn(y,x) \wedge books(employer(y),x))$$

The logical formula expresses additional knowledge that is not captured in the graph representation. It states that, for every trip, there must be an employee that participates in this trip while the employer of this participant is the company that booked the flight.

Rules can also be formalised with logic. An IF-THEN rule can be represented as a logical implication with universally quantified variables. For example, a common formalisation of the rule

IF *a trip's source and destination cities are close to each other*
THEN *the trip is by train*

is the translation to the logical formula

$$\forall x, y, z : (Trip(x) \wedge startsFrom(x,y) \wedge endsIn(x,z) \wedge close(y,z) \rightarrow TrainRide(x)).$$

However, the typical rule-based systems do not interpret such a formula in the classical sense of first-order logic but employ different kinds of semantics, which are discussed in Sect. 3.2.

Since a precise axiomatisation of domain knowledge is a prerequisite for processing knowledge within computers in a meaningful way, we focus on logic as the dominant form of knowledge representation. Therefore, we investigate different kinds of logics and formal semantics more closely in a subsequent section.

In the context of the Semantic Web, two particular logical formalisms have gained momentum, reflecting the semantic network and rules forms of knowledge representation. The graph notations of semantic networks have been formalised through *description logics*, which are fragments of first-order logic with typical

Tarskian model-theoretic semantics but restricted to unary and binary predicates to capture the notions of concepts, an relations. On the other hand, rules have been formalised through *logic programming* formalisms with minimal model semantics, focusing on the derivation of simple facts about individual objects. Both description logics and logic programming can be found as underlying formalisms in various knowledge representation languages in the Semantic Web, which are addressed in Sect. 3.4.

3.1.3 Reasoning about Knowledge

The way in which we, as humans, process knowledge is by reasoning, i.e. the process of reaching conclusions. Analogously, a computer processes the knowledge stored in a knowledge base by drawing conclusions from it, i.e. by deriving new statements that follow from the given ones.

The basic operations a knowledge-based system can perform on its knowledge base are typically denoted by `tell` and `ask` [43]. The `tell` operation adds a new statement to the knowledge base, whereas the `ask` operation is used to query what is known. The statements that have been added to a knowledge base via the `tell` operation constitute the *explicit knowledge* a system has about the domain of interest. The ability to process explicit knowledge computationally allows a knowledge-based system to reason over a domain of interest by deriving *implicit* knowledge that follows from what has been told explicitly.

This leads to the notion of logical consequence or *entailment*. A knowledge base *KB* is said to entail a statement α if α "follows" from the knowledge stored in *KB*, which is written as $KB \models \alpha$. A knowledge base entails all the statements that have been added via the `tell` operation plus those that are their logical consequences. As an example, consider the following knowledge base with sentences in first-order logic.

$$\begin{aligned} KB = \{ \; & Person(MisterX), participates(MisterX, FL4711), \\ & Flight(FL4711), books(UbiqBiz, FL4711), \\ & \forall x,y,z : (Flight(y) \wedge participates(x,y) \wedge books(z,y) \rightarrow employedAt(x,z)), \\ & \forall x,y : (employedAt(x,y) \rightarrow Company(x) \wedge Employee(y)), \\ & \forall x : (Person(x) \rightarrow \neg Company(x)) \quad \} \end{aligned}$$

The knowledge base *KB* explicitly states that "*MisterX is a person who participates in the flight FL4711 booked by UbiqBiz*", that "participants of flights are employed at the company that booked the flight", that "the employment relation holds between companies and employees" and that "persons are different from companies". If we ask the question "Is MisterX employed at UbiqBiz?" by saying

$\texttt{ask}(KB, employedAt(MisterX, UbiqBiz))$

the answer will be yes. The knowledge base *KB* entails the fact that "MisterX is employed at UbiqBiz", i.e. $KB \models employedAt(MisterX, UbiqBiz)$, although it was not "told" so explicitly. This follows from its general knowledge about the domain. A further consequence is that "UbiqBiz is a company", i.e. $KB \models Company(UbiqBiz)$, which is reflected by a positive answer to the question

`ask`$(KB, Company(UbiqBiz))$.

This follows from the former consequence together with the fact that "employment holds between companies and employees".

Another important notion related to entailment is that of consistency or *satisfiability*. Intuitively, a knowledge base is consistent or satisfiable if it does not contain contradictory facts. If we would add the fact that "UbiqBiz is a person" to the above knowledge base *KB* by saying

`tell`$(KB, Person(UbiqBiz))$,

it would become unsatisfiable because persons are said to be different from companies. We explicitly said that UbiqBiz is a person while at the same time it can be derived that it is a company.

In general, an unsatisfiable knowledge base is not very useful, since in logical formalisms it would entail any arbitrary fact. The `ask` operation would always return a positive result independent from its parameters, which is clearly not desirable for a knowledge-based system.

The inference procedures implemented in computational reasoners aim at realising the entailment relation between logical statements [43]. They derive implicit statements from a given knowledge base or check whether a particular statement is entailed by a knowledge base.

An inference procedure that only derives entailed statements is called *sound*. Soundness is a desirable feature of an inference procedure, since an unsound inference procedure would potentially draw wrong conclusions. If an inference procedure is able to derive every statement that is entailed by a knowledge base then it is called *complete*. Completeness is also a desirable property, since a complex chain of conclusions might break down if only a single statement in it is missing. Hence, for reasoning in knowledge-based systems we desire sound and complete inference procedures.

3.2 Logic-Based Knowledge-Representation Formalisms

First-order (predicate) logic is the prevalent and single most important knowledge representation formalism. Its importance stems from the fact that basically all current symbolic knowledge representation formalisms can be understood in their relation to first-order logic. Its roots can be traced back to the ancient Greek philosopher Aristotle, and modern first-order predicate logic was created in the 19th century, when the foundations for modern mathematics were laid.

First-order logic captures some of the essence of human reasoning by providing a notion of *logical consequence* as already mentioned. It also provides a notion of *universal truth* in the sense that a logical statement can be universally valid (and thus called a *tautology*), meaning that it is a statement which is true regardless of any preconditions.

Logical consequence and universal truth can be described in terms of *model-theoretic semantics*. In essence, a model for a logical theory[3] describes a state of affairs which makes the theory true. A tautology is a statement for which all possible states of affairs are models. A logical consequence of a theory is a statement which is true in *all* models of the theory.

How to derive logical consequences from a theory – a process called *deduction* or *inferencing* – is obviously central to the study of logic. Deduction allows to access knowledge which is not explicitly given but implicitly represented by a theory. Valid ways of deriving logical consequences from theories also date back to the Greek philosophers, and have been studied since.

At the heart of this is what has become known as *proof theory*. Proof theory describes syntactic rules which act on theories and allow to derive logical consequences without explicit recurrence to models. The notion of universal truth can thus be reduced to syntactic manipulations. This allows to abstract from model theory and enables deduction by symbol manipulation, and thus by automated means.

Obviously, with the advent of electronic computing devices in the 20th century, the automation of deduction has become an important and influential field of study. The field of automated reasoning is concerned with the development of efficient algorithms for deduction. These algorithms are usually required to be sound, and completeness is a desired feature.

The fact that sound and complete deduction algorithms exist for first-order predicate logic is reflected by the statement that first-order logic is *semi-decidable*. More precisely, semi-decidability of first-order logic means that there exist algorithms which, given a theory and a query statement, terminate with positive answer in finite time whenever the statement is a logical consequence of the theory. Note that for semi-decidability, termination is not required if the statement is *not* a logical consequence of the theory and, indeed, termination (with the correct negative answer) cannot be guaranteed in general for first-order logical theories.

For some kinds of theories, however, sound and complete deduction algorithms exist which always terminate. Such theories are called *decidable*, and they have certain more-or-less obvious advantages, including the following.

- Decidability guarantees that the algorithm always comes back with a correct answer in finite time.[4] Under semi-decidability, an algorithm which runs for a considerable amount of time may still terminate, or may not terminate at all, and thus the user cannot know whether he has waited long enough for an answer. Decidability is particularly important if we want to reason about the question of whether *or not* a given statement is a logical consequence of a theory.

[3] A logical theory denotes a set of logical formulas, seen as the axioms of some theory to be modelled

[4] It should be noted that there are practical limitations to this due to the fact that computing resources are always limited. A theoretically sound, complete and terminating algorithms may thus run into resource limits and terminate without an answer

- Experience shows that practically efficient algorithms are often available for decidable theories due to the effective use of heuristics. Often, this is even the case if worst-case complexity is very high.

3.2.1 Description Logics

Description logics [3] are essentially decidable fragments of first-order logic,[5] and we have just seen why the study of these is important. At the same time, description logics are expressive enough such that they have become a major knowledge representation paradigm, in particular for use within the Semantic Web.

We will describe one of the most important and influential description logics, called $\mathcal{ALC}$. Other description logics are best understood as restrictions or extensions of $\mathcal{ALC}$. We introduce the standard description logic notation and give a formal mapping into standard first-order logic syntax.

The Description Logic $\mathcal{ALC}$

A description logic theory consists of statements about concepts, individuals and their relations. Individuals correspond to constants in first-order logic, and concepts correspond to unary predicates. In terms of semantic networks, description logic concepts correspond to general concepts in semantic networks, while individuals correspond to individual concepts. We deal with concepts first, and will talk about individuals later.

Concepts can be *named concepts* or *anonymous (composite) concepts*. Named concepts consist simply of a name, say "human", which will be mapped to a unary predicate in first-order logic. Composite concepts are formed from named concepts by use of concept constructors, similar to the formation of complex formulas out of atomic formulas in first-order logic. In $\mathcal{ALC}$, we have the *boolean constructors*

- conjunction $\sqcap$, which is binary
- disjunction $\sqcup$, which is binary
- negation $\neg$, which is unary.

Hence, if C and D are concepts, then $C \sqcap D$, $C \sqcup D$ and $\neg C$ are also concepts. Concept constructors can be nested arbitrarily. The translation of boolean constructors to first-order predicate logic is obvious. To give an example, the statement $C \sqcap \neg D$ translates to the formula $C(x) \wedge \neg D(x)$.

$\mathcal{ALC}$ statements relate named or anonymous concepts by means of one of the following:

- inclusion $\sqsubseteq$
- inverse inclusion $\sqsupseteq$
- equivalence $\equiv$.

[5] To be precise, there do exist some description logics which are not decidable. And there exist some which are not straightforward fragments of first-order logics. But for this general introduction, we will not concern ourselves with these

Their meaning in first-order logic are implication $\rightarrow$ inverse implication $\leftarrow$ and equivalence $\leftrightarrow$. Occurring free variables are universally quantified. To give an example, the statement $C \sqsubseteq D \sqcup \neg E$ translates to $\forall x : (C(x) \rightarrow (D(x) \vee \neg E(x)))$.

$\mathcal{ALC}$ provides two special classes as shortcuts, namely $\bot$ and $\top$. They are defined by means of the equivalences $\bot \equiv C \sqcap \neg C$ and $\top \equiv C \sqcup \neg C$, where C is some arbitrary concept. That is, $\bot$ is the empty concept, and $\top$ is the concept under which everything falls.

$\mathcal{ALC}$ allows the restricted further use of quantifiers by means of the so-called *role restrictions*. A *role* is a named entity which translates to a binary predicate in first-order logic. In the semantic network paradigm, roles are relations between concepts. Given such a role r and a (named or anonymous) concept C, the composite concepts $\forall\, r.C$ and $\exists\, r.C$ can be formed. Role restrictions and boolean constructors can be nested arbitrarily with each other to form anonymous concepts. The composite concept $\forall\, r.C$ translates to $\forall\, y : (r(x,y) \rightarrow C(y))$ in first-order logic, while $\exists\, r.C$ translates to $\exists\, y : (R(x,y) \wedge C(y))$.

An $\mathcal{ALC}$ *TBox*, finally, consists of a set of statements of the form $C \sqsubseteq D$, $C \sqsupseteq D$ or $C \equiv D$, where C and D are named or composite concepts. Obviously, any TBox can be translated to first-order logic, and thus inherits a logical consequence relation from it.

To give some examples for TBox statements from the business trips domain,

$$Employee \sqsubseteq Person$$

encodes the knowledge that every employee is a person, while

$$Trip \sqsubseteq \exists\, bookedBy.(Company \sqcup Person)$$

states that every Trip is booked by a company or a person.

We now come to individuals, which correspond to constants in first-order logic. $\mathcal{ALC}$ allows to state that some individuals belong to (named or composite) concepts, e.g. $C(a)$ states that the individual a belongs to concept C. Similarly, a statement $r(a,b)$, where r is a role, means that the individuals a and b stand in relation r. The translation to first-order logic is obvious.

An $\mathcal{ALC}$ *ABox* consists of a set of statements of the form $C(a)$ or $R(a,b)$, where C is a named or anonymous concept, R is a role and a, b are individuals. An $\mathcal{ALC}$ *knowledge base* consists of an $\mathcal{ALC}$ ABox and an $\mathcal{ALC}$ TBox.

Examples for ABox statements are $Flight(FL4711)$ and $bookedBy(FL4711, UbiqBiz)$, with the obvious meanings.

$\mathcal{ALC}$ allows to define a basic form of knowledge bases. We have already mentioned that it appears to be somewhat akin to semantic networks, but differs in two important respects: $\mathcal{ALC}$ comes with a precise formal semantics via first-order logic, and it is more expressive due to the use of concept constructors.

Nevertheless, $\mathcal{ALC}$ is very restricted in expressiveness in comparison with other knowledge representation formalisms. This is apparent, e.g., by the very restricted kinds of first-order logical statements which are expressible in $\mathcal{ALC}$. In order to meet the requirements of practice, it is therefore necessary to extend expressiveness of $\mathcal{ALC}$. These extensions are not necessarily of a kind such that a larger fragment of first-order logic is obtained. This is indeed just one of the ways of extending $\mathcal{ALC}$ which we will examine.

Decidability-Preserving Extensions to $\mathcal{ALC}$

We have seen before that decidability is a desirable property, and so the natural question arises, which extensions of $\mathcal{ALC}$ retain its decidability. Indeed, extending $\mathcal{ALC}$ while staying within first-order logic on the one hand, and while retaining decidability on the other, has been one of the driving forces behind description logic research in the recent past. We briefly describe some of these extensions. For a comprehensive treatment of description logics, see [3].

The following additions can be made to $\mathcal{ALC}$ while retaining decidability.[6]

- Roles (i.e. binary predicates) can have additional properties such as being transitive, symmetric or inverse to other roles.
- A role can be described as the inverse of another role.
- Roles can be arranged hierarchically, i.e. a statement such as $r \sqsubseteq s$ is allowed between roles, which translates to $\forall x, y : (r(x, y) \rightarrow s(x, y))$ in first-order logic.
- Individuals can be compared, e.g. by stating explicitly that two individuals are identical ($a = b$), or different ($a \neq b$).
- It is allowed to use the so-called *nominals* in the TBox. Nominals are classes which consist of an enumeration of exactly those elements which are in the class. For example, the statement $C \equiv \{a, b, c\}$ says that the class C contains exactly the elements a, b and c.
- Quantifiers can be generalised to *number restrictions*, which yields anonymous concepts such as $\leq n\, r$ and $\geq n\, r$, where r is a role, and n is a positive integer. The first of these describes the set of all individuals x for which less than or equal to n individuals y are in relation $r(x, y)$ to x. The meaning of the second construction is analogous. Note, e.g., that $\geq 1\, r$ is equivalent to $\exists\, r.\top$.
- Roles such as the ones described so far are also called *abstract roles*. Some description logics additionally allow the use of *concrete roles*, which allow to assign datatype values such as integers or strings to individuals.

$\mathcal{ALC}$, together with the above-mentioned additions, roughly constitutes the description logic $\mathcal{SHOIN}(\mathbf{D})$. The strange acronym comes from a certain agreed-upon standard for naming description logics, where each letter stands for a specific (group of) allowed constructor(s). The $\mathcal{S}$ stands for $\mathcal{ALC}$ together with transitivity for roles. $\mathcal{H}$ stands for role hierarchies. $\mathcal{O}$ and $\mathcal{I}$ stand for nominals and for the use of inverse roles, respectively. $\mathcal{N}$ stands for number restrictions. The $\mathbf{D}$, finally, stands for the use of concrete roles and datatypes.

[6] Some minor restrictions need to be respected, which we do not include here

Non-classical Semantics

$\mathcal{SHOIN}$(**D**) is essentially still a decidable fragment of first-order predicate logic.[7] Certain expressive features, however, cannot be conveniently described by means of first-order logic. The study of such expressive features is motivated by Artificial Intelligence applications and has a long history in knowledge representation and reasoning, and most recently corresponding extensions and alterations of description logics are also being developed.

From a very general perspective, such expressive features are obtained by altering the notion of logical consequence. Recall that for first-order predicate logic a statement is a logical consequence of a theory if it is true in *all* models of the theory. Models of the theory, in turn, are interpretations (i.e. states of affairs) which make the theory true. An alternative notion of logical consequence can thus be derived by not selecting *all* interpretations which make the theory true, but only *some*, *more* or simply *other* such interpretations, and by calling those statements logical consequences, which are true in all these selected interpretations.

This endeavour, although it appears to be somewhat dubious at first, provides a general perspective on many expressive features in knowledge representation and reasoning. Important for this is certainly that the corresponding selections of interpretations are clearly defined and meaningful. Often, this selection is done most conveniently by means of additional syntax and, in the following, we will cover some additional expressive features which are most important for the Semantic Web context.

Let us remark that reasoning with expressive features is computationally expensive, and this fact is a well-known obstacle for developments in symbolic Artificial Intelligence. By means of description logics and the fact that they show reasonable scalability despite high worst-case complexities, expressive knowledge representation features become attractive for practical purposes. Of obvious importance is thus the identification of tractable description logics, as done e.g. in [18, 9, 2, 27].

3.2.2 Closed-World Assumption

The Closed-World Assumption (CWA) can be understood as a computational reinterpretation of *negation*. Roughly speaking, it is the assumption that *what cannot be proven is wrong*. Assume, e.g., the statement “if an employee is not booked on a trip at a certain date, then (s)he is available for internal meetings that day”, and assume furthermore that there is no knowledge available whether the employee MisterX is booked on a trip on a certain day. Then, under the CWA, we would conclude that MisterX is available for an internal meeting on that particular day.

A CWA perspective is particularly natural from a database point of view. An employee is assumed to be *not* booked on a trip, unless the booking can be found in the database. Thus, the database describes a *closed world*, in which all statements are either the case (if they are explicitly known) or not the case (otherwise).

[7] More precisely, it corresponds to first-order predicate logic with equality. Care needs to be taken with the encoding of number restrictions, and datatypes must be allowed as required

Treating Semantic Web knowledge under CWA, however, is conceptually difficult in some cases. This comes from the open nature of the World Wide Web, where data is constantly added and changing. Thus, if a particular piece of knowledge cannot be retrieved from the Semantic Web, then it cannot safely be assumed to be false: the information may be contained on a web page which has not been included yet, but which will be crawled next. Such a situation should be treated under the *Open-World Assumption* (OWA), which assumes that only such conclusions should be drawn which will remain valid if new information is added.

The semantics of first-order predicate logic – and thus also of description logics – operates under the OWA. If we have no knowledge about whether a person is booked on a flight, then under the OWA we cannot conclude anything on this person's availability for an internal meeting from the example statement given above.

It is safe to assume that knowledge from databases will play a natural role in the realisation of the Semantic Web, and will come alongside knowledge from other sources, like the open web. Restricting knowledge representation to pure OWA or pure CWA settings is thus insufficient: while the basic framework for the open Semantic Web should be based on the OWA, a restricted use of the CWA should be possible at the same time. This integration has become known as *Local Closed World* (LCW) [16], and is currently being researched from several perspectives. We will say more about this in the next section on non-monotonicity.

3.2.3 Non-monotonicity

The original motivation for the study of non-monotonic reasoning comes from the observation that humans tend to *jump to conclusions* when making every day practical and commonsense decisions. If we book a train trip, then we conclude that we will not be arriving by bus, and in case we have to base further decisions on the knowledge, we simply assume the conclusion to be true. However, our knowledge about the real world is never complete. It may turn out, e.g., that there is a large power outage on the day of the trip so that the trains will not run – and as a substitute, we are being transported by bus on short notice.

When *jumping to conclusions*, it may be necessary to withdraw the conclusions if further knowledge becomes available. In the example just given, we withdraw the knowledge about not arriving by bus as soon as we learn about the special circumstances. In this sense, commonsense reasoning is *non-monotonic*.

More formally, a knowledge representation formalism is called *monotonic* if a larger theory implies *more conclusions* or, in other words, if the addition of knowledge never invalidates conclusions drawn before the addition. A knowledge representation formalism is *non-monotonic* if it is not monotonic.

First-order predicate logic – and thus also description logics – are monotonic. Formalisms operating under the CWA are usually non-monotonic: if a database does not contain a booking information for MisterX being on a business trip at a certain date, then it could be concluded that MisterX is available for internal meetings at this date by an appropriate rule; if, however, such a booking information becomes known and is added to the database, then the earlier conclusion must be withdrawn.

The strong relation between CWA and non-monotonicity is well known and has inspired many lines of research in these areas. Historically, there are three major approaches to non-monotonicity, which we briefly list in the following.

Default Logic [42] uses the so-called *default rules* of the form $(\alpha : \beta)/\gamma$ for expressing the following condition for formulas α, β and γ: if α is the case and β is possible, then conclude γ. To give an example, α could be the statement "FL4711 is a trip to a foreign country", β could be the statement "FL4711 is not a train ride", and γ could be the statement "FL4711 is a flight". We further assume that we indeed know that FL4711 is a trip to a foreign country. Without any further knowledge whether FL4711 is a flight or a train ride, we conclude by the default rule that FL4711 is a flight. If we add further knowledge that FL4711 is indeed a train ride, then the conclusion must be withdrawn. In this sense, a default rule is a rule that allows for exceptions.

Circumscription [33] realises non-monotonicity by means of a condition over logical predicates which ensures that in some cases truth or falsity of a statement is enforced although this would not be the case in classical first-order predicate logic. Circumscription is expressed by means of second-order logic (see Sect. 3.2.5), and does not require any extension of syntax.

Autoepistemic Logic [35] employs a modal logic operator to represent that something is *believed* (but not necessarily known).

All three historic approaches are being studied in the context of description logics, and central references are [4], [6] and [14], respectively. It is still an open quest to find out which of these is most suitable for Semantic Web applications. Of particular importance – besides the obvious scalability requirements – is the question how the formalism realises LCW reasoning in a practically useful way.

Historically, the area of non-monotonic reasoning received decisive impulses in the 1980s and 1990s from logic programming research, which we discuss next.

3.2.4 Logic Programming

Logic programming was originally conceived as a way to use (first-order predicate) logic as a programming language. In order to allow for efficient computation, formulas were syntactically restricted to the so-called *Horn clauses*. Additionally, only certain kinds of logical consequences are being considered.

Syntactically, Horn clauses can be understood as rules. For example, the expression $\mathit{Trip}(t) \vee \neg\, \mathit{Flight}(t)$ is a Horn clause, which is semantically equivalent (with respect to FOL) to $\forall t : \mathit{Trip}(t) \leftarrow \mathit{Flight}(t)$. This, in turn, can also be interpreted as the rule `Trip(?t) :- Flight(?t)` from page 55.

Note, however, that the semantics of the Horn clause is given by means of first-order logic semantics, whereas logic programming rules are usually understood in a different sense. One of the differences stems from the fact that in a logic programming system only certain types of logical consequences are being considered, namely ground[8] instances of predicates. In the example, the addition of a fact `Flight(FL4711)` would allow to conclude `Trip(FL4711)` both in FOL and in a logic programming system. A conclusion such as `Trip(FL4711)` $\vee$ $\neg$ `Flight(FL4711)`, however, would be possible only in FOL, and not derivable using logic programming semantics.

The second difference between the semantics concerns the handling of negative information. In the example above, we could be interested in whether the statement `Trip(FL2306)` holds. In FOL, neither truth nor falsity of this statement is derivable. In logic programming, however, the statement would be considered false. The handling of negative information in logic programming in this sense is based on the CWA: as no information on `FL2306` is available, it is considered to be *not* a trip.

Logic programming semantics is thus non-monotonic: just consider adding the single fact `Flight(FL2306)` to the knowledge base, by which `Trip(FL2306)` turns true. This insight triggered substantial research efforts on relating logic programming and non-monotonic reasoning, which led to the introduction of non-monotonic kinds of negation into the logic programming paradigm, see [1].

How to combine logic programming or other rules formalisms with description logics constitutes a recent research issue. Prominent approaches include the creation of hybrid systems by interfacing logic programming systems with description logic systems, as e.g. in [15]. Other approaches simply go back to Horn clauses and add them as FOL statements to description logic knowledge bases [26].

3.2.5 Higher-Order Logic

Another feature which is considered important for knowledge representation in the Semantic Web is what has become known as *metamodelling*. This occurs, e.g., whenever description logic classes should be considered as individual members of other (meta-)classes, or if properties shall be attached to entire classes by means of roles. Logically, this corresponds to using high-order logics, and generally results in the loss of decidability. Decidable fragments, however, can be described, as in [36].

To give an example, consider an international company using a semantics-based knowledge management system for business trips, which requires that different languages spoken within the company are supported by the system. It may thus be necessary to represent the knowledge that the concept *Flight* is called "*Flug*" in German. This could be represented by using a concrete role statement like *germanName*(*Flight*, "*Flug*"). Here, "*Flug*" would be a data value of type string, while the concept *Flight* actually appears syntactically as an individual. Notice that here a data value is directly assigned to a concept rather than to its instances.

3.2.6 Treatment of Inconsistencies

A point of particular importance for the Semantic Web lies in a sensible treatment of inconsistencies in knowledge bases. This comes from the fact that in Semantic

[8] A ground (instance of a) predicate is an atomic formula which does not contain any variable symbols

Web applications it is very often necessary to merge different knowledge bases from different sources, and it can be expected that in many cases some parts of the respective knowledge bases may conflict with each other, resulting in inconsistency. In a classical FOL setting, a single inconsistency causes a knowledge base to be entirely useless. For practical purposes, however, it should be possible to rescue at least some of the knowledge in a constructive way in order to draw meaningful conclusions from the knowledge.

There exist two basic approaches to dealing with inconsistency. The first one is based on the intuition that inconsistencies point to mistakes in modelling, and thus should be repaired. Technically, such repairs can be done by identifying, e.g., maximal consistent subsets of the knowledge base and using those for drawing conclusions, see e.g. [48]. The other approach is based on using the so-called *paraconsistent logics* with an additional truth value which represents contradiction, see e.g. [50].

3.2.7 Uncertainty

Knowledge is often acquired by machine learning techniques. Knowledge base statements obtained this way are usually uncertain, e.g. in a probabilistic sense or in the sense of fuzzy logic. Recent efforts are thus under way to provide methods and tools for the representation and the reasoning with uncertainty in description logics.

To give an example, consider a business trips booking Internet portal which uses a knowledge base for providing personalised content to the user. From the usage patterns of *UbiqBiz* customers the knowledge base knows with a probability of 80% that a *UbiqBiz* customer browsing the portal will be interested in booking a flight, and is thus able to provide appropriate personalised content. As part of a sophisticated personalisation knowledge base, the treatment of such probabilities and other uncertainty values becomes important.

3.3 Ontologies in Information Systems

Recently, the notion of ontologies as computational artefacts has appeared in Artificial Intelligence and Computer Science, while "ontology" originally denotes the study of existence in philosophy. In information systems, ontologies are conceptual models of what "exists" in some domain, brought into machine-interpretable form by means of knowledge representation techniques. In this section we start from a general definition of the notion of ontology and elaborate on its appearance and usage in computer science.

3.3.1 Ontology

In its original meaning in philosophy, *ontology* is a branch of metaphysics and denotes the philosophical investigation of existence. It is concerned with the fundamental questions of "what is being?" and "what kinds of things are there?" [11].

Dating back to Aristotle, the question of "what exists?" lead to studying general categories for all things that exist. Ontological categories provide a means to classify all existing things, and the systematic organisation of such categories allows to analyse the world that is made up by these things in a structured way. In ontology, categories are also referred to as *universals*, and the concrete things that they serve to classify are referred to as *particulars*.

Philosophers have mostly been concerned with general top-level hierarchies of universals that cover the entire physical world. Examples of universals occurring in such top-level hierarchies are most general and abstract concepts like "substance", "physical object", "intangible object", "endurant" or "perdurant". Philosophers have argued about the appropriateness of different such abstract categorisations and about the general properties of everything existing. Transferred to knowledge representation and computer science, information systems can benefit from the idea of ontological categorisation. When applied to a limited domain of interest in the scope of a concrete application scenario, ontology can be restricted to cover a special subset of the world. Examples of ontological categories in the business trips domain are "Person", "Company", "Trip" or "Flight", whereas examples for particular individuals that are classified by these categories are the person "MisterX", the company "UbiqBiz" or the particular flight "FL4711".

In general, the choice of ontological categories and particular objects in some domain of interest determines the things about which knowledge can be represented in a computer system [45]. In this sense, ontology provides the labels for nodes and arcs in a semantic network or the names for predicates and constants in rules or logical formulas that constitute an *ontological vocabulary*. By defining "what exists" it determines the things that can be predicated about. The terms of the ontological vocabulary are then used to represent knowledge, forming statements about the domain.

3.3.2 Ontologies

While "ontology" studies what exists in a domain of interest, "an ontology" as a computational artefact encodes knowledge about this domain in a machine-processable form to make it available to information systems.

Definition of an Ontology

In various application contexts, and within different communities, ontologies have been explored from different points of view, and there exist several definitions of what an ontology is. Within the Semantic Web community the dominating definition of *an ontology* is the following, based on [19].

> An *ontology* is a formal explicit specification of a shared conceptualisation of a domain of interest.

This definition captures several characteristics of an ontology as a specification of domain knowledge, namely the aspects of formality, explicitness, being shared, conceptuality and domain-specificity, which require some explanation.

- *Formality*
  An Ontology is expressed in a knowledge representation language that provides a formal semantics. This ensures that the specification of domain knowledge in an ontology is machine-processable and is being interpreted in a well-defined way. The techniques of knowledge representation help to realise this aspect.
- *Explicitness*
  An ontology states knowledge explicitly to make it accessible for machines. Notions that are not explicitly included in the ontology are not part of the machine-interpretable conceptualisation it captures, although humans might take them for granted by common sense.[9]
- *Being shared*
  An ontology reflects an agreement on a domain conceptualisation among people in a community. The larger the community the more difficult it is to come to an agreement on sharing the same conceptualisation. Thus, an ontology is always limited to a particular group of people in a community, and its construction is associated with a social process of reaching consensus.
- *Conceptuality*
  An ontology specifies knowledge in a conceptual way in terms of symbols that represent concepts and their relations. The concepts and relations in an ontology can be intuitively grasped by humans, as they correspond to the elements in our mental model. (In contrast to this, the weights in a neural network or the probability measures in a Bayesean network would not fit such a conceptual and symbolic approach.) Moreover, an ontology describes a conceptualisation in general terms and does not only capture a particular state of affairs. Instead of making statements about a specific situation involving particular individuals, an ontology tries to cover as many situations as possible, that can potentially occur [21].
- *Domain specificity*
  The specifications in an ontology are limited to knowledge about a particular domain of interest. The narrower the scope of the domain for the ontology, the more an ontology engineer can focus on axiomatising the details in this domain rather than covering a broad range of related topics. In this way, the explicit specification of domain knowledge can be modularised and expressed using several different ontologies with separate domains of interest.

Technically, the principal constituents of an ontology are *concepts*, *relations* and *instances*. Concepts map to the generic nodes in semantic networks, or to unary

[9] Notice that this notion of explicitness is different from the distinction between explicit and implicit knowledge, introduced earlier. Implicit knowledge that can be derived by means of automated deduction does not need to be included in an ontology for a computer system to access it. However, knowledge that is neither explicitly stated nor logically follows from what is stated can by no means be processed within the machine, although it might be obvious to a human. Such knowledge remains implicit in the modeller's mind and is not represented in the machine

predicates in logic, or to concepts as in description logics. They represent the ontological categories that are relevant in the domain of interest. Relations map to arcs in semantic networks, or to binary predicates in logic, or to roles in description logics. They semantically connect concepts, as well as instances, specifying their interrelations. Instances map to individual nodes in semantic networks, or to constants in logic. They represent the named and identifiable concrete objects in the domain of interest, i.e. the particular individuals which are classified by concepts.

These elements constitute an ontological vocabulary for the respective domain of interest. An ontology can be viewed as a set of statements, expressed in terms of this vocabulary, which are also referred to as *axioms*. A simple axiom would, e.g., state that "Mister X is an employee", involving an instance and a concept. A more complex axiom could state that "only employees of a particular company can be on trips booked by this company", imposing a restriction on a relation between two concepts.

Conceptual modelling with ontologies seems to be very similar to modelling in object-oriented software development or to designing entity-relationship diagrams for database schemas. However, there is a subtle twofold difference. First, ontology languages usually provide a richer formal semantics than object-oriented or database-related formalisms. They support encoding of complex axiomatic information due to their logic-based notations. Hence, an ontology specifies a semantically rich axiomatisation of domain knowledge rather than a mere data or object model. Second, ontologies are usually developed for a different purpose than object-oriented models or entity-relationship diagrams. While the latter mostly describe components of an information system to be executed on a machine and a schema for data storage, respectively, an ontology captures domain knowledge as such and allows to reason about it.

In summary, an ontology used in an information system is a conceptual yet executable model of an application domain. It is made machine-interpretable by means of knowledge representation techniques and can therefore be used by applications to base decisions on reasoning about domain knowledge.

Appearance of Ontologies

When engineered for or processed by information systems, ontologies appear in different forms related to the forms of knowledge representation which we discussed. A knowledge engineer views an ontology by means of some graphical or formal visualisation, while for storage or transfer it is encoded in an ontology language with some machine-processable serialisation format. A reasoner, in turn, interprets an ontology as a set of axioms that constitute a logical theory. We illustrate these different forms of appearance in ontology engineering, machine-processing and reasoning by an example.

Our business trips scenario, introduced earlier, involves several domains of interest. On the one hand, reasoning about business trips requires knowledge about travelling infrastructure for trains, flights and rental cars, while on the other hand it involves financial knowledge about prices, different currencies and methods of payment when it comes to comparing different offers. Yet another related domain is that of geographic knowledge about locations of sources and destinations for trips, which we pick up as an example to illustrate appearance of ontologies. All these different domains of interest can be thought of as being captured by a modularised set of ontologies to which an information system in the business trips scenario can have access.

A geographic ontology suitable for a business trips booking system encodes countries and continents with their geographic regions, as well as geographic features like rivers, roads, rail tracks or cities. It relates geographic features to their regions, stating, e.g., that a city occupies a certain region, and it defines containment between such regions; the geographic region of a European city is, e.g., contained in that of Europe. Besides these general geographic concepts and their relations, such an ontology also determines concrete instances, such as particular cities, countries and continents, and relates them appropriately.

To a knowledge engineer an ontology is often visualised as some form of semantic network. Figure 3.2 shows the graphical visualisation of an example geographic ontology.

As common to most ontology development environments,[10] the visualisation in Fig. 3.2 presents to the knowledge engineer a taxonomy, i.e. a subsumption hierarchy, of the concepts in the ontology, which is indicated by $\xrightarrow{isa}$ links. The two taxonomies exposed in the graph are those for *GeographicRegion* with subconcepts

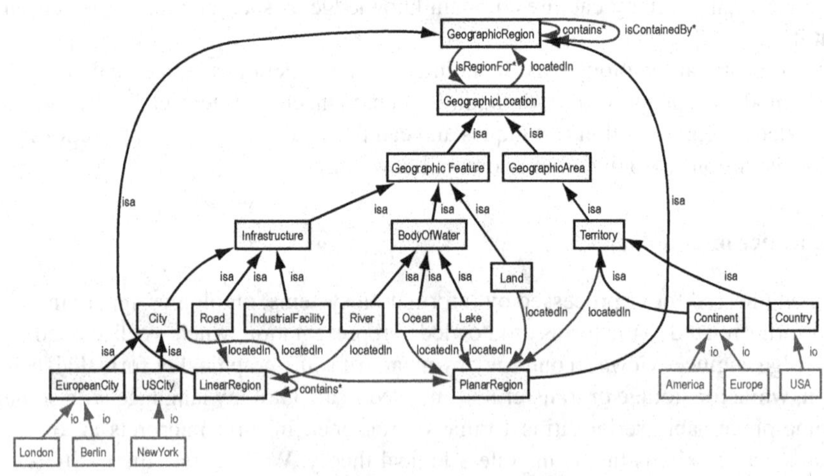

Fig. 3.2. A graphical visualisation for a geographic ontology

[10] The ontology graph in Fig. 3.2 has been produced with the OntoViz-plugin for the Protégé environment (`http://protege.stanford.edu/plugins/owl/`)

for linear and planar regions, and for *GeographicLocation* with subconcepts for geographic features, like cities or rivers, and geographic areas, like continents or countries. In the visualisation, the knowledge engineer can also see conceptual relations as arcs pointing from their domain concept to their range concept. By the relation $\xrightarrow{locatedIn}$ between *GeographicLocation* and *GeographicRegion* a location, such as a city or a country, is associated to some region in which it is actually located. A *Road* or *River* is further restricted to be located in a *LinearRegion*, whereas a *City* or *Lake* is located in a *PlanarRegion* encompassing a surface area. The graph also shows some concrete cities and countries, modelled as instances of their respective concepts, which here serve as representatives for all the particular geographic places such an ontology would be populated with.

Not all the information in an ontology can easily be visualised in a graph as the one shown in Fig. 3.2. For some more detailed information, such as complex axioms and restrictions on concepts, there does not exist to date any appropriate visualisation paradigm other than exposing such fragments of the ontology in a formal language. Therefore, ontology engineering environments usually provide extra means for displaying and editing such complex axiomatic information, using a special-purpose ontology language or logical formal notation. When the environment exports the ontology for storage on a disk or for transfer over the wire, all of its information is expressed in the ontology language supported by the tool. Hence, the way an ontology appears to a developer of an ontology editor, storage facility or reasoner is in the form of ontology language constructs in some serialisation format suitable for machine processing.

There are various ontology languages, based on different knowledge representation formalisms, and we investigate the most prevalent of them in Sect. 3.4. For illustrating a fragment of our example geographic ontology, we choose the OWL[11] ontology language. The following listing displays a part of the ontology encoded in the OWL RDF serialisation format.

```
...
<owl:Class rdf:ID="City">
    <rdfs:subClassOf>
        <owl:Restriction>
            <owl:onProperty rdf:resource="#locatedIn"/>
            <owl:allValuesFrom rdf:resource="#PlanarRegion"/>
        </owl:Restriction>
    </rdfs:subClassOf>
    <rdfs:subClassOf rdf:resource="#Infrastructure"/>
    <owl:disjointWith rdf:resource="#Road"/>
    <owl:disjointWith rdf:resource="#IndustrialFacility"/>
</owl:Class>
<owl:ObjectProperty rdf:ID="locatedIn">
    <rdf:type rdf:resource="&owl;FunctionalProperty"/>
    <rdfs:domain rdf:resource="#GeographicLocation"/>
    <rdfs:range rdf:resource="#GeographicRegion"/>
    <owl:inverseOf rdf:resource="#isRegionFor"/>
</owl:ObjectProperty>
<EuropeanCity rdf:ID="London"/>
...
```

[11] The DL-based Web Ontology Language (OWL) is popular in the Semantic Web context, and it is described in Sect. 3.4 among other languages

The listing shows an excerpt of the geographic ontology as it is serialised and parsed by tools and transferred over the network. It exhibits the specification of OWL classes (concepts), properties (relations) and individuals (instances), all expressed by tags and attributes of a customised XML serialisation. The *City* concept is defined as a subconcept of *Infrastructure* with the restriction that the relation $\xrightarrow{locatedIn}$ can only have instances of *PlanarRegion* as values. The relation $\xrightarrow{locatedIn}$ is defined as functional (having a unique value) and as being inverse to $\xrightarrow{isRegionFor}$, with proper domain and range concepts. *London* is introduced as an instance of *EuropeanCity*.

As ontology languages like OWL are based on logical formalisms, the formal semantics of the language precisely defines the meaning of an ontology in terms of logic. To a reasoner, therefore, an ontology appears as a set of logical formulas that express the axioms of a logical theory. It can verify whether these axioms are consistent or derive logical consequences. This form of appearance of an ontology is free of syntactical or graphical additions or ambiguities and reflects the pure knowledge representation aspect.

We use the description logic notation for OWL to exemplify some of the axioms in our example geographical ontology in their logical form. The following DL formulas constitute the definition of a European city.

$$\begin{array}{rcl}
\exists\, locatedIn.\top & \sqsubseteq & GeographicLocation \\
\top & \sqsubseteq & \forall\, locatedIn.GeographicRegion \\
\exists\, contains.\top & \sqsubseteq & GeographicRegion \\
\top & \sqsubseteq & \forall\, contains.GeographicRegion \\
GeographicLocation & \sqsubseteq & =1\ locatedIn \\
Continent & \sqsubseteq & GeographicLocation \\
Continent & (Europe) & \\
PlanarRegion & \sqsubseteq & GeographicRegion \\
City & \sqsubseteq & GeographicLocation \sqcap \forall\, locatedIn.PlanarRegion \\
EuropeanCity & \equiv & City \sqcap \forall\, locatedIn.\exists\, contains^{-}.\exists\, locatedIn^{-}.\{Europe\}
\end{array}$$

The last, quite sophisticated formula defines the concept of a European city by its geographical region being contained in the geographical region of the European continent. It has the following translation to first-order logic.

$$\begin{array}{l}
\forall x : (EuropeanCity(x) \leftrightarrow \\
\qquad City(x) \wedge \forall y : (locatedIn(x,y) \rightarrow \exists z : (contains(z,y) \wedge locatedIn(Europe,z))))
\end{array}$$

In prose, its reading is as follows: "European cities are cities for which all geographic regions they are located in are contained in some geographic region in which Europe is located." This allows a knowledge-based system to decide whether a city is European by reasoning over containment of geographic regions.

In this logical form, an ontology is the set of axioms that constitutes the explicit knowledge represented about its domain of interest. By means of automated deduction, implicit knowledge of the same form can be derived but is not part of the ontology's explicit specification.

3.3.3 Usage of Ontologies

Often, an ontology is distinguished from a knowledge base in that it is supposed to describe knowledge on a schema level, i.e. in terms of conceptual taxonomies and general statements, whereas the more data-intensive knowledge base is thought of containing instance information on particular situations. We take a different perspective and perceive the relation between an ontology and a knowledge base as the connection between an epistemological specification of domain knowledge and a technical tool for reasoning. From this point of view, an ontology is a piece of knowledge that can be used by a knowledge-based application among other pieces of knowledge, e.g. other ontologies or meta data. To properly cover its domain of interest, it can make use of both schema level and instance level information. Whenever the knowledge-based system needs to consult the ontology, it loads (parts of) its specification into a knowledge base, most likely together with other pieces of knowledge, to take it into account for reasoning. The business trips booking system, e.g., would probably make combined use of a geographical ontology, a financial one, and one for public transportation, when comparing offers for trips, loading all relevant domain knowledge in its knowledge base. In this sense, a knowledge-based application uses an ontology via its knowledge base.

The computational domain model of an ontology can be used for various purposes, depending on the application scenario. We distinguish the different cases of usage on diverse levels, as follows.

- Level of knowledge connectivity
  An application can view an ontology as its single and isolated source of knowledge in a stand-alone fashion. This is the way an expert system maintains a highly specialised knowledge base to answer questions in its domain of interest, simulating expert knowledge.

  In contrast to this, an ontology can also be viewed in relation to other sources of knowledge, such as other ontologies or meta data that is aligned to the ontology's conceptual model. In an information integration scenario, e.g., an ontology supports interoperability among different systems on the knowledge or data level, providing a basic domain vocabulary.
- Level of knowledge abstraction
  On the one hand, an application can process an ontology on the schema level of knowledge about categories. Examples for this are applications which need to automatically classify user-defined concepts in an existing taxonomy or which build upon answers to general domain questions.

  On the other hand, an ontology can be used as a schema for data-intensive instance retrieval on large knowledge or databases.
- Level of automation in knowledge processing
  An application can make intensive use of automated reasoning techniques in order to derive implicit knowledge from the axioms in an ontology, answering sophisticated domain questions.

At the same time, ontologies can also be used for documentation and reference purposes, targeting humans to read their specifications rather than machines. This way, the documentation of domain models benefits from precise specification through the formal semantics of ontology languages.

In Artificial Intelligence research, some typical types of applications have evolved that make use of ontologies in different ways. We list some of them as examples of how applications can leverage the formalised conceptual domain models that ontologies provide.

- Information integration
  A promising field of application for ontologies is their use for integrating heterogeneous information sources on the schema level. Often, different databases store the same kind of information but adhere to different data models. An ontology can be used to mediate between database schemas, allowing to integrate information from differently organised sources and to interpret data from one source under the schema of another.

  Our example geographic ontology could be used to integrate geographic databases with different schemas; for example, one relating cities directly to their countries as different entities and another modelling a single entity for geographic places which have the property of being either a city or a country. In either schema, the local entities and relations can be mapped to the respective notions of *City*, *Country*, *GeographicRegion* and $\xrightarrow{locatedIn}$ in the ontology, realising unified querying and reasoning over both information sources.
- Information retrieval
  Motivated by the success and key role of Google[12] in the World Wide Web, information retrieval on web documents is a major field of application for ontologies. The idea behind ontology-based information retrieval is to increase the precision of retrieval results by taking into account the semantic information contained in queries and documents, lifting keywords to ontological concepts and relations.

  When interpreted according to our example geographic ontology, a query like "capital of Germany" would yield documents that are about Berlin, the capital of Germany. Some of the false positive matches that keyword-based retrieval systems typically produce, such as documents about the German venture capital market, can be filtered out this way.
- Semantically enhanced content management
  In many areas of computation, the data that is actually computed is annotated with meta data for various purposes. Ontologies provide the domain-specific vocabulary for annotating data with meta data. The formality of ontology languages allows for an automated processing of this meta data and their grounding in knowledge representation facilitates machine-interpretability.

  The geographic concepts and relations provided by our example ontology could be used to annotate manifold geographic content, such as geographic books and articles in an electronic library to better find and archive them or 3D-models

[12] `http://www.google.com`

of geographic sites in surveying and mapping, in order to better group and relate them, providing easier access to their content.

- Knowledge management and community portals
  In companies or other organised associations, or in communities of practice, individual knowledge can be viewed as a strategic resource that is desirable to be shared and systematically maintained, which is referred to as *knowledge management*. Ontologies provide a means to unify knowledge management efforts under a shared conceptual domain model, connecting technical systems for navigating, storing, searching and exchanging community knowledge.

  Our example ontology could serve as the backbone for a geographic knowledge portal in the Internet, through which land surveying offices, urban planning institutions and other interested community members provide access to geography-related resources.
- Expert systems
  In various domains, such as medical diagnosis or legal advice in case-law, it is desirable to simulate a domain expert who can be asked sophisticated questions. In an expert system, this is achieved by incorporating a thoroughly developed domain ontology that formalises expert knowledge. Domain-specific questions can then be answered by reasoning over such highly specialised knowledge.

  An expert system for the geographical domain could answer questions like "Which is the German city closest to the French border? "or "Through which cities does the river Rhein flow? ".

3.3.4 Types of Ontologies

Since the beginning of ontology research in Computer Science, ontologies have been considered as a means to foster reuse within knowledge-based system engineering, and it turned out that different types of ontologies exhibit a different potential for reuse.

A categorisation of ontologies can be made according to their subject of conceptualisation. The most prominent insights in this respect have been published in [20] and are summarised in Fig. 3.3.

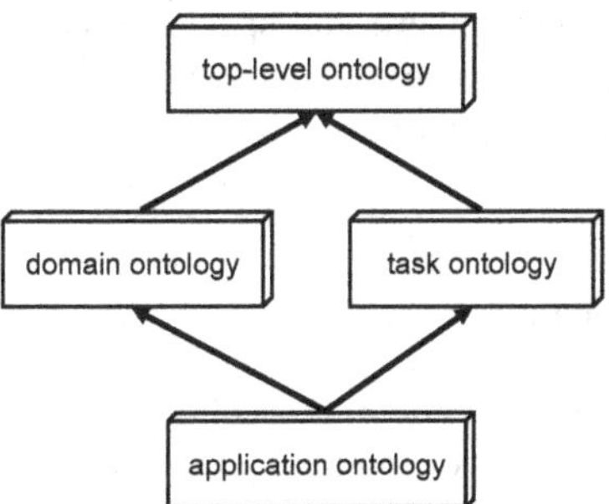

Fig. 3.3. Types of ontologies

The categorisation in Fig. 3.3 distinguishes the following types of ontologies.

- Top-level ontologies
  Top-level ontologies – also called upper ontologies or foundational ontologies – attempt to describe very abstract and general concepts that can be shared across many domains and applications. They borrow from philosophical notions, describing top-level concepts for all things that exist, such as "physical object" or "abstract object", as well as generic notions of common-sense knowledge about phenomena as time, space, processes, etc. They are usually well thought out and extensively axiomatised. Due to their generality, they are typically not directly used in applications but for other ontologies to be aligned to. Prominent examples for top-level ontologies are DOLCE [17] and SUMO [39].
- Domain ontologies and task ontologies
  These types of ontologies capture the knowledge within a specific domain of discourse, such as medicine or geography, or the knowledge about a particular task, such as diagnosing or configuring. In this sense, they have a much narrower and more specific scope than top-level ontologies. In the ideal case, the conceptualisation in a domain ontology is kept strictly task independent, while the notions in a task ontology are described neutrally with respect to a domain. Much work has been done in the development of domain ontologies in medicine, genetics, geographic and environment information, tourism, as well as cultural heritage and museum exhibits. Task ontologies have been devised, e.g., for scheduling and planning tasks, monitoring in a scientific domain, intelligent computer-based tutoring, missile tracking, execution of clinical guidelines, etc.
- Application ontologies
  Further narrowing the scope, application ontologies provide the specific vocabulary required to describe a certain task enactment in a particular application context. They typically make use of both domain and task ontologies, and describe, e.g., the role that some domain entity plays in a specific task. For example, a particular physical entity in some engineering domain may play the role of a replaceable unit in a machine diagnosis and maintenance task, and at the same time play the role of a spare resource in a configuration or production process.

Altogether, we can say that the lattice indicated in Fig. 3.3 represents an inclusion hierarchy: the lower ontologies inherit and specialise concepts and relations from the upper ones. The lower ontologies are more specific and have thus a narrower application scope, whereas the upper ones have a broader potential for reuse.

3.3.5 Ontologies in the Semantic Web

In the context of the Semantic Web, ontologies play a particularly important key role. The idea of the Semantic Web is to annotate web content by machine-interpretable meta data such that computers are able to process this content on a semantic level. Ontologies provide the domain vocabulary in terms of which semantic annotation is formulated. Meta statements about web content in such annotations refer to a commonly used domain model by including the concepts, relations and instances of a domain ontology. The formality of ontology languages allows to reason about semantic annotation from different sources, connected to background knowledge in the domain of interest. There are a couple of characteristics of the web which affect the use of ontologies for semantic annotation.

One aspect is the natural distributedness of content in the Semantic Web. The knowledge captured in semantic annotation and ontologies is not locally available at a single node but spread over different sites. This poses additional constraints on the use of ontologies in the Semantic Web, taking into account distributedness of knowledge. To avoid the need to transfer relevant knowledge to a central location, there should be techniques that allow for a modularisation of the reasoning process by handling partial results that are computed locally, based on a subset of all relevant information. This issue is addressed by current research on *distributed reasoning*.

Another related aspect is that content on the web is created in an evolutionary manner and maintained in a decentralised way. There is no central control over semantic annotation and ontologies that evolve in the Semantic Web, and information in one ontology can conflict with information in another one. To deal with conflicting pieces of knowledge, there should be techniques that resolve such situations by, e.g., preferring one or another consistent sub view, similar to how humans would do. Such techniques are subject to investigation in current research on *paraconsistent reasoning*, as mentioned in Sect. 3.2.6.

There is an extra chapter dedicated to the topic of semantic annotation, namely Chap. 5, in which the usage of ontologies for annotating web content with meta data in the Semantic Web context is further elaborated on.

3.4 Ontology Languages

To make ontologies available to information systems, various concrete ontology languages have been designed and proposed for standardisation. In this section, we give an overview of the most prevalent ontology languages that are important in the context of the Semantic Web, and present some of them in detail.

3.4.1 Hierarchy of Languages for the Semantic Web

In the light of widespread impact and industrial usability, the standardisation of ontology languages is of great importance to the Semantic Web community. Various different aspects are considered for language standardisation, such as issues of the underlying knowledge representation formalism in terms of expressiveness and computational properties, web-related features like global unique identification and XML serialisation syntax, or usability add-ons like the inclusion of strings and numbers or non-functional meta data. The influence of different research and user communities with manifold requirements have resulted in a complex landscape of a multitude of languages backed by different past and ongoing standardisation efforts. Which languages are best suited for what purpose, how they can be efficiently implemented and realised in a user-friendly way, or technically and semantically made interoperable is still an open topic stimulating lively discussions in current research.

In Fig. 3.4 we make an attempt to sketch this landscape of languages, giving an overview of the most important ontology languages with respect to current trends in the Semantic Web. Since some languages build on others and on formerly achieved standards, this landscape can be perceived as a hierarchy of languages for the Semantic Web. However, besides a hierarchical structure with some languages being clearly layered on top of others, there are also parallel branches and cross-relations between languages and formalisms.[13]

One of the major distinctions of Semantic Web languages is by the knowledge representation paradigm they follow. On the left-hand side in Fig. 3.4 there is the description logic family of languages that build on various DL dialects and their rule-extensions. They adhere to the classical model-theoretic semantics of first-order predicate logic and to the open-world assumption. On the right-hand side there is the family of logic programming languages that build on rules with

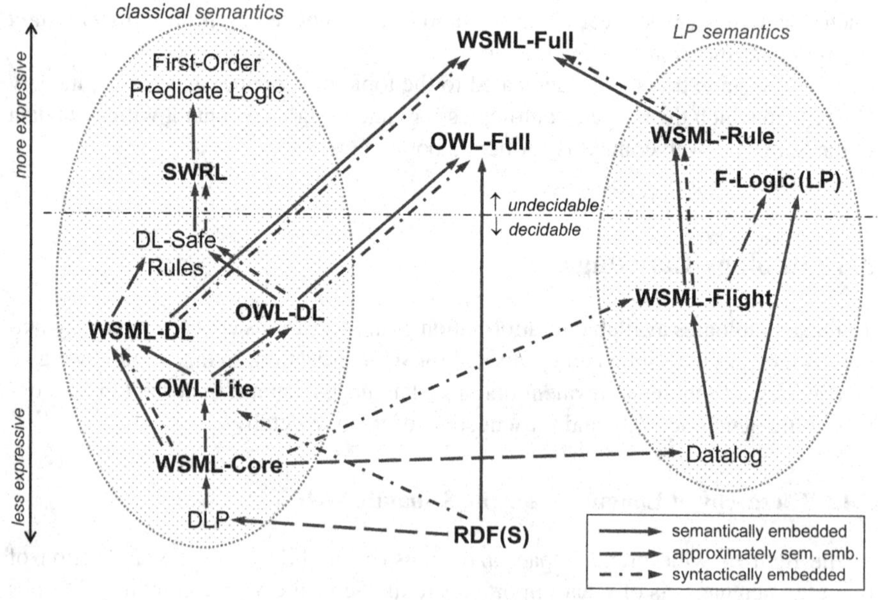

Fig. 3.4. An overview of Semantic Web languages

[13] This figure shall convey a rough intuition about the relationships between major languages with respect to their underlying knowledge representation formalisms and paradigms. It therefore abstracts from certain language details and is necessarily imprecise and vague in some aspects

negation-as-failure. They typically follow a semantics of minimal or preferred models and adhere to the closed-world assumption. There are also languages in between these two main strands, which cannot be clearly assigned to either paradigm. These have been designed with a focus set on aspects other than a logically clear semantics, or are attempts to combine features from both worlds, while the pure DL and LP family languages have well understood properties in terms of computability and inferential behaviour.

Languages that are placed near to the top in Fig. 3.4 are more expressive than languages that are placed close to the bottom, meaning that they allow for expressing more complex knowledge and for richer inferencing through more sophisticated logical consequences than less expressive languages do. Accordingly, high expressivity of a language is traded for higher computational complexity of decision procedures for reasoning. Within recent standardisation efforts, it is considered highly desirable to at least maintain decidability as a design goal for a Semantic Web ontology language, and Fig. 3.4 shows a boundary for decidability, above of which languages do not meet this goal.

Three different kinds of arrows in Fig. 3.4 express a relationship of embedment between languages. A solid arrow denotes complete semantic containedness of a less expressive language in a more expressive one, meaning that anything that can be expressed in the former can also be expressed in the latter by means of a direct mapping of languages constructs. A dashed arrow denotes a weaker form of embedding, where not all the features of the less expressive language do completely fit the more expressive target language, meaning that the former is in principle (approximately) covered by the latter, apart from moderate deficiencies in some language constructs and their semantic interpretation. A dash-dotted arrow denotes a syntactic embedding such that the language constructs of the (syntactically) less expressive language can be directly used in the more expressive one, although they may semantically be interpreted in a different way.

An early initiative to standardise a language for semantic annotation of web resources by the World Wide Web consortium (W3C) resulted in *RDF* and *RDFS*, which form now a well established and widely accepted standard for encoding meta data. The *RDF(S)* language is described in more detail in Sect. 3.4.2. It can be used to express class-membership of resources and subsumption between classes but its peculiar semantics does fit neither the classical nor the LP-style. If semantically restricted to a first-order setting, RDF(S) can be mapped to a formalism named description logic programs (*DLP*) [18], which is sometimes used to interoperate between DL and LP by reducing expressiveness to their intersection.

On top of RDF(S), W3C standardisation efforts have produced the *OWL* family of languages for describing ontologies in the Semantic Web, which comes in several flavours with increasing expressiveness. Only the most expressive language variant, namely *OWL-Full,* has a semantically proper layering on top of RDF(S), allowing for features of metamodelling and reification. The less expressive variants *OWL-Lite* and *OWL-DL* map to certain description logic dialects and fit the classical semantics as subsets of *first-order logic*. Besides the class membership and subsumption relations inherited from RDF(S), OWL offers the construction of complex classes from simpler ones by means of DL-style concepts constructors. Among ongoing standardisation efforts, OWL-DL is currently the most prominent Semantic Web ontology language following the description logic paradigm, and in Sect. 3.4.3 the OWL family is described in more detail.

A current trend in research on knowledge representation formalisms in the context of the Semantic Web is to integrate DL-style ontologies with LP-style rules to be interoperable on a semantic level. One attempt to do so is the Semantic Web Rule Language *SWRL*)[14] that extends the set of OWL axioms to include Horn-like rules interpreted under first-order semantics. Interoperability with OWL ontologies is realised by referring to OWL classes and properties within SWRL rules; however, the combination of OWL-DL and SWRL rules results in an undecidable formalism. Another approach to amalgamate OWL ontologies and rules are the so-called *DL-safe rules* [38], which extend DL knowledge bases in a way similar to SWRL. However, DL-safe rules preserve decidability of the resulting language by imposing an additional safety restriction on SWRL rules which ensures that they are only applied to individuals explicitly known to the knowledge base.

Languages that follow the logic programming paradigm mainly stem from deductive database systems, which apply rules on the facts stored in a database to derive new facts by means of logical inferencing. A common declarative language used in deductive databases is *Datalog* [47], which is syntactically similar to *Prolog* [31]. In the Semantic Web context, *F-Logic* is a more prominent rule language that combines logical formulas with object-oriented and frame-based description features. In its logic programming variant *F-Logic (LP)*, it adopts the semantics of Datalog rules. In Sect. 3.4.4 we investigate F-Logic in more detail.

Finally, the Web Service Modeling Language (*WSML*) family is the most recent attempt to standardise ontology languages for the web, with a special focus on annotating Semantic Web Services. Since WSML tries to cover all the major aspects of different knowledge representation formalisms, its various language variants are spread over the scheme of Fig. 3.4. They fit semantically in between existing languages by being based on similar formalisms in both the DL and the LP strands. We will have a closer look at the WSML family of languages in Sect. 3.4.5.

3.4.2 RDF(S)

The Resource Description Framework (RDF) [30] is a language recommended by the W3C standardisation body for representing information about resources in the World Wide Web. It is particularly intended for the representation of meta data about identifiable web resources, such as title and author of a web page, topic and copyright information of an electronic document retrievable from the web or functionality and access conditions of a Web Service.

Abstracting from retrievable or electronically processable web resources to anything that has identity, RDF can be used to represent information about just anything.

[14] `http://www.w3.org/Submission/SWRL/`

In this sense, RDF can serve as a language to represent knowledge as meta data about entities in, e.g., the business trips domain.

The RDF Vocabulary Description language RDF Schema (RDFS) [7] is an extension to RDF which facilitates the formulation of vocabularies for RDF meta data. While RDF is used to relate resources by means of properties, RDFS introduces the notions of resource classes and their hierarchies. The combined use of both RDF and RDFS is often referred to as RDF(S) and provides a simple ontology language for conceptual modelling with some basic inferencing capabilities.

Basic Elements of RDF

The approach for representing meta data about resources in RDF is based on a few main ideas.

Identity through URIs

Uniform Resource Identifiers (URIs) are used for naming entities. They exhibit some naming conventions that allow for partitioning of names into namespaces. For modelling ontologies in RDF, URIs may be used to identify the following kinds of entities: individuals, such as the person MisterX or the company UbiqBiz; kinds of things, such as Employee or Company; properties of those things, such as mailbox; and values of those properties, such as the string "`mailto:mrX@ubiqbiz.com`".

By URIs, resources are uniquely identified throughout the web, which allows for a decentralised organisation of knowledge about commonly referenced resources.

Sentences with Subject, Predicate and Object

Statements in RDF have the form of subject–predicate–object sentences, which are also referred to as RDF *triples*. A triple

`[subject] --predicate--> [object]`

relates a *subject* to an *object* via a *predicate*, while the roles of subject, predicate and object are played by resources identified by URIs. The subject is the resource to be described, the predicate is a specific property of this resource, and the object serves as a value of this property for this resource.

Examples for triples in RDF are[15]

`[btr:MrX] --btr:employedAt--> [btr:UbiqBiz]`,

stating that MisterX is employed at UbiqBiz, or

`[http://ubiqbiz.com/web/MrX.html] --btr:hasAuthor--> [btr:MrX]`,

stating that MisterX is the author of his web page at the UbiqBiz website.

[15] In the examples, `btr:` refers to a namespace abbreviation for the business trips domain

Graph Representation

Several triples taken together form an RDF *graph*, whose nodes are resource URIs and whose arcs are properties. A node in an object position can be either a resources or an RDF *literal*, which represents a data value like the string "`mailto:mrX@ubiqbiz.com`" or some number. Furthermore, RDF graphs support *blank nodes*, which represent anonymous resources. From a knowledge representation view, an RDF graph can be seen as a semantic network, similar to the one depicted in Fig. 3.1.

Since RDF is a web language, the various triples in an RDF graph can originate from different sites, with the idea that anybody can state anything about any resource. In this sense, RDF is designed to capture knowledge and meta data that is spread over the web.

XML Serialisation

Another web-related aspect of RDF is its XML serialisation format in which RDF graphs are encoded for machine processing and for transport over the wire. An example of the above triples encoded in RDF/XML syntax is the following.

```
<rdf:Description rdf:about="http://ubiqbiz.com/web/MrX.html">
    <btr:hasAuthor rdf:resource="btr:MisterX"/>
</rdf:Description>
<rdf:Description rdf:about="btr:MisterX">
    <btr:employedAt rdf:resource="btr:UbiqBiz"/>
</rdf:Description>
```

Descriptions of resources are encoded using special XML tags from the RDF-predefined vocabulary.

Reification

RDF allows one to make statements about statements, which is referred to as reification. A reified statement is a resource that represents an occurrence of an RDF triple. In this way, meta statements can be formulated, which can be illustrated as follows.

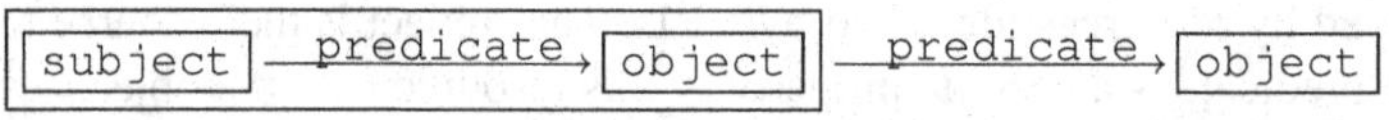

```
[ [subject] --predicate--> [object] ] --predicate--> [object]
```

Here, the subject role is played by a resource that represents a whole statement.

Reification is particularly interesting in the context of the Semantic Web, where it can be used to make statements about things that have been stated elsewhere by referring them as resources.

Data Structuring Facilities

Furthermore, RDF specifies elements to represent basic data structures as known from programming languages, namely *containers* and *collections*. Containers can be used to realise open data structures, such as ordered and unordered sequences, whereas collections allow for list structures that can be closed by stating that there are no more members.

Typing Resources with RDFS

RDFS facilitates the specification of application-specific ontological vocabularies in the form of class and property hierarchies on top of RDF resources. For this purpose, it defines a set of reserved keywords that can be used in RDF triples to relate resources to classes.

Classes

RDFS defines a type system for RDF resources by introducing the concept of a *class*. The reserved predicate `rdf:type` is used to indicate class membership, i.e. that a resource is of a certain type. RDFS classes are organised in a hierarchy of types for RDF resources. The reserved predicate `rdfs:subClassOf` is used to state a subclass relationship between two types. The following RDF(S) graph illustrates the typing of resources.

```
[btr:MrX] --rdf:type--> [btr:Employee] --rdfs:subClassOf--> [btr:Person]
```

Here, the resource that represents MisterX is stated to be of type `btr:Employee`, i.e. MisterX is a member of the class of employees, which is itself a subclass of persons.

These RDF(S) constructs for typing allow for the formulation of subsumption hierarchies and for the distinction between instances and concepts in the ontological sense. However, in RDF(S) there is no clear separation between classes and their members. Instead, RDF(S) allows self-reference and classes being members of (meta) classes. Any resource can be tagged as a class by relating it to the predefined meta type `rdfs:Class`.

Properties

By the semantics of RDF(S), any resource used in the predicate position of an RDF triple is a member of the class `rdfs:Property`. Besides classes, properties can also be organised in a hierarchy by means of the keyword `rdfs:subPropertyOf`. An example is the following triple,

```
[btr:employedAt] --rdfs:subPropertyOf--> [btr:worksFor]
```

which reflects the fact that anybody employed at some company works for this company.

With the predefined predicates `rdfs:domain` and `rdfs:range`, one can define the domain and range for a property. By setting the range of the property `btr:employedAt` in the above example to `btr:Company`, any resource that fills the object position of an RDF triple with this property as predicate is a member of the company class.

Semantics of RDF(S)

RDF(S) comes with a formal semantics that is specified in a model-theoretic way in [24]. Here, we only sketch the basic ideas of the semantics defined there, giving an intuition on the inferencing characteristics of RDF(S).

In logical terms, RDF is an assertional language in which each triple expresses a positive ground proposition. An RDF graph, as a set of triples, makes up a logical theory that consists of positive ground assertions. Since there is no concept of negation, one cannot express contradictory information in the language. Although it is possible to express or infer that, e.g., a person is both male and female, there is no way of stating that the classes of males and females cannot have common resources as their members.

In [24], the semantics of RDF(S) is characterised in the form of axiomatic triples and entailment rules that derive new, inferred triples. To yield the set of all entailed statements for an RDF graph G_{RDF}, the rules are exhaustively applied to the triples of G_{RDF} together with all axiomatic triples. In this sense, the RDF(S) semantics determines which implicit knowledge is derived from explicitly stated assertions in a graph. To illustrate the most essential parts of the RDF(S) semantics, we give examples of some of these entailment rules and their application to triples.

For example, the semantics for class membership and inheritance is determined by the following two entailment rules applied to the triples of an RDF graph G_{RDF}.

(1) IF G_{RDF} contains (C, `rdfs:subClassOf`, D) and (R, `rdf:type`, C)
THEN derive (R, `rdf:type`, D)

(2) IF G_{RDF} contains (C, `rdfs:subClassOf`, D) and (D, `rdfs:subClassOf`, E)
THEN derive (C, `rdfs:subClassOf`, E)

Their reading is to derive the triple in the THEN part for any instantiation of triples in the IF-part. The variables occurring inside the triples range over RDF resource URIs. Rule (1) entails the membership of resources in superclasses, while rule (2) ensures the transitivity of the subclass relationship. From the previous triple about MisterX being an employee as a special kind of person, rule (1) would entail the following triple.

`btr:MrX` —`rdf:type`→ `btr:Person`

Thus, an implementation of an RDF system would include MisterX in the result for the query asking for all persons.

As another example, the semantics for domains and ranges of properties is determined by the following two entailment rules.

(3) IF G_{RDF} contains (P, `rdfs:domain`, C) and (R, P, S)
THEN derive (R, `rdf:type`, C)

(4) IF G_{RDF} contains (P, `rdfs:range`, C) and (R, P, S)
THEN derive (S, `rdf:type`, C)

By setting the domain and range of the property `btr:employedAt` to `btr:Employee` and `btr:Company`, as follows,

`btr:Employee` ←`rdfs:domain`— `btr:emp.At` —`rdfs:range`→ `btr:Company`

the rules (3) and (4) apply to the triple

`btr:MrX` —`btr:employedAt`→ `btr:UbiqBiz`,

deriving that MisterX is an employee and that UbiqBiz is a company.

The entailment rules also apply to the RDF(S) meta vocabulary, determining the relationship between predefined vocabulary resources like `rdfs:Class` or `rdfs:Property`. For example, the axiomatic triple

`[rdf:type]` —`rdfs:range`→ `[rdfs:Class]`,

already triggers rule (4) for any class membership assertion, deriving that the referred type resource is a class.

Software Support for RDF(S)

The RDF(S) language is used by various web-based applications for describing meta data, and a number of tools are available that support visual editing and programmatic handling of RDF(S) descriptions.

One of the most common visual editors for RDF(S) is Protégé,[16] although recently its focus has been shifted towards OWL. Protégé allows to navigate and edit an RDF(S) class hierarchy and has special support for populating an RDF Schema with instances using customisable input forms. Other ontology editors that support RDF(S) are WebODE[17] [10], OntoEdit[18] [46] and KAON[19] OI-Modeller.

For in-memory processing and database storage of RDF(S) descriptions, common tool suites are Sesame[20] [8] and Jena[21] [32], which provide software libraries that enable software developers to process RDF(S) descriptions within their applications. They comprise parsing and serialisation for the RDF XML format, an in-memory object representation for RDF(S) descriptions as well as database persistency and querying functionality including reasoning capabilities. Recently, also oracle include RDF(S) support in their database solutions. [22]

3.4.3 OWL

The Web Ontology Language (OWL) [40] has been standardised by the W3C consortium as a language for semantic annotation of web content and is widely accepted within the Semantic Web community.

An important issue for the design of OWL was the trade-off between expressivity of the language on the one hand and scalability of reasoning on the other. To this end, OWL comes in three different flavours, namely OWL-Lite, OWL-DL and OWL-Full, reflecting different degrees of expressiveness. The design of OWL-Lite and OWL-DL has been significantly influenced by descriptions logics, and hence these two

[16] `http://protege.stanford.edu/`

[17] `http://webode.dia.fi.upm.es/WebODEWeb/index.html`

[18] Meanwhile OntoStudio – `http://ontoedit.com/`

[19] `http://sourceforge.net/projects/kaon`

[20] `http://sourceforge.net/projects/sesame/`

[21] `http://jena.sourceforge.net/`

[22] See the technical whitepaper at `http://www.oracle.com/technology/tech/semantic_technologies/pdf/semantic_tech_rdf_wp.pdf`

variants correspond to the description logic dialects $\mathcal{SHIF}(\mathbf{D})$[23] and $\mathcal{SHOIN}(\mathbf{D})$, respectively. OWL-Full, on the contrary, departs from description logic semantics in order to provide compatibility with RDF(S). The DL-based OWL variants benefit from well understood computational properties and decidability of description logic, while OWL-Full has shown to be undecidable [36]. In our presentation of OWL, we focus on OWL-DL as the most prominent language variant with the most support by the Semantic Web community.

Syntax and Intuitive Semantics

The OWL standard defines different syntaxes based on RDF(S), XML and proprietary text format. The *OWL RDF/XML syntax* allows for an encoding of an OWL ontology within the RDF(S) framework in RDF/XML serialisation. The *OWL XML presentation syntax* provides a more compact XML format for OWL ontologies, independent from RDF(S). In contrast to these machine-oriented serialisations, the *OWL abstract syntax* serves as a human readable text format to present OWL ontologies to knowledge engineers. Yet another popular way to present OWL content to a reader in a more scientific context is to make use of DL formulas. We choose to present examples in OWL abstract syntax as well as in the more compact description logic formal notation.

Similar to RDF(S), OWL provides syntactic modelling constructs for the basic elements of an ontology, i.e. concepts, relations and instances. In OWL these are called *classes*, *properties* and *individuals*, respectively, and they correspond to concepts, roles and individuals in description logics. In contrast to RDF(S), OWL-DL strictly separates classes from individuals and allows for building complex classes out of simpler ones by means of class *constructors*. In the following we go over a selection of the syntactic elements of OWL including various such constructors. For each example statement, taken from the geographic ontology depicted in Fig. 3.2, we give its intuitive meaning in natural language as well as notations in OWL abstract syntax and DL formulas.

OWL by Examples

Named classes are usually introduced by means of class declarations that correspond to DL inclusion axioms with an atomic concept on the left-hand side, as in the following example.

① "*A continent is a geographic location different from a country.*"	

`Class(`*Continent* `partial`
    `intersectionOf(`*GeographicLocation*
 	
`complementOf(`*Country*`))`
	$\mathit{Continent} \sqsubseteq \mathit{GeographicLocation} \sqcap \neg \mathit{Country}$

Here the class *Continent* is introduced through a *partial* declaration, which specifies (some of) its necessary conditions. By means of the constructors `intersectionOf`

[23] The $\mathcal{F}$ stands for functional roles, i.e. it can be stated that role relationships must be functional

and `complementOf`, a continent is declared to be a geographic region but not a country. Hence, this syntactic construct states both subclass relationship and disjointness, according to the respective DL inclusion axiom. "Necessary" here means that any continent is also a geographic location and not a country. However, not any geographic location that is not also a country is necessarily a continent; the partial class declaration only works in one direction and does not impose a "sufficient" condition, which can be achieved by using the keyword `complete` instead of `partial`. The keyword `complete` specifies class equivalence.

Individuals are introduced based on class descriptions, as in the following example.

② *"Europe is a particular continent."*	
`Individual(`*Europe* `type(`*Continent*`))`	$Continent(Europe)$

Here the individual *Europe* is introduced as an instance of the class *Continent*. Although this example shows the instantiation of a previously declared named class, the class description for the `type`-clause can be arbitrarily complex using class constructors.

An alternative way to define a class is to enumerate all its individuals, as shown in the following example.

③ *"The continents are America, Europe, Africa, Asia and Australia."*	
`EnumeratedClass(`*Continent* *America Europe Africa Asia Australia*`)`	$Continent \equiv \{America, Europe, Africa, Asia, Australia\}$

Here the class *Continent* is defined by listing all its known members, i.e. all the different continents.

Similar to classes, properties are introduced through explicit declarations with optional domain and range classes and other modifiers, as shown in the following example.

④ *"Geographic regions in general contain geographic regions."*	

`ObjectProperty(`*contains*
`domain(`*GeographicRegion*`)`
`range(`*GeographicRegion*`)`
`inverseOf(`*isContainedBy*`)`
`Transitive)`
	$\exists\, contains.\top \sqsubseteq GeographicRegion$,
	$\top \sqsubseteq \forall\, contains.GeographicRegion$,
	$locatedIn \equiv isContainedBy^{-}$
	$\mathsf{Trans}(contains)$

Here the object property *contains* is declared as a transitive containment relation between geographic regions. It is linked to its inverse property *isContainedBy*. The `domain` and `range` clauses are mapped to appropriate DL inclusion axioms: anything that contains something is a geographic region, as well as anything that is being contained. In addition to the domain of individuals OWL also offers the so-called *concrete domains* [3], i.e. properties can alternatively range over datatypes such as integer, float or string.

Once properties have been introduced, complex class descriptions can be formed by imposing restrictions on them. The following example shows a general subclass statement including a restriction on the previously introduced property.

⑤ *"A planar region only contains planar or linear regions."*	
SubClassOf (*PlanarRegion* restriction (*contains* allValuesFrom (unionOf (*PlanarRegion* *LinearRegion*))	$PlanarRegion \sqsubseteq \forall contains.(PlanarRegion \sqcup LinearRegion)$

Here planar regions are restricted to only contain planar or linear regions by means of the `restriction` constructor. The `allValuesFrom` clause requires that all values for the restricted property are of a certain type, which is specified as a disjunction by means of the `unionOf` constructor. Although this example states subclass relationship for a named class, both parameters of the `subClassOf`-clause can be arbitrarily complex class descriptions made up of constructors.

Statements of class equivalence can also be quite sophisticated as in the following example.

⑥ *"A European city is a city whose geographic region is contained in that of Europe."*	
EquivalentClasses (*EuropeanCity* intersectionOf (*City* restriction (*locatedIn* allValuesFrom (restriction (*isContainedBy* someValuesFrom (restriction *isRegionFor* someValuesFrom (oneOf (*Europe*))))))))	$EuropeanCity \equiv City \sqcap \forall locatedIn.\exists isContainedBy.\exists isRegionFor.\{Europe\}$

Here the class *EuropeanCity* is set equivalent to a complex class description with nested restrictions on properties and their inverses. By this, a city can be concluded to be European if its geographic region is contained by that of the European continent. The `someValuesFrom` clause restricts a property such that there must exist a value of a certain type, while the `oneOf` constructor creates a class from an explicitly named individual, similar to the enumerated class in ③.

Another way to restrict properties is to constrain their cardinality, as shown in the following example.

⑦ *"A city is a geographic location governed by a single country."*	
SubClassOf (*City* restriction (*governedBy* maxCardinality 1))	$City \sqsubseteq \leq 1\ governedBy$

Here cities are restricted to be governed by at most one country by means of the `maxCardinality` clause. Similarly, minimal cardinality can be realised with the `minCardinality` clause, while both can be combined to require a fixed cardinality.

Another usage of introduced properties is to connect individuals to other individuals or data values, as shown in the following example.

⑧ *"Munich is a German city with 1288307 inhabitants."*	
Individual (*Munich* type (*City*) value (*governedBy Germany*) value (*numberOfInhabitants* 1288307))	$City(Munich)$, $governedBy(Munich, Germany)$ $numberOfInhabitants(Munich, 1288307)$

Here the individual Munich is stated to be a city that lies in Germany by an appropriate connection to the individual *Germany*. It is asserted an integer value for the property *numberOfInhabitants*.

Model-Theoretic Semantics

The exact semantics of the DL-based OWL variants is determined by the model-theoretic semantics of the underlying description logic formalism. An OWL ontology consists of a collection of statements as the ones shown in the examples ① – ⑧. These statements are interpreted as axioms of a DL knowledge base, as described in Sect. 3.2, and thus OWL employs the open-world assumption. Table 3.1 shows the mapping of OWL abstract syntax constructs to their corresponding description logic axioms.

Table 3.1. Translation of OWL abstract syntax to description logic formal notation

OWL abstract syntax	DL syntax
Axioms	
`Class(`A `partial` $C_1 \dots C_n$`)`	$A \sqsubseteq C_1 \sqcap \dots C_n$
`Class(`A `complete` $C_1 \dots C_n$`)`	$A \equiv C_1 \sqcap \dots C_n$
`EnumeratedClass(`$A\ a_1 \dots a_n$`)`	$A \equiv \{a_1\} \sqcup \dots \sqcup \{a_n\}$
`SubClassOf(`$C\ D$`)`	$C \sqsubseteq D$
`EquivalentClasses(`$C_1 \dots C_n$`)`	$C_1 \equiv \dots \equiv C_n$
`DisjointClasses(`$C_1 \dots C_n$`)`	$C_i \sqsubseteq \neg C_j$, $(1 \leq i < j \leq n)$
`ObjectProperty(`r `super(`r_1`)...super(`r_n`)`	$r \sqsubseteq r_1 \sqcap \dots \sqcap r_n$
`domain(`C_1`) ... domain(`C_n`)`	$\exists\, r.\top \sqsubseteq C_1 \sqcap \dots \sqcap C_n$
`range(`C_1`) ... range(`C_n`)`	$\top \sqsubseteq \forall\, r.C_1 \sqcap \dots \sqcap \forall\, r.C_n$
`[inverseOf(`s`)]`	$r \equiv s^-$
`[Symmetric]`	$r \equiv r^-$
`[Functional]`	$\top \sqsubseteq\ \leq 1\, r$
`[InverseFunctional]`	$\top \sqsubseteq\ \leq 1\, r^-$
`[Transitive])`	Trans(r)
`SubPropertyOf(`$r\ s$`)`	$r \sqsubseteq s$
`EquivalentProperties(`$r_1 \dots r_n$`)`	$r_1 \equiv \dots \equiv r_n$
`Individual(`a `type(`C_1`) ... type(`C_n`)`	$C_1 \sqcap \dots \sqcap C_n(a)$
`value(`$r_1\ a_1$`) ... value(`$r_n\ a_n$`))`	$r_1(a, a_1), \dots, r_n(a, a_n)$
`SameIndividual(`$a_1 \dots a_n$`)`	$a_1 = \dots = a_n$
`DifferentIndividuals(`$a_1 \dots a_n$`)`	$a_i \neq a_j$, $(1 \leq i < j \leq n)$
Descriptions	
`Class(`A`)`	A
`Class(`*owl:Thing*`)`	$\top$
`Class(`*owl:Nothing*`)`	$\bot$
`intersectionOf(`$C_1\ C_2$ `...)`	$C_1 \sqcap C_2$
`unionOf(`$C_1\ C_2$ `...)`	$C_1 \sqcup C_2$
`complementOf(`C`)`	$\neg C$
`oneOf(`$a_1\ a_2$ `...)`	$\{a_1\} \sqcup \{a_2\}$
`restriction(`r `someValuesFrom(`C`))`	$\exists\, r.C$
`restriction(`r `allValuesFrom(`C`))`	$\forall\, r.C$
`restriction(`r `hasValue(`a`))`	$\exists\, r.\{a\}$
`restriction(`r `minCardinality(`n`))`	$\geq n\, r$
`restriction(`r `maxCardinality(`n`))`	$\leq n\, r$

Working with OWL Ontologies

Due to the connection of OWL to description logics, the basic reasoning services available for DL knowledge bases also apply to OWL ontologies. Thus, an OWL ontology can be checked for consistency or it can be queried for implicit knowledge.

Ontology Inconsistency

Consider the following OWL ontology consisting of three statements.

```
{ subClassOf(City restriction(governedBy maxCardinality(1))),
  Individual(Nicosia type(City) value(governedBy Greece) value(governedBy Turkey)),
  DifferentIndividuals(Greece Turkey)                                              }
```

The first statement is taken from ⑦ and says that cities are uniquely governed by a single country. The second statement says that the city of Nicosia[24] is governed by both Greece and Turkey, while the third statement assures that these are two different countries. This is clearly a contradiction and this OWL ontology is therefore *inconsistent*. This can be verified by using the reasoning service of *knowledge base satisfiability*, offered by common description logic reasoners. Notice that for practical reasons an inconsistent ontology is quite useless, since it allows to conclude any arbitrary statement.

Ontology Coherency

Another kind of "problematic modelling" in ontologies is to introduce classes that cannot have instances, which is the case in the following OWL ontology.

```
{ subClassOf(City restriction(governedBy maxCardinality(1))),
  class(SplitCity complete
      intersectionOf(City restriction(governedBy minCardinality(2)))) }
```

Again, the first statement, taken from ⑦, restricts cities to be governed by at most one country. The second statement introduces a class *SplitCity*, requiring that split cities are cities governed by at least two countries. However, by the first statement, this is not possible and thus the class *SplitCity* cannot have an instance in any valid model of the corresponding description logic knowledge base. In DL-terms this means that the concept *SplitCity* is unsatisfiable. Common description logic reasoners offer the service of checking concepts for their satisfiability. An ontology that contains an unsatisfiable concept/class is said to be *incoherent*. In contrast to inconsistent ontologies, an incoherent ontology is not useless and many reasoning tasks might not be affected by the unsatisfiability of a particular class. However, incoherence of an ontology indicates erroneous modelling, and once an unsatisfiable class is assigned an individual as an instance the ontology becomes inconsistent.

[24] Nicosia is the capital of Cyprus and is split into a Greek and a Turkish part

Querying for Subsumption

Besides checking an ontology for consistency or coherency, its main usage is to be queried for implicit knowledge. Based on the notion of entailment, for any OWL statement we can ask whether it follows from an OWL ontology, i.e. whether its corresponding DL axiom is entailed by the respective DL knowledge base. Querying for subsumption between two classes underlies the most important usage of reasoning in the OWL language, namely *classification*. The following OWL ontology allows for the automatic classification of two classes that are not explicitly put in subsumption relation.

```
{ class(SplitCity complete
      intersectionOf(City restriction(governedBy minCardinality(2)))),
  class(GreekTurkishCity partial
      intersectionOf(City
                     restriction(governedBy someValuesFrom(oneOf(Greece)))
                     restriction(governedBy someValuesFrom(oneOf(Turkey))))),
  DifferentIndividuals(Greece Turkey)                                          }
```

The first statement introduces split cities as before, while the second statement introduces a class *GreekTurkishCity* for cities which are governed by both Greece and Turkey. The third statement assures the two involved countries to be distinct, as before. Notice that this time the ontology does not restrict cities to be governed by a single country. From the knowledge specified in the ontology, *GreekTurkishCity* is a subclass of *SplitCity* and a DL reasoner would derive the statement `subClassOf(GreekTurkishCity SplitCity)` as a logical consequence.

By checking subsumption between all the named classes in an OWL ontology, an inferred class hierarchy can be established.

Querying for Assertion

The other kind of statements an OWL ontology can be queried for are assertion axioms. For both role assertions and concept assertions, we can ask whether they hold with respect to an OWL ontology, as illustrated by the following example.

```
{ subClassOf(EUCountry restriction(officialCurrency hasValue(Euro))),
  Individual(Germany type(EUCountry),
  class(GermanCity partial
      intersectionOf(City restriction(governedBy hasValue(Germany)))),
  Individual(Munich type(GermanCity)                                  }
```

This ontology states that in countries in the EU, as e.g. Germany, the official currency is Euro, and that German cities, as e.g. Munich, are cities governed by Germany. From the knowledge specified in the ontology, it follows that *Munich* is governed by *Germany*, and a DL reasoner would derive the statement `Individual(Munich value(governedBy Germany))` as a logical consequence, since *Munich* is assigned to be a *GermanCity*. Furthermore, the ontology allows to conclude that in Munich one can pay with Euro, i.e. Munich is governed by a country that has Euro as official currency. A reasoner would derive the statement `Individual(Munich type(restriction(governedBy` someValuesFrom(restriction(*officialCurrency* hasValue(*Euro*))))), since, as a *GermanyCity*, *Munich* is governed by *Germany* whose official currency is *Euro*.

By iterating over all the individuals in an OWL ontology, querying for subsets of named individuals with certain properties can be achieved. For example, in the above query *Munich* can be subsequently replaced by other named individuals to retrieve all cities in which one can pay with Euro.

Software Support for OWL

Since OWL is technically built on top of RDF(S), some RDF(S) specific tools can be readily applied, e.g. for parsing and serialisation in the OWL RDF/XML format, while others have also been upgraded to OWL versions.

The ontology editor Protégé [22] also supports OWL and comes with a variety of plugins that allow for visualisation and management of OWL ontologies. In addition to different graphical views of the explicit class and property hierarchies, it facilitates the visual editing of OWL axioms and enables the embedding of reasoning tools for computing inferred subsumption hierarchies. Other visual editors for OWL ontologies that offer similar functionality are SWOOP[25] [28] or the commercial tools Altova Semantic Works[26] and TopBraid.[27]

For the programmatic handling of OWL ontologies, the OWL API[28] [5] as well as Jena [32] can be used by software developers to process OWL descriptions within their applications. They provide means for parsing and serialisation of the different OWL syntax formats and for in-memory manipulation of ontologies.

As OWL is an expressive knowledge representation language, reasoning plays an important role, and there are a number of description logic reasoners available that can be used for querying OWL ontologies with respect to inferred knowledge or for verifying their consistency. The most common description logic reasoners in the Semantic Web context are based on the tableau calculus, and available systems that support the OWL language are Racer[29] [23], FaCT[30] [25] and Pellet[31] [44]. Recently, new DL reasoning algorithms – based on deductive database technology – were devised for the development of the KAON2[32] [37] system, which is particularly optimised for querying ontologies with large A-Boxes.

3.4.4 F-Logic

Frame Logic (F-Logic) [29] is a deductive, object-oriented database language which aims at combining the declarative semantics and expressiveness of logic program-

[25] http://www.mindswap.org/2004/SWOOP/
[26] http://origin.altova.com/products_semanticworks.html
[27] http://www.topbraidcomposer.com/
[28] http://owl.man.ac.uk/api.shtml
[29] Meanwhile RacerPro – http://www.racer-systems.com/
[30] Meanwhile FaCT++ – http://owl.man.ac.uk/factplusplus/
[31] http://www.mindswap.org/2003/pellet/
[32] http://kaon2.semanticweb.org/

ming with rich and intuitive conceptual modelling capabilities, as provided by frame-based systems. The most significant language features of F-Logic comprise object identity, complex objects, classes, inheritance, polymorphic types, rules and queries. Besides the aspects of a frame-based language for conceptual modelling, it can also be perceived as a logic with model-theoretic semantics and a sound and complete resolution-based proof theory.

We give a short overview on syntax and informal semantics of the most important features of F-Logic. In the original specification [29], F-Logic is given several semantics and in its full version it is an extension of first-order logic. However, systems that support the language do not implement full F-Logic but a logic programming variant based on the well-founded semantics. Thus, we present F-Logic as a rule-based LP-style language, as it is widely perceived.

F-Logic by Examples

Frame-Based Modelling

F-Logic allows to describe *objects* – identified by an object ID – by grouping related information about the object in the so-called *F-molecules*. The following example illustrates the use of F-molecules to describe some objects from our business trips scenario.

```
UbiqBiz[hasLegalName    ->  'Ubiquitous Business Ltd.',
        hasOfficesIn    ->> {NewYork, London, Singapore},
        hasPhones       ->> {0017324747123, 00654564458},
        hasEmployees    ->> {MrX, MrY, MsZ}].

MrX[hasName        -> 'Mister X',
    hasAddress     -> AddressMrX[hasStreet -> 'Fifth Avenue',
                                 hasNumber -> 521,
                                 hasCity   -> NewYork].

BookingUbiqMrX[bookedBy    ->   UbiqBiz,
               bookedFor   ->   MrX,
               issuedFor   ->   FL4711].
```

In the example, objects, such as `UbiqBiz`, are described in terms of F-molecules that assign them values for certain attributes, such as legal name, locations of offices, phone numbers and associated employees. As values for attributes, F-Logic allows objects as well as data values, such as strings or numbers. The symbol `->` denotes an assignment of a single value, while the symbol `->>` indicates the assignment of multiple values for set-valued attributes. As illustrated by the attribute `hasAddress`, attribute assignments in F-molecules can be nested.

From an ontology point of view, the objects in the example can be seen as instances. Besides these, F-Logic also provides language features for describing *classes* of objects with attached *attributes* and relating them in class hierarchies, as shown next.

```
Company :: LegalEntity.
Company[hasLegalName    =>  STRING,
        hasOfficesIn    =>> City,
        hasPhones       =>> NUMBER,
```

```
        hasEmployees    =>> Person].

Person :: LegalEntity.
Person[hasName          => STRING,
       hasAddress       => Addresss].

Employee :: Person.
Employee[isEmployedAt => Company].

Booking[bookedBy    =>  LegalEntity,
        bookedFor   =>  Person,
        issuedFor   =>  Flight].

UbiqBiz : Company.
MrX : Person.
FL4711 : Flight.
BookingUbiqMrX : Booking.
```

In the example, the object `Company` is described as a class for company objects with appropriate attribute ranges. The symbol `=>` indicates a single-valued range, while the symbol `=>>` assigns a set-valued range for attributes with multiple values.

Both `Company` and `Person` are declared as subclasses of `LegalEntity` by means of the symbol `::`, which denotes class inheritance and is used to build class hierarchies. The class `Employee` is, in turn, a subclass of `Person` with an additional attribute for employment; it inherits the attributes from its parent class `Person`.

Objects can be assigned to classes using the symbol `:`. In the ontological view, this means to relate an instance to a concept. Here, the symbol `:` is used to state that UbiqBiz is a company, that MisterX is a person, etc. Since any object can serve as a class, classes can be declared as instances of other classes, and thus F-Logic supports metamodelling facilities.

Rules

In the Semantic Web context, F-Logic is primarily perceived as a language following the rule-based paradigm. Indeed, LP-style rules form the essential language feature for the deductive aspects of F-Logic.

The keyword `FORALL` – to indicate universal quantification of involved variables – is used together with the symbol `<-` to construct rules in F-Logic. A rule

```
FORALL  <variables> <head>   <-   <body>.
```

has the typical reading: for any possible instantiation of variables in the rule body, derive the corresponding instantiation of the rule head. By deriving new information, rules extend an F-Logic object base by intensional knowledge, forming its deductive closure.

The following is an example of a rule that operates on the descriptions of the classes and objects given before.

```
FORALL  C,E  C[hasEmployees ->> E]  <-   E : Employee[isEmployedAt -> C].
```

It captures a part of the inverse relationship between the attributes `hasEmployees` and `isEmployedAt`. Whenever an employee can be derived to be employed at a certain company, the rule derives that this employee is among the list of employees of that particular company.

Another, more complex example of a rule is the following, taken from Sect. 3.1.

```
FORALL  B,C,P  P : Employee[isEmployedAt -> C] <- P : Person AND
                                                  C : Company AND
                                                  B : Booking[bookedBy -> C,
                                                          bookedFor -> P].
```

It concludes a person to be an employee of a certain company whenever there is a booking for this person by that particular company. From the concrete booking `BookingUbiqMrX` for flight FL4711, specified before, this rule would derive the F-molecule

```
MrX : Employee[isEmployedAt -> UbiqBiz].
```

stating that MisterX is an employee of UbiqBiz.

Queries

F-Logic provides queries as a language element for the retrieval of (tuples of) objects. Objects are bound to possible instantiations of variables that occur in the query. Syntactically, queries in F-Logic are a special kind of rules with an empty head and have the following form.

```
FORALL  <variables>   <-   <body>.
```

As with rules, the variables that occur in the body of a query are universally quantified. Whenever a tuple of objects is a possible instantiation of variables that conform with the deductive closure of the object base, this tuple is part of the result for the query.

An example for an F-Logic query is the following,

```
FORALL E,A   <-   E : Employee[isEmployedAt -> UbiqBiz,
                           hasAddress -> A[hasCity -> NewYork]].
```

asking for all UbiqBiz employees who live in New York. Applied to the formerly described objects and rules, the answer to this query would be the object `MrX` because MisterX is assigned an address in New York and he can also be derived to be an employee.

Queries can also ask for schema elements and bind variables to classes. The following query asks for all classes which MisterX belongs to.

```
FORALL C   <-   MrX : C.
```

The answer to the query is the set {`Person`, `Employee`, `LegalEntity`} of classes.

Negation as Failure

Under the semantics of the logic programming variant, F-Logic makes the closed-world assumption for the evaluation of queries and for the deductive closure on an object base. For example, the query

```
FORALL E   <-   E : Employee.
```

that asks for all employees only yields `MrX` as a result. For `MrY` and `MsZ`, it has not been stated that they are employees, nor can this information be derived from the specified knowledge. Therefore, MisterY and MissZ are assumed to be no employees.

Furthermore, the negation operator NOT, used in the bodies of rules and queries, is interpreted as negation-as-failure. The following is an example of a query that contains a negation operator, combined with a rule.

```
FORALL P  P : FlightParticipant   <-   F : Flight AND
                                      B : Booking[bookedFor -> P,
                                                  issuedFor -> F].
FORALL E   <-   UbiqBiz[hasEmployee ->> E] AND
                NOT E : FlightParticipant.
```

It asks for all the employees of UbiqBiz who do not participate in any known flight, which yields the set {MrY, MsZ}.

Software Support for F-Logic

Since F-Logic sets a focus on rule-based inferencing rather than on web aspects, it does not come in a web-style XML serialisation format like other ontology languages in the Semantic Web. Its syntax rather resembles the style of typical programming languages and is human-readable for people with a software development background. To this end, there is not much support in graphical editing tools and F-Logic ontologies are typically developed using text editors. An exception is OntoStudio,[33] which provides graphical editing capabilities for F-Logic rules, while some other ontology editors also support F-Logic export features.

There are two major inference engines available that perform reasoning on F-Logic rules: the freely available $\mathcal{F}$LORA-2[34] [49] and the commercial OntoBroker[35] [12]. Recently, also the KAON2[36] system has included some support for F-Logic.

3.4.5 WSML

The WSMO[37] initiative aims at providing an overarching framework for handling Semantic Web Services (SWS). It comprises the WSMO conceptual model, as an upper-level ontology for Semantic Web Services, the WSML language and the WSMX execution environment. WSMO (Web Service Modelling Ontology) is described in Part III Chap. 7 in more detail, while here we are concerned with ontology language aspects. WSML (Web Service Modeling Language) is a language to formally describe the elements defined in the WSMO conceptual model, providing syntax and formal semantics for them.

WSML is particularly designed for describing Semantic Web Services and is therefore not a mere ontology language. Besides typical ontological notions, it also provides SWS-specific language constructs, such as "goal", "web service", "interface", "choreography" or "capability", to capture different aspects of Web Service

[33] http://www.ontoprise.de/content/e1171/e1249/index_eng.html

[34] http://flora.sourceforge.net/florahome.php

[35] http://ontobroker.semanticweb.org/

[36] http://kaon2.semanticweb.org/

[37] http://www.wsmo.org

semantics. One of the corner stones in WSMO are the domain ontologies used to semantically annotate Web Services. Hence, WSML also provides means to describe such ontologies, as any ordinary ontology language does. Since here we are interested in the description of ontologies in general, we present the ontology-related part of WSML only.

Syntax

The Syntax of WSML is split into a *conceptual* part and a *logical expression* part. The conceptual syntax allows typical conceptual modelling with concepts, relations and instances, known from frame-based systems where information about a certain entity is specified locally in a single syntactic construct. The logical expression syntax allows the formulation of complex axiomatic information using logical formulas. It is very similar to F-Logic syntax and provides the typical logical symbols as well as different forms of negation and implication, LP-style rules and constraints. WSML also supports datatypes like integer, float or string, up to user-defined datatypes.

The following listing shows a fragment of our example geographic ontology in WSML syntax in its *human readable* serialisation.

```
concept GeographicRegion
    isRegionFor inverseOf(locatedIn) ofType GeographicLocation
    contains inverseOf(isContainedBy) transitive impliesType GeographicRegion
    boundedBy ofType (2 *) SurfacePoint

concept SurfacePoint
    hasLongtitude ofType _float
    hasLatitude ofType _float

concept City subConceptOf Infrastructure
    locatedIn ofType PlanarRegion
    officialName ofType _string
    numberOfInhabitants ofType _integer

concept EuropeanCity subConceptOf City

instance Europe memberOf Continent

instance Munich memberOf City
    officialName hasValue "München"
    numberOfInhabitants hasValue 1288307

axiom EuropeanCity_sufficient_condition definedBy
    ?c memberOf EuropeanCity :- ?c memberOf City and
                ?c[locatedIn hasValue ?rc] and
                ?rc[containedBy hasValue ?re] and
                ?re[isRegionFor hasValue Europe].
```

The upper part shows the conceptual syntax with bold-faced keywords for defining concepts, instances and their membership relations. *Attributes*, i.e. relations defined in the scope of a concept, are further restricted or filled with concrete values. They can be declared as being transitive or as the inverse of another attribute, and they can be constrained by their range type or cardinality. With the distinction between the **ofType** and **impliesType** constructs, WSML offers both range constraints that ensure attribute values to be of a certain type, and range restrictions in the style of OWL that allow to conclude information about attribute values. Attribute ranges can be concepts or datatypes, such as _integer, _float or _string. The lower part of the listing shows an axiom defined by a logical expression in form of an LP-style rule with variables preceded by a ? symbol. The rule concludes a city to be European if its geographic region lies within that of Europe, referring to the elements declared in the conceptual part.

Besides the human readable form, there are other forms of serialisation for the WSML syntax, similar to the different serialisation formats for OWL. These cover serialisation in XML as well as in RDF.

Semantics

Similar to OWL, WSML comes in various language variants that have different expressiveness and that reflect different knowledge representation paradigms. The most basic and least expressive variant is WSML-Core, which is based on DLP [18] as a least common denominator for description logic formalisms on the one hand and logic programming and rule-based systems on the other hand. WSML-Core is separately extended in the directions of these two paradigms by the variants WSML-DL and WSML-Flight/Rule, respectively. Ultimately, the vision of WSML-Full is to semantically amalgamate the two paradigms in a language with first-order model-theoretic semantics augmented by non-monotonic extensions and typical LP-style features like default negation or constraints. At the current stage, however, the WSMO initiative is an ongoing effort and the semantics of WSML-Full is yet to be defined.

In Fig. 3.5 the WSML language variants are positioned with respect to different knowledge representation formalisms.

WSML-Core

This variant is based on the DLP fragment described in [18]. It offers basic conceptual modelling with concepts, attributes and instances, as well as taxonomic hierarchies and the use of datatypes. Its semantics is defined by a mapping to function-free horn logic interpreted in the classical model-theoretic way. Similar to RDF, it does not allow to express any form of negative information, and thus no contradictory statements can be formulated.

WSML-DL

This variant extends WSML-Core to a description logic formalism, namely to the logic $\mathcal{SHIQ}$(D). In this sense, WSML-DL is very similar to the OWL language. The WSML syntax does not provide the variable-free constructs that are typical for DLs. Thus, in WSML-DL logical expressions with variables and logical connectives are interpreted as in first-order logic, with the restriction to only allow unary and binary predicates for DL concepts and roles.

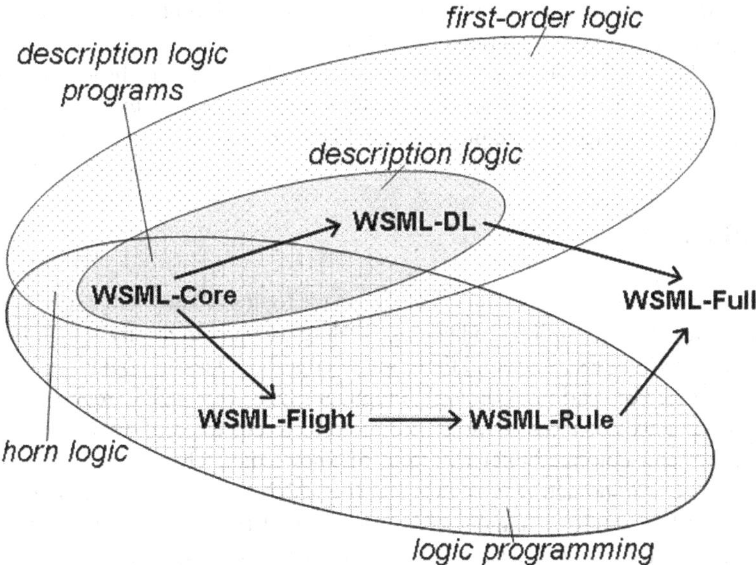

Fig. 3.5. WSML language variants in knowledge representation

WSML-Flight

This variant extends WSML-Core to an LP-style rule language with a closed-world semantics. It is similar to F-Logic (LP) and offers features like negation-as-failure, constraints and meta-modelling. The semantics of WSML-Flight is defined by a mapping to F-Logic formulas interpreted under perfect model semantics.

WSML-Rule

This variant further extends WSML-Flight with more expressive logic programming features, such as function symbols or unsafe rules. Its semantics is based on the well-founded semantics.

WSML-Full

The still-to-be-defined semantics of WSML-Full is envisioned to combine WSML-DL and WSML-Rule. A candidate formalism to achieve integration of the two paradigms is autoepistemic logic.

Software Support for WSML

Since WSML is a relatively new language, tool development is in an early stage. However, there are some tools available for handling and editing WSML ontologies, all driven by the WSMO initiative.

The WSMO4J[38] framework enables parsing, serialisation and in-memory processing of WSML ontologies an other WSML elements.

The Web Services Modelling Toolkit (WSMT)[39] is a graphical editor that allows for visualisation and manipulation of WSML ontologies. Other tools for editing WSML elements are WSMO Studio[40] [13] and DOME.[41]

3.5 Outlook

In this chapter we have presented an overview on the topics of knowledge representation, ontologies and Semantic Web languages. Here we want to briefly sketch future research and usability issues around these knowledge-based technologies.

Having reviewed various ontology languages and knowledge representation paradigms, we have seen that there are multiple different ways of approaching the representation and computational handling of knowledge. There is still room for research on which approach is most suitable for which kind of application context. A current trend in ontology languages is to perceive LP-based approaches as particularly suitable for data-intensive retrieval tasks with rule-based inferencing on the one hand, and DL-based approaches for automated classification and for satisfiability problems on the other hand.

To achieve wide-spread use of ontologies, they have to be established as usable software artefacts that are interchanged and traded between parties, similar to computer programs or other forms of electronic content. As such, they can principally be plugged in systems that make use of knowledge-based technology. However, the logic-based notions in which ontologies are described are typically too technical and too onerous to handle to be widely accepted. To overcome this deficiency, design methodologies and higher-level descriptive languages should be introduced that abstract from the surfeit of logical details, presenting the user a more intuitive view on domain knowledge. An analogous level of abstraction has been achieved in the field of software engineering, where more and more abstract higher-level languages have been build on machine codes and assembler languages.

In the Semantic Web context, also other techniques from the field of Artificial Intelligence are used, such as lexical methods for natural language processing or statistics-based methods for machine learning. There, the symbolic knowledge representation in ontologies should used complementarily to exploit synergies with such techniques in Semantic Web applications. Moreover, there is a trend to forbear from the heavy-weight semantics of logical formalisms, moving to the light-weight semantics of languages with decreased expressive power in applications where precision and exactness is not the main focus. In this sense, some applications prefer, e.g., RDF(S) over the semantically richer OWL due to simplicity or scalability issues.

---

[38] `http://wsmo4j.sourceforge.net/`

[39] `http://wsmt.sourceforge.net`

[40] `http://www.wsmostudio.org/`

[41] `http://dome.sourceforge.net/`

Finally, there is much space for research on finding the right degree of formality in semantics for a particular application scenario.

References

1. G. Antoniou. *Nonmonotonic Reasoning*. MIT Press, 1996.
2. F. Baader, S. Brandt, , and C. Lutz. Pushing the EL Envelope. In *Proceedings of the 19th Int. Joint Conference on Artificial Intelligence (IJCAI-05), Edinburgh, UK*. Morgan Kaufmann, 2005.
3. F. Baader, D. Calvanese, D. McGuinness, D. Nardi, and P. Patel-Schneider, editors. *The Description Logic Handbook*. Cambridge University Press, January 2003.
4. F. Baader and B. Hollunder. Embedding Defaults into Terminological Knowledge Representation Systems. *Journal of Automated Reasoning*, 14:149–180, 1995.
5. S. Bechhofer, R. Volz, and P. Lord. Cooking the Semantic Web with the OWL API. In *Proc. of the First International Semantic Web Conference 2003 (ISWC 2003), October 21-23, 2003, Sanibel Island, Florida*, 2003.
6. P. Bonatti, C. Lutz, and F. Wolter. Description Logics with Circumscription. In *Proceedings of the 10th Int. Conference on Principles of Knowledge Representation and Reasoning, KR-06*, 2006.
7. D. Brickley and R.V. Guha. RDF Vocabulary Description Language – RDF Schema. `http://www.w3.org/TR/rdf-schema/`, 2004.
8. J. Broekstra, A. Kampman, and F. van Harmelen. Sesame: A Generic Architecture for Storing and Querying RDF and RDF Schema. In *ISWC '02: Proceedings of the First International Semantic Web Conference on The Semantic Web*, pages 54–68, London, UK, 2002. Springer.
9. D. Calvanese, G. de Giacomo, D. Lembo, M. Lenzerini, and R. Rosati. DL-Lite: Tractable Description Logics for Ontologies. In *Proceedings of the 20th National Conference on Artificial Intelligence (AAAI-2005)*, 2005.
10. Ó. Corcho, M. Fernández-López, A. Gómez-Pérez, and Ó. Vicente. WebODE: An Integrated Workbench for Ontology Representation, Reasoning, and Exchange. In *EKAW*, p. 138–153, 2002.
11. E. Craig. Ontology. In E. Craig, editor, *Routledge Encyclopedia of Philosophy*, pages 117–118. Routledge, New York, 1998.
12. S. Decker, M. Erdmann, D. Fensel, and R. Studer. Ontobroker: Ontology Based Access to Distributed and Semi-Structured Information. In *Semantic Issues in Multimedia Systems. Proceedings of DS-8*, pages 351–369, 1999.
13. M. Dimitrov, A. Simov, V. Momtchev, and D. Ognyanov. WSMO Studio - An Integrated Service Environment for WSMO. In *Proc. of the 2nd WSMO Impl. Workshop, Innsbruck, Austria*, 2005.
14. F.M. Donini, D. Nardi, and R. Rosati. Description Logics of Minimal Knowledge and Negation as Failure. *ACM Transactions on Computational Logic*, 3(2):177–225, 2002.
15. T. Eiter, G. Ianni, R. Schindlauer, and H. Tompits. A Uniform Integration of Higher-Order Reasoning and External Evaluations in Answer Set Programming. In L. P. Kaelbling and A. Saffiotti, editors, *Proceedings of the 19th International Joint Conference on Artificial Intelligence (IJCAI-05)*, 2005.
16. O. Etzioni, K. Golden, and D. Weld. Tractable Closed World Reasoning with Updates. In *Proceedings of the 4th International Conference on Knowledege Representation and Reasoning (KR-1994)*, pages 178–189. Morgan Kaufmann, 1994.

17. A. Gangemi, N. Guarino, C. Masolo, A. Oltramari, and L. Schneider. Sweetening Ontologies with DOLCE. In *EKAW-02: Proceedings of the 13th Int. Conference on Knowledge Engineering and Knowledge Management. Ontologies and the Semantic Web*, pages 166–181. Springer, 2002.
18. B. Grosof, I. Horrocks, R. Volz, and S. Decker. Description Logic Programs: Combining Logic Programs with Description Logics. In *Proceedings of WWW-2003, Budapest, Hungary*, pages 48–57. ACM, 2003.
19. T.R. Gruber. A Translation Approach to Portable Ontology Specifications. *Knowledge Acquisition*, 6(2):199–221, 1993.
20. N. Guarino. Semantic Matching: Formal Ontological Distinctions for Information Organization, Extraction, and Integration. In M.T. Pazienza, editor, *Information Extraction: A Multidisciplinary Approach to an Emerging Information Technology*, number 1299 in LNCS, pages 139–170. Springer-Verlag, 1997.
21. N. Guarino. Formal Ontology and Information Systems, Preface. In N. Guarino, editor, *Proceedings of the 1st International Conference on Formal Ontologies in Information Systems, FOIS-98, Trento, Italy*, pages 3–15. IOS Press, 1998.
22. N. Noy M. Musen H. Knublauch, R. Fergerson. The Protege OWL Plugin: An Open Development Environment for Semantic Web Applications. *Proceedings of the 3rd International Semantic Web Conference (ISWC)*, 2004.
23. V. Haarslev and R. Möller. Description of the RACER System and its Applications. In *International Workshop on Description Logics*, 2001.
24. P. Hayes. RDF Semantics. `http://www.w3.org/TR/rdf-mt/`, 2004.
25. I. Horrocks. Using an Expressive Description Logic: FaCT or Fiction? In *Proceedings of the 6th International Conference on Knowledege Representation and Reasoning (KR1998)*, pages 636–645. Morgan Kaufmann, 1998.
26. I. Horrocks and P. F. Patel-Schneider. A Proposal for an OWL Rules Language. In *Proceedings of the 13th International World Wide Web Conference (WWW-2004)*. ACM, 2004.
27. U. Hustadt, B. Motik, and U. Sattler. Data Complexity of Reasoning in Very Expressive Description Logics. In *Proceedings of the 19th International Joint Conference on Artificial Intelligence (IJCAI-05), Edinburgh, UK*, pages 466–471. Morgan Kaufmann, 2005.
28. A. Kalyanpur, B. Parsia, E. Sirin, B. Cuenca Grau, and J. Hendler. Swoop: A Web Ontology Editing Browser. *Journal of Web Semantics*, 4(2):144–153, 2006. `http://dx.doi.org/10.1016/j.websem.2005.10.001`.
29. M. Kifer, G. Lausen, and J. Wu. Logical Foundations of Object-Oriented and Frame-Based Languages. *Journal of the ACM*, 42(4):741–843, July 1995.
30. G. Klyne and J. Carroll. RDF Concepts and Abstract Syntax. `http://www.w3.org/TR/rdf-primer/`, 2004.
31. J.W. Lloyd. *Foundations of Logic Programming*. Springer-Verlag, 1988.
32. B. McBride. Jena: Implementing the RDF Model and Syntax Specification. In *SemWeb*, 2001. `http://CEUR-WS.org/Vol-40/mcbride.pdf`.
33. J. McCarthy. Circumscription – A Form of Non-Monotonic Reasoning. *Artificial Intelligence*, 13(1):27–39, 1980.
34. J. Minker. Logic and Databases: Past, Present, and Future. *AI Magazine*, 18(3):21–47, 1997.
35. R. Moore. Semantical Considerations on Nonmonotonic Logic. *Artificial Intelligence*, 25(1), 1985.

36. B. Motik. On the Properties of Metamodeling in OWL. In Y. Gil, E. Motta, V.R. Benjamins, and M. Musen, editors, *Proceedings of the 4th International Semantic Web Conference (ISWC-2005)*, volume 3729 of *LNCS*, pages 548–562. Springer-Verlag, 2005.
37. B. Motik and U. Sattler. A Comparison of Reasoning Techniques for Querying Large Description Logic ABoxes. In Miki Hermann and Andrei Voronkov, editors, *Proc. of the 13th Int. Conf. on Logic for Programming Artificial Intelligence and Reasoning (LPAR 2006)*, LNCS, Phnom Penh, Cambodia, November 13–17 2006. Springer.
38. B. Motik, U. Sattler, and R. Studer. Query Answering for OWL-DL with Rules. In S. A. McIlraith, D. Plexousakis, and F. van Harmelen, editors, *Proc. of the 3rd Int. Semantic Web Conf. (ISWC 2004)*, pages 549–563, Hiroshima, Japan, November 7–11 2004. Springer.
39. I. Niles and A. Pease. Towards a Standard Upper Ontology. In C. Welty and B. Smith, editors, *Proceedings of the 2nd International Conference on Formal Ontology in Information Systems (FOIS-2001)*, 2001.
40. P.F. Patel-Schneider, P. Hayes, and I. Horrocks. OWL Web Ontology Language; Semantics and Abstract Syntax. `http://www.w3.org/TR/owl-semantics/`, November 2002.
41. S. Pepper and G. Moore. XML Topic Maps (XTM) 1.0. `http://www.topicmaps.org/xtm/1.0/`.
42. R. Reiter. A Logic for Default Reasoning. *Artificial Intelligence*, 13:81–132, 1980.
43. S. Russel and P. Norvig. *Artificial Intelligence – A Modern Approach.* Prentice-Hall, 1995.
44. E. Sirin, B. Parsia, B. Cuenca Grau, A. Kalyanpur, and Y. Katz. Pellet: A Practical OWL-DL Reasoner. Technical report, University of Maryland Institute for Advanced Computer Studies (UMIACS), 2005. `http://mindswap.org/papers/PelletDemo.pdf`.
45. J.F. Sowa. *Knowledge Representation.* Brooks Cole Publishing, Pacific Grove, CA, USA, 2000.
46. Y. Sure, M. Erdmann, J. Angele, S. Staab, R. Studer, and D. Wenke. OntoEdit: Collaborative Ontology Development for the Semantic Web. In *ISWC '02: Proceedings of the First International Semantic Web Conference on The Semantic Web*, pages 221–235. Springer-Verlag, 2002.
47. Jeffrey D. Ullman. *Principles of Database and Knowledge-Base Systems: Volumes I and II.* Computer Science Press, 1989.
48. F. van Harmelen, Z. Huang, H. Stuckenschmidt, and Y. Sure. A Framework for Handling Inconsistency in Changing Ontologies. In Y. Gil, E. Motta, V.R. Benjamins, and M. Musen, editors, *Proceedings of the 4th International Semantic Web Conference (ISWC-2005)*, volume 3729 of *LNCS*, pages 353–367. Springer-Verlag, 2005.
49. G. Yang, M. Kifer, and C. Zhao. Flora-2: A Rule-Based Knowledge Representation and Inference Infrastructure for the Semantic Web. In *CoopIS/DOA/ODBASE*, pages 671–688, 2003.
50. M. Yue and L. Zuoquan. Infering with Inconsistent OWL DL Ontology: a Multi-valued Approach. In *Proceedings of the International Conference on Semantics in a Networked World, ICSNW-2006, Munich, Germany*. Springer-Verlag, 2006.

4

Ontology Development

Methodologies for Ontology Engineering

Gábor Nagypál

FZI Research Center for Information Technologies at the University of Karlsruhe, Germany, nagypal@fzi.de

Summary. The development of ontologies is comparable in complexity with the development of a complex software. Therefore, it is not enough just to be familiar with the available ontology formalisms to build high-quality ontologies. Development methodologies are needed, which structure the steps of the ontology development process. This chapter will introduce two popular methodologies – On-To-Knowledge and METHONTOLOGY – which show most of the major ideas behind ontology methodologies. Creating the conceptual ontology model – which is one of the steps in the ontology development process – is a highly complex task, and methodologies alone do not provide solutions how to perform it. This chapter therefore also provides an overview of best-practice ontology design principles, which provide standard solutions for the most common problems. A discussion about the modularisation of big ontologies closes this chapter.

4.1 Introduction

The development of ontologies is comparable in complexity with the design and development of a complex software. As it is unrealistic to except someone who knows only the basics of a programming language will be able to design a good software architecture using that language, similarly it is not enough just to know the available ontology formalisms to build good ontologies.

To remain by the analogy of software development; a software analyst first of all needs lots of analysis and design experience to be able to design high-quality software applications. Unfortunately, experience cannot be described in books. There are, however, various software development methodologies which provide a framework for the various software development activities, together with various analysis and design patterns which communicate some general rules how a good analysis or design model should look like.

Similarly, an ontology engineer needs first of all lots of ontology building experience which cannot be described in books. There are, however, various ontology development methodologies available. They provide guidance through the complex process of ontology development. Based on existing ontology development experience some philosophical and practical design principles were also reported in the literature. Unfortunately, these principles are not yet organised in the form of patterns, as ontology engineering is still a nascent field compared to software engineering.

After the previous chapter described the concept of ontologies and the various popular ontology formalisms available today, this chapter provides an overview of the activities of a typical ontology development process, describes the main ideas of two popular methodologies for organising these activities into a consistent framework, provides an overview of some generally accepted ontology design principles and finally discusses some issues which are relevant for large ontologies.

4.2 Activities of the Ontology Development Process

An ontology development process consists of various activities and tasks. In this section we give an overview of the most typical activities. We base the discussion on [14], where a comprehensive list of ontology development activities is described.

Activities are categorised in [14] as *management activities*, *development-oriented activities* and *support activities*. This categorisation is motivated by the relevant IEEE standard on software processes [1], whereas support activities are termed as *integral activities* in the IEEE document.

Management activities include activities which are common to all kinds of projects. Development-oriented activities form the core of the development process, and are normally conducted sequentially. These type of activities are further categorised as *pre-development*, *development* and *post-development* activities. Finally, support (or integral) activities are crucial for the success of the development activities (and such for the whole project), and they are conducted parallel with one or more development activities. Many of them (like documentation) are performed continuously throughout the whole project. A summary of these activities is shown in Fig. 4.1 and they are discussed in detail in the following.

4.2.1 Management Activities

These kind of activities are common for all kinds of projects, and they are by no means specific for the ontology development process. They are enumerated here only for the sake of completeness.

Scheduling: Scheduling identifies the tasks to be performed, their order, dependencies and allocates time and resources for them.

Control: This activity guarantees that the tasks are performed in a way that was specified by the scheduling activity. Adjustments in the plan are made if needed.

Quality Assurance: This activity assures that the quality of each produced artefact (in our case the ontology, its documentation and eventually supporting software) is satisfactory.

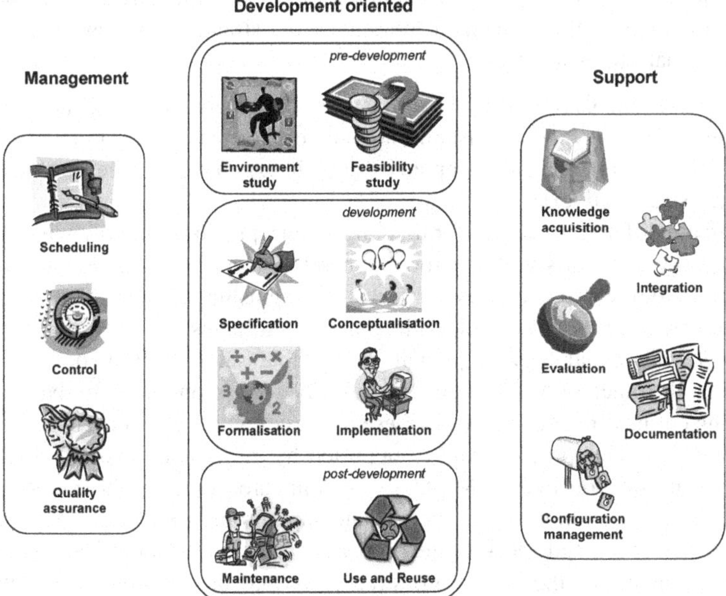

Fig. 4.1. Activities of the ontology development process

4.2.2 Development-Oriented Activities

These activities form the core of the ontology development process.

Pre-development Activities

Environment study: Identifies where the ontology will be used, in which technical environment (software platform, applications), by which types of users, etc.

Feasibility study: Checks whether it is possible and whether it is feasible to build the ontology in the given environment. Perhaps the project goals can also be achieved without building a new ontology, or the costs of building an ontology would outweigh the benefits provided by using an ontology. In this case the ontology development project should be cancelled.

Development Activities

Specification: This activity normally results in the ontology specification document. This document can be informal (natural language description, informal competency questions) or formal (formal competency questions). The document should define at least the goal and the scope of the ontology clearly and give clear criteria for ontology evaluation. It should also list the major information sources (domain experts, documents, external ontologies) for the ontology. It can optionally also list the most important entities of the domain (if the middle-out strategy is followed, see below the Conceptualisation activity).

Conceptualisation: Creates a model of the relevant domain knowledge at the knowledge level [32]. This model is usually not suitable for reasoning and can be in any form which is understood and accepted by domain experts (e.g. Excel sheets, a mind map, semi-structured text).

There are different strategies for defining a conceptualisation. Following the *top-down* strategy one starts with the most general concept (e.g. THING) and tries to refine the ontology structure along different distinguishing notions. This strategy is usable mostly in case of top-level, philosophical ontologies.

The *bottom-up* strategy starts with a suitable set of information resources (databases, documents) which should be described by an ontology. In the first step, interesting entities are collected from these resources which are worth to be included to the ontology. This process can be supported by information extraction (IE) and ontology learning tools like Text-to-Onto[1] or Amilcare.[2] Later on the ontology engineer tries to find common superconcepts and superproperties of the identified concepts and properties, and specifies the proper concepts for the identified instances.

The advantage of the bottom-up strategy is that the ontology will definitely describe the target document corpus or database(s) properly, i.e. it will describe the "information supply" well. On the other hand, with this approach there is a danger that the ontology will be too focused on a specific information resource, thus it will not be reusable. Experience also shows that semi-automatically generated ontologies are (yet) of lower quality than manually engineered ones. It is also important to note that this strategy can be used only for very low-level ontologies, where a specific information resource should be semantically described. This approach thus cannot be used for high-level ontologies, which should be developed independently from specific databases or document corpora.

Finally, the *middle-out* strategy starts with a list of most important ontology entities (concept, properties) which can be collected during a brain-storming session. This approach can be used for both low-level, application ontologies, and medium-level ontologies where a list of most important concepts can be easily identified at the beginning.

Generally speaking, we can say that both the top-down and middle-out strategies can result in high-quality ontologies which represents the "information need" in the domain quite well. There is a danger, however, that the ontology will not describe a specific collection of documents or a database adequately.

Formalisation: This phase includes choosing a suitable formalism (e.g. first order logic (FOL), F-Logic , description logic (DL)) and transform the conceptual model into that formalism. This formal representation is semi-computable, i.e. it can be rewritten into a suitable syntax quite easily, which can serve as an input for a reasoner.

[1] http://sourceforge.net/projects/texttoonto/

[2] http://nlp.shef.ac.uk/amilcare/

Implementation: Codifying the formal representation using a specific ontology language (such as OWL-DL) which can be executed in a suitable reasoner.

Post-development Activities

Maintenance: No ontology is ever complete as our understanding of the world (i.e. our conceptualisation) evolves constantly. It is also possible that the needs of the ontology users or applications change with the time, i.e. other parts of the domain will be relevant. To reflect those changes the ontology should be continuously evolved.

There are two types of ontology maintenance strategies [42, 43]: *centralised* and *decentralised*. In the centralised case, one person (or a group of people) is responsible for ontology changes. In the decentralised case, everyone can make changes to the ontology. In this case, tool support for ontology change management is crucial. The centralised strategy should be followed if high quality is important. On the other hand, the decentralised strategy is cheaper, faster and more flexible. As part of the maintenance activity, clear guidelines should be provided, which describe the maintenance strategy that is followed by the project.

Use and reuse: The ontology is used by various applications and users, and can be reused as part of other ontologies.

Ontology reuse is a very important aspect, as one of the main motivation for developing ontologies is the hope that knowledge formalised in such form is more amenable for reuse than in other forms (like relational database schemas or rule sets in expert systems). An ontology can reuse an other ontology in many ways. It can *reference* elements of an other ontology in its axioms. It can *include* the axioms of the other ontology. Finally, it can serve as a semantical basis during the development of the new ontology. In this case reuse happens at the knowledge level in the heads of ontology engineers. The axioms of the original ontology are adapted according to the needs of the new ontology, so it is even possible that almost none of the original axioms are taken in a syntactically unchanged form. Still, in many cases, it is simpler to adapt an existing ontology in the same domain than to develop a completely new one from scratch.

Ontology reuse during the ontology development process happens as part of the *integration activity* which will be discussed later.

4.2.3 Support Activities

These activities are important for the success of the development process, and they are performed in parallel with the development-oriented activities.

Knowledge acquisition: Knowledge has to be extracted from the various knowledge sources. Those sources can include domain expert knowledge, existing books and external ontologies. As mentioned at the conceptualisation activity, parts of the knowledge acquisition can happen automatically. In this case we speak of ontology learning [27].

Evaluation: Evaluation includes *verification*, i.e. judgement of ontology correctness with respect to a frame of reference (e.g. the ontology specification document). It also includes *validation*, i.e. judgement of the ontology with respect to the real-world domain it is supposed to represent. From a different point of view evaluation can be categorised in three categories [42, 43], as follows:

- Technology-focused evaluation: This includes checking the syntactical correctness and semantical consistency of the ontology, its performance, modularity, maintainability, etc.
- User-focused evaluation: This includes checking whether the ontology contains all of the information which was identified in the ontology specification document. A usage pattern–based evaluation is also part of this process, where it is checked that all parts of the ontology are really used, i.e. there are no unnecessary parts in it.
- Ontology-focused evaluation: This checks the semantical correctness of the ontology. Both philosophical methods (such as OntoClean [21]) and ontology evaluation rules [13] can be used to find incorrect conceptualisations.

Integration: It is strongly recommended to search for related ontologies which could be reused in our ontology before we start building a new ontology from scratch. If a suitable ontology is identified, it must be integrated in our new ontology. This integration process can be supported by two subactivities: ontology merging and ontology alignment. Ontology merging (e.g. [41]) aims at obtaining a new ontology by merging several ontologies from the same domain. The resulting ontology unifies elements of the source ontologies. Ontology alignment [35] only identifies mappings between the source ontologies, but does not create a new ontology. It is important to note that a prerequisite for a successful ontology merging is that proper mappings between the ontologies to be merged are already found in a previous alignment step.

Documentation: Proper documentation of an ontology is crucial for later maintenance and reuse [12]. One of the most serious hindrance in ontology reuse nowadays is that most of the ontologies available on the Web are not properly documented. Both the meaning of ontology entities and the design decisions which led to a specific ontology must be documented, otherwise the ontology cannot be judged objectively, when someone wants to decide about the integration of the ontology into a new one.

Configuration management: Configuration management means recording versions of the ontology, of the ontology documentation and of the supporting software (if it exists). Mainly in the case of big ontologies, which are developed collaboratively, configuration management is crucial for the success of the project, similarly to big software development projects. For this activity, the tools of Software Engineering can be used,[3] and also some ontology editing environments provide such features.[4]

---

[3] For example, Subversion, see `http://subversion.tigris.org/`

[4] For example, the Protege editor, see `http://protege.stanford.edu/`

4.2.4 The Rationale for Separating Conceptualisation, Formalisation and Implementation

Some of the existing methodologies, and many practitioners, do not separate the conceptual model and the ontology implementation in a formal ontology language, but propose to develop the ontology at once in the target language. This raises the question whether it is meaningful to separate the conceptualisation, formalisation and implementation activities at all.

First of all we examine the reasons for separating conceptualisation from the formalisation and implementation steps. There are basically two motivations for doing this. One is the *limited expression power* of most of the ontology formalisms, the other is the *need for communication* between domain experts and ontology engineers.

Most formal ontology languages are designed with the motivation to provide for several reasoning constructs. A natural requirement from the user side is that these reasoning operations should be calculated efficiently, or at least the reasoning should be decidable. Clearly, the more expressive an ontology language is, the more complicated the reasoning will be, and it is easy to reach the point where the reasoning will not be decidable any more. Therefore, these languages make various compromises in the area of expressiveness in favour of efficiency. This means that in many cases the knowledge required to properly represent the target domain requires constructs which are not supported by the target ontology language. As a result, it is possible that changes in the conceptual structure are required because of the limitations of the target formalism. For example, description logic usually supports only binary relations and many formalisms do not allow metaclasses, i.e. entities that are instances and concepts at the same time. It is also possible that some elements of the full conceptual model are lost completely. For example, information about the uncertainty of some facts and axioms cannot be represented in most of the popular ontology formalisms.

Because for an intermediate conceptual model reasoning support is not a requirement, we can include any knowledge representation constructs which seem to be natural for the problem at hand. This has many advantages.

First, even if some of the constructs can be represented in the target formal language using a workaround (e.g. representing n-ary relations as concept instances), this makes the understanding of the model for humans much more complicated, and thus practically eliminates the possibility of ontology reuse. On the other hand, a natural representation of the ontology is available at the conceptual level; therefore, people do not have to "parse" the low-level formal representation.

Second, if some information cannot be represented in the target formalism at all, we still have it in the conceptual model. If we later switch to a more powerful formalism, we can readily reuse this information. Moreover, if the information loss causes any problems during ontology usage (e.g. non-intuitive inferences), the cause of the problem can be found more easily, as all of the lost information is properly documented in the conceptual model.

Finally, because the conceptual model uses constructs that naturally describe the domain of discourse, it is easier to communicate it towards the domain experts. It is sometimes even possible that domain experts can edit parts of the model, without active participation of the ontology engineer. This helps to solve the common dilemma: Who should develop an ontology? The domain experts who understand the domain, but have only a little or absolutely no idea of good ontology design; or the ontology engineer, who has extensive knowledge about proper ontology constructs, but only a limited knowledge of the domain of discourse? By using intermediate models, the domain experts can edit those representations, and the ontology engineer can devise the best ways to map that non-computable conceptual representations into formal ontology constructs. In most cases, it is possible to find ways to generate parts of the formal ontology out of parts of the conceptual model fully automatically.

The use of intermediate models was already proved in many real-world systems (such as Galen [38], VICODI [31] or in the OTK use cases [43]). It is also interesting to note that the idea of separating the conceptual model from the implementation (i.e. the concrete ontology formalism) is very similar to the vision of *Model Driven Architecture* (MDA), a movement which became popular recently in the software engineering field.[5]

The only cases where the development of intermediate conceptual models cannot be advised are when

- the expressing power of the target ontology formalism is adequate to represent all of the relevant information of the domain in a natural way
- the domain experts have no problems in understanding the target ontology formalisms (e.g. when ontology engineers develop an ontology describing the knowledge engineering domain).

There are much less reasons for the separation of the formalisation and implementation steps. The transformation from an abstract formal representation to a specific syntactical representation required by a specific reasoner can be usually made fully automatically, as in most cases no more semantical changes are needed. If it is possible to devise algorithms to transform the conceptual model to a formal representation automatically, it is advisable to perform the transformation into the implementation language at once.

There are some cases, however, when a separation of formalisation and implementation can be advantageous.

- It is not possible to fully automatise the transformation from the conceptual to the formal model, but human intervention is required. In this case, it is better to have an explicit formal model, and it can be transformed completely automatically into the various ontology implementation languages.
- Even if a fully automated transformation from the conceptual to the formal model is possible, it is a good idea to keep the formal model separate from the implementation model, if there are lots of target implementation languages which we should support. For example, we have to support OIL, DAML+OIL and

[5] See `http://www.omg.org/mda/` for details

OWL-DL versions of our ontology. By separating the formal model from the implementation language we have to write the potentially difficult mapping from the conceptual to the formal model only once, and we can easily add new trivial mappings from the formal model to a new implementation language later.

4.3 Ontology Building Methodologies

As ontology development is a very complex, creative process, a methodology which co-ordinates the various activities involved, is crucial for its success. Ontology development is comparable with software engineering in complexity, a field where already lots of matured methodologies exist like the Rational Unified Process [23] or Extreme Programming [3]. Unfortunately, as the field of ontologies is not so matured yet as the field of software engineering, presently there is no set of established, generally accepted methodologies. There were numerous methodologies proposed, however, and some of them are quite elaborated.

The main purpose of a methodology is to define the life cycle of the ontology development process, i.e. the order in which the activities (described in the previous section) should be executed. Most of the methodologies propose the *evolving prototypes* approach, where changes in the developed ontology are always possible, i.e. it is always possible to switch between various phases of the development, like conceptualisation and implementation.

Another important criterion of a methodology is its application dependency. A methodology can be *application dependent*, which means that the ontology is built on the basis of an existing application. This is not typical, and presently only the KACTUS methodology [40] is known which proposes such a strategy. *Application semi-dependent* methodologies start with concrete scenarios of future ontology usage as part of their specification activity. This definitely helps to make the decision later on during the conceptualisation activity whether a piece of information about the domain of discourse is relevant for the ontology or not. Actually, there is a debate in the ontology engineering community whether it is possible to develop meaningful ontologies at all without considering their future application scenarios [46, 18] (it is the so-called *interaction problem* [7]). On the other hand, if the ontology engineer focuses too much on the target application, the ontology will not be reusable. The methodologies which follow this strategy include the methodology of Grüninger and Fox [16] and On-To-Knowledge [42, 43]. Finally, application-independent methodologies do not make any assumptions about the future applications of the ontology. Examples in this category include the methodology of Uschold and King [45] and METHONTOLOGY [26, 12].

Yet another categorisation is based on whether a proposed methodology depends on an existing core ontology. For example, the SENSUS approach [44] proposes to design a domain ontology by pruning and extending the highly complex SENSUS ontology. This approach is not usual, however, and most of the methodologies do not depend on specific core ontologies.

Based on recent studies [9, 14], the two most matured and detailed methodologies presently exist are METHONTOLOGY [12] and the On-To-Knowledge methodology [43]. Both build strongly on the best ideas of other, older methodologies. Therefore, we will discuss only these here and recommend reading one of the detailed studies about other methodologies for the interested reader. Some good studies and overviews which can be recommended are the following: [9], Chap. 3 in [14] and [24].

4.3.1 The On-to-Knowledge Methodology

The *On-to-Knowledge methodology (OTK)* concentrates on building knowledge-based systems, where ontologies form an important part of the system. This methodology defines two orthogonal processes, the *Knowledge Process* and the *Knowledge Meta Process*. The former describes the process of ontology usage, the latter guides the ontology creation. Therefore, here we are interested only in the Knowledge Meta Process.

OTK defines the following steps as part of the Knowledge Meta Process (see also Fig. 4.2 taken from [43]):

Feasibility study: OTK follows the CommonKADS methodology [39] in order to decide whether it makes sense to start the project, i.e. to build the ontology.

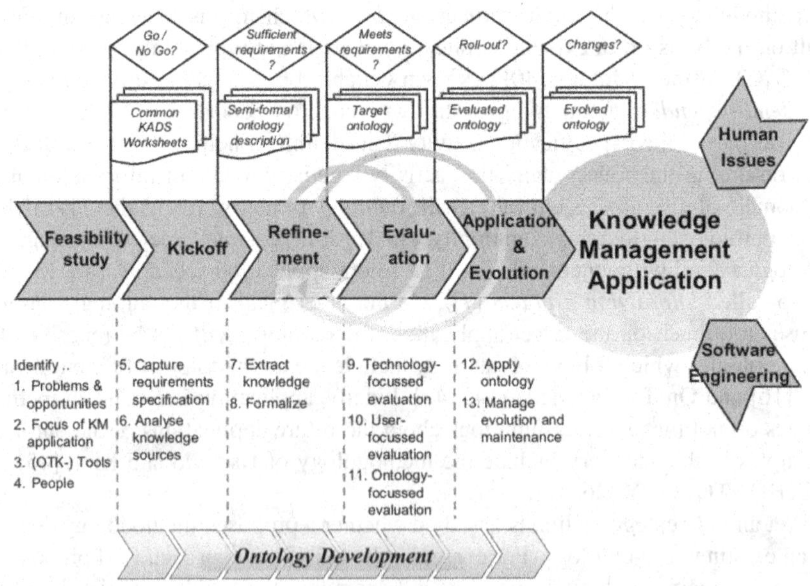

Fig. 4.2. OTK steps

Kickoff: During this phase the ontology requirements are finalised: the exact goal and the scope of the ontology is determined. According to the middle-out strategy during a brainstorming session, an initial list of important entities is collected and a list of relevant experts and knowledge sources is compiled. Design guidelines are also made which will guide the development process. Competency questions are collected which can be used later to validate the ontology. This step corresponds to the Specification activity in Sect. 4.2.

Refinement: In this phase relevant knowledge is extracted from the identified knowledge sources (and from human experts) and formalised. This phase is a combination of the Conceptualisation, Formalisation and Implementation activities in Sect. 4.2.

Evaluation: OTK describes all the three types of evaluation which were described in Sect. 4.2 (technology-focused, user-focused and ontology-focused evaluation). It is interesting to note that in the case of OTK the evaluation activity is a main development activity and not just a supporting one. This shows that the categorisation of activities into "development" and "support" is somewhat subjective.

Application and evolution: This is practically the Maintenance activity described in Sect. 4.2, using a different name.

OTK proposes a cyclic ontology development process, i.e. the Refinement and Evaluation phases are iterated until a stable, high-quality ontology version is reached, and the lessons learned during the "Application & Evolution" phase can initiate a new cycle.

OTK was used in various use cases during the On-To-Knowledge project.[6] The most important lessons learned during these use cases were the following:

- "Human Issues" can dominate other forces during a Knowledge Management (KM) project.
- Domain experts in industrial context need pragmatic development guidelines (which we also provide in this chapter).
- Collaborative ontology engineering requires physical presence and advanced tool support.
- Brainstorming is very helpful for early stages of ontology engineering, especially for domain experts not familiar with modelling. In OTK, mind maps[7] were used quite successfully.

4.3.2 The METHONTOLOGY Methodology

The METHONTOLOGY methodology [26, 12] describes a similar process than OTK, but it focuses more on the ontology development (it does not address the issue of Knowledge Process) and describes the conceptualisation activity in

[6] See `http://www.ontoknowledge.org`

[7] See `http://en.wikipedia.org/wiki/Mind_mapping`

much more detail. METHONTOLOGY defines an evolutionary type of life cycle (similar to most of the other methodologies) which is shown on Fig. 4.3. This means that the development activities are executed iteratively throughout the development process. From the project management activities, planning is done at the very beginning, control and quality assurance are continuous. All of the integral activities are done continuously, although the amount of knowledge acquisition, integration and evaluation decreases as the ontology matures and its structure stabilises.

As it can be seen on Fig. 4.3, this methodology specifies exactly the same activities that were described in Sect. 4.2, using the same names, but it does not mention the *environmental study* and *feasibility study* steps.

As it was already mentioned, the main strength of METHONTOLOGY is the detailed description of the conceptualisation activity. In the remaining part of this section we therefore will concentrate on this activity.

As it was already described in Sect. 4.2, the main task of the conceptualisation activity is the construction of an intermediate conceptual model. This model is (usually) not suitable for reasoning and can be in any form which is understood and accepted by domain experts (e.g. Excel sheets, a mind map, semi-structured text or combinations thereof). On the other hand, the intermediate model should be machine processable, i.e. it must be possible to automatise the generation of the formal model out of the conceptual model, at least partially.

METHONTOLOGY describes various artefacts which specify different aspects of the conceptual model:

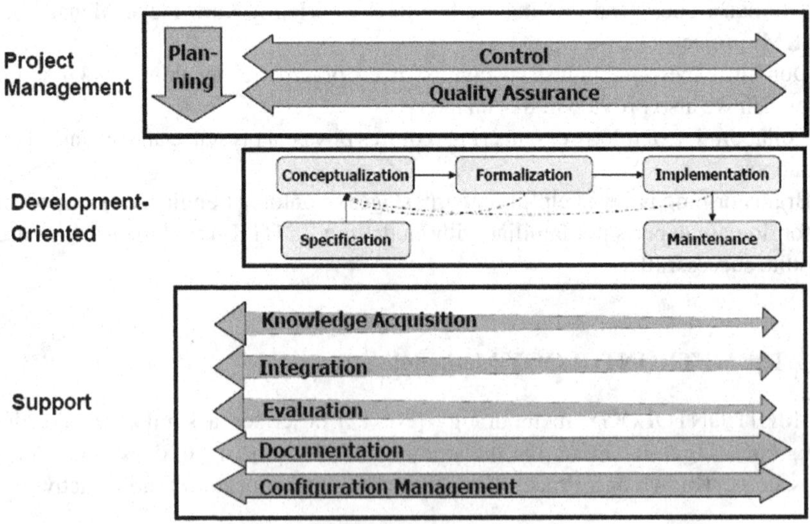

Fig. 4.3. Methodology life cycle

- Glossary of terms
- Concept taxonomy
- Ad hoc binary relation diagrams
- Concept dictionary
- Descriptions (tables) of relations, instance and class attributes and constants
- Descriptions of formal axioms and rules
- Table of instances

According to METHONTOLOGY, the conceptualisation process is a controlled development of the described artefacts. The list of artefacts shows the order of their creation. First, a glossary of relevant terms of the domain is built. Terms representing concepts are identified, and the taxonomy of those concepts is devised. As the next step, ad hoc binary relations are defined. After that, the concept dictionary is constructed, which exactly defines which properties belong to which concepts. Next, tables are created where properties of binary relations, instance and class attributes, constants, formulas, axioms and rules are exactly specified. Finally, a table of ontology instances is also created, if the ontology contains instances.

Clearly, the documents are in close relationship to each other. For example, only such concept names can appear in the concept dictionary, which are also mentioned in the glossary of terms. According to the "evolving prototypes" life cycle that METHONTOLOGY defines, it is always possible to add new information to any of the documents, but care must be taken that the whole model remains consistent. For example, if a new concept is added to the concept dictionary, its name should also be described in the glossary of terms, and it should also be added to the concept taxonomy.

Listing conceptualisation steps and artefacts is only a possible way to define a conceptual model. It can vary from project to project which is the most suitable formalism for the domain which is also understood by the domain experts. For example, METHONTOLOGY commits strongly to a frame-based conceptual model with binary relations, n-ary relations can be defined only as axioms or rules. This may not be appropriate for all application domains.

More detailed descriptions of the documents forming the intermediate conceptual model of METHONTOLOGY and the steps that should be taken can be found in Sect. 3.3.5 of [14] and in [12]. A detailed practical example using METHONTOLOGY is described in [26].

Other useful guides which describe possible tasks to take during the conceptualisation activity are [34] and [5], although these papers do not mention the utility of intermediate conceptual models.

4.4 Ontology Design Principles

As we have seen, the conceptualisation activity is one of the most important ones and it is definitely the most complex one. Practical guidelines and techniques are definitely useful, if not crucial, to carry out this task.

Unfortunately, there is no standard catalog of "ontology design patterns", "knowledge patterns" or "semantic patterns". Although there is already some preliminary work in this area (e.g. [8, 37, 33]), ontologies are still immature in comparison to software development, where a significant body of analysis and design patterns are available (see e.g. [10, 11]). Therefore, we think that it is a valuable contribution to list some of the best-practice principles which were collected from state-of-the-art ontology-related literature (including [21, 14, 12, 36, 38, 24, 15, 28, 42, 37, 33, 9, 43, 34]) and are validated by many ontology building projects (e.g. [31, 43]).

For the sake of consistency, we will use the domain of train travel in all of the examples in this section. A part of the ontology is shown on Fig. 4.4.

4.4.1 Philosophical Principles

The following principles describe high-level rules which describe at a general, philosophical–epistemological level how a good ontology design should look like.

The first five principles, namely clarity, coherence, extendibility, minimal encoding bias and minimal ontological commitment, are identified by Gruber and are described in his seminal paper [15].

Clarity: What this principle states informally is that it is important that ontologies are understandable. With other words, not only machines but also human beings should understand the content of an ontology. Gruber defines clarity as follows:

> An ontology should communicate effectively the intended meaning of defined terms. Definitions should be objective. Definitions can be stated on

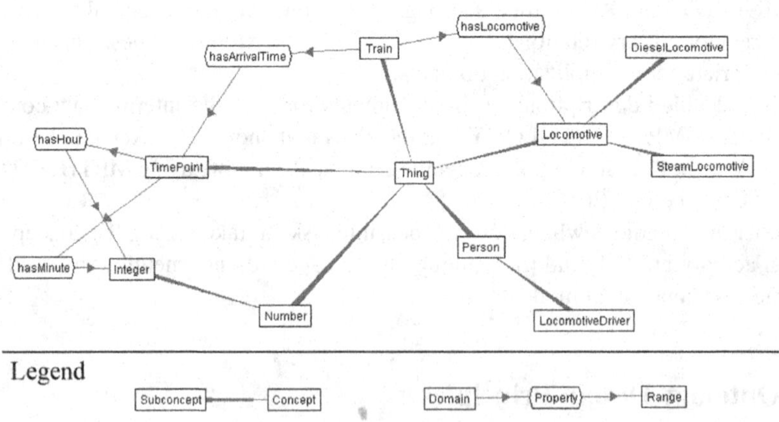

Fig. 4.4. Excerpt from the train ontology

> formal axioms, and a complete definition (defined by necessary and sufficient conditions) is preferred over a partial definition (defined by only necessary or sufficient conditions). All definitions should be documented with natural language.

For example, if we know that steam locomotives are exactly those locomotives which have steam propulsion, we should describe that fact with the proper logical axioms, and also paraphrase this fact in natural language as part of the ontology documentation, instead of simply inserting a STEAMLOCOMOTIVE concept into the ontology as subconcept of LOCOMOTIVE, without any other axioms, constraints or documentation.

Coherence: This principle deals with the consistency of the formal and informal layers of the ontology (axioms vs natural language documentation and labels). The principle states that the formal and informal layers of the ontology should make the same statements. Gruber expresses this as follows:

> An ontology should be coherent: that is, it should sanction inferences that are consistent with the definitions. [...] If a sentence that can be inferred from the axioms contradicts a definition or example given informally, then the ontology is incoherent.

For example, if we define the STEAMLOCOMOTIVE concept with logical axioms as locomotives that have diesel engines, our ontology is incoherent, because our logical level contradicts the natural language label we have chosen for the concept.

Extendibility: This is a very abstract principle which states that an ontology should be designed in a way which allows us to add new definitions without revising or modifying old ones. Gruber's definition is the following:

> One should be able to define new terms for special uses based on the existing vocabulary, in a way that does not require the revision of the existing definitions.

As this is a very abstract and general principle, it is hard to give a simple example here, but we refer to Sect. 4.5 where we show a technique to achieve extendibility in huge ontologies, and we also give numerous examples there.

Minimal encoding bias: This principle states that when we specify ontologies we should remain at the knowledge level [32] if it is possible. With Gruber's words,

> The conceptualisation should be specified at the knowledge level without depending on a particular symbol-level encoding.

Typical examples for the symbol level are the built-in datatypes, functions and predicates which can be found in many database or logic programming languages. If we use those symbols in the definition of our ontology (say, we state that the range of the HASWHEELS property of locomotives is `integer`), the ontology will be clearly system dependent and thus less reusable. The ideal solution would be to avoid using system-dependent symbols in the ontology definition at all, and specify everything with proper logical axioms at the knowledge level.[8] Unfortunately, practical considerations normally prohibit that approach, e.g. nobody would define and manage 100000 number instances in their ontology, instead of simply using some built-in integer datatype. From a practical point of view we can therefore say that probably a standardised set of primitive datatypes is a better solution, as it provides for ontology interoperability, while making also ontology management and reasoning more efficient. Indeed, most of the web ontology standards today support the XML Schema datatypes [4].

Minimal ontological commitment: This principle states that we should define our conceptualisation in more detail which is absolutely needed for our purposes. As Gruber writes;

> Since ontological commitment is based on the consistent use of the vocabulary, ontological commitment can be minimised by specifying the weakest theory and defining only those terms that are essential to the communication of knowledge consistent with the theory.

As an example, consider the HASARRIVALTIME property of the TRAIN concept. We can say that the range of HASARRIVALTIME is a TIMEPOINT, but what is a time point? The minimal commitment depends on our needs. For example, if we need to record only hours and minutes, we could attach the required information to time points by defining the HASHOUR and HASMINUTE properties on the TIMEPOINT concept. This keeps the definition general, and if later someone also needs to define years, seconds or time zones,[9] these new definitions can be added to the ontology without disturbing the existing axioms. On the other hand, if we would have fixed everything in our definition,[10] our ontology could not be reused in other applications without changes.

Similarly, if the colour of various locomotives is not interesting for us at the moment, we should not include various colour information to our ontology just to make it more "complete".

Proper subconcept taxonomies: In many ontologies, subconcept relations are misused to represent part of subtopic or other relations [21]. Even if we avoid such apparently wrong cases, there are still a number of situations where it is hard to decide whether a proper subconcept relationship exists between two concepts.

Guarino and Welty propose their *OntoClean* method for evaluating such decisions. The main idea of the method is to annotate concepts in the ontology with philosophical meta-properties like *identity*, *unity* or *rigidity*. After annotating the concepts, several rules can be applied, which validate the existing subconcept relationships from a ontological–philosophical point of view. Unfortunately, because of space limitations, we cannot give a deep discussion of this method here. We will give

---

[8] For example, by introducing an INTEGER concept as a subconcept of NUMBER with 1, 2, etc. as instances

[9] That is, our definition is not adequate for the purposes of that new ontology any more

[10] For example, stating that we use two digit years with Western European time zone

here only a short motivating example, and recommend studying the pretty extensive literature available on the topic (e.g. [20, 19, 22, 21, 47] and also Sect. 3.8.3 of [14]).

Let us consider the question whether PERSON can be a subconcept of LOCOMOTIVEDRIVER or not. To answer that question, first we have to define one of the meta-properties used by the OntoClean method, namely *rigidity*. The OntoClean method uses the term "property" in its discussion, and we also adopt that terminology here for the sake of simplicity. It must be stressed, however, that this property has nothing to do with properties in RDFS, OWL and similar ontology formalisms. If an entity "has a property *X*" in OntoClean speak, it is roughly synonymous with the sentence "the entity is an instance of the concept *X*".

A property is *rigid* if it is essential for all of its instances. Something is essential if it is always true for an entity. For example, being a person is essential as we are persons throughout our whole lives, and it cannot change. Therefore PERSON is rigid; as if something is a member of the concept, it will remain a member forever.

A property is *non-rigid* if it is not rigid. Finally, a property is anti-rigid if it is non-essential for all of its instances. For example, being a locomotive driver is non-rigid, as a locomotive driver can cease to be one (e.g. when he is retired). Furthermore, being a locomotive driver is anti-rigid, as nobody exists who is essentially a locomotive driver, i.e. who was always a locomotive driver and will remain one forever.

Now, that we defined rigidity, we are ready to apply a rule of OntoClean which says "An anti-rigid property cannot subsume a rigid property" [19]. In our example, it means that LOCOMOTIVEDRIVER cannot subsume PERSON: therefore the answer to our question is "no". On the other hand, none of the rules forbid us to make LOCOMOTIVEDRIVER a subconcept of PERSON, which meets our intuition.

4.4.2 Technical Principles

The following principles contain concrete, practical advices, which can make the conceptualisation process easier. Some of the described principles, like using naming conventions, and the importance of scoping and documentation are not ontology specific. They are also valid for software development, or for the development of any complex system. The other principles are, however, specific for ontology development.

Define and use naming conventions [2, 34]: To achieve a consistent, and meaningful ontology, it is extremely important to define naming conventions, and obey to them throughout the development process. Probably the most important areas, where clear guidelines are needed, are the following (Fig. 4.5):

- Capitalisation: It is a common convention to begin concept names with capital, instance and property names with non-capital letters.
- Delimiters: Common conventions are using space or the "-" character as delimiters, or writing names in CamelCase which eliminates the need for delimiters. As the Wikipedia writes:[11]

[11] See also `http://en.wikipedia.org/wiki/CamelCase`

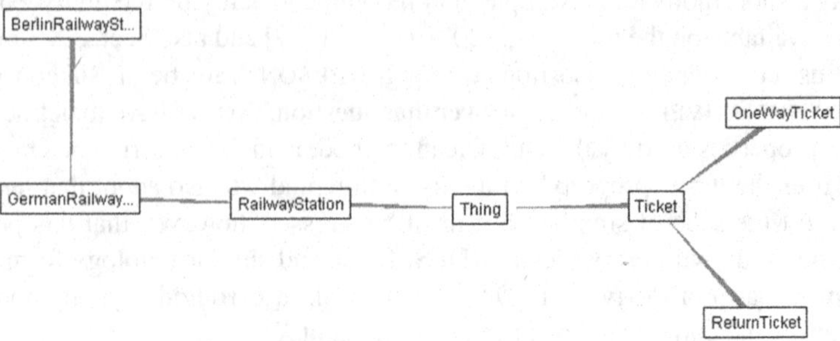

Fig. 4.5. Using naming conventions

> CamelCase is the practice of writing compound words or phrases where the words are joined without spaces, and each word is capitalised within the compound. The name comes from the uppercase "bumps" in the middle of the compound word, suggesting the humps of a camel.

Note that CamelCase is also suitable for ontology URIs, therefore it is frequently used in web ontologies.

- Singular or plural: It is important to decide whether to use singular or plural form of names. It is a common convention to use the singular form in concept names.
- Prefix and suffix conventions: These conventions are mainly important for property names. A usual solution is to use "has" and "is" as prefixes for properties, with an additional "of" suffix for the "is" form. In case of an inverse property pair, one of them should follow the 'has' scheme and the other should follow the "is" scheme.
- Avoid abbreviations: Abbreviations should be avoided in names, except from some very well established ones, like URI for Uniform Resource Identifier.
- Consistently exclude/include superconcepts in names: The name of superconcepts or superproperties should be consistently included or excluded in the name of subconcepts or subproperties throughout the ontology. For example, both ONEWAYTICKET, RETURNTICKET or ONEWAY, RETURN can be used as names for subconcepts of the TICKET concept, but ONEWAYTICKET and RETURN should not be used together.
- Standardisation of names: To make the ontology more comprehensible, the same naming conventions should be used for related terms [2]. For example, STATIONINBERLIN and GERMANSTATION do not follow the same naming convention.

Scope Your ontology: [34, 43] Scoping means that an ontology should not contain all of the imaginable distinctions of the target domain but, on the other hand, it should contain all of the important distinctions of the domain. Without defining a clear scope it is hard/impossible to decide whether a specific fact or axiom should go to the ontology or not. Note that for high-level ontologies it is not easy to decide what is relevant and what is not. In this case, scoping means deciding about the generality level where the ontology should stop.

Introducing new entities: [34] Introduce a new concept or property only if it is significant for the problem domain, i.e., we can say something about that very entity which is not true for any of the other entities in the ontology. For example, typically you should introduce new concepts only if they will have a different set of properties than other concepts in the ontology. On the other hand, you should introduce a new entity whenever that distinction is important for you, even if the formal entity definition does not (yet) differ from other definitions.

Formal concept hierarchy: [34] Always define a formal concept hierarchy: if D is subconcept of C, all instances of D must be also instances of C.

Do not mix concepts with topics! A good example for an informal topic hierarchy is the Yahoo Directory.[12] An example hierarchy path in this directory is COMPUTERS AND INTERNET > SOFTWARE > INTERNET > WORLD WIDE WEB > HTML EDITORS. This hierarchy of informal topics may be meaningful for humans if they would like to browse Yahoo, but it is by no means a formal concept hierarchy. For example, we can clearly say that a specific HTML editor (instance of HTML EDITORS) is not a kind of "World Wide Web", therefore it is not an instance WORLD WIDE WEB.

Further examples are as follows:

- All RETURNTICKETs are TICKETS. (Good)
- All LOCOMOTIVEs are TRANSPORTATION. (Bad, it is a topic hierarchy, as a locomotive is not a transportation, but belongs to the transportation topic.)

If you are unsure about a subclass relationship, the OntoClean evaluation methodology [21] can help to validate the decision, as it was described at the "Proper taxonomies" principle.

Optimal number of subconcepts: The optimal number of subconcepts is between 2 and 12 (according to [34]). If you have only one subconcept, it is a good indication that either the subconcept, is unnecessary, or siblings of that concept are missing from the ontology, and they should be added. If you have more than twelve subconcepts, introducing an intermediate classification level may be useful, otherwise human users will have serious problems comprehending your ontology.

New concept or property value: The following decision has to be made quite often during ontology development: Should I represent something by introducing a new concept, or is it enough to fill in the right value for a property at the instance level? For example, the distinction between slow and fast locomotives can be represented by introducing new SLOWLOCOMOTIVE and FASTLOCOMOTIVE concepts, or by filling the proper values of a HASSPEED property (SLOW or FAST) at the instances of LOCOMOTIVE.

If a distinction makes entities to participate in different relations, make the new entities concepts, otherwise a property value is probably enough [34]. For

[12] `http://dir.yahoo.com/`

example, if there is a concept HIGHSPEEDLINE and we know that only fast locomotives are allowed to travel on such lines, it is probably a good idea to define FASTLOCOMOTIVE as a concept.

Another indicator for using a property value instead of defining new concepts is if the value would change often [34]. For example, if locomotives are newly painted each year with different colours, probably it is not the best idea to define the concepts BLUELOCOMOTIVE and REDLOCOMOTIVE, as locomotive instances would change their concept frequently (Fig. 4.6). Of course, if our target ontology formalism supports axiomatic concept definitions, and thus automatic categorisation of instances (like description logic-based formalisms), this is not a real problem, and such concepts can be defined even if concept membership often changes.

From a more philosophical point of view, we can also check whether an entity can exist alone, or it is always dependent on other entities. For dependent entities, it is better to define a new property instead of a new concept [5]. For example, it makes sense to speak of "arrival time" if we know the entity whose arrival time we talk about (e.g. a specific train). In this case, it is probably a good decision to have a HASARRIVALTIME property instead of an ARRIVALTIME concept. Of course in many cases the distinction is not so clear. For example, the colour "red" exists also without considering other entities, but it is also clear that in many cases we are interested in the connection between this colour and other objects.

Concept or instance: If it is meaningful to speak of a "kind of X" in the target domain, i.e. the entity represents a set of something, make X a concept. Otherwise X should be an instance [5, 34]. A good intuitive test for instances if you ask your-

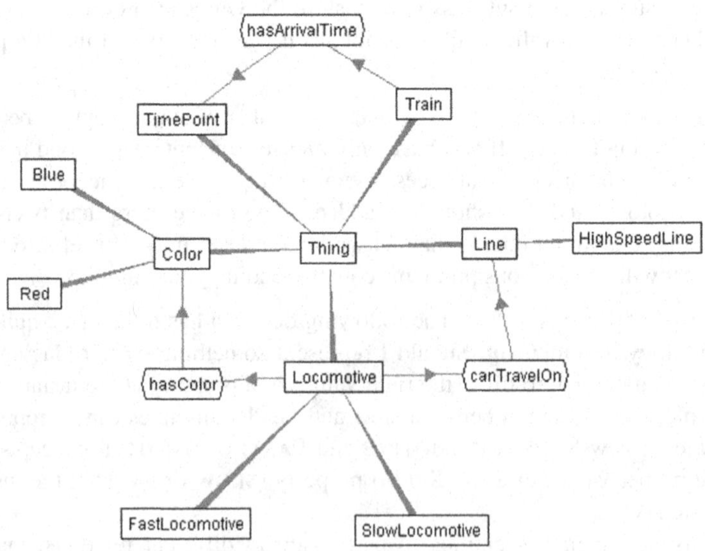

Fig. 4.6. Concepts vs properties

self whether it makes sense to count that entity [5], because normally instances are countable, while concepts are usually not. If you are unsure, make X a concept, that is the safer strategy [37].

For example, consider the case when you have a LOCOMOTIVE concept. The question is, whether STEAMLOCOMOTIVE and DIESELLOCOMOTIVE should be subclasses or instances of this concept. From a conceptual point of view, both options are possible, the choice depends on whether we want to model concrete instances of steam or diesel locomotives (e.g. STEAMLOC234543534). If locomotive instances are not interesting for us, we can have STEAMLOCOMOTIVE and DIESELLOCOMOTIVE as instances of LOCOMOTIVE, in which case LOCOMOTIVE represents the set of locomotive types. If we are unsure whether we will ever need to represent LOC234543534, it is better to have STEAMLOCOMOTIVE and DIESELLOCOMOTIVE as concepts. It is important to note that in this case LOCOMOTIVE will represent a set of locomotive instances (and not locomotive types, as before), i.e. the ontology will have a different semantics. If we represent STEAMLOCOMOTIVE and DIESELLOCOMOTIVE as concepts, we will always be able to define new subconcepts and instances of them, what would not be possible for an instance any more. (Fig. 4.7).

Generally speaking, we can say that the concept vs instance distinction is unnatural for human beings, and in many cases the answer is that an entity is both a concept (a set of something) and an instance (a member of a set). Consider the situation described in [30]. There is a concept SPECIES (representing the set of all species), with instances such as APE. However, APE may be also viewed as a set of all apes. It

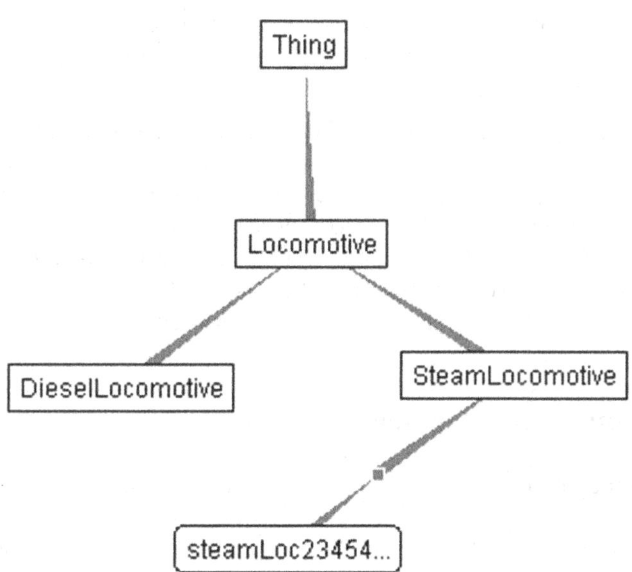

Fig. 4.7. Concepts vs instances

may be argued that APE may be modelled as a subconcept of SPECIES. However, if this is done, other irregularities arise. Since APE is a set of all apes, SPECIES, being a superconcept of APE, must contain all apes as their members, which is conceptually clearly wrong. Further, when talking about the APE species, there are many properties that may be attached to it, such as habitat, type of food, etc. This is impossible to do if APE is a subconcept of SPECIES, since concepts cannot have properties (in most ontology formalisms). This shows the need for ontology formalisms supporting metaclasses, i.e. where concepts can be viewed as instances at the same time. KAON [30], OWL-Full [29] or F-Logic [27] are examples for such ontology formalisms.

Document your ontologies: Documentation is crucial for the reuse of ontologies [12]. You should always document ontology entities in natural language also[13] [15]. While logical axioms are very useful for logic reasoners, usually human beings[14] have problems interpreting and understanding them. On the other hand, simple labels are usually ambiguous,[15] and therefore paraphrasing the exact meaning of the ontology entity with one or more sentences, is needed in the most cases. It is also possible to express design considerations in natural language, which are not expressible in the target modelling language, but are important when someone tries to reuse the ontology.

Represent disjoint and exhaustive knowledge explicitly: If a set of subconcepts are disjoint, or cover the superconcept completely, this information should always be represented explicitly via logical axioms [2, 34], if supported by the ontology formalism. Explicitly representing this information allows applying powerful sanity checking rules on the ontology. For example ONEWAYTICKET and RETURNTICKET form a disjoint decomposition of the concept TICKET because no ticket can be one-way and return at the same time. If the railway company provides only one-way and return tickets, this is also an exhaustive decomposition, because every ticket instance is either one-way or return.

Minimise syntactic difference among siblings To improve the clarity of the ontology, you should always strive to minimise the syntactic difference among sibling concepts, i.e. represent them using the same ontological primitives [2]. For example, if you define STEAMLOCOMOTIVE stating that steam locomotives are LOCOMOTIVEs which HASPROPULSION STEAM, and in the same ontology you define DIESELLOCOMOTIVE simply as a subconcept of LOCOMOTIVE without any further axioms or constraints, it is syntactically inconsistent.

4.5 Developing Large Ontologies

Especially in the case of very big ontologies that are developed collaboratively, it is useful to split the ontology into independent modules. A possible technique for doing that is described in [36] by Rector, based on his more than fifteen years of ontology

[13] see also the principle of "Clarity" above
[14] especially domain experts with no or minimal background in logic
[15] For example, consider "wing" in an airplane or in a bird ontology

building experience. In terms of the ontological principles presented in Sect. 4.4, this technique is concerned mainly with the "Extendibility" principle. We overview this technique here informally, and recommend the interested reader to read the referred paper for more details.

Before we can start discussing the modularisation technique, we have to introduce some new terminology. Let A denote a logical formula, let C and D denote concept names and i an ontology instance. $A(i)$ means that the formula A is true on instance i, $C(i)$ means that i is an instance of C. Let $\rightarrow$ denote the usual logical implication and $\leftrightarrow$ the logical equivalence.

Axioms in the form $A(i) \rightarrow C(i)$ define a sufficient condition on C. Axioms in the form $C(i) \rightarrow A(i)$ define a necessary condition on C. Axioms in the form $A(i) \leftrightarrow C(i)$ define a necessary and sufficient condition on C. It is important to note that $C(i)$ is also a logical formula itself, which is true if i is an instance of C. Therefore, a subconcept axiom $C \in D$ which can be written in an equivalent form as $C \rightarrow D$ is also a necessary condition on C.[16]

A concept which is defined by a sufficient and necessary condition is called *defined*. A non-defined concept is called *primitive*.

The main ideas of this modularisation technique are the following:

- The ontology should be split into *independent modules*, containing only *primitive concepts*. As a primitive concept is not defined fully by necessary and sufficient conditions in the ontology, it is transparent for the reasoner. In other words, the reasoner does not "understand" the meaning of the concept. As we have seen, simple subconcept axioms do not fully define concepts, therefore organising primitive concepts into hierarchies still does not fully define them. For example, we can state that LOCOMOTIVE is a subconcept of VEHICLE, which is enough information for the reasoner to infer that all locomotives are vehicles, the but the reasoner still does not have any information about what are locomotives and vehicles exactly, i.e. what is the exact difference between them.
- In a module, a *tree taxonomy of primitive concepts* should be defined where
  - each concept has a maximum of one parent concept (i.e. the taxonomy forms a tree)
  - children of a concept are always pairwise disjoint
  - the whole taxonomy is based on only one differentiating notion, such as speed, colour, functionality or structure. That is, RED and FAST should not be part of the same module, RED and BLUE should be.
- The *modules should be connected by defined concepts* which are defined by axioms using primitive concepts from the various modules. These defined concepts should be always subconcepts of exactly one primitive concept, and connected by properties with other primitive concepts. For example, we can define FASTREDLOCOMOTIVE as LOCOMOTIVE which HASSPEED FAST and HASCOLOR RED.

[16] and therefore a sufficient condition on D

The consequences of this procedure are the following:

- The place for new instances are easily identified even for huge ontologies, as
  - all leaf concepts in a module's tree hierarchy are pairwise disjoint (i.e. the instance should belong only to one of them)
  - the modules describe independent aspects and therefore it is easy to choose the right module for the instance
- Updates (new axioms and instances) have minimal or absolutely no impact on already existing parts of the ontology.
- The modules can be developed independently from each other, possibly by different expert groups.

As an example demonstrating the advantage of the approach, consider the following. We would like to define the FASTREDSMALLLOCOMOTIVE concept in a big railway ontology. Using a naive conceptualisation, this concept could be defined as a subconcept of FASTLOCOMOTIVE, REDLOCOMOTIVE and SMALLLOCOMOTIVE, which are again subconcepts of LOCOMOTIVE.

What happens if we later also want to make a distinction in the ontology, based on the propulsion type of locomotives? How to add the FASTREDSMALLSTEAMLOCOMOTIVE concept? Of course, we could add this new concept as the subconcept of FASTREDSMALLLOCOMOTIVE, but this would cause two problems. First of all, because we did not define clearly what is the difference between FASTREDSMALLLOCOMOTIVE and FASTREDSMALLSTEAMLOCOMOTIVE,[17] it is not possible to classify existing (and possibly quite numerous) locomotive instances automatically, but we have to examine all(!) of them manually, and declare them as FASTREDSMALLSTEAMLOCOMOTIVE when it is appropriate.

Second, it is an open question, who is responsible for adding this new concept and doing the job of manual classification. The experts dealing with colours? With speed? Or with vehicle types? Most likely, the result will be a deadlock, where nobody will do anything. Alternatively, many experts will try to add the new concept simultaneously. You should never underestimate human issues in a big ontology development project, as it was already mentioned in Sect. 4.3.

Using the modularisation approach, expert groups can develop modules of vehicle types (containing LOCOMOTIVE), speed (containing FAST), colour (containing RED) independently (Fig. 4.8), and the ontology engineer can define the new concept FASTREDSMALLLOCOMOTIVE as a LOCOMOTIVE which is red, fast and small. Responsibilities for adding new instances can be clearly defined. For example, the vehicle expert group adds new locomotives, and defines their properties (speed and colour). If it is not possible, e.g. because the required colour does not yet exist in the "colour" module, it notifies the other expert group, responsible for the maintenance of that module. The instances are categorised automatically and properly as FASTREDSMALLLOCOMOTIVE when it is appropriate.

What happens, if we also want to use propulsion types? It is easy, we just create a new expert group which defines a new "propulsion types" module containing,

[17] Because those are primitive concepts

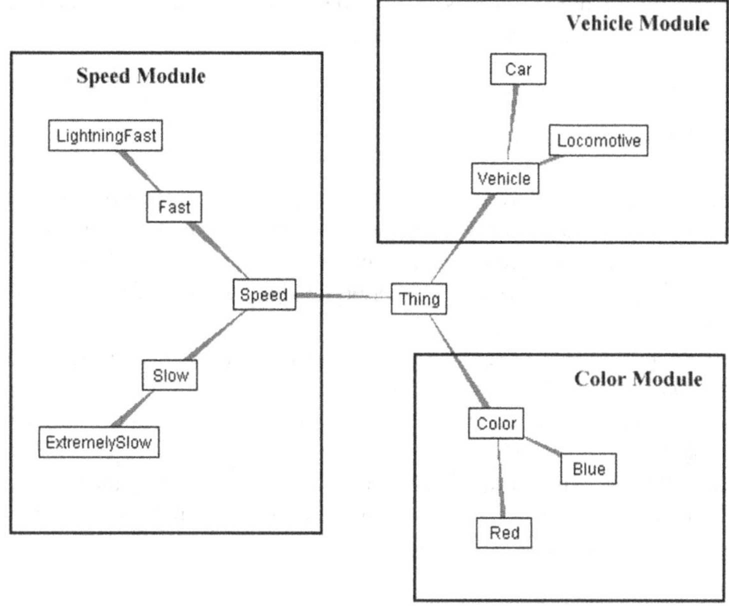

Fig. 4.8. The modularised train ontology

e.g., the STEAM concept.[18] When they are finished with the "propulsion" module, the vehicle expert group can extend the locomotive instances with their propulsion information. The ontology engineer defines the FASTREDSMALLSTEAMLOCOMOTIVE concept as the set of all Locomotives which are fast, small, red and have steam propulsion. After defining that concept, all of the existing (and new) instances of locomotives are categorised automatically and properly.

Based on this discussion, it should be clear that this approach provides the maximum benefit, if the ontology formalism provides some possibilities to infer the membership of an instance in a concept automatically. Rector proposed this approach specifically for description logic-based formalisms (such as OWL-DL), and those formalisms support that type of inference. But there exist many other formalisms, where such an inference can be expressed (such as F-Logic), although sometimes with slightly different semantics (closed-world vs open-world semantics).

Interestingly, independently of Rector, Gu and her colleagues also proposed to partition complex, semi-formal taxonomies into disjoint tree structures [17]. In this case, concepts connecting the modules[19] must be defined at the meta-level, using special kinds of the subconcept relations. Although in this case the automatic classification benefit is clearly lost, they argue that the resulting structure is much more

[18] or the STEAM instance of the PROPULSION concept

[19] Gu and her colleagues speak of "contexts" in their paper

comprehensive for human beings. This shows that the idea of tree partitioning is viable also for ontologies using less powerful ontology formalisms.

4.6 Summary

This chapter provided an overview of some important issues of ontology development. First, we enumerated the activities of a typical ontology development process. After that we described the main ideas of two popular methodologies (On-To-Knowledge and METHONTOLOGY) for organising these activities into a consistent framework.

Later, we provided an overview of some generally accepted ontology design principles based on a careful review of relevant ontology literature. Finally, we discussed the tree partitioning technique which can be useful for developing and maintaining large ontologies.

Because of space limitations and because of the complexity of the topic, we could only provide an overview of the field, but we gave many useful references throughout the discussion for the interested reader.

References

1. IEEE Standard for Developing Software Life Cycle Processes. IEEE Std 1074-1995, IEEE Computer Society, New York, 1996.
2. J.C. Arpírez, A. Gómez-Pérez, A. Lozano-Tello, and H.S. Pinto. $(\mathrm{ONTO})^2$Agent: An Ontology-Based WWW Broker to Select Ontologies. In A. Gómez-Pérez and R.V. Benjamins, editors, *Proceedings of ECAI'98 Workshop on Applications of Ontologies and Problem-Solving Methods*, pages 16–24, Brighton, UK, 1998.
3. K. Beck. *Extreme Programming Explained: Embrace Change*. Addison-Wesley, 2000.
4. P.V. Biron and A. Malhotra (eds.). XML Schema part 2: Datatypes. W3C Recommendation, May 2001.
5. R.J. Brachman, D.L. McGuiness, P.F. Patel-Schneider, and L.A. Resnick. Living with CLASSIC: When and How to Use a KL-ONE-like Language. In J. Sowa, editor, *Principles of Semantic Networks*. Morgan Kaufmann, San Mateo, USA, 1990.
6. D. Brickley and R.V. Guha (eds.). RDF Vocabulary Description Language 1.0: RDF Schema. Recommendation, World Wide Web Consortium, 2004. Available from `http://www.w3.org/TR/rdf-schema/`.
7. T. Bylander, and B. Chandrasekaran. Generic Tasks for Knowledge-Based Reasoning: The "Right" Level of Abstraction for Knowledge Acquisition, *International Journal of Man-Machine Studies*, issn 0020-7373, 26(2):231–243, Academic Press Ltd, 1987.
8. P. Clark, J. Thompson, and B. Porter. Knowledge Patterns. In A.G. Cohn, F. Giunchiglia, and B. Selman, editors, *KR2000: Principles of Knowledge Representation and Reasoning*, pages 591–600, San Francisco, 2000. Morgan Kaufmann.
9. M. Fernández-López and A. Gómez-Pérez. Deliverable 1.4: A Survey on Methodologies for Developing, Maintaining, Evaluating and Reengineering Ontologies. Technical Report, EU IST Project IST-2000-29243 OntoWeb, 2002.
10. M. Fowler. *Analysis Patterns: Reusable Objects Models*. Addison Wesley, 1997.

11. E. Gamma, R. Helm, R. Johnson, and J. Vlissides. *Design Patterns: Elements of Reusable Object-Oriented Software*. Addison-Wesley, Massachusetts, 1994.
12. A. Gómez-Pérez. *Handbook of Applied Expert Systems*, chapter Knowledge Sharing and Reuse. CRC Press, 1997.
13. A. Gómez-Pérez. Evaluation of Ontologies. *International Journal of Intelligent Systems*, 16(3):391–409, 2001.
14. A. Gómez-Pérez, M. Fernández-López, and O. Corcho. *Ontological Engineering With Examples From the Areas of Knowledge Management, e-Commerce and the Semantic Web*. Advanced Information and Knowledge Processing. Springer-Verlag, 1st edition, 2004.
15. T.R. Gruber. Toward Principles for the Design of Ontologies Used for Knowledge Sharing. In N. Guarino and R. Poli, editors, *Formal Ontology in Conceptual Analysis and Knowledge Representation*, Deventer, The Netherlands, 1993. Kluwer Academic Publishers.
16. M. Grüninger and M.S. Fox. 7methodology for the design and evaluation of ontologies.
17. H. Gu, Y. Perl, J. Geller, M. Halper, and M. Singh. A Methodology for Partitioning a Vocabulary Hierarchy into Trees. *Artificial Intelligence in Medicine*, 15(1):77–98, 1999.
18. N. Guarino. Understanding, Building and Using Ontologies. *International Journal of Human-Computer Studies*, 46(2-3):293–310, 1997.
19. N. Guarino and C. Welty. A Formal Ontology of Properties. In *Proceedings of 12th International Conference on Knowledge Engineering, Modeling and Management*, LNCS, pages 97–112. Springer-Verlag, 2000.
20. N. Guarino and C. Welty. Ontological Analysis of Taxonomic Relationships. In *International Conference on Conceptual Modeling / the Entity Relationship Approach (ER-2000)*, pages 210–224, 2000.
21. N. Guarino and C. Welty. Evaluating Ontological Decisions With OntoClean. *Communications of the ACM*, 45(2):61–65, February 2002.
22. N. Guarino and C. Welty. An Overview of OntoClean. In S. Staab and R. Studer, editors, *Handbook on Ontologies*. Springer-Verlag, 2004.
23. J. Hunt. *Guide to the Unified Process featuring UML, Java and Design Patterns*. Springer Professional Computing. Springer-Verlag, September 2003.
24. D. Jones, T. Bench-Capon, and P. Visser. Methodologies for Ontology Development. In *Proc. IT&KNOWS Conference, XV IFIP World Computer Congress*, Budapest, Hungary, August 1998.
25. M. Kifer, G. Lausen, and J. Wu. Logical Foundations of Object-Oriented and Frame-Based Languages. *Journal of the ACM*, May 1995.
26. M.F. Lopez, A. Gomez-Perez, J.P. Sierra, and A.P. Sierra. Building a Chemical Ontology Using Methontology and the Ontology Design Environment. *IEEE Intelligent Systems*, 14(5):37–45, January/February 1999.
27. A. Maedche. *Ontology Learning for the Semantic Web*. Kluwer Academic Publishers, 2002.
28. K. Mahesh. Ontology Development for Machine Translation: Ideology and Methodology, 9 June 1997.
29. D.L. McGuinness and F. van Harmelen. OWL Web Ontology Language Overview. Recommendation, W3C, february 2004. available from `http://www.w3.org/TR/owl-features/`.
30. B. Motik, A. Maedche, and R. Volz. A Conceptual Modeling Approach for Semantics-driven Enterprise Applications. In *Proc. 1st International Conference on Ontologies, Databases and Application of Semantics (ODBASE-2002)*, October 2002.

31. G. Nagypál. Creating an Application-Level Ontology for the Complex Domain of History: Mission Impossible? In *Proceedings of Lernen - Wissensentdeckung - Adaptivität (LWA 2004), FGWM 2004 Workshop*, pages 287–294, Berlin, Germany, 4–6 October 2004.
32. A. Newell. The Knowledge Level. *Artificial Intelligence*, 18:87–127, 1982.
33. N. Noy. Representing Classes As Property Values on the Semantic Web. Working draft, W3C, July 21 2004.
34. N.F. Noy and D.L. McGuinness. Ontology Development 101: A Guide to Creating Your First Ontology. Technical Report KSL-01-05 and SMI-2001-0880, Stanford Knowledge Systems Laboratory and Stanford Medical Informatics, 2001.
35. N.F. Noy and M.A. Musen. Evaluating Ontology-Mapping Tools: Requirements and Experience. In J. Angele and Y. Sure, editors, *EKAW'02 Workshop on Evaluation of Ontology-based Tools (EON2002)*, CEUR Workshop Proceedings, Sigüenza, Spain, 2002.
36. A. Rector. Modularisation of Domain Ontologies Implemented in Description Logics and Related Formalisms Including OWL. In *Proceedings of the International Conference on Knowledge Capture*, pages 121–128. ACM Press, 2003.
37. A. Rector. Representing Specified Values in OWL: "Value Partitions" And "Value Sets". Working draft, W3C, 3 August 2004.
38. A. Rector, C. Wroe, J. Rogers, and A. Roberts. Untangling Taxonomies and Relationships: Personal and Practical Problems in Loosely Coupled Development of Large Ontologies. In *Proceedings of the International Conference on Knowledge Capture*, pages 139–146. ACM Press, 2001.
39. G. Schreiber, H. Akkermans, A. Anjewierden, R. de Hoog, N. Shadbolt, W. van de Velde, and B. Wielinga. *Knowledge Engineering and Management–The CommonKADS Methodology*. MIT Press, 2000.
40. G. Schreiber, B. Wielinga, and W. Jansweijer. The KACTUS View on the 'O' Word. In *Proceedings of the IJCAI-95 Workshop on Basic Ontological Issues in Knowledge Sharing*, pages 15.1–15.10, 1995.
41. G. Stumme and A. Maedche. FCA-MERGE: Bottom-Up Merging of Ontologies. In B. Nebel, editor, *Proceedings of the 17th International Conference on Artificial Intelligence (IJCAI-01)*, pages 225–234, San Francisco, CA, USA, August 4–10 2001. Morgan Kaufmann.
42. Y. Sure. *Methodology, Tools & Case Studies for Ontology Based Knowledge Management*. PhD thesis, University of Karlsruhe, May 2003.
43. Y. Sure and R. Studer. On-To-Knowledge Methodology. On-To-Knowledge Project Deliverable 18, Institute AIFB, University of Karlsruhe, 2002. Available at `http://www.aifb.uni-karlsruhe.de/WBS/ysu/publications/OTK-D18_v1-0.pdf`.
44. B. Swartout, R. Patil, K. Knight, and T. Russ. Toward Distributed Use of Large-Scale Ontologies. In *AAAI'97 Spring Symposium on Ontological Engineering*, pages 138–148. Stanford University, 1997.
45. M. Uschold and M. King. Towards a Methodology for Building Ontologies. In *IJCAI'95 Workshop on Basic Ontological Issues in Knowledge Sharing*, Montreal, Canada, 1995.
46. G. van Heijst, A. Th. Schreiber, and B. J. Wielinga. Using Explicit Ontologies in KBS Development. *International Journal of Humand-Computer Studies*, 46(2-3):183–292, 1997.
47. C. Welty and N. Guarino. Supporting Ontological Analysis of Taxonomic Relationships. *Data and Knowledge Engineering*, 39:51–74, 2001.

5

Semantic Annotation of Resources in the Semantic Web

Siegfried Handschuh

National University of Ireland Galway, Ireland, Siegfried.Handschuh@deri.org

Summary. In this chapter, we give a brief introduction into the main idea of the Semantic Web, namely making better use and enabling more intelligent applications for Web-accessible information by accompanying them with machine-understandable, semantic meta data; we sketch the major methodological framework behind, consisting of two intertwined, orthogonal processes, the knowledge process and the knowledge meta process–the latter is concerned with ontology engineering, the former uses ontologies for ontology-based meta-data assignment to Web resources, i.e. for semantic annotation. The major part of the chapter is devoted to the idea of semantic annotation, requirements and functionalities of annotation tools, an example implementation and an overview of the state of research and practice in semantic annotation.

5.1 The Semantic Web: Goals and Solution Approach

Before we focus on semantic annotation, this section will introduce the main ideas of the Semantic Web and Semantic Web technology.

The Semantic Web aims at machine-processable information. The step from the current Web to the Semantic Web is the step from the manual to the automatic processing of information. This step is comparable to the step from the manual processing of goods to the machine processing of goods at the beginning of the industrial revolution. Hence, the Semantic Web can be seen as the dawn of the informational revolution.

The Semantic Web enables automated intelligent services such as information brokers, search agents, information filters, etc. The Semantic Web, which contains machine-processable information, will enable further levels of software-system interoperability.

Technology and standards need to be defined not only for the syntactic representation of documents (like HTML), but also for their semantic content. Semantic interoperability is facilitated by recent W3C standardisation efforts, notably XML/XML Schema [7], RDF/RDF Schema [8] and OWL (cf. [2, p. 70], [42]). The technology stack envisioned by the W3C is depicted in Fig. 5.1.

Apparently, XML as well as XML Schema are the second layer above URIs and Unicode. The third layer is RDF and RDFS. The next layer is the ontology language.

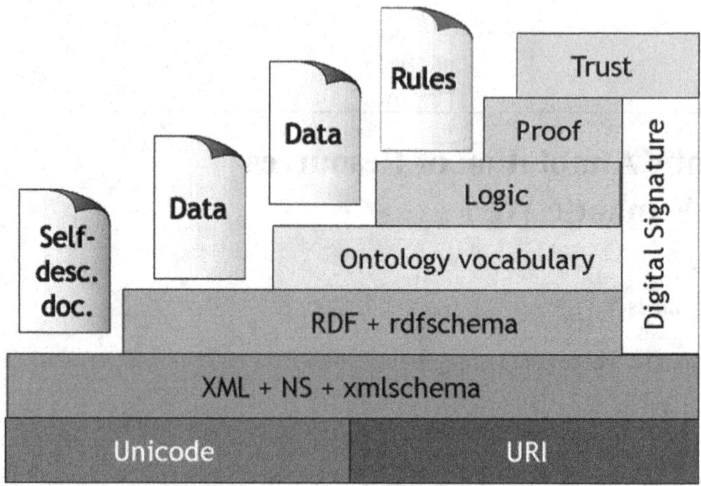

Fig. 5.1. Semantic Web layer cake

On top of the ontology language, there is a need for a language to express logic, so that information can be inferred and better put into relation. Once there is logic, it makes sense to use it to prove things. The proof layer enables everyone to write logic statements, and an agent can follow these semantic "links" to construct proofs, so that validity of a statement, especially an inferred statement, can be checked. The proof layer combined with digital signatures will lead to trust. Consequently, ontology and ontology-based meta data are the basic ingredients for the Semantic Web layer cake. An important question is therefore how to create and use ontology and ontology-based meta data.

5.1.1 Infrastructure for the Semantic Web: The Information Food Chain

Figure 5.2 depicts the *information food chain for the Semantic Web* introduced in [12] as a visionary infrastructure for the Semantic Web and its related applications which are required, e.g., for ontology engineering or for meta-data creation.

The food chain starts with the construction of an ontology describing the knowledge structures in the application domain about which we want to process Web-based information–preferably using a supporting tool for ontology construction.[1] The ontology is the foundation for a set of data items. The next part of the information food chain is a tool to support the task of structuring the HTML pages. A Web page annotation tool (cf. Sect. 5.2) provides the means for browsing an ontology and for selecting appropriate terms of the ontology and mapping them to sections of a Web page. The Web-page annotation process creates a set of annotated Web pages, which are availableto an automated agent to achieve his task. Of course, the anno-

[1] For example, the Ontology Engineering environment, OntoEdit (cf. [46])

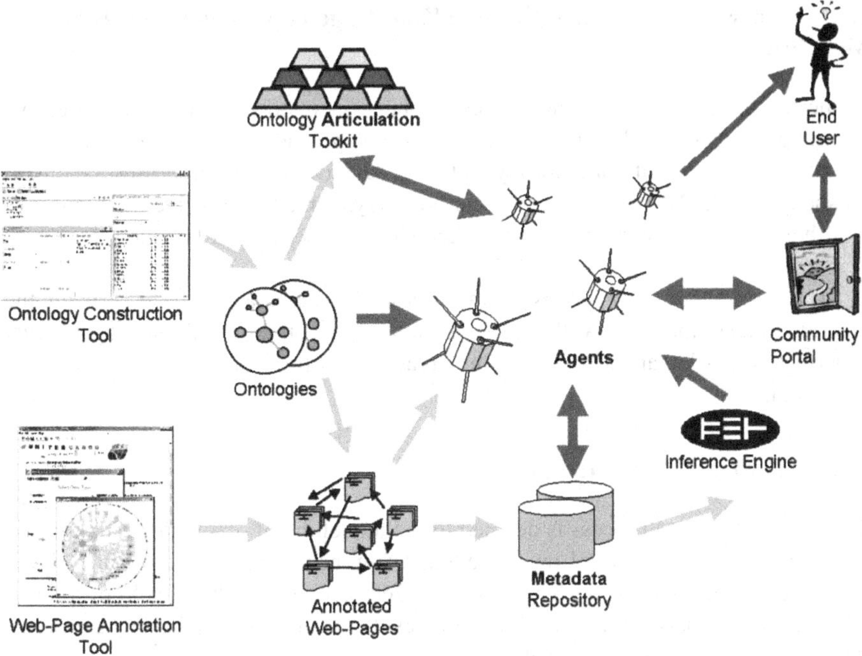

Fig. 5.2. Information food chain for the Semantic Web

tation process itself has a human component: Although the effort to generate the annotation of a Web page is of an order lower in magnitude than the creation of the Web page itself, there has to be some incentive to expend the extra effort. The incentive for the creation of the annotation (which is meta data for the Web page) is visible on the Web for a community Web portal, which presents a community of interest distributed on the Web to the outside world in a concise manner. The data collected from the annotated Web pages simplifies to a significant extent the task of maintaining a community Web portal because changes are incorporated automatically, without any manual work. An automated agent itself needs several sub-components: An important task of the agent is the integration of data from several distributed information sources. Because of the need to describe the relationships between the data in a declarative way (otherwise the agent has to be programmed for every new task), an agent needs an inference engine for the evaluation of rules and queries. The inference engine is coupled with a meta-data repository–the memory of an agent as to where retrieved information is cached. Furthermore, if an automated agent browses the Web, it will usually encounter data formulated in unknown ontologies. Therefore, it needs the facility to relate unknown ontologies to ontologies with which it is already familiar. This facility is an Ontology Articulation Toolkit for information mediation.

5.1.2 Processes for the Semantic Web: Knowledge Process and Knowledge Meta Process

While the information food chain presents necessary tools and infrastructure, this section presents the underlying processes of ontology and meta-data creation.

Based on the duality of ontology and meta data, two central processes are distinguished in [47]: The development of an ontology, named knowledge meta process, and then the subsequent creation of a knowledge base, named knowledge process (Fig. 5.3).

The *knowledge meta process* comprises all aspects that are necessary for the creation of an ontology as well as its extension and adaption. The *knowledge process* describes in particular the steps for the creation and processing of ontology-based meta data.

5.1.3 Knowledge Meta Process

The knowledge meta process is devoted to the modelling of ontologies. The process can be regarded as a form of reverse-engineering, because the structure underlying the resources needs to be derived from the Web resources with the help of domain experts. But this derivation is not exact: the result, the ontology, and also the process, the steps to an ontology are variable.

Considering the result, since each ontology designer has a certain application in mind for which he designs his ontology and has another understanding of the considered domain, a multitude of ontologies can be created for one domain. The dependence on an application, however, should be not so strong that it limits the re-usability of an ontology [41, p. 4]. With regard to the process "no single correct ontology-design methodology" exists [41, p. 4] which describes the steps for designing an ontology. Proposals for methodologies, however, have been developed by various researchers such as the Buchanan-Methodology, the Uschold-Methodology [55]

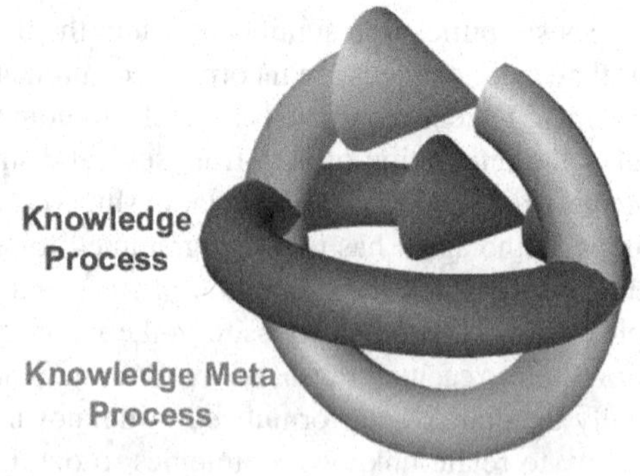

Fig. 5.3. Two orthogonal processes with feedback loops

and Methontology by López et al. [51]. The methodologies have in common approximately the following four steps: specification, conceptualisation/refinement, implementation and evaluation. More steps which can be added are a feasibility study (preceding the four steps mentioned above) and a maintenance phase (following the four steps mentioned above) [45, p. 2]. The feasibility study should support the decision if the creation of an ontology is useful in a certain domain of knowledge. The maintenance phase is important, so that ontologies keep track of the changes in the real world and are evolving over time.

5.1.4 Knowledge Process

In the *knowledge process* (Fig. 5.4), which is orthogonal to the knowledge meta process, meta data is created to describe the relevant information of some resources with the use of ontology. The resulting meta data consists of instances of a specific concept connected with properties (attributes and relations) and axioms. The output of the meta-data creation process is the knowledge base, viz. a collection of this meta data in a specified formal representation language. In the case that Web resources are described, the knowledge base or a part of it can be embedded in the existing Web-page description to provide semantic information for intelligent agents in the WWW. The knowledge base can be extended by inferring "new" facts on the basis of defined axioms. This creation process is the topic of this chapter.

As we have seen above and in Chap. 4, much work has been done for developing agreed-upon, practically useful and scientifically valid ontology-engineering methods. Compared to this, not much work has already been done, up to now, regarding methodological support for the design of meta data.

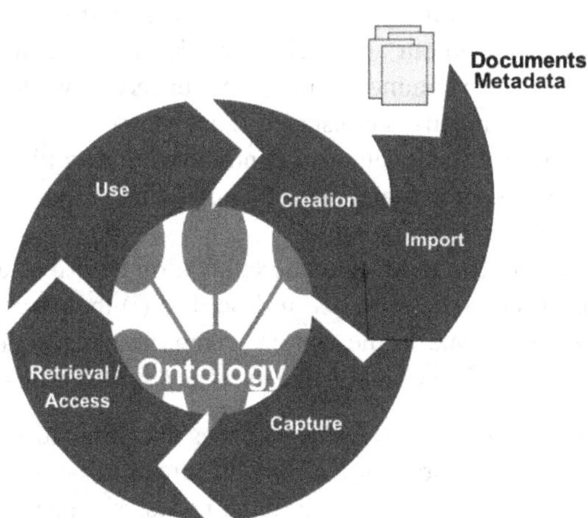

Fig. 5.4. The knowledge process

5.2 Basics of Semantic Annotation

In the following, we define the terminology, the semantics and the content of meta-data creation as envisioned in this chapter.

5.2.1 Terminology

The terminology used here has been elaborated because many of the terms that are used with regard to meta-data creation tools carry several, ambiguous, connotations that imply conceptually important decisions.

- Ontology: An ontology is a formal, explicit specification of a shared conceptualisation of a domain of interest [25, p. 1]. In our case, an ontology is defined in RDF(S) or OWL. Hence, an ontology is constituted by statements expressing definitions of OWL classes–RDF(S) resources, respectively–and properties ([42], [8]).
- Annotations: An annotation in our context is a set of instantiations attached to an HTML document. We distinguish (i) instantiations of OWL classes, (ii) instantiated properties from one class instance to a data-type instance–henceforth called attribute instance (of the class instance), and (iii) instantiated properties from one class instance to another class instance–henceforth called relationship instance.

  Class instances have unique URIs.[2] They frequently come with attribute instances, such as a human-readable label like "Steffen" .
- Meta data: Meta data are data about data. In our context, the annotations are meta data about HTML documents.
- Relational meta data: We use the term relational meta data to denote the annotations that contain relationship instances.

  Often, the term "annotation" is used to mean something like "private or shared note", "comment" or "Dublin Core meta data". This alternative meaning of annotation may be emulated in our approach by modelling these notes with attribute instances. For instance, a comment note "I like this book" would be related to the URL of the paper via an attribute instance "hasComment".

  In contrast, relational meta data also contain statements like "Siegfried cooperates with Steffen", i.e. relational meta data contain relationships between class instances rather than only textual notes.
- Semantic annotation: The term semantic annotation describes a process as well as the outcome of the process. Hence it describes (i) the process of addition of semantic data or meta data to the content given an agreed ontology and (ii) it describes the semantic data or meta data itself as a result of this process.

Figure 5.5 illustrates our use of the terms "ontology", "annotation" and "relational meta data". It depicts some part of the SWRC[3] (Semantic Web Research Community) ontology. Furthermore, it shows two home pages, viz. pages about Siegfried[4]

---

[2] For instance, like `http://www.aifb.uni-karlsruhe.de/WBS/sst/#Steffen`

[3] `http://ontoware.org/projects/swrc/`

[4] `http://www.aifb.uni-karlsruhe.de/WBS/sha`

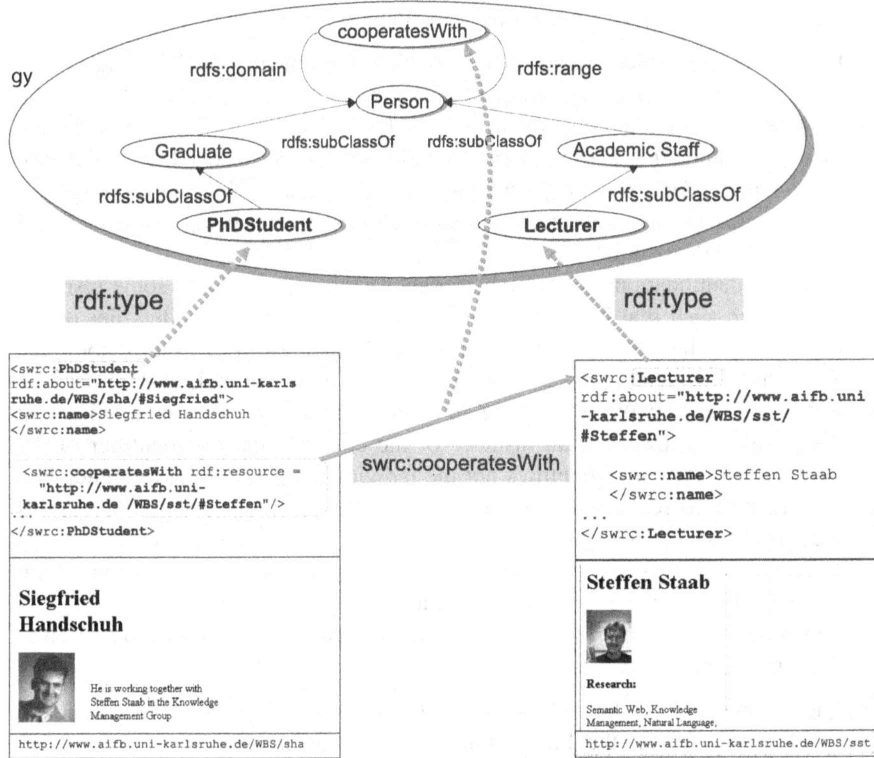

Fig. 5.5. Annotation example

and Steffen[5] with annotations given in an XML serialisation of RDF facts. The two persons, Steffen[6] and Siegfried[7] are denoted by their corresponding URIs. Hence, the swrc:name of the latter URI is "Siegfried Handschuh". In addition, there is a relationship instance between the two persons, viz. they cooperate. This cooperation information "spans" the two pages.

5.2.2 The Semantics of Semantic Annotation

There are two players in the annotation game, the annotation *provider* and the annotation *consumer*. The key is, as Bechhofer et al. point out [4], that consumer and provider *share underlying assumptions* about the annotation. Part of this assumption is the common ontology, but part of it is how the terms of the ontology are to be used.

In the literature about semantic annotation, it is evident that different assumptions exist about the nature and the scope of semantic annotation.

[5] `http://www.aifb.uni-karlsruhe.de/WBS/sst`
[6] URI: `http://www.aifb.uni-karlsruhe.de/WBS/sst/#Steffen`
[7] URI: `http://www.aifb.uni-karlsruhe.de/WBS/sha/#Siegfried`

Bechhofer et al. [4] differentiate between the following:

- Decoration: Is the idea of creating a kind of user comment about Web pages. This is the view that Annotea has adopted for their annotation (cf. [34]).
- Linking: To annotate a document with further links. The provision of dynamic linking as annotation is used by the COHSE project (cf. Sect. 1.1 in [4]). Annotation within COHSE can be seen as a mechanism that allows the user to specify possible link anchors within a document, with the anchor being associated with a conceptual description.
- Instance identification: We are making an assertion that there is some resource in the Web such that it is an instance of an concept, and the identifier of the instance, viz. the URI, identifies the resource. This means the instance about the annotation that is being made is clearly accessed by the given URI.
- Instance reference: We are making an assertion that there is some individual in the world, such that it is an instance of the concept, and the identifier of the instance, viz. the URI, identifies not the individual itself, but the reference in a document to the real world individual. This is the semantic of annotation that is used by our annotation framework.
- Aboutness: A user expresses that a particular resource (i.e. a Web page) is about a certain concept, but not an instance of an concept.
- Pertinence: A user expresses that a particular resource (i.e. a Web page) gives further useful information about a concept.

Our viewpoint of annotation is based on *instance reference* (cf. Sect. 5.2.1), but we can emulate most of the other annotation types with our framework.

5.2.3 Layering of Annotation

As shown before, there exist different notions of the semantics of semantic annotation. Additionally, [43] presents a layering of annotation which reflects different aspects of content to be represented:

- Structural annotation: Used to define the physical structure of the document, its organisation into head and body, into sections, paragraphs and sentences.
- Linguistic annotation: Associated to a short span of text (smaller than a sentence), and identify lexical units. They could be referred to also as *Textual Annotations* or *Lexical Annotation*. This corresponds to the *grammatical structure* in ([20]).
- Semantic annotation: Corresponds to our view of semantic annotation. Similar to the representation of the *logical structure* ([20]) of the document.

As mentioned before, our focal point lays on the *semantic annotation*. However, we aim to present a generic annotation model that is able to deal with most of the semantics of semantic annotation, as well as with the aspects or layers of annotation.

5.2.4 Requirements for Semantic Annotation

Given the problems with syntax, semantics and pragmatics in earlier annotation experiences, e.g. the KA2 initiative [5] for providing semantic markup on HTML pages for the knowledge acquisition community, we list here a set of requirements for semantic annotation:

Consistency: Semantic structures should adhere to a given ontology in order to allow for better sharing of knowledge. For example, it should be avoided that annotators use an attribute instance, whereas the ontology requires a concept instance.

Proper reference: Identifiers of instances, e.g. of persons, institutes or companies, should be unique. In fact, in most real-world situations the same object will be given many URIs, since people create them independently. For instance, the meta data generated in the KA2 case study contained three different identifiers for the particular person "Dieter Fensel". Thus, knowledge about this person could not be grasped with a straightforward query. To remedy this problem, there are technical ("smushing") and logical (e.g. OWL:sameAs) solutions.

Avoid redundancy: Decentralised knowledge provisioning should be possible. However, when annotators collaborate, it should be possible for them to identify (parts of) sources that have already been annotated and to reuse previously captured knowledge in order to avoid laborious redundant annotations.

Relational meta data: Like HTML information, which is spread on the Web, but related by HTML links, knowledge markup may be distributed, but it should be semantically related. Current annotation tools tend to generate template-like meta data, which is hardly connected, if at all. For example, annotation environments often support Dublin Core [16, 17], providing means to state, e.g., the name of authors of a document, but not their IDs.[8] Thus, the only possibility to query for all publications of a certain person requires the querying for some attribute like fullname–which is very unsatisfying for frequent names like "John Smith".

Dynamic documents: A large percentage of the Web pages are not static documents. For dynamic web pages (e.g. ones that are generated from a database), it does not seem to be useful to annotate every single page. Rather one wants to "annotate the database" in order to reuse it for its own Semantic Web purpose.[9]

Maintenance: Knowledge markup needs to be maintained. An annotation tool should support the maintenance task.

Ease of use: It is obvious that an annotation environment should be easy to use in order to be really useful. However, this objective is not easily achieved, because meta-data creation involves intricate navigation of semantic structures, e.g. taxonomies, properties and concepts.

Efficiency: The effort for the production of meta data is an important restraining threshold. The more efficiently a tool supports meta-data creation, the more meta-data users tend to produce. This requirement is related to the ease of use. It also depends on the automation of the meta-data creation process, e.g. on the preprocessing of the document.

[8] In the web context, one typically uses the term 'URI' (uniform resource identifier) to speak of a "unique identifier"

[9] The huge amount of Web accessible content stored in databases and available through dynamic Web pages is often called "deep Web" or "hidden Web". Consequently, the semantic annotation of dynamic Web pages is usually called "deep annotation" [28]

Multiple ontologies: HTML documents in the semantic web may contain information that is related to different ontologies. Therefore, the annotation framework should cater for concurrent annotations with multiple ontologies.
These requirements can be tackled by combining advanced mechanisms for inferencing, fact crawling, document management, meta ontology definitions, meta-data re-recognition, content generation and information extraction. These components are explained in following, showing the CREAM framework, an exemplary software framework for semantic annotation.

5.3 Design of the CREAM Framework for Semantic Annotation

The difficulties sketched before directly feed into the design rationale of an exemplary annotation framework. The design rationale links the requirements with the modules. This results in an N:M matrix (neither functional nor injective). A tabular overview of such a matrix can be found in [26].

Document editor: The document editor may be conceptually–though not practically–divided into a viewing component and the component for generating content.

The *document viewer* visualises the document contents. The annotator may easily provide new meta data by selecting pieces of text and aligning it with parts of the ontology. The document viewer should support various formats (HTML, PDF, XML etc.). For some formats, the following component for content generation may not be available.

The document viewer highlights the existing semantic annotation and server-side markup of the Web page. It distinguishes visually between semantic annotation and markup that describes the information structure of an underlying database.

The editor also allows the conventional authoring of documents, viz. the *content generation*. In addition, instances already available may be dragged from a visualisation of the content of the annotation inference server and dropped into the document. Thereby, some piece of text and/or a link is produced taking into account the information from the meta ontology (cf. module meta ontology).

The newly generated content is already annotated and the meta ontology guides the construction of further information, e.g. further XPointers [14, 24] are attached to instances.

Ontology guidance and fact browser: The framework needs guidance from the ontology. In order to allow for sharing of knowledge, newly created annotations must be consistent with a community's ontology. If meta-data creators instantiate arbitrary classes and properties, the semantics of these properties remains void. Of course, the framework must be able to adapt to multiple ontologies in order to reflect different foci of the meta-data creators. In the case of concurrent annotation with multiple ontologies, there is an ontology guidance/fact browser for each ontology.

Crawler: The creation of relational meta data must take place *within* the Semantic Web. During meta-data creation, subjects must be aware of which entities already exist in their part of the Semantic Web. This is only possible if a crawler makes relevant entities immediately available.

Annotation inference server: Relational meta data, proper reference and avoidance of redundant annotation require querying for instances, i.e. querying whether and which instances exist. For this purpose as well as for checking of consistency, we provide an annotation inference server. The annotation inference server reasons on crawled and newly created instances and on the ontology. It also serves the ontological guidance and fact browser, because it allows to query for existing classes, instances and properties.

Meta ontology: The purpose of the meta ontology is the separation of ontology design and use. It is needed to describe how classes, attributes and relationships from the domain ontology should be used by the annotation framework. Thus, the ontology describes how the semantic data should look like, and the meta ontology connected to the ontology describes how the ontology is used by the annotation environment to actually create semantic data. This is explained in more detail in [26].

Deep annotation module: This module enables the deep annotation scenario. It manages the generation of mapping rules between the database and the client ontology. For this purpose, it combines the generic annotation stored in the annotation inference server and the server-side markup provided with the content [28]. On demand it publishes the mapping rules derived from the generic annotations.

Document management: Considering the dynamics of HTML pages on the web, it is desirable to store foreign Web pages one has annotated together with their annotations. Foreign documents for which modification is not possible may be remotely annotated by using XPointer as a addressing mechanism.

Meta-data re-recognition and information extraction: Even with sophisticated tools it is laborious to provide semantic annotations. A major goal thus is semi-automatic meta-data creation taking advantage of information extraction techniques to propose annotations to meta-data creators and, thus, to facilitate the meta-data creation task. Concerning our environment we envisage three major techniques.

First, meta-data re-recognition compares existing meta-data literals with newly typed or existing text. Thus, the mentioning of the name "Siegfried Handschuh" in the document triggers the proposal that the corresponding URI[10] is co-referenced at this point. Secondly, "Wrappers" may be learned from given markup in order to automatically annotate similarly structured pages. Thirdly, Message extraction systems may be used to recognise named entities, propose co-reference and extract some relationship from texts (cf. e.g. [40, 48]). This component can be realised by using an information extraction system, e.g. Amilcare (cf. [27]).[11]

Besides the requirements that constitute single modules, one may identify functions that cross module boundaries, such as storage and replication. The CREAM annotation framework supports two different ways of *storage*. The annotations will be stored inside the document, i.e. in the document management component. Alternatively or simultaneously, it is also possible to store them in the annotation inference

[10] http://www.aifb.uni.de/WBS/sha/#Siegfried

[11] http://www.dcs.shef.ac.uk/~fabio/Amilcare.html

server. We provide a simple *replication* mechanism by crawling annotations into our annotation inference server. Then inferencing can be used to rule out formal inconsistencies.

Exemplary Architecture and Implementation of an Annotation Framework

The architecture of the CREAM annotation framework is depicted in Fig. 5.6. The design pursues the idea to be flexible and open. Therefore, OntoMat, the reference implementation of the framework, comprises a plug-in structure, which is flexible with regard to adding or replacing modules.

The core OntoMat (screenshot in Fig. 5.7), which is downloadable[12], consists of an Ontology Guidance and Fact browser (left hand side), a document viewer/editor (right hand side) and an internal memory data-structure for the ontology and meta data. However, one only gets the full-fledged semantic capabilities (e.g. Datalog reasoning or subsumption reasoning) when one uses a plug-in connection to a corresponding annotation inference server.

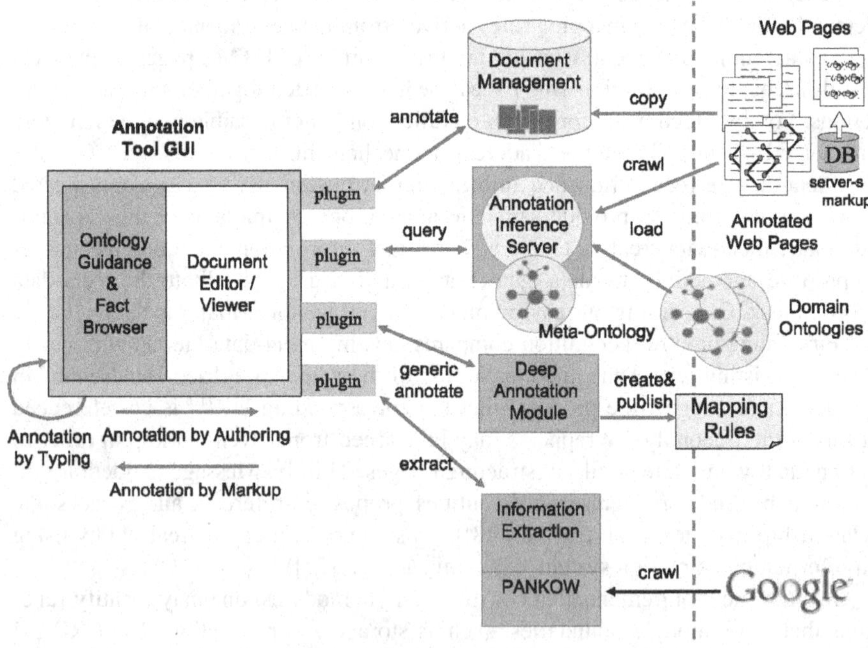

Fig. 5.6. Architecture of the CREAM annotation framework

[12] `http://annotation.semanticweb.org/`

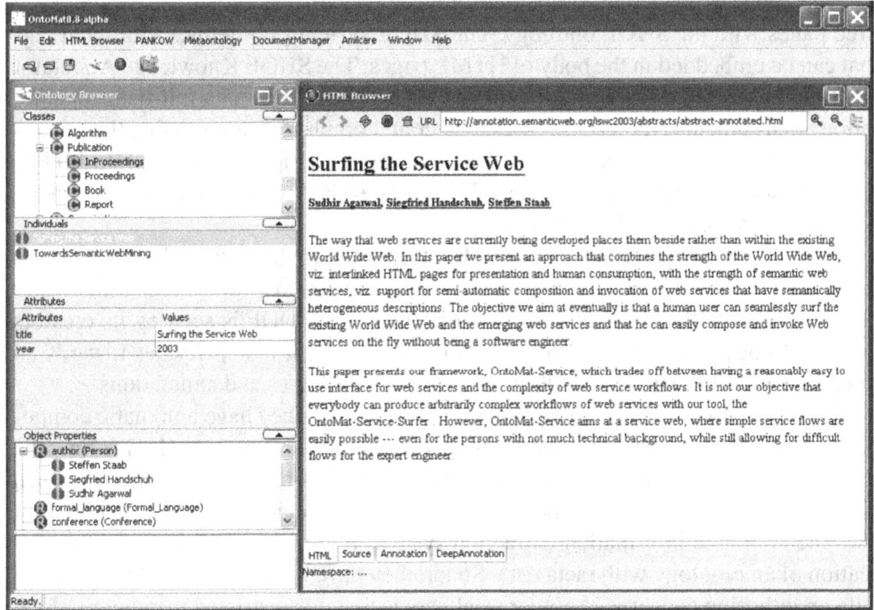

Fig. 5.7. Screenshot of OntoMat

5.4 Relevant Inputs for Semantic Annotation

Semantic annotation, as we presented it here, is a cross-sectional endeavour. There is a number of research communities that have contributed towards achieving the objectives of semantic annotation. We distinguish four major areas of relevant related work.

First, there are frameworks for markup in the Semantic Web. Secondly, semantic annotation may be considered as a particular knowledge acquisition task, where the most prominent tool is Protégé [18]. Thirdly, there are annotation frameworks, with a focus on note taking, such as Annotea [34]. And finally, semantic annotation is achieved by authoring frameworks with an emphasis on meta-data creation.

5.4.1 Knowledge Markup in the Semantic Web

We know of three major early systems that use knowledge markup intensively in the Semantic Web, viz. SHOE [30], Ontobroker [11] and WebKB [38]. All three of them rely on markup in HTML pages. They all started with providing manual markup by editors. However, our experiences (cf. [19]) have shown that text-editing knowledge markup yields extremely poor results, viz. syntactic mistakes, incorrect references and all the problems outlined in the scenario section.

The SHOE Knowledge Annotator is a Java program that allows users to mark-up Web pages with the SHOE ontology. The SHOE system [37] defines additional tags that can be embedded in the body of HTML pages. The SHOE Knowledge Annotator is a little helper (like our earlier OntoPad [21], [11]) rather than a full-fledged annotation environment. WebKB [38] uses conceptual graphs for representing the semantic content of Web documents. It embeds conceptual-graph statements into HTML pages. Essentially, it offers a Web-based template-like interface such as knowledge acquisition frameworks described below.

A more recent contribution is the RDF annotator SMORE.[13] SMORE allows markup of images and emails, as well as HTML and text markup. A tool with similar characteristics is the Open Ontology Forge (OOF) [9]. OOF is seen by its creators as an ontology editor that supports annotation, taking it a step further towards an integrated environment for handling documents, ontologies and annotations.

The next group of markup tools is semi-automatic: They have automatic components, but assume intervention by the user in the annotation process. In this line, the tool which is most similar to the presented OntoMat is the system from The Open University [50] and the corresponding MnM [56] annotation tool. MnM [56] also uses the Amilcare information-extraction system. It allows the semi-automatic population of an ontology with meta data. So far, they have not dealt with relational meta data or authoring concerns. Another weakness is that it is restricted to either marking up the slots for a single concept at a time or marking up all the concepts on a single hierarchical level of a single ontology (but not their slots).

AeroSWARM[14] is an automatic tool for annotation using OWL ontologies, based on the DAML annotator AeroDAML [35]. This has both a client–server version and a Web-enabled demonstrator in which the user enters a URI, and the system automatically returns a file of annotations on another Web page. To view this in context, the user would have to save the RDF to an annotation server and view the results in an annotation-friendly browser such as Amaya. AeroDAML is therefore not in itself an annotation environment. SemTag is another example of a tool which focuses only on automatic mark-up [15]. It is based on IBM's text-analysis platform Seeker and uses similarity functions to recognise entities which occur in contexts similar to marked-up examples. The key problem of large-scale automatic markup is identified as ambiguity, e.g. identical strings, such as "Niger" which can refer to different things, a river or a country. A Taxonomy-Based Disambiguation (TBD) algorithm is proposed to tackle this problem. SemTag is proposed as a bootstrapping solution to get a semantically tagged collection off the ground. AeroSWARM and SemTag, as the most large-scale automatic markup systems, focus on class instantiation, in the goal comparable to another Karlsruhe University approach [10], called PANKOW. However, AeroSWARM and SemTag also have not dealt with the creation of relation meta data.

KIM [53] uses information extraction techniques to build a large knowledge base of annotations. The annotations in KIM are meta data in the form of named entities

---

[13] `http://www.mindswap.org/~aditkal/editor.shtml`
[14] `http://ubot.lockheedmartin.com/ubot/hotdaml/aeroswarm.html`

(people, places, etc.) which are defined in the KIMO ontology and identified mainly from reference to extremely large gazetteers. This is restrictive, and it would be a significant research challenge to extend the KIM methodology to domain specific ontologies. However, named entities are a class of meta data with broad usage, and the KIM platform is well placed to showcase the kinds of retrieval and data analysis services that can be provided over large knowledge bases of annotations.

5.4.2 Knowledge Acquisition Frameworks

Semantic annotation targets a roughly similar objective to the instance-acquisition phase in the Protégé framework [18] (the latter needs to be distinguished from the ontology-editing capabilities of Protégé). The obvious difference between a semantic annotation framework and Protégé is that the latter does not (and was not intended to) support the particular Web setting, viz. managing and displaying Web pages–not to mention Web page authoring. From Protégé we have adopted in our CREAM design the principle of a meta ontology that allows a distinction between different ways that classes and properties are treated.

Another recent knowledge acquisition framework with particular applications in mind is TRELLIS [23]. It is designed to support argument analysis in decision-making scenarios. It demonstrates the additional support that can be given to users when an annotation environment is designed for a specific purpose. For example, annotations in TRELLIS are in the form of free-text statements. This presents a problem since statements about the same thing can be phrased differently and consequently not matched up by the user. Therefore a component called ACE has been built which helps users to formulate statements in ways which are consistent with terms in the ontology [6]. The annotations in TRELLIS can be output as RDF. However, perhaps because it is designed as a tool for analysing a wide range of document formats, the authors do not discuss whether it is possible to anchor annotations to a particular part of a text.

5.4.3 Note Taker Annotation Frameworks

There is a lot of–also commercial–annotation tools like ThirdVoice[15], Yawas [13], CritLink [58] and Annotea (Amaya) [34]. These tools all share the idea of creating a kind of user comment about Web pages. The term "annotation" in these frameworks is understood as a remark assigned to an existing document.

Annotea actually goes one step further. It allows an RDF schema to be used as a kind of template that is filled by the annotator. For instance, Annotea users may use a schema for Dublin Core and fill the author-slot of a particular document with a name. This annotation, however, is again restricted to attribute instances. The user may also decide to use complex RDF descriptions instead of simple strings for filling such a template. However, he then has no further support from Amaya that helps him provide syntactically correct statements with proper references.

[15] `http://www.thirdvoice.com`

5.4.4 Authoring Frameworks

An approach interesting to authoring is the Briefing Associate of Teknowledge [54]. The tool is an extension of Microsoft PowerPoint. It pursues the idea of producing PowerPoint documents with meta-data coding as a by-product of document composition. For each concept and relation in the ontology, an instantiation button is added to the PowerPoint toolbar. Clicking on one of these buttons allows the author to insert an annotated graphical element into his/her presentation. Thus, a graphic element in the presentation corresponds to an instance of a concept, and arrows between the elements correspond to relationship instances. In order to use an ontology in PowerPoint, one must assign graphic symbols to the concepts and relations, which is done initially by the visual-annotation ontology editor (again a kind of meta-ontology assignment). The Briefing Associate is available for PowerPoint documents.

The authoring of hypertexts and the authoring with concepts are topics in the COHSE project [24]. They allow for the automatic generation of meta-data descriptions by analysing the content of a Web page and comparing the tokens with concept names described in a lexicon. They support ontology reasoning, but they do not support the creation of relational meta data. It is unclear to what extent COHSE considers the synchronous production of document and meta data by the author.

The latest contribution to the authoring and annotation of web documents are Semantic Wikis. Semantic Wikis allow users to make formal descriptions of resources by annotating the pages that represent those resources. Where a regular Wiki enables users to describe resources in natural language, a Semantic Wiki enables users to additionally describe resources in a formal language. By adding meta data to ordinary Wiki content, users get added benefits such as improved retrieval, information exchange and knowledge reuse. The most prominent systems under ongoing development are WikSAR [3], Semantic MediaWiki [57], IkeWiki [44] and SemperWiki [52]. Most existing Semantic Wikis only allow statements about the current page. The subject of an annotation is never explicitly stated, but always implicitly assumed to be the page on which the statement appears.

5.5 Conclusions

Semantic Meta data are, simply expressed, facts that are related to a domain ontology. Though this may appear trivial at first, it easily conflicts with several other requirements. We also need a *meta ontology* describing how the domain ontology should be used by the annotation framework. Furthermore, there is the requirement for remote storage of annotation, which leads to the need for a robust referencing scheme, viz. *XPointer*. Also, there is the need for the provision of *meta-meta data*, e.g. author, date, time and location of annotation. In addition, different requirements exist for different *semantics* of semantic annotation as well as the need to express different aspects of the content in meta data, viz. a *layering* of the annotation (e.g. structural annotation, lexical annotation and semantic annotation).

Automatisation is vital to ease the knowledge acquisition bottleneck. To achieve this, the integration of knowledge extraction technologies into the annotation environment has been undertaken. This is used to semi-automatically identify entities in text that are instances of a particular class and relations between the classes. As the evaluation in [29] showed, HCI implications are also important here, so that a semi-automated tool can be used effectively by Web users without expertise in natural-language processing methods.

Annotation is a potential knowledge acquisition bottleneck as discussed above. To ease the constriction, annotation has to be carried out by people who are not specialist annotators. To facilitate the annotation task is especially important for the success of the Semantic Web. The annotation interfaces must, therefore, bridge the gap between formal descriptions of knowledge and Web users who understand their domains of interest. A good approach is therefore a semantic authoring environment, so that the environment in which users annotate documents is the same as the one in which they create, read and edit them.

The general problem of meta-data creation remains interesting. In the following, the open questions that are not yet answered satisfactorily by research are identified:

- First, the question of *scalability* to more and larger dimensions. Like "what happens if there are 100,000 people known in your annotation inference server?." Even for scientific evaluation experiments, it is still often necessary to prune the ontology in order to make it feasible for the annotation task.
- Secondly, semantic annotation takes place within the Semantic Web. For the proper creation of relational meta data, we need *unique identifiers* of persons, institutes or companies. While crawling of existing meta data helps to *reduce* this problem, it is not solved and possibly may never be.
- Thirdly, we are still in the early stages with respect to providing *methodological guidelines* for the purposes of semantic annotation.
- Fourthly, probably the most important for the Semantic Web: How to create *incentives* for annotation?

Documents created by Semantic Annotation bring the advantages of semantic search and interoperability. These benefits, however, come at the cost of an increased authoring effort. In this chapter, we have, therefore, presented a comprehensive framework which supports users in dealing with the documents, the ontologies and the annotations that link documents to ontologies.

Future research challenges include further improvements to automatic annotation components, such as relation extraction, and developing support systems for ontology evolution. There are also important human–computer interaction challenges inherent in building integrated systems of this complexity.

As is shown in [1], the notion of semantic annotation is easily lifted from Web pages to Web services, and software tools for annotation support can be provided, as well. Similar to the approach presented in this chapter, there are, for instance, also proposals to use machine learning for semi-automatic semantic annotation of Web services [33]. In Chap. 11, we also see an example of a Web Service annotation tool.

References

1. S. Agarwal, S. Handschuh, and S. Staab. Annotation, Composition and Invocation of Semantic Web Services. *Journal on Web Semantics*, 2(1):1–24, 2005.
2. G. Antoniou and F. van Harmelen. Web Ontology Language: OWL. In S. Staab and R. Studer, editors, *Handbook on Ontologies*, Handbooks in Information Systems, pages 67–92. Springer-Verlag, 2004.
3. D. Aumueller. Semantic Authoring and Retrieval Within a Wiki. In *2nd European Semantic Web Conference ESWC-2005, Heraklion, Greece*. May 2005.
4. S. Bechhofer and C. Goble. Towards Annotation using DAML+OIL. In *Proceedings of the Knowledge Markup and Semantic Annotation Workshop 2001 (at K-CAP 2001)*, pages 13–20, Victoria, BC, Canada, October 2001.
5. R. Benjamins, D. Fensel, and S. Decker. KA2: Building Ontologies for the Internet: A Midterm Report. *International Journal of Human Computer Studies*, 51(3): 687–713, 1999.
6. J. Blythe and Y. Gil. Incremental Formalization of Document Annotations through Ontology-Based Paraphrasing. In Proceedings of the 13th International Conference on World Wide Web (WWW 2004), New York, NY, USA, 2004, pages 17–22.
7. T. Bray, J. Paoli, and C.M. Sperberg-McQueen. Extensible Markup Language (XML) 1.0. Technical report, W3C, 2004. `http://www.w3.org/TR/REC-xml`.
8. D. Brickley and R.V. Guha. RDF Vocabulary Description Language 1.0: RDF Schema. Technical report, W3C, February 2004. W3C Working Draft. `http://www.w3.org/TR/rdf-schema/`.
9. N. Collier, A. Kawazoe, A. A. Kitamoto, T. Wattarujeekrit, T. Y. Mizuta, and A. Mullen. Integrating Deep and Shallow Semantic Structures in Open Ontology Forge. *Special Interest Group on Semantic Web and Ontology. JSAI (Japanese Society for Artificial Intelligence)*, 2004.
10. P. Cimiano, S. Handschuh, and S. Staab. Towards the Self-Annotating Web. In Stuart I. Feldman, Mike Uretsky, Marc Najork, and Craig E. Wills, editors, *Proc. of the WWW-2004*, pages 462–471, New York, USA. ACM, May 2004.
11. S. Decker, M. Erdmann, D. Fensel, and R. Studer. Ontobroker: Ontology Based Access to Distributed and Semi-Structured Information. In R. Meersman et al., editors, *Database Semantics: Semantic Issues in Multimedia Systems*, pages 351–369. Kluwer Academic Publisher, 1999.
12. S. Decker. *Semantic Web Methods for Knowledge Management*. PhD thesis, University of Karlsruhe, 2002.
13. L. Denoue and L. Vignollet. An Annotation Tool for Web Browsers and its Applications to Information Retrieval. In *Proceedings of RIAO-2000*, Paris, April 2000. `http://www.univ-savoie.fr/labos/syscom/Laurent.Denoue/riao2000.doc`.
14. S. DeRose, E. Maler, and R. Daniel. XML Pointer Language (XPointer). Technical report, W3C, 2001. Working Draft 16 August 2002.
15. S. Dill, N. Eiron, D. Gibson, D. Gruhl, R. Guha, A. Jhingran, T. Kanungo, S. Rajagopalan, A. Tomkins, J.A. Tomlin, and J.Y. Zien. SemTag and Seeker: Bootstrapping the Semantic Web via Automated Semantic Annotation. In *Proceedings of the 12th International Conference on World Wide Web*, pages 178–186. ACM Press, 2003.
16. Dublin Core Metadata Initiative, April 2001. `http://purl.oclc.org/dc/`.
17. Dublin Core Metadata Template, 2001. `http://www.ub2.lu.se/metadata/DC_creator.html`.

18. H. Eriksson, R. Fergerson, Y. Shahar, and M. Musen. Automatic Generation of Ontology Editors. In *Proceedings of the 12th International Workshop on Knowledge Acquisition, Modelling and Management (KAW-99), Banff, Canada*, October, 1999.
19. M. Erdmann, A. Maedche, H.-P. Schnurr, and S. Staab. From Manual to Semi-Automatic Semantic Annotation: About Ontology-Based Text Annotation Tools. In *P. Buitelaar & K. Hasida (eds). Proceedings of the COLING 2000 Workshop on Semantic Annotation and Intelligent Content*, Luxembourg, August 2000.
20. J. Euzenat. Eight Questions about Semantic Web Annotations. *IEEE Intelligent Systems*, 17(2):55–62, Mar/Apr 2002.
21. D. Fensel, J. Angele, S. Decker, M. Erdmann, H.-P. Schnurr, S. Staab, R. Studer, and A. Witt. On2broker: Semantic-Based Access to Information Sources at the WWW. In *Proceedings of the World Conference on the WWW and Internet (WebNet-99), Honolulu, Hawaii, USA*, pages 366–371, 1999.
22. D. Fensel, K.P. Sycara, and J. Mylopoulos, editors. *ISWC-2003 — Proceedings of the 2nd International Semantic Web Conference*, LNCS 2870. Springer-Verlag, 2003.
23. Y. Gil and V. Ratnakar. Trellis: An Interactive Tool for Capturing Information Analysis and Decision Making. In Knowledge Engineering and Knowledge Management. Ontologies and the Semantic Web, 13th International Conference (EKAW-2002), pages 37–42.
24. C. Goble, S. Bechhofer, L. Carr, D. De Roure, and W. Hall. Conceptual Open Hypermedia = The Semantic Web? In S. Staab, S. Decker, D. Fensel, and A. Sheth, editors, *The 2nd International Workshop on the Semantic Web*, CEUR Proceedings, Volume 40, `http://www.ceur-ws.org`, pages 44–50, Hong Kong, May 2001.
25. T.R. Gruber. A Translation Approach to Portable Ontology Specifications. *Knowledge Acquisition*, 6(2):199–221, 1993.
26. S. Handschuh and S. Staab. Authoring and Annotation of Web Pages in CREAM. In *Proceedings of the 11th WWW 2002, Honolulu, Hawaii, USA*, pages 462–473. ACM Press, 2002.
27. S. Handschuh, S. Staab, and F. Ciravegna. S-CREAM — Semi-automatic CREAtion of Metadata. In *Proceedings of EKAW-02*, LNCS 2473, pages 358–372, Sigüenza, Spain, Springer-Verlag, 2002.
28. S. Handschuh, S. Staab, and R. Volz. On Deep Annotation. In *Proceedings of the WWW-2003*, Budapest, Hungary, May 2003.
29. S. Handschuh. *Creating Ontology-based Metadata by Annotation for the Semantic Web.* Dissertation, University Karlsruhe, 2005.
30. J. Heflin and J. Hendler. Searching the Web with SHOE. In *Artificial Intelligence for Web Search. Papers from the AAAI Workshop. WS-00-01*, pages 35–40. AAAI Press, 2000.
31. J. Heflin and J. Hendler. Dynamic Ontologies on the Web. In *AAAI-2000 – Proceedings of the National Conference on Artificial Intelligence. Austin, TX, USA*, 2000.
32. J. Hendler and I. Horrocks, editors. *ISWC-2002 – Proceedings of the 1st International Semantic Web Conference*, LNCS 2342. Springer-Verlag, 2002.
33. A. Heß, E. Johnston, and N. Kushmerick. ASSAM: A Tool for Semi-Automatically Annotating Semantic Web Services. In *Proceedings International Semantic Web Conference ISWC-04*, 2004.
34. J. Kahan, M. Koivunen, E. Prud'Hommeaux, and R. Swick. Annotea: An Open RDF Infrastructure for Shared Web Annotations. In *Proceedings of the 10th International World Wide Web Conference, WWW 10, Hong Kong, China, May 1-5, 2001*, pages 623–632. ACM Press, 2001.
35. P. Kogut and W. Holmes. AeroDAML: Applying Information Extraction to Generate DAML Annotations from Web Pages. 2001.

36. M.-R. Koivunen and R.R. Swick. Collaboration through Annotations in the Semantic Web. In S. Handschuh and S. Staab (eds.): *Annotation for the Semantic Web*, IOS Press, 2003.
37. S. Luke, L. Spector, D. Rager, and J. Hendler. Ontology-Based Web Agents. In *Proceedings of the 1st International Conference on Autonomous Agents, Marina del Rey, CA, USA, February 1997*, pages 59–66, 1997.
38. P. Martin and P. Eklund. Embedding Knowledge in Web Documents. In *Proceedings of the 8th International World Wide Web Conference (WWW8), Toronto, May 1999*, pages 1403–1419. Elsevier Science B.V., 1999.
39. S. A. McIlraith, D. Plexousakis, and F. van Harmelen, editors. *ISWC-2004 – Proceedings of the 3rd International Semantic Web Conference*, LNCS 3298. Springer-Verlag, 2004.
40. *MUC-7 – Proceedings of the 7th Message Understanding Conference*, 1998. `http://www.muc.saic.com/`.
41. N.F. Noy and D.L. McGuinness. Ontology Development 101: A Guide to Creating Your First Ontology. Technical Report SMI-2001-0880, Stanford Medical Informatics, 2001.
42. OWL Web Ontology Language Reference. `http://www.w3.org/TR/owl-ref`, 2004.
43. F. Rinaldi, J. Dowdall, M. Hess, J. Ellman, G.P. Zarri, A. Persidis, L. Bernard, and H. Karanikas. Multilayer Annotations in Parmenides. In *Proceedings of the Knowledge Markup and Semantic Annotation Workshop, Sanibel, Florida , USA*, pages 33–40, 2003.
44. S. Schaffert, A. Gruber, and R. Westenthaler. A Semantic Wiki for Collaborative Knowledge Formation. In *Semantics-2005*. 2005.
45. S. Staab, H.-P. Schnurr, R. Studer, and Y. Sure. Knowledge Processes and Ontologies. *IEEE Intelligent Systems*, 16(1), 2001.
46. Y. Sure, M. Erdmann, J. Angele, S. Staab, R. Studer, and D. Wenke. OntoEdit: Collaborative Ontology Development for the Semantic Web. ISWC-2002 – Proceedings of the 1st International Semantic Web Conference, pages 221–235.
47. Y. Sure. *Methodology, Tools and Case Studies for Ontology based Knowledge Management*. PhD thesis, University of Karlsruhe, 2003.
48. M. Vargas-Vera, E. Motta, J. Domingue, S. Buckingham Shum, and M. Lanzoni. Knowledge Extraction by using an Ontology-based Annotation Tool. In *Proceedings of the Knowledge Markup and Semantic Annotation Workshop 2001 (at K-CAP-2001)*, pages 5–12, Victoria, BC, Canada, October 2001.
49. M. Vargas-Vera, E. Motta, J. Domingue, S. Buckingham Shum, and M. Lanzoni. Knowledge Extraction by Using an Ontology-Based Annotation Tool. In *Proceedings of the Knowledge Markup and Semantic Annotation Workshop 2001 (at K-CAP-2001)*, pages 5–12, Victoria, BC, Canada, October 2001.
50. Y. Lei, E. Motta, and J. Domingue. An Ontology-Driven Approach to Web Site Generation and Maintenance. In Knowledge Engineering and Knowledge Management. Ontologies and the Semantic Web, 13th International Conference, EKAW-2002.
51. Fernández-López, M. (1999). Overview of Methodologies for Building Ontologies. In *Proceedings of the IJCAI-99 Workshop on Ontologies and Problem-Solving Methods: Lessons Learned and Future Trends*. CEUR Publications.
52. E. Oren. SemperWiki: A Semantic Personal Wiki. In Proceedings of the 1st Workshop on The Semantic Desktop, 4th International Semantic Web Conference, Galway, Ireland. Available at `http://www.m3pe.org/publications.html`. November 2005.
53. B. Popov, A Kiryakov, D. Ognyanoff, D. Manov, A. Kirilov, and M. Goranov. Towards Semantic Web Information Extraction. ISWC-2003 – Proceedings of the 2nd International Semantic Web Conference, LNCS 2870. Springer-Verlag, 2003.

54. M. Tallis, N. Goldman, and R. Balzer. The Briefing Associate: A Role for COTS Applications in the Semantic Web. In *Semantic Web Working Symposium (SWWS)*, Stanford, California, USA, August 2001.
55. M. Uschold and M. Grüninger, (1996). Ontologies: Principles, Methods and Applications. *Knowledge Sharing and Review*, 11(2).
56. M. Vargas-Vera, E. Motta, J. Domingue, M. Lanzoni, A. Stutt, and F. Ciravegna. MnM: Ontology Driven Semi-Automatic and Automatic Support for Semantic Markup. In Knowledge Engineering and Knowledge Management. Ontologies and the Semantic Web, 13th International Conference, EKAW-2002, pages 379–391.
57. M. Völkel, *et al.* Semantic Wikipedia. In *Proceedings of the 15th International Conference on World Wide Web, WWW 2006, Edinburgh, Scotland*, May 2006.
58. K.-P. Yee. CritLink: Better Hyperlinks for the WWW, 1998. `http://crit.org/~ping/ht98.html`.

Part III

Semantic Web Services

6

Goals and Vision

Combining Web Services with Semantic Web Technology

Chris Preist

HP Laboratories, Bristol, UK, chris.preist@hp.com

Summary. This chapter introduces the combination of the formerly described Web Services and Semantic Web technologies to Semantic Web Services. It outlines the vision and goals in the Semantic Web Services area and clarifies terminology in this field. It defines an abstract Semantic Web Service architecture and introduces a life cycle of the relationship between a requester and a provider party. This motivates the subsequent chapters for description, discovery, mediation and invocation of semantically annotated services in the web.

6.1 Semantic Web Services Vision

As we have seen from previous chapters, the technologies provided by the Semantic Web are working towards a web which is machine-interpretable; a web where computer algorithms are able to process and reason with information which currently is only available in a human readable form. Web Services technologies, on the other hand, are working towards an environment where organisations can make some of their abilities accessible via the Internet. This is done by 'wrapping' some computational capability with a Web Service interface, and allowing other organisations to locate it (via UDDI) and interact with it (via WSDL). Web Service technology provides a standard and widely accepted way of defining these interfaces.

The Semantic Web Services vision [1, 2] is to combine these two technologies, and through this to enable automatic and dynamic interaction between software systems. Web Service technology allows the description of an interface in a standard way, but says nothing (in machine-interpretable form) about what the software system does, or what sequence of messages is used to interact with it. We can overcome this lack using Semantic Web technology. We can annotate software being offered via Web Service interfaces with machine interpretable descriptions describing what the software does (namely the service it provides a potential user) and how it does it. Furthermore, with ontologies able to describe the services that can be provided, we can bring about 'advertising' of services in a way which is both rich and machine-interpretable. This allows more sophisticated discovery of services than is currently possible with UDDI.

Combining these technologies enables many new things to be done. 'Services' as varied as protein analysis, bookselling, translation and animation rendering could be advertised and discovered automatically on the Internet. A company needing a service could locate a provider they were previously unaware of, set up a short-term business relationship and receive the service in return for a payment. All this could be done automatically and at high speed. Furthermore, several services could be combined into a more complex service, possibly automatically [3]. If one of the component services is unavailable, a replacement could be rapidly found and inserted, so the complex service can still be provided.

Note that we used the word 'enable' in the previous paragraph. Semantic Web Services technology is an enabling technology, so it is necessary but not sufficient to bring about the vision we have just described. It provides a means for describing services, and also infrastructural capabilities to discover services and to enable interoperation. However, it does not provide the reasoning to decide which service you want, which provider is 'best', how to negotiate the parameters of a service and what actions to take when using a service. If a service is simple and used in a straightforward way, this reasoning will also be simple. However, in some of the more ambitious scenarios, complex reasoning such as negotiation or dynamic planning will be necessary. Hence, Semantic Web Services alone will not bring about this brave new world – it can do so only in conjunction with other computer science disciplines.

6.2 Example Scenarios

The real value that Semantic Web Services can enable is best illustrated through some example scenarios which this technology, together with appropriate reasoning techniques, can bring about. In this section, we introduce four scenarios. Initially, we present a 'storyboard' for each. In subsequent sections, these example scenarios will be used to illustrate different features of Semantic Web Services.

6.2.1 Scenario A: Overdraft Notification Service

A bank provides an 'overdraft notification service' to its customers to help them manage their account, and to warn them when they are at risk of going overdrawn. Software at the bank monitors the behaviour of a customer's account, and keeps track of when regular payments are made into or out of it. Based on the expected future transactions in an account, and the current balance, banking software can predict if the customer is likely to go overdrawn. If this is about to happen, the customer is warned via an email, text or voice message. To send the warning message, the bank's software component uses some message-sending service. It does not have a pre-selected provider of this service, but instead automatically makes a decision at the time a message must be sent. To do this, it looks in a directory of available service providers and the message services they offer, and selects one based on factors such as cost, reliability and the preferences of the customer receiving the message. It then sends the message to the provider of that service, which in turn sends a text or voice message to the customer.

This scenario is described in [4] in more detail.

6.2.2 Scenario B: Intelligent Procurement

A large manufacturing company makes regular purchases of supplies from a variety of on-line companies. Supplies essential for manufacturing, such as components, are purchased through a fixed supply chain from providers who have been carefully vetted to meet the companys requirements. However, less business-critical supplies, such as stationery, anti-static foot straps or reference books, can be purchased from any reputable supplier. This provides opportunity for shopping around to get the best deal. A software agent acting on behalf of the company is given a list of stationery equipment needed over the next month. It looks in a directory of suppliers the company considers acceptable for those which are able to supply stationery. The suppliers provide purchasing websites which use a 'shopping trolley' model similar to Amazon's – a customer browses a catalog, places items it wants onto a list and goes to a checkout to get a quote for the total package, including postage. They provide a Web Service front end to these portals, allowing programs to interact with them as well as people. The software agent visits several such sites simultaneously. It interacts with them, discovering if they have the specific items in stock, and builds up a 'shopping trolley' of purchases. On reaching 'checkout', it receives a quote for each as to the total cost of the bundle, including volume discounts. Based on these quotes, it selects the cheapest and completes the transaction with that supplier, cancelling the other requests. The supplier then ships the order.

6.2.3 Scenario C: Provision of a Logistics Supply Chain

A company requires the transport of a crate from Bristol to Moscow. It already has long-term contracts in place for land transportation of crates from Bristol to Portsmouth, and from St Petersburg to Moscow. However, its usual supplier of shipping services is for some reason unavailable and it needs to rapidly locate and agree a replacement freight forwarder. A software agent acting on behalf of the company has detailed information about the transportation task which must be carried out. It contacts a discovery agent which has access to descriptions of services various organisations are able to provide, and asks for providers able to ship between Portsmouth and St Petersburg. The discovery agent responds with a list of possible freight forwarders likely to be able to meet these requirements. The software agent then selects one or more of the possible freight forwarders, and sends a more detailed description of the task it requires to be performed, including the date the shipment will arrive at Portsmouth, and the date it must reach St Petersburg. The freight forwarders respond with lists of services they can offer which meet these requirements. For example, one forwarder may say that it has a ship leaving Portsmouth on the required day which will arrive in St Petersburg the day before the deadline. It will also give the cost of placing a crate on that ship. The requesting agent then selects one of the proposed services (possibly by interacting with a user to make the final decision) and informs the provider of the decision. Effectively, the two parties enter into an agreement at this point.

As the shipment takes place, it is coordinated by an exchange of messages between the two parties. The messages use an industry standard, RosettaNet, which describes the format and order of the messages. The exchange starts when the crate is about to arrive in Portsmouth, with a RosettaNet Advanced Shipment Notification being sent by the requester to the freight forwarder, and ends with the sending of a Proof of Delivery and Invoice by the freight forwarder when the crate arrives in St Petersburg.

This scenario is described in [5] in more detail.

6.2.4 Scenario D: Free Stock Quote Web Service

A small-time investor has a software package to keep track of his/her share portfolio. He/she is able to receive updated share prices via Web Services technology. When he/she connects to the internet, the software searches for services able to provide share prices. It locates two possible services, and asks the user to select one. One service gives prices delayed by 1 minute, and requires a subscription of € 10 /per month to use. The other gives prices delayed by 30 minutes and is free. The investor chooses the latter, because he/she does not engage in real-time trading, and the software package then updates his/her portfolio information whenever he/she is online.

6.3 Key Concepts in Semantic Web Services

We now introduce some key concepts in Semantic Web Services, and show how these inter-relate. In each case, we illustrate this with examples from the scenarios introduced in Sect. 6.2. The work presented in this section follows the Semantic Web–enabled Web Services conceptual architecture [6].

6.3.1 Notion of Service

First, let us define the key concept of *service*. Intuitively, one party provides a service to another when the first party does something for the benefit of the second. A service may be freely given, but is often done for payment. A window cleaner performs the service of cleaning windows; a hairdresser performs the service of cutting hair. In Scenario A above, the bank provides the overdraft warning service to its customer; in Scenario B, the stationery supplier provides the service of sale and shipment of stationery to the manufacturing company; in Scenario C, the freight forwarder provides the service of transferring a crate from one port to another. Formally, we can summarise this by saying that a service is the performance of some actions by one party to provide some value to another party. Note that it makes sense to talk about a service in a certain domain. (In Scenario C, the domain would be transport and logistics.) We refer to this as the *domain of value* of the service. We call the party which performs the service the *service provider* and the party which receives the benefit of the service the *service requester*. Services can be considered at different levels of abstraction. A *concrete service* is a specific performance of actions at a given time by one party for another. (In Scenario C, a concrete service would be the shipping of crate 246 on the ship departing from Portsmouth at 9.25 on 11/12/04 and arriving in St Petersburg at 22.00 on 14/12/04.) However, often when we are reasoning about services, we do not want to be so specific. In particular, when discussing a hypothetical service to be performed in the future, we cannot be specific about all of its details. Hence, we use an abstraction. An *abstract service* corresponds to some set or class of concrete services, and allows us to discuss these hypothetical future services without being precise about all aspects of them. (In Scenario C, the service requester may want to talk about a hypothetical service which will carry crate 246, departing from Portsmouth sometime on 11/12/04 and arriving in St Petersburg before 17/12/04.)

6.3.2 Service Representation

One goal of Semantic Web Services is to bring about a computational machine-readable representation of the service, in terms of the value it provides. This is referred to as the *service description*. Usually, a service description will describe an abstract service, in which case it can be referred to as an *abstract service description*. Less often, a concrete service description is used to describe a concrete service.

To describe services, the Semantic Web approach uses techniques based on knowledge representation, a discipline which has developed a set of formal languages and techniques for describing knowledge in a way which permits reasoning with it. When describing a service, there are two key design decisions which must be made initially. First, what formal language is going to be used to describe it? Should it be described using horn clause logic, description logic, non-monotonic logic or some other approach? Different formalisms can be used, and this will be further discussed in Chap. 7. Secondly, what specific concepts and relations are going to be permitted in descriptions, and what is the meaning of these? This involves the creation or selection of an ontology, which provides a structured ontological vocabulary: a set of concepts and relations which can be used to describe things in the domain of interest. It is important that the terms the ontology provides allow a specification of the actions the service consists of, and/or the outcomes it brings about, in the terminology of the domain of value of the service.

When two parties describe services, they make different choices with regard to the language and ontology used. As a result, if one party is to reason with a description produced by the other party, then some additional reasoning will be necessary to translate between the two approaches. This additional reasoning is termed *mediation*, specifically ontology mediation. Other forms of mediation may also be necessary, and we will discuss this further below.

6.3.3 Agents

Having discussed the representation of services, we need to consider the online representation of the service requester and provider. If the providing and receiving of a service is to be automated, then these two parties must have some online presence. We refer to the software components which represent the parties as *agents*, with a service provider agent representing a service provider and a service requester agent representing a service requester.

These software components are agents in a very precise sense; they act as representatives online on behalf of some party. (This is the same sense of the word 'agent' as in 'estate agents', who act on behalf of a house seller.) Hence, the agent property is a role the component takes, rather than some intrinsic property of the component. Hence, these software entities are not necessarily agents in the sense used in Multi Agent Systems research [7]. Often, they will be reactive not proactive, and will be hardwired to follow some pre-determined process. For example, a set of Web Services provided by Amazon make up a service provider agent able to sell books on behalf of Amazon. However, as these entities become more sophisticated, and take on further tasks from the party they represent, they will make use of technology developed by the Multi Agent Systems community. For example, they may use negotiation algorithms [8] to allow them to agree details of services and prices; they may use distributed planning [9] to allow complex service composition and they may use utility theoretic reasoning to decide between possible alternative courses of action [10] as a service is delivered.

Another consequence of 'agent' being a role that a software component takes is that it can behave as a requester agent at one time, and a provider agent at another. This can be seen in Scenario A; the bank's software system acts as a service provider agent to its customer, providing the service of account warnings. However, to get the warning message to its customer, the bank's system behaves as a service requester and enters into an arrangement with a provider of a message delivery service.

If we are to be precise, we need to make a clear distinction between the service requester (or provider) and the service requester agent (or provider agent) which represents it. However, in practice this is not necessary in our subsequent discussions and we will use 'service provider/requester' to refer to the agent also.

6.3.4 Communication

Choreography

When a service is provided online, there must be some interaction between the provider and the requester. This interaction will require some exchange of messages. The exchange of messages within an interaction must follow certain constraints if they are to make sense to both parties. In other words, the message exchange must proceed according to a certain communication protocol known to both parties. In the Semantic Web Services world, a communication protocol, which can be multi-party, is often referred to as a *choreography*. For consistency with this existing literature, we will adopt this terminology subsequently. When some exchange of messages takes place according to the constraints provided by some choreography, we refer to this as a *conversation* between two parties which satisfies the choreography.

Interactions about a service may involve more than two parties, playing different roles. In general, many multi-party interactions can be reduced to a set of two-party interactions. However, there are some cases where this is not possible. For the purposes of this book, we focus only on two-party interactions; however, many of the concepts generalise straightforwardly to the multi-party case.

When two parties engage in a conversation, they must each have one or more communication endpoints to send and receive the messages according to some transport protocol. This is referred to as the *grounding* of the choreography. In many cases, service providers will interact via an interface specified in terms of Web Service operations. This is particularly the case for simple service provider agents with no internal state, where their choreography consists simply of a call–response interaction. The free stock quote service in Scenario D is of this type. However, there are other possibilities; the freight forwarder interacts using a complex set of RosettaNet messages with implicit state information in their sequencing, and these messages will be transported between the business partners using the RNIF standard.

Semantics in Choreography

As we discussed above, the first technical goal of Semantic Web Services is to provide machine-readable descriptions of service, to allow them to be reasoned with by different parties. The second technical goal of Semantic Web Services is to describe the different choreographies, which parties can use to interact, in a machine-readable form. This form should represent not only the messages which are exchanged, but also provide some model for the underlying intention behind the exchange of messages on the part of both parties. In other words, it should represent the semantics of the message exchange. In Scenario D, messages are exchanged to build up a stationery order; semantic representation of this will show that a certain sequence of messages corresponds to adding an item to the order, another sequence corresponds to getting a quote for the order, and another sequence corresponds to a final agreement that the order will be processed and payment made.

Doing this will allow software entities to reason about choreographies. For example, an entity could use an explicit model of a choreography to dynamically decide which action to take or message to send next.

6.3.5 Orchestration and Service Composition

As explained above, choreography determines the constraints on the ordering of messages sent between the service requester and service provider. However, the constraints alone are not enough to determine exactly which message is sent when. This is the role of an *orchestration*. An orchestration is a specification, within an agent, of which message should be sent when. Hence, the choreography specifies what is permitted of both parties, while an orchestration specifies what each party will actually do.

The real power of orchestration becomes evident when we look at multiple simultaneous relationships between agents. So far in this discussion, we have focussed on a single interaction, with one agent taking the role of service requester and the other the role of service provider. However, it is clear that in many circumstances an agent will be involved in multiple relationships; in some, it will be acting as a service provider, while in others it will be acting as a service requester. For example, in Scenario A, the bank's overdraft notification service agent acts as a provider to the bank's customer. However, it outsources the task of delivering the notification to other parties. Hence, it acts as a service requester in relationship with these parties.

Often, such an agent will communicate with several service providers and coordinate the services they provide to produce some more complex service – as, e.g., the logistics coordinator does in Scenario C. This act of combining and coordinating a set of services is referred to as *service composition*. When a requester agent is interacting simultaneously with many service providers, an orchestration can specify the sequencing of messages with all of these, including appropriate dependencies. The orchestration can be specified in several different ways. The most straightforward, and least flexible, is to make a design time choice of which service providers to use, and hard-code the integration logic in the service requester agent. A more flexible way is to use a declarative workflow language to describe the process of integrating the interactions with the chosen service providers. This is the approach taken by BPEL [14]. This is more easily maintainable, but suffers from the drawback that if one of the chosen service providers is unavailable, then the overall service orchestration will fail. A more robust approach, advocated by WSMF [11], is not to select the service providers in advance within the orchestration, but instead merely include descriptions of their required functionality. When the orchestration is executed, appropriate service providers are dynamically discovered and selected at run-time.

Having an explicit description of a service orchestration in terms of some process language has a further advantage. It means that the orchestration can exist independently of a specific requester agent, and be passed between agents as a data structure. This approach is used to a great extent by the OWL-S virtual machine [12]. Rather than the service requester being responsible for generating an orchestration, any party can produce one, showing how several services can be combined to produce a more complex service. In particular, in the case where a single service provider offers a variety of services, it is more appropriate for the provider to take responsibility to show how they can be combined in different ways. If this is done in some agreed standard process language, such as the OWL-S process model [13], and a service requester has access to a means to interpret that process language, such as the OWL-S virtual machine, then any such service requester can make use of the complex service.

6.3.6 Mediation

When an interaction between two parties takes place, there may be further need for mediation. There are four forms of mediation which could be necessary: *data mediation*, *ontology mediation*, *choreography mediation* and *process mediation*. We will now briefly introduce each.

Data Mediation

A message or fragment of data represents the information it carries in some specific syntactic format. Different service providers may expect different syntactic formats for their messages, even though the information carried is equivalent. Data mediation consists of transforming from one syntactic format to another.

Ontology Mediation

When two parties describe services, they make different choices with regard to the vocabulary of terms, and therefore ontology, used to do so. As a result, if one party is to reason with a description produced by the other party, then some additional reasoning will be necessary to translate between the two approaches. This additional reasoning is termed ontology mediation.

Protocol Mediation

Two components which are to interact with each other (such as a service requester and service provider) may each have been designed with a particular interaction choreography in mind. Unless agreement was reached between the two designers (either directly or indirectly through the adoption of a standard) then it is unlikely that the two choreographies will be identical. Protocol mediation is mediation which reconciles these two choreographies, by translating a message sequence used by one into a different message sequence used by the other to accomplish the same end.

Process Mediation

Behind any interaction, each party has some internal process which manages the reasoning and resources necessary to bring about that interaction. (In many domains of application, this will correspond to a business process.) In some cases, even though the two parties are able to interact via some protocol, there may be some difference between their processes which means this interaction will not succeed. Process mediation is mediation which reconciles the differences in such processes. This is the hardest form of mediation, and may in many cases be impossible without engaging in process re-engineering.

Mediation of these four different kinds is only possible automatically if the messages and choreographies are annotated semantically. It is key to enabling service interaction to take place automatically, and so forms a core part of the Semantic Web Services research programme. Further discussion will be provided in Chap. 10.

Up to now, we have discussed interactions between service provider and service requester in general terms, without considering the underlying goals of the interaction. This is because there are several different goals an interaction can have behind it. As the relationship between service provider and service requester progresses, different goals are required. For that reason, we now turn to this relationship.

6.3.7 Life cycle

The life cycle of the relationship between service requester and service provider goes through four phases: *modelling*, *discovery*, *service definition* and *service delivery*. During discovery, a requester attempts to locate possible providers able to give it the service it requires. During service definition, the requester and provider interact to define the details of the service which is to be provided. During service delivery, different kinds of interactions can occur which are associated with the provision of the service.

Service Modelling Phase

At the outset of the discovery phase, a service requester prepares a description of the service it is interested in receiving. Because it is unlikely that all details of the service will be known at the outset (e.g., the provider of the service is not known, and the cost of the service may not be known), the description will be of an abstract service. This abstract service description makes up the service requirement description of the service requester. Similarly, service providers create abstract service descriptions representing the service they are able to provide. This is referred to as the service offer description. Note that both the service requirement description and the service offer description are simply descriptions of a service, and hence use the same concepts and relations in the description. However, in each case, the service description plays a different role. In the first case, it describes a service which is being looked for, and in the second case it describes a service which is being provided.

Service Discovery Phase

If the requirement description of a requester and the offer description of a provider are in some sense compatible, then there is a match and the two parties could go on to the service definition phase. There are different ways of deciding whether two descriptions are compatible; these will be discussed in Chap. 8.

To illustrate this, consider Scenario A. The bank is looking for a service provider able to send a message to the customer. Let us say the customer has chosen to receive the message via text. The bank's requester agent creates a service requirement description stating that it wants to send a text message of length 112 characters to a number on Telefonica Movistar, a Spanish mobile network. A provider advertises a service offer description stating that it is able to send text messages of maximum length 120 characters to Telefonica Movistar numbers at a cost of € 0.1. These two are potentially compatible, so a match should be made during discovery.

There are also different architectures which can be used to carry out discovery. The most common is a centralised discovery 'service' which is contacted by the requester using a simple message exchange protocol.

Service Definition Phase

During discovery, a requester may identify several providers which are potentially able to meet their needs. From the set of providers identified, the requester may contact one or more of these and enter into a service definition conversation with them. Selection of which to contact may simply be random, or may involve some analysis of the service providers and choice of which appear in some sense 'best'. (Recall in Scenario D, the investor chose the cheaper but older service for stock quotes, because low cost was more important than having immediate information.) If service definition fails with those selected, the requester has the option to later contact others which were not initially selected, and try with those.

The service definition phase involves taking an abstract service description of a provider and refining it so that it describes a specific service which meets the requester's needs. One way of conceptualising this is to think of the abstract service as having attributes which must be instantiated. In Scenario C, the shipment service would have attributes including weight of crate, departure and arrival ports, departure and arrival times, and price. The selection of the values these attributes take is the role of the service definition phase. Sometimes, it is not necessary to specify a specific value, but some constraint on a value is adequate. (In Scenario C, the arrival time might be specified as between 18.00 and 22.00.) This process takes place through a conversation governed by a service definition choreography.

When a requester enters into service definition phase with several possible providers, it will often be in an attempt to explore what options the different parties provide in order to select the best. (Recall in Scenario B, the service requester agent making a stationery purchase goes through the motions of preparing an order and receiving a quote with several providers.) The requester will complete the service definition phase with only one of them, terminating the conversations with those it has not selected.

If the service definition phase is successfully completed between two parties, they have agreed a service to be delivered by the provider to the requester, and can enter into the service delivery phase. Some of the attributes may not be fully defined, merely constrained. (In Scenario C, the freight forwarder may specify that the crate must be lighter than 500 Kg.) In this case, it means that one party (usually the provider) will allow the other to make a selection of attribute value during the delivery phase. (In Scenario C, the requester will inform the freight forwarder of the final crate weight in the advance shipment notification message it sends just before dispatch.) There may be a formal representation of the agreed service description, which can form part of a contract between the two parties [16].

In many cases, a service definition conversation will not be necessary. The description of the service by the provider will define fixed values for all the attributes the provider cares about. The only flexibility in the description will be where a provider is willing to allow a requester to freely choose. Effectively, the provider gives a 'take it or leave it' description of the service it provides, and the requester simply selects one. This can be seen in Scenario D. There is no service definition conversation between the investment software and the service provider agents. Instead, the investor simply selects which to use based on his/her preferences.

In some cases, the conversation will involve iterative definition of the service, selecting from options to create a complete description piece-by-piece. This can be seen in Scenario B, where the shopping-trolley metaphor is used during service definition. Through an exchange of messages between the two parties, the requester browses the wares, selects some, gets a final quote and agrees (or not) to purchase them.

Less often, the conversation may involve negotiation of certain parameters, such as price. Negotiation involves the iterative relaxing of constraints on values until some agreement is reached. Negotiation is an important area of agent technology research,but detailed discussion is beyond the scope of this chapter.

Service Delivery Phase

When the definition of a service has been agreed, then service delivery can take place. It may be immediate, as in Scenario A where the text message is sent as soon as the bank confirms its selection. Alternatively, it may take place a while after service definition has been completed, as in Scenario C where the agreement to carry a crate in a certain ship may be made days or weeks before the actual voyage. Service delivery may take place entirely off-line, with no communication, as in Scenario A where the text message is sent by the provider without any further exchange of messages. Alternatively, it may involve communication between the two parties. If communication takes place, this is again governed by an interaction choreography.

Several different types of interaction can occur during service delivery, and each is governed by a choreography:

1. The service delivery choreography covers the exchange of messages associated directly with the delivery of the service. In some cases, the service is provided directly by this exchange of messages, as in Scenario D where the stock quote data will be carried within a reply message from the quotation Web Service. In other cases, the exchange of messages is linked with activities occurring in the real world, as in Scenario C where the messages initiate and control (to a limited extent) the movement of a crate from Portsmouth to St Petersburg.
2. A monitoring choreography covers the exchange of messages which allow the service requester to receive information regarding the progress of the service from the provider. In Scenario C, there is a RosettaNet message exchange, 'Shipment Status Message', which allows the service requester to get information about the progress of the shipment from the freight forwarder. This is an example of a monitoring choreography.
3. A cancellation/renegotiation choreography allows the service requester, in certain circumstances, to cancel or alter the service which they are receiving from the provider. In Scenario B, we can imagine (as in Amazon) that the purchaser has the option to review, modify or cancel their order through an exchange of messages, provided the order has not entered the dispatching process.

6.4 Architecture for Semantic Web Services

Having introduced the concepts used in Semantic Web Services, we now consider an architecture which can be used to develop and deploy applications. Inevitably, by moving from a conceptual level to an architecture, certain design decisions will be made. We do not claim that this is the only way to make such decisions.

In Multi Agent Systems research, a distinction is made between a micro-architecture and a macro-architecture. A micro-architecture is the internal component-based architecture of an individual entity within a community. A macro-architecture is the structure of the overall community, considering each entity within it as a black box. It is also helpful to consider this distinction in Semantic Web Services. In an open community, it is necessary to standardise the macro-architecture to some extent, but the micro-architecture can be more flexible, with differences in design between various community members.

6.4.1 Macro-Architecture

Initially, we will present the macro-architecture for our community. In our community, there are three possible roles that a software entity can have: service requester agent, service provider agent and discovery provider agent. In general, an entity may have more than one role; however, for clarity we will consider each role separately.

To recap from the previous section, a service requester agent acts on behalf of an individual or organisation to procure a service. It receives a service requirement description from its owner, and interacts with other agents in an attempt to fulfil the requirement it has been given. It has some model, in an ontology, of the domain of the service and also has some model of the kind of actions that can be taken (through message exchange) in this domain.

A service provider agent is able to provide a service on behalf of an organisation. It has a service offer description in some domain ontology (ideally, the same as the requester agent), which describes at an abstract level the kind of services it can provide. It also has a means to generate more concrete descriptions of the precise services it can deliver. Furthermore, it has a formal description of the message protocol used to deliver the service. This includes mappings from the content of messages into concepts within the domain ontology. It also includes mappings from message exchange sequences into actions. In Scenario C, a field in the initial Advance Shipment Notification (ASN) message might map onto the 'weight' attribute of the 'crate' concept within the domain. The sequence consisting of one party sending the ASN and the other party acknowledging receipt may correspond to a 'notify shipment' action in the domain ontology.

A discovery provider agent has access to descriptions of service offers, together with references to provider agents able to provide these services. These service offer descriptions are all in some domain ontology associated with the discovery provider agent. Within this ontology is a 'service description' concept which effectively acts as a template for the descriptions of services that the discovery provider can contain.

We illustrate the macro-architecture by specifying the interactions which can take place between the different agents. These interactions are roughly in order of the life cycle progression introduced in the previous section.

1. Provider agent registering a service offer description

   A simple message exchange protocol is used between a provider agent and a discovery agent. The provider agent sends a register message to the discovery agent, containing a service offer description in the ontology of the discovery agent and a URI for the provider agent. The discovery agent replies with an accept message if it is able to accept and store the description, reject otherwise. It will only reject a description if the description is not a valid concept in its ontology, or there is some practical reason it can't accept it, such as lack of memory. Prior to this, if the provider agent is not aware of the ontology used by the discovery agent, it can send a requestOntology message to the discovery agent. The agent replies with an informOntology message containing the section of the ontology relevant to the service description. If this is a different ontology from that used by the service provider agent, then ontology mediation will be necessary. We assume this takes place within the provider agent. However, in general it could take place using a third party or within the discovery agent.

2. Requester agent finding possible providers

   Discovery takes place through a simple exchange protocol between a service requester agent and a discovery agent. The requester agent sends a request-Providers message containing a service requirement description in the ontology used by the discovery agent. (As above, it can find out what this is using a requestOntology/informOntology exchange. It may then require ontology mediation, which we assume takes place within the requester agent.) The discovery agent responds with an informProviders message containing a list of URIs of service provider agents. These correspond to those provider agents which have offer descriptions stored within the discovery agent which match (using the discovery agent's algorithm) with the service requirement description.

3. Requester and provider agents define service

   Following discovery, the requester agent exchanges messages with one or more provider agents to define the service it will receive, and to select which provider agent to use. In our architecture, we assume a single simple service definition protocol is used by all requester and provider agents. This protocol is adequate for very many service definition tasks; however, in the general case this assumption is unrealistic and multiple protocols (and possibly protocol mediation) would be necessary. The FIPA standards [17] provide various possible negotiation protocols which could be used at this stage. Our simple protocol consists of two rounds of message exchange. Initially, the service requester agent sends a requestServices message to each provider agent. The message contains a service requirement description. The provider agent replies with an informServices message, which contain (almost) concrete service descriptions of the services it is able to provide that meet the needs of the requester. If the requester wishes to select one of these, it replies with a selectService message containing the required service, and the provider responds with confirm. The confirm message contains a URI referencing where the description of the choreographies which will be used during service delivery are to be found. If the requester does not select one within a certain time window, sending no response to the provider, this is taken as cancelling. Note that this protocol does not allow negotiation–it simply allows the service provider to list a set of potentially interesting concrete services to the requester, and allows the requester to select one of these. Note also that our protocol does not capture Scenario B, intelligent procurement. The service selection protocol used in this example is a shopping-trolley protocol. While this is a natural protocol for human users (who are interested in browsing, and looking at one item at a time), it is less essential for software entities interacting with the service provider. We can imagine an alternative access protocol to shopping sites, similar to the one described here, where a requester agent submits a list of product descriptions it is interested in, receives a list back of relevant available products, selects a subset and places an order. However, in practice, many sites will continue to use the shopping-trolley metaphor meaning that protocol mediation will be important at this stage. For the purposes of the architecture presented here, we ignore this additional complexity and assume all parties use the same service specification protocol.

4. Service delivery

   Service delivery starts when one party (depending on the choreography used) sends an initiating message. Unlike previous stages, many different choreographies can be used depending on the domain of application of the service. In Scenarios A and D, the choreography is simply a single message exchange corresponding to 'do the service', with a reply being 'I have done the service and here is the result.' Scenario B is similar, except the response is 'I will do the service' (and it takes place off-line, via mail.) In Scenario C, the choreography used at this stage will correspond to the sequence of messages specified by the RosettaNet standard.

Because of the large variety of choreographies which are possible during service delivery, it is at this stage that protocol mediation will play the largest role. This will particularly be the case where the choreography can be more complex, as in Scenario C. For the purposes of this architecture, we assume that any protocol mediation that is required will take place in the service requester agent and use the choreography descriptions referenced by the provider agent. However, mediation can equally well take place within the provider or within a third party.

Given this assumption, then the macro-architecture appears as follows. Each service provider has a description of the service delivery choreography associated with each service it can provide. At the end of the service definition protocol, as a parameter of the confirm message, it informs the requester of a URI which references this description. The requester is then responsible for accessing this description, interpreting it and engaging in a message exchange with the provider which satisfies the requirements of the choreography described.

6.4.2 Micro-Architecture

Having described the macro-architecture, we now turn to the micro-architecture of the system. We look at two of the three roles that software entities can have – requester agent and provider agent – and present a micro-architecture for each. The micro-architecture of the discovery service provider agent will be covered in Chap. 8. Note that, unlike the macro-architecture, a micro-architecture is not normative within a community. The macro-architecture defines the exchange of messages between entities of different roles, and if the community is to function effectively, this must be agreed and adhered to (though the provision of protocol mediation within the macro-architecture allows some flexibility). The micro-architecture of each agent, however, need not follow some pre-agreed structure. The community can function perfectly well with any internal structure, provided the functionality the micro-architecture implements does indeed correspond to the requirements of the macro-architecture.

Figure 6.1 illustrates our architecture for the service requester agent. At the heart of the agent is the application logic, which is responsible for decision-making with

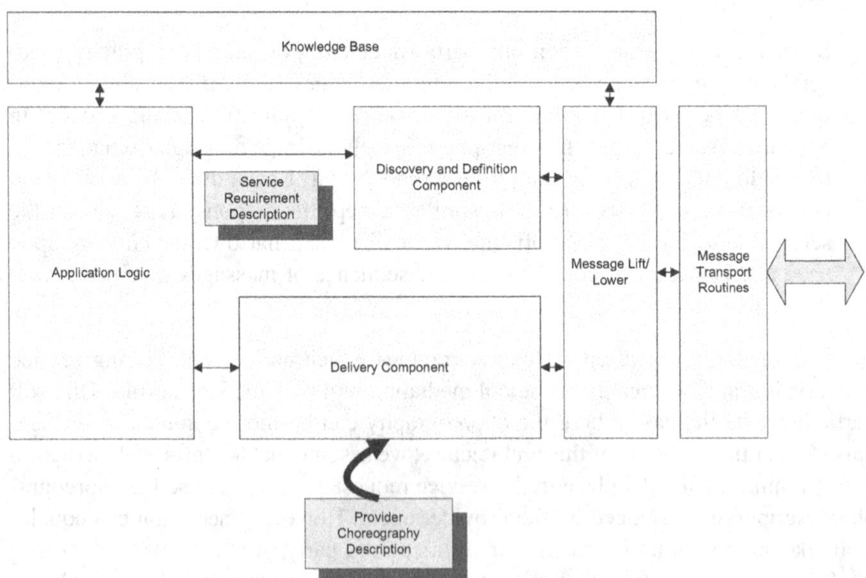

Fig. 6.1. Architecture of service requester agent

regard to which service to select and how to make use of it. This can include integration with other back-end systems within the organisation which the service requester agent represents. It may also access and assert information in the knowledge base. In other cases, the application logic will be provided by a user interacting through a user interface; the requester agent effectively acts as an online proxy for the user, and relays any important decision-making problems to them, acting on their choice.

The first role of the application logic is to define a service requirement description for the service it needs. When this has been done, it passes the description to the discovery and definition component. This component is responsible for managing the discovery and service definition choreographies, and sends appropriate messages to do this as described in the macro-architecture above. The message format and contents are prepared using the messaging lift/lower component and passed to the transport routines for transmission via an appropriate transportation protocol. Often, but not exclusively, these transportation routines will use WSDL Web Service technology for communicating with the service provider. At points where a decision is required – namely when one or more provider is to be chosen to contact after discovery and when a service is to be chosen during the selection process – the decision is passed for the application logic to be made. The message lift/lower component performs data mediation. When it receives incoming messages, it translates their contents into semantic information according to an ontology and stores these in the Knowledge Base. It generates the content of outgoing messages by using facts in the Knowledge Base to fill fields according to some message schema. When a service has been defined, the application logic initiates the delivery process by passing the URI identifying the delivery choreography to the delivery component. Unlike the discovery and selection component, which contains hard-wired logic for a single protocol, the delivery component is able to carry out protocol mediation. It accesses the description of the choreography given by the service provider. This shows how message contents map onto the domain ontology of the knowledge base, and also shows how sequences of messages correspond to actions within this domain ontology. State machines describe the order in which actions can take place. The application logic can request the execution of an action. This will result in the delivery component initiating an exchange of messages with the service provider. The content of a message will be instantiated by accessing the knowledge base and 'lowering' the relevant information into the required message format using the lift/lower component. The message can then be passed to the transport routines for transmission. When a message is received as part of such an exchange, the contents of the message will be 'lifted' into the knowledge base using the lift/lower component and the delivery component will note the progress of the message exchange. When an exchange terminates (either through successful completion or through some failure) the application logic is informed of this. The delivery component also handles messages from the provider which are not part of an exchange initiated by the requester. These correspond to actions within the domain which the provider is initiating. The delivery component identifies which action they are initiating, 'lifts' the message content to the knowledge base and informs the application logic. It replies (possibly after a decision from the application logic of how to respond) by 'lowering' content into a message, which is then passed to the transport routines. Full details of this process, and the architecture used, are given in Chap. 10.

We now turn our attention to the provider agent (Fig. 6.2). Because, in our architecture, we assume that protocol mediation takes place within the requester, the provider can be simpler. It also has an application logic component at its heart, which is responsible for deciding which services to offer a given requester and also for the provisioning of the service itself. As in the case of the requester, this will often involve integration with a variety of back-end systems belonging to the service provider's organisation. Initially, the application logic prepares a service offer description and registers this with the discovery service provider. It also prepares a choreography description associated with this service, and publishes it on the web, giving it a URI. From that point on, in our architecture, the provider agent is reactive. The service definition component has an interface (often, though not exclusively, provided by Web Service WSDL technology) which allows a requester to submit a service requirement description. On receipt of this, the application logic prepares a set of possible services which satisfy the requirement, and this is sent to the requester through the definition component interface. If the definition component receives a selection message from the requester, it responds with a confirm containing the URI of the choreography description which it obtains from the application logic. The service delivery protocol is executed by the service delivery component, again via an interface which may or may not use WSDL Web Service technology. Unlike the requester agent, the provider agent does not need to carry out protocol mediation so the protocol can be hard-wired in the component. Message contents are still lifted into the knowledge base, for access by the application logic. The application logic is informed of the progress of the conversation, requested to initiate internal actions

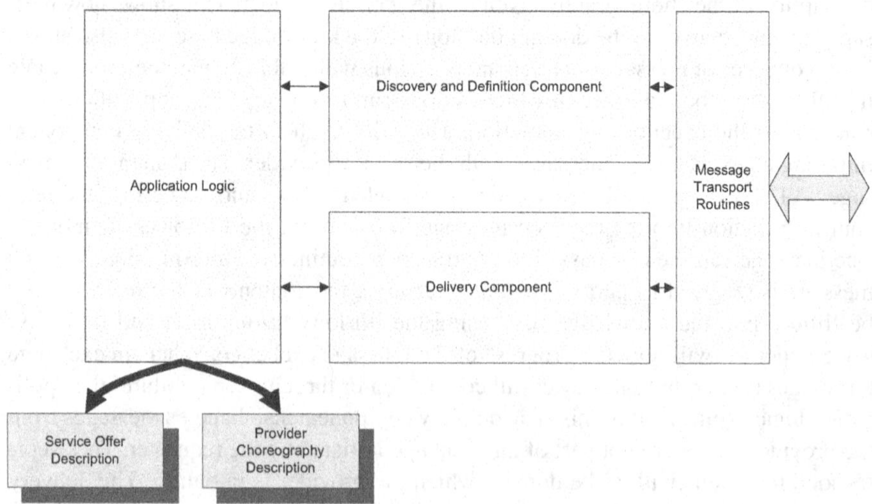

Fig. 6.2. Architecture of service provider agent

to bring about the service, and also consulted if a decision is necessary during the execution of the protocol. In this way, the micro architectures of the two types of actor can animate the conversations required by the macro-architecture. The macro-architecture in turn embodies the concepts introduced in our conceptual model of Semantic Web Services.

6.5 Outlook

In this chapter, we have presented a conceptual model for Semantic Web Services which is driven from a requirements analysis of several scenarios. Using this conceptual model, we have developed a technical architecture which could be used to deploy applications of Semantic Web Services. We have introduced the key notions of discovery, service description, mediation and composition, and shown how they form part of a service life cycle within our conceptual model. Subsequent chapters will provide more details of these ideas, and present the techniques available to make them real.

The architecture presented in this chapter is one possible embodiment of the conceptual model, but others are possible. This particular embodiment has been implemented as part of the EU Semantic Web–enabled Web Services program, and has been used to create a demonstrator of Semantic Web Services technology in the domain of logistics supply chain management [5]. If Semantic Web Services are to be deployed effectively on a large scale, it will be necessary for the community to reach agreement about how to do this. A conceptual model and flexible architecture will be a necessary part of this agreement. We believe the ideas presented in this chapter are a step in this direction.

References

1. S. McIlraith and D. Martin. Bringing Semantics to Web Services. *IEEE Intelligent Systems*, 18(1):90–93, 2003.
2. M. Paolucci and K. Sycara. Autonomous Semantic Web Services. *IEEE Internet Computing*, September 2003:34–41.
3. S. McIlraith and T.C. Son. Adapting Golog for Composition of Semantic Web Services. *Proceedings 8th International Conference on Knowledge Representation and Reasoning*, 482–493, 2002.
4. J.M. Lopez-Cobo, S. Losada, O. Corcho, R. Benjamins, M. Nino and J. Contreras. Semantic Web Services for Financial Overdrawn Alerting. *Proceedings of the 3rd International Semantic Web Conference (ISWC-2004)*, 782–796, Hiroshima, Japan, 2004.
5. C. Preist, J. Esplugas-Cuadrado, S.A. Battle, S. Grimm and S.K. Williams. Automated Business-to-Business Integration of a Logistics Supply Chain using Semantic Web Services Technology. *Proceedings of the 4th International Semantic Web Conference (ISWC-2005)*, Galway, Ireland, 2005.
6. C. Preist. A Conceptual Architecture for Semantic Web Services. *Proceedings of the 3rd International Semantic Web Conference (ISWC-2004)*, 395–409, Hiroshima, Japan, 2004.

7. M. Wooldridge and N.R. Jennings. Agent Theories, Architectures, and Languages: A Survey. *in Intelligent Agents, Proceedings of the ECAI-94 Workshop on Agent Theories, Architectures, and Languages*, Springer-Verlag, Lecture Notes in Artificial Intelligence, Vol. 890, Pages 1–39, 1995.
8. N.R. Jennings, P. Faratin, A.R. Lomuscio, S. Parsons, C. Sierra and M. Wooldridge. Automated Negotiation: Prospects, Methods and Challenges. *International Journal of Group Decision and Negotiation*, 10(2):199–215, 2001.
9. E.H. Durfee. Planning in Distributed Artificial Intelligence. *Foundations of Distributed Artificial Intelligence*:231–245, John Wiley, 1996.
10. M. Barbuceanu and W. Lo. A Multi-Attribute Utility Theoretic Negotiation Architecture for Electronic Commerce. *Proceedings Fourth International Conference on Autonomous Agents (AGENTS 2000)*:239–246, 2000.
11. D. Fensel and C. Bussler. The Web Service Modeling Framework WSMF *Electronic Commerce: Research and Applications*, 1:113–137, 2002.
12. M. Paolucci, A. Ankolekar, N. Srinivasan and K. Sycara. The DAML-S Virtual Machine *Proceedings of the 2nd International Semantic Web Conference (ISWC-2003)*, 290–305, Florida, USA, 2003.
13. `http://www.daml.org/services/owl-s/`
14. T. Andrews, F. Curbera, H. Dholakia, Y. Goland, J. Klein, F. Leymann, K. Liu, D. Roller, D. Smith, S. Thatte, I. Trrickovic and S. Weerawarana. Business Process Execution Language for Web Services - Version 1.1. BEA Systems, IBM, Microsoft, SAP AG and Sibel Systems Whitepaper, 5 May 2003.
15. D. Trastour, C. Bartolini and C. Preist. Semantic Web Support for the B2B E-Commerce Pre-Contractual Lifecycle *Computer Networks*, 42(5):661–673, 2003.
16. B. Grosof and T. Poon. SweetDeal: Representing Agent Contracts with Exceptions Using Semantic Web Rules, Ontologies and Process Descriptions. *International Journal of Electronic Commerce*, 8(4):61–98, 2004.
17. The Foundation for Intelligent Physical Agents `http://www.fipa.org/`

7

Description

Semantic Annotation for Web Services

Holger Lausen[1], Rubén Lara[2], Axel Polleres[3], Jos de Bruijn[1] and Dumitru Roman[1]

[1] Digital Enterprise Research Institute (DERI), Innsbruck, Austria
<name>.<surname>@deri.org
[2] Tecnología, Información y Finanzas (TIF), Madrid, Spain, rlara@afi.es
[3] Universidad Rey Juan Carlos, Madrid, Spain, axel.polleres@urjc.es

Summary. Web Services have added a new level of functionality to the current Web, making the first step to achieve seamless integration of distributed components. Nevertheless, current Web Service technologies only address the syntactical aspects of a Web Service and, therefore, only provide a set of rigid services that cannot adapt to a changing environment without human intervention. The human programmer has to be kept in the loop and scalability as well as economy of Web Services are limited. The description of Web Services in a machine-understandable fashion is expected to have a great impact in areas of e-Commerce and Enterprise Application Integration, as it can enable dynamic and scalable cooperation between different systems and organisations. These great potential benefits have led to the establishment of an important research activity, both in industry and in academia, which aims at realising Semantic Web Services. This chapter outlines aspects of the description of semantic Web Services.

7.1 Modelling Semantic Web Services

Web Services technologies as they stand now provide an abstraction of existing invocation mechanisms. Essentially they are a set of standards that provide a wrapper on top of an existing software component. The Web Service Description Language (WSDL) provides means to describe the operations that can be invoked with their input and output, their name and their endpoint. Those information are sufficient in order to abstract from the operating system and the programming language used for a specific component. For an entity using some functionality of a Web Service, those aspects of the underlying software component are totally transparent.

However, despite the achievements, several aspects remain open. With the technology described it is only possible to model the functionality of a component by giving its operation an identifier and to type the associated messages according to XML-schema data types. For example, a service offering temperature information for airports might be described by a mandatory input of the type string and a second optional of the type date and the return value of the type float. The fact that the string represents a three letter airport code, that the optional date is specified in Central

European Time and that the result is a temperature measured in degrees of Celsius can only be described by using "meaningful" identifiers or as textual comment in the interface description. In both cases the information can help a human developer using his common sense to use the service in a meaningful way, but for computers this information is not interpretable.

If we extend this simple example by a second operation that searches airport codes given the name of a city, additional requirements become obvious. By only stating the operations by their name and input and output parameters, the order in which they can be invoked remains open. In order to give the invoking entity this information, the protocol of the service needs to be described, i.e. that the search airport code operation can be optionally invoked before the get temperature operation and that the result of the first can be used as location input for the latter. We refer to this external behaviour as choreography.

In business scenarios additional needs arise. For example, the transactional behaviour of the service becomes important, e.g. if and when which transactional protocol it supports. Some service may support a truly transactional behaviour according to a well known protocol such as the two phase commit protocol, other may just offer operations for compensating the effect of a previous invocation. A money transfer of a banking Web Service may serve as example for the first and a hotel booking service offering cancellation of reservation as example for the latter.

There are many more aspects to be considered that we will mention during the description of concrete proposals for the modelling of Web Services. For now we can already resume that the current standards such as WSDL are mainly concerned about the syntactic modelling of Web Service, thereby abstracting from low-level aspects such as a programming language. However, additional semantic aspects need to be modelled to enable a further automatisation of the use of Web Services.

A natural candidate for such descriptions are logics. They have well-defined semantics, not determined by a natural language text description, but through a model theory that exactly specifies which statements are true and which not. Chapter 3 already provided an overview of existing approaches. In this chapter, we will present two of the conceptual models for the description of semantic Web Services.

7.1.1 Existing Approaches

Major initiatives in the area are documented by recent W3C member submissions: WSMO [8], OWL-S [30], SWSF [2] and WSDL-S [1]. The proposals defer in scope, modelling approach and the concrete logical languages used. We will give a short introduction to all of them; however, due to space limitations we will only describe two approaches in more detail: OWL-S and WSMO. We selected these proposals because they represent the two conceptually different approaches and both are backed by several existing implementations.

- WSMO: Web Service Modeling Ontology [8] is an initiative to create an ontology for describing various aspects related to Semantic Web Services, aiming at solving the integration problem. WSMO is developed by the Semantic Web

Services working group[1] of the ESSI cluster,[2] which includes more than 50 academic and industrial partners. We describe WSMO in more detail in Sect. 7.2.

- OWL-S [30], an effort by BBN Technologies, Carnegie Mellon University, Nokia, Stanford University, SRI International and Yale University to define an ontology for semantic markup of Web Services. OWL-S is intended to enable automation of Web Service discovery, invocation, composition, interoperation and execution monitoring by providing appropriate semantic descriptions of services. A more detailed analysis follows in Sect. 7.3.
- SWSF; the Semantic Web Services Framework [2], is a relatively recent attempt towards a Semantic Web Service annotation framework that greatly benefits from previous work with its roots in OWL-S and the Process Specification Language (PSL), standardised by ISO 18269. This framework is a joint proposal by the Semantic Web Services Language Committee and was also submitted to the W3C in September 2005. SWSO can be seen as an extension or refinement of OWL-S. There are many similarities with the OWL-S ontologies, but the important difference is the expressiveness of the underlying language which is, instead of OWL, a richer language called the Semantic Web Service Language (SWSL). However, as opposed to other approaches, we are unaware of any serious SWS tools and ongoing implementation efforts based on SWSF so far.
- WSDL-S [1] is a rather minimalist approach which aims at a direct extension of existing "traditional" Web Service descriptions in WSDL with Semantics (indicated by the last letter of the acronym). WSDL-S augments Web Service descriptions in WSDL with semantics by adding respective annotation tags to the XML schema of WSDL, the proposal picks aspects similar to those in WSMO capability definitions or OWL-S profiles, such as precondition and effects. This method keeps the semantic model outside WSDL, making the approach impartial to any ontology representation language. Hence, WSDL-S does not fix a specific formalism for semantic descriptions and accordingly also does not claim to be a fully-fledged description framework/ontology, but rather simply adds some useful attributes to WSDL's XML tags in order to reference semantic annotations. However, without a certain degree of commitment to a specific language, or at the very least a definition of how different semantics of usable languages relate to one another, it is impossible to formally define requests, queries or notions of "match" between service requests and service descriptions. Therefore, we see it more as a complementary effort to the other "fully-fledged" frameworks.

In the following, we discuss both OWL-S and WSMO in more detail. Conceptually, SWSF can be seen similar to OWL-S and thus for a general introduction the explanation of OWL-S should give the reader a sufficient understanding of both frameworks. WSDL-S can be seen as orthogonal effort to the fully-fledged frameworks; since it does not define the semantics of the referenced descriptions, one needs an additional framework for the definition of the semantic information. Since this is the major focus of the chapter, we deem the previous introductory explanation sufficient.

[1] `http://www.wsmo.org/`
[2] `http://www.essi-cluster.org/`

7.2 WSMO

The Web Service Modeling Ontology (WSMO) describes all relevant aspects related to general services which are accessible through a Web Service interface with the ultimate goal of enabling the (total or partial) automation of the tasks (e.g. discovery, selection, composition, mediation, execution, monitoring, etc.) involved in both intra- and inter-enterprise integration of Web Services. WSMO has its conceptual basis in the Web Service Modeling Framework (WSMF) [12], refining and extending this framework and developing a formal ontology and set of languages.

WSMO Top-Level Elements

Following the key aspects identified in the Web Service Modeling Framework, WSMO identifies four top-level elements as the main concepts which have to be described in order to define Semantic Web Services (Fig. 7.1).

1. *Ontologies* provide the terminology used by other WSMO elements to describe the relevant aspects of the domains of discourse.
2. *Services* represent services that could be requested, provided or agreed on by service requesters and service providers. These descriptions comprise the capabilities, interfaces and internal working of the service. All these aspects of a service are described using the terminology defined by the ontologies.
3. *Goals* describe aspects related to user desires with respect to the requested functionality; again Ontologies can be used in order to define the used domain terminology to describe the relevant aspects of goals. Goals model the user view in the Web Service usage process and therefore are a separate top–level entity in WSMO.
4. *Mediators* describe elements that handle interoperability problems between different WSMO elements. Mediators are the core concept to resolve incompatibilities on the data, process and protocol level, i.e. in order to resolve mismatches between different used terminologies (data level), in how to communicate between services (protocol level) and on the level of combining Web Services (process level).

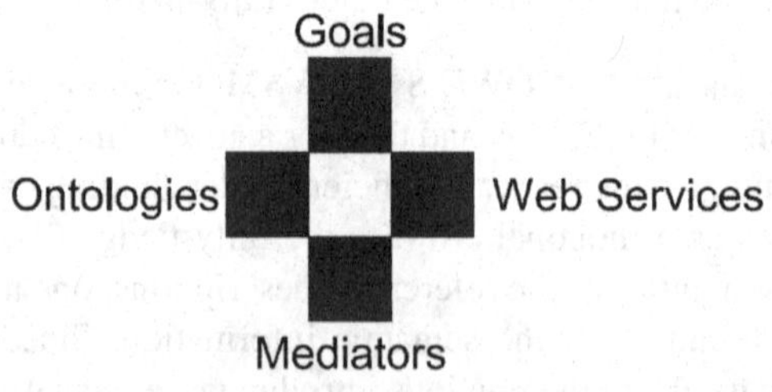

Fig. 7.1. WSMO core elements

Language for Defining WSMO

WSMO is meant to be a meta-model for Semantic Web Services–related aspects. For defining this model we make use of Meta Object Facility (MOF) [22] specification which defines an abstract language and framework for specifying, constructing and managing technology neutral meta-models. MOF defines a metadata architecture consisting of four layers:

1. The *information layer* comprises the data we want to describe.
2. The *model layer* comprises the metadata that describes data in the information layer.
3. The *meta-model layer* comprises the descriptions that define the structure and semantics of the metadata.
4. The *meta-meta-model layer* comprises the description of the structure and semantics of meta-metadata.

In terms of the four MOF layers, the language in which WSMO is defined corresponds to the meta-meta-model layer. WSMO itself constitutes the meta-model layer, the actual ontologies, services, goals, and mediators specifications constitute the model layer, and the actual data described by the ontologies and exchanged between Web Services constitute the information layer. Figure 7.2 shows the relation between WSMO and the MOF layered architecture.

The most used MOF meta-modelling construct in the definition of WSMO is the *Class* construct (and implicitly its class generalisation (*sub-Class*) construct), together with its *Attributes*, the *type* of the *Attributes* and their *multiplicity* specifications. When defining WSMO, the following assumptions are made:

- Every *Attribute* has its *multiplicity* set to multi-valued by default; when an *Attribute* requires its *multiplicity* to be set to "single-valued", this will be explicitly stated in the listings where WSMO elements are defined.
- Some WSMO elements define *Attributes* taking values from the union of several types, a feature that is not directly supported by the MOF meta-modelling constructs; this can be simulated in MOF by defining a new *Class* as *super-Class* of all the types required in the definition of the *Attribute*, representing the union

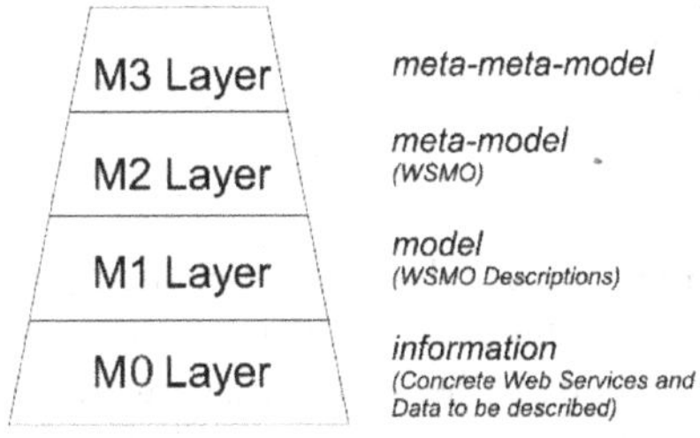

Fig. 7.2. The relation between WSMO and MOF

of the single types, with the *Constraint* that each instance of this new *Class* is an instance of at least one of the types which are used in the union; to define this new *Class* in WSMO, we use curly brackets, enumerating the *Classes* that describe the required types for the definition of the attribute.

In the following, we use listings with the MOF metamodel to illustrate the structure of WSMO where it supports the understanding of the overall structure. To be brief some listings are shortened or omitted; the complete specification of WSMO in terms of MOF can be found in [28].

Illustrating Example

In order to illustrate WSMO, we will adopt the Scenario B introduced in Chap. 6. In this scenario, shipment services are modelled that offer transportation of goods. The corresponding domain ontologies respectively define concepts like packages, routes and locations.

7.2.1 Ontologies

An ontology is a formal explicit specification of a shared conceptualisation [14]. From this conceptual definition we extract the essential components which constitute an ontology. They define a common agreed upon terminology by providing concepts and relationships among the concepts.

Although there are currently several standardisations efforts for ontology languages [16] [10] [17], none of them has the desired expressivity and computational properties that are required to describe Web Services at a sufficient level of granularity. In the following, we will define an epistemological model which is general enough to intuitively capture existing languages.

In the following, we will present the conceptual model along with concrete examples. We will now introduce the elements that constitute an ontology using MOF notation, defining the class ontology with the following attributes.

```
Class ontology
    hasNonFunctionalProperty type nonFunctionalProperty
    importsOntology type ontology
    usesMediator type ooMediator
    hasConcept type concept
    hasRelation type relation
    hasFunction type function
    hasInstance type instance
    hasAxiom type axiom
```

In the following subsections, we will describe all elements in more detail. The illustrating examples are given in WSML [9], a language specifically designed to express the WSMO meta model. Although other concrete languages might be used to express our model, we chose WSML for its close relationship to the meta model. A general introduction to the WSML language can be found in Chap. 3. Necessary explanation are given throughout the text, however, some general remarks beforehand: WSML identifiers are URIs, for readability they are abbreviated using the QName [4] mechanism. URIs in the default namespace do not need a prefix, other namespaces will be introduced in the explaining text sections. A QName is written in the format prefix#localPart and will be expended to the full URI during processing.

Non-functional Properties

Non-functional properties are allowed in the definition of all WSMO elements. They are mainly used to describe non-functional aspects such as creator, creation date, natural language descriptions, etc. We take the elements defined by the Dublin Core Metadata Initiative [31] as a starting point and introduce other elements, e.g. the version of the ontology (other elements necessary for the description of other elements of WSMO, e.g. Web Services, are introduced in their corresponding sections).

```
namespace {_"http://example.org/wsmo#",
  loc _"http :// wsmo.org/ontologies/location#",
  dc _"http :// purl.org/dc/elements/1.1#"}

ontology _"http :// example.org/Routes"
  nonFunctionalProperties
    dc# title hasValue "An ontology describing trips and reservations"
    dc#creator hasValue "DERI Innsbruck"
    dc#publisher hasValue "DERI International"
    dc#format hasValue "text/x-wsml"
  endNonFunctionalProperties}
```

The example above illustrates the use of namespace declaration to QNames for readability. Note that those identifiers are only logical identifiers and not physical ones. The metadata in the non-functional properties can also refer to URIs.

Imported Ontologies

Building an ontology for some particular problem domain can be a rather cumbersome and complex task. One standard way to deal with the complexity is modularisation. Imported ontologies allow a modular approach for ontology design and can be used as long as no conflicts need to be resolved between the ontologies. By importing ontologies all statements of the imported ontology will be virtually included in the importing ontology. Every WSMO top-level entity may use this import facility to include the logical definition of the vocabulary used.

Used Mediators

When importing ontologies in realistic scenarios, some steps for aligning, merging and transforming imported ontologies in order to resolve ontology mismatches are needed. For this reason and in line with the basic design principles underlying the WSMF, ontology mediators (ooMediator), which are described in detail in Sect. 7.2.4, are used when an alignment of the imported ontology is necessary. Such an alignment can be, e.g., the renaming of concepts or attributes. Just like the *importsOntology* statement the *usesMediator* statement is applicable to all top-level elements; however depending on the element different mediators may be used.

Concepts

Concepts constitute the basic elements of the agreed terminology for some problem domain. From a high-level perspective, a concept – described by a concept definition – provides attributes with names and types. Furthermore, a concept can be a subconcept of several (possibly none) direct superconcepts as specified by the "isA" relation.

In the WSMO model, each concept can have a finite number of concepts that serve as a superconcept for some concept. Being a subconcept of some other concept in particular means that a concept inherits the signature of this superconcept and the corresponding constraints. Furthermore, all instances of a concept are also instances of each of its superconcepts. In the example given, a route in Europe is defined as subconcept of a general route.

```
concept routeInEurope subConceptOf route
  origin ofType loc#location
  destination ofType loc#location

axiom routeInEruope
  definedBy
    forall ?x (?x memberOf routeInEurope equivalent
       ?x[destination hasValue ?dest,
          origin hasValue ?orig] memberOf trip and
       ?dest[locatedIn hasValue loc#Europe] and
       ?orig[locatedIn hasValue loc#Europe]).
```

A concept provides a (possibly empty) set of attributes that represent named slots for the data values for instances. An attribute specifies a slot of a concept by fixing the name of the slot as well as a logical constraint on the possible values filling that slot, which in the simple case can be another concept. Within the example the domain of the possible attribute values for *origin* is restricted to instances of the concept location (loc# abbreviates the full logical identifier of this external ontology). Note that in WSMO/WSML we do not restrict ourselves to typing constraints but also allow the types of slot fillers to be implied by the definition. This can be modelled in WSML by means of the keyword `impliesType` replacing `ofType`. For a more in-depth discussion we refer the reader to [7, 9].

As every element in WSMO, a concept can be refined by a logical expression. Additionally to the conceptual model, logical expressions can be asserted to a concept that refines its meaning, e.g. with nuances that are not expressible by attributes or the "isA" hierarchy. A logical expression can be used to refine the semantics of the concept. More precisely, the logical expression defines (or restricts) the extension (i.e. the set of instances) of the concept. Within the example the expression refines a route to a route in Europe, i.e. restricts all attribute values of origin and destination to locations that have a *locatedIn* attribute value indicating them being located in Europe.

Relations

Relations are used in order to model interdependencies between several concepts (respectively instances of these concepts). The arity of relations is not limited.

```
relation airLineDistance subRelationOf distance
  from ofType loc#location
  to ofType loc#location
  distanceInMeter ofType _integer
```

Every relation can have a finite set of super relations. Being a subrelation of some other relation in particular means that the relation inherits the signature of this superrelation and the corresponding constraints. Furthermore, the set of tuples belonging to the relation (the extension of the relation) is a subset of each of the extensions of the superrelations. In the example given, we define air-line distance as a sub-relation of the general distance relation.

Similar to attributes for concepts, each relation has a possible empty set of named parameters. In case no named parameters are given, a unnamed, ordered list is assumed. Each parameter is single valued and can have a range restriction in the form of a concept.

Functions

A function is a special relation, with a unary range and a n-ary domain (parameters inherited from relation), where the range specifies the return value. Functions can be used, for instance, to represent and exploit built-in predicates of common datatypes. Their semantics can be captured externally by means of an oracle or it can be formalised using logical expressions. In WSML there are no extra keywords for modelling functions, but relations can be used with corresponding refining axioms.

Instances

Instances are either defined explicitly or by a link to an instance store, i.e. an external storage of instances and their values. An explicit definition of instances of concepts is as follows:

```
instance Innsbruck memberOf loc#location
  locatedIn hasValue loc#austria
```

Besides the identifier of the instance (*Innsbruck*), the concept and the attribute values are given. These values have to be compatible with the corresponding type declaration in the concept definition. Instances of relations (with arity n) can be seen as n-tuples of instances of the concepts which are specified as the parameters of the relation.

In general, instances do not need to be specified using the explicit notation presented above. Especially for the case when a huge number of instances exist, a link to a data store can be used [20]. Basically, the approach is to integrate large sets of instances which are already existing on some storage devices by means of sending queries to external storage devices or oracles.

Axioms

An axiom is considered to be a logical expression together with its non-functional properties. Generally the conceptual model does not assume a particular logical language, although it does suggest a language.

7.2.2 Services

The *Service* element of WSMO provides a conceptual model (a meta model in MOF terms) for describing in an explicit and unified manner all the aspects of a service, including its non-functional properties, functionality and the interfaces to obtain it. An unambiguous model of services with well-defined semantics can be processed and interpreted by computers without human intervention, enabling the automation of the tasks involved in the usage of Web Services, e.g. discovery, selection, composition, mediation, execution or monitoring.

As discussed in Chap. 6, the word *service* can be understood in different ways, with slightly different meanings: as provision of value in some domain, as a software entity able to provide something of value and as a means of interacting online with a service provider.

WSMO provides a unifying view of a service; the value the service can provide is captured by its *capability*, and the means to interact with the service provider to request the actual performance of the service, or to negotiate some aspects of its provision, is captured by the service *interfaces*. The software entity able to provide the service is transparent to us, and we are only concerned with its interaction style and with what other services are used to actually provide the value described in the capability. The distinction made between abstract service and concrete service in Chap. 6 is not built into WSMO; however, a WSMO capability can be used to model abstract services, whereas a concrete service is determined during the execution of a choreography.

Notice that in WSMO the interaction with a service can be realised by using Web Services in the WSDL [3] sense. However, we are not restricted to WSDL as the grounding of services.

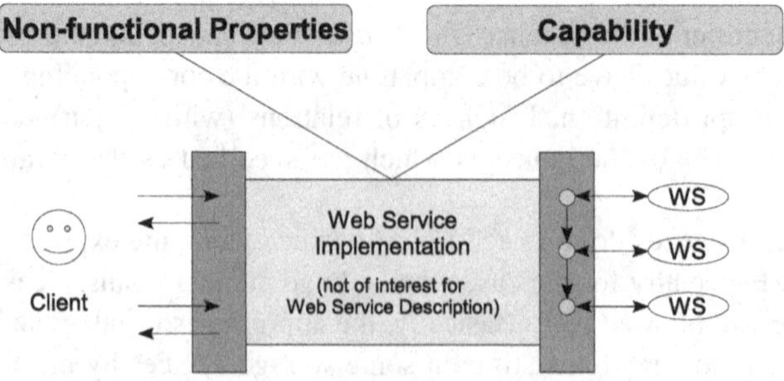

Fig. 7.3. WSMO service – general description

Figure 7.3 shows the core elements that are part of the description of a WSMO service. The main elements of a service description are a capability describing the value the service can provide and one or more interfaces in which the choreography and the orchestration of the service are described. The choreography specifies how the service achieves its capability by means of interactions with its user – i.e. the communication with user of the service; the orchestration specifies how the service achieves its capability by making use of other services – i.e. the coordination of other services.

More precisely, the WSMO *service* element is defined as follows:

```
Class service
  hasNonFunctionalProperty type nonFunctionalProperty
  importsOntology type ontology
  usesMediator type {ooMediator, wwMediator}
  hasCapability type capability multiplicity = single-valued
  hasInterface type interface
```

The *non-functional properties* of a service are aspects of the service that are not directly related to its functionality; besides the non-functional properties presented in Sect. 7.2.1, they consist of Web Service specific elements like Accuracy (the error rate generated by the service), Financial (the cost-related and charging-related properties of a service [23]), Network-related QoS (QoS mechanisms operating in the transport network which are independent of the service), Owner (the person or organisation to which the service belongs), Performance (how fast a service request can be completed), Reliability (the ability of a service to perform its functions, i.e. to maintain its service quality) and others.[3] The non-functional properties are to be mainly used for the discovery and selection of services; however, they contain information that is also suitable for negotiation.

Imported Ontologies are used to import the explicit and formal vocabulary used in the specification of a service (see Sect. 7.2.1).

A service *uses mediators* in the following situations: (1) When using heterogeneous terminologies and conflicts between them arise; in these cases, a service can import ontologies using ontology mediators (ooMediators), as explained in Sect. 7.2.1. (2) When it needs to cope with process and protocol heterogeneity when interacting with other services; in this case a *wwMediators* is used. For a more detailed description of mediators, see Sect. 7.2.4.

Capability

The functionality offered by a given service is described by its capability; it is expressed by the state of the world before the service is executed and the state of the world after successful service provision. The service capability is meant primary for discovery and selection purposes, i.e. the capability is used by the requester to determine whether the service meets its needs.

[3] For a detailed description of the non-functional properties we refer the reader to [28]

```
Class capability
  hasNonFunctionalProperty type nonFunctionalProperty
  importsOntology type ontology
  usesMediator type ooMediator
  hasPrecondition type axiom
  hasAssumption type axiom
  hasPostcondition type axiom
  hasEffect type axiom
```

The set of *non-functional properties* that can be attached to a capability is the one presented in Sect. 7.2.1. *Imported Ontologies* and *used mediators* are defined as in Sect. 7.2.1.

Preconditions in the description of the capability specify the required state of the information space before the service execution, i.e. they specify what information a Web Service expects to provide its service. Preconditions constrain the set of states of the information space such that each state satisfying these constraints can serve as a valid starting state (in the information space) for executing the service in a defined manner.

We extend the already described example and use the ontology presented in Sect. 7.2.1. The following example requires that the information sent to the service must be an instance of the transportRequest concept together with a credit card information. The service only accepts such request that require a transport between a location in England to anywhere in Europe. Note that the restriction on the destination of the route is inherited from the axiom in the ontology given in the previous section.

```
precondition
  definedBy
    exists {?origin, ?destination}
    (request[
      hasRoute hasValue ?route
      hasPackage hasValue ?package
      hasCreditCard hasValue ?creditCard
    ]memberOf transportRequest and
    ?route[origin hasValue ?origin] memberOf routeInEurope and
    ?origin[locatedIn hasValue England])
```

Assumptions in the description of the capability describe the state of the world which is assumed before the execution of the service. Otherwise, the successful provision of the service is not guaranteed. As opposed to preconditions, assumptions are not necessarily to be checked by the service. We make this distinction in order to allow an explicit notion of conditions on the world state but outside the information space.

Within our example we present an assumption saying that the service will be provided only if the provided credit card is valid. The validity of the credit card is specified using the *valid* relation.

```
assumption
  definedBy
    valid(?creditCard).
```

PostConditions in the description of the capability describe the state of the information space that is guaranteed to be reached after the successful execution of the service; it also describes the relation between the information that is provided to the service and its results.

The following example presents a postcondition saying that the information that the service provides is an instance of the confirmation concept, with the condition that the item that is confirmed is the trip initially requested.

```
postcondition
  definedBy
    confirmationInstance[confirmationItem hasValue request] memberOf confirmation
```

Effects in the description of the capability describe the state of the world that is guaranteed to be reached after the successful execution of the service, i.e. if the preconditions and the assumptions of the service are satisfied.

The following example presents an effect saying that, after the execution of the service, the balance of the credit card given as input will be deducted by the costs of the shipment and a contract exists for shipping a package according to the request specified.

```
effect
  definedBy
    creditCardInstance[po#balance hasValue (initialBalanceInstance – transportationCost)]
    and shipmentContract(request,package).
```

Interfaces

An interface describes how the functionality of the service can be achieved (i.e. how the capability of a service can be fulfilled) by providing a twofold view on the operational competence of the service: (1) *choreography* decomposes a capability in terms of interaction with the service. (2) *orchestration* decomposes a capability in terms of functionality required from other services.

This distinction reflects the difference between communication and cooperation. The choreography defines how to communicate with the service in order to consume its functionality. The orchestration defines how the overall functionality is achieved by the cooperation of more elementary service providers.

The Web Service interface is meant primarily for behavioural description purposes of Web Services and is presented in a way that is suitable for software agents to determine the behaviour of the service and reason about it; it might also be useful for discovery and selection purposes and in this description the connection to some existing Web Services specifications, e.g. WSDL [3] could also be specified.

```
Class interface
    hasNonFunctionalProperty type nonFunctionalProperty
    importsOntology type ontology
    usesMediator type ooMediator
    hasChoreography type choreography
    hasOrchestration type orchestration
```

Choreography provides the necessary information to communicate with the service. The general model for representing choreographies is a state-based mechanism and is inspired by the Abstract State Machines [15, 3] methodology. The reason for choosing ASMs as a basis for WSMO choreography is that ASMs provide a high flexibility in modelling systems, being at the same time theoretically well founded. A choreography defines a state signature that is given by elements of the WSMO Ontology, and it remains unchanged during the execution of the service, a state that is given by a set of instance statements, and guarded transitions that express changes of states by means of rules, similar to ASM transition rules. For a more detailed description of WSMO choreography we refer the reader to [27].

Orchestration describes how the service makes use of other services in order to achieve its capability. In many real scenarios, a service is provided by using and interacting with services provided by other applications or businesses. For example, the booking of a trip might involve the use of another service for validating the credit card and charging it with the correspondent amount and the user of the booking service may want to know which other business organisations he she is implicitly going to deal with.

WSMO introduces the orchestration element in the description of a service to reflect such dependencies. WSMO orchestration allows the use of statically or dynamically selected services. In the former case, a concrete service will be selected at design time. In the latter case, the service will only describe the goal that has to be fulfilled in order to provide its service. This goal will be used to select at run-time an available service fulfilling it (i.e. the service user could influence this choice).

7.2.3 Goals

Goals are used in WSMO to describe user's desires. They provide the means to specify the requester-side objectives when consulting a Web Service, describing at a high-level a concrete task to be achieved.

Goals are representations of objectives for which fulfillment is sought through the execution of Web Services; they can be descriptions of services that would potentially satisfy the user desires.

Notice that WSMO completely decouples the objectives a requester has, i.e. his goal, from the services that actually can fulfil such goal. Goals are to be resolved by selecting available services that describe service provision that satisfies the goal. The definition of a goal is given below:

```
Class goal
    hasNonFunctionalProperty type nonFunctionalProperty
    importsOntology type ontology
    usesMediator type {ooMediator, ggMediator}
    requestsCapability type capability multiplicity = single-valued
    requestsInterface type interface
```

Given the fact that a goal can represent the service that would potentially satisfy the user desires, the set of *non-functional properties* that can be attached to a goal is similar to the one attached to Web Services (see Sect. 7.2.2). An extra non-functional property can be attached to a goal, the *Type of Match*, which represents the type of match desired for a particular goal (under the assumption of a set-based modelling this can be an exact match, a match where the goal description is a subset of the Web Service description or a match where the Web Service description is a subset of the goal description; for a detailed discussion refer to [18]). A goal uses *imported ontologies* as the terminology to define the other elements that are part of the goal as long as no conflicts are needed to be resolved.

A goal *uses mediators* in the following situations: (1) When using heterogeneous terminologies, conflicts between them might arise; in these cases, a service can import ontologies using ontology mediators (*ooMediators*), as explained in Sect. 7.2.1. (2) When a goal reuses already existing goals, e.g. by refining them; for this, *ggMediators* are used (they are explained in more detail in Sect. 7.2.4).

The *requested Capability* in the definition of the goal describes the capability of the services the user would like to have.

The *Interface* in the definition of the goal describes the interface of the service the user would like to have and interact with.

The following example presents the goal having a contract for a shipment. It only specifies between which locations some good has to be shipped, but leaves other details open.

```
goal havingATransportationContract
  capability
    effect definedBy
      shipmentContract(myRoute,myPackage) and
      myRoute[origin hasValue Bristol, detination hasValue Hamburg].
```

7.2.4 Mediators

Mediation is concerned with handling heterogeneity, i.e. resolving possibly occurring mismatches between resources that ought to be interoperable. Heterogeneity naturally arises in open and distributed environments, and thus in the application areas of Semantic Web Services; WSMO defines the concept of Mediators as a top-level notion.

Mediator orientated architectures as introduced in [33] specify a mediator as an entity for establishing interoperability of resources that are not compatible a priori by resolving mismatches between them at runtime. The aspired approach for mediation relies on declarative description of resources whereupon mechanisms for resolving mismatches work on a structural, semantic level, in order to allow defining generic, domain independent mediation facilities as well as reuse of mediators. Concerning the needs for mediation within Semantic Web Services, the WSMF [12] defines three levels of mediation:

1. Data-level mediation – mediation between heterogeneous data sources; within ontology-based frameworks like WSMO, this is mainly concerned with ontology integration.[4]
2. Protocol-level mediation – mediation between heterogeneous communication protocols; in WSMO, this mainly relates to choreographies of Web Services that are ought to interact.
3. Process-level mediation – mediation between heterogeneous business processes; this is concerned with mismatch handling on the business logic level of Web Services (related to the orchestration of Web Services).

WSMO Mediators realise a mediation-orientated architecture for Semantic Web Services, providing an infrastructure for handling heterogeneities that possibly arise between WSMO components and realising the design concept of strong decoupling and strong mediation. A WSMO Mediator connects WSMO components and resolves mismatches between them with the following specifying the general definition:

```
Class mediator
    hasNonFunctionalProperty type nonFunctionalProperty
    importsOntology type ontology
    hasSource type {ontology, goal, webService, mediator}
    hasTarget type {ontology, goal, webService, mediator}
    hasMediationService type {webService, goal, wwMediator}
```

As a mediator can be provided as a service, the same *non-functional properties* as for services are used (see Sect. 7.2.2 for what these non-functional properties consist of).

Imported ontologies are used to import the explicit and formal vocabulary used in the specification of a mediator (see Sect. 7.2.1).

The *source* component of a mediator defines the resources wherefore heterogeneities are resolved; a mediator can have several source components.

The *target* component of a mediator is the component that receives the mediated source components.

The *mediation service* defines the mediation facility applied for resolving mismatches. This can be defined in different ways: directly (i.e. explicitly linking to a mediation service); via a goal that specifies the desired mediation facility which is then detected by a discovery mechanism; or via another mediator when a mediation service is to be used that is not interoperable to the mediator.

WSMO Mediator Types

In order to allow resolving heterogeneities between the different WSMO components, WSMO defines different types of mediators for connecting the different WSMO components and overcome heterogeneities that can arise between the components: OO Mediators, GG Mediators, WG Mediators and WW Mediators. All mediators are subclasses of the general WSMO Mediator class defined above,

[4] One can further refine this (e.g. as done in Chap. 10) into a syntactic (data) and semantic (ontology) layer

whereby a prefix indicates the components connected by the mediator type. The following explains the different WSMO Mediator types, while a general example for using mediators is provided in the next section.

OO Mediators resolve mismatches between ontologies and provide mediated domain knowledge specifications to the target component. The source components are ontologies or other OO Mediators that are heterogeneous and to be integrated, while the target component is any WSMO top-level notion that applies the integrated ontologies. The following shows the description specialisation of an OO Meditator:

```
Class ooMediator sub−Class mediator
    hasSource type {ontology, ooMediator}
```

OO Mediators are used to import the terminology required for a resource description whenever there is a mismatch between the ontologies to be used. The mediation technique related to OO Mediators is mainly ontology integration, i.e. merging, aligning and mapping ontology definitions in order to retrieve integrated, homogeneous terminology definitions.

A GG Mediator connects goals, allowing to create a new goal from existing goals and thus defining goal ontologies. GG Mediators are defined as follows:

```
Class ggMediator sub−Class mediator
    usesMediator type ooMediator
    hasSource type {goal, ggMediator}
    hasTarget type {goal, ggMediator}
```

A GG Mediator might use an OO Mediator to resolve terminology mismatches between the source goals. Mediation services for GG Mediators reduce or combine the descriptions of the source goals into the newly created target goal.

A WG Mediator links a Web Service to a Goal, resolves terminological mismatches, and states the functional difference (if any) between both. WG Mediators are defined as follows:

```
Class wgMediator sub−Class mediator
    usesMediator type ooMediator
    hasSource type {service, wgMediator}
    hasTarget type {goal, ggMediator}
```

WG Mediators are used to prelink Services to existing Goals, or for handling of partial matches within Web Service discovery. As within GG Mediators, OO Mediators can be applied for resolving terminological mismatches.

A WW Mediator is used to establish interoperability between Web Services that are not interoperable a priori. Its definition in the language of WSMO is as follows:

```
Class wwMediator sub−Class mediator
    usesMediator type ooMediator
    hasSource type {service, wwMediator}
    hasTarget type {service, wwMediator}
```

A WW Mediator mediates between the choreographies of Web Services that are ought to interact, wherefore mediation might be required on the data, the protocol, and the process level. As within the other WSMO mediator types, OO Mediators can be applied for resolving terminological mismatches.

7.2.5 Logical Language

A framework for describing the semantics of Web Services needs a solid basis on some logical formalism which allows to express ontological structures in the used terminology, conditions over effects, relations between inputs and outputs, etc. in order to describe the functionality of a service and to allow formal reasoning based on these descriptions.

As an ongoing effort, the Web Service Modeling Language (WSML) Working Group[5] is working on the specification of a family of languages for the specification of Ontologies and Web Services, based on the WSMO conceptual model. The family of languages, called WSML [9], considers Description Logics as well as Logic Programming and conceptual modelling as a basis for different language variants.

WSML consists of five different variants. These variants differ in logical expressiveness and in the underlying language paradigms and allow users to make the trade-off between provided expressiveness and the implied complexity for ontology modelling on a per-application basis.

1. WSML-Core is based on the intersection of the Description Logic $\mathcal{SHIQ}$ and Horn Logic, based on Description Logic Programs [13]. It has the least expressive power of all the WSML variants. The main features of the language are concepts, attributes, binary relations and instances, as well as concept and relation hierarchies and support for datatypes.
2. WSML-DL captures the Description Logic $\mathcal{SHIQ}(\mathbf{D})$, which is a major part of the (DL species of) OWL [10].
3. WSML-Flight is an extension of WSML-Core which provides a powerful rule language. It adds features such as meta-modelling, constraints and nonmonotonic negation. WSML-Flight is based on a logic programming variant of F-Logic [19] and is semantically equivalent to Datalog with inequality and (locally) stratified negation.
4. WSML-Rule extends WSML-Flight with further features from logic programming, namely the use of function symbols, unsafe rules and unstratified negation under the Well-Founded semantics.
5. WSML-Full unifies WSML-DL and WSML-Rule under a First-Order umbrella with extensions to support the nonmonotonic negation of WSML-Rule. The semantics of WSML-Full is currently an open research issue.

The variants follow two alternative layerings, namely WSML-Core $\Rightarrow$ WSML-DL $\Rightarrow$ WSML-Full and WSML-Core $\Rightarrow$ WSML-Flight $\Rightarrow$ WSML-Rule $\Rightarrow$ WSML-Full.

[5] `http://www.wsmo.org/wsml/`

For both layerings, WSML-Core and WSML-Full mark the least and most expressive layers. The two layerings are to a certain extent disjoint in the sense that interoperation between the Description Logic variant (WSML-DL) on the one hand and the Logic Programming variants (WSML-Flight and WSML-Rule) on the other is only possible through a common core (WSML-Core) or through a very expressive superset (WSML-Full).

7.3 OWL-S

In this section, we introduce each of the description elements of OWL-S. We will identify the equivalent or similar concepts in WSMO (if any). OWL-S defines an upper ontology for services with four major elements (Fig. 7.4).

1. Service: This concept serves as an organisational point of reference for declaring Web Services; every service is declared by creating an instance of the Service concept.
2. Service Profile: The profile describes what the service does at a high level, describing its functionality and other non-functional properties that are used for locating services based on their semantic description.
3. Service Model: The model of a service describes how the service achieves its functionality, including the detailed description of its constituent processes.
4. Service Grounding: The grounding describes how to use the service, i.e. how a client can actually invoke the service.

7.3.1 OWL-S Service

The *Service* concept in OWL-S links the profile, service model and grounding of a given service through the properties *presents*, *describedBy* and *supports*, respectively. As an example of the use of the *Service* concept in OWL-S, the BravoAir service[6] from a fictitious airline is modelled as follows:

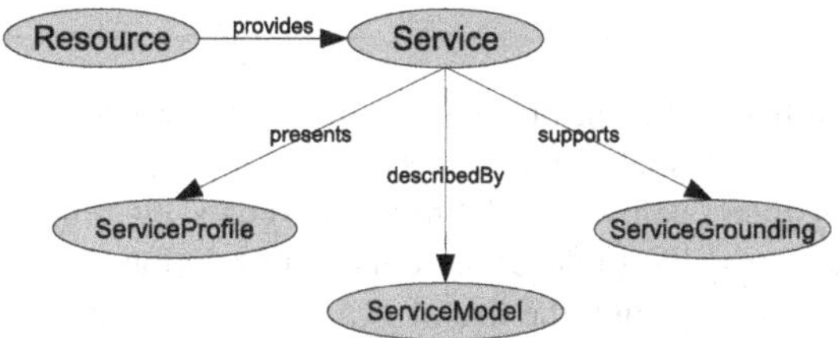

Fig. 7.4. OWL-S upper ontology

[6] `http://www.daml.org/services/owl-s/1.1B/BravoAirService.owl`. This example is part of the OWL-S specification

```
<service:Service rdf:ID="BravoAir_ReservationAgent">
  <service:presents rdf:resource="BravoAirProfile.owl#Profile_BravoAir_ReservationAgent"/>
  <service:describedBy rdf:resource="BravoAirProcess.owl#BravoAir_Process" />
  <service:supports rdf:resource=BravoAirGrounding.owl#Grounding_BravoAir_ReservationAgent"/>
</service:Service>
```

WSMO also provides a direct link between a Web Service, its capability and its interfaces (containing the service choreographies and groundings). However, WSMO explicitly decouples the requester point of view from the provider point of view: goals are defined independently from Web Services and they are linked through *wgMediators*. In addition, the requester and the provider can use different terminologies, as the difference is resolved by the *ooMediators* used by the *wgMediator*.

7.3.2 OWL-S Service Profile

In OWL-S, the service profile describes the intended purpose of the service, both describing the service offered by the provider and the service desired by the requester. In the following, we go through the details of the OWL-S service profile and describe their counterparts in WSMO.

Profile Hierarchy

The profile of a Web Service can be positioned in a hierarchy of profiles.[7] Positioning a given service profile in a profile hierarchy is though optional, and a concrete profile can be directly defined as an instance of the profile class.

As an example, the BravoAir service is categorised as an airline ticketing service in a hierarchy defining, among others, e-commerce service profiles[8]:

```
<owl:Class rdf:ID="AirlineTicketing">
 <rdfs:subClassOf rdf:resource="#E_Commerce"/>
 <rdfs:subClassOf>
  <owl:Restriction>
   <owl:onProperty rdf:resource="#merchandise"/>
   <owl:allValuesFrom rdf:resource="#CommercialAirlineTravel"/>
  </owl:Restriction>
 </rdfs:subClassOf>
</owl:Class>
```

In the example, airline ticketing profiles are defined as a subclass of e-commerce profiles where the commercialised products are commercial airline travels.

WSMO *ggMediators* allow the definition of goals by refining existing ones. Therefore, it is also possible to describe refinement relations between goals, building a hierarchy of goals through the use of *ggMediators*. Similarly, OWL-S service profiles can be positioned in a previously defined hierarchy, WSMO services can be linked to a goal using a *wgMediator*.

[7] http://www.daml.org/services/owl-s/1.1B/ProfileHierarchy.html

[8] http://www.daml.org/services/owl-s/1.1B/ProfileHierarchy.owl

Service Name, Contact, Description and Category

The OWL-S service profile includes human-readable information, contained in the properties serviceName (of type string; maximum one service name), textDescription (of type string; maximum one description) and contactInformation (of class *Actor*, including information such as name, phone, fax or e-mail). A service categorisation is also given, although the classification schemas are not fixed and, therefore, the range of this property is not specified.[9] There are no cardinality restrictions for the categorisation, i.e. a service can be assigned to none or multiple categories in different categorisation schemes. The BravoAir example is defined as follows:

```
<profile:serviceName>BravoAir_ReservationAgent</profile:serviceName>
< profile:textDescription >This service...</ profile:textDescription >
<profile:contactInformation>
  <actor:Actor rdf:ID="BravoAir-reservation">
   <actor:name>BravoAir Reservation department</actor:name>
   <actor:phone>412 268 8780</actor:phone>
   <actor:email>Bravo@Bravoair.com</actor:email>
   [...]
  </actor:Actor>
</profile:contactInformation>
<profile:serviceCategory>
 <addParam:UNSPSC rdf:ID="UNSPSC-category">
  <profile:value>Travel Agent</profile:value>
  <profile:code>90121500</profile:code>
 </addParam:UNSPSC>
</profile:serviceCategory>
[...]
```

This information is expressed in WSMO by using non-functional properties, such as title, description, identifier, creator, publisher or type. WSMO uses commonly accepted terminology for these properties (the Dublin Core Metadata Element Set [32]). Notably, non-functional properties can be defined for any of the core WSMO elements, and for other elements such as ontology concepts or attributes, while in OWL-S non-functional properties can be associated only with the service profile.

Profile Parameters

In addition to the above non-functional properties, the OWL-S profile also includes an expandable list of non-functional properties expressed as *service parameters*. The range for the service parameters is not specified.[10] For example, the BravoAir profile is described below:

[9] Some examples of possible categorisation such as NAICS or UNSPC are given in `http://www.daml.org/services/owl-s/1.1B/ProfileAdditionalParameters.owl`

[10] Examples of such properties are geographic radius or response time (see `http://www.daml.org/services/owl-s/1.1B/ProfileAdditionalParameters.owl`)

```
<profile:serviceParameter>
 <addParam:GeographicRadius rdf:ID="BravoAir–geographicRadius">
  <profile:serviceParameterName>BravoAir Geographic Radius</profile:serviceParameterName>
  <profile:sParameter rdf:resource="Country.owl#UnitedStates" />
 </addParam:GeographicRadius>
</profile:serviceParameter>
```

Functionality Description

The OWL-S profile specifies what functionality the service provides. The functionality description is split into the *information transformation* performed by the service and the *state change* as a consequence of the service execution. The former is captured by defining the *inputs* and *outputs* of the service, and the latter is defined in terms of *preconditions* and *effects*. Inputs, outputs, preconditions and effects are normally referred to as IOPEs. Effects are defined as part of a *result*. The schema for describing IOPEs is not defined in the profile, but in the OWL-S process. Instances of IOPEs are created in the process and referenced from the profile, and it is envisioned that the IOPEs of the profile are a subset of those published by the process [30].

Inputs and outputs. OWL-S inputs and outputs describe what information is required and what information is produced by the service. Inputs and outputs are modelled as subclasses of parameter, which is in turn a subclass of SWRL variable [17] with a property indicating the class or datatype the values of the parameter belong to. Local variables can also be used, and they are modelled in the ontology as subclasses of parameter. Inputs, outputs and local variables have as scope the process where they appear. The inputs and outputs defined in the service model are referenced from the profile via the *hasInput* and *hasOutput* properties, respectively, and there are no cardinality restrictions for inputs and outputs Local variables can be referenced via the *hasParameter* property. For the BravoAir example, inputs and outputs are declared in the profile as follows:

```
<profile:hasInput rdf:resource="BravoAirProcess.owl#DepartureAirport"/>
<profile:hasInput rdf:resource="BravoAirProcess.owl#ArrivalAirport"/>
<profile:hasInput rdf:resource="BravoAirProcess.owl#OutboundDate"/>
<profile:hasInput rdf:resource="BravoAirProcess.owl#InboundDate"/>
<profile:hasInput rdf:resource="BravoAirProcess.owl#RoundTrip"/>
 [...]
```

The inputs and outputs are defined in the process[11] as part of the different atomic processes where they appear:

```
<process:Input rdf:ID="DepartureAirport">
 <process:parameterType rdf:datatype="&xsd;anyURI">Concepts.owl#Airport</process:parameterType>
</process:Input>
<process:Input rdf:ID=" ArrivalAirport ">
 <process:parameterType rdf:datatype="&xsd;anyURI">Concepts.owl#Airport</process:parameterType>
</process:Input>
 [...]
<process:Output rdf:ID="FlightsFound">
```

[11] http://www.daml.org/services/owl-s/1.1B/BravoAirProcess.owl

```
<process:parameterType rdf:datatype="&xsd;anyURI">Concepts.owl#FlightList
 </process:parameterType>
</process:Output>
<process:Output rdf:ID="ReservationID">
 <process:parameterType rdf:datatype="&xsd;anyURI">
   Concepts.owl#ReservationNumber
 </process:parameterType>
</process:Output>
[...]
```

Preconditions and effects. Preconditions are conditions on the state of the world that have to be true for successfully executing the service. They are modelled as conditions, a subclass of expression. Expressions in OWL-S specify the language in which the expression is described[12] and the expression itself is encoded as a (string or XML) literal. Effects describe conditions on the state of the world that are true after the service execution. They are modelled as part of a result. A result has an *inCondition*, a *ResultVar*, an *OutputBinding* and an *Effect*. The *inCondition* specifies the condition for the delivery of the result. The *OutputBinding* binds the declared output to the appropriate type or value depending on the *inCondition*. The *effects* describe the state of the world resulting from the execution of the service. The *ResultVars* play the role of local variables for describing results. Conditions, i.e. preconditions defined in the service model, are referenced from the profile via the *hasPrecondition* property and results via the *hasResult* property, with no cardinality restrictions. The BravoAir example does not specify any precondition, but one result:

```
<profile:hasResult rdf:resource="BravoAirProcess.owl#HaveSeatResult"/>
```

The result is declared in the service process, as part of the atomic process where it appears. However, the definition of this result is not complete in the example. Therefore, we illustrate the definition of results with a more detailed example taken from [30]. This result declares that the effect of the service is that a purchase is confirmed, the object purchased is owned by the requester and the credit limit of the credit card is decreased by the amount of the purchase. The condition for such effect to happen is that the credit limit of the credit card is bigger or equal to the purchase amount. The output is a confirmation number for the purchase:

```
<process:hasResult>
 <process:Result>
  <process:hasResultVar>
   <process:ResultVar rdf:ID="CreditLimH">
    <process:parameterType rdf:resource="&ecom;#Dollars"/>
   </process:ResultVar>
  </process:hasResultVar>
  <process:inCondition expressionLanguage="&expr;#KIF" rdf:dataType="&xsd;#string">
     (and (current-value (credit-limit ?CreditCard)
                          ?CreditLimH)
                         (>= ?CreditLimH ?purchaseAmt))
  </process:inCondition>
  <process:withOutput>
   <process:OutputBinding>
    <process:toParam rdf:resource="#ConfirmationNum"/>
```

[12] The use of SWRL [17], KIF [11] or DRS [21] is recommended

```
      <process:valueFunction rdf:parseType="Literal">
       <cc:ConfirmationNum xsd:datatype="&xsd;#string"/>
      </process:valueFunction>
     </process:OutputBinding>
    </process:withOutput>
    <process:hasEffect expressionLanguage="&expr;#KIF" rdf:dataType="&xsd;#string">
       (and (confirmed (purchase ?purchaseAmt) ?ConfirmationNum)
             (own ?objectPurchased)
             (decrease (credit−limit ?CreditCard)
                         ?purchaseAmt))
    </process:hasEffect>
   </process:Result>
  </process:hasResult>
```

State change is described in WSMO by using assumptions and effects. The goal only defines effects, as the state of the world that is desired. The capability defines both assumptions (similar to preconditions, but referencing aspects of the state of the world beyond the actual input) and effects (the state of the world after the execution of the service). As for preconditions and postconditions, no cardinality restrictions are placed for assumptions and effects.

The relation between the input and the output, and between the preconditions and the effects of a Web Service have to be captured in order to accurately describe the service functionality. If such relation is not provided, then the service only characterises the input and the output, but does not model the function that transforms one into the other. This relation can be described in OWL-S when defining the *result* of the execution of the service, where the (logical) relation between the input, output and effects is described. In the example above, the *inCondition* and the *effect* states that the credit limit of the credit card given as input will be decreased if the limit was bigger or equal than the purchase amount before invoking the service. In WSMO, this relation is described in the definition of postconditions and effects, as can be seen in the examples.

7.3.3 OWL-S Service Model

In OWL-S, a service model represents how the service works, i.e. how to interoperate with the service. The service is viewed as a process, and the class *ProcessModel* is the root class for its definition. The process model describes the functional properties of the service, together with details of its constituent processes (if the service is a composite service), describing how to interact with the service. The functionality description contained in OWL-S service models corresponds with the capability of a WSMO Web Service, while the descriptions of how to interact with the Web Service correspond to WSMO choreographies.

Functionality Description

The functionality description, as for the service profile, is split into information transformation and state change and is expressed in terms of IOPEs (see Sect. 7.3.2). IOPEs are linked to any process via the properties *hasInput*, *hasOutput*, *hasPrecondition* and *hasResult*, with no cardinality restrictions.

Composite process, i.e. processes which contain other processes, can define the functionality of each individual or (partially) aggregated process. Capabilities in WSMO provide the functional description described in OWL-S using IOPEs of the process. Notice that the OWL-S functionality description in the profile (from the provider point of view) and in the model are merged into a single specification in WSMO: the Web Service capability. However, the WSMO capability only defines the overall functionality of the Web Service; for multi-step services, where each step will provide a particular part of the overall functionality, these partial functionalities are not reflected in the Web Service capability. The concrete specification of WSMO choreography clarifies how the steps of complex services are described and whether the functionality of each individual step, or groups of such steps, is part of these descriptions.

Atomic Processes

OWL-S distinguishes between atomic, simple and composite processes. OWL-S atomic processes can be invoked, have no subprocesses and are executed in a single step from the requester's point of view. They are a subclass of *process* and, therefore, they specify their inputs, outputs, preconditions and effects. The BravoAir service describes several atomic processes. The atomic processes for getting flight details and for selecting an available flight are listed below:

```
<process:AtomicProcess rdf:ID="GetDesiredFlightDetails">
   <process:hasInput rdf:resource="#DepartureAirport"/>
   <process:hasInput rdf:resource="#ArrivalAirport"/>
   <process:hasInput rdf:resource="#OutboundDate"/>
   <process:hasInput rdf:resource="#InboundDate"/>
   <process:hasInput rdf:resource="#RoundTrip"/>
   <process:hasOutput rdf:resource="#FlightsFound"/>
</process:AtomicProcess>

<process:AtomicProcess rdf:ID="SelectAvailableFlight">
   <process:hasInput rdf:resource="#FlightsAvailable" />
   <process:hasOutput rdf:resource="#SelectedFlight" />
</process:AtomicProcess>
```

Simple Processes

OWL-S simple processes are not invocable and they are viewed as executed in a single step. They are used as elements of abstraction, although this kind of processes is not illustrated in the BravoAir example. The functionality of a simple process, when it is the only process of the service, can be described by a WSMO capability as part of a Web Service description with no grounding information, i.e. not invocable.

Composite Processes

OWL-S composites are decomposable into other processes. OWL-S provides a set of control constructs such as *sequence* or *split* (for a complete account of the available control constructs we refer the reader to [30]) which are used to define the control flow inside the composite process. In addition to the control constructs, means to declare the data flow between processes are provided in the latest version of OWL-S. Processes are annotated using the *binding* class. A binding is declared as a process which consumes data from other processes which declares what other process and which concrete process parameter the data comes from. The example below defines one of the composite processes of BravoAir for booking a flight. It is a sequence of processes, from which the first one is to perform the login, and the second one is to complete the reservation. The process for completing the reservation takes data from the parent process (the *ChosenFlight* input to the parent process) and uses it as the input for its own *ChosenFlight* input:

```
<process:CompositeProcess rdf:ID="BookFlight">
 <process:composedOf>
  <process:Sequence>
   <process:components>
    <process:ControlConstructList>
     < list:first >
      <process:Perform rdf:ID="PerformLogin">
       <process:process rdf:resource="#LogIn"/>
      </process:Perform>
     </ list:first >
     < list:rest >
      <process:ControlConstructList>
       < list:first >
        <process:Perform>
         <process:process rdf:resource="#CompleteReservation"/>
         <process:hasDataFrom>
          <process:Binding>
           <process:toParam rdf:resource="#ChosenFlight"/>
           <process:valueSource>
            <process:ValueOf>
             <process:theVar rdf:resource="#ChosenFlight"/>
             <process:fromProcess rdf:resource="Process.owl#TheParentPerform"/>
[...]
```

WSMO can model OWL-S composite processes by defining complex (multi-step) service choreographies. One important difference between OWL-S and WSMO is that the former only defines the externally visible behaviour of the Web Service, while WSMO also models how the service makes use of other services to provide its functionality. While WSMO choreographies describe how to interact with the service from a requester perspective, WSMO orchestrations describe how the service acts as a requester for other services in order to complete the functionality declared in its capability. The orchestration defines what Web Services will be invoked or what goals have to be fulfilled (enabling automatic location of suitable services), together with how to interact with such services.

7.3.4 OWL-S Service Grounding

The grounding in OWL-S provides the details of how to access the service, mapping from an abstract to a concrete specification of the service.

OWL-S links a Web Service to its grounding by using the property *supports*. A Web Service can have multiple groundings and a grounding must be associated with exactly one service. These groundings are associated with the atomic processes defined in the service model, although this association is not described in the model but only in the grounding. Therefore, the groundings for the atomic processes of the model can be located only by navigating from the service model to the service (via the *describes* property), and from there to the service grounding (via the *supports* property).

OWL-S does not dictate the grounding mechanism to be used. Nevertheless the current version of OWL-S provides a predefined grounding for WSDL, mapping the different elements of the Web Service to a WSDL interface. An OWL-S atomic process is mapped to a WSDL operation, and its inputs and outputs to the WSDL input and output message parts, respectively. Such mappings are also established in the WSDL description, using the WSDL 1.1 [3] extensibility elements.

7.3.5 OWL-S Languages

OWL-S is an ontology specified in OWL. Actual OWL-S Web Service specifications are created by subclassing and instantiating the classes of OWL-S. Thus one can say that the OWL language together with the OWL-S vocabulary makes up the OWL-S Web Service specification language.

However, it has been recognised that OWL alone is not enough for the specification of the behaviour of Web Services. The major problem is that OWL does not allow chaining variables over predicates, which makes it impossible to, e.g., specify the relationship between input and output, which is necessary to formally describe the behaviour of any software component [26]. Therefore, OWL-S allows the user a choice of different languages for the specification of preconditions and effects. However, the interface between the input and the output, which are described in OWL, and the formulae in the precondition and the effect, is not clear. It is especially important to know how these interact, because it is already possible to specify conditions on the input and the output through complex OWL descriptions. The OWL-S coalition recommends the use of either SWRL, KIF or DRS for the specification of preconditions and effects.

SWRL

The Semantic Web Rule Language [17] is an extension of OWL, which adds support for Horn rules over OWL DL ontologies. Instead of arbitrary predicates, SWRL allows arbitrary OWL DL descriptions in both the head and the body of the rule, where a unary predicate corresponds with an OWL class and a binary predicate corresponds with an OWL property. Predicates with higher arity are not allowed. However, *n*-ary predicates can always be encoded in a description logic knowledge base by "emulating" relation parameters through the introduction of a number of functional properties.

The authors of SWRL have demonstrated that the language is undecidable. This undecidability is mainly caused by allowing existential quantification in the head of the rule (inherited from OWL), combined with chaining variables over predicates (inherited from Horn logic).

KIF

The Knowledge Interchange Format (KIF) is a standards-proposal from the 1990s for the interchange of knowledge between knowledge bases. The language is constructed in such a way that it can be used to capture the semantics of most knowledge bases. As such, it is an extension of the first-order logic with reification.

KIF currently has only a normal text syntax and thus each KIF expression in an OWL-S description consists of text and thus does not benefit from validation and parsing services offered by XML and RDF parsers/validators.

DRS

DRS (Declarative RDF System) is an OWL ontology, which provides a vocabulary for writing down arbitrary formulas. DRS does not prescribe the semantics of formulas written down using its vocabulary. Thus, when using DRS to specify Web Services, the user will have to find a way outside the language to agree on the semantics of the description.

7.4 Summary and Outlook

We have presented in detail two of the Semantic Web Service frameworks that are proposed by academic and industrial research. Despite different origins and backgrounds, both frameworks share a number of similarities. First of all they are using formal logics to define the meaning of Web Services. Both frameworks have some notion of precondition and postcondition as well as dynamic aspects.

However, while WSMO explicitly defines the orchestration of the service, describing what other services have to be used or what other goals have to be fulfilled to provide its functionality, OWL-S does not model this aspect of a Web Service, but does define the choreography of a service.

While an OWL-S request is formulated as the description of a profile which characterises the service being sought and thus uses a single modelling element for both views, WSMO explicitly reflects the separation of providers and requesters concerns by defining goals and Web Service capabilities separately.

WSMO relies on loose coupling with strong mediation. Different kinds of mediators are used to link together the core WSMO elements, dealing with the heterogeneity problems inherent to a distributed environment. OWL-S does not explicitly consider the heterogeneity problem in the language itself, treating it as an architectural issue, i.e. mediators are not an element of the ontology but are part of the underlying Web Service infrastructure [25].

From a more conceptual point of view, the most striking difference is the way the meta models of the respective approaches are defined: WSMO follows a language specification similar to MOF (Meta-Object Facility) [29], in the sense that the language specification layers are clearly separated and different languages can be used to express WSMO. In OWL-S, the meta-meta model is specified using OWL and actual descriptions consist of subclasses and instances of the OWL-S ontology.

It has been recognised that OWL is not expressive enough for all description aspects and thus in the OWL-S approach other languages are syntactically integrated (such as SWRL, KIF or DRS). Combinations with SWRL or the purely syntactic framework of DRS lead to inherent undecidability or leave semantics open from the start.

WSMO has designed from the beginning a set of layered languages. The layered logical analysis of decidable semantic fragments combining conceptual modelling with rules in the WSML Core, DL, Rule and Flight species seems more focused than the current suggestions in OWL-S.

Although work in the area of an overall framework for Semantic Web Services is now already a research issue for a couple of years, maturity is not yet reached: In summer 2005, the W3C organised a workshop on *Frameworks for Semantics in Web Services*[13] to clarify the different views of the community and explore current chances for standardisation. Over 80 participants from industry and academia presented their proposals, but despite many conceptual overlaps, one intent of the workshop did not yet succeed: In the details of the deployed technologies the community is still far from agreement and therefore not ready for a rapid move towards standardisation.

Although activities towards standardising an overall Semantic Web Services framework have been stalled by W3C for the moment, standardisation organisations such as the *Organisation for the Advancement of Structured Information Standards (OASIS)*[14] and also W3C itself have in between established several working groups or technical committees to develop and standardise particular aspects around Semantic Web Service technologies.

Within the W3C a more light weight approach has been chartered: The *Semantic Annotations for WSDL Working Group* aims to add minimal semantic extensions to WSDL. WSDL itself only specifies a way to describe the abstract functionalities of a service and concretely how and where to invoke it. The WSDL 2.0 specification does, however, not include semantics in the description; thus two services can have similar descriptions with totally different meanings or similar meanings with completely different descriptions. The objective of the Semantic Annotations for WSDL Working Group is to develop a mechanism to enable semantic annotation of WSDL descriptions. This mechanism will take advantage of the WSDL 2.0 extension mechanisms to build a simple and generic support for semantics in Web Services.

References

1. R. Akkiraju et al. Web Service Semantics - WSDL-S. W3C Member Submission. November 2005. Available from `http://www.w3.org/Submission/WSDL-S/`.
2. S. Battle et al. Semantic Web Services Framework (SWSF). W3C Member Submission. May 2005, Available from `http://www.w3.org/Submission/2005/07/`.

[13] `http://www.w3.org/2005/01/ws-swsf-cfp.html`
[14] `http://www.oasis-open.org`

3. E. Börger. High Level System Design and Analysis using Abstract State Machines. In D. Hutter and W. Stephan and P. Traverso and M. Ullmann, editor, *Current Trends in Applied Formal Methods (FM-Trends 98)*, number 1641 in LNCS, pages 1–43. Springer-Verlag, 1999.
4. T. Bray, D. Hollander, and A. Layman. Namespaces in XML. W3C Recommendation. January 1999, Available from `http://www.w3.org/TR/REC-xml-names`.
5. D. Brickley and L. Miller. *FOAF Vocabulary Specification*, 2004. Available from `http://xmlns.com/foaf/0.1/`.
6. E. Christensen, F. Curbera, G. Meredith, and S. Weerawarana. Web Services Description Language (WSDL) 1.1. `http://www.w3.org/TR/wsdl`, March 2001.
7. J. de Bruijn, A. Polleres, R. Lara, and D. Fensel. OWL DL vs. OWL Flight: Conceptual Modeling and Reasoning for the Semantic Web. Technical Report DERI-TR-2004-11-10, DERI, November 2004.
8. J. de Bruijn et al. Web Service Modeling Ontology (WSMO). W3C Member Submission 3 June 2005, Available from `http://www.w3.org/Submission/WSMO/`.
9. J. de Bruijn, editor. *The WSML Family of Representation Languages*. 2005. WSMO Deliverable D16, WSMO Working Draft, 2005, latest version available at `http://www.wsmo.org/TR/d16/d16.1/`.
10. M. Dean and G. Schreiber, editors. *OWL Web Ontology Language Reference*. 2004. W3C Recommendation 10 February 2004.
11. KIF. Knowledge Interchange Format: Draft Proposed American National Standard. Technical Report NCITS.T2/98-004, 1998. available from `http://logic.stanford.edu/kif/dpans.html`.
12. D. Fensel and C. Bussler. The Web Service Modeling Framework WSMF. *Electronic Commerce Research and Applications*, 1(2), 2002.
13. B.N. Grosof, I. Horrocks, R. Volz, and S. Decker. Description Logic Programs: Combining Logic Programs With Description Logic. In *Proc. Intl. Conf. on the World Wide Web (WWW-2003)*, Budapest, Hungary, 2003.
14. T.R. Gruber. A Translation Approach to Portable Ontology Specifications. *Knowledge Acquisition*, 5:199–220, 1993.
15. Y. Gurevich. *Evolving Algebras 1993: Lipari Guide*, pages 9–36. Oxford University Press, Inc., 1995.
16. P. Hayes. RDF Semantics. W3C Recommendation, February 2004, Available from `http://www.w3.org/TR/rdf-mt/`.
17. I. Horrocks et al. SWRL: A Semantic Web Rule Language Combining OWL and RuleML. W3C Submission, May 2004, Available from `http://www.w3.org/Submission/2004/SUBM-SWRL-20040521/`.
18. U. Keller, M. Stollberg, and D. Fensel. Woogle Meets Semantic Web Fred. In *Proceedings of the Workshop on WSMO Implementations (WIW 2004)*, volume Vol-113, 2004.
19. M. Kifer, G. Lausen, and J. Wu. Logical Foundations of Object-Oriented and Frame-Based Languages. *Journal of the ACM*, 42(4):741–843, 1995.
20. A. Kiryakov, D. Ognyanov, and V. Kirov. A Framework for Representing Ontologies Consisting of Several Thousand Concepts Definitions. DIP Deliverable D2.2, Ontotext Lab, 2004.
21. D. McDermott. DRS: A Set of Conventions for Representing Logical Languages in RDF. Available from `http://www.daml.org/services/owl-s/1.1B/DRSguide.pdf`, January 2004.
22. Object Management Group Inc. (OMG). Meta Object Facility (MOF) Specification v1.4, 2002.

23. J. O'Sullivan, D. Edmond, and A. ter Hofstede. What is a Service?: Towards Accurate Description of Non-Functional Properties. *Distributed and ParallelDatabases*, 12(2-3):117–133, 2002.
24. M. Paolucci, A. Ankolekar, N. Srinivasan, and K. Sycara. The DAML-S Virtual Machine. In *International Semantic Web Conference (ISWC 2003)*, 2003.
25. M. Paolucci, N. Srinivasan, and K. Sycara. Expressing WSMO Mediators in OWL-S. In D. Martin, R. Lara, and T. Yamaguchi, editors, *Proceedings 1st International Workshop SWS'2004 at ISWC-2004*, volume 119, `CEUR-WS.org/Vol-119/`, November 2004. CEUR-WS.org.
26. J. Penix and P. Alexander. Towards Automated Component Adaptation. In *Proceedings of the 9th International Conference on Software Engineering and Knowledge Engineering*, June 1997.
27. D. Roman, editor. *WSMO Choreography*. WSMO Choreography Working Draft D14v0.3. April 2006, Available from `http://www.wsmo.org/TR/d14/`.
28. D. Roman, H. Lausen, and U. Keller, editors. *Web Service Modeling Ontology (WSMO)*. WSMO Working Draft D2v1.2, April 2005. Available from `http://www.wsmo.org/TR/d2/`.
29. The Object Management Group. Meta-Object Facility. Technical Report, 2004. Available from `http://www.omg.org/technology/documents/formal/mof.htm`.
30. D. Martin et al. OWL-S: Semantic Markup for Web Services. W3C Member Submission, November 2004, Available from `http://www.w3.org/Submission/2004/07/`
31. S. Weibel, J. Kunze, C. Lagoze, and M. Wolf. Dublin Core Metadata for Resource Discovery. RFC 2413, IETF, September 1998.
32. S. Weibel, J. Kunze, C. Lagoze, and M. Wolf. *RFC 2413 - Dublin Core Metadata for Resource Discovery*, September 1998.
33. G. Wiederhold. Mediators in the Architecture of the Future Information Systems. *Computer*, 25(3):38–49, 1994.

8

Discovery

Identifying Relevant Services

Stephan Grimm

FZI Research Center for Information Technologies, University of Karlsruhe, Germany
stephan.grimm@fzi.de

Summary. Web Services expose machine-processable interfaces that provide flexible access to their functionality in network environments for realising application integration scenarios. As any other web resource, it is desirable to locate and get access to Web Services by specifying relevant properties in the form of a request, similar to how websites are located via search engines. When annotated with semantic information about their functionality, Web Services can be located based on their actual capabilities rather than on their interfaces only. Discovery is the task of locating Web Services by means of their semantic annotations. This typically involves matching of semantic capability descriptions for requested service against those for advertised services. This chapter discusses the notion of discovery of services in the Semantic Web. It gives an overview on approaches to realise discovery by different matching techniques and elaborates on matching of service annotations within the description logic formalism. This particular approach is illustrated by an example taken from the logistics domain.

8.1 Notion of Discovery

In the vision of the Semantic Web, human users are replaced by computational agents which are supposed to access the content and service functionality offered in the web on their behalf. Since these agents can not interpret webpages and Web Service documentation as humans can, web content and service endpoints are semantically annotated with machine-interpretable meta data. To be an effective surrogate for the human, the agent must be able to reason about this meta data. One of the tasks that involves such reasoning is for the agent to discover relevant service providers, i.e. to decide whether a certain service endpoint can be used to fulfil its current mission. With respect to Semantic Web Services this means that parties who offer their services via the Internet semantically annotate the Web Services that provide access to these services by means of machine-interpretable meta data that tells an agent "what the service does". Hence, Web Services are the technical means to realise the services offered in some domain of value and the semantic annotation of Web Services describes the capabilities of these services, as motivated in Chap. 6. On the other hand, parties who request services via the Internet need to locate the means to access provided services which meet their requirements. Discovery of services in the

Semantic Web is the process of locating the means to access provided services with relevant capabilities, based on semantic annotation.

In the vision sketched above, discovery is to be performed fully automated, since there is no human in the loop who could help the agent in judging whether a service offer is relevant or not. To this end, all the pieces of semantic annotation involved must be machine-understandable in order for the agent to put them together and to draw the correct conclusions. To achieve this, discovery of services in the Semantic Web exploits expressive knowledge representation formalisms and sophisticated automated reasoning techniques.

8.1.1 Discovery Based on Semantic Annotation

We call the annotation that specifies the semantics of a service a *semantic service description*, or *service description* for short. In general, such a semantic service description covers many different aspects of the service, ranging from the actual capabilities in the domain of value to the ontological grounding of service parameters at the message exchange level. In any of the phases of discovery, execution, composition, etc., different subsets of these aspects are taken into account. Since, in the first place, the finding of relevant service offers should be based on "what the service does" while details about how to communicate with the service's interface play a minor role, we base our notion of discovery on the specification of the capabilities a service provides in its domain of value. In the context of discovery, we therefore understand a semantic service description also as *semantic capability description*.

Figure 8.1 depicts the role of semantic capability descriptions in a generic discovery scenario. In this scenario, providers of services make use of capability

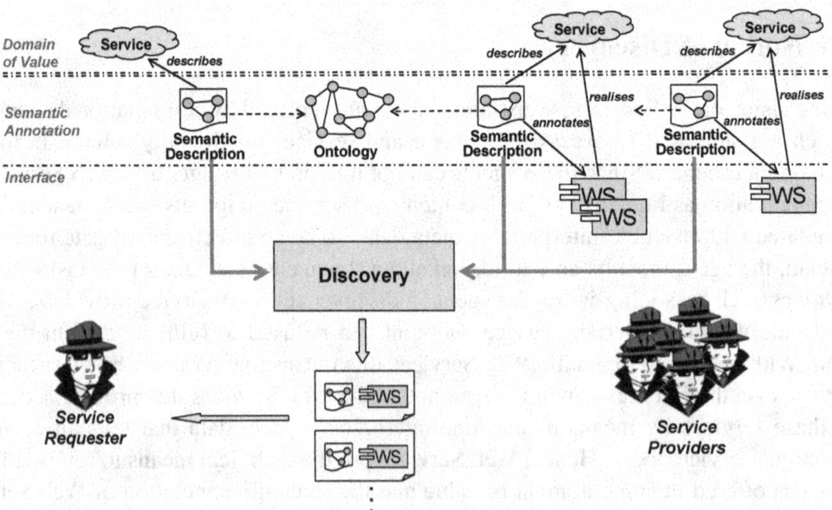

Fig. 8.1. Discovery based on semantic service descriptions

descriptions to publish their service offers, while a requester party issues a service request in the same way. In their semantic descriptions, they both refer to services in some domain of value. On the interface level, the providers implement Web Services that realise these services as a technical means to access their functionality and to make use of the value they provide. Inline with the Semantic Web idea, a service description annotates a Web Service interface and it describes the service in the domain of value which this interface provides access to.

The Web Services and semantic descriptions on the levels of interface and semantic annotation are computational objects that reside within the scope of the machine's information space. Contrarily, the entities in the domain of value cannot be directly processed within this information space but have their representation through the ontological descriptions involved. Ontologies play a major role in describing the meaning of content in the Semantic Web. In our discovery scenario they have a twofold use: on the one hand upper-level service ontologies, like WSMO or OWL-S introduced in Chap.7, form the basis for modellers to express service semantics in terms of generic service-related constructs; on the other hand domain ontologies are plugged in to describe service capabilities in terms of the domain of value of a service. By making use of knowledge representation techniques and methodologies described in the Chaps. 3 and 4, semantic capability descriptions try to capture "what a service does" in the form of ontological descriptions.

The semantic capability descriptions serve as input for the discovery process, which compares the requester's description with those of providers to figure out which service offer is relevant for the request. This means that discovery operates on the ontological descriptions of the capabilities of a service rather than on specifications of Web Service interfaces. As a result, the discovery process returns references to service descriptions considered relevant, together with references to their associated Web Service interfaces. The requester agent has then the possibility to further investigate the relevant service offers either by looking at their semantic descriptions in more detail or by directly calling the Web Service interface.

8.1.2 Discovery and Pre-contractual Negotiation

According to Chap. 6 there is a point in time in the lifecycle of service usage when a contract between the requester and the provider of the service is established. Prior to this point the phases of service discovery and service definition aim towards establishing the contract, being the requirement for the delivery of the service to be carried out. The phase of discovery is distinct from the phase of service definition and chronologically precedes it. The service definition can also be seen as *pre-contractual parameter negotiation*, since to define the concrete service to be carried out the service parameters have to be negotiated and fixed. This distinction is depicted in Fig. 8.2 and characterised in the following paragraphs.

Discovery Phase

The parties involved in discovery are a requester and several providers of services. During the discovery process the capability descriptions for abstract services of these

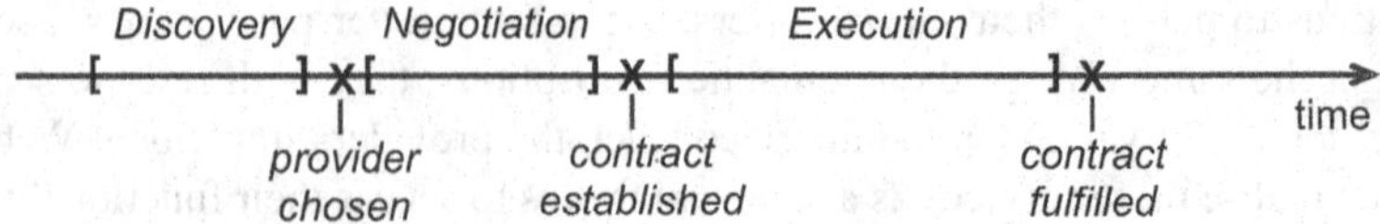

Fig. 8.2. Different phases around discovery

parties are consulted. As a result, discovery leads to the selection of service offer descriptions of providers that are relevant with respect to the service requirement description of the requester. In this sense, discovery aims towards the choice of the service provider. This means that successful discovery does not necessarily lead to a contract between the two parties – service definition due to pre-contractual parameter negotiation can still fail after potential service providers have been successfully identified. On the other hand, failure of discovery means that there are no potential providers who could meet the requester's requirements.

Negotiation Phase

The parties involved in parameter negotiation are a requester and one single provider whose service offer description has been identified as relevant. In general, pre-contractual negotiation can require the requester to negotiate with several potential providers; however, the actual process of negotiation can be seen as bilateral. During this process there is communication between the two parties, which already involves invocation of the provider's Web Service interface. As a result, parameter negotiation finally leads to the choice of the service provider and to a contract between the requester and this provider, if successful. Failure of pre-contractual negotiation with a particular service provider means that the two parties could not establish a contract. Failure of pre-contractual negotiation as a whole means that finally none of the potential providers was feasible to establish a contract with the requester.

8.1.3 Different Interpretations of Discovery

Based on the distinction between the phases of discovery and pre-contractual negotiation, the notion of discovery is that of "identifying service offers that meet a requester's needs". This notion can be interpreted in different ways. A weak interpretation is to assume that the capability descriptions of services are specified on a very abstract level which does not detail enough information to assure successful service definition. According to the terminology introduced in Chap. 6, this would result in capability descriptions describing *abstract services*. A strong interpretation is to assume that capability descriptions provide access to detailed information about the contracts that can finally be agreed on by requesters and providers, respectively. This would result in capability descriptions describing *concrete services*. One can think of cases in between these two extremes and gradually move from abstract to concrete descriptions, including more and more detailed information about service definition.

In [17] the authors distinguish between "correct" and "complete" service descriptions. Applying this idea to our capability descriptions, a description is "correct" if any concrete service it allows is also covered by the abstract service that the modeller intends to describe with it. On the other hand, a description is "complete" if it allows any concrete service the modeller intends to be covered. Achieving correctness here means to interpret the notion of discovery in the strong sense, assuring successful service definition. However, [17] states that correctness cannot be achieved often and that a natural interpretation for discovery, therefore, is to have complete but not necessarily correct capability descriptions.

For the presentation in this chapter, the notion of discovery is interpreted in a rather weak sense. This way it is clearly separated from pre-contractual negotiation and the two problems of discovery and parameter negotiation can be tackled independently from each other. For an agent, this means that discovery is only part of its job in achieving the fulfillment of its goal. Once a service has been discovered, the agent still needs to communicate to the interface that realises this service in order to figure out if it is the right one to consult.

8.2 Discovery in Case Study Scenarios

This section illustrates the notion of discovery by revisiting the example case studies listed in Chap. 6. For each of the example scenarios, discovery is identified and characterised in the context of the particular use case.

8.2.1 Scenario A

In the first scenario, customers of a bank are notified when they are at risk of going overdrawn. Here the requested service is that of notification via email or voice message. The overdraft controlling software running at the bank acts as the service requester agent that issues a request to a central discovery service in the web. Provider agents of notification services and others register their service offers with this central discovery service. The capability descriptions of both requester and providers describe the kind of notification they require or offer with some details about the way of notification, cost, reliability, etc. The discovery service sorts out those service offers that are suitable for the currently issued request. The requester agent then gets in contact with one or more of the potential notification service providers to negotiate about the details and picks the one that best fits its preferences.

8.2.2 Scenario B

In the second scenario the purchase of non-critical supplies is automated in an electronic procurement setting. Here, online sales services for certain supplies are requested by the company's e-procurement software, acting as the requester agent.

To maximally benefit from the dynamic market situation, the requester agent should be provided with the currently available sales service offers at any time it requests a certain kind of purchase. Therefore, it issues a request to a central discovery service whenever a new purchase is to be made. Via semantic matchmaking of capability descriptions, discovery detects the currently available service providers that could deliver the purchase. The capability descriptions here capture the type of online shop and some details on the products covered by the purchase. In this scenario, discovery precedes a more complex pre-contactual service definition phase with extensive parameter negotiation.

8.2.3 Scenario C

In the third scenario, logistics providers in a transport chain shall be replaced on demand. Here the requested service is conveyance of goods from one location to another. The requester agent is the software that puts together the pieces of the transportation chain, running at the site of the customer company. Logistics providers register their service offers to a central discovery service accessible to customers and suppliers in the logistics domain. The capability descriptions involved specify the kind of transportation, locations of origin and destination, the type of cargo and vehicle, etc. Discovery detects which of the logistics providers currently registered could fill in the broken part of the transportation chain, by looking at the specified capabilities. By pre-contractual negotiation with the potential candidates the requester agent then picks the most preferable one to fix the chain.

8.2.4 Scenario D

In the fourth scenario, a share portfolio management software updates stock prices with recent Information looked up in the Internet. Here the requested service is retrieving online stock quote information. The requester agent that looks up this service is the portfolio management software. It has a fixed capability description requiring stock quote prices, although it might be possible to parameterise details on the conditions about price and delay time. Discovery looks up the stock quote services currently available in the web. Here pre-contractual service definition contains a manual step, leaving the final decision of which service to use to the human, after having collected all information that is necessary to support this decision.

8.3 Discovery Frameworks

The former sections have introduced the notion of service discovery in the Semantic Web and have shown discovery by example in different case study scenarios. A *discovery framework* is the conceptual frame that allows to realise such scenarios. It describes all the methods and components needed to operationalise discovery. An implementation of a discovery framework needs to instantiate these methods and components, and to interrelate them in a discovery architecture. This section characterises a discovery framework on a general level, while Sect. 8.4 describes an example for a concrete discovery framework realised with the description logics formalism and applied to the logistics-centred Scenario C.

Basically, a discovery framework needs to specify the following two essential things:

1. How capability descriptions of services are modelled.
2. How capability descriptions are compared in terms of relevance.

These two aspects are intertwined with each other and for both of them a discovery framework must define precise methods and the components to support these methods. Defining the relevance comparison mechanism alone is not sufficient, since it is then not clear what kind of descriptions serve as input. Instead, the comparison method must take into account the specifics of the chosen way of modelling and the modelling method must be suitable for the chosen way of how comparison is performed.

8.3.1 Modelling Service Semantics with Respect to Discovery

A discovery framework not only determines which formalism is used to represent service semantics but also specifies the way of how to utilise this formalism to model capability descriptions. This means that the modeller has to adhere to certain rules of modelling that might restrict him in freely using what the formalism offers.

Fixing an Ontological Vocabulary

In particular, a discovery framework should define the domain-independent part of the ontological vocabulary in terms of which capability descriptions are to be defined. This determines the general service model that discovery processes can assume when interpreting capability descriptions. This part of the ontological vocabulary is usually being fixed by choosing an upper-level ontology for services, such as WSMO or OWL-S (see Chap. 7). In opposite to a domain ontology, an upper-level ontology provides a very general conceptual model, e.g. for services, that is independent from any application domain. In fact, an upper-level service ontology can be seen as an ontology whose domain is that of "services". Therefore it provides basic concepts, as e.g. "Service", "ServiceParameter", "ServiceCondition", etc., which form the foundation of any capability description.

To completely describe the capability of a service, additional vocabulary is required, originating in an ontology for a particular domain of value. For a service within the logistics domain, e.g., a capability description would include concepts like "Transportation", "Container" or "Location". Several domain ontologies modelling different aspects can be combined, such as a logistics ontology together with an ontology for geographic knowledge about the regions and locations that are relevant for the transportation of goods. In opposite to the service-specific vocabulary, such domain-specific knowledge is not fixed by the discovery framework – modellers can refer to arbitrary domain ontologies.

The way in which such a combined ontological vocabulary for service and domain knowledge can be used is manifold. It can, e.g., be extended on the conceptual level by introducing new concepts in relation to existing ones, or existing concepts can be instantiated and their relations filled with values. Depending on the underlying knowledge representation formalism, capability descriptions can be modelled at the conceptual level, at the instance level, as a mix of both or in terms of complex logical formulas. In any case the discovery framework should fix this modelling choice and precisely define how a capability description, modelled in the chosen way, is to be interpreted for discovery purposes.

Abstracting from Concrete Services

In the sense of a weak interpretation of discovery, as introduced in Sect. 8.1, capability descriptions describe abstract services that generalise from the concrete services to be performed. In the modelling phase, requesters and providers do not want to explicitly list all the concrete services they are willing to accept. Instead they want to use a narrow set of modelling constructs, based on the underlying knowledge representation formalism, to represent the set of all these concrete services. An example of how to abstract from concrete services is given by the following DL expression

$$D \equiv \mathit{Shipping} \sqcap \forall\, \mathit{item}.\mathit{CargoContainer} \sqcap \exists\, \mathit{payment}.\mathit{CreditCard}$$

Here the capability description D is defined as a concept representing a shipping service for which all conveyed items must be cargo containers and for which the required way of payment is via credit card. It can be interpreted such that all instances of the concept D are the concrete services this description abstracts from. One such concrete service would ship two cargo containers to be paid with VISA card, another one three cargo containers to be paid with Master card, etc. The domain and service specific terms are supposed to be defined in appropriate domain and upper-level ontologies.

A similar service is modelled by the following WSML expression, describing an effect within the capability description for a WSMO Web Service.

```
effect
  definedBy
    ?service memberOf Shipping[item hasValue ?i, payment hasValue ?p]
      and ?i memberOf CargoContainer
      and ?p memberOf CreditCard.
```

Here the respective service is required to be of type *Shipping* and to have values of type *CargoContainer* and *CreditCard* for the properties *item* and *payment*, respectively.

Meeting the Modeller's Intuition

Providing a formalism together with a restricting set of rules for how to use it still leaves the modeller with the difficult task of formulating capability descriptions in logical expressions or other formal means of description. This strategy is often not feasible in a real world setting, especially when modelling is to be performed by end-users with no expertise in knowledge representation. For this reason, a discovery framework would also benefit from providing a methodology for modelling capability descriptions that allows modelling on an intuitive level. The modeller's intuition can be better met abstracting from knowledge representation formalisms and building layers on top of them.

A first step in this direction is to paraphrase formal modelling constructs, as done in the context of [19] for the OWL ontology language. There, the OWL-DL class constructors are paraphrased with natural language sentences that capture their exact meaning. This helps the modeller in understanding the underlying expression but does not ease the burden of its sometimes non-intuitive complexity. Here a discovery framework could define a set of intuitive modelling primitives that map to formal constructs, layered on top of the chosen formalism. While this is difficult to do for a certain formalism, like OWL-DL, in general, it seems to be feasible when the specific features of modelling service semantics can be taken into account. The intuitive modelling primitives are then tailored for describing the capabilities of a service.

8.3.2 Matching Capability Descriptions

As described in Sect. 8.1, discovery is performed by comparing capability descriptions to figure out which provided service is relevant for a specific request. This comparison is also referred to as *matching*. As its core functionality, a discovery framework must specify how the matching of capability descriptions is carried out.

Matching Behaviour

Discovery can be seen as a retrieval problem where all the service offers relevant for a service request are to be returned. To realise this retrieval task, the matching functionality needs to decide for any service offer whether it is relevant for the service requirement. Therefore, the input parameters of the matching process are the capability description of the service requirement and a capability description of a single service offer. In addition, the domain knowledge which the two capability descriptions refer to must also be input to the matching process, since the decision is to be made with respect to the ontologies used. In the simple case, the outcome of the matching process is a boolean result, i.e. the service offer is either relevant or not.

In frameworks which try to rank the potential service offers according to their relevance, the outcome of the matching process reflects a degree of matching. Since the description of capability semantics is based on symbolic knowledge representation formalisms, it is hard to measure the degree of matching in terms of numbers. In [15] there has been proposed a discrete scale with four partially ordered degrees of matching, which are detailed in Sect. 8.4.

Realisation of Matching

In knowledge representation and automated reasoning, the way of processing knowledge and reasoning about descriptions under consideration of domain-level facts is to apply logical inferencing. A discovery framework must specify how logical inferences are applied to realise matching. This, in turn, strongly depends on the chosen way of modelling capability descriptions. For example, if service offers are modelled in the form of ontological instances, the matching process will probably perform some kind of instance retrieval. If, on the other hand, all capability descriptions are modelled in the form of ontological concepts, some kind of conceptual matchmaking has to be carried out, as described later in Sect. 8.4. Logical inferences are executed by a reasoner as a separate component of the discovery framework used in the matching process.

The problem of matching can either be fully solved within the underlying logical formalism or partly outside. In the first case, capability descriptions are directly represented with elements of the formalism, e.g. concepts, and in the matching process inferences are applied on these elements, e.g. a single inference whose outcome reflects the desired relevance. An example of this approach is given in Sect. 8.4. Alternatively, inferences can be applied to parts of capability descriptions, e.g. to single parameters of a service, and in the matching process the partial results are combined using application logic algorithms. This approach is, e.g., followed in [15].

Matching Abstract Descriptions

Following Sect. 8.3.1, modellers abstract from concrete services in their capability descriptions. The basic idea of matching an abstract capability description of a service request against an abstract capability description of a service offer is to determine whether there is a concrete service that is captured by both these descriptions. If so, the requester and provider can potentially agree on at least one of the concrete objects to be delivered by the service, i.e. their descriptions have some overlap. In [17] this is stated as the "minimal functionality" required by a discovery system.

Recalling the distinction between the service discovery and service definition phases, this minimal functionality assures those providers to match for which there is at least the possibility to meet the specified requirements. At the same time, it filters out those who can by no means meet the request since there is no overlap of the descriptions.

8.3.3 Architectural Issues

When semantic descriptions of services are publicly advertised, issues of architectural organisation of the involved service repositories or registries arise. Most discovery approaches investigated in the context of Semantic Web technologies focus on the actual matching of service descriptions and take a centralised architectural view, with a single service registry. Other approaches, in particular those investigated in the context of distributed information systems, take scalability issues into account and investigate scenarios in which repositories of service descriptions are spread over a multitude of nodes in a peer-to-peer network.

In the following paragraphs, three such architectural views are sketched and characterised according to their degree of distributedness.

Centralised Discovery

In a centralised architectural view, there is a single service registry and repository as entry point for requester and provider agents who participate in discovery. Providers publish semantic descriptions of their service offers with this central repository, while requesters query it on the basis of semantic descriptions of their requirements. This central registry/repository can be a (semantically annotated) Web Service itself. Whenever a request is issued, the respective semantic service description is iteratively matched against the descriptions of all the registered service offers.

In the light of costly matching techniques based on logical inferencing, such a strategy is feasible only in controlled environments with a small number of available services, such as company-internal intranet applications or closed community portals. In open environments where service repositories grow large quickly, it is desirable to distribute the registry or repository functionality over several nodes, which allows for parallelisation of matching or for pre-selection of appropriate sub-repositories.

Hierarchical Discovery

A first step towards scalability by distribution is to spread service offer descriptions over several thematically clustered repositories, while a single registry still serves as the central entry point for requesters and providers. The single repositories can be organised in a hierarchy of topics, similar to the taxonomic classification schemes used in UDDI[1] (see Chap. 2). An incoming request is then directed to a repository that fits its specific topic, and the full logical matchmaking is only applied locally to thematically relevant service offer descriptions.

Distributed Discovery in Peer-To-Peer Networks

In a fully distributed architectural view, the functionality of both repository and registry for service offer descriptions is organised in a decentralised way. Service advertisements are published in a peer-to-peer network of registries, and requesters can query for services using any registry as their entry point. The peer-to-peer based registries then take care of routing the request to the peer that can answer it.

[1] `http://www.uddi.org`

References to approaches that consider peer-to-peer aspects in the context of the Semantic Web and service discovery are [26, 20, 25, 22].

8.3.4 Predominant Discovery Approaches

There are various efforts that investigate different techniques for matching semantic service descriptions in the context of discovery. Many of them are tightly coupled to one of the prevalent Semantic Web Services annotation frameworks, such as OWL-S, WSMO or WSDL-S, and exploit framework-specific description characteristics. This subsection gives a brief overview on such existing approaches for discovery frameworks, before the following section describes a particular approach based on matching through description logic inferencing in detail.

Matching Service Descriptions with DL Inferencing

Principally independent from any of the Semantic Web Services annotation frameworks mentioned in Chap. 7, the matching of concept-based descriptions by using description logic inferencing has been investigated in the context of e-Business service discovery in [24, 4, 23]. The basic idea behind this discovery approach is to represent service descriptions as DL concepts and to check whether two such descriptions intersect or show even stronger overlap.

The general matching technique has been applied to OWL-S service profiles in [10], extended by the ideas of different degrees of matching from [15]. Also in the context of WSMO discovery, this technique is described as one of several alternatives in [7, 6]. Peculiarities of the involved DL inferencing have been studied in more detail in [5], while standard inferences have been extended towards more finer-grained ranking strategies in [13] and [3]. Recently, in [21] the same matching technique has been investigated in the light of non-monotonic extensions to DL that allow to overcome some problems due to the open-world assumption.

In Sect. 8.4, this approach to matching semantic service descriptions is investigated in detail.

Retrieval of WSDL-S Descriptions

Within the Semantic Web Services activities around the METEOR-S[2] project, the MWSDI (METEOR-S Web Services Discovery Infrastructure)[25] realises a discovery approach for WSDL-S descriptions in a UDDI-based environment. In comparison to the discovery efforts in other frameworks, like OWL-S or WSMO, this approach uses rather light-weight semantics for matching, based on the semantic tags in WSDL-S descriptions and on UDDI-specific search facilities. It follows a bottom-up strategy by starting from existing Web Service technologies, namely WSDL and UDDI, extending them by ontological lifting of input and output parameters.

[2] `http://lsdis.cs.uga.edu/projects/meteor-s/`

Since WSDL-S does not commit to a specific Web Service ontology or language, as do OWL-S or WSMO, one of its characteristics is that semantic information in WSDL-S tags can be expressed in a wide range of standards, languages and formalisms including, e.g., RDF(S) or even legacy UML descriptions. This is possible because the matching techniques employed in MWSDI mostly work on the labels (and some taxonomic and property-related structure) of ontological elements, using various concept similarity measures. Mappings from service parameters to ontological concepts are captured in UDDI-specific tModels and UDDI's retrieval facilities are used to perform discovery. On the other hand, these techniques do not fully exploit logical inferencing with ontologies that have some richer axiomatisation.

An elaborate description of this approach to discovery can be found in [14], where the different similarity measures that affect the matching are also detailed.

Matching of OWL-S Service Profiles

In the scope of the OWL-S[3] framework, an algorithm [15] has been devised for the matching of OWL-S service profiles based on inferencing with input and output parameters. Within this algorithm, the characteristics of the state-transformation-based description model [12] (see also Chap. 7) in the service profile is implicitly taken into account by handling inputs and outputs of requesters and providers differently.

The algorithm applies logical inferencing separately to pairs of input and output concepts. It recognises different degrees of match (described in Sect.8.4.3) by detecting the taxonomic relation between an input and an output concepts with respect to the involved domain ontologies. In contrast to how service descriptions are handled in the DL-based matching approach mentioned before, here the service profile is not (logically) reasoned about as a whole; it is rather interpreted in the sense of a container whose elements point to concepts in an ontology.

This strategy for matchmaking has also been combined with UDDI, in that a separate matching module works on top of a UDDI registry. The details of the matching algorithm and its use with service registries is described in detail in [15].

Discovery in WSMO

In the WSMO Semantic Web Services annotation framework, efforts on discovery are rather following a top-down strategy, starting from the WSMO conceptual model for services. Here, discovery operates on WSMO capability elements (see Chap. 7) as abstract semantic service descriptions, while concrete input and output parameters and other communication details are treated in a separate interface element. Thus, the grounding of service descriptions in WSDL specifications does not affect discovery.

Due to this separation, and to the conceptual top-down nature of the approach, WSMO discovery is currently farther away from integration with concrete Web Service technologies (e.g. WSDL and UDDI) and from implementation in tools than

---

[3] `http://www.daml.org/services/owl-s/1.0/`

MWSDI or OWL-S matchmaking. An overview on the conceptualisation of discovery frameworks building on WSMO is given in [7]. Similar to the distinction made in [12] for OWL-S service profiles, this overview work supports discovery strategies for both an abstract concept-based description model as envisioned for the DL-based discovery approach described in Sect. 8.4, and a state-transition-based description model. However, the focus within WSMO is clearly set to a description of pre- and post-states with respect to service execution, and publications that follow this line for discovery and matching are [6, 9, 8]. In contrast to OWL-S matchmaking, but similar to the DL-based matching elaborated in Sect. 8.4, this work tries to capture the meaningful processing of logical expressions in capability descriptions within the underlying knowledge representation formalism rather than in an explicit algorithm.

Rule-Based Discovery within SWSF

The SWSF initiative (see Chap. 7) is a very recent effort to establish a Semantic Web Services annotation framework, and due to its early stage there is not much work on discovery published. The material available at [2] describes a discovery use case where service descriptions are expressed in the SWSL-Rules formalism and discovery is realised by executing rule-based queries. Details on the idea of how querying is performed with transaction logic – a rule-based formalism that supports the explicit representation of change – can be found in [9], which describes early work on discovery in the context of WSMO.

8.4 Discovery by Description Logic Inferencing

This section describes an approach to discovery based on capability descriptions formulated in description logic (DL). Consequently, DL inferences are used to perform matching of capability descriptions. The usage of DL as a knowledge representation formalism is motivated by its close relation to OWL [16], the proposed ontology language for the Semantic Web (see Chap. 3).

The subsequent subsections describe how the modelling and matching of capability descriptions, i.e. the two corner stones of a discovery framework, can be realised using DL description and inferencing techniques.

8.4.1 DL-Based Modelling of Service Semantics

It is important to precisely define the way how capability descriptions are modelled and how these descriptions are to be interpreted, i.e. what their intuitive meaning is. This subsection describes how the constructs of the DL formalism can be used to formulate capability descriptions. The intuitive meaning of these descriptions is based on the distinction between abstract and concrete services, as mentioned in Sect. 8.3.

Capability Descriptions in DL

Within the DL-based approach we call the concrete services to be delivered *service instances*. A service instance can be seen as a contract between a requester and a provider, defining all the necessary details to perform the business interaction associated with the service. In the logistics scenario, such a service instance would exactly specify the information about which item to be shipped, together with its size and weight, the date and time when shipping is to be performed, the locations of origin and destination, etc. This reflects the instantiation of all the parameters of the shipping business transaction in form of articles of agreement which the two parties want to appear in their contract. Such a service instance can be understood as a graph whose nodes and arcs represent the concrete service properties. In Fig. 8.3, there are two examples of service instances depicted as graphs: $shipping_1$ represents a service instance for shipping a package of 50 kg from Plymouth to Bremen, while $shipping_2$ captures the shipping of a 25 kg barrel from Dover to Hamburg. In the DL formalism, such a service instance graph maps to the relational structure in an interpretation $\mathcal{I}$, connecting individuals of a domain $\Delta^{\mathcal{I}}$ through roles. (For an introduction to DL interpretations and semantics, see e.g. [1].)

In their capability descriptions, requesters and providers of services want to express which service instances they are willing to accept, i.e. which ones they request or provide, respectively. However, they do not want to list all the different service instances explicitly; instead they want to make use of semantically rich constructs provided by the DL-based modelling framework for expressing requests and offers in a compact way – i.e., they want to describe an abstract service. Describing a set of objects in DL is done by using concepts. Thus, the set of service instances acceptable to a requester or provider maps to the extension $S^{\mathcal{I}}$ of a DL concept S that represents the abstract service to be described. A feature of DL is that complex concepts can be formed out of simpler ones. In this sense S is described by a DL concept expression that is composed from the basic concepts of, e.g., the logistics domain. More generally, the concept S is specified by a set of DL axioms D which we associate with the capability description of a service.

Figure 8.3 shows an example of a capability description for a service offer for some provider as a set of DL axioms D_p specifying the service concept S_p. ${S_p}^{\mathcal{I}}$ is the extension of the service concept S_p and contains all the service instances this provider is willing to accept. To specify which service instances belong to ${S_p}^{\mathcal{I}}$, the capability description D_p consists of two axioms: the first one restricts the concept S_p to shipping of items with a weight less than or equal to 50 kg from cities in the UK to cities in Germany, while the second one assures that instances of shipping services actually specify locations for origin and destination (exactly one for each). By the capability description D_p the provider accepts the set of service instances in the extension ${S_p}^{\mathcal{I}}$ of the service concept; among others, the two service instances for shipping a 50 kg package from Plymouth to Bremen and for shipping a 25 kg barrel from Dover to Hamburg both belong to this set. Hence, the provider would agree on contracts that meet the constraints on the service parameter configurations as specified in the capability description ${D_p}^{\mathcal{I}}$.

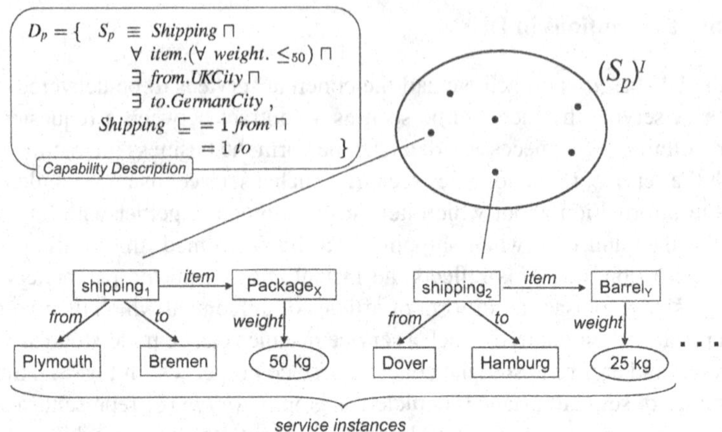

Fig. 8.3. DL concepts for expressing service capability descriptions

The concept expressions in the axioms of D_p are build up from basic concepts and roles taken from the logistics domain, such as *Shipping*, *Container*, *item*, etc. These concepts and roles are defined in domain ontologies which the requesters and providers commonly refer to. In DL such domain ontologies map to a DL knowledge base *KB* that contains the axioms which capture the domain knowledge stated there.

Incomplete Capability Descriptions

By describing an abstract service, the main purpose of a capability description is to capture a set of service instances which vary on several parameters. Hence, capability descriptions introduce variance on service properties. In [5] two different kinds of variance have been identified that are desirable to be modelled in capability descriptions:

1. Variance due to intended diversity: The modeller of a capability description intends to accept a variety of different service instances. For example, a logistics provider offers shipping between various different pairs of cities in the UK and Germany, i.e. they want to cover shipping service instances for all possible such pairs.
2. Variance due to incomplete Knowledge: The modeller of a capability description wants to leave details about certain properties of a service unspecified. For example, a logistics provider does not specify which kind of containers they support, since this might be dependent on a complex business logic which shall not be captured by the capability description but off-loaded to a parameter negotiation phase.

With its model-theoretic interpretations inherited from first-order logic, the DL formalism adheres to an open-world semantics. This means that for things not fully specified in a knowledge base there are several ways of how to interpret the situation, which map to the different models (i.e. valid interpretations) of the knowledge base. With any of these models we associate a *possible world* in which incomplete knowledge is resolved in a different way.

Due to its open-world semantics, a feature of DL is to deal with incomplete information. This allows a DL-based discovery framework to support capability descriptions that do not fully specify all of the service details. Thus, the capability descriptions formulated in terms of DL axioms and concept expressions can capture the variance introduced before in a compact way.

Figure 8.4 depicts the two different kinds of variance along two dimensions. The vertical dimension reflects variance due to intended diversity by a multitude of service instances within one possible world. The horizontal dimension reflects variance due to incomplete knowledge by several possible worlds in each of which unspecified information is resolved in a different way.

In DL, a possible world that resolves incomplete knowledge in a certain way maps to an interpretation $\mathcal{I}$ that is a model of $KB \cup D$. Variance due to intended diversity is reflected by the service concept $S^{\mathcal{I}}$ containing several instances, whereas variance due to incomplete knowledge is reflected by $KB \cup D$ having several models $\mathcal{I}_1, \mathcal{I}_2, \ldots$. In the example, the logistics provider does not want to miss any pair, of UK and German cities in the variety of accepted service instances. At the same time they are indifferent about the type of item to be shipped, such as package or barrel.

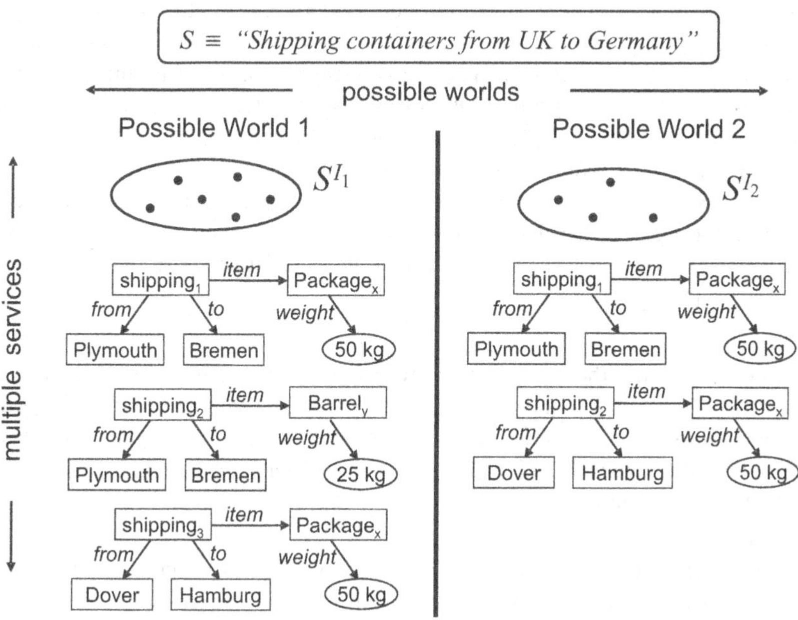

Fig. 8.4. Two different kinds of variance in capability descriptions along two dimensions

Sometimes it is difficult, or even impossible, to exactly specify the desired set of acceptable service instances, while leaving things unspecified at the same time. For example, if the provider wants to exclude possible worlds in which not all cities are covered by some service instance, this has to be stated explicitly by the axioms in the description D_p. One possible way to do this is through a special kind of range-coverage axioms [5] introduced in a subsequent section.

Another possibility to avoid undesired variance due to incomplete knowledge has been investigated in [21]. There a non-monotonic extension to DL in the form of an epistemic operator is used to realise a local closed-world assumption for capability descriptions. In this way, parts of a description can be prevented from varying over all possible worlds where desired.

Methodology for Intuitive Modelling

Having determined the intuitive meaning of different elements in the DL formalism for modelling capability descriptions, it is still not straightforward for a modeller to describe the capabilities of a service. The DL-based discovery framework should also provide some methodological guidelines of how to apply the different constructs to certain cases to meet the modeller's intuition, as mentioned in Sect. 8.3.

Unfortunately, finding such a modelling methodology has not been paid much attention to in the work around the predominant Semantic Web Services annotation frameworks in general, and also not for the presented DL-based capability descriptions in particular. However, as a first step towards an intuitive methodology for modelling capability semantics in DL, a characterisation of service property restrictions has been suggested in [5]. The idea is to provide a set of intuitive modelling primitives that map to underlying DL constructs, introducing a layer of abstraction in between the modeller and the details of the logical formalism.

The axioms in a capability description D constrain the set of acceptable service instances in $S^{\mathcal{I}}$ by restricting various properties of the service. In our DL-based capability descriptions, such service properties map to DL roles and can be restricted with respect to certain characteristics. The following is a list of possible characteristics according to [5].

- Variety
  A property can either be restricted to a *fixed* value or it can be *ranging* over instances of a certain concept. This can be expressed with qualifying DL concept constructors, such as $\forall\, r.\{i\}$ and $\forall\, r.C$, respectively. For any acceptable service instance, the value of such a property must either be a certain individual or a member of a certain class.
- Availability
  A property can either be *obligatory*, requiring all acceptable service instances to have a value for it, or *optional*, allowing service instances without a property value. By using existential quantification of the form $\exists\, r.\top$ service instances are required to have a value for r.

- Multiplicity
  A property can either be *multi-valued*, allowing service instances with several different property values, or *single-valued*, requiring service instances to have at most one value for the property. By the number restriction $\leq 1\ r$, a property can be marked as single valued.
- Coverage
  A property can be explicitly known to cover a range. If it is *range-covering*, the service description enforces that in every possible world, for any value in the range, there is an acceptable service instance with this property value. This introduces variance due to intended diversity and can be expressed by including an additional axiom of the form $C \sqsubseteq \exists\ r^{-}.S$ in D, where the concept C is the range of the property r to be covered.[4] Conversely, a non-range-covering property induces variance due to incomplete knowledge, as in different possible worlds different subsets of the range will be covered.

Building on such a characterisation, a next step would be to a set of intuitive modelling primitives which combine the different kinds of property restrictions and give them an intuitive interpretation. Domain experts could then formulate capability descriptions on an intuitive level, abstracting description logic–specific technicalities.

8.4.2 DL Inferences for Matching Capability Descriptions

To carry out the task of discovery, a capability description for a requested service has to be matched against a capability descriptions for a provided service. Within a DL-based discovery framework this matching is based on DL inferences such as satisfiability or subsumption checks. Since the matching has to be done with respect to the domain knowledge, the inferences to be applied operate on concepts S specified in capability descriptions D as well as on the knowledge base KB. Matching a requester's capability description D_r against a provider's capability description D_p with respect to a domain knowledge base KB is formally captured by a boolean function $match(KB, D_r, D_p)$ that specifies the way of how to apply DL inferences.

In the literature three different DL inferences relevant for discovery have been proposed [24, 15, 5], based on the notions of intersection, subsumption and non-disjointness. Subsumption is sometimes counted for two different inferences, since it can be applied in two directions.

On an intuitive level the different behaviour of these inferences is grounded in the different ways of how to treat variance due to intended diversity and variance due to incomplete knowledge during the matching process. Variance due to intended diversity can be treated such that either all or just some of the intended

[4] This is obtained by transforming the axiom $\forall x\ :\ C(x)\ \rightarrow\ \exists y\ :\ [r(y,x) \wedge S(y)]$ into description logic by standard manipulation of first-order formulas

alternatives are considered relevant, which maps to subsumption or intersection of concepts, respectively. Variance due to incomplete knowledge can be treated such that a match can either be established regardless of how incomplete knowledge is resolved or such that the existence of some way to resolve incomplete knowledge is sufficient, which maps to entailment or satisfiability inferences. The following paragraphs explain how these ways of treating variance are combined in the different inferences.

Inferences for Matching

Intersection: Intersection matching directly follows the intuition of checking for a non-empty intersection of the sets of service instances associated to the requester's and provider's capability descriptions, as suggested in [24].

Inference:	*Satisfiability of Concept Conjunction*
Function:	$match_{int}(KB, D_r, D_p)$
Formula:	$S_r \sqcap S_p$ is satisfiable w.r.t. $KB \cup D_r \cup D_p$
Situation:	$(S_p)^{\mathcal{I}_1}$ $(S_r)^{\mathcal{I}_1}$ $(S_p)^{\mathcal{I}_2}$ $(S_r)^{\mathcal{I}_2}$ ...
Intuition:	Is there a way to resolve unspecified issues such that D_r and D_p specify some common service instance?

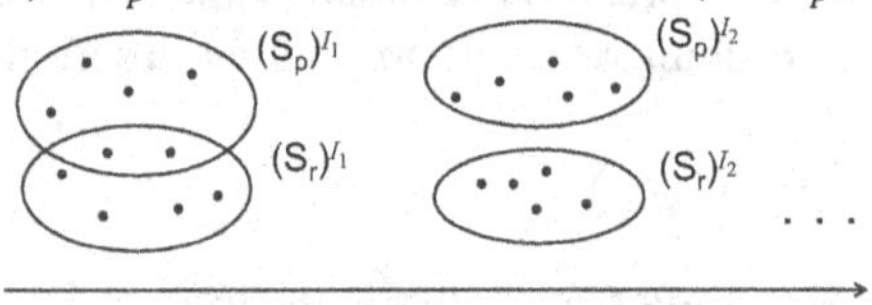

Intersection matching uses concept satisfiability as a standard DL inference supported by any DL reasoner. The function $match_{int}(KB, D_r, D_p)$ adds all the axioms in the requester's and the provider's capability descriptions to the domain knowledge and checks, with respect to this extended knowledge base, whether the concept formed by the conjunction of S_r and S_p is satisfiable. In DL a concept is satisfiable with respect to a knowledge base if there exists a model of the knowledge base in which the concept has a non-empty extension. Since the conjunction of S_r and S_p in fact intersects the two associated sets of acceptable service instances, this inference checks whether these sets can have at least one element in common, i.e. whether there is *some* possible world $\mathcal{I}$ in which $S_r^{\mathcal{I}} \cap S_p^{\mathcal{I}} \neq \emptyset$ holds. Thus, if $match_{int}(KB, D_r, D_p) = true$, the capability descriptions of the requester and the provider allow at least one service instance on which they both agree. According to [17] this is the minimum requirement for a discovery matching procedure – i.e., if $match_{int}(KB, D_r, D_p) = false$ then discovery must definitely filter out this provider because there is no possible overlap in the descriptions.

Subsumption: The idea behind subsumption matching is to check whether the requested service capability is a specialisation of the provided one or vice versa. Therefore, it comes in two flavours, $\Rightarrow$ and $\Leftarrow$, as the subsumption relation is not symmetric and can be applied in two directions.

Inference: *Entailment of Concept Subsumption*
Function: $match_{sub_{\Rightarrow}}(KB, D_r, D_p)$
Formula: $KB \cup D_r \cup D_p \models S_r \sqsubseteq S_p$
Situation: $(S_p)^{I_1}$ $(S_r)^{I_1}$ $(S_p)^{I_2}$ $(S_r)^{I_2}$ . . .
Intuition: Do the service instances of D_p encompass the service instances of D_r, regardless of how unspecified issues are resolved?

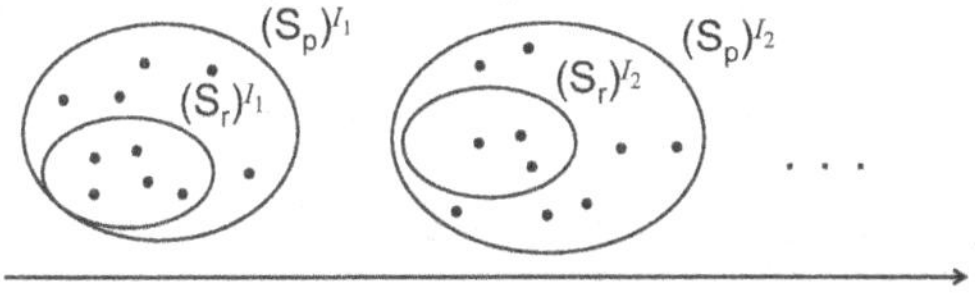

Inference: *Entailment of Concept Subsumption*
Function: $match_{sub_{\Leftarrow}}(KB, D_r, D_p)$
Formula: $KB \cup D_r \cup D_p \models S_p \sqsubseteq S_r$
Situation: $(S_r)^{I_1}$ $(S_p)^{I_1}$ $(S_r)^{I_2}$ $(S_p)^{I_2}$ . . .
Intuition: Do the service instances of D_r encompass the service instances of D_p, regardless of how unspecified issues are resolved?

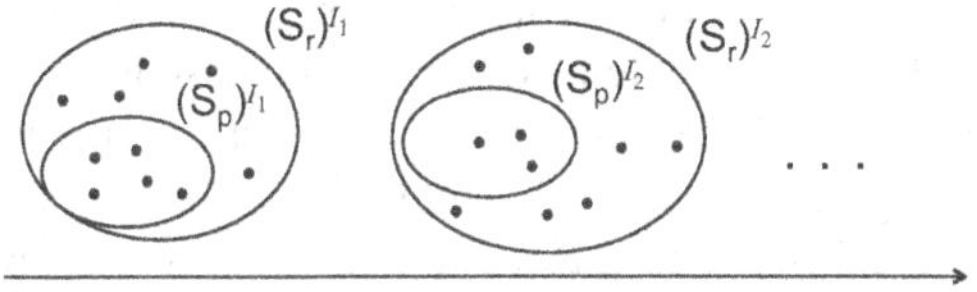

Also subsumption matching directly maps to a standard DL inference provided by DL reasoners, namely entailment of concept subsumption. The function $match_{sub}(KB, D_r, D_p)$ adds all the axioms in the requester's and the provider's capability descriptions to the domain knowledge and checks whether from this extended knowledge base it follows that one of the concepts S_r and S_p is subsumed by the other one. In DL a concept A is subsumed by a concept B if, for any model of the knowledge base, all the individuals that belong to A also belong to B. If $match_{sub_{\Rightarrow}}(KB, D_r, D_p) = true$ then in *every* possible world the requester's set of acceptable service instances is fully contained in the provider's – that is ${S_r}^{\mathcal{I}} \subseteq {S_p}^{\mathcal{I}}$. In this case the requester can be assured that each of their acceptable service instances is also acceptable to the provider, regardless of how incompleteness in capability descriptions is interpreted. In [15] this is called a plugin-match. If $match_{sub_{\Leftarrow}}(KB, D_r, D_p) = true$ then in *every* possible world the provider's set of acceptable service instances is fully contained in the requester's – that is ${S_p}^{I} \subseteq {S_r}^{I}$. In this case the requester can be assured that each service instances acceptable to the provider is covered by their request, regardless of how incomplete capability descriptions are interpreted. In [15] this is called a Subsumes-match. An equivalence-match according to [15] denotes the situation when both $match_{sub_{\Leftarrow}}(KB, D_r, D_p)$ and $match_{sub_{\Leftarrow}}(KB, D_r, D_p)$ return a positive result, such that the two sets coincide.

Non-Disjointness: The idea behind non-disjointness matching is to combine the weak intersection match with the strong notion of entailment [5].

Inference:	*Entailment of Concept Non-Disjointness*
Function:	$match_{ndj}(KB, D_r, D_p)$
Formula:	$KB \cup D_r \cup D_p \cup \{S_r \sqcap S_p \sqsubseteq \bot\}$ is unsatisfiable
Situation:	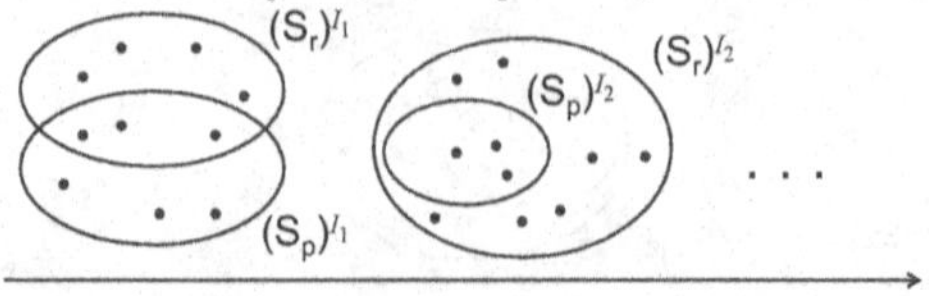 (Sr)I1 (Sr)I2 (Sp)I2 (Sp)I1 . . .
Intuition:	Do D_r and D_p specify some common service instance, regardless of how unspecified issues are resolved?

Non-Disjointness matching does not directly match to a standard DL inference but it can be realised with common DL reasoners via a disjointness axiom and knowledge base satisfiability. The function $match_{ndj}(KB, D_r, D_p)$ adds all the axioms in the requester's and the provider's capability descriptions to the domain knowledge together with an additional axiom that assures the concepts S_r and S_p to be disjoint. It then checks whether this extended knowledge base is unsatisfiable. In DL a knowledge base is unsatisfiable if there does not exist any model for it – that is, it contains contradictory statements. Like intersection matching, non-disjointness matching checks for a non-empty intersection of the two sets of acceptable service instances. However, in contrast to intersection matching, here the intersection must be non-empty regardless of how incomplete knowledge is resolved – that is, it checks whether $S_r^{\mathcal{I}} \cap S_r^{\mathcal{I}} \neq \emptyset$ is true in *every* possible world. Thus, if $match_{ndj}(KB, D_r, D_p) = true$ then the capability descriptions of the requester and the provider allow at least one common service instance, independent from the interpretation of incompleteness in the descriptions.

Discussion of Inferences by Example

In this paragraph the three different inferences are discussed by applying them to an example scenario taken from the logistics domain. In this scenario a requester looks for a logistics services that supports shipping from certain cities in the UK. There are two providers, A and B, one offering shipping from cities in the UK and another one offering shipping from cities in the US. The example is very reduced since it is supposed to serve a comprehensive analysis of the behaviour of the different inferences. The situation is described by the following specifications of capability descriptions and domain knowledge in DL.

$$KB = \{ \; UKCity(Plymouth) \; , \; \; Shipping \sqsubseteq \, = 1 \, from \; \}$$

$$\begin{aligned} D_r = \{ \; & S_r \equiv Shipping \sqcap \forall from.\{Plymouth, Dublin\} \; , \\ & \exists \, from^{-}.S_r(Plymouth) \; , \\ & \exists \, from^{-}.S_r(Dublin) \qquad \qquad \} \end{aligned}$$

$$D_{p_A} = \{ \; S_{p_A} \equiv Shipping \sqcap \forall from.UKCity \; , \; UKCity \sqsubseteq \exists from^{-}.S_{p_A} \; \}$$

$$D_{p_B} = \{ \; S_{p_B} \equiv Shipping \sqcap \forall from.USCity \; , \; USCity \sqsubseteq \exists from^{-}.S_{p_B} \; \}$$

Our intuition tells us that provider A should match with the request, since one of the alternatives for the city of origin is covered by what they offer – namely Plymouth is a city in the UK. On the other hand, provider B should not match, since neither alternative for the requested city of origin is covered by what they offer – neither Plymouth nor Dublin are cities in the US. The following paragraphs discuss whether the different inferences yield the intuitively desired matching behaviour.

Intersection: Applied to the example, $match_{int}(KB, D_r, D_{p_A})$ yields a positive result because the concept $S_r \sqcap S_{p_A}$ is satisfiable with respect to $KB \cup D_r \cup D_{p_A}$. Fig. 8.5a depicts one possible world $\mathcal{I}$ describing the situation of the example scenario. In DL terms $\mathcal{I}$ is a model of $KB \cup D_r \cup D_p$. In this possible world, there is one service instance for shipping from Plymouth and another one for shipping from Dublin – the two alternatives specified by the requester – both of which belong to the requester's set of acceptable service descriptions. Since in $\mathcal{I}$ Plymouth is a UK city, the first of these two service instances is also contained in the set S_{p_A} of provider A; thus the sets $S_r{}^{\mathcal{I}}$ and $S_{pA}{}^{\mathcal{I}}$ have a non-empty intersection. The existence of this one possible world $\mathcal{I}$ is already sufficient for provider A to match the request.

On the other hand, $match_{int}(KB, D_r, D_{p_B})$ also yields a positive result, which does not meet our intuition formulated before. Again, Fig. 8.5a gives the answer for why this behaviour is correct in the sense of how intersection matching is defined. In the particular possible world $\mathcal{I}$, the individual Plymouth happens to be both a UK and a US city. Indeed, the facts in the knowledge base given by $KB \cup D_r \cup D_{p_A}$ do not prevent Plymouth from being a US city, such that the possible world depicted in Fig. 8.5a is a perfectly valid model of this extended knowledge base.

To overcome this problem, modellers should impose additional constraints to reduce variance due to incomplete knowledge. In this particular example, an additional disjointness axiom $UKCity \sqcap USCity \sqsubseteq \bot$ in the domain knowledge base KB would prevent any individual from being a UK city and a US city at the same time.

Subsumption: When applying subsumption matching to the example, neither $match_{sub_{\Rightarrow}}(KB, D_r, D_{p_A})$ nor $match_{sub_{\Leftarrow}}(KB, D_r, D_{p_A})$ do yield a positive result. In the

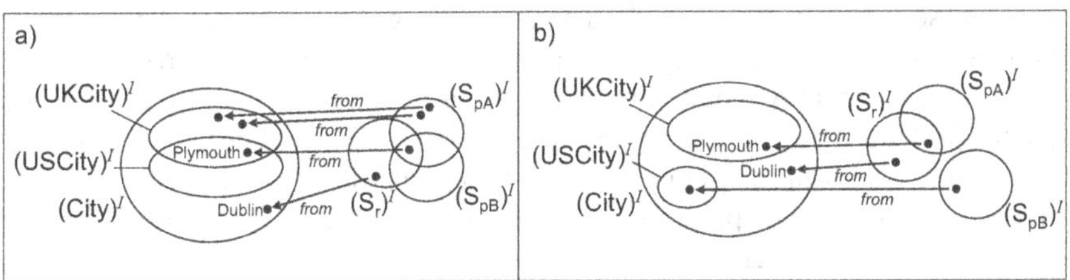

Fig. 8.5. Model-theoretic situations for shipping services

possible world of Fig. 8.5a, neither of the two sets ${S_r}^{\mathcal{I}}$ and ${S_{p_A}}^{\mathcal{I}}$ does fully contain the other. (The same holds for provider B.) The existence of this one possible world is already enough to let subsumption matching fail here, since it requires set containment in *every* possible world.

It seems to be difficult to apply the subsumption inference in the general case, where neither one of the two capability descriptions involved is likely to be subsumed by the other as a whole. One possibility to overcome this problem would be to avoid combining several alternatives for a property value in a disjunctive way, as done in D_r by the requester here. Instead, the requester could have separated the two alternative cities of origin in two distinct capability descriptions in order to issue them independently from each other and to combine the results in a post-processing step.

Non-disjointness: Applying non-disjointness matching to the example achieves the desired discovery behaviour, since $match_{ndj}(KB, D_r, D_{p_A})$ yields a positive result whereas $match_{ndj}(KB, D_r, D_{p_B})$ does not. Figure 8.5b depicts a situation that is prototypical for all the models of $KB \cup D_r \cup D_p$. By specifying that the property *from* is range-covering, provider A ensures that there is a service instance for shipping from each UK city in every possible world. Thus, a service instance for shipping from Plymouth yields a match since Plymouth is a UK city in each possible world. Furthermore, there is at least one possible world in which Plymouth is not a US city, since it has not been explicitly specified as such. Therefore, the capability description of provider B does not match with the capability description of the requester. The existence of one such possible world where Plymouth is not a US city is already sufficient for provider B to not match, since entailment here checks for non-empty intersections in *every* possible world.

Although in this particular example non-disjointness matching works out well, it has some deficiencies which make it problematic to use in a DL-based discovery framework. The reason is that it requires modellers to make use of range-covering property restrictions in order to reduce variance due to incomplete knowledge, as introduced earlier in this section. As described in [5], however, problems arise if several range-covering property restrictions need to be combined in one capability description. To give an example, suppose that provider A would also include the city of destination in the description and require it to be a UK city as well, covering the same range as the city of origin. This would be achieved by including the two axioms $S_{p_A} \sqsubseteq \exists\ to.UKCity$ and $UKCity \sqsubseteq \exists\ to^{-}.S_{p_A}$, yielding the description D'_{p_A}. In this way, the ranges of the two properties *from* and *to* would be covered separately but not in combination – i.e., not all pairs of values (f, t) with $f, t \in UKCity^{\mathcal{I}}$ would be covered by service instances in ${S_{p_A}}^{\mathcal{I}}$. There exists, e.g., a valid model of $KB \cup D'_{p_A}$ in which there is no service instance for shipping from Plymouth to Dover, even if both these cities are explicitly required to be UK cities by appropriate A-Box assertions. What the provider really would like to express is the coverage of the combined range $UKCity \times UKCity$ for the combination of the two properties. To express the coverage of a range $C_1 \times C_2$ for two properties at once, one needs the following formula stated in first order predicate logic:

$$\forall x_1, x_2 : C_1(x_1) \wedge C_2(x_2) \rightarrow \exists y : [r_1(y, x_1) \wedge r_2(y, x_2) \wedge S(y)].$$

Unfortunately, this formula cannot be translated to DL as it is no longer in the two-variable fragment of first-order predicate logic.

8.4.3 Possible DL-Based Discovery Frameworks

Regarding Sect. 8.3, a discovery framework should relate modelling and matching of capability descriptions. Thus, a DL-based discovery framework should specify the way in which the modelling techniques from Sect. 8.4.1 are to be combined with the inferences from Sect. 8.4.2. The discussion of the behaviour of the different inferences by an example has already shown that their usefulness depends on the way in which capability descriptions and domain knowledge are modelled.

There are several possibilities of how the matching of capability descriptions can be realised by applying the inferences introduced before. In the following two paragraphs, they are discussed with regard to the way of how capability descriptions and domain ontologies are modelled.

Using a Single Inference

Applying a single inference tries to solve the problem of matching within the scope of DL by solely using logical inferencing. Some remarks on the single usage of each inference follow.

Intersection: As discussed in Sect. 8.4.2, intersection matching is the weakest check that can be performed. It is very good in telling us that two capability descriptions do not match. If $match_{int}(KB, D_r, D_p) = false$ then we can be sure that D_r and D_p are incompatible. On the other hand, it gives less information about whether two capability descriptions match; if $match_{int}(KB, D_r, D_p) = true$ then we know that the two parties can potentially agree on a common service instance only under certain circumstances.

A DL-based discovery framework that realises matching by intersection alone, therefore, needs to require modellers of capability descriptions and domain knowledge to exclude some undesirable cases of matching by formulating additional constraints that reduce variance due to incomplete knowledge. Such constraints can be disjointness axioms or maximum cardinality restrictions, as exemplified in the discussion of the intersection inference. Since intersection matching is based on satisfiability, the existence of one possible world for the intersection is sufficient for yielding a positive result. Therefore, modellers have to make sure that no such possible world exists accidentally. One way of introducing a rather restricting way of modelling is to replace subsumption by disjoint partitioning as, e.g., suggested in [19]. Applied to a taxonomy of cities as in the example, this technique makes sure that any two sibling city concepts in the hierarchy are disjoint by default.

A remaining problem, however, is that intersection matching is vulnerable to including externally specified domain knowledge in the matching process. For example, if some provider introduces a concept that is neither known to the requester nor to the commonly used domain ontology, then this concept is likely to produce an undesired positive matching result. Neither the requester nor the commonly used domain ontology have the chance to put any constraints on this concept, e.g. by making it disjoint from other concepts. A discovery framework using intersection matching together with disjoint partitioning of taxonomies must therefore specify a way of how to handle external domain ontologies or it must prohibit their inclusion.

Subsumption: The natural direction in which to apply subsumption seems to be $match_{sub_{\Rightarrow}}(KB, D_r, D_p)$, requiring that the requested capability is more specific than the provided capability. Naturally, the provider offers many options of which only some have to be of interest for the requester. Due to the strong notion of entailment, a discovery framework using subsumption would not have the problem of yielding false positive matches based on externally specified domain knowledge, as intersection matching has. However, it is arguable whether subsumption can provide a natural way of matching when capability descriptions represent sets of acceptable service instances. The discussion of the behaviour of the subsumption inferences has shown that there are cases in which desired positive matches are not recognised by the matching procedure. In frameworks where subsumption has been used, it has been applied to parts of a service description only [13, 15], as e.g. to the types of input and output parameters. Thus, it seems to better fit in frameworks where the matching problem is tackled by a combination of logical inferences with algorithmic processing outside logical reasoning, as discussed below.

Non-disjointness: As seen in the discussion of the inferences, non-disjointness matching is also based on the strong notion of entailment. Therefore, it requires modellers to make sure that the service characteristics they encode in their capability descriptions hold in every possible world. One way to do this is by making use of range-covering property restrictions, as described in Sect. 8.4.1. However, a DL-based discovery framework based on non-disjointness matching in combination with a requirement for range-covering property restrictions in capability descriptions would lack expressivity due to the limitations of DL. A naive way of overcoming this problem would be to replace axioms for range-coverage by appropriate A-Box assertions, assuring that all individuals within the range are covered one by one. Although these A-Box assertions could possibly be generated automatically out of range-covering property restrictions and the domain knowledge, this would lead to exponential blow-up in the number of A-Box assertions. Therefore, it would make sense to extend such discovery frameworks by moving towards a more expressive knowledge representation formalism.

Using a Combination of Inferences

A DL-based discovery framework can also combine the different inferences instead of using just a single one. In this way, the problem of matching is no longer tackled within logical reasoning alone but involves some algorithmic processing, yielding a more complex matching process. Variants of this approach apply DL inferences to match (parts of) capability descriptions and combine the intermediary results from a DL reasoner by means of algorithmically formulated steps.

In [15, 10], there has been proposed a degree of matching by defining an order on the different inferences. The following five degrees of matching have been identified:

1. *fail* – the intersection between two descriptions is empty
2. *intersect* – the intersection between two descriptions is non-empty
3. *subsume* – subsumption between two descriptions holds in the $\Leftarrow$ direction
4. *plugin* – i.e. subsumption between two descriptions holds in the $\Rightarrow$ direction
5. *exact* – i.e. subsumption between two descriptions holds in both directions ($\Leftrightarrow$)

Obviously, if two descriptions are equivalent, i.e. their degree of matching is *exact*, then they also subsume each other pairwise . Furthermore, if one description subsumes another one, i.e. their degree of matching is either *plugin* or *subsume*, then their intersection cannot be empty. Therefore, the order for the degrees of matching is $fail \prec intersect \preceq subsume - plugin \preceq exact$ with *exact* being the most desirable match. There have been proposed matching algorithms that determine the degree of match for parts of service descriptions [15] as well as for the whole description [10].

8.4.4 DL-Based Discovery Applied to a Logistics Scenario

This section describes the application of a DL-based discovery framework on a more elaborate example taken from the logistics domain. In opposite to the mini example in Sect. 8.4.2, here the focus is set on how the different parts of the discovery framework interact rather than on the technicalities of the inferences used for matchmaking. The framework uses DL-based intersection matching together with a modelling strategy that puts sufficient constraints on domain-level knowledge, including disjointness between siblings in a taxonomy. The example is taken from an industrial scenario described in [18], corresponding to Scenario C.

Example Setting

In this scenario, a requester requires a logistics service to ship a cargo freight between certain locations. There are several providers of logistics services who are being matched against the request by the discovery system. Two of them are potential candidates to agree on a contract for the shipping order. After refining the request such that no aircrafts are allowed to convey the freight, one of these potential providers is dropped out due to a company-internal policy for aircraft transportation between certain regions. This conclusion, drawn by the discovery system, involves some complex reasoning in which several independent sources of knowledge need to be combined.

Domain knowledge – The domain knowledge used in this example is captured in the logistics ontology O_{log}. It refers itself to two more general domain ontologies, one for geographical knowledge O_{geo} and one for technical knowledge about vehicles O_{tec}. For reasoning, all the referred domain ontologies must be included in the knowledge base, i.e. $KB = O_{log} \cup O_{geo} \cup O_{tec}$. The following set of DL axioms shows an excerpt of the geographic knowledge about cities in O_{geo}.

$$\begin{aligned} O_{geo} \supset \{ \; & City \sqsubseteq \top \,, \;\; EUCity \sqsubseteq City \,, \;\; ContinentalEUCity \sqsubseteq EUCity \,, \\ & UKCity \sqsubseteq EUCity \,, \;\; ContinentalEUCity \sqcap UKCity \sqsubseteq \bot \,, \\ & GermanCity \sqsubseteq ContinentalEUCity \,, \;\; EnglishCity \sqsubseteq UKCity \,, \\ & EnglishCity(Plymouth) \,, \;\; GermanCity(Hamburg) \quad \} \end{aligned}$$

The top-level concept *City* is split in *EUCity* and others are not listed here. *EUCity* is partitioned in *ContinentalEUCity* and *UKCity*, since geographically the UK forms an island which is not connected to the European continent. For each of these two subregions, a representative country is chosen to further specialise it, i.e. *EnglishCity* and *GermanCity*. For both of these two countries, there is one exemplary city modelled as an individual, i.e. Plymouth and Hamburg. This forms the geographic knowledge which the logistics ontology O_{log} will refer to. The other external source of knowledge for O_{log} is given by the following excerpt of the technical ontology about vehicles.

$$\begin{aligned} O_{tec} \supset \{ \; & Vehicle \sqsubseteq \top \,, \; OverlandVehicle \sqsubseteq Vehicle \,, OverseaVehicle \sqsubseteq Vehicle \,, \\ & GroundVehicle \sqsubseteq OverlandVehicle \,, \;\; Aircraft \sqsubseteq OverlandVehicle \,, \\ & OverseaVehicle \sqcap GroundVehicle \sqsubseteq \bot \,, \;\; Ship \sqsubseteq OverseaVehicle \,, \\ & Ship \sqcap Aircraft \sqsubseteq \bot \;\; OverseaVehicle \equiv Ship \sqcup Aircraft \quad \} \end{aligned}$$

The top-level concept *Vehicle* is split in *OverseaVehicle*; and *OverlandVehicle*; however, these two are not disjoint. In fact, an *Aircraft* can be used to transcend both solid ground and water, whereas a *Ship* can only be used on waterway. Notice that $O_{tec} \models Aircraft \sqsubseteq OverseaVehicle$.

The logistics domain ontology O_{log} uses the concepts defined in O_{geo} and O_{tec} to form new knowledge based on them and also introduces new concepts and roles. The following axioms describe containers to be used as items for shipping.

$$\begin{aligned} O_{log} \supset \{ \; & Container \sqsubseteq \top \,, \;\; CargoContainer \sqcap TankContainer \sqsubseteq \bot \,, \\ & CargoContainer \sqsubseteq Container \,, \;\; TankContainer \sqsubseteq Container \; \} \end{aligned}$$

There are two different kinds of containers, one for cargo and one for liquid goods. The following fragment connects the already defined concepts in O_{geo}, O_{tec} and O_{log} to a central concept for a shipping service by introducing roles with appropriate domain and range restrictions.

$$\begin{aligned} O_{log} \supset \{ \; & \top \sqsubseteq \forall\, location.City \,, \;\; \exists\, location.\top \sqsubseteq Shipping \,, \\ & from \sqsubseteq location \,, \;\; to \sqsubseteq location \,, \\ & \top \sqsubseteq \forall\, vehicle.Vehicle \,, \;\; \exists\, vehicle.\top \sqsubseteq Shipping \,, \\ & \top \sqsubseteq \forall\, item.Container \,, \;\; \exists\, item.\top \sqsubseteq Shipping \quad \} \end{aligned}$$

The top-level concept *Shipping* acts as the domain for all the roles introduced. The *location* role splits into the subroles *from* and *to*. By setting *City* as the range of the *location* role and *Vehicle* as the range of the *vehicle* role, the external ontologies O_{geo} and O_{tec} are referred to within O_{log}. Setting *Container* as the range of the *item* role refers to an internal concept, introduced within O_{log} itself. As the most important concept, O_{log} defines *Shipping*, which is further characterised by the following axioms.

$$\begin{aligned} O_{log} \supset \{ \ & \mathit{Shipping} \sqsubseteq =1\, \mathit{from} \sqcap \ =1\ \mathit{to} \sqcap \ =2\ \mathit{location}\ , \\ & \mathit{Shipping} \sqsubseteq \forall\ \mathit{location.UKCity} \sqcup \forall\ \mathit{location.\neg UKCity} \sqcup \\ & \ (\exists\ \mathit{location.UKCity} \sqcap \exists\ \mathit{location.\neg UKCity} \sqcap \exists\ \mathit{vehicle.OverseaVehicle})\ \} \end{aligned}$$

The *Shipping* concept represents the actual Service to be carried out, describing its capability. The locations of origin and destination are required to be unique and there cannot be any other specialised locations than these two. The second of the axioms shown above ensures that an *OverseaVehicle* is used whenever shipping is conducted between the UK and locations outside the UK as, e.g., continental Europe. It captures three cases in a disjunctive clause: either all locations are UK cities or none of the locations is a UK city or one of them is and the other is not, in which case the *vehicle* role is restricted appropriately.

Requested service: The capability description describing the service requirement issued by the requester is specified by the following axiom.[5]

$$\begin{aligned} D_r = \{ \ \ S_r \equiv \ & \mathit{Shipping} \sqcap \ =1\ \mathit{item} \sqcap \\ & \exists\ \mathit{from}.\{\mathit{Plymouth}\} \sqcap \exists\ \mathit{to}.\{\mathit{Hamburg}\} \sqcap \\ & \exists\ \mathit{item}.(\mathit{CargoContainer} \sqcap \forall\ \mathit{weight}.\ =_{200})\ \} \end{aligned}$$

The required service is shipping cargo from Plymouth to Hamburg. There is just one item to be shipped and this freight weighs 200 kg. For refinement of this request, the use of aircraft as vehicle is prohibited by adding the following axiom, yielding the description D_r'.

$$D_r' = D_r \cup \{ \ \ S_r \sqsubseteq \forall\ \mathit{vehicle}.\neg \mathit{Aircraft}\ \}$$

Provided services: There are four service providers involved in this scenario, named A, B, C and D. The capability descriptions of the services they offer are given by the following sets of axioms.

$$\begin{aligned} D_{P_A} = \{ \ \ S_{P_A} \equiv \ & \mathit{Shipping} \sqcap \forall\ \mathit{location.EUCity} \sqcap \\ & \forall\ \mathit{item}.(\mathit{TankContainer} \sqcap \forall\ \mathit{weight}.\ \leq_{1000})\ \} \end{aligned}$$

$$\begin{aligned} D_{P_B} = \{ \ \ & S_{P_B} \equiv \mathit{Shipping} \sqcap \forall\ \mathit{location.EUCity}\ , \\ & S_{P_B} \sqsubseteq \forall\ \mathit{location.UKCity} \sqcup \forall\ \mathit{location.ContinentalEUCity} \sqcup \\ & (\exists\ \mathit{location.UKCity} \sqcap \exists\ \mathit{location.ContinentalEUCity} \sqcap \\ & \ \forall\ \mathit{vehicle}.\neg \mathit{Ship}) \qquad \} \end{aligned}$$

$$\begin{aligned} D_{P_C} = \{ \ \ S_{P_C} \equiv \ & \mathit{Shipping} \sqcap \forall\ \mathit{location.City} \sqcap \\ & \forall\ \mathit{item.CargoContainer} \sqcap \forall\ \mathit{vehicle}.\neg \mathit{Aircraft}\ \} \end{aligned}$$

[5] In these descriptions, the discovery framework exploits the concrete domain approach (see e.g. [11]) to include reasoning with numbers. Expressions like $=_{200}$ and $\leq_{1000}$ are concrete domain predicates which express, in this case, numbers equal to 200 and numbers less or equal to 1000, respectively

$$D_{P_D} = \{ \;\; S_{P_D} \equiv Shipping \sqcap \forall\, location.UKCity \sqcap \exists\, item.(\forall\, weight.\leq_{100}) \sqcap =1\, item \;\}$$

Provider A ships between any EU cities but only tank containers with a maximum weight of 1000 kg. Provider B also ships between any EU cities without a restriction on the item to be conveyed. However, for some reasons provider B follows a company-internal policy according to which shipping between the UK and continental Europe is not to be carried out by ship. Provider C ships cargo containers worldwide but does not offer transportation by aircraft. Provider D ships within the UK only and conveys anything in small single units weighing at most 100 kg.

Discovery Results

In this example scenario, the discovery system retrieves D_r as a request and consults a repository containing the capability descriptions of the services offered by the providers. For each of these descriptions, the intersection matching function is used to check whether this particular offer is relevant for the request. The result of discovery here is the set

$$\{X \in \{A, B, C, D\} \mid match_{int}(KB, D_r, D_{P_X}) = true\}.$$

In the first step of the scenario, this is the set $\{B, C\}$, meaning that the providers B and C match the request formulated in D_r. After refining the request and replacing D_r by D'_r in a second step, the result is reduced to the set $\{C\}$, leaving provider C as the only one matching the request.

Provider A is ruled out in both cases because they do not support cargo containers. The request description requires any instance of the concept S_r to point to an instance of *CargoContainer* via the *item* role. On the other hand, via the *item* role any instance of the concept S_{P_A} can only point to instances of *TankContainer*. Since the two concepts *CargoContainer* and *TankContainer* are declared to be disjoint in O_{log}, the extension of $S_r \sqcap S_{P_A}$ must be empty in every model of $KB \cup D_r \cup D_{P_A}$.

Provider D is ruled out for two reasons: they neither support locations outside the UK nor items weighing more than 100 kg. Notice that the axiom $Container \sqsubseteq\, =1\, weight$ in O_{log} prohibits models in which there is no weight specified for a container, such that the two universal restrictions in D_r and D_{P_D} cannot be satisfied trivially.

Provider C matches in both cases. The concept $S_r \sqcap S_{P_C}$ allows models in which a cargo container is shipped between the requested cities and in which *vehicle* points to anything but an aircraft. In consequence, this vehicle must be a ship in these models because from the characterisation of *Shipping* in O_{log}, together with the axioms in O_{tec} and O_{geo}, it can be derived that transportation between the UK and continental Europe can be conducted only via ship or aircraft.

Provider B matches with the original request D_r but not with the refined request D'_r . Its description D_{P_B} is split in the definition of the service concept S_{P_B} and an additional policy that further constrains this concept. The restriction of locations to EU cities is compatible with the restrictions in D_r, since both Plymouth and Hamburg are cities in the EU. The policy, on the other hand, prohibits the vehicle to be a ship in cases where one of the two *location* roles points to a UK city and the other one to a non-UK city, as required by D_r. Figure 8.6 depicts the situations of the two matching cases involving (a) D_r and (b) D'_r. Part (a) of Fig. 8.6 shows a model of $KB \cup D_r \cup D_{p_B}$ in which the intersection of $S_r{}^{\mathcal{I}}$ and $S_{p_B}{}^{\mathcal{I}}$ is non-empty. The concept *OverseaVehicle* is modelled such that it is exhaustively partitioned by the disjoint concepts *Aircraft* and *Ship*. The existence of this model is sufficient for $match_{int}(KB, D_r, D_{p_B})$ to be true. On the other hand, the model shown in part (b) of Fig. 8.6 is characteristical for all the models of $KB \cup D'_r \cup D_{p_B}$. In all of them, instances of S_r point to oversea-vehicles that are not-aircrafts, whereas instances of S_{p_B} point to oversea-vehicles that are not-ships. Hence, there is no model in which the extensions $S_r{}^{\mathcal{I}}$ and $S_{p_B}{}^{\mathcal{I}}$ have a common instance.

Characteristics of the DL-Based Logistics Example

There are some aspects worth mentioning about the presented logistics-centred discovery example, characterising the applied discovery framework in a more general view.

Due to the choice of the intersection matching inference, together with the compact form of abstract capability descriptions with open-world semantics, discovery here realises a pre-filtering of relevant services, as discussed in Sect. 8.1. The requester and provider agents need to negotiate about the logistics-specific parameters of shipping contracts, which probably also requires sophisticated AI techniques, either similar or complementary to the automated reasoning that is performed during discovery.

Furthermore, the peculiarities of the chosen intersection matching inference shifts some of the effort necessary to separate out the relevant services to the modeller of capability descriptions. In the example, sibling concepts in taxonomies, such as various concepts for cities, explicitly need to be declared disjoint in order to prevent false positive matches, as discussed in Sect. 8.4.2.

On the other hand, the example shows that there can be variety in independently modelled sources of knowledge even within a relatively small set of ontologies build up according to a predetermined way of modelling. In the example, most of the par-

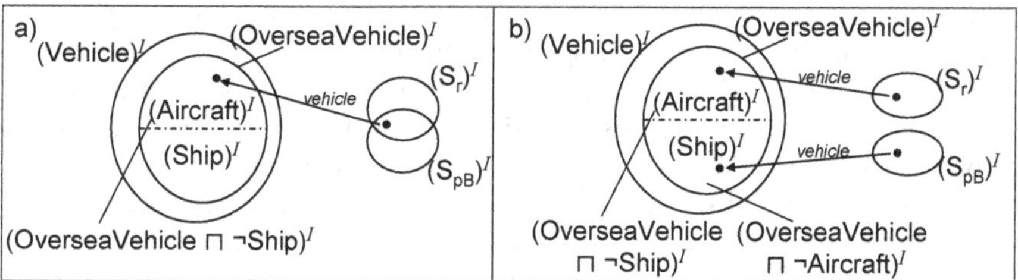

Fig. 8.6. Model-theoretic situations for matching D_{p_B} with a) D_r and b) D'_r

ties involved formulate their ontologies or capability descriptions without knowledge of each other. The geographic ontology, as well as the ontology about vehicles, are independent domain ontologies that can be reused in many scenarios. The logistics domain ontology depends on these two but it can itself be reused in related scenarios. Requesters and providers of services formulate capability descriptions with respect to the logistics domain ontology but independently from each other. Moreover, a single party, like provider B in the example, can combine several independently formulated pieces of knowledge to form their capability descriptions: the company-internal policy is being combined with any capability description issued by provider B. The benefit of independently formulated ontological descriptions is that different knowledge engineers can focus on the conceptualisation of the domain they are the experts for. Synergy arises from putting together these pieces of knowledge, when the system carries out complex reasoning which no single knowledge engineer had in mind at the time of modelling.

8.5 Outlook

Adding semantics to descriptions of services offered in the web allows for high precision finding of relevant services by applying logics-based matching techniques. However, matching based on logical inferencing is computationally costly and demands high-quality semantic service descriptions. To realise a practical discovery framework for large-scale real-world scenarios, the different techniques for matching and retrieval need to be combined appropriately with regard to architectural issues. Discovery could be approached in a two (or multi) step way, starting with conventional keyword-based filtering or pre-selection of thematically scoped service repositories based on taxonomies for service classification; then, logics-based matching techniques are applied on a reduced set of remaining capability descriptions that focus on a particular fine-grained domain of interest.

Concerning the quality of service annotation, practical discovery frameworks need to specify precise guidelines of how to formulate capability descriptions. Moreover, they should provide the user with a more intuitive way of modelling, introducing layers of abstraction in between the technical details of logical formalisms and a more service-based view.

The logics-based description and matching of service capabilities is still an issue of current research activities. This involves the selection of a knowledge representation formalism together with appropriate inferencing schemes, as well as the choice of which kind of information to include in descriptions. Both the open-world and closed-world paradigms are being investigated for service discovery in approaches using description logic and rule-based inferencing, respectively. For capability descriptions of services, various annotation frameworks include information about input and output parameters, state-transition-based notions, explicit taxonomic classification or high-level abstract properties of a service.

References

1. F. Baader, D. Calvanese, D. McGuinness, D. Nardi, and P. Patel-Schneider, editors. *The Description Logic Handbook.* Cambridge University Press, January 2003.
2. S. Battle, A. Bernstein, H. Boley, B. Grosof, M. Gruninger, R. Hull, M. Kifer, D. Martin, S. McIlraith, D. McGuinness, J. Su, and S. Tabet. Semantic Web Services Framework (SWSF). W3C Member Submission. Available at `http://www.w3.org/Submission/2005/07/`, May 2005.
3. B. Benatallah, M.-S. Hacid, A. Leger, C. Rey, and F. Toumani. On Automating Web Service Discovery. *VLDB Journal*, 14(1), 2005.
4. J. Gonzales-Castillo, D. Trastour, and C. Bartolini. Description Logics for Matchmaking of Services. In *Proceedings of the KI-2001 Workshop on Applications of Description Logics*, volume 44. CEUR Workshop Proceedings (`http://ceur-ws.org`), 2001.
5. S. Grimm, B. Motik, and C. Preist. Variance in e-Business Service Discovery. In *Proceedings 1st International Workshop SWS'2004 at ISWC-2004*, November 2004.
6. U. Keller, R. Lara, H. Lausen, A. Polleres, and D. Fensel. Automatic Location of Services. In *Proceedings of the 2nd European Semantic Web Conference (ESWC)*, 2005.
7. U. Keller, R. Lara, and A. Polleres. WSMO D5.1 discovery. `http://www.wsmo.org/TR/d5/d5.1/v0.1/`, 2004.
8. U. Keller, H. Lausen, and M. Stollberg. On the Semantics of Functional Descriptions of Web Services. In *Proceedings of the 3rd European Semantic Web Conference (ESWC)*, 2006.
9. M. Kifer, R. Lara, A. Polleres, C. Zhao, U. Keller, H. Lausen, and D. Fensel. A Logical Framework for Web Service Discovery. In *Proceedings of the 1st International Workshop SWS'2004 at ISWC-2004*, November 2004.
10. L. Li and I. Horrocks. A Software Framework For Matchmaking Based on Semantic Web Technology. In *Proceedings of the 12th International World Wide Web Conference (WWW-2003)*, pages 331–339. ACM, 2003.
11. C. Lutz. Description Logics with Concrete Domains—A Survey. In *Advances in Modal Logics*, volume 4. King's College Publications, 2003.
12. D.L. Martin, M. Paolucci, S.A. McIlraith, M.H. Burstein, D.V. McDermott, D.L. McGuinness, B. Parsia, T.R. Payne, M. Sabou, M. Solanki, N. Srinivasan, and K.P. Sycara. Bringing Semantics to Web Services: The OWL-S Approach. In J. Cardoso and A.P. Sheth, editors, *Semantic Web Services and Web Process Composition, First International Workshop, SWSWPC 2004, San Diego, CA, USA, July 2004, Revised Selected Papers*, volume 3387 of *LNCS*, pages 26–42. Springer-Verlag, 2004.
13. T.D. Noia, E.D. Sciascio, F.M. Donini, and M. Mogiello. A System for Principled Matchmaking in an Electronic Marketplace. *International Journal of Electronic Commerce*, 2004.
14. S. Oundhakar, K. Verma, K. Sivashanmugam, A. Sheth, and J. Miller. Discovery of Web Services in a Multi-Ontology and Federated Registry Environment. *International Journal of Web Services Research*, 1(3), 2005.
15. M. Paolucci, T. Kawamura, T. Payne, and K. Sycara. Semantic Matching of Web Service Capabilities. In *Proceedings of the 1st International Semantic Web Conference (ISWC)*, pages 333–347, 2002.
16. P.F. Patel-Schneider, P. Hayes, and I. Horrocks. OWL Web Ontology Language; Semantics and Abstract Syntax. `http://www.w3.org/TR/owl-semantics/`, November 2002.
17. C. Preist. A Conceptual Architecture for Semantic Web Services. *Proceedings of the 3rd International Semantic Web Conference (ISWC)*, 2004.

18. C. Preist, J. Esplugas-Cuadrado, S. Battle, S. Grimm, and S. Williams. Automated B2B Integration of a Logistics Supply Chain Using Semantic Web Services Technology. In *Proceedings of the 4th International Semantic Web Conference (ISWC)*, 2005.
19. A. Rector, N. Drummond, M. Horridge, J. Rogers, H. Knublauch, R. Stevens, H. Wang, and C. Wroe. OWL Pizzas: Common errors & common patterns from practical experience of teaching OWL-DL. In *Proceedings of the Eleventh International Conference on World Wide Web*, pages 89–98, 2002.
20. M. Schlosser, M. Sintek, S. Decker, and W. Nejdl. A Scalable and Ontology-Based P2P Infrastructure for Semantic Web Services. In *P2P-02: Proceedings of the Second International Conference on Peer-to-Peer Computing*, page 104, Washington, DC, USA, 2002. IEEE Computer Society.
21. S. Grimm, B.Motik, and C.Preist. Matching Semantic Service Descriptions with Local Closed-World Reasoning. In *Proceedings of the 3rd European Semantic Web Conference (ESWC)*, 2006.
22. I. Toma, B. Sapkota, J. Scicluna, J.M. Gomez, D. Roman, and D. Fensel. A P2P Discovery mechanism for Web Service Execution Environment. *Proceedings of the 2nd International WSMO Implementation Workshop (WIW-2005)*, June 2005.
23. D. Trastour, C. Bartolini, and J. Gonzales-Castillo. A Semantic Web approach to service description for Matchmaking of Services. In *Proceedings of the First Semantic Web Working Symposium*. `http://www.semanticweb.org/SWWS/program/`, 2001.
24. D. Trastour, C. Bartolini, and C. Preist. Semantic Web Support for the Business-to-Business e-Commerce Lifecycle. In *Proceedings of the 11th International Conference on World Wide Web*, pages 89–98, 2002.
25. K. Verma, K.Sivashanmugam, A. Sheth, A. Patil, S. Oundhakar, and J. Miller. METEOR-S WSDI: A scalable P2P infrastructure of registries for semantic publication and discovery of web services. *Information Technology and Management*, 6(1):17–39, 2005.
26. L. Hung Vu, M. Hauswirth, and K. Aberer. Towards P2P-based Semantic Web Service Discovery with QoS Support. *Workshop on Business Processes and Services (BPS), in conjunction with the Third International Conference on Business Process Management*, 2005.

9

Composition

Combining Web Service Functionality in Composite Orchestrations

Laurent Henocque and Mathias Kleiner

LSIS laboratory, University of Saint-Jerome, France
ILOG S.A, France
laurent.henocque@gmail.com, mathias.kleiner@lsis.org

Summary. This chapter deals about Semantically annotated Web Service (SWS) composition, one of the main challenges for the Semantic Web. We define the principles of SWS composition as well as the difficulties it raises. We follow with an overview of the different approaches envisioned in the research community. We also present an efficient solving method for this problem based on configuration. This technic uses a constrained object model as knowledge representation, which we precisely define in this chapter.

9.1 Definition of SWS Composition

Composition is defined in Chap.6 as the "act of combining and coordinating a set of Semantic Web Services (SWS)". Under such a definition, *composition* naturally refers to the process involved in computing such a combination. On the other hand, the product of "service composition" is called an "orchestration". This chapter hence considers issues that arise when addressing the task of automatically or manually designing an orchestration from a set of available Web Services.

We place ourselves in the scope of automatic or computer-aided, goal-oriented SWS composition, with immediate applications to Business Process Modelling or the Semantic Web. The basic assumptions for composing SWS is that there exists a form of directory listing of SWS that document their choreography using a workflow ontology, as well as a directory listing of transformations that are usable to mediate between workflows having incompatible message-type requirements. How and when a proper list of elementary workflows and transformations can be produced is beyond the scope of this chapter, and is treated as if it was available to the program from the start. In other words, we do not consider here the functionalities involved in helping an end-user to produce, document and/or publish the related elements. The corresponding issues about the description of SWS are presented in Chap. 7.

9.1.1 Goal-Oriented Semantic Web Service Composition

We assume the composition process to be *goal oriented.* On low-level grounds, this can be understood as follows: a user describes his/her overall goal by specifying the list of message types he/she can possibly input to the system (e.g. credit card number, expiry date, budget, yes/no answer, etc.) involving restrictions on their types and attributes, and the precise (set of) message(s) that must be output by the system (e.g. a plane ticket reservation electronic confirmation, his/her "objective"), again involving restrictions on their types and attributes. Based upon these elements, an automatic or assisted composer will attempt to produce an orchestration, which at least produces all expected outputs, and at most expects all possible input messages. According to this viewpoint, the *goal* is essentially formulated as a list of expected outputs.

This option cannot be sustained in the general case, because there are too many candidate Web Services that can expect or produce target messages, specifically if mediation comes into play. Mediation indeed broadens the scope of search for candidate Web Services to a composition. The complexity of producing valid compositions from such requirements, in a real life, scalable situation, is simply too high.

There also exists at least one other reason why composition cannot be achieved simply from the statement of required outputs/possible inputs. Although a composer may perfectly match input/output messages based on their types and restrictions, it cannot be expected that such a process remains possible in the presence on semantic ambiguities. Just consider a simple example. Imagine the process of generating a composite virtual travel agency Web Service. The target service combines flight reservation WS, hotel reservation WS for all travel locations, and activity WS for booking activities in all locations. An automated composer cannot discover by itself that the city for the first hotel night is the same as the arrival city for the flight. Indeed, all the Web Services involved here have cities as essential input or output items.

We therefore claim that the user of a composition tool must be able to formulate a composition request by manipulating, organising and placing constraints on abstractions of Web Services and their I/O messages. This is required to remove semantic ambiguities on the one hand, and obviously results in reducing the complexity. This claim is supported by other authors as in [38]. Under such settings, we have the following definitions:

- An *atomic goal* is an abstraction of all the Web Services that expect/produce messages that belong to exactly the same ontologies. The corresponding Web Services may differ in the restrictions they impose to I/O data, and also in the non-functional properties. They may also significantly differ in their choreographies (for instance, an online payment Web Service may expect the credit card number before the purchase pricing details, or the opposite).
- A *role* is the abstraction of the messages exchanged by goals (the counterpart of inputs/outputs of the matching SWSs). Roles have names, and may be bound to ontologies.
- A *composition goal* is a set of atomic goals together with the inter-connection and constraints that apply to roles and goal properties.

It may first be noticed that atomic goals, bound by further constraints in a composition goal, can be readily exploited to query Semantic Web Service discovery engines. We will give further details on how to express composition goals in Sect. 9.6.

9.1.2 A Glance at the Composition Process

Based upon what precedes, composing can be best viewed as a two-stage operation.

In the first step, the user designs a composition goal by selecting appropriate atomic goals from a goal repository. It is possible that an automatic composer automatically completes a partially valid composition goal to help the user build his/her request. The composition goal can be exploited to generate requests to the discovery engine. The main input received from this discovery is the set of choreographies bound to the target Web Services.

In the second step, the composer creates an orchestration of SWSs by replacing atomic goals with matching SWSs, taking into account their messages exchange patterns (choreographies). Among other possibilities covered later in this chapter in the state of the art section, this can be achieved using configuration techniques, as was shown feasible in [1] and [2]. The binding to actual SWS and messages may then either be performed by the composition program or be left open for runtime (lazy) evaluation. Indeed, all the SWS that match a given goal and have the same choreography can be freely interchanged in a valid orchestration. This optionally allows for runtime selection based upon non-functional properties, for instance.

9.1.3 Context for Goal-Oriented SWS Composition

SWS Descriptions

We will consider Semantic Web Services to be described on three levels:

1. The *capability* states the mandatory inputs, outputs, preconditions and effects of the service (all taken from a specific given ontology), as well as its non-functional properties.
2. The *choreography* describes how the service can be consumed from a user point of view (messages exchange patterns).
3. The optional *orchestration* describes the workflow of the service, including internal computations and calls to external SWSs (especially in composed SWSs). Orchestration is generally hidden to the user.

The focus of such descriptions is on interfaces, meaning that the service functionality does not need to be mentioned further from the published orchestration. This three fold viewpoint over SWS interfaces is commonly accepted in the Semantic Web, although there exists other ways to describe Semantic Web Services (most often, only names differ but the basic elements are the same). We will thus use this representation in the following sections.

In the rest of the chapter, we have chosen to illustrate various notions using the rather complex "producer/shipper" example from [38]. This example assumes the

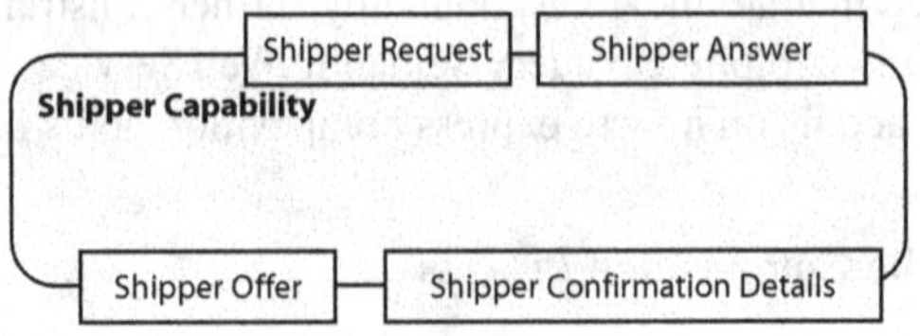

Fig. 9.1. The shipper service capability

existence of two elementary SWS, one being responsible for giving a product quote from a product description, and the other having the capability to produce a shipping quote (and organise the shipping of course) if possible. The usefulness of this example stems from the fact that the participant's choreographies are tightly interleaved in a solution. This results from the fact that neither the producer WS nor the shipper WS are "one shot" Web Services. Instead, in both cases, the WS remains "alive" during the whole execution. Using these elements, we illustrate SWS description in Fig. 9.1 and 9.2. The choreography is expressed using a subset of the UML2 activity diagrams presented in [2], and we will use the same language for orchestrations.

Atomic Goals

A user looking for a particular SWS will express requirements allowing to discover a target candidate. Such requirements are called *atomic goals*. A goal is more general than a SWS, in that it may match a number of registered SWSs and can hence be seen as a SWS abstraction. Defining a goal is like designing a query that can be used to

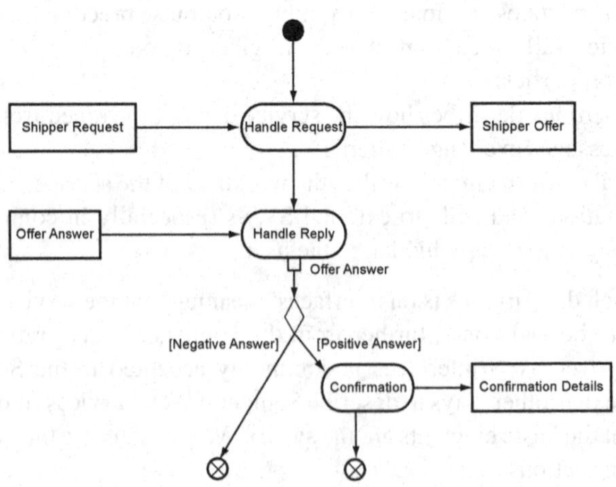

Fig. 9.2. The shipper choreography

retrieve concrete SWSs from a repository (a process known as *discovery*). Therefore, an atomic goal is defined in the same way as a SWS capability, specifying what we want to realise and what we will provide. In what follows, we call *input* and *output roles* the abstraction of input and output messages mentioned at the goal level. Roles do not need to pertain to an ontology,[1] though they can be constrained to.

Figure 9.3 illustrates an atomic goal where we specify a destination city the matching SWS has to provide.

Choice of a Workflow Language

We consider SWS choreographies and orchestrations defined using a variant of extended workflow nets, as are UML2 activity diagrams [20] or the YAWL language [51]. In order to adapt to market trends, the choice made focused on a relevant subset of UML2 activity diagrams as a language for describing choreographies and orchestrations. The underlying semantic model is close to that of *coloured*[2] Petri nets, under specific "traverse-to-completion" semantics.[3] UML diagrams generally receive poor acceptance from the scientific community, because of patent ambiguities,at both the syntactic and semantic levels. By isolating a useful subset of UML2AD, we have the possibility to wipe out all ambiguities. At the syntactic level, this is enforcing appropriate restrictions to the graphic language wherever needed, and documenting them by constraints. In order for the model constraints to be unquestionable, we are using the Z mathematical (relational) language instead of the - again controversial – OCL (UML's Object Constraint Language). At the semantic level, the translation from activity diagrams to abstract state machines [7] results in applying unambiguous operational semantics to the chosen subset.

We do not need, however, to consider here operational semantics for the selected workflow language, since we solely need to syntactically deal with workflows (i.e. reason about how to combine, extend, interleave them). We hence focus on the properties of the corresponding metamodel. Indeed, we treat workflow composition as the

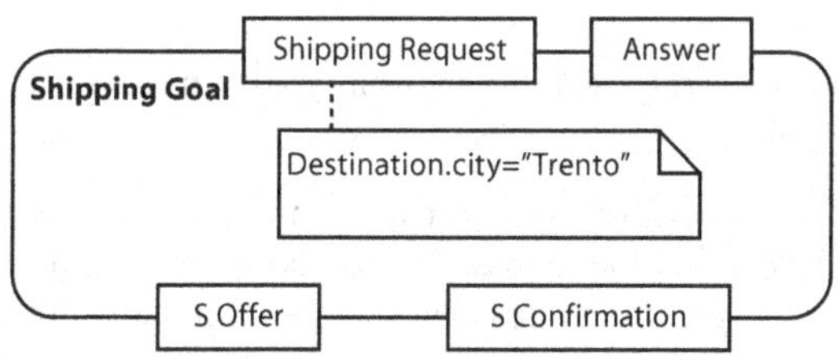

Fig. 9.3. The shipping atomic goal

[1] Often, role names suffice to define the appropriate bindings

[2] In a CPN (coloured Petri net), messages (tokens) have types

[3] Essentially, these semantics as introduced in the UML superstructure aim at preventing flow starvation in case of token competition

process of connecting input and output message flows to pre-existing or added workflow items, like fork, join nodes or auxiliary user input handling actions. Hence, the only elements retained for composition are the structural properties of workflows, messages and transformations. We do not need to emulate workflows in any case, but can formulate some constraints that to some extent guarantee the viability of the result (some constraints guarantee that a composite workflow will not be subject to starvation).

A Test Case: The Producer–Shipper Problem

The previously described general context for SWS composition is envisioned in several research papers [12, 38]. As an archetypal problem, the "producer–shipper" use case which originates from [38] was selected to introduce the required notions. The problem there is to compose a valid workflow from a producer workflow and a shipper workflow. One difficulty is that the execution of both workflows must be interleaved. Briefly stated, the producer outputs results that must be fed into the shipper so that both their "offers" can be aggregated and presented to the user. This interconnection remains unknown to the external user. Experimental evidence on the possibility to address this problem using constraint-based configuration was published in [2]. The producer–shipper example is interesting in many points:

- Both the shipper and the producer make an offer corresponding to the user request, which are aggregated to make a global offer that may later be accepted or rejected by the user. Note that the shipper needs input data from the producer to build its offer.
- Both the producer and the shipper are specified using full-fledged partial[4] workflows, and do not simply amount to simple isolated activities.
- The two workflows cannot be executed one after the other, but they must be interleaved, as each one must wait for the other offer to obtain an OfferAcceptance and therefore complete the transaction.
- The ShipperWorkflow needs a data as input (here a "size"), which can only be obtained by extraction (i.e transformation) on the ProducerOffer, a very frequent situation.
- Finally, the goal is decomposed into two sub-goals: the producer and the shipper order confirmations.

The user of an SWS composition system expects in return for his/her input a complete "composite" SWS, that interleaves the execution of several of the elementary argument SWS choreographies, while ensuring that all possible integrity constraints remain valid. Among such constraints are those that stem from the metamodel itself: for instance, some constraints state that two or more choreographies should not be

[4] Here, "partial" means that the diagram is not complete in the UML sense, since it lacks actual connections to the external participants. Normally, a diagram where input/output pins are not connected is not valid

inter-blocking, all waiting for some other to send a message for instance. Other constraints are more problem specific, like those stating for instance that an item being shipped is indeed the one that was produced.

9.1.4 Brief Introduction to Configuration

A configuration task consists in building (a simulation of) a *complex product* from *components* picked from a catalog of *types*. Neither the number nor the actual types of the required components are known beforehand. Components are subject to *relations*, and their types are subject to *inheritance* relationships. *Constraints* (also called well-formedness rules) generically define all the valid products. A configurator expects as input a fragment of a target object structure, and expands it to a solution of the configuration problem, if any, adding necessary elements during search. This problem is semi-decidable in the general case. The reader can refer to [30] for an extensive introduction to configuration.

A configuration program is well described using a *constrained object model* in the form of a standard class diagram (as illustrated by the simplified UML2AD metamodel fragment in Fig. 9.4), together with well-formedness rules or constraints. Technically, solving the associated enumeration problem can be made using various formalisms or technical approaches: extensions of the CSP paradigm [34, 16], knowledge-based approaches [48], terminological logics [35], logic programming (using forward or backward chaining, and non-standard semantics) [46], object-oriented approaches [30, 48]. Our experiments were conducted using the object-oriented configurator Ilog JConfigurator [30].

Currently, there exists no universally accepted language for specifying constrained object models. The choice of UML/OCL is advocated [14], and is realistic in many situations, but has some drawbacks due to a number of weaknesses. As shown in [2, 23], the Z relational language has enough expressive power and extensibility to properly address the task of specifying a constrained object model, without requiring to use an ad hoc object-oriented extension of Z.

Chapter 3 introduces logical formalisms used for describing ontologies in the scope of the Semantic Web. A natural question is why do we need another language here (i.e. UML + Z) and cannot use the existing. Ontology languages usually bear strong relationships with description logics, and thus belong to the broad category of "predicate calculus". Ontology languages of practical use (as OWL or WSML) are generally restricted to match the properties of the associated theorem provers. In contrast to this, the choice of UML + Z addresses several issues:

- preserve the possibility of using widely accepted graphical notations
- do not commit to a logical style (e.g. description logics in the case of OWL)
- take advantage of the expressiveness of Z as a set theoretic-based relational language for specification, not being bound by the limitations of some or another predicate calculus variant.

A configurator can be used to find valid instances of a constrained object model. An object-oriented configurator like Ilog JConfigurator represents its catalog of types using an object model involving classes, attributes and relations between these classes. Class relations are inheritance or associations. Class to class associations are implemented using roles on objects on each opposite side. Each object role is implemented using a set variable. A complete search procedure enumerates all the model instances that are compatible with the constraints.

Fig. 9.4 illustrates a simplified constrained object model, here a meta-model for workflow activities, using a UML class diagram. UML diagrams mention some of the model constraints, most notably relation cardinalities. Figure 9.4, for instance, states that a message relates to at most one activity. There is, however, no possibility in the general case to graphically cover the whole range of constraints that may occur in an object model, thus advocating the use of an additional constraint language as Z.

9.1.5 From Configuration to Workflow/SWS Composition

Configuration emerges as an AI technique with applications in many different areas, where the problem can be formulated as the production of a finite instance of an object model subject to constraints. Reasoning about workflows falls into this category, because a workflow description is an instance of a given metamodel (as

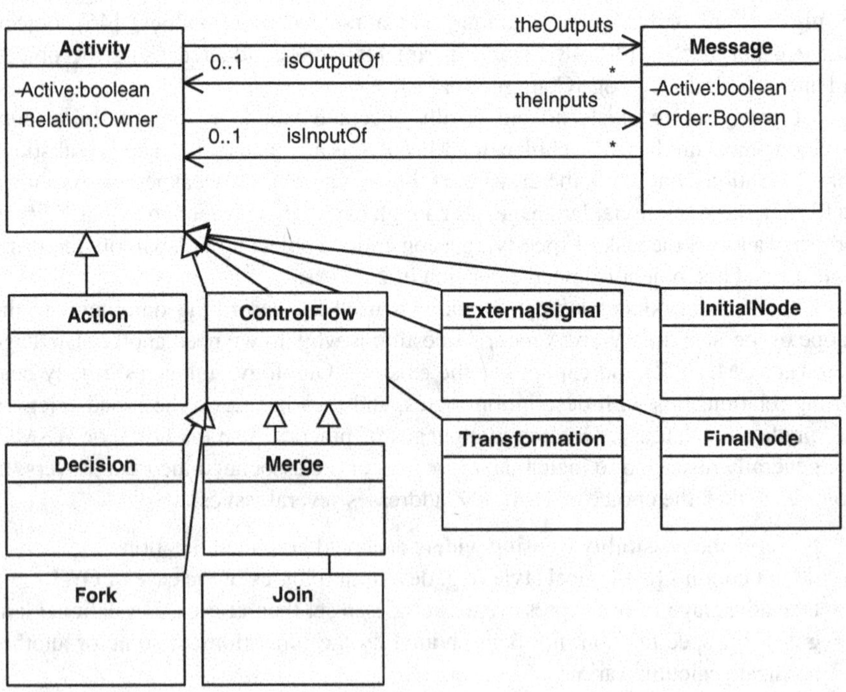

Fig. 9.4. Simplified meta-model for workflow activities

is the UML metamodel for activity diagrams [20]). Composing workflows is a configuration problem in that in so doing one must introduce an arbitrary number of previously non-existent transitions ("fork", "join", "split", "merge", "transformations", predefined user-interactions sequences), and interconnect input and output message pins provided they have compatible types.

An SWS composition system in our sense expects

- a list of potentially usable workflows
- the ontologies for the data types
- a goal to be satisfied by the result composition
- a list of the data input the end-user can provide.

In our approach, the simplest form of a composition request is defined as a single message, according to an appropriate/specific ontology, connected to the final node of the composite workflow (the objective). The inputs provided by the user are modelled as available external signals. A more elaborated language for expressing composition goals is presented in Section sec:corel allowing to place additional constraints on the requested composite SWS.

9.2 Composition in Case Study Scenarios

From the scenarios introduced in Chap. 6, only B and C involve composition.

9.2.1 Scenario B

Here, each supplier considered by the purchasing software agent may have a distinct choreography. We are now used to see such supplier sites behave as standard Internet sites, hence may feel that their behaviour is fairly comparable. The shopping-trolley metaphor is indeed a must in this area. There may exist differences though, in the way some interactions are handled. For instance, payment data may be asked for according to a given sequence on one site, or payment interaction may be kept internal or redirected to another specific web site, etc. In that case, the purchasing agent must adapt to the variety of choreographies of its suppliers so as to enter valid conversations with them. Generating such a valid conversation (i.e. by adapting one's orchestrations to a remote's choreography) can be viewed as a simple form of composition. Indeed, it may not be the case that the client software agent has enough knowledge to perform such computations, in which case external "composition" skills may be required.

9.2.2 Scenario C

This scenario involves semantic discovery and process/protocol mediation as in Scenario B for the first "shipper selection" phase. Then, in the second phase, that we will refer to as a "tracking" phase, the shipper Web Service and the company's tracking Web Service enter a complex interaction, based upon Rosetta net messages. It is realistic to imagine that both services obey to their own choreographies. Organising this interaction hence is not an easy task, which can be viewed as a first class composition problem. A realistic viewpoint over the resulting situation is the following: the coordinator process that actually executes is an orchestration involving both existing "tracking" software on the client side, and the shipper's tracking software on the other side. Such a coordination obviously requires the execution of various mediators, and the capacity to adapt distinct and complex choreographies on either side. This is a composition problem.

9.3 State of the Art

Automated workflow or SWS composition is a field of intense activity, with applications to at least two wide areas: Business Process Modelling and (Semantic) Web Services. Tentative techniques to address these problems are experimented using many formalisms and techniques, among others Situation calculus [32], Logic programming [44], Type matching [11, 10], coloured Petri nets [12], Linear logic [40], Problem-solving methods [4, 19, 49], AI Planning [9, 38], Markov decision processes [13] and constraint-based configuration [1, 2].

The current section attempts to present in greater detail the viewpoints and scientific options considered by the scientific community on this subject.

9.3.1 Essential "Design by Composition" Issues

Web Service design requires the description of a complex process in the presence of asynchronous (web based) communication , parallel execution of tasks or subservices, external events, arbitrary interruption points, exception handling, etc. In order to specify such a composite Web Service, it is necessary to define the chaining and parallelisation of activities (the workflow), to describe the dynamic production and transfer of data (the data flow), to define states (asynchronous systems may conditionally remain forever in a given state with no ongoing activity) to deal with explicit time for timeout events of activity duration, for instance.

Promoting of the reusability of services is an issue long studied in the field of Business Process Reengineering. Data flows must be adapted to accommodate distinct yet compatible specifications of input/output data. Equally, when Web Services are seen as asynchronous agents that are to be combined, their externally published behaviour (called their *choreography*) must be compatible in order to allow composition. Finally, in order to design a Web Service by combining others, it is necessary to know what to combine. Hence, there must exist semantically enriched databases of Web Services that describe their capabilities in the most abstract manner, and are queried according to practical goals.

Workflows and Workflow Patterns

A workflow is the chaining of elementary activities required to perform a task. Workflows are usually modelled using graph-related diagrams or structures, with/without support for a notion of state (as in Petri nets or UML state diagrams). Workflow editing and executing tools are numerous, either in the field of Business Process Management or more recently in the field of Web Service design. The properties of workflow systems differ in general, and their expressive power can be compared against the list of workflow patterns. The workflow patterns site proposes a comparison of Web Service composition languages and tools with respect to the 20 identified workflow patterns in [53]. One essential contribution of the workflow patterns has been to demonstrate that stateless workflow languages cannot support several important patterns, such as "milestone" or "interleaved parallel execution", for example. This advocates the use of Petri nets, for instance the Petri net extension YAWL [51], designed to explicitly support all of the 20 patterns, a strong requirement in SWS composition.

Data Flows, Data Creation and Deletion

Processes transport, transform, use, create or delete *data*. Data flows map onto the workflow by adding details about the kind of data that is being processed. Useful known extensions to Petri nets are "coloured" Petri nets [24], where structured data is referred to by a colour. Each token carries some piece of data. Tokens may appear or disappear as a result of firing transitions. Also, transitions may or may not be fired depending on the token(s) colour(s) and the valuation of their incoming arcs. The latest version of UML2 activity diagrams has taken the change to token-flow semantics.

States

States are essential in modelling workflows, and proved to be mandatory in order to implement all the workflow patterns. A process or Web Service may wait forever in a state, whereas transitions may be instantaneous (although most languages now have abandoned the instantaneous semantics for transitions in favour of the "Run To Completion" semantics where transitions, actions and events may last till their completion, as, e.g., in the UML semantics for state diagrams). However, there is a strict difference in the status of a "state" in Harel statecharts for instance[22], or in Petri net–based semantics. In the former, states have names and are first-class constructs. In Petri nets, the state is implicit, characterised by an a priori unknown number and locations of tokens. It is now well understood that state machines (as are UML2 Harel Statechart–based state diagrams) are not fully adapted to implement workflows, hence to reason about SWS composition.

Explicit Time

Explicit time is required in workflows for several reasons, like timeouts for instance. In order to compose workflows, it is necessary to account for such time information. Most workflows, however, can abstract time in favour of explicit, time unaware dependencies (sequence, split, join). Note that composite Web Service description must abandon the concept of a global time, since processes run on distant and non-synchronised machines.

Data Adaptation: Adapters and Bridges

Data adaptation is a key issue in workflow composition, since process/service optimal reuse may lead to services having compatible, yet non-identical corresponding data types. It is thus essential to mediate between data formats to ensure that Web Services can be composed.

Discovery: Capabilities and Goals

In order to compose Web Services, it is necessary to find candidates for composition. This issue is covered in detail in Chap. 8 about discovery. Web Services are advertised (roughly) by their programming interface in WSDL. Semantic Web Services are advertised by a formal description of their capability, using a language like WSML or OWL, for instance. Finding a candidate Web Service for composition (i.e. for solving a given, maybe intermediate, goal) amounts to finding a Web Service's capability which can provably be shown to address the goal. This issue is much more general than the one currently addressed by tools that simply exploit the WSDL information published by Web Services (e.g. DAML-S Matchmaker [37]) and, depending upon the language chosen for implementing goal and capability, ontologies may require the intervention of a reasoner.

9.3.2 Essential "Automatic Composition" Issues

In order to automatically compose a Web Service from others, it is necessary to reason about the logical properties of their descriptions. The chosen service capabilities must be adequate with respect to the target goal, and must also be compatible. Automated reasoning about capabilities and their compatibility remains as a challenging problem in the general case. Reasoning requires that the Web Service specifications are formulated in one or a combination of formal methods. A formal method requires: the following

- a formal language: syntax and semantics that allow formal specification,
- a proof system allowing formal reasoning.

A proof system often does not capture the entirety of the underlying language because of tractability[5] or decidability[6] issues. Even though in one sense or another, all formal methods are "logical", and they fall into several more specific categories,

[5] Tractability – some problem instances yield combinatorial explosion, the space search remains finite, but no answer can be expected in an acceptable time frame

[6] Decidability – the search space is infinite, and not finitely representable, no program can ever span it

depending on whether they are logic oriented (based upon an extension of predicate, modal or higher-order logic + predefined axioms), algebraic (based upon the definition of operations and equations over a set) or model based (allowing the reuse of predefined components, e.g. Petri nets).

Formal Language

In order to reason about data and processes, formalisms endowed with both syntax and semantics are required. Reasoning about workflows, for instance, disqualifies a language like BPEL[7] (which still remains a choice when execution must be performed) or other such business process flow representation languages since they are programming languages, and operate at the execution level, even though attempts exist to give them a logical foundation, at least to a restricted subset.

Reasoning about Time

If the formalism used to describe the Web Services involves time, then there must be support for reasoning about such a "time". Even though explicit (absolute) time is apparently not an issue, temporal relationships may occur. Many constraints involving time (e.g. precedence constraints) can be efficiently handled, while others render the problems intractable (e.g. "no overlap" constraints).

Reasoning About Actions and State Change

An inherent difficulty in workflows stems from the fact that transitions affect the world's state. Data (such as resources) may be created, deleted or modified, which must be accounted for by the formal language and reasoning system. Formalisms like linear logic, situation calculus or Petri nets account for this to a variable extent. As a consequence of the desirable modular expression of actions and their effects, a problem emerges called the "frame problem": how does the world state behave when a transition occurs that solely mentions its immediate effects (for instance, if an action describes its effects on an object, it normally says nothing about the rest of the world, which normally, but not always, remains unaffected). The problem has attracted the attention of many researchers, and generally requires some form of non-monotonic reasoning.[8] A typical solution to the frame problem is to consider that what is unmentioned remains unchanged, if compatible with the theory axioms.

---

[7] `http://www-128.ibm.com/developerworks/library/specification/ws-bpel/`

[8] A form of reasoning is *non-monotonic* when some consequences of a theory need to be withdrawn if the theory is incrementally updated, this is what happens when default or preferred inferences are performed

Reasoning About Objects and Concepts

As Web Services are to be semantically advertised, their description will be made using various ontologies. Matching a goal against the capabilities of advertised Web Services requires reasoning about the data described by the used ontologies. In the most general case, the level of reasoning required is that of first-order theorem proving.

Reasoning About Graphs

A workflow is a graph. In order to compose workflows, it is necessary to compose graphs. The work in [12] addresses this in a very pertinent way, even though it provides no hints whatsoever as to how to "automatically" do this in the presence of data flows.

Proof Procedure or Reasoning Tool

The language chosen to model the capabilities of Web Services, as well as the goals used to query them, must come along equipped with a reasoning tool if one ever wants to automate the composition process.

9.3.3 Formal Foundations to Web Service Composition

This section lists known scientific approaches to Semantic Web Service composition. Each subsection briefly presents the folllowing:

- core features and expressive power of the formalism
- tools that implement it, either in isolation or in combination (e.g. as a subset of the language)
- experiments conducted in the field of automatic Web Service composition

and concludes with a tentative critical analysis of the pros and cons of using the technology (availability of reasoners, complexity, expressive power, etc.).

The present subsection attempts to produce an exhaustive list of the logical formalisms considered or used for SWS composition in recent publications. To give quick hints of the broad category to which each formalism or technique belongs, we attach to the names a category among First-Order Logic, Modal Logic, Algebras, Higher order calculus, Graphical/Semi formal methods, Meta models, Constraint programming.

Situation Calculus (First-Order Logic)

In the Situation Calculus (SC) [41], originally proposed by McCarthy and Hayes in 1969, first-order logic is applied to the description of world states (or situations) and side effect actions. Situation Calculus allows one to reason about valid moves, reachable situations and raises issues of strong concern in AI planning such as the frame problem. The essential idea in Situation Calculus is to replace predicates by *fluents*, predicates indexed with situations. SC introduces special predicates like “poss” (can an action be performed in a given situation?), “holds” (is a formula true in a given situation) and “do” (perform an action provided its preconditions are met). Preconditions are naturally stated using “poss”. Standard Situation Calculus does not allow reasoning about explicit time, nor about concurrent or continuous actions. It is very well suited, however, to deal with change.

Golog [29] is a high-level specification language built on top of the situation calculus, with knowledge and sensing actions. Golog introduces a number of extra logical constructs for assembling primitive actions, defined in SC, so as to form complex actions that may be viewed as programs. These constructs are familiar to process designers: sequences, tests, non-deterministic choice of actions or arguments, non-deterministic iteration, conditional and loops. Existing Golog interpreters are Prolog based. In [32], the Golog extension ConGolog (“concurrent” Golog) is shown to be suitable for Web Service composition with two extensions. To circumvent the fact that the “sequence” Golog construct is static, and allows for no insertion of actions, [32] introduces an extraneous “Order” construct, which allows the dynamic insertion of an action so as to fulfil precondition conditions. The authors warn that the new construct potentially introduces important combinatorial overhead and should be used with care. However, they claim their translation introduces no extra overhead with respect to the original problem. The approach exhibits significant customisation and reasoning possibilities.

Process Specification Language (First-Order Logic)

Among applications of first-order logic relevant to Web Service composition, we must cite the Process Specification Language (PSL) [42]. PSL also builds on situation calculus and defines a neutral representation for manufacturing processes. Process data is used throughout the life cycle of a product, from early indications of manufacturing process flagged during design, to process planning, validation, production scheduling and control. In addition, the notion of process also underlies the entire manufacturing cycle, coordinating the workflow within engineering and shop floor manufacturing. The PSL language is formally based upon the Knowledge Interchange Format, used to formally define ontologies of processes. PSL-Core is based upon first-order theory, with four basic classes (Object, Activity, Activity Occurrence and Timepoint) and four basic relations (Participates-in, Before, BeginOf, and Endof). Objects can come into existence (e.g. be created) and go out of existence, e.g. be “used up” as a resource) at certain points in time. PSL provides explicit time, and the full language incorporates Situation Calculus. PSL statements being logical, any process specification in this language can be logically exploited, manually or using a theorem prover. Although no scientific account has yet been provided on using PSL in the scope of Web Service modelling, the language offers the potential to design Web Services by composition, or automate the process.

Description Logic (First-Order Logic)

Description logics are knowledge representation languages tailored for expressing knowledge about concepts and concept hierarchies, in a sub language of predicate calculus. Description logics have had strong connections with the Semantic Web since its inception, as they provide the formal foundations to ontologies and ontology reasoning, as implemented in OIL and later OWL. Description logics can be viewed as allowing a form of object-oriented knowledge representation while benefiting from the soundness of a logical formalism. The composition of Web Services described via OWL ontologies hence depend upon various forms of description logic–based ontology reasoning. Description logics are irrelevant to Web Service composition beyond the fact that they may be chosen to represent goal/capability ontologies. DL formalisms build a common foundation for frame-based systems, semantic networks and KL-ONE-like languages, object-oriented representations, semantic data models and type systems. Their basic building blocks are concepts, roles (binary relations) and individuals. Each description logic language defines constructs (intersection, union, role quantification, etc.) used to define new concepts and roles. The main reasoning tasks in DLs are classification, satisfiability, subsumption and instance checking. A whole family of knowledge representation systems have been built using these languages and for most of them complexity results for the main reasoning tasks are known. Constraint-based configurators [26], as used in the area of SWS composition, also have strong connections with description logics.

Frame Logic (First-Order Logic)

Frame logics [27] provide a formalism for object-oriented logic programs. A formal account for object identity, inheritance and methods vs functions is achieved in the language, which is hence suitable not only for various object-oriented database reasoning schemes on the one hand, but also for ontology reasoning in the context of the Semantic Web. F-Logic allows for the description of method and function signatures. The semantics of Frame logic rely upon skolemisation and Herbrand structures, with an extension to account for object equality. Reasoning about F-Logic programs is possible using Prolog-based approaches as in the program Flora-2.[9]

Transaction Logic (First-Order Logic)

Transaction logic (TR) accounts in a declarative fashion for logical theory update, with applications to databases and logic programs [6]. Transaction logic allows one to specify and execute procedures that permanently update a logic program. The Horn version of TR supports SLD resolution and can be easily automated. What really differs with respect to other logics for change is that transactions are natively executable as logic programs. In combination with F-Logic, TR lets the user formalise the behaviour of methods that change the internal state of objects. This combination is implemented in the Flora-2 system. No research report to date accounts

[9] `http://flora.sourceforge.net/`

for Web Service composition using F-logic + Transaction logic. A difficulty with using this combination of languages stems from the necessity to fit the descriptions within a Horn subset of logic, which often requires expert intervention.

Logic Programming (First-Order Logic – Horn Clauses)

The work in [44] illustrates the possibility of using Prolog to interactively generate Web Service compositions based on their semantic descriptions (originally in WSDL). This approach emphasises the possibility of viewing Web Service composition as a recursive process, and advocates the use of well-known AI techniques in the field. Specifically, the possibility offered by Prolog for an end-user to interactively control a composition program is interesting. Such a system can efficiently exploit semantic conditions, and can also explore an entire combinatorial search space. The authors of [44] claim their system gives a straightforward account of WSDL specifications. The prototype implementation performs on the basis of previously discovered Web Services, hence does not contribute to the discovery process. The limitations of using (standard) logic programming are as usual: because of the Horn clause (rule like) subllanguage, direct support for some logical expressions turns out to be difficult, such as those involving disjunctions or existential quantifiers. Such a system can, however, non-deterministically explore the complete search space of possible compositions and account for many constraints. The work in [11, 10] uses recursive algorithms in a forward/backward chaining spirit closely related to logic programming.

Type Matching (Type Systems)

The cost of Web Service discovery queries, together with expected non-availability of advertised choreographies and capabilities offering exact matches, induces a promising way of composing Web Services on the basis of partial matches of their input/output data types. Type description/reasoning itself can be performed in one or another language, from description logics to "mixins"-based languages. In that case composition algorithms themselves range from ad hoc recursive procedures to standard logic programming forward/backward chaining. Type matching–based composition hence deserves a separate section in this review. The work in [11, 10] details an algorithm for Web Service composition with partial type matches, and shows that such an approach significantly improves the number of successful compositions. Interestingly enough, the composition algorithm interleaves the composition task with Semantic Web Service discovery, which addresses two practical problems:

1. The discovery process should be as efficient as possible, and type inference can in many cases be made very efficient (for that purpose, [11] uses numeral representations of types).
2. The number of discovery queries should be limited as much as possible, due to the significant overload induced by complex remote queries performed on potentially huge databases.

Partial type-matching approaches to Web Service composition reinforce the intuition that an essential issue regarding this problem has to do with the type of data exchanged between peer services (this is also a leading intuition in problem-solving methods). Partially matching inputs/outputs can be adapted, reorganised, grouped together, so as to build a working system from disparate and literally incompatible elements. In that sense, reasoning about type compatibility appears as a central requirement to Web Service composition, prior to more advanced forms of reasoning.

Petri Nets (First-Order Logic – Model Based)

Petri nets provide distributed operational semantics for processes, and unlike most processes algebraic options offer techniques for quantitative analysis. Petri nets are useful for their computational semantics, ease of implementation and ability to address both offline analysis tasks such as Web service composition and online execution tasks such as deadlock determination, resource satisfaction and quantitative performance analysis. Compared to other stateless workflow languages, Petri nets allow for modelling states (an essential issue concerning two important workflow patterns as advocated in [53]). Also, compared with other formalisms (e.g. Situation Calculus), Petri nets offer an interesting account of the frame problem. Mapping to and from Petri net representations and process languages is often acknowledged. However, [50] argues that the usability of Petri nets exceeds that of (current) process languages because the graph structure of workflows is more easily rendered with this formalism than using algebraic descriptions which are linear or tree structured by construction. Petri nets are suitable for modelling, analysing and prototyping dynamic systems with parallel activities, so distributed planning lends itself very well to this approach. The main contribution we expect from Petri nets is their ability to improve the representation of complex services and to allow their dynamic coordination and execution. The Petri net model mainly offers the following advantages:

- natural and graphical expression of the synchronisation of parallel activities
- clear decomposition of processing (transitions) and sharing data (places)
- scheduling of actions (causal and temporal relationships) of services
- dynamic allocation of tasks
- qualitative and quantitative analysis of Petri net models.

Useful Petri nets in the field of Web Service description and composition are hierarchical high-level Petri nets: the tokens are "coloured", which means that they carry data (the net hence offers both the data flow and the work flow views), they account for time, and they are hierarchical: a transition can represent an entire (sub) Petri net. A generalisation known as Recursive Coloured Petri nets could be found in [43, 31]. The usefulness of high-level Petri nets in the field of Web Service composition is assessed by several recent results. Reference [57] practically illustrates how coloured Petri nets can be generated from BPEL specifications, which allows detailed accounting for the compatibility of the choreographies. Reference [12] details the viewpoints one can have when composing Petri net–based choreographies and orchestrations, and the level of control that can be achieved.

Petri nets easily support variants without losing their elegance. For instance, [51] presents an extension to high-level Petri nets called YAWL that implements in a straightforward way all of the workflow patterns described in [53]. Considering the expressivity of YAWL together with the interesting Petri net-based contribution to Web Service composition in [12], Petri nets and their extensions clearly are a potentially major option for Web Service composition.

Temporal Logic of Actions (Modal Logic)

The temporal logic of actions (TLA) is a logical formalism for specifying and reasoning about concurrent systems. Systems and their properties are represented in the same logic, so the assertion that a system meets its specification and the assertion that one system implements another are both expressed by logical implication. TLA+ is presented in [28]. This extension to TLA offers a logic with sets and structures, plus action and temporal operators. The logic does not allow the modelling of explicit time. TLA+ was shown to be useful in formally specifying a Web Service protocol called the Web Service transaction protocol [25]. TLA+ is suitable for model checking, for instance, when using the TLC program. Dealing with the composition of Web Services when specified in TLA+ has not been proposed to date, as far as we know.

Modal Action Logic (Modal Logic)

Multi agent systems [56] share a lot in common with the Semantic Web. Formal agent conversation languages may be applied in some cases to workflow composition problems because they also deal with protocols. The full interaction of several agents can be perceived as a complex choreography in a SWS sense. As an example of the proximity of the two fields, in [3] Web Services are viewed as actions, either simple or complex, characterised by preconditions and effects. Also, interaction is interpreted as the effect of communicative action execution, so that it can be reasoned about. The formal language used is a modal action and belief logic DyLog. DyLog is well suited for reasoning about world change and actions, and being based upon logic programming the reasoning possibilities offered by the language are real. However, the combination of modal operators and logic programming makes it a tool for experts, which could be a challenging issue to SWS composition.

Process Algebras, CCS and Pi Calculus (Algebras)

The use of process algebraic languages (like CCS [33] or Pi Calculus, but also CSP (Constraint Satisfaction Problem) and LOTOS) which originate from the rich field of concurrent programming and systems has been advocated for Web Service composition. The constructs of several process languages for the Semantic Web (XLANG, WSCI) have been "a posteriori" formally grounded on process algebras. The work in [8] details a possible formal account of WSCI using CCS, and points to accurate bibliography in the field. Model checking methods can be used to automate or assist the composition/validation process.

CCS [33] is the simplest process algebra. A CCS grammar is defined using "processes", "channels", data items and sequences of values. A process can be prefixed by an atomic action, or composed with other processes, either in parallel'||' or by means of the choice'+' operator. Atomic actions are either the internal (or silent) action "T", input actions (a message "x" is received from a channel "a") or output actions (a message is sent through a channel). The operational semantics of CCS is defined by a transition system where standard rules model parallel and choice operators, and synchronisation is produced by the parallel composition of two complementary actions.

In spite of its simplicity, CCS presents a high expressive power, capable of capturing WSCI as illustrated in [8]. Ad hoc and more complex process algebras than CCS can be designed to formally define core subsets of process languages. The work in [54] illustrates this, giving precise formal description of the semantics of a core subset of BPEL. The originality of the process algebra in [54] is that besides standard process algebra constructs (e.g. choice, sequence) it provides notations for iterative cycles and variable assignment (that stem from standard programming languages).

The *Cashew* [36] language offers interesting compositionality properties, together with explicit support for several workflow patterns, as well as external vs internal choice.

Linear Logic (Higher-Order Calculus)

Linear logic (LL) [18] is an extension of classical logic to model a notion of evolving state by keeping track of resources. Other resource aware logics were developed before, but LL has attracted a lot of research attention. Specifically, LL has well defined semantics and provers are available. The paper [40] proposes an application of LL to Web Service composition. The authors claim that the WSDL presentation of a Web Service can be automatically translated to a set of LL axioms. Then, they use a prover for the multiplicative propositional fragment of LL to infer the composition of a Web Service. The target Web Service is described as a sequent in LL, to be proved by the proof system. The context is a restrictive case (the "core" Web Service is known, but not some of its value added sub services). Being complete, the system can generate all possible compositions. Each composition, available as a sequent proof, can be translated to a BPEL workflow. This original approach still faces several limitations, acknowledged by the authors themselves ("the full automation of the composition process is a difficult problem"), like the fact that the logic used is "only" propositional.

Coordination Languages (Higher-Order Calculus)

Coordination languages are an active field of research in the scope of multi agent systems. Mobile agents bear some resemblance with Web Services. They communicate through protocols and require a form of discovery mechanism. The language KLAIM (Kernel Language for Agent Interaction and Mobility) is a higher order calculus for mobile processes, inspired by the LINDA model, which relies on the concept of tuple space (the tuple space is a common store used to synchronise data and processes) and O'Klaim (Object-Oriented Klaim) [5] is a linguistic extension of Klaim with object-oriented features. One issue of potential significance with respect to Web Service discovery/composition is the fact that the language models mobile "mixins". A *mixin* is a form of dynamically resolved subclass. The essence of a mixin is to describe a fraction of a programming interface, which can be treated as a type in its own right. Mixins can be statically simulated by multiply inherited interfaces in UML/Java/C++, for instance. The fact that a Web Service offers some type of data or functionality in its capability could be achieved by the object representing that capability being an instance of a given mixin, no matter what its actual type is. Mixins appear as a useful concept in relation to data adaptation or mediation: they describe the fact that a data structure of a "don't care" type holds a specific data item (for instance, a "date" or a "price").

Problem-Solving Methods (Meta-Model)

The problem-solving method (PSM) [4] describes the foundational ontologies for the UPML language [15]. As such, PSM is not a formal system, but forms a model of processes that can be used to compose semantically described Web Services. The work in [19] describes a possible framework for using PSM in that objective. The essence of PSM is to provide a distinction between methods and their abstraction called tasks, and to focus on the inputs and outputs of tasks and methods, described using ontology-based pre/post conditions. This approach treats workflows as secondary relative to the logical conditions necessarily matched by viable processes. For instance, the preconditions satisfied by composite tasks must match the preconditions of their starting subtasks. This viewpoint is essential to Web Service composition, where determining whether Web Services are I/O compatible is necessary even before testing that their choreographies are compatible.

The intuitions underlying the PSM model can be related with practical experimentations conducted with the Ariadne mediator system, as documented in [49]. This work shows how input/output requirements for Web Services can be exploited using a simple forward chaining algorithm, according to the following idea: the user feeds in the system with a description of the data they can provide, plus a description of the data they request from the (dynamically composed) system. The composition algorithm recursively loops adding Web Services that produce some of the desired information. Each new required input not currently available is further treated as desired. The system stops when a set of Web Services has been constructed that produces the expected output from the available initial input. Although [49] does not account for the compatibility of Web Services choreographies, the proposed working system validates several important intuitions regarding Web Service composition.

(AI) Planning (FOL, Constraint Programming)

Beyond complex compatibility issues, Web Service composition can obviously be viewed as a planning problem: we look for a plan of actions (i.e. Web Services) which guarantees that the target objective will be reached. This particular view of the composition problem is covered by the work in [9], where state descriptions are ambiguous and operator definitions are incomplete. The same viewpoint is chosen in the library for interactive Web Service composition SWORD [39] where the plans are generated using a rule-based forward chaining algorithm.

Hierarchical Task Network (HTN) planning is an AI planning methodology that creates plans by task decomposition. This is a process in which the planning system decomposes tasks into smaller and smaller subtasks, until primitive tasks are found that can be performed directly. SHOP2 is a domain-independent HTN planning system. An application of Shop2/BPEL to Web Service composition is presented in [45] and [55].

SAT (Satisfiability Problem)- based planning is largely studied, because of the possibility to exploit efficient heuristics and cuts (as, e.g., in Graphplan), and also thanks to recent improvements in SAT solving alone. The system Blackbox uses Graphplan as a front-end to the most efficient SAT solver to date. Modern planners read their input in (a subset of) the "Planning Domain Definition Language" (PDDL), a language for describing planning problems. PDDL supports conditional effects, dynamic universes (object creation and destruction), universal quantification and domain axioms over stratified theories, but limited support to object oriented constructs beyond simple types. Actions are defined not only in terms of their preconditions and effects, but also by their expansion: possible subactions that can be used to implement the action itself. PDDL also allows the statement of goals as function free first-order predicate logic statements. Although translating arbitrary PDDL planning descriptions to SAT may yield significant formula expansion, SAT-based planning deserves some interest if Web Service composition is to be performed using constraint programming techniques.

Non-linear Discrete Optimisation (Constraint Programming)

An original viewpoint over Web Service composition is advocated in [17] where the composition problem is viewed as a non-linear discrete optimisation problem, called Activity Resource Assignment problem (ARA), in the presence of an optimisation criterion. The requester for a composite Web Service expects to maximise their utility. The model involves activities, resources, activity constraints (temporal and/or preferences) and relationships. Despite the fact that the given problem is NP-complete, the authors claim that the structure inherent to the problem renders the computations easier. It also does not seem to be possible by this method to address first-level logic issues, like the dynamic creation of data. Nevertheless, this appears as an interesting, constraint programming–based contribution to the composition problem.

Other approaches explicitly referring to constraint satisfaction, to some extent related to constraint-based configuration are advocated in [16, 48]. These approaches clearly influenced our own proposal, presented further in the chapter.

Configuration (Constraint Programming)

As presented earlier, configuration is an evolution of constraint programming dealing with constrained object models. Using configuration was proved useful to composing workflows in [1]. The present chapter will enter into greater detail about the possibilities offered by this kind of techniques.

9.4 A Language for Choreography and Orchestration

We choose a comprehensive subset of UML2AD[10] as a language for expressing choreographies and orchestrations. This choice is a pragmatic compromise meant to ensure sufficient coverage of workflow patterns [53] and business usage compliance. This decision is also backed by several significant moves made by the Business Process Modelling community recently, including the merger of BPMI and OMG.

Among other workflow languages exists YAWL [52], certainly the best choice with respect to workflow pattern coverage, but still lacking widespread editor support. YAWL diagrams also end up not being easily readable to untrained eyes which introduces an extra difficulty: users would have to learn YAWL in addition to what they already know. YAWL authors themselves acknowledge the fact that UML2AD, although with some ambiguities, provides good support for all workflow patterns.

We are aware of a number of difficulties raised by ambiguities in the UML2 specifications. The chosen subset solves these issues both at the denotational level and at the operational level.

At the denotational level, we are using a subset of the Z language [47] to document the diagram restrictions that we have chosen to enforce. Although these restrictions do not impair expressiveness, they significantly enhance the rigour of the associated diagrams. Z allows for a fully formal and unquestionable specification of metamodel constraints which replaces equivalent – but less readable – OCL statements.

9.4.1 Token-Flow Semantics: Introduction

UML2 Activity Diagrams being built on token-flow semantics, we will give here its main principles[11] to help the reader understand the following sections. Diagrams are composed of nodes and edges. Upon execution, an information going through an edge (we will say "traversal" of an edge) is called a "token", and multiple tokens can traverse the same edge at different times. When a token is removed, we will say it is "consumed" (most often by a node, but some constructs allow to consume tokens in

---

[10] The UML documentation is available at `http://www.uml.org/`, and more specifically at `http://www.omg.org/technology/documents/modeling\_spec\_catalog.htm\#UML`

[11] Further explanations can be found in the UML2AD specification

an entire region). Tokens which do not contain any data are called "control" tokens. The arrival of tokens in a node fires its execution depending on the node type (some will require all incoming edges to receive tokens while others start when at least one incoming edge receives a token). This formalism is very natural in the sense that a user can easily simulate the execution by tracking creations and traversals of tokens in the diagram.

9.4.2 The UML2AD Subset as a Constrained Abstract Model

This section describes the precise UML2AD subset used in both choreography and orchestration. This description is presented using a subset of the UML metamodel, involving class diagrams as usual to introduce the concepts. The specification below only slightly differs from the corresponding subset of the official UML specification [21]. It restricts it in some places, and introduces a limited number of extra classes.

In order to produce an unquestionable specification, we have chosen not to use the UML constraint language OCL (as in [1]), but instead a fragment of the Z language, as shown in [2, 23]. This offers several advantages:

- The limitations brought by the exclusive use of the dotted notation in OCL are overcome using Z, a language with extremely rich expressiveness.
- All workflow well formedness rules can be stated unambiguously.
- The constraints as listed in Z receive a direct translation to configuration rules in ILOG JConfigurator.
- Z is extensible: it allows the declaration of user defined operators that complement the syntax. We use this feature to introduce the largely accepted dotted notation. As often as required and possible, Javascript or OCL like dotted statements will be used.

Each diagram introduces a number of classes, their relations, and attributes. Together with the diagram are the following points:

- Classes – the formal declaration of diagram classes.
- Attributes – the formal declaration of attributes as Z functions.
- Relations and roles: the formal declaration of relations (as Z relations) and roles as Z functions.
- Semantics – the operational semantics of the workflow constructs, which impact the ASM (Abstract State Machines) translation but are not presented other than textually here.
- Constraints – the structural (well-formedness) constraints. They are presented as Z axioms using the previously declared classes and relations, preceded by a textual version of the constraint.

Before entering the metalanguage description, we present the logical constructs used for the Z specification. We use Z in the sole purpose of formulating the object model constraints, which complements the UML class diagrams. Extra definitions required to properly type check the document can be kept invisible because they are implicit from the class diagrams. These definitions merely duplicate the class, relation and multiplicity declarations, as well as any constraint made explicit or implicit in the UML diagrams.

We are using a specific prelude file[12] which defines an enumerated type called *UNIVERSE* (the set of all objects) and three dereferencing operators, which can be used for the statement of linear dereferencing chains, as is common in languages like JavaScript or UML's OCL. Dereferencing a role or attribute on a single object occurs as a ".". Dereferencing a set to obtain a set occurs as a " $\rightarrow$". Dereferencing a set to obtain a bag occurs as a "$\leadsto$". Using these definitions, roles in the standard sense (the opposite viewpoints of a binary relation) as well as relations can be dereferenced. Apart from this, all possible Z constructs can be used to formulate model constraints, among which: $|$ denotes a restriction on the domain of the variables the constraint applies to, $\bullet$ denotes the core of the constraint, applying to the domain defined in the head.

Activity Groups

The class diagram for activity groups is presented in Fig. 9.5.

Semantics

- *Groups* have no special semantics. They just enable grouping together a part of an activity. Web Service choreographies can be represented as a group.
- *InterruptibleRegions* are used to model external choices, as required in the shipper choreography example. The operational semantics of this construct are that

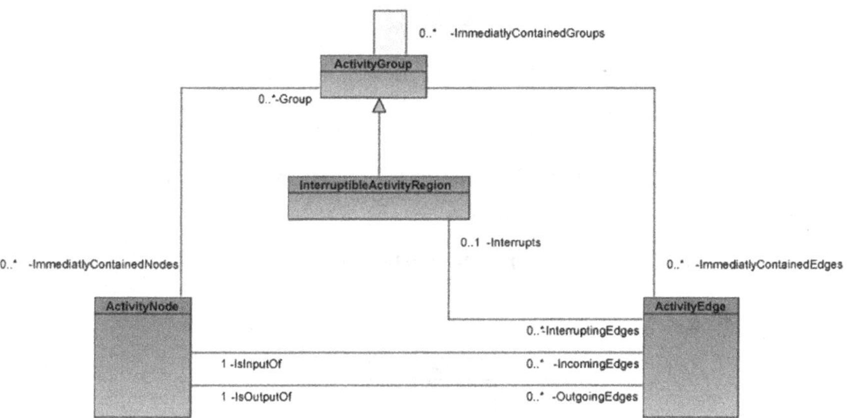

Fig. 9.5. Overview – activity groups

[12] The prelude file "umzprelude.tex" can be obtained at `http://www.esil.univ-mrs.fr/~henocque/umz/umzprelude.tex`

whenever a token traverses an interrupting edge (an edge pointed by the "interrupts" relation), all other tokens of the region are consumed.

Constraints

- InterruptibleRegions: Interrupting edges have source in the region and target outside the region

$$\forall x : ActivityEdge; y : InterruptibleActivityRegion \mid y = x.interrupts \bullet \\ x.isOutputOf.nodeGroup = y \wedge \\ x.isInputOf.nodeGroup \neq y$$

Activity Nodes and Edges

The class diagrams for activity nodes and edges are presented in Figs. 9.6 and 9.7. The operational semantics of object and control flows are described in the UML as "traverse-to-completion" semantics. The aim of these semantics is to allow workflow not to enter undue self-blocking states, which could be caused, for instance, by tokens mistakenly sent to an alternative outgoing path, and thus missing for a synchronisation to occur via an other outgoing path.

The currently presented subset of UML2AD diagrams overcomes most difficulties by disallowing random alternative routes, outgoing actions. In other words, when a token is produced by an action, it is presented to an output pin that has no more than one edge connected.

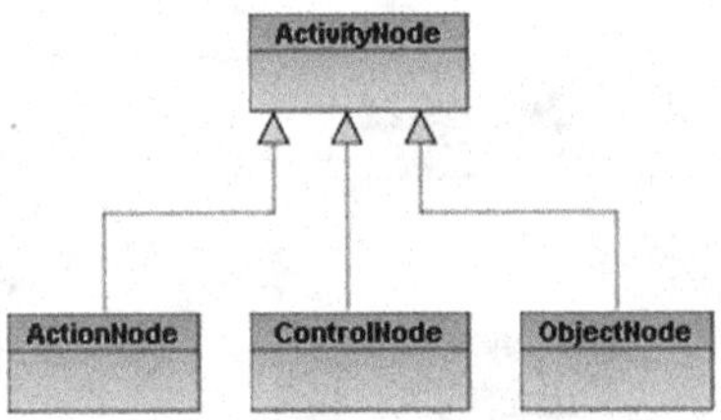

Fig. 9.6. Activity nodes

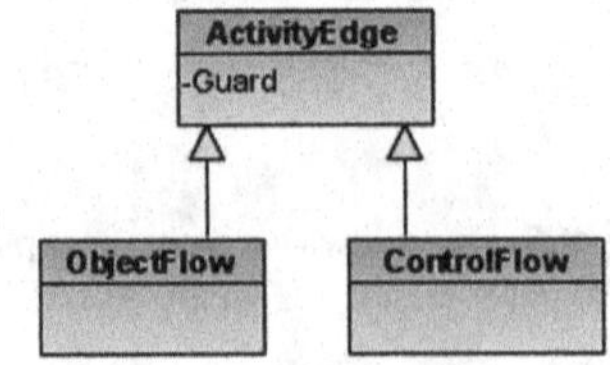

Fig. 9.7. Activity edges

- Object Flows – carry data tokens.
- Control Flows – carry control tokens.
- Guards – conditions expressing which decision node's outgoing edge will receive a token.

Constraints

- Only edges outgoing from a decision node can have a guard. Decision nodes are visually and formally presented with the other control nodes later in the document in Fig. 9.8:

$$\forall e : ActivityEdge;\ g : Guard \mid g = e.guard \bullet e.isOutputOf \in DecisionNode$$

- Only one edge outgoing from the same decision node can have an else condition as the guard:

$$\forall n : DecisionNode \bullet \\ \#\{e : ActivityEdge \mid n = isOutputOf(e) \wedge e.guard = else\} = 1$$

- Control flows may not have object nodes at either end:

$$\forall e : ControlFlow \bullet \\ e.isInputOf \notin ObjectNode \wedge e.isOutputOf \notin ObjectNode$$

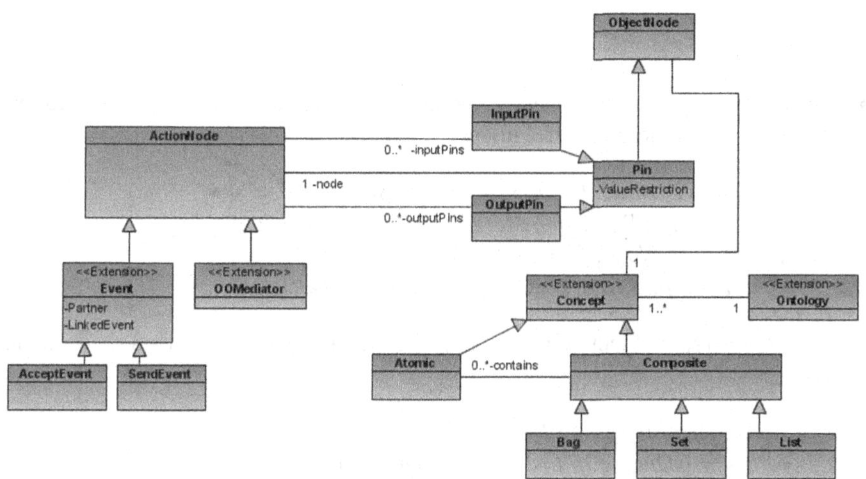

Fig. 9.8. Control nodes

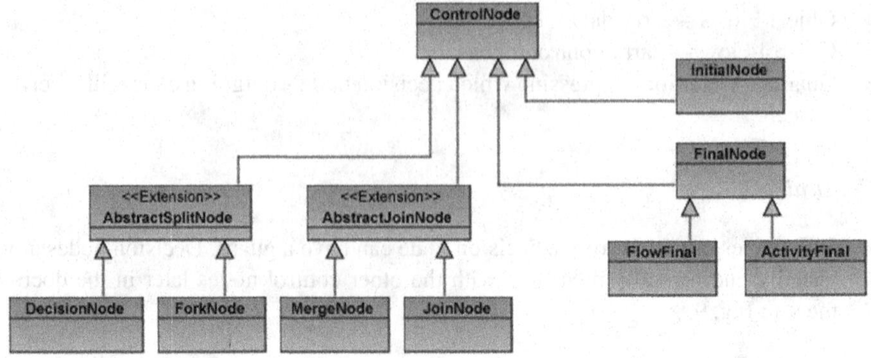

Fig. 9.9. Action nodes and object nodes

Action and Object Nodes

The class diagram for action and object nodes is presented in Fig. 9.9. Action nodes denotes that a local action is realised at this node. Pins are used to receive and send data tokens. The inputs are synchronised (all incoming edges and input pins have to carry a token for the action to start).

OOMediator does not belong to the original UML2AD specification. They are introduced here as a special sub-type of ActionNode having no side effects: such mediators are required to transform data.

AbstractEvent does not either occur in the original UML2AD specification. Being non-executable, an AbstractEvent has to be specialised in a concrete model.

Constraints

- ObjectFlow connects exclusively an output pin to an input pin (with the exception of decision and merge control nodes).

$$\begin{aligned}
&\forall n : ActivityNode; f : ObjectFlow \mid f.isOutputOf = n \bullet \\
&\quad n \in InputPin \vee n \in MergeNode \vee n \in DecisionNode \\
&\forall n : ActivityNode; f : ObjectFlow \mid f.isInputOf = n \bullet \\
&\quad n \in InputPin \vee n \in MergeNode \vee n \in DecisionNode
\end{aligned}$$

- The downstream object node type must be the same of the upstream object node type

$$\begin{aligned}
&\forall f : ObjectFlow; s, t : Pin \mid \\
&\quad s = isOutputOf(f) \wedge t = isInputOf(f) \bullet \\
&\qquad s.ontology = t.ontology
\end{aligned}$$

- AcceptEvent instances have no incoming activity edge

$$\forall e : ActivityEdge \bullet e.isInputOf \notin AcceptEvent$$

- SendEvent instances have no outgoing activity edge

$$\forall e : ActivityEdge \bullet e.isOutputOf \notin SendEvent$$

Control Nodes

Semantics

- AbstractSplit – this is an additional construct from UML2AD specification. Not executable: any AbstractSplit has to be specialised
- AbstractJoin – this is an additional construct from UML2AD specification. Not executable: any AbstractJoin has to be specialised
- MergeNode – any token offered on any incoming edge is offered to the outgoing edge
- DecisionNode – each token arriving can traverse to only one outgoing edge
- ForkNode – incoming token duplicated to outgoing edges
- JoinNode – when all incoming edges have tokens, one is created on outgoing edge. Only one incoming edge can be an object flow. Outgoing edge can be an object flow only if there is an object flow among the incoming edges (in this case, the incoming data token is sent to the outgoing edge)
- Flow Final – consumes one token
- Activity Final – all tokens in the activity are consumed

Constraints

- AbstractSplit – 1 incoming edge only

$$\forall x : AbstractSplit \bullet \#(x.incomingEdges) = 1$$

- AbstractJoin – 1 outgoing edge only

$$\forall x : AbstractJoin \bullet \#(x.outgoingEdges) = 1$$

- JoinNode – Only one incoming edge is an object flow

$$\forall x : JoinNode \bullet \#((x.incomingEdges) \cap ObjectFlow) \leq 1$$

- InitialNode – no incoming edge

$$\forall x : InitialNode \bullet x.incomingEdges = \varnothing$$

- FinalNode – no outgoing edge

$$\forall x : FinalNode \bullet x.outgoingEdges = \varnothing$$

- DecisionNode – the edges coming into and out of a decision node must be either all object flows or all control flows
- MergeNode – the edges coming into and out of a decision node must be either all object flows or all control flows

$$\begin{aligned}&\forall x : ActivityNode \mid x \in DecisionNode \cup MergeNode \bullet\\&\quad (x.incomingEdges \cup x.outgoingEdges) \subset ObjectFlow \vee\\&\quad (x.incomingEdges \cup x.outgoingEdges) \subset ControlFlow\end{aligned}$$

Graphical Representation

The graphical representation of all the workflow constructs presented so far is sketched in Fig. 9.10. These graphics mostly respect the UML2 superstructure specification.[13]

Usage and Tool Support

Concluding this section, we outline the already existing tool support for UML2 activity diagrams allowing it to be used as the user language for behaviour interface descriptions. A facility for editing, browsing and maintaining choreography and orchestration descriptions as UML2 Activity Diagrams is intended to be integrated within Web Service editing and management environments. In order to allow usage of existing infrastructure for managing choreography and orchestration descriptions as UML2 activity diagrams, these can be stored as WSML ontologies. Hence, UML2 descriptions can be stored, retrieved and interchanged by ontology infrastructures.

9.5 Composing Workflows Using Configuration

As shown in [1, 2], SWS choreographies can be efficiently composed using the subset of UML2AD presented previously. Rather than explaining the whole process in detail (the reader can refer to those papers for further explanations), we will outline here its main principles through the "producer–shipper" example.

A configuration tool uses a library of available elements to construct a valid instance of the constrained object model it is based on. The configuration-based composer is launched with the following input:

- output (objective and root object for configuration) of the composed workflow: a confirmation of a product being purchased and shipped
- inputs the user can provide to the system: a product name, a shipping destination, acceptance and rejection upon receiving offers
- a library of available mediators
- a library of available SWSs, among which we find the shipper (its capability is presented in Fig. 9.1 and its choreography is presented in Fig. 9.2) and the producer (its capability and choreography are similar to the shipper's capability and choreography modulo the ontology of inputs/outputs)

The composer uses all those elements to create a workflow composed of the needed choreographies adding during the process all necessary elements in order to obtain a valid workflow. This composed workflow instance follows the presented abstract model, with the following additions:

13 `http://www.uml.org/`

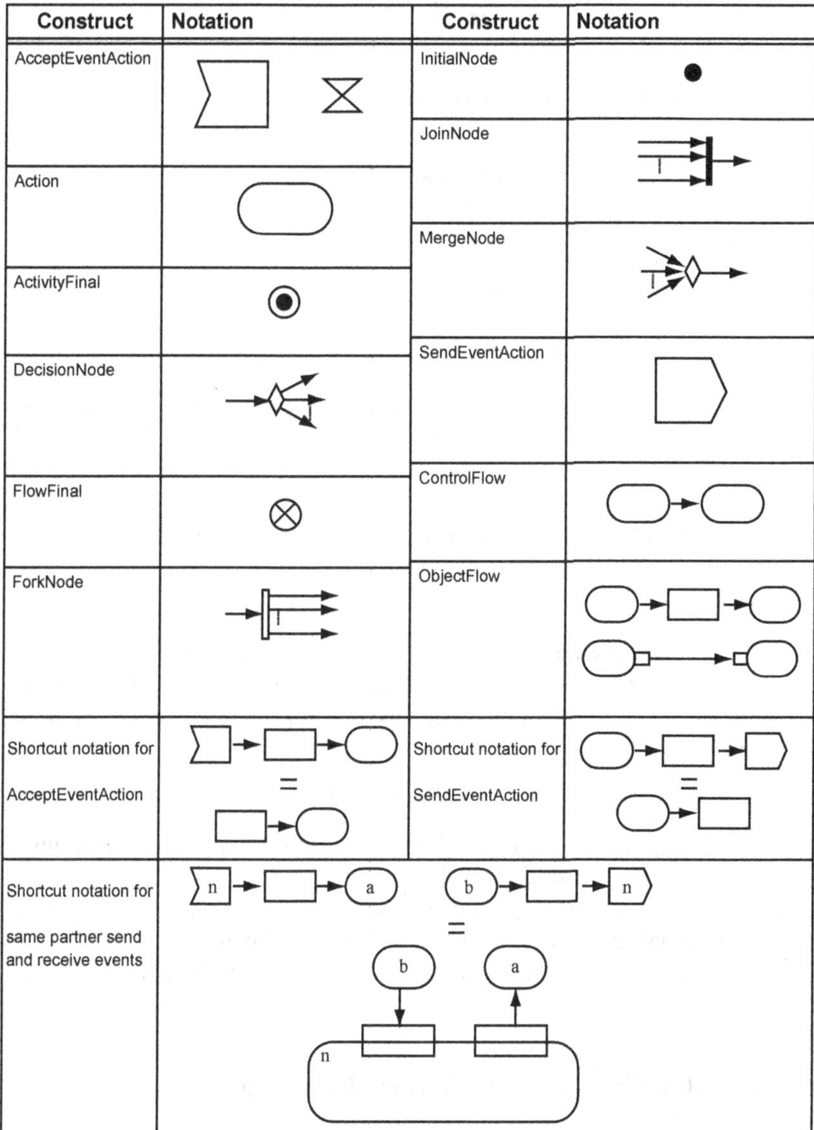

Fig. 9.10. Graphical representation for the UML2AD adapted subset constructs

- The tool propagates an "activity" attribute to all nodes and edges which denotes whether this part of the workflow is used during execution. Indeed, some execution paths of the choreographies may not be needed for the desired behaviour, and thus it is not needed to find elements providing their incoming tokens.

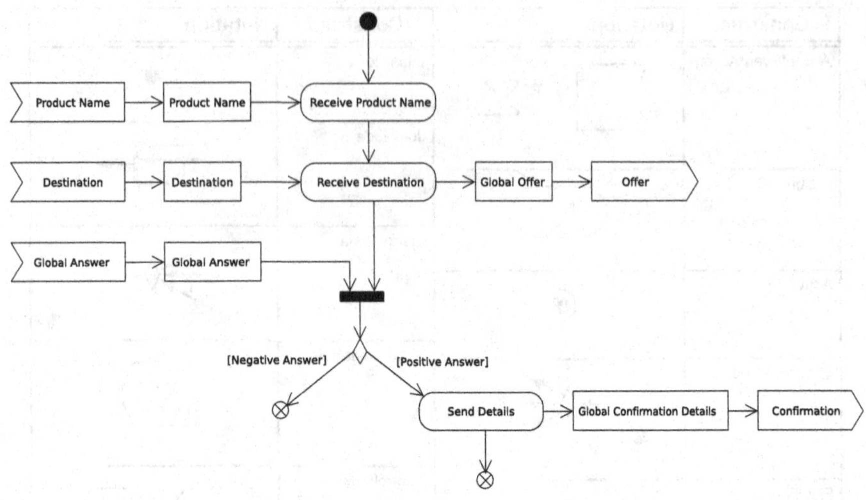

Fig. 9.11. Choreography of the producer-shipper composed Web Service

- In order to link choreographies exchanged messages between them, a new constraint states that a necessary(active) "ReceiveEvent" has to be linked to a corresponding "SendEvent" of the same type (i.e. consuming tokens from the same concept).

From this composed workflow it is then possible to extract

- the choreography of the composed Web Service (only elements regarding user interaction) as presented in Fig. 9.11
- the orchestration of the composed Web Service (not including SWSs choreographies but signals pointing to them) as presented in Fig. 9.12
- the capability of the composed Web Service, constructed from the user request.

9.6 A Flexible Composition Request Language

9.6.1 Aims and Requirements of a Request Language

In the previous section, we have used a sole message as the goal for composition. However, as discussed in Subsect.9.1.1, a composer will often need more precise requests in order to directly create the truly desired composed Web Service, thus avoiding many valid but unrealistic solutions. Let us take a virtual travel agency Semantic Web Service as example, which uses external SWSs to book hotels and trips. Those external SWSs may take a "city" message as input to know the location of the desired hotel, or the departure and destination locations. If we let the composer

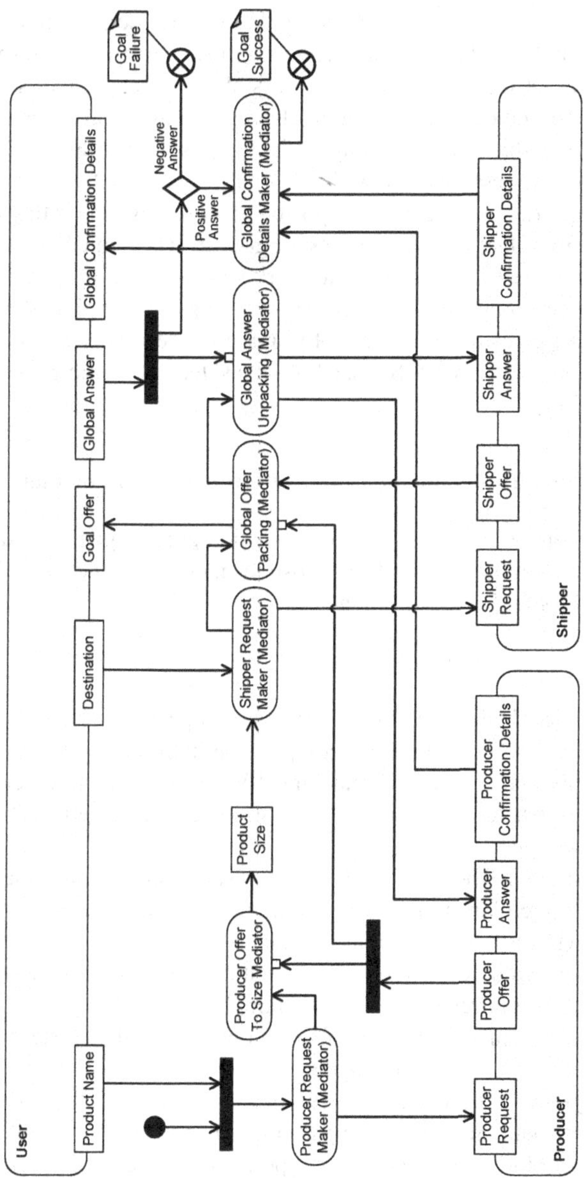

Fig. 9.12. Orchestration of the producer-shipper composed Web Service

compute any possible solutions, we will obtain some workflows where departure is used as the hotel city, which certainly is not the intended behaviour.

In order to express such internal requirements, we present in this section a flexible composition request language. Flexible means it should be possible for a user to express simple requests (which need to be extended) or precise ones. This allows end-users (as individuals using a web-based "on-the-fly" composition service), who do not necessarily have skills to manipulate complex constructs, to formulate a minimal request and let the tool extend it to possible complete requests among which he/she can choose the desired behaviour. However, it also leaves the possibility for middle-users (as industrials designing their composite Web Service) to precisely specify how the composed workflow should behave.

Another important feature of a composing request language is that it should stay at the most possible abstract level, such as the goal level presented in sect. 9.1.1. Staying at this abstract level allows users to work solely on the semantic relations and properties of their composed Web Service, ignoring the technical details of choreographies. It also gives the advantage of pruning the search space in the workflows composition phase, as only SWSs matching the selected atomic goals will be taken into consideration.

9.6.2 An Abstract Model for the Composition Request Language

We present in Figs. 9.13 and 9.14 the composition goal language used to formulate requests to the composer, as an UML abstract model together with Z constraints specifying well formed composition goals.

Semantics

- Atomic goals: Abstractions of SWS's. Used to perform discovery thus making the matching SWS's available for composition in the solution workflow.
- Roles: Inputs and outputs of matching SWS's. Internal roles can be used to denote intermediate objects in the orchestration. Each role has a concept taken from an ontology.
- Value Constraints: The solution workflow respects any given value constraints.
  - Unary Value Constraints: The solution workflow ensures that the specified object will respect given (ranged) values.
  - Relational Value Constraints: The solution workflow ensures that the specified objects will respect given constraint between them.
- Dataflow Constraints: The solution workflow ensures the existence of a specific dataflow between sources and targets.
  - IdentityFlow: The dataflow between the source and the targets makes no change to data. Source and targets concepts must be the same.
  - OperationFlow: The dataflow will perform an operation on sources' tokens values to obtain targets. Only applicable to integers and floats.
  - MediationFlow: The dataflow between sources and targets needs to use a specific mediator.
  - AggregationFlow: The dataflow will aggregate sources into the composite concept target.
  - ExtractionFlow: The dataflow will extract parts of the composite concept source into the targets.

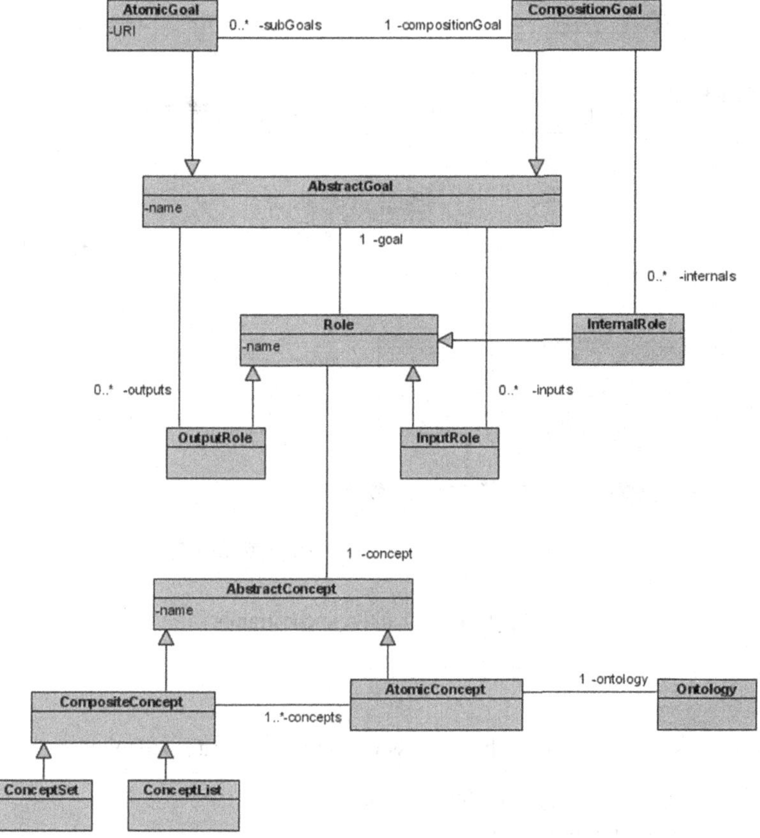

Fig. 9.13. Goals, roles and concepts

- DecisionFlow: The dataflow will go from source to different targets depending on the constraint text. Source and targets concepts must be the same.
- MergeFlow: The dataflow takes any incoming source and delivers it to target. Source and targets concepts must be the same.

Constraints

- Goals to roles relations reciprocity:

$$\forall n : AbstractGoal \bullet$$
$$\quad inputs(n) = \{e : Role \mid e.goal = n\}$$
$$\forall n : AbstractGoal \bullet$$
$$\quad outputs(n) = \{e : Role \mid e.goal = n\}$$
$$\forall n : AbstractGoal \bullet$$
$$\quad internals(n) = \{e : Role \mid e.goal = n\}$$

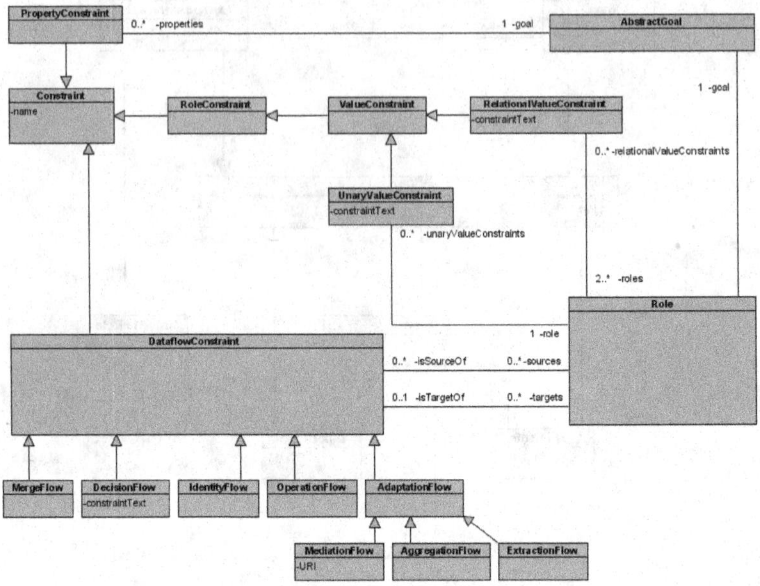

Fig. 9.14. Goal and role constraints

- Sources of dataflows must be of class OutputRole or InternalRole:

$$\forall n : Role \mid \#(n.isSourceOf) > 1 \bullet \\ n \in OutputRole \vee \\ n \in InternalRole$$

- Targets of dataflows must be of class InputRole or InternalRole:

$$\forall n : Role \mid \#(n.isTargetOf) > 1 \bullet \\ n \in InputRole \vee \\ n \in InternalRole$$

- Sources and targets of IdentityFlow, DecisionFlow and MergeFlow must share same concept type:

$$\forall n : DataflowConstraint \mid (n \in IdentityFlow \vee n \in MergeFlow \vee n \in DecisionFlow) \bullet \\ (sources(n) \rightarrow concept = targets(n) \rightarrow concept$$

- DecisionFlow has only one source:

$$\forall n : DecisionFlow \bullet \\ \#(n.sources) = 1$$

- MergeFlow has only one target:

$$\forall n : MergeFlow \bullet \\ \quad \#(n.targets) = 1$$

- ExtractionFlow has only one source, which concept is composite and targets have atomic concepts included in the source:

$$\forall n : ExtractionFlow \bullet \\ \quad \#(n.sources) = 1 \wedge sources(n) \rightarrow concept \in CompositeConcept \\ \quad \wedge\ targets(n) \rightarrow concept \in AtomicConcept \\ \quad \wedge\ targets(n) \rightarrow concept \subset sources(n) \rightarrow concept \rightarrow concepts$$

- AggregationFlow has only one target, which concept is composite and sources have atomic concepts included in the target:

$$\forall n : ExtractionFlow \bullet \\ \quad \#(n.targets) = 1 \wedge targets(n) \rightarrow concept \in CompositeConcept \\ \quad \wedge\ sources(n) \rightarrow concept \in AtomicConcept \\ \quad \wedge\ sources(n) \rightarrow concept \subset targets(n) \rightarrow concept \rightarrow concepts$$

Graphical Representation

We provide a graphical representation based on UML2 activity diagrams in order to draw composition goals in a user-friendly environment. Figure 9.15 lists all constructs and their graphical notation.

Construct	Notation	Construct	Notation
Composition Goal with input & output roles	name:concept name:concept composition goal name:concept	Dataflow Constraint	<<DecisionFlow>> Constraint1
		Value Constraint	<<UnvaryValueConstraint>> Constraint1
Atomic Goal with input & output roles	name:concept atomic goal name:concept name:concept	Constraint Text	constraint: constraint text <<RelationalValueConstraint>> name
Internal Role	name:concept		
isSourceOfRelations	Role <<IdentityFlow>> DataflowConstraint	Targets, roles, role relations	Role <<UnvaryValueConstraint>> Constraint1

Fig. 9.15. Graphical representation for composition goal constructs

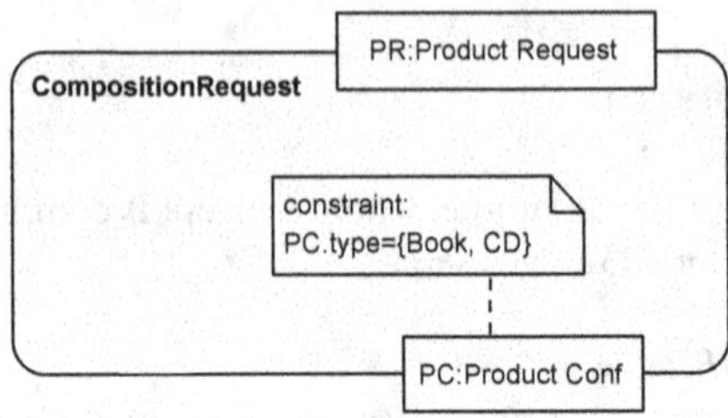

Fig. 9.16. Graphical example of a composition request (partial composition goal)

9.6.3 Overall Composition Process

We are now able to identify a complete process for efficient SWS composition. In the first step, the composer receives a request which might need to be extended to a full and valid composition goal, following the abstract model presented in the present section. This solving is efficiently done using configuration technics. We give an

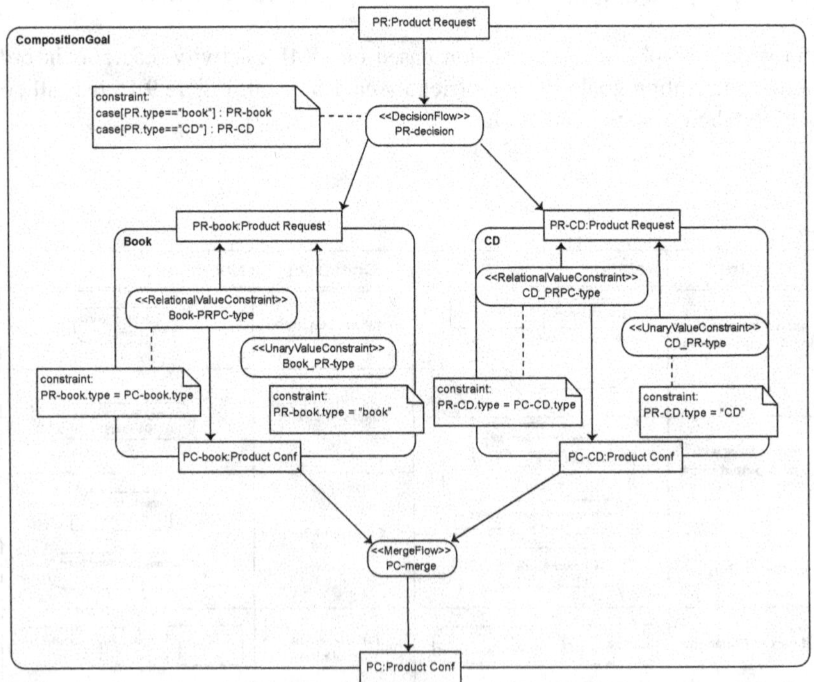

Fig. 9.17. Graphical example of a full and valid composition goal

example of a simple request and its extension to a full-composition goal in Figs. 9.16 and 9.17. This configuration process is similar to the one presented in Sect. 9.5. The tool searches for a valid instance of the constrained abstract model, using the outputs of the request as root objects. The available elements are the ones given in the request, as well as a library of atomic goals, mediators and operations.

Discovery is then executed on the basis of the atomic goals present in the final composition goal in order to retrieve matching SWSs and their choreographies.

Finally, the composer is able to compose those workflows as shown in Sect. 9.5, following the additional constraints and objectives of the composition goal, and extract the orchestration, choreography and capability of the composed Semantic Web Service.

9.7 Outlook

To summarise this chapter, we may say SWS composition is a field of intense research and one of the most challenging problem for the Semantic Web. We have shown it is well viewed and efficiently solved as a constraint-based configuration problem. We isolated a constrained abstract model for composing workflows in such a way. We have also pointed out the necessity of a flexible request language and presented an abstract model for it. The research community is going to face many issues in the future about composition, among which we can see scalability (the high number of SWSs expected to be available on the web might require the addition of local search technics), reliability of composed Web Services, compensation (foresee possible execution problems and create relevant alternative paths) and trust between partners in the composition.

References

1. P. Albert, L. Henocque, and M. Kleiner. Configuration Based Workflow Composition. In *Proceedings of International Conference on Web Services ICWS'05*, pages 285–292, Orlando, Florida, USA, 2005.
2. P. Albert, L. Henocque, and M. Kleiner. A Constrained Object Model for Configuration Based Workflow Composition. In *Revised Selected papers of the Third International Conference on Business Process Management Workshops BPM-05-WSCOBPM*, pages 102–115, Nancy, France, September 2006.
3. M. Baldoni, C. Baroglio, A. Martelli, and V. Patti. Reasoning About Interaction Protocols for Web Service Composition. In *Proceedings of 1st International Workshop on Web Services and Formal Methods (web service-FM 2004)*, Pisa, Italy, February 2004.
4. V.R. Benjamins and D. Fensel. Editorial: Problem Solving Methods. *Special Issue on Problem-Solving Methods. International Journal of Human-Computer Studies (IJHCS)*, 49(4):305–313, 1998.
5. L. Bettini, V. Bono, and B. Venneri. O'klaim: A Coordination Language with Mobile Mixins. In *Proceedings of COORDINATION-2004*, pages 20–37. LNCS, Springer-Verlag 2004.

6. A. J. Bonner and M Kifer. Transaction Logic Programming. Technical Report CSRI-323. Technical report, CSRI, November 1995.
7. E. Börger and R. Stärk. *Abstract State Machines. A Method for High-Level System Design and Analysis*. Springer-Verlag, 2003.
8. A. Brogi, C. Canal, and A. Pimentel, E.and Vallecillo. Formalizing Web Services Choreographies. In *Proceedings of 1st International Workshop on Web Services and Formal Methods (web service-FM 2004)*, Pisa, Italy, February 2004.
9. M. Carman, L. Serafini, and P. Traverso. Web Service Composition as Planning. In *Proceedings of ICAPS-03 International Conference on Automated Planning and Scheduling*, Trento, Italy, June 2003.
10. I. Constantinescu, W. Binder, and B. Faltings. Flexible and Efficient Matchmaking and Ranking in Service Directories. In *2005 IEEE International Conference on Web Services (ICWS 2005)*, pages 5–12, Florida, USA, July 2005. IEEE Computer Society.
11. I. Constantinescu, B. Faltings, and W. Binder. Large Scale, Type-Compatible Service Composition. In *IEEE International Conference on Web Services (ICWS 2004)*, pages 506–513, San Diego, USA, July 2004. IEEE Computer Society.
12. R. Dijkman and M. Dumas. Service-Oriented Design: A Multi-Viewpoint Approach, CTIT Technical Report Series No. 04-09. Technical Report, Centre for Telematics and Information Technology, University of Twente, The Netherlands, February 2004.
13. D. Prashant, R. Goodwin, R. Akkiraju, and K. Verma. Dynamic Workflow Composition Using Markov Decision Processes. *International Journal of Web Services Research*, 2(1):1–17, January – March 2005.
14. A. Felfernig, G. Friedrich, D. Jannach, and M. Zanker. Configuration Knowledge Representation Using UML/OCL. In *Proceedings of the 5th International Conference on The Unified Modeling Language*, pages 49–62. Springer-Verlag, 2002.
15. D. Fensel, E. Motta, F. van Harmelen, V. R. Benjamins, M. Crubézy, S. Decker, M. Gaspari, R. Groenboom, W. E. Grosso, M. A. Musen, E. Plaza, G. Schreiber, R. Studer, and B. J. Wielinga. The Unified Problem-Solving Method Development Language UPML. *Knowledge and Inference Systems*, 5(1):83–131, 2003.
16. G. Fleischanderl, G. Friedrich, A. Haselböck, H. Schreiner, and M. Stumptner. Configuring Large-Scale Systems With Generative Constraint Satisfaction. *IEEE Intelligent Systems, Special issue on Configuration*, 13(7), 1998.
17. R. Ginis and K.M. Chandy. Service Composition Issues for Distributed Business Processes. In *Proceedings of the 2003 International Conference on Web Services (ICWS 2003)*, pages 27–33, Las Vegas, Nevada, USA, June 23 - 26 2003.
18. J.-Y Girard. Linear Logic. *Theoretical Computer Science*, 50:1–102, 1987.
19. A. Gómez-Pérez, R. González-Cabero, and M. Lama. A Framework for Design and Composition of Semantic Web Services. In *Semantic Web Services, 2004 AAAI Spring Symposium Series*, pages 113–120, March 2004.
20. Object Management Group. *UML v. 2.0 Specification*. OMG, 2003.
21. Object Management Group. UML 2 Superstructure. Technical Report 2.0, OMG, 2004.
22. D. Harel. Statecharts: A Visual Formalism for Complex Systems. *Science of Computer Programming*, 8:231–274, 1987.
23. L. Henocque. Modeling Object Oriented Constraint Programs in Z. *RACSAM (Revista de la Real Academia De Ciencias serie A Mathematicas), Special Issue about Artificial Intelligence and Symbolic Computing*, pages 127–152, 2004.
24. K. Jensen. *Coloured Petri Nets, Basic Concepts, Analysis Methods and Practical Use. Volume 1 and 2*. Springer-Verlag, 1997.

25. J.E. Johnson, D.E Langworthy, L. Lamport, and F.H. Vogt. Formal Specification of a Web Services Protocol. In G. Zavattaro and M. Bravetti, editors, *Proceedings of the 1st International Workshop on Web Services and Formal Methods*, Pisa, Italy, February 2004.
26. U. Junker and D. Mailharro. The Logic of ILOG (j)Configurator: Combining Constraint Programming With a Description Logic. In *Proceedings of Workshop on Configuration, IJCAI-03*, pages 13–20, 2003.
27. M. Kifer, G. Lausen, and J. Wu. Logical Foundations of Object-Oriented and Frame-Based Languages. *Journal of the ACM*, 42(4):741–843, 1995.
28. L. Lamport. Specifying Concurrent Systems with TLA+. *Calculational System Design*, 173:183–247, March 1999.
29. H. Levesque, R. Reiter, Y. Lesperance, F. Lin, and R. Scherl. Golog: A Logic Programming Language for Dynamic Domains. *Journal of Logic Programming*, 31(1-3):59–84, 1997.
30. D. Mailharro. A Classification and Constraint Based Framework for Configuration. *AI-EDAM, Special Issue on Configuration*, 12(4):383 – 397, 1998.
31. S. Marcus and J. McDermott. SALT: A Knowledge Acquisition Language for Propose and Revise Systems. *Journal of Artificial Intelligence*, 39(1):1–37, 1989.
32. S. McIlraith and T. Son. Adapting Golog for Composition of Semantic Web Services. In *Proceedings of Conference on Knowledge Representation and Reasoning*, April 2002.
33. R. Milner. *Communication and Concurrency*. Prentice Hall, 1989.
34. S. Mittal and B. Falkenhainer. Dynamic Constraint Satisfaction Problems. In *Proceedings of AAAI-90*, pages 25–32, 1990.
35. B. Nebel. Reasoning and Revision in Hybrid Representation Systems. *LNAI* 422, Springer-Verlag, 1990.
36. B. Norton, S. Foster, and A. Hughes. A Compositional Operational Semantics for OWL-S. In *Proceedings 2nd Workshop on Web Services and Formal Methods (WS-FM 2005)*, 2005.
37. M. Paolucci, T. Kawamura, T.R. Payne, and K. Sycara. Semantic Matching of Web Services Capabilities. In *Proceedings of the 1st International Semantic Web Conference (ISWC)*, 2002.
38. M. Pistore, F. Barbon, P. Bertoli, D. Shaparau, and P. Traverso. Planning and Monitoring Web Service Composition. In *Proceedings of the Workshop on Planning and Scheduling for Web and Grid Services held in conjunction with ICAPS-2004*, Whistler, British Columbia, Canada, June 2004.
39. S.R. Ponnekanti and A. Fox. Sword: A Developer Toolkit for Web Service Composition. In *Proceedings of the 11th International WWW Conference*, pages 83–107, Hawaii, May 2002.
40. J. Rao, P. Kungas, and M. Matskin. Logic-Based Web Service Composition: From Service Description to Process Model. In *Proceedings of the 2004 IEEE International Conference on Web Services, ICWS 2004*, San Diego, California, USA, July 2004.
41. R. Reiter. *Knowledge in Action: Logical Foundations for Specifying and Implementing Dynamical Systems*. MIT Press, 2001.
42. C. Schlenoff, M. Gruninger, M. Ciocoiu, and J Lee. The Essence of the Process Specification Language. *Transactions of the Society for Computer Simulation International, Special Issue on Modeling and Simulation in Manufacturing Systems*, 16, No. 4:204–216, December 1999.
43. A.E.F. Seghrouchni and S Haddad. A Recursive Model for Distributed Planning. In *Proceedings of the 2nd International Conference on Multi-Agent Systems (ICMAS-96)*, pages 307–314, Kyoto, Japan, 1996. IEEE.

44. E. Sirin, J. Hendler, and B. Parsia. Semi Automatic Composition of Web Services Using Semantic Descriptions. In *Proceedings of the ICEIS-2003 Workshop on Web Services: Modeling, Architecture and Infrastructure*, Angers, France, April 2003.
45. E. Sirin, B. Parsia, D. Wu, J. Hendler, and D. Nau. HTN Planning for Web Service Composition Using SHOP2. *Journal of Web Semantics*, 1(4):377–396, 2004.
46. T. Soininen, I. Niemelõ, J. Tiihonen, and R. Sulonen. Unified Configuration Knowledge Representation Using Weight Constraint Rules. In *ECAI-2000 Configuration Workshop*, 2000.
47. J. M. Spivey. *The Z Notation: A Reference Manual.* Prentice Hall originally, now J.M. Spivey, 2001.
48. M. Stumptner. An Overview of Knowledge-Based Configuration. *AI Communications*, 10(2):111–125, June 1997.
49. S. Thakkar, C.A. Knoblock, J.L. Ambite, and C. Shahabi. Dynamically Composing Web Services From On-Line Sources. In *Proceedings of AAAI-02 Workshop on Intelligent Service Integration*, Edmonton, Canada, July 2002.
50. W. van der Aalst. Pi Calculus Versus Petri Nets: Let us Eat Humble Pie Rather Than Further Inflate the Pi Hype. *BPTrends*, 3(5):1–11, May 2005.
51. W.M.P. van der Aalst, L. Aldred, and M. Dumas. Design and Implementation of the YAWL System. QUT Technical Report, FIT-TR-2003-07. Technical report, Queensland University of Technology, Brisbane, 2003.
52. W.M.P. van der Aalst and A.H.M. ter Hofstede. YAWL: Yet Another Workflow Language. *Information Systems*, 30(4):245–275, 2005.
53. W.M.P. van der Aalst, A.H.M. ter Hofstede, B. Kiepuszewski, and A.P. Barros. Workflow Patterns. *Distributed and Parallel Databases*, 14(3):5–51, July 2003.
54. M. Viroli. Towards a Formal Foundation to Orchestration Languages. In *Proceedings of 1st International Workshop on Web Services and Formal Methods (web service-FM 2004)*, Pisa, Italy, February 2004.
55. M. Vukovic and P. Robinson. Adaptive, Planning Based, Web Service Composition for Context Awareness. In *Proceedings of the 2nd International Conference on Pervasive Computing*, Vienna, Austria, 2004.
56. M. Wooldridge. *Introduction to Multi Agent Systems.* Wiley, 2002.
57. X. Yi and K. Kochut. A CP-Nets-Based Design and Verification Framework for Web Services Composition. In *proceedings of 2004 IEEE International Conference on Web Services, July 2004*, San Diego, California, USA, July 2004.

10

Mediation

Bridging between Heterogeneous Web Service Systems

Oscar Corcho, Silvestre Losada and Richard Benjamins

Intelligent Software Components, S.A. (iSOCO), Madrid, Spain,
{ocorcho, slosada, rbenjamins}@isoco.com

Summary. This chapter covers the mediation aspect in a Semantic Web Services environment. Mediation components should allow any service to speak with any other service in a scalable manner, overcoming the heterogeneity of data formats, terminologies, interaction styles, etc. In this chapter, we decompose mediation in three levels, according to the classification provided in Chap. 6: (1) data mediation, concerned with the transformation of the syntactic format of the messages exchanged by Web Services; (2) ontology mediation, concerned with the transformation of the terminology used inside the messages exchanged and (3) protocol or choreography mediation, concerned with the problem of non-matching message interaction patterns. Business process mediation is not considered, since it requires to perform a task of process re-engineering that is outside the context of research in Semantic Web Services.

10.1 Notion of Mediation

The interaction of Semantic Web Services in an application is centred on two complementary principles [7].

1. Strong de-coupling of the various components that realise the application, including the hiding of information based on the difference of internal business intelligence and public message exchange protocol interface descriptions.
2. Strong mediation services enabling anybody to speak with everybody in a scalable manner, including the mediation of different data formats, terminologies, interaction styles, etc.

This chapter is focused on the second architectural principle. According to it, mediation can be described as a process for settling a dispute between two parties where a third one is employed whose task is to try to find common ground that will resolve inconsistencies between their respective conceptualisations of a given domain.

The mediation problem has been widely addressed in the literature in the context of system integration. For example, component-based software development introduced the so-called *adapters* [10], aimed at enabling the reuse of descriptions of objects by making it possible to combine objects that differ in their syntactical input and output descriptions. Also in software engineering, the notion of connectors is introduced [11]. Connectors are software pieces that establish the relationships between different components and mediate between their interaction styles, i.e. between their different business logics.

We can find similar examples in the knowledge engineering area. Adapters [8] were introduced in knowledge-based systems so as to facilitate knowledge reuse. The objective of adapters in this context is to decouple the elements of a knowledge model, by encapsulating them and explicitly modelling their interactions. In the context of heterogeneous and distributed information systems, the notion of mediators appears, together with the notion of wrappers [22]. Mediators translate user queries into sub-queries on the different information sources that are accessed through the use of wrappers and integrate the sub-answers received from each of the information sources. In other words, mediators are defined as entities for establishing interoperability of resources that are not compatible a priori by resolving mismatches between them at runtime.

In summary, mediators are used to overcome the heterogeneity problems between different sources of information, different software components and different knowledge elements. These problems are usual in current system integration, and especially in more open contexts such as those of service-oriented architectures (together with one of their common deployments: Web Services).

As described in Chap. 6, the heterogeneity problem must be handled at different levels. These levels of heterogeneity are usually classified as follows:

- Data mediation : It is concerned with the transformation of the syntactic format of the messages exchanged by different services. That is, the service requester may provide an input for the service provider that is not in the format that the latter is expecting, and vice versa. For instance, the parameter values in a SOAP message may appear in different places of the message body or header, with different orders, etc.
- Ontology mediation : It is concerned with the transformation of the semantic models used by the service requester and provider to express the messages that they exchange. It is likely that the service requester and the service provider will use different ontologies (with different degrees of complexity) to refer to the content of their messages.[1]
- Protocol mediation : Also known as choreography mediation, it is concerned with the problem of non-matching message interaction patterns. That is, two or more services exchanging messages may use different interaction patterns (e.g. one of them sends only one message while the other expects two).[2]

[1] In the context of WSMO, described in Chap. 7, this type of mediators would correspond to the so-called *ooMediators*

[2] In the context of WSMO, this type of mediators would correspond to the so-called *wwMediators*. The other types of mediators (ggMediators and wgMediators) do not correspond to this classification

- Process mediation : Also known as business process mediation, it is concerned with the alignment of business processes that have different conceptual models, although the effect or result of executing the processes may be compatible. For example, a marketplace service may implement the notion of "shopping basket" while one of its clients may implement the notion of "one-stop shop" for buying and selling products.

10.1.1 Mediation in the Macro-Architecture and Micro-Architecture

Section 6.4 of chap. 6 described an architecture for the deployment of applications using Semantic Web Services. Following some of the proposals in Agent Technology research, it identified two types of architecture: macro-architecture and micro-architecture, each of them focused on different aspects of the general framework. We will follow the same approach to describe the role of mediation in the context of Semantic Web Service applications.

From a macro-architectural point of view, the role of the different types of mediation in each of the possible interactions is described in Table 10.1.

The table shows that data mediation is only used in the case of service delivery, i.e. when the actual service is executed. The reason for this is that for other aspects like discovery or negotiation of the service provision there is no need to specify the concrete values for the parameters that will be inside each of the messages exchanged.

On the contrary, ontology mediation is needed for all the possible interactions identified in the macro-architecture. It may be needed in the process of registration with a discovery agent, because the latter may be using a different ontology for service description. It may also be needed in the process of discovering available services, since the ontology used by the service requester might be different to those of the service providers registered in the discovery agent. It may be needed in the definition of the service provision made by the service requester and provider, for the same reason given above. And it may be needed during the service delivery, i.e. during the service execution.

Protocol mediation is not needed for the service registration and discovery, since the process to be followed for registering and querying is already known by all the parties. But it may be needed for service definition, where the protocol is negotiated,

Table 10.1. The role of mediation in the SWS macro-architecture defined in Sect. 6.4 of Chap. 6

	data mediation	ontology mediation	protocol mediation
1. service offer registration		X	
2. service request		X	
3. service definition requester-provider		X	X
4. service delivery	X	X	X

and for service delivery, where the existence of different message exchange patterns has to be overcome in the communication.

Let us now see how the different levels of mediation are applied in the context of the micro-architectures presented in Sect. 6.4 of Chap. 6.

Figure 10.1 summarises the role of mediation from the point of view of the service requester. Data mediation is performed by the message lift/lower component, which transforms incoming and outgoing messages to a canonical format that can be used by the rest of the modules. Ontology mediation takes place between the discovery/definition component and the application logic component, and between the delivery component and the application logic. Finally, protocol mediation takes place in the delivery component, using the choreography descriptions referenced by the provider agent during the service definition interaction.

Figure 10.2 summarises the role of mediation from the point of view of the service provider. Data and ontology mediation take place in the same locations of the architecture as in the service requester case. The only difference is related to the role of protocol mediation, as aforementioned: the service provider just provides descriptions of its choreography to the service requester, and hence no mediation takes place here at the protocol level.

In the following sections, we will provide a general overview of the current state of the art in mediation in the first three of the aforementioned levels. We start positioning mediation in the context of the case study scenarios defined in Chap. 6. Then we will describe some of the existing approaches to data, ontology and protocol mediation. We exclude process mediation from this chapter because it is out of the scope of current research in Semantic Web Services. As aforementioned, process

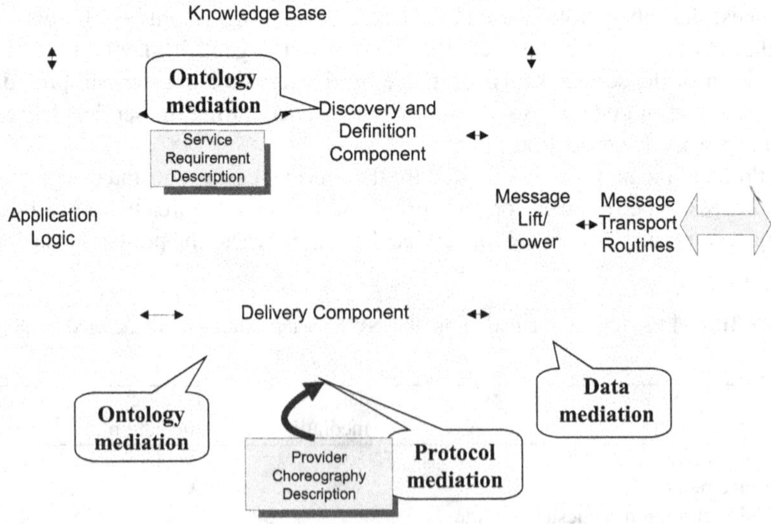

Fig. 10.1. Mediation from the point of view of the service requester

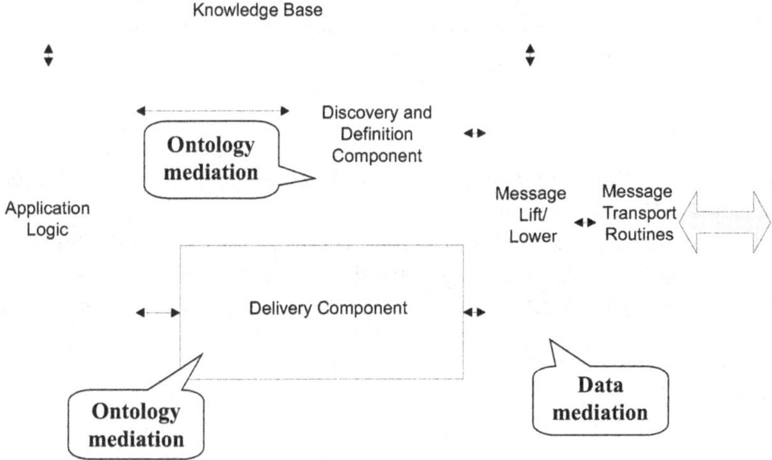

Fig. 10.2. Mediation from the point of view of the service provider

mediation normally needs of a process re-engineering task to achieve a successful interaction between the services involved in a conversation. Some of the concrete approaches described in each of the following sections are taken from the work performed in the context of the SWWS project. Finally, we provide the conclusions to the work presented and describe what we think will be the future trends in mediation in the Semantic Web Services domain.

10.2 Mediation in Case Study Scenarios

This section illustrates the notion of mediation by revisiting the example case studies listed in Chap. 6. For each of the example scenarios, mediation is identified and characterised in the context of the particular case study.

10.2.1 Scenario A

In this scenario, the needs of the customer notification agent will be mainly related to data and ontology mediation. Data mediation will be needed because the information obtained from the banks with respect to the current balance of different accounts, the information about consumer good companies with respect to future payments to be done, and the data sent through any of the different user notification means (SMS, e-mail, etc.) will be available in different formats (services from different banks and consumer good companies will use different formats for dates and currency amounts, and different notification means will need different types of formats for sending the text of the notification, among others). Ontology mediation will be needed because each service will probably be using a different terminology to refer to the customer information (a bank may classify its customers according to their age while another may classify them according to their employment status, and have different information in each case), to the payment details, etc.

10.2.2 Scenario B

In this scenario, there are similar needs for data and ontology mediation. Each stationery provider will be using different terms to refer to the same object, and the formats used in each case will be different. There is no need for more types of mediation since the protocol used for defining the sequence of messages is clear (that of a shopping basket) and all the services that participate in a conversation share that model.

10.2.3 Scenario C

In this scenario, besides the need for data and ontology mediation already pointed out for the other scenarios, we may need to perform some kind of protocol mediation. Though the scenario is defined in Chap. 6 as one where all the services involved in the communication use the same model for exchanging messages (RosettaNet), we could easily imagine that one of them uses a different one, such as EDIFACT, for receiving and forwarding logistic requests. In that case, the exchange of messages between different services will be different (one message in RosettaNet can correspond to several messages in EDIFACT and vice versa, one message may not need to be sent in the another protocol, etc.)

10.2.4 Scenario D

Finally, this scenario will be one where, again, data and ontology mediation will be needed, with no clear role for protocol or process mediation.

10.3 Data Mediation

Data mediation is specific of the syntax transformation that takes place during message exchange between a service requester and the service provider, or between a set of cooperating parties participating in a choreography. Hence, its main function is to provide syntax transparency that guarantees information flow between them, transforming the input and output data of the Web Services so that they can be handled by the corresponding parties.

As described in the introduction to this chapter, data mediation is only used during the service delivery phase (i.e. on service invocation), which is the moment when actual data is transported from one service to another.

The mismatches that can appear in the data mediation layer are of many different types: the message generated by the service requester may contain more or less information than the information needed by the service provider, the information may be provided with a different structure, using a different encoding scheme, etc.

There are mainly two alternatives to perform transformations in the data mediation layer:

1. **One-step transformation approaches**: This type of transformation deals at the same time with all the transformations to be made to the syntax, structure, encoding, etc. of the messages exchanged.
2. **Multi-step transformation approaches**: This type of transformation divides the transformation process in several steps: (1) extract data from the native source message syntax into a data mediation syntax and structure (normally known as lifting); (2) perform the ontology mediation (described in the next section) in that common syntax; (3) write the mediated data to the native target message syntax (normally known as lowering).

From both approaches, the second one is normally easier to build (and especially to maintain), even if it requires more programming effort than the first one. However, most of the existing implementations of data mediation components rely on ad hoc solutions based on the first approach. That is, the data mediation component is implemented specifically for each pair of service requester and provider, all the transformations are done in one step, making them more difficult to maintain when there is a change in the requester or provider and less reusable, and finally the corresponding code is generated in a general-purpose programming language.

In the next section, we describe one possible implementation of a data mediation component,[3] based on a multi-step transformation approach. This implementation has been created and evaluated in the context of the SWWS project.

10.3.1 An Implementation of a Data Mediation Component

As commented above, this section presents a possible implementation of a data mediation component based on a multi-step approach. This component, which can be used both by the service requester and by the service provider, consists of two subcomponents:

1. A lifting component, which transforms the content of the incoming message (normally available in XML format) into a normalised format (e.g. a set of RDF statements). The RDF statements generated are related to an ontology, which may be available either in RDF Schema or in OWL. The RDF statements represent instances of that ontology and values for the properties defined for that ontology, and this information comes from the original message received by the component.
2. A lowering component, which concretises outgoing messages following a symmetric process to that of the lifting component. This component transforms RDF code that has been used or generated by the service (for instance, as a result of its execution) into another format usable by the service provider or requester (normally XML).

[3] The contents of this section are based on an earlier version from Steve Battle – HP labs

Though the subsequent use of the RDF statements generated during the lifting process is not a matter of the data mediation component, it is important to mention that normally these statements will be inserted into a knowledge base, which can then be used by the service during its execution (e.g. for ontology mediation purposes).

Let us describe now with more detail how we implemented each of these components in the context of the SWWS project.

The Lifting Subcomponent

The subcomponent described in this section is a generic piece of software that can take a message in XML and generates the corresponding set of RDF statements according to a set of mapping rules specified by a user. These mapping rules determine how each of the parameters and values inside the XML message have to be transformed into RDF statements according to a RDF Schema or OWL ontology.

The lifting process performed by this subcomponent consists of two consecutive stages:

1. The XML message is transformed to RDF according to an OWL ontology that resembles the message structure (i.e. it can be considered as an ontology of XML Schema). This means that every XML element and XML attribute corresponds to a RDF property, that every XML sequence corresponds to an rdf:Seq, etc.
2. The RDF model is transformed into another RDF model that is in conformity with the domain ontology that is going to be used to describe the message content. This second stage can be performed by means of rules.

We describe the two stages in the following in more detail by giving examples.

1st Stage – XML Transformation to RDF

Transformation of XML Elements and Attributes. The central idea of the first stage of the lifting process is *that every XML element name and every XML attribute name maps to an RDF property*, viewing the XML structure as a relational model between parent nodes and their children. Pragmatically, this first transformation process brings the message data into the RDF realm, allowing subsequent inference to take place.

Alternative approaches have been proposed to this idea, including the transformation of element names into RDF Schema class names, and then only XML attributes would be identified with RDF properties. However, this transformation is not uniformly applied and neither can it be recovered from the schema.

Transformation of XML Schema Simple and Complex Types. Furthermore, properties can be further classified into object and datatype properties (this is not possible in RDF Schema, but in OWL). XML Schema describes them in terms of simple and complex types. *Simple XML Schema datatypes are mapped onto OWL datatype properties*, which relate a resource and a typed literal. *Untyped simple XML Schema types are interpreted as plain literals.* For derived simple types, the property definition uses only the base type from which it is derived. The content of enumerations can be preserved as property restrictions.

XML Schema ComplexTypes are described using sequence, all and choice compositors. *For each XML Schema complex type, we create a new resource that represents the class and use it to define the rdf:type of the product information* (where the type has a global name). Complex types may also support mixed content models with interspersed text. In this case, the rdf:value property is used where a singular literal will not do.

XML is not strictly a tree, but a tree with pointers as described by IDs and IDREFs. Rather than preserve the IDREF datatype, we interpret it as a URI–defined relative to the document base. IDREFs are an exception where a simple type does not refer to a literal value.

Preservation of the XML Sequencing. A naive translation of XML into RDF has the side effect of losing the sequencing implicit in the XML. From the two approaches that could be taken to represent sequencing with RDF containers (RDF lists and RDF sequences), we choose sequences, using the rdf:Seq primitive.

Summary of Transformations. The XML Schema–based mapping is summarised in Table 10.2.

Example

As a simple example, let us consider the XML message below (a response to a request to add an item to the order). This reports on the status of an operation to add an item to the order (addToOrder).

```
<?xml version="1.0"?> <ns:addLineToOrder
 xmlns:ns="http://ontology.hpl.hp.com/slms/addLineToOrderResponse.xsd">
        <STATUS><![CDATA[TRUE]]></STATUS>
        <ErrorFlag><![CDATA[False]]></ErrorFlag>
</ns:addLineToOrder>
```

Assuming that the base URI of the previous XML document is `http://example.com/slms/addlinetoorder1.xml`, after the first stage of lifting the following RDF code is generated:

```
<rdf:RDF
 xmlns:rdf="http://www.w3.org/1999/02/22-rdf-syntax-ns#"
 xmlns:j.0=
 "http://ontology.hpl.hp.com/slms/addLineToOrderResponse.xsd/addLineToOrder/"
```

Table 10.2. Summary of transformations from XML to RDF

XML Schema	RDF
Element	Property
Attribute (except ID)	Property
Attribute (ID)	Resource URI
Predefined simpleType (not IDREF)	Typed literal
Untyped simpleType	Plain literal
Complextype (named)	Resource type
Sequence compositor	Rdf:Seq
Literals in mixed content	Rdf:value properties
Restriction (base type)	Typed literal
Attribute group	Resource type

```
xmlns:j.1="http://ontology.hpl.hp.com/slms/addLineToOrderResponse.xsd/">
 <rdf:Description rdf:about="http://example.com/slms/addlinetoorder1.xml">
   <j.1:addLineToOrder rdf:parseType="Resource">
     <j.0:ErrorFlag rdf:datatype="http://www.w3.org/2001/XMLSchema#string"
     >False</j.0:ErrorFlag>
     <j.0:STATUS rdf:datatype="http://www.w3.org/2001/XMLSchema#string"
     >TRUE</j.0:STATUS>
   </j.1:addLineToOrder>
 </rdf:Description>
</rdf:RDF>
```

Observe that all of the elements that appeared in the original XML message (addLineToOrder, STATUS, ErrorFlag) are mapped to RDF properties. The type information for these properties (xsd:string) has been recovered from the XML Schema referenced from the XML message.

2nd Stage – Transformation of the Canonical RDF Model into a Domain Model. The second stage consists in manipulating the raw RDF output obtained in the previous stage so that it conforms to a specific domain ontology, which defines the content of the original message. This may involve changes to the structure of the output as well as name changes.

Example
Below we show an example of a set of rules[4] (variables are preceded by a question mark '?'). These rules replace the values 'TRUE', 'FALSE', 'True' and 'False' with lowercase equivalents. They also cast the property names into a different namespace as it is irrelevant that they are defined locally within the 'addLineToOrder' element (see 'j.0'). Finally, they skip over the property that corresponds to the document element ('addLineToOrder'), which contains no additional content.

```
@prefix ns:
<http://ontology.hpl.hp.com/slms/addLineToOrderResponse#>

@prefix j.0:
<http://ontology.hpl.hp.com/slms/addLineToOrderResponse.xsd/
              addLineToOrder/>
@prefix j.1: <http://ontology.hpl.hp.com/slms/addLineToOrderResponse.xsd/>

(?x j.1:addLineToOrder ?y) -> (?y eg:lift ?x).
(?x eg:lift ?z), (?x j.0:STATUS 'TRUE') -> (?z ns:status 'true').
(?x eg:lift ?z), (?x j.0:STATUS 'FALSE') -> (?z ns:status 'false').
(?x eg:lift ?z), (?x j.0:ErrorFlag 'True') -> (?z ns:errorFlag 'true').
(?x eg:lift ?z), (?x j.0:ErrorFlag 'False') -> (?z ns:errorFlag 'false').
```

Once, that this transformation has been done, we want to obtain only the properties with the 'ns' prefix (which corresponds to `http://ontology.hpl.hp.com/slms/addLineToOrderResponse\#`). The final result for the original XML message is as follows:

---

[4]These rules are defined using the Jena rule language. Jena is a library for the management of OWL and RDF(S) ontologies, developed by HP Labs (see `http://jena.sourceforge.net/`). This is just an implementation option and any other alternative could have been used

```
<rdf:RDF
    xmlns:ns="http://ontology.hpl.hp.com/slms/addLineToOrderResponse#"
    xmlns:rdf="http://www.w3.org/1999/02/22-rdf-syntax-ns#">
  <rdf:Description
   rdf:about="http://ontology.hpl.hp.com/slms/addlinetoorder1.xml">
    <ns:status>true</ns:status>
    <ns:errorFlag>false</ns:errorFlag>
  </rdf:Description>
</rdf:RDF>
```

This message contains the RDF statements that can now be used by the service to execute its business logic. A summary of the transformations that have been performed in this example is given in Fig. 10.3.

Lowering

The lowering subcomponent is also a generic piece of software that can be considered as the reverse of the lifting one. That is, it takes a model in RDF and generates the corresponding XML message, according to a set of mapping rules specified by a user and to an XML Schema that defines how the resulting XML message has to be created.

As in the case of lifting, the lowering process consists of two consecutive stages: the first one where the original RDF model, based on a domain ontology, is transformed into an RDF model that resembles the XML Schema of the message that has

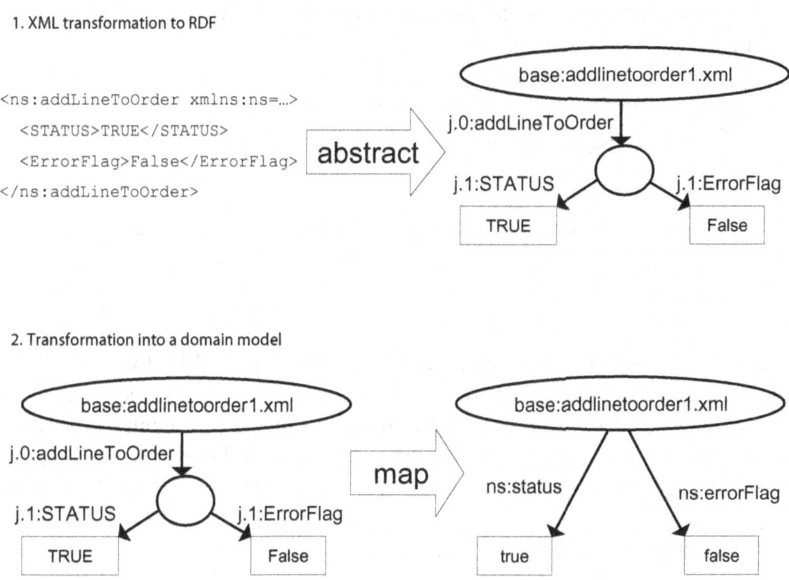

Fig. 10.3. Lifting process for an incoming XML message

to be output; and a second step where that canonical RDF model is transformed to XML according to the XML Schema that it has to follow.

The first stage is based on the use of mapping rules as the ones presented in the case of lifting. In the second stage, the lowering process navigates RDF statements downstream (moving from subject to object) so as to construct an XML document object model from the root element. The local names of the matched properties must match the local names of attributes and elements defined in the XML Schema. Furthermore, the namespaces must follow the conventions defined by the mapping that preserve the scope of XML Schema components.

Since the basis of these processes is very similar to the one used in the lifting component, we will not give too much details about it but just an example of how it can be used.

Example

For this example, we will construct the outgoing message representing the request to add a line to an order. This line specifies that the cost centre has the value 999. The raw RDF input representing this message is shown below.

```
<rdf:RDF
    xmlns:rdf="http://www.w3.org/1999/02/22-rdf-syntax-ns#"
    xmlns:ns="http://ontology.hpl.hp.com/slms/addLineToOrder#">
  <rdf:Description rdf:about="http://example.com/slms/addlinetoorder.xml">
    <ns:costCentre>999</ns:costCentre>
  </rdf:Description>
</rdf:RDF>
```

The XML Schema which the output message must comply with is shown below. It shows that we need to specify an XML element called Field1 and its corresponding value using an XML element called Value1.

```
<?xml version="1.0" encoding="UTF-8"?> <xs:schema
  targetNamespace="http://ontology.hpl.hp.com/slms/addLineToOrder.xsd"
  xmlns:xs="http://www.w3.org/2001/XMLSchema">
    <xs:element name="addLineToOrder" form="qualified">
        <xs:complexType>
          <xs:sequence>
            <xs:element name="Field1" type="xs:string" minOccurs="0"/>
            <xs:element name="Value1" type="xs:string" minOccurs="0"/>
          </xs:sequence>
        </xs:complexType>
    </xs:element>
</xs:schema>
```

The first stage consists in obtaining an RDF model that resembles the XML Schema that we want to comply with. This will be done by means of the rule specified below. The left-hand side of the rule detects the presence of the cost-centre property and translates this into the appropriate document structure including the document element property ‘addLineToOrder’ and the separate ‘Field1’ and ‘Value1’ properties.

```
@prefix ns: <http://ontology.hpl.hp.com/slms/addLineToOrder#>
@prefix j.0: <http://ontology.hpl.hp.com/slms/addLineToOrder.xsd/>
@prefix j.1:
<http://ontology.hpl.hp.com/slms/addLineToOrder.xsd/addLineToOrder/>

(?x ns:costCentre ?c) -> (?x j.0:addLineToOrder ?y), (?y j.1:Field1
'COST CENTER'), (?y j.1:Value1 ?c).
```

As a result of the application of this rule, the following piece of RDF code is obtained:

```
<rdf:RDF
  xmlns:j.0="http://ontology.hpl.hp.com/slms/addLineToOrder.xsd/"
  xmlns:rdf="http://www.w3.org/1999/02/22-rdf-syntax-ns#"
  xmlns:j.1="http://ontology.hpl.hp.com/slms/addLineToOrder.xsd/addLineToOrder/">
 <rdf:Description rdf:about="http://example.com/slms/addlinetoorder.xml">
   <j.0:addLineToOrder rdf:parseType="Resource">
       <j.1:Field1>COST CENTER</j.1:Field1>
       <j.1:Value1>999</j.1:Value1>
   </j.0:addLineToOrder>
 </rdf:Description>
</rdf:RDF>
```

Now the second stage starts. The property names in the RDF statements above are defined relative to the target namespace of the XML Schema `http://ontology.hpl.hp.com/slms/addLineToOrder.xsd`. The response from this call is the corresponding XML that has to be output, conforming with the XML Schema.

```
<?xml version="1.0"?> <ns1:addLineToOrder
   xmlns:ns1="http://ontology.hpl.hp.com/slms/addLineToOrder.xsd">
  <Field1>COST CENTER</Field1>
  <Value1>999</Value1>
</ns1:addLineToOrder>
```

10.4 Ontology Mediation

The objective of ontology mediation in the context of Semantic Web Services is to produce mappings between the conceptualisations of the service provider and requester (or in a more general way, among the services involved in a choreography). It differs from data mediation both in the scope of the mediation performed (focused on overcoming the heterogeneity of semantic models instead of the message syntax) and in the tools used for that purpose, as we will explain later.

As described in the introduction to this chapter, ontology mediation is normally needed in all of the Semantic Web Service interactions identified in our macro-architecture: on service offer registration by a service provider, on service request by a service requester, on the definition of a service provision between the service requester and provider and on service delivery.

The reason for this is that the services involved in a choreography may use different semantic models to represent the data that they are exchanging. While the service requester may use the parameter departurePlace as the departure port name for a freight service, the service provider receiving the message may be expecting that the departurePlace is the name of the city and the name of the country from which the freight service will be done.

As specified in Chap. 3, ontologies are shared models of a domain, which means that if the services involved in a choreography share the same ontology then there will be no problems on understanding the content of the messages that they are exchanging (after data mediation in the case of service invocation or for service discovery, registration, etc.). However, this is not always the case when any set of services exchange messages. That is, there are cases where the service requester and provider do not share the same ontology. In that case, there are differences in the conception of the domain that may affect the effective communication between them. These differences are commonly known as mismatches, which are overcome by ontology mediation.

According to the literature, ontology mediation can be accomplished following at least two different strategies: alignment and merge. Ontology alignment is defined as "a set of correspondences between two or more (in case of multi-alignment) ontologies (by analogy with DNA sequence alignment)" [2]. Ontology merge is defined as "the creation of a new ontology from two or more (possibly overlapping) source ontologies; this concept is closely related to that of integration in the database community" [2]. In other words, ontology alignment is accomplished by establishing links between the different source ontologies, which are kept separated, while ontology merge consists in joining the source ontologies into a single ontology that comprises all the information of the sources.

Although they have different purposes (keeping source ontologies separated or transforming them to a single ontology), ontology alignment and merge can be performed with similar algorithms, techniques and tools. Among them we can cite the PROMPT tool suite [19], the MAFRA framework [15], the Chimaera tool [16], RDFT [20], GLUE [5], OntoMap [14] and Semantic Matching [6]. There are also integrated systems that cover the problem of ontology alignment and merge and that propose algorithms and techniques as well, such as InfoSleuth [9], ONION [18], OBSERVER [17] and MOMIS [1], among others.

It is not the objective of this section to provide an extensive discussion about the current state of the art on ontology alignment and merge, but to comment on the solutions to the ontology mediation problem in the context of Semantic Web Services. For extensive surveys of the state of the art on ontology alignment and merge, we recommend reading [12], [13] and [4]. They all provide a good overview and classification of the state of the art on ontology mediation methods and tools, as well as a characterisation of the different types of ontology mismatches that can be found between heterogeneous ontologies. Besides these readings, in the EON2004 workshop[5] proceedings we can find ontology alignment and merge experiments that have been carried out with some of these tools.

10.4.1 An Implementation of an Ontology Mediation Component for Semantic Web Services

Ontology mediation methods, techniques and tools usually consist of two steps. First the mappings between the concepts and relations of the ontologies used by the services are established. These mappings are usually known as mapping rules, even though they are not necessarily implemented as rules. Then these mapping rules are executed to transform the messages that are being exchanged or the goals and capabilities of the service requesters and providers. Figure 10.4 illustrates this process,

[5] `http://km.aifb.uni-karlsruhe.de/ws/eon2003`

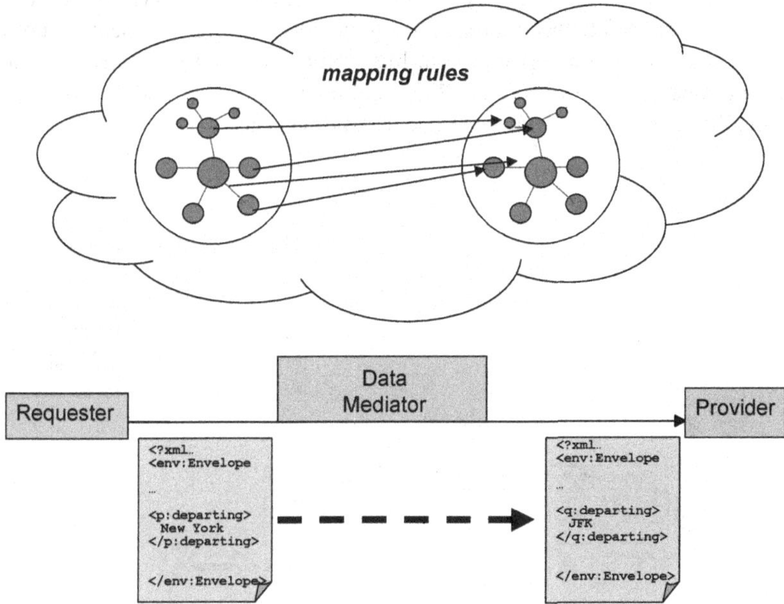

Fig. 10.4. Ontology mediation for the exchange of messages between Web Services

showing how the message content would be transformed according to the mapping rules defined between two services.

As described in Chap. 8, the goals of a service requester can be described either as instances of the requester ontologies, where the specific values for the service parameters are specified, or as class expressions based on the requester ontologies, which define in a more abstract way the requester goal without specifying the actual values for the service parameters.

We will show now an ontology mediation approach that has been implemented in the context of the SWWS project, following the first approach. That is, we assume that goals are described as instances of the requester ontologies, with specific values for their properties. In this context, ontology mediation consists in transforming the instances of the service requester ontologies into instances of the service provider ontologies. These transformations are executed from the mappings between the service requester and provider ontologies, which may have been derived using any of the ontology merge and alignment approaches aforementioned or specified manually.

Let us assume that we are in the context of the first case study described in Chap. 6, the one about a financial overdraft notification service. We will focus on the notification part of the service. Let us also consider that there are a set of Semantic Web Services that provide different types of notification services for users (notification by e-mail, phone, SMS, etc.).

Figure 10.5 shows graphically part of the ontology that the service requester (the system that decides whether notifying users or not) uses for representing notifications. This ontology contains concepts like notification, notificationByFax, notificationByPhone, notificationByPostalMail, etc. Besides this, it models more general concepts like users, postal addresses, dates and times, etc.

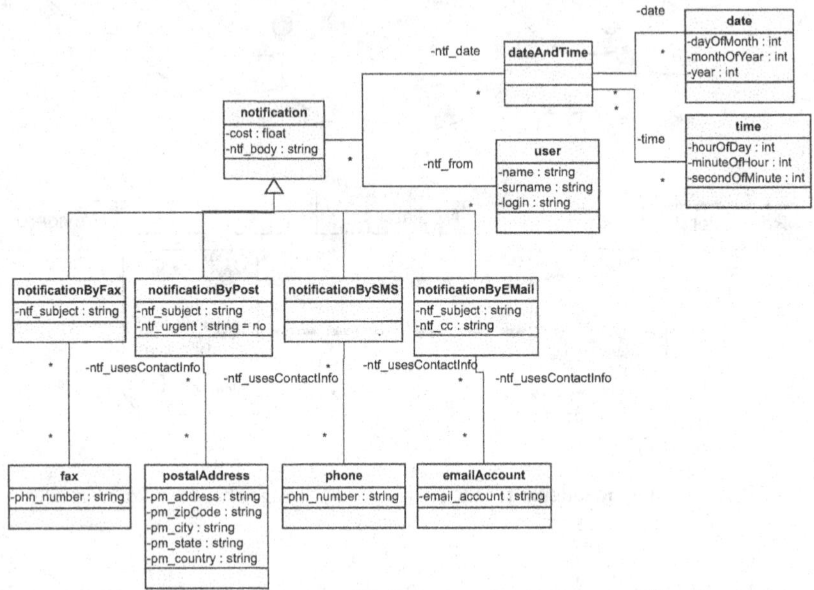

Fig. 10.5. Notification ontology of the service requester (*source ontology*)

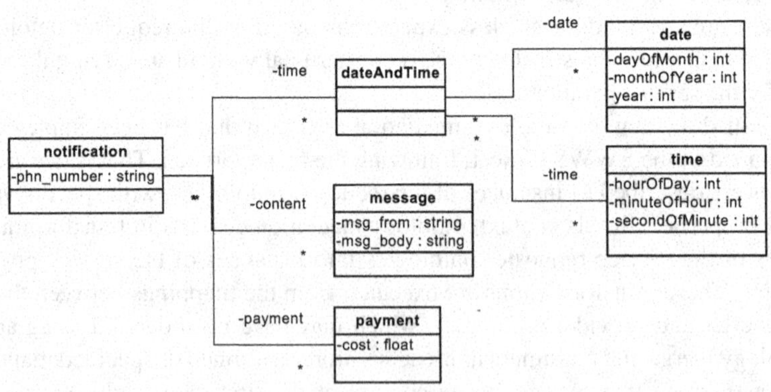

Fig. 10.6. Notification ontology of the service provider (*target ontology*)

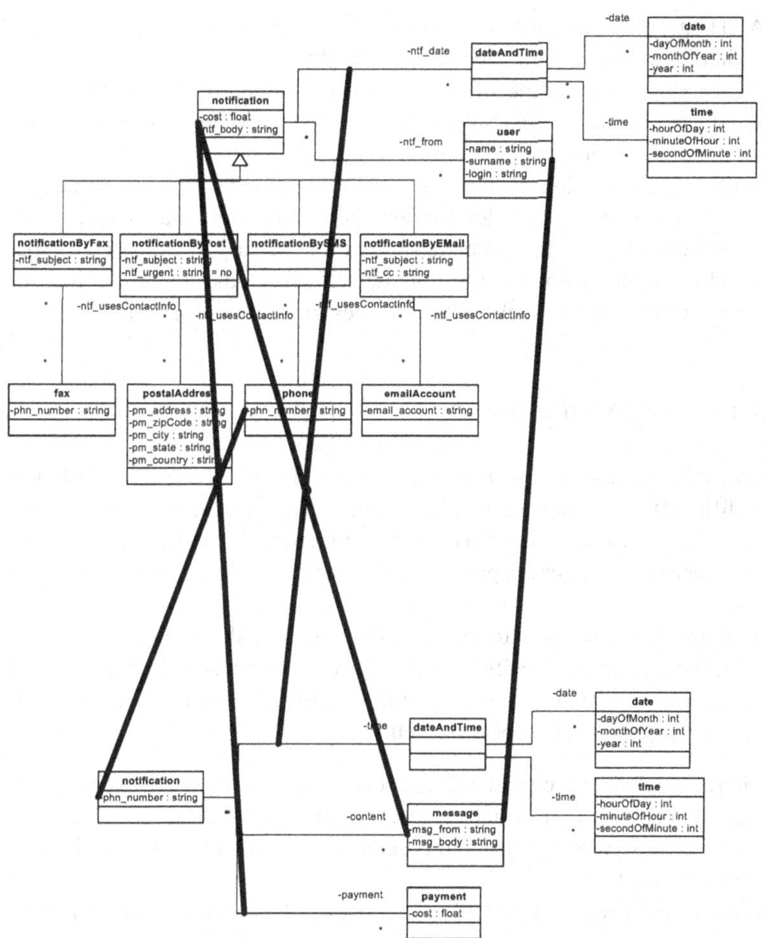

Fig. 10.7. Mapping rules for mediation between the two notification ontologies

Figure 10.6 shows graphically part of the ontology used by the service provider (in this case the service in charge of notifying users by SMSs). We can see that both services use the concept notification to refer to the notification to be sent. However, the properties of this concept are not exactly the same in both ontologies (they use different names in some cases, the structure is different for some of them, where a set of datatype properties in one case is transformed into an object property where the range is another concept, etc.). Besides this, in the source ontology there is a classification of different types of notifications, according to the type of medium used to send it, while in the target ontology there is only one type of notification considered, since the service provider only deals with messages sent by SMS. Finally, we can see that both services use the same representation for timestamps (represented by the dateAndTime, date and time concepts in both ontologies), so there will be no need for mediation in this specific piece of information.

Figure 10.7 shows some of the mediation rules needed to generate instances of the concept notificationBySMS of the service provider ontology given a set of instances from the service requester ontology.

In the current version of the software that is in charge of the ontology mediation process, the mediation rules are specified in an ad hoc language, which is not presented here since we have not considered it necessary to explain the process followed. These rules can be easily implemented using other more common mapping specification formalisms, such as the ones described in [2] or [4].

10.5 Protocol Mediation

Protocol mediation intends to map the patterns of conceptually similar but mechanically different interaction protocols sharing a similar conceptual model of a given domain. It can happen either between two functionally similar protocols or on the part of a service requester adapting its behaviour to the interface offered by a service provider.

A protocol is a set of activities and transitions with conditions for such transitions. Depending on the specific process, these tasks are a combination of distributed services, which can themselves be composite. In the context of Semantic Web Services, they are used for the following purposes:

- Choreography, where protocols are seen as a set of message exchanges between participants which are bound to occur in given sequences.
- Orchestration, where a protocol is seen as a partial order of operations that need to be executed.
- Collaboration, where protocols are considered as relations between participants of the service with the aim to combine their capabilities and solve complex problems via composition.

The interaction patterns of several Web Services involved in a communication do not always have a precise match, i.e. do not always follow exactly the same pattern in realising a complex process. Sometimes there can be mismatches like the ones identified in [3] and summarised in Fig. 10.8:

- Unexpected messages: One of the parties does not expect to receive a message issued by another. For instance, in a commercial transaction with a credit card a service sends the credit card type, the credit card number, the expiration date, the full name and the pin code, while the service that receives those messages does not expect to receive a pin code, since it does not use it.
- Messages in different order: The parties involved in a communication send and receive messages in different orders. In the previous case the sender may send the messages in the order specified above while the receiver expects first the full name and then the rest of the messages.

- Messages that need to be split: One of the parties sends a message with multiple information inside it, which needs to be received separately by the party with which it is communicating. In the previous example, the sender sends the expiration date in one message, while the receiver expects it as two messages, indicating the expiration month and the expiration year, respectively.
- Messages that need to be combined: One of the parties sends a set of messages that the receiver expects as a single message with the multiple information. In the previous example we can think of the inverse situation to the one presented (the expiration date is sent in two different messages and the receiver expects it in a unique message).
- Dummy acknowledgements or virtual messages that have to be sent: One of the parties expects an acknowledgement for a certain message, but the receiver does not issue such acknowledgement; or the receiver expects a message that the sender is not prepared to send.

All these mismatches can be combined to form other types of mismatches, hence adding more complexity to the task of dealing with mismatches. In fact, after the definition of a complex service one must determine the compatibility of the external visible behaviours of the Web Services involved in the communication, and determine the correctness and validity of the resulting complex service.

Reference [21] describe the implementation and use of a solution in the logistics domain. This solution is based on the existence of a general abstract state machine that represents the overall state of the communication between parties, and a set of abstract machines for each of the parties in the conversation, which specify their state and the sets of actions to be performed when they receive a set of messages or when they have to send a set of messages.

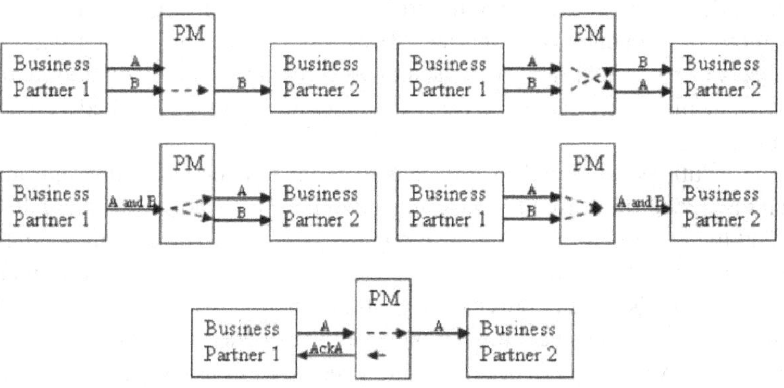

Fig. 10.8. Set of message interaction mismatches that can appear in a Web Service communication (from [3])

In the context of the WSMO initiative, [3] describe the approach taken for the design and implementation of the process mediator for the Semantic Web Service execution engine WSMX. This approach is similar to the one described in [21], since it is based on the use of an abstract machine with guarded transitions that are fired by the exchange of messages and the definition of choreographies for each of the parties involved in the communication.

10.6 Outlook

This chapter has covered the current major trends on mediation in the context of Semantic Web Services. According to the conceptual architecture presented in Chap. 6, mediation and decoupling are the most important principles to be considered in the development of Semantic Web Service architectures. Mediation services are those that resolve inconsistencies between two or more parties involved in a conversation (a sequence of message exchanges in order to achieve a goal).

Mediation can be considered at many different levels, from simpler transformations between formats to more complex transformations of message exchange patterns. However, all of these transformations have to be coordinated and most of them are usually necessary in any message exchange between two heterogeneous services. This chapter has been structured according to a classification of mediation layers that considers mediation problems at the data, ontology, protocol and process levels. We have described the current state of the art in mediation approaches and we have given some indications on possible solutions to this problem, most of them based on the work done in the context of the SWWS project. Process mediation has not been considered in this chapter because it falls outside the current context of Semantic Web Service research.

The notion of mediation appeared a long time ago and much effort has been done to date in order to solve the mediation problems that appear in open environments such as those of Semantic Web Services. However, there is still a long way to go in all aspects of mediation in order to achieve a fully automatic mediation platform that is able to make any set of services interoperate without any need of manual intervention.

All the solutions presented in this chapter require much user intervention: the lifting and lowering rules used for data mediation have to be specified manually and are difficult to derive automatically; the mappings between ontology components are normally supervised by human users, although some of the current ontology alignment and merge tools already provide suggestions about possible mappings; and the choreographies used in protocol mediation have to be created with the help of choreography editors. As a consequence of the high degree of user intervention needed to create the appropriate mediation services, the process of building an application out of several pre-existing Web services still requires an important amount of effort, and mediators are still difficult to build and maintain.

We think that the future trends in mediation in the Semantic Web Services environment will go in the following directions:

- Providing more degree of automation in the generation of mediation rules, mappings and choreographies.
- Facilitating the debugging and maintenance of previously generated mediation rules, mappings and choreographies.
- Facilitating the reuse of existing mediation components by the use of mediation patterns.

Only if these aspects are considered in the following years, it will be possible to completely automate the process of combining different Semantic Web Services and hence exploiting the full potential of adding semantics to current Web Services.

References

1. S. Bergamaschi, S. Castano, and M. Vincini. Semantic Integration of Semistructured and Structured Data Sources. *SIGMOD Record, Special Issue on Semantic Interoperability in Global Information*, 28(1), March 1999.
2. P. Bouquet, J. Euzenat, E. Franconi, L. Serafini, G. Stamou, and S. Tessaris. Specification of a Common Framework for Characterizing Alignment. KnowledgeWeb Project Deliverable D2.2.1, 2004.
3. E. Cimpian and A. Mocan. Process Mediation in WSMX. WSMO Working Draft D13.7 v0.1, 2005.
4. J. de Bruijn, F. Martín-Recuerda, D. Manov, and M. Ehrig. State-of-the-Art Survey on Ontology Merging and Aligning. SEKT Project Deliverable D4.2.1, 2004.
5. A. Doan, J. Madhaven, P. Domingos, and A. Halevy. *Ontology Matching: A Machine Learning Approach*, pages 397–416. Springer-Verlag, 2004.
6. F. Giunchiglia and P. Shvaiko Semantic Matching. *Knowledge Engineering Review*, 18(3), 2003.
7. D. Fensel and C. Bussler. The Web Service Modeling Framework WSMF. *Electronic Commerce Research and Applications*, 1(2):113–137, 2002.
8. D. Fensel and R. Groenboom. Specifying Knowledge-Based Systems with Reusable Components. In *Proceedings of the 9th International Conference on Software Engineering & Knowledge Engineering (SEKE-97)*, Madrid, Spain.
9. J. Fowler, M. Nodine, B. Perry, and B. Bargmeyer. Agent-Based Semantic Interoperability in Infosleuth. *SIGMOD Record*, 28(1), 1999.
10. E. Gamma, R. Helm, R. Johnson, and J. Vlissides. *Design Patterns*. Addison-Wesley, 1995.
11. D. Garlan and D.E. Perry. Introduction to the Special Issue on Software Architecture. *IEEE Transactions on Software Engineering*, 21(4), 1995.
12. A. Gómez-Pérez, M. Fernández-López, and O. Corcho. *Ontological Engineering: With Examples From the Areas of Knowledge Management, e-Commerce and the Semantic Web*. Springer-Verlag, 2004.
13. J. Euzenat et al. State of the Art on Current Alignment Techniques. KnowledgeWeb Project Deliverable D2.2.3, 2004.
14. A. Kiryakov, K. Simov, and M. Dimitrov. OntoMap: Ontologies for Lexical Semantics. In G. Angelova, K. Bontcheva, R. Mitkov, N. Nicolov, and N. Nikolov, editors, *Proceedings of the Euroconference Recent Advances in Natural Language Processing (RANLP-2001)*, pages 142–148, Tzigov, Bulgaria, 2001.

15. A. Maedche, B. Motik, N. Silva, and R. Volz. MAFRA: A Mapping Framework for Distributed Ontologies. In A. Gómez-Pérez and R. Benjamins, editors, *Proceedings of the 13th European Conference on Knowledge Engineering and Knowledge Management (EKAW-2002)*, Sigüenza, Spain, 2002.
16. D. McGuinness, R. Fikes, J. Rice, and S. Wilder. The Chimaera Ontology Environment. In P. Rosenbloom, H.A. Kautz, B. Porter, R. Dechter, R. Sutton, and V. Mittal, editors, *Proceedings of the 17th National Conference on Artificial Intelligence (AAAI00)*, pages 1123–1124, Austin, Texas, 2000.
17. E. Mena, A. Illarramendi, V. Kashyap, and A. Sheth. OBSERVER: An Approach for Query Processing in Global Information Systems Based on Interoperation Across Pre-Existing Ontologies. *Distributed and Parallel Databases*, 8(2):223–271, 2000.
18. P. Mitra, G. Wiederhold, and M. Kersten. A Graph-Oriented Model for articulation of Ontology Interdependencies. In *Proceedings of Conference on Extending Database Technology (EDBT 2000)*, Konstanz, Germany, March 2000.
19. N.F. Noy and M.A. Musen. PROMPT: Algorithm and Tool for Automated Ontology Merging and Alignment. In *Proceedings 17th National Conference on Artificial Intelligence (AAAI-2000)*, Austin, Texas, USA, July/August 2000.
20. B. Omelayenko. RDFT: A Mapping Meta-Ontology for Business Integration. In *Proceedings of the Workshop on Knowledge Transformation for the Semantic Web at the 15th European Conference on Artificial Intelligence (KTSW-2002), pages.*
21. C. Preist, J.E. Cuadrado, S. Battle, S. Williams, and S. Grimm. Automated Business-to-Business Integration of a Logistics Supply Chain using Semantic Web Services Technology. In *Proceedings of the 4th International Semantic Web Conference (ISWC-2005)*, Galway, Ireland, 2005.
22. G. Wiederhold. Mediators in the Architecture of Future Information Systems. *IEEE Computer*, 25(3):38–49, March 1992.

Part IV

Tools and Use Cases

11

Tools for Semantic Web Services

Support for Development and Deployment

Anupriya Ankolekar[1], Massimo Paolucci[3], Naveen Srinivasan[2] and Katia Sycara[2]

[1] AIFB University of Karlsruhe, Germany, ankolekar@aifb.uni-karlsruhe.de
[2] Carnegie-Mellon University, Pittsburgh PA, USA, paolucci@docomo.com
[3] NTT DoCoMo Eurolabs, München, Germany, {naveen, katia}@cs.cmu.edu

Summary. In this chapter, we present an overview of selected tools and systems available for developing Semantic Web Services. We examine five prominent tools for developing Semantic Web Services and align them to the Semantic Web Service deployment lifecycle presented in Chap. 6. In particular, we describe the development of OWL-S services using tools, such as the OWL-S IDE and the OWL-S Editor; the development of WSMO services, through the WSMO set of tools and IRS-III; and finally, the annotation of services in WSDL-S through the tool MWSAF. Each of these tools cover the steps in the Semantic Web Services deployment and usage lifecycle to varying extents. Some of them, such as MWSAF, focus on only one stage of the lifecycle, whereas other tools, such as the OWL-S IDE and WSMO set of tools, cover all stages.

11.1 Introduction

Semantic Web Services promise to facilitate the discovery and composition of Web Services. However, the development and deployment of Semantic Web Services is quite complex and its adoption within the industry has been relatively slow. A prime factor in this is the significant human effort required to create semantic service offer and request descriptions and then to monitor the invocation and execution of the Web Services. The widespread availability of usable and comprehensive tools can mitigate this by supporting developers in creating semantic service descriptions from the code they write and in simulating Web Service execution. A number of tools and systems have therefore been developed within the Semantic Web Services community to support, in particular the semantic annotation of Web Services and their deployment. In this chapter, we review five prominent tools and discuss how they support the Semantic Web Service deployment lifecycle discussed in Chap. 6. The first two tools support the annotation of Web Services in OWL-S, namely the OWL-S IDE[1] and the OWL-S Editor[2]; the next two support the deployment of WSMO-annotated services,

[1] http://projects.semwebcentral.org/projects/owl-s-ide
[2] http://owlseditor.semwebcentral.org/

namely WSMX[3] and Internet Reasoning Service (IRS) III[4]; and finally, we examine the METEOR-S Web Service Annotation Framework[5] (MWSAF), which supports the addition of WSDL-S annotation to Web Services.

While certain tools such as the OWL-S IDE and WSMX attempt to provide a complete environment for Web Service developers, from modelling the service to executing it, other tools focus on a few stages of the lifecycle, e.g. MWSAF and the OWL-S Editor which primarily focus on semantic annotations of Web Services. Before we examine each of these tools in detail and their support of the Semantic Web Service deployment lifecycle, we first discuss a number of Web Service 'tool-lets', freely available small programs, which primarily perform syntactic transformations between Web Service descriptions in various languages. Many of the tools we will discuss build on these small programs, which are useful tools in their own right.

11.1.1 Web Service Tools

Since Semantic Web Services essentially add semantic annotations to Web Services, many Semantic Web Service tools build on established Web Services tools. In most cases, they are 'tool-lets' rather than tools, being small programs that perform a narrowly defined task, such as automatically generating sample WSDL descriptions from Java classes. Table 11.1 lists these existing Web Service tools, which primarily convert one kind of service description into another. In the following, we go through each of these tools in detail.

Java2WSDL

The Java2WSDL tool generates WSDL descriptions from Java classes. It is part of the Apache Axis SOAP toolkit [2], originally developed by IBM and now an Apache open source software development project. The same toolkit also provides the WSDL2Java tool, which generates Java proxies and skeletons for to-be-implemented

Table 11.1. An overview of freely available tools that convert between various forms of Web Service descriptions

Tool-let	Description
Java2WSDL	Converts Java interfaces and classes into WSDL descriptions
WSDL2Java	Generates Java stubs from WSDL descriptions
WSDL2OWL-S	Converts WSDL descriptions into OWL-S Profile, Process Model and Grounding
Java2OWL-S	Converts Java classes into WSDL files
OWL-S2UDDI	Converts OWL-S Profiles to UDDI advertisements

[3] `http://www.wsmx.org/`

[4] `http://kmi.open.ac.uk/projects/irs/`

[5] `http://lsdis.cs.uga.edu/projects/meteor-s/mwsaf/`

services described in WSDL. To develop a Web Service, a developer can first write a Java interface of the Web Service, which can then be used to develop WSDL descriptions for the Web Service using the Java2WSDL tool. The WSDL descriptions can be used to develop stubs, skeletons and bindings for useful Java classes using the WSDL2Java tool. For a flavour of the transformation, the Java function below:

```
String addWidget(String name, Double price)
```

generates the following WSDL fragment:

```
<operation name="addWidget"
           returnType="xsd:string"
           xmlns:xsd="http://www.w3.org/2001/XMLSchema">
    <parameter name="name" type="xsd:string"/>
    <parameter name="price" type="xsd:double"/>
</operation>
```

and the WSDL fragment [6]

```
<service name="AddressBookService">
    <port name="AddressBook"
          binding="tns:AddressBookSOAPBinding">
    <soap:address location="http://localhost:8080/axis/
                                 services/AddressBook"/>
    </port>
</service>
```

will generate the following Java interface:

```
public interface AddressBookService
                       extends javax.xml.rpc.Service {
  public String getAddressBookAddress();

  public AddressBook getAddressBook()
                        throws javax.xml.rpc.ServiceException;

  public AddressBook getAddressBook(URL portAddress)
                        throws javax.xml.rpc.ServiceException;
}
```

WSDL2OWL-S

The WSDL2OWL-S tool,[7] developed as part of the OWL-S, toolsuite,[8] converts WSDL Web Service interface descriptions into OWL-S, generating a complete OWL-S Grounding, a partial OWL-S Process Model and Profile for the WSDL service. In addition, the tool generates OWL classes for user-defined Java classes used

[6] taken from the Axis User Guide at http://ws.apache.org/axis/java/user-guide.html

[7] http://www.daml.ri.cmu.edu/wsdl2owls/

[8] http://www.daml.ri.cmu.edu/tools

in the Java service class.[9] The generated Grounding is clearly complete, because the WSDL file contains all the information necessary to invoke the Web Service. However, the WSDL file is only a partial description of the Web Service, so the generated OWL-S Process Model and Profile are stubs and need to be manually enriched with semantic information. This includes defining composite processes in the Process Model, describing the service capability descriptions within the Profile and XSLT transformations from the WSDL XSD types to OWL ontologies. Note that a tool converting process descriptions in the opposite direction, namely using the OWL-S Grounding to generate WSDL descriptions of the Web Service, would also be useful, e.g., if the Web Service is semantically specified before being actually implemented. Such a tool is however yet to be developed to our knowledge.

Java2OWL-S

The Java2OWL-S tool,[10] also part of the OWL-S toolsuite, combines the Apache Axis Java2WSDL converter and the WSDL2OWL-S converter to provide a partial translation from Java classes to OWL-S descriptions. As with the WSDL2OWL-S tool, this tool generates a complete OWL-S Grounding, and a partial OWL-S Process Model and Profile for the service implemented by the Java class. In addition, the tool generates OWL classes for user-defined Java classes used in the Java service class.

OWL-S2UDDI

The OWL-S toolsuite also contains a OWL-S2UDDI Converter,[11] which embeds OWL-S profile descriptions in the corresponding UDDI advertisements. These UDDI advertisements can then be published in any UDDI registry and then discovered by service requesters. A matchmaker that understands OWL-S can use the UDDI registry to discover Web Services and then make use of any additional OWL-S semantic annotations that may exist to describe them.

OWL-S API

In addition to these tools, most Semantic Web Service tools also make use of an OWL-S API, developed independently by both CMU[12] and University of Maryland, [13] which provides programmatic access to OWL-S service descriptions. The OWL-S API provides Java classes and methods to extract information from an

[9] The OWL-S ontology defines classes that are required for the description of the Web Service, such as the `Processes` it contains and their `Inputs` and `Outputs`. In addition to these, a semantic service description refers to OWL ontologies that describe the data being exchanged by the Web Service, such as `Book` or `Ticket`

[10] `http://projects.semwebcentral.org/projects/java2owl-s/`

[11] `http://owl-s2uddi.projects.semwebcentral.org/`

[12] `http://www.daml.ri.cmu.edu/owlsapi/`

[13] `http://www.mindswap.org/2004/owl-s/api/`

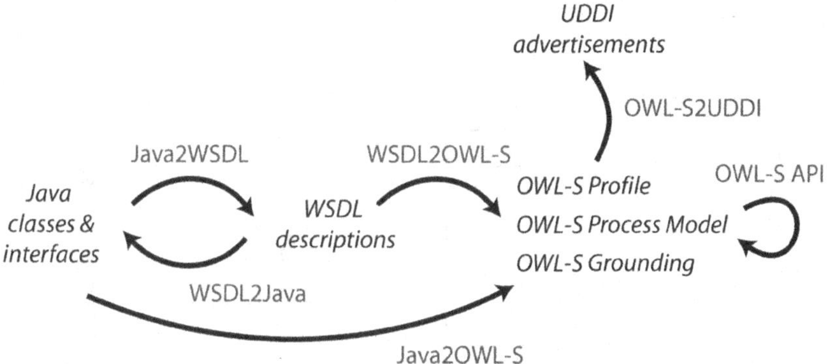

Fig. 11.1. An overview of tools for generating annotations from Java code and vice versa

OWL-S description or to generate an OWL-S description. The CMU OWL-S API is based on the Jena [9] OWL models and API.

The functionality of the tools described above is depicted in Fig. 11.1.

11.2 Lifecycle of Semantic Web Services

The deployment and usage of Semantic Web Services follows a particular lifecycle of interactions between service requester and service provider as described in Chap. 6. The lifecycle begins with the modelling of the service and request by the service provider and requester, respectively, in the *service modelling* stage. Then service requests and service offers[14] are matched in the *service discovery* phase, possibly through a third-party matchmaker. Once a set of potential service providers have been identified for a service request, the *service definition* stage takes place, where the selected services are configured to result in concrete services that can be delivered. There is an additional pruning of service providers that takes place at this stage, resulting in a single concrete service, which is eventually delivered to the service requester in the *service delivery* stage. A developer developing a Web Service would need to go through the service modelling stage to develop a semantic description of the Web Service, simulate the service discovery and definition phases to ensure the Web Service can be discovered and configured correctly. Finally, the developer may wish to simulate the service delivery to verify that the developed Web Service functions correctly in all stages of the Web Service lifecycle. A service requester, user or developer would typically need to go through all four stages in order to develop and use a Web Service.

Most Semantic Web Service tools focus on the service modelling stage, since adding semantic annotations to a service description require most human effort. The

[14] Note: In the following, when we refer to Web Service or service descriptions, we will be referring specifically to semantic service offer descriptions. Similarly, semantic service request descriptions will be referred to as service requests or simply requests

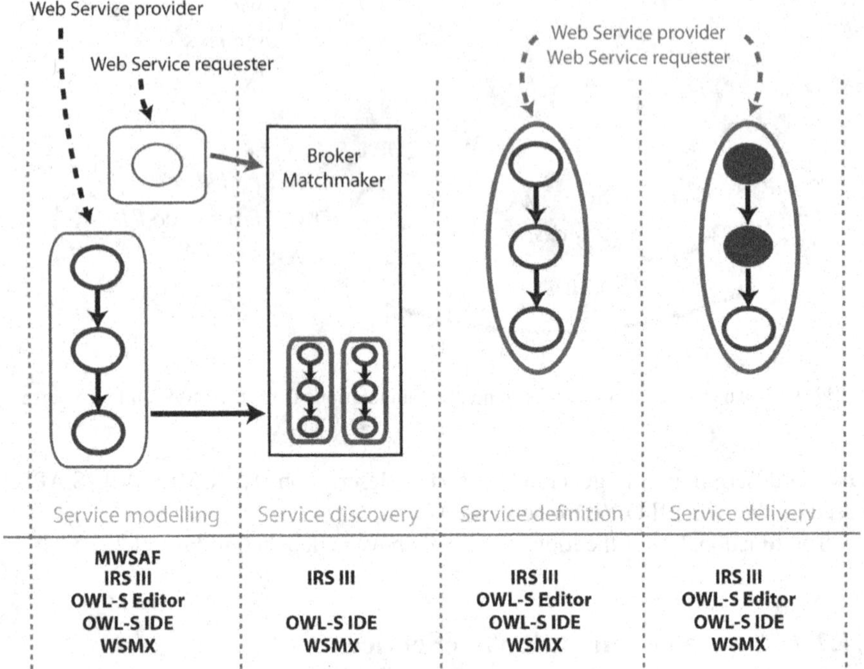

Fig. 11.2. Semantic Web Service tool support for the various stages of the Semantic Web Service deployment lifecycle

other stages are generally less well supported. Accordingly, our discussion of the tools will be most detailed for the first stage. Figure 11.2 shows the Semantic Web Service lifecycle and classifies prominent tools with respect to the lifecycle stages they support. The five tools are the OWL-S IDE, the OWL-S Editor, the METEOR-S Web Service Annotation Framework (MWSAF), the IRS-III and the WSMX toolsuite. The first two tools, the OWL-S IDE and the OWL-S Editor support OWL-S service description creation, the MWSAF supports developing WSDL-S descriptions and the last two tools, IRS-III and WSMX support WSMO service description creation.

11.3 Service Modelling

In the service modelling stage, both service provider and service requester prepare service offer descriptions and service requirement descriptions respectively. There are two ways in which a developer may construct a service offer description. On the one hand, the developer may first develop a Web Service and then describe the functionality provided within a service offer description. In this case, the developer first implements the Web Service, then generates a WSDL [3] specification to describe the invocation interface of the Web Service. If the Web Service is to be annotated semantically, then the developer will define additional OWL-S or WSMO specifications to describe the Web Service in terms of its goals and process flow. To describe the semantics of the data exchange during the Web Service invocation, the developer will choose ontologies, specifically concepts and relations in certain ontologies. Finally, the service description will be published with a registry or directory service. We call this approach the *code-driven approach*, as it uses an existing Web Service implementation as the starting point to derive a service offer description. This is commonly the case when Web Services are being developed to expose the functionality of legacy systems, where most of the functionality of the system has already been implemented, but is unavailable to the outside world.

If, on the other hand, the Web Service is to be developed from scratch, another possibility is to treat the service offer description as a high-level description of the required functionality of the Web Service and then partially generate the code required to implement the Web Service. This could be termed the *model-driven approach*. In this case, first the service offer description is developed using appropriate ontologies, then the orchestration or process model is used to define stubs and skeletons for the implementation of the Web Service. This implementation is in turn used to generate a WSDL grounding and as in the code-driven approach, the service description is finally published with a registry or some form of directory service.

Ideally, tools that support the creation of service offer descriptions and the corresponding Web Service need to support both approaches, since most developers will go through a combination of a code-driven and model-driven approach to arrive at the final semantic description and Web Service. As described in Sect. 11.1.1, several tools have been developed to automate some of the steps of each approach. In the code-driven approach, for instance, the tools Java2WSDL, WSDL2OWL-S and Java2OWL-S can support the creation of partial OWL-S specifications from Java code. Similarly, for the model-driven approach, a tool such as WSDL2Java can assist in the implementation of the Web Service. The set of stubs and skeletons generated by the tool can be instantiated by the Web Service developer into concrete classes that perform the functionalities promised by the service description. A smart tool could even exploit the interaction protocol specified in the OWL-S description to define implementation classes within generated Java code, reducing the burden of implementation on the Web Service developer.

Developing the service requirement description is considerably simpler than developing the service description. In order to produce a service requirement description, a service requester needs to first decide which capabilities of the desired Web Service to discover. The desired capabilities then need to be represented to a directory service, such as a UDDI server, in order for the service discovery to take place. These capabilities are described at a high level by making use of appropriate OWL ontologies. This requires support in the form of making ontologies available and findable. In addition, we require a user interface to allow people to express goals and requirements. Having developed the service requirement description, the service requester finally needs to publish the request to a registry.

This stage is the most fundamental in the Semantic Web Service lifecycle and is supported by all the five tools. The OWL-S IDE and OWL-S Editor support the modelling and specification of the Web Service in OWL-S, WSMX and IRS-III support the same in WSMO and MWSAF supports annotating WSDL files with additional lightweight semantics, such as UML. We now examine each of the tools and their support for service modelling in detail.

11.3.1 OWL-S IDE

The OWL-S IDE [11] is an Eclipse [8] plug-in providing an integrated development environment (IDE) to support Web Service developers in both the implementation of Web Services and in the generation of OWL-S descriptions of their Web Services. As an Eclipse plug-in, the OWL-S IDE can make use of Eclipse's Java IDE and community-built software development tools to enable the design of a Web Service using UML, the implementation of the Web Service in Java and the deployment of the Web Service, all within a single uniform environment. The OWL-S IDE augments the available Eclipse tools and extends the current Web Service development process by allowing a developer to additionally construct OWL-S semantic descriptions of the Web Service. The OWL-S IDE supports both Web Service developers and Web Service requesters: Web Service developers can generate the OWL-S service descriptions directly from the Java code that implements the Web Service and then deploy and register the Web Service with a UDDI server. Web Service requesters can define an OWL-S Profile of the desired Web Service and use it to query a UDDI server, all within Eclipse. Furthermore, the OWL-S IDE can also assist Web Service requesters develop the client-side code for interaction with the Web Service.

In particular, the OWL-S IDE supports Web Service developers in performing the following tasks:

1. Code-driven approach
   a) Develop and modify the implementation of a Web Service through the Eclipse environment.
   b) Generate a WSDL description of the service from the complete Web Service implementation.
   c) Generate an OWL-S description of the Web Service from WSDL.
   d) Develop an OWL-S ontology to describe the Web Service using OWL ontologies.
   e) Publish a service description with UDDI.
   f) Deploy the Web Service by publishing the Web Service implementation, WSDL and OWL-S descriptions on a Web server.
2. Model-driven approach
   model-driven approach, Given OWL-S descriptions of a Web Service to be built:
   a) Automatically derive Web Service code through the OWL-S Process Model.
   b) Develop and modify the implementation of a Web Service through the Eclipse environment.
   c) Publish a service description with UDDI.
   d) Deploy the Web Service by publishing the Web Service implementation, WSDL and OWL-S descriptions on a Web server.

Support for developing and modifying the Java implementation of the Web Service in Step 1a is not really part of the OWL-S IDE, but is provided in the Java plug-in for Eclipse and is well-integrated with the OWL-S IDE plug-in. Assuming the developer has defined a Java interface to expose particular capabilities of the Web Service, Steps 1b and 1c can be accomplished through the Axis Java2WSDL converter and the WSDL2OWL-S converter, respectively. The result of these two steps is a complete WSDL description, and schematic OWL-S Profile, Process Model and Grounding. These schematic descriptions contain placeholders for OWL-S atomic processes, a mapping between atomic processes and WSDL operations, and placeholders for inputs and outputs in the Profile. However, since WSDL does not provide any semantic annotations, these descriptions do not have any semantic descriptions of the inputs and outputs. In addition, since WSDL does not impose any order on the invocation of operations, the OWL-S descriptions also do not contain any specification of the Web Service control flow.

A screenshot of the OWL-S IDE in Fig. 11.3 shows four different panes of the plugin. The tree pane labelled A presents the elements of an OWL-S description in a hierarchical fashion, allowing the user to browse through the hierarchical structure and select an element to edit or to add an attribute to an element. The action pane and the form pane marked as B and C respectively are responsive to the selection

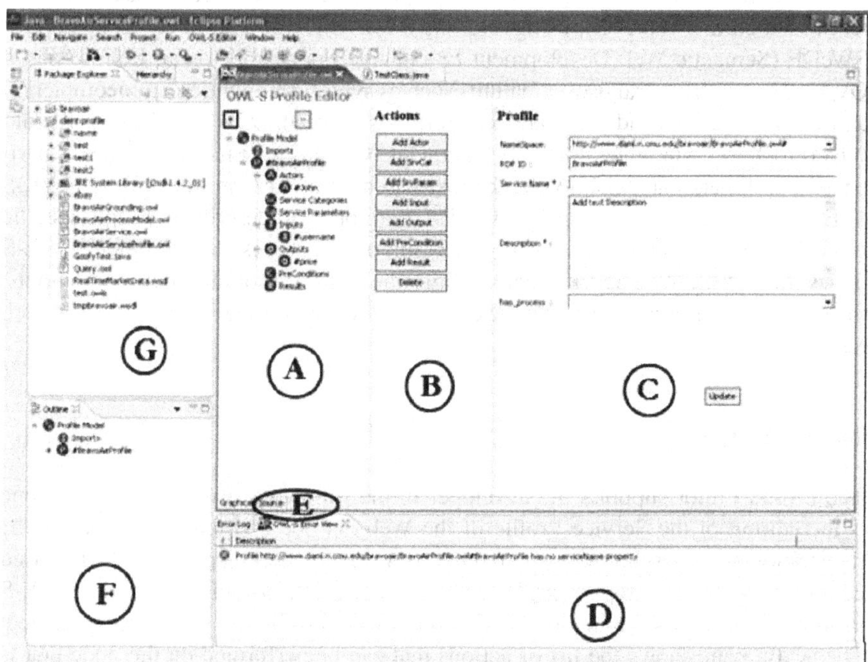

Fig. 11.3. Main layout of the OWL-S IDE

in the tree pane. The action pane displays the controls such as adding and deleting of attributes that are pertinent to the element selected in the tree pane. Similarly, the form pane displays the attributes of the element in a form-like manner, which may be modified. Pane G is a file navigation window contributed directly by the Eclipse framework and is used to browse and manipulate the file system and manage projects in the Eclipse workspace. The outline pane marked as F displays a tree-based synopsis of the file that is being edited. Finally, error pane labelled D displays information of about the errors in the OWL-S file that is being edited.

The main editor pane (with labels A–C) displays four editors to support the manipulation of different fragments of the OWL-S descriptions, namely the Profile Editor, the Process Model Editor, the Grounding Editor and the Service Editor. For each, it provides two modes for editing OWL-S files: form-based editing and text-based editing. The form editor provides guidance to the developer on what information should be added at each stage of the compilation of the OWL-S description. For instance, in the compilation of a process, it requires the developer to enter the inputs, outputs, preconditions and effects. Each of these is, in turn, a form that requires the developer to enter the appropriate information. If the information entered is not correct the developer is flagged an error that he/she can immediately fix.

Within the OWL-S IDE, the service descriptions can either be generated from scratch or by editing an existing OWL-S description. The latter case (Step 1d) may involve editing the schematic service descriptions generated in the previous step from WSDL descriptions. The OWL-S Editor provides form-based editing or text-based editing (label E), using, e.g. the SWeDE OWL plug-in for Eclipse [13]. SWeDE (Semantic Web Development Extendable Framework) is an Eclipse-based OWL editor with several useful features such as syntax highlighting, autocompletion and error-detection, and integrates existing tools like the OWL Validator, Kazuki (OWL to Java code generator) and DumpOnt (Ontology Visualiser). More experienced developers may wish to use the text-based editing capabilities of the OWL-S IDE to more expeditiously develop OWL-S ontologies to describe concepts specific to the Web Service being annotated. The result of this process is a complete OWL-S description of the Web Service that specifies the semantics of all inputs and outputs, the preconditions and effects, and the complete control flow and data flow of the Web Service.

The Profile Editor

The Profile Editor supports the developer in the following two tasks: the first one is the editing of the Service Profile of the Web Service and the second one is the registration and querying with an UDDI server. Figure 11.4 displays the form-based editor that is used to compile an OWL-S Profile. The leftmost selection of the OWL-S Profile Editor shows the hierarchal structure of the profile file that is being Edited. The action pane shows the list of actions that can be performed on the node that is selected, in this case a profile is selected in the tree structure. The form pane displays the attributes of the node that is selected.

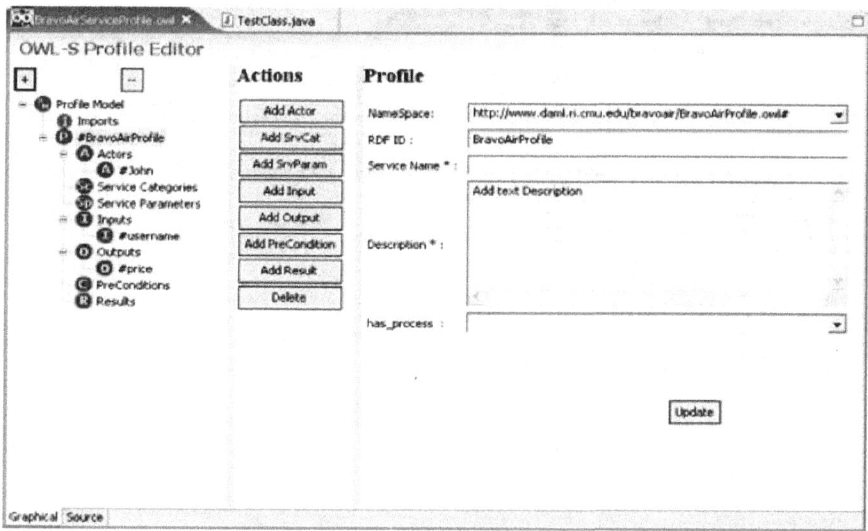

Fig. 11.4. The OWL-S IDE Profile Editor

Process Model Editor

The Process Model Editor supports the developer in the generation of the Process Model using the same approach as the Profile Editor. It also provides a form-based editor to define processes and their control flow and data flow. The tree structure in the form editor supports drag and drop operations, to facilitate the definition of control flow and dataflow in composite processes. When adding a new composite process, we add the components of the process which constitutes the control flow of a process. Figure 11.5 displays a screenshot of the Process Editor, as a composite process is being defined. When displaying a composite process in the process tree, its components are displayed in a nested manner, so that the control flow of the process model can be understood just by following the process tree structure. A dataflow link between two components of the composite process is added by selecting one of the components and selecting the appropriate action from the action pane, such as adding an input or output. In order to add a dataflow link between two components, we need three pieces of information: first the name of the input of the component that needs the data, second the name of the component that generates the data and finally the name of the input or output in the other component that actually has the data.

Grounding Editor

The Grounding Editor supports the compilation of OWL-S grounding descriptions. In order to compile the grounding description, two files are required: an OWL-S Process Model description file, containing information about atomic processes of the

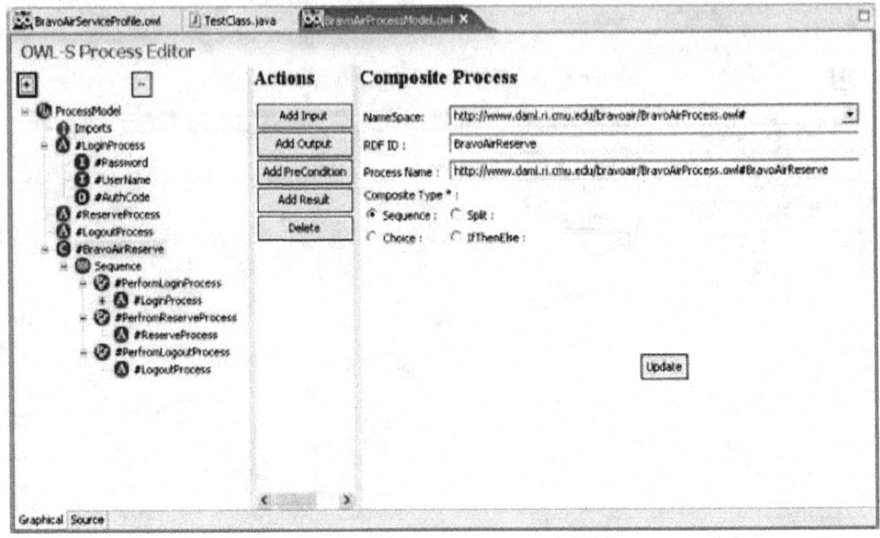

Fig. 11.5. The OWL-S IDE Process Editor

Web Service, and a WSDL file that contains information about the operations and messages exchanged. Once these two files are loaded into the editor, the Grounding Editor generates OWL-S grounding descriptions, essentially information, such as which process in the process model description maps to which operation in the WSDL file, which input/output of a process maps to which message in the WSDL file. OWL-S service descriptions generated by the WSDL2OWL-S converter already have a reasonably comprehensive Grounding, but if otherwise, the OWL-S IDE supports a developer in manually defining the Grounding through the Grounding Editor. Fig. 11.6 displays a screenshot of the Grounding Editor.

Service Editor

The service editor assists the developer in compiling OWL-S service descriptions. The function of the service description is to bind the Profile, the Process Model and the Grounding descriptions of a Web Service explicitly, since the links between them, e.g. between the inputs in the Profile and in the Process Model, are only implicit otherwise. To build a service description in the OWL-S IDE, a Profile, Process Model and Grounding for the service are all loaded independently and then linked with the service description.

11.3.2 OWL-S Editor

The OWL-S Editor [6] takes a slightly different approach to supporting Semantic Web Service development. The OWL-S Editor is being developed as a plug-in for

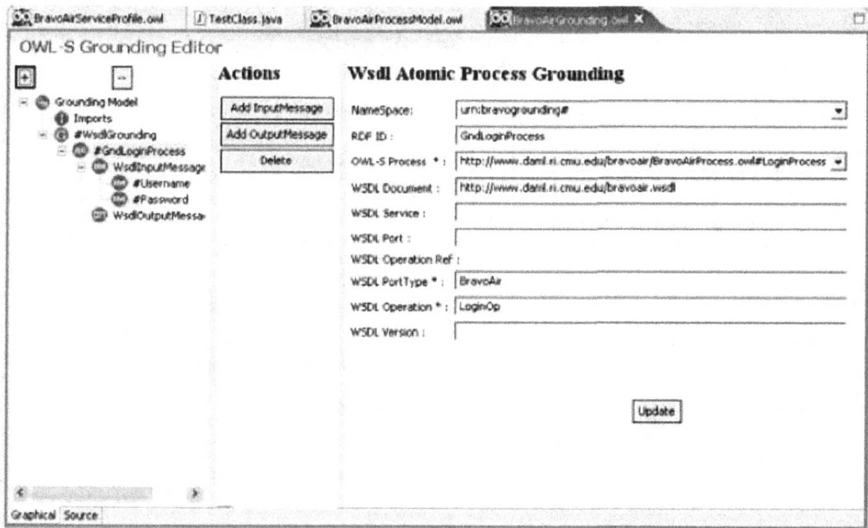

Fig. 11.6. The OWL-S IDE Grounding Editor

Protégé [10], on top of the existing Protégé OWL plug-in. Due to its foundations in Protégé, an ontology editor, the OWL-S Editor provides good support for the creation of service domain ontologies in OWL and the development of valid service descriptions in OWL-S based on these ontologies. In particular, it provides support for constructing mutually consistent OWL-S service profiles and OWL-S service process models, such that, e.g., they refer to the same input parameters. The control flow of an OWL-S process model can be visualised and edited in a UML-like Activity Diagram (Fig. 11.7). The left pane of the screenshot displays the top-level OWL-S Process in a hierarchical tree structure, while the right pane displays the same process workflow graphically. Similarly, the data flow of the process model can also be visualised and defined graphically (Fig. 11.8).

The inputs, outputs, preconditions and results of an OWL-S description are defined using a Protégé-like interface (Fig. 11.9). The OWL-S Editor provides basic support for mapping an OWL-S Grounding to a WSDL file. Given a WSDL file for a Web Service, the OWL-S Editor uses the WSDL2OWLS tool[15] to generate an OWL-S description for the Web Service.

The OWL-S Editor provides good support for the service modelling phase, primarily the service offer description creation. Although it follows the code-driven approach, assuming that the implementation and possibly WSDL description of the Web Service already exists, unlike the OWL-S IDE, it does not interface with the actual implementation code of a Web Service, relying on at most the WSDL file. The WSDL description need only be annotated appropriately to make it useful in the OWL-S world. Interestingly, the OWL-S IDE and the OWL-S Editor

[15] This tool is part of the OWL-S API from the University of Maryland

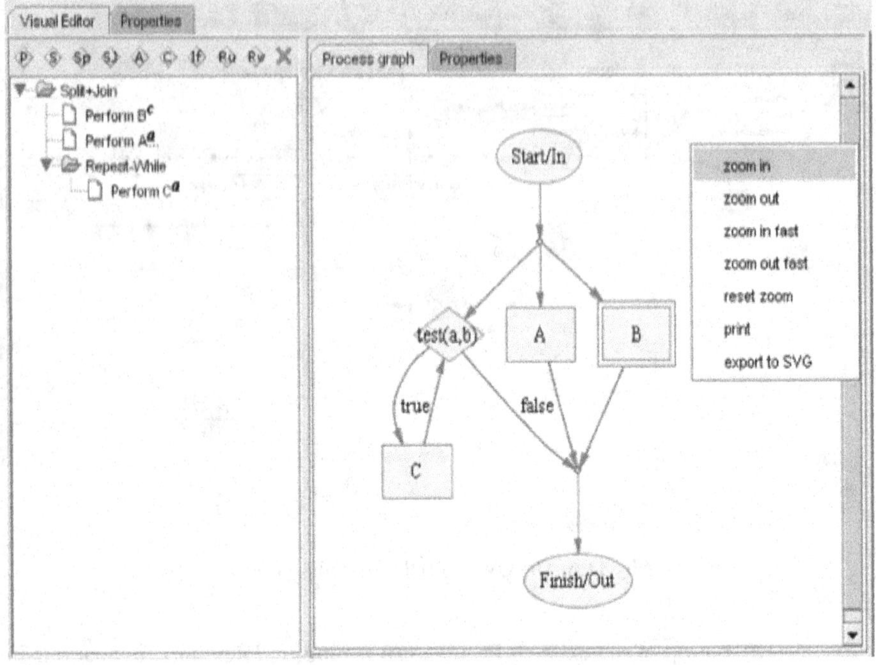

Fig. 11.7. Defining a composite process in the OWL-S Editor

have complementary perspectives: the former focusses on deriving OWL-S service descriptions from the implementation code of a Web Service, the latter on modelling OWL-S service descriptions as ontology-based descriptions. Combining the two perspectives in a single tool would enable developers to model OWL ontologies, OWL-S service descriptions and Web Service implementation in one coherent environment. However, there is currently no such tool in existence.

Moving to the WSMO world, there are two tools that support creating WSMO annotations for Web Services: the WSMO Studio and IRS-III. We next examine these two tools, albeit in less detail than the previous two.

WSMO Studio

The WSMO initiative supports a detailed form of service discovery, which is implemented in the WSMX execution environment. WSMX provides a reference implementation of the WSMO framework for Semantic Web Services and supports the development of WSMO-based Web Services from modelling (through WSMO Studio) to orchestration and choreography. It provides a set of APIs and UIs to allow developers to interact with WSMX across the different phases of the Semantic Web Service deployment lifecycle.

The focus of WSMX and IRS-III (discussed later) is on various kinds of mediation to reduce or remove interoperability problems between service requesters and

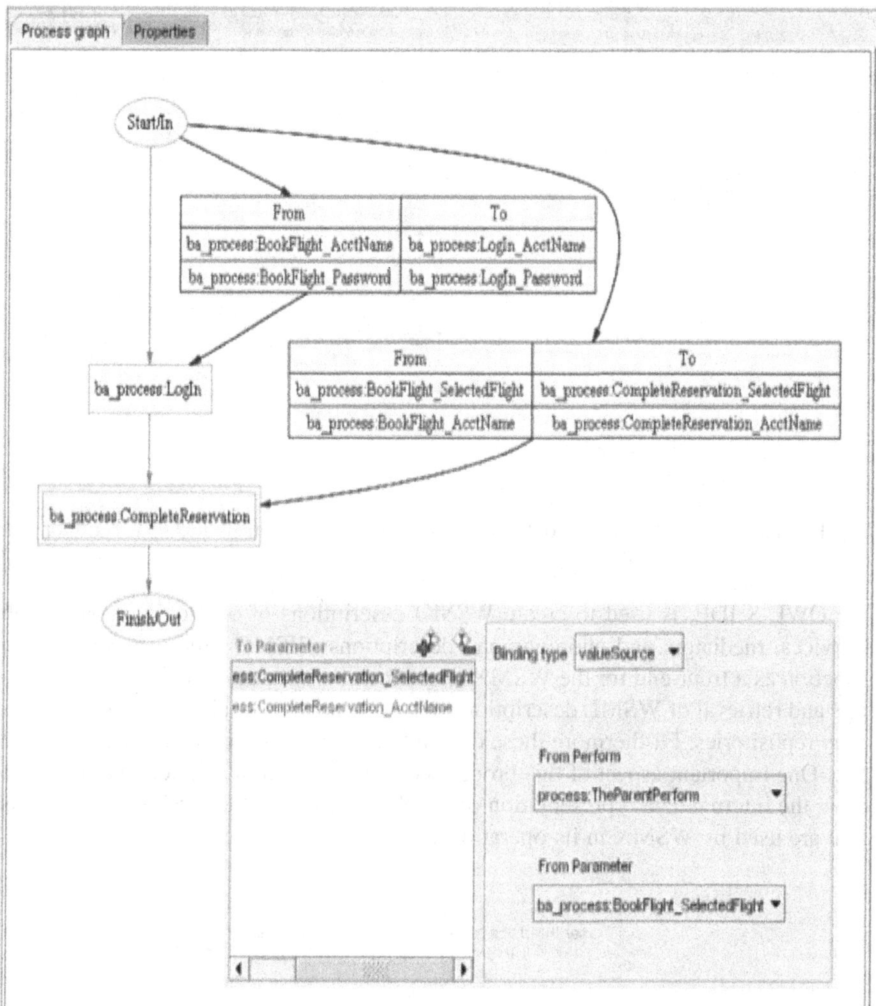

Fig. 11.8. Defining dataflow within the OWL-S Editor

service providers. Not surprisingly, the tools that have been produced by these two projects facilitate the creation and use of mediators, components that mediate between two Web Services or between a Web Service and a service requester. Architecturally, WSMX provides a broker between a set of Web Services and any potential client (Fig. 11.10). As a broker, WSMX not only mediates between the client and the services, but also provides a number of interfaces that support the client and the services in their activities. The WSMO *registration process* allows a service provider to advertise its service with WSMX. With respect to the lifecycle, the registration process is within the service modelling phase. Essentially, in this phase, the Web Services Modelling Ontology Studio (WSMO Studio), an Eclipse plug-in similar to

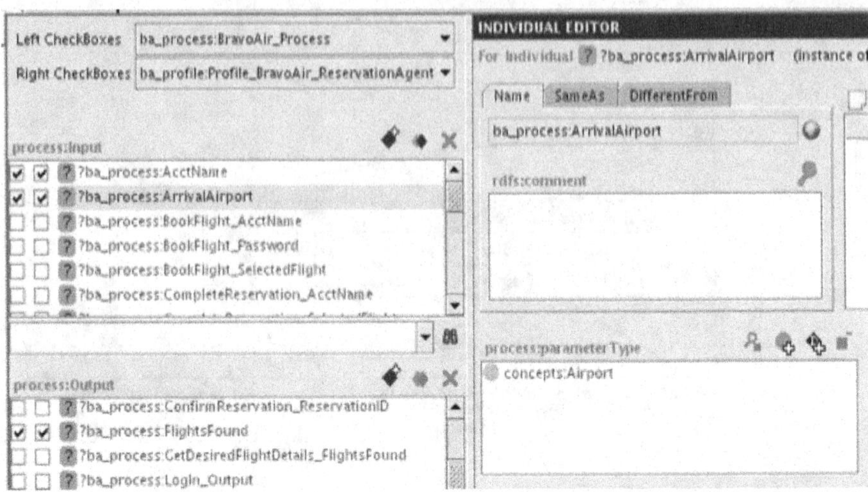

Fig. 11.9. Specifying inputs, outputs, preconditions and results in the OWL-S Editor

the OWL-S IDE, is used to create WSMO descriptions of ontologies, goals, Web Services, mediators and choreography descriptions. WSMO Studio is intended to function as a front-end for the WSMX execution environment and supports the storage and retrieval of WSML descriptions in remote service, goal, mediator and ontology repositories. Furthermore these descriptions are validated and stored for future use. One important aspect of this process is the generation of adapters that translate from the internal data representation of the Web Service to the WSML descriptions that are used by WSMX in its operations. One important result of using adapters is

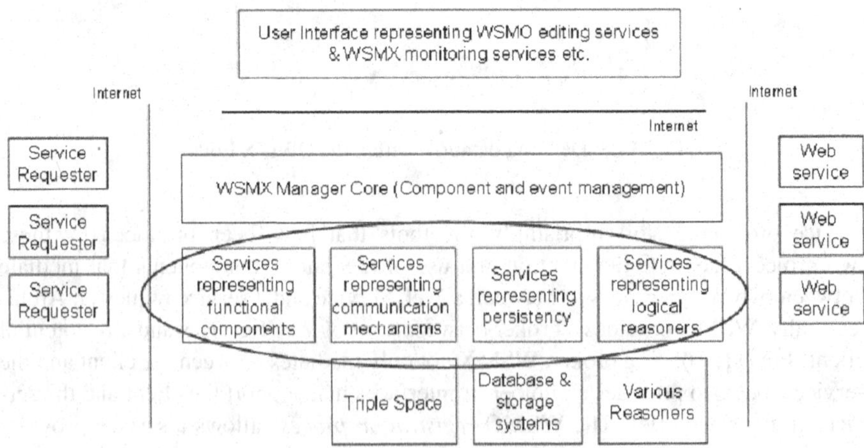

Fig. 11.10. Services in the WSMX architecture

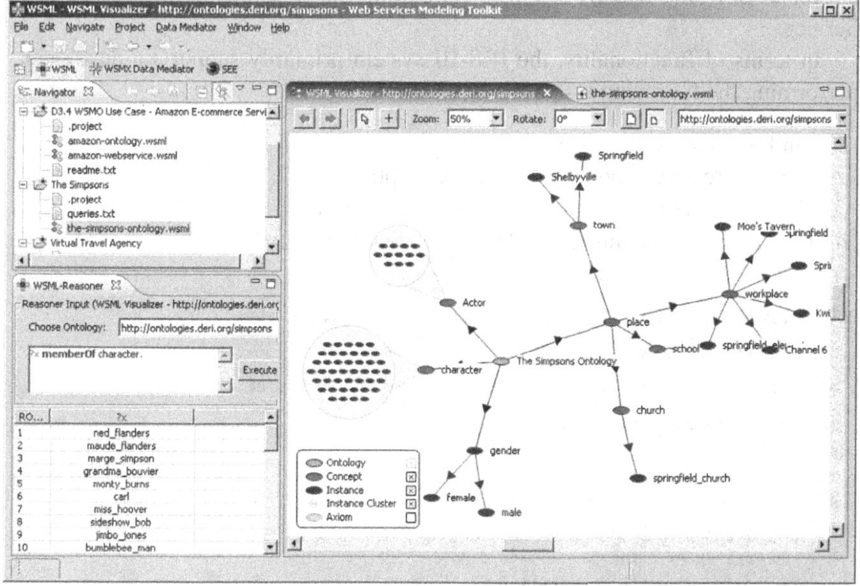

Fig. 11.11. The WSMO Studio concept editor

the abstraction from the actual implementation of the Web Service, to the abstract description of the service in the WSML semantic language.

Figure 11.11 displays a screenshot of the Web Services Modelling Toolkit (WSMT) (which builds on WSMO Studio), in particular an editor that allows the editing of concepts in WSML ontologies. WSMO Studio has several other editors, such as a service editor to edit service descriptions, a repository editor and a choreography editor (Fig. 11.15).

IRS-III

Through its long evolution, the IRS system [7] converged on an architecture in which clients interoperate directly with a broker that selects the most appropriate service to satisfy the client's needs. In turn, each Web Service essentially exposes a Problem Solving Method (PSM) which performs the actions that are required to satisfy the requirements of the client. The tools that are available for IRS-III, the WSMO-compliant version of IRS, facilitate the retrieval and registration of ontologies, Web Services and goals with the IRS server. In this sense, the IRS-III tools support the developer through the whole development process by providing an implicit checklist of tasks that the developer needs to perform.

A screenshot of the IRS-III browser is shown in Fig. 11.12. The top pane displays a WSMO ontology and the goals, Web Services and mediators defined through the ontology. The lower pane displays details on a chosen element of the ontology, in this case the `European-exchange-rate-web-service`. Fig. 11.13 presents a screenshot of the IRS-III interface for editing the semantic description of a Web Service.

In terms of functionality, the IRS-III system primarily supports a developer in performing the following tasks:

1. Find or create an appropriate ontology.
2. Find or create an appropriate goal description.
3. Find or create an appropriate mediator description.
4. Find or create a number of related Web Services.

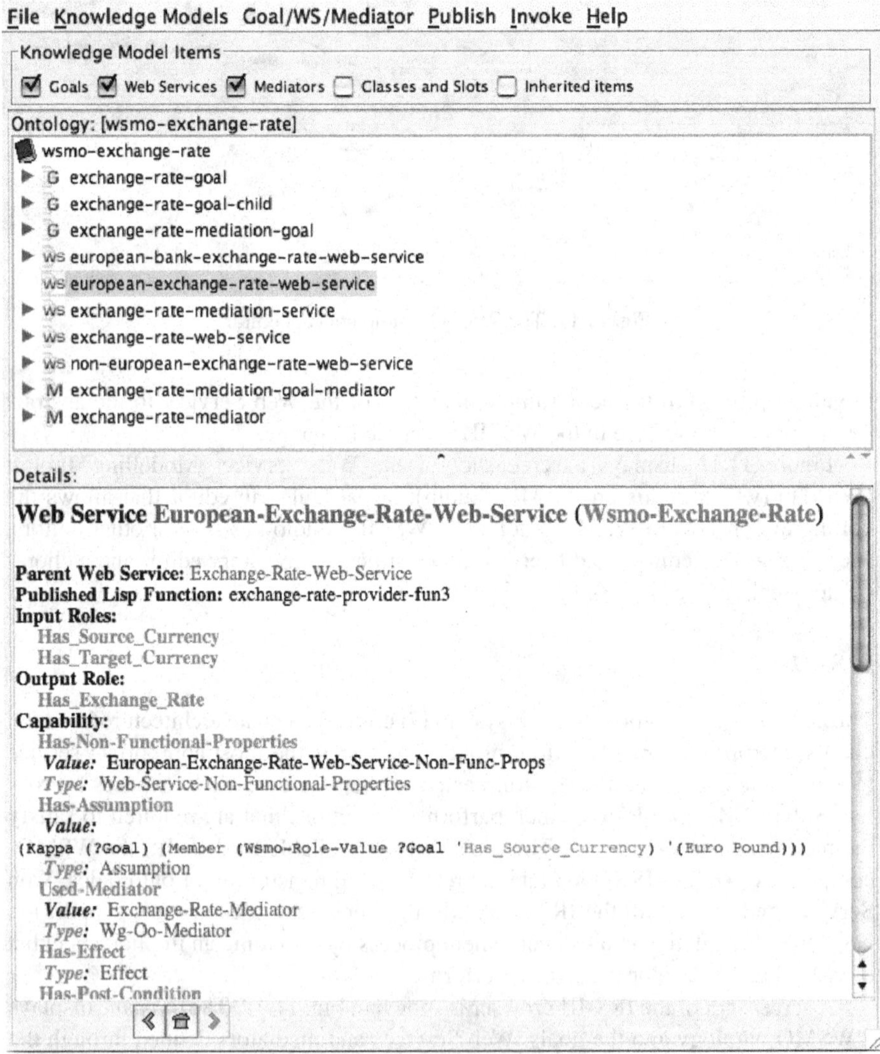

Fig. 11.12. The main IRS-III browser window

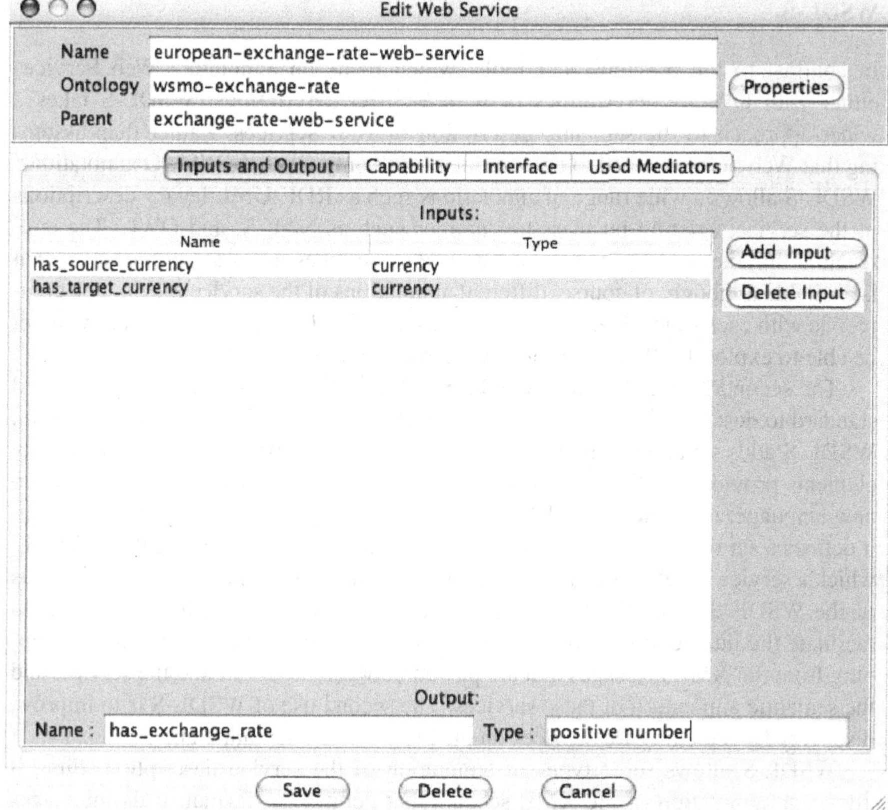

Fig. 11.13. Defining a Web Service in IRS-III

5. Link the Web Services to the goal created in 2 through mediators
6. Use the Web Services for publishing services (Java or Lisp code).
7. Invoke services through the invocation of the Goal.

The actual implementation of some of these tasks is delegated to other tools. Specifically, the implementation of the Web Service may be done through LISP or Java[16] development environments. In addition, the IRS-III system provides a means to link these implementations to their semantic service descriptions in IRS-III.

11.3.3 MWSAF

MWSAF (METEOR-S Web Service Annotation Framework) addresses the problem of annotating WSDL documents to compile them into WSDL-S [1]. WSDL-S is a relative newcomer on the semantic service description scene. We first present a brief description of WSDL-S before describing MWSAF in detail.

[16] IRS-III supports services implemented in these two languages only

WSDL-S

In contrast to the previous four tools, which focus on annotating Web Services either with OWL-S descriptions or with WSMO descriptions, WSDL-S takes a wider approach to the semantic description of Web Services. Rather than assuming that Web Services need to be described using only OWL or WSMO annotations, WSDL-S allows a wide range of annotations such as RDF, UML legacy descriptions of the service, existing business taxonomies such as NAICS, and OWL. The end-result is that the developer can annotate his/her services using any information that is available although, of course, different annotations of the service may not be compatible with each other. Thus, a client that is using OWL to describe services will not be able to exploit UML annotations of the Web Service.

The second intuition behind WSDL-S is that WSDL is such a widely accepted standard to describe Web Services that it should necessarily be exploited. Therefore, WSDL-S adds semantic annotations to Web Services by exploiting the extensibility elements provided by WSDL. As a consequence, WSDL-S does not really invent a new language, in the sense of the language invented by OWL-S or WSML. Rather, it defines a set of "standard" tags to be used in the extensibility elements of WSDL, which a service developer can use to annotate the semantics of the different elements of the WSDL description. In principle, WSDL-S has two uses: the first one is to facilitate the interaction between Web Services and their clients by defining a mapping from the XML messages that are passed between the client and the service, and the semantic annotation of these services. The second use of WSDL-S is to improve discovery by searching for services on the basis of their semantic annotation.

WSDL-S allows three types of annotation of the service description. First, it allows an annotation of the XML schema that defines the format of the messages that are exchanged between the client and the server (representing the inputs and outputs of relevant operations). These annotations, in turn, take two forms: the user may directly annotate the elements of the XML schema, defining therefore the semantics of the individual atomic elements, or it can annotate the entire XML schema. In the latter case, WSDL-S allows the use of XSLT scripts to specify how the semantics of the individual pieces compose in the semantics of the complete structure. The second annotation is at the level of operations, in which the developer can specify the *preconditions* to the use of an operation, and the *effects* that result from the use of that operation. The third and last type of annotation is the specification of the type of service on the basis of some taxonomy of services.

Because WSDL-S is used at both discovery and invocation time, it comes out as an hybrid of the OWL-S Profile and Grounding. In principle, the information that it provides can be used to improve the automatic generation of both the OWL-S Profile and Grounding given the WSDL-S description of the service. Superficially, the use of WSDL-S could help tools such as WSDL2OWL-S (which would then become WSDL-S2OWL-S) that translate WSDL into OWL-S. But this gain would come at the cost of a more expensive generation of WSDL specifications. The current WSDL generation tools, such as Java2WSDL, perform a syntactic translation from the programmer's code written in Java to the corresponding XML specification. Still, this translation would fail to generate the annotation of the message types or the preconditions and effects of operations. The automatic generation of such annotation from the plain Java code is a very challenging problem. Ultimately, a tool like WSDL2OWL-S should be defined in two steps: the first one a translation from WSDL to WSDL-S and the second one a translation from WSDL-S to OWL-S. To the extent that OWL is used as annotation language, the second step may be reduced to a simple syntactic re-writing of the OWL-S functional properties,[17] the first step however requires active annotation on the side of the developer.

The MWSAF Tool

The goal of MWSAF is to facilitate the annotation task, rather than generating the annotation automatically. MWSAF proposes three panes to the developer, as shown in Fig. 11.14. On the left side, the WSDL description of the Web Service is shown, on the left side the ontology is displayed and in the centre pane the mappings are displayed. The developer can perform the semantic annotation directly by using the select buttons at the bottom of the Web Service and ontology panes and then adding an annotation, or by asking the tool to propose an annotation automatically. In the latter case, the tool would display one such annotation and its degree of confidence in the correctness of the annotation. For instance, the derivation shown in Fig. 11.14 shows that the tool suggested an association between the element *High* in the Web Service definition with the concept *trade_high* in the ontology with a confidence level equal to 0.38333. The developer can then either accept the suggestion or reject it by clicking on the select box next to it. In terms of the Web Service deployment lifecycle of Sect. 11.2, MWSAF primarily helps a service provider develop semantic annotations for a WSDL Web Service, in the service modelling phase.

Furthermore, it is critical for the subsequent matchmaking process that both the service offer description and the service requirement description use the same ontology concepts and relations in the descriptions. This necessitates some method for the service requester and provider to find commonly used ontologies and express their descriptions within them. Typically, this might be accomplished by querying a registry service, e.g. a UDDI server, for its ontologies. However, the ontologies used by services registered with the UDDI server may not always correspond to the ontologies used by a service requester in his/her own context. In this case, ontology mediation (see Chap. 10) needs to take place to relate the service requester's own ontologies to the ontologies she must express her service request in. When there are multiple possible ontologies for service requests, this situation can be problematic, since one does not know which ontology to map to, to get desired or desirable services.

---

[17] Still some care has to be taken here. First, OWL-S defines conditional outputs and effects to account for the fact that the outputs of the service may not be deterministic and always predictable. Second, the annotation would not help with the specification of non-functional properties

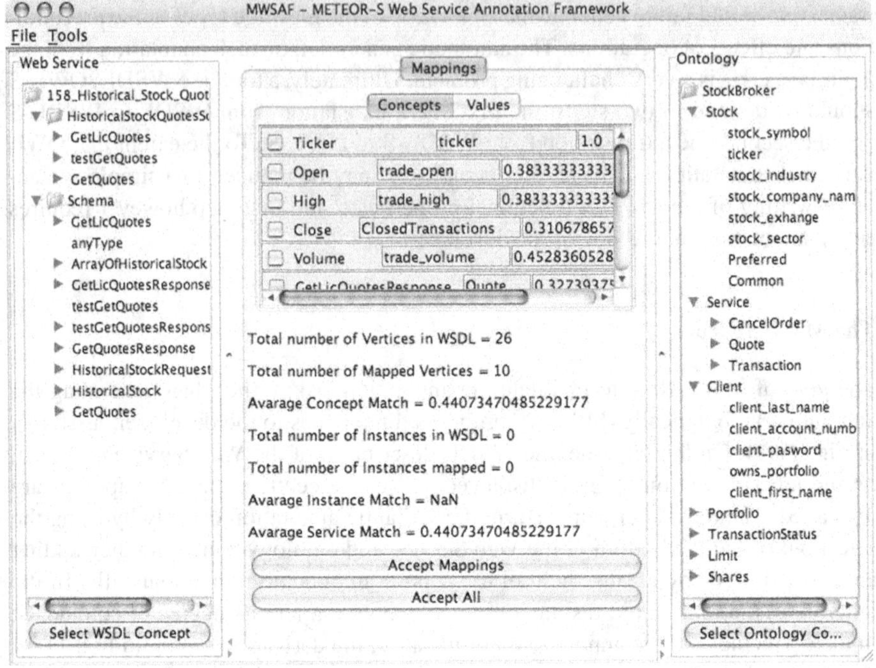

Fig. 11.14. The MWSAF tool for annotating Web Services in WSDL-S

11.4 Service Discovery

In this phase, one or more service offer descriptions have been found to match a service requirement description by a matchmaking service. In this case, the service requester must be notified of the match. It is possible that the matched service may not match the service requester's requirements exactly or that there may be no matches for the service request. In this case, the service requester may need to refine or reformulate the service requirement description or proceed to another matchmaking service. The service discovery process may itself be a multi-stage process, as the requester may evaluate how well matched services fit his/her requirements and based on his/her analysis modify him/her service request and initiate service discovery again. Most of the tools discussed thus far provide only minimal support for a single-step discovery process and no support for a multi-stage service discovery process.

The OWL-S IDE supports publishing a developed Web Service with a UDDI server (a kind of registry service) and deploying it on a Web server. The OWL-S Profiles are first translated into UDDI service descriptions using OWL-S2UDDI. The UDDI descriptions are then published to a UDDI registry using a UDDI client. Similarly, a Web Service requester could define a profile of a desired Web Service within the OWL-S IDE Profile Editor, describing the inputs it should take and the outputs it should return. Essentially, the developer compiles the profile of the "perfect" Web service he/she would like to work with. This profile is translated into a UDDI representation and used to query a UDDI registry, which returns a set of matching services. The OWL-S Editor does not support service discovery.

To support service discovery, WSMX provides the facilities that allow the requester to describe the capabilities that it needs, and the matching process that perform the selection of the most appropriate service. Discovery is performed in two phases: first a *Matchmaker* is called to locate all the existing services that match the requirements of the requester and second a *Selector* is called to select the service that more closely fits the requirements of the requester. In this process, the Matchmaker and the Selector can invoke *Data Mediators* to resolve eventual mismatches between the goals of the service and the requirements of the requester. Although technical details on both the Matchmaker and the Selector are scant, since both components are still under development, the Selector seems to cover the service definition phase that allows WSMX to evaluate how the service meets the requirements of the requester. Nevertheless, WSMX provides a very different discovery process than the process proposed by UDDI [14] or its semantic derivatives [15, 12] in which the broker goes beyond finding services and extends into making important decisions on which service the requester is going to use.

MWSAF itself does not support service discovery. A proposal to incorporate WSDL-S annotations within UDDI descriptions has been described in [15] and [4], but, as far as we know, it is not yet integrated with WSDL-S. WSDL-S could be mapped to UDDI by exploiting the WSDL to UDDI mapping [5], but it will still require a mapping of the semantic annotations to UDDI elements. One way to do such a mapping has been proposed in [15], but it is restricted only to inputs and outputs, and no description is provided on how to map preconditions and effects (though such a generalisation is quite straightforward). The second aspect of the service discovery that must be specified is the matchmaking mechanism, since the native mechanisms in UDDI will not be able to support the inferences required by WSDL-S.

11.5 Service Definition

This is one of the most complex stages of the Web Service interaction lifecycle, where a service requester is faced, as a result of the service discovery stage, with several providers who could potentially meet the requester's needs. The service requester now selects one or more service providers and enters into a service definition conversation with them. During the Web Service definition, the abstract service description of each selected service provider is instantiated with concrete values for the required attributes and parameters of the service. This yields a concrete Web Service for each of the service providers that the service requester can compare in order to find the most appropriate Web Service for his/her requirements. There may be some negotiation of price and other attributes before the Web Service can be finally chosen. If the service requester is a human user, the list of service providers needs to be presented to the user, with some of the key distinguishing attributes of the Web Services highlighted. Once a Web Service has been chosen, the service definition conversations with the rest of the service providers are terminated. The configuration of the chosen service description may then be formally represented within a contract between the service provider and requester. Tool support for this stage would need to include support for managing the multiple conversations of the client with multiple service providers.

Tool support for this stage is rudimentary, since most of the tools cover development of the Web Service rather than actual deployment. Thus, they try to ensure that the Web Service being developed can be discovered in the previous stage and then at best, just present the list of discovered services in this stage, relying on the user to select one manually. This is the case for the OWL-S IDE, since once again the discovery process will select Web services that are only 'similar enough' to the Web service that was originally requested. The client developers can use the descriptions of these services to decide which one to use and to decide whether he/she needs to gather additional information by invoking additional Web services. Knowing which service to use is still only part of the story. Code to interact correctly with the found Web Service must still be written. The problem here is that the Process Model specifies the order in which the Web service expects information and what type of information the Web service needs. Any violation of such order, or a violation of the type of information expected by the Web service, would lead to a failure of the inter action. To control the interaction process, the OWL-S IDE supports the automatic generation of Web service specific interfaces to the OWL-S Virtual Machine (VM), which executes OWL-S Process Models. The OWL-S VM takes the OWL-S specification and executes it, but it has to ask to the client what information to send, and which non-deterministic choices to make. By implementing the interface, the developer is obliged to provide the functionalities that support the OWL-S VM in its interaction with the Web service.

Since the OWL-S Editor does not support service discovery, this stage is also trivial, in that only one service is present anyway, the Web Service being described. The OWL-S Editor does allow the user to select values for input parameters of the Web Service, which is then subsequently executed. Since both WSMX and IRS-III are broker-based architectures, it is somewhat unclear how this stage is supported within WSMX and IRS-III, since service definition is not an explicit component of the WSMO Semantic Web Services framework.

11.6 Service Delivery

Once a service definition has been agreed upon, the last stage in the lifecycle, service delivery, can take place. When the service delivery involves the exchange of multiple messages between the service provider and the requester, an interaction choreography is required. This is particularly so when the solution of the problem of the requester may involve more than one service, and may therefore result in more than one service being involved. This stage is currently somewhat ill-defined. There are several issues that need to be resolved about the role of choreography in Semantic Web Services, who defines the choreography or orchestration of a service and how to monitor the execution of a choreography and orchestration. It is therefore supported to varying extents by Semantic Web Services tools.

From the point of view of OWL-S, the interaction choreography is the responsibility of the client. The service definition and choreography essentially occur on the part of the client and are enabled by OWL-S, but not modelled explicitly within it. OWL-S thus describes the orchestration of a Web Service. In fact, since OWL-S has a well-defined scope in describing a Web Service and how to interact with it, choreography is out of bounds for OWL-S. Accordingly, both the OWL-S IDE and the OWL-S Editor have little or no support for choreography.

On the other hand, choreography is critical in the WSMO world and WSMO Studio Choreography Editor (Fig. 11.15), in particular, supports it extensively. WSMX also provides a *Choreography Engine*, which is used to manage the communication patterns required by the Web Service. Because WSMX is a brokered architecture, it can make strong assumptions about the interaction and deployment of Web Services that are not made by other development environments such as the OWL-S IDE or the OWL-S Editor. The centralised structure of WSMX provides, at least in principle, the ability to control the composition of Web Services so that choreography languages provided by the WSMO framework can be applied. In a totally distributed architecture, such languages are very difficult to apply or outright impossible. As a sidenote, one aspect that is left unclear is how the assumptions that are built into WSMX carry over to WSMO. Whereas WSMX imposes a centralised architecture, presumably, WSMO may be implementable also in totally distributed architectures.

With respect to the actual service invocation, this is supported to some extent by all of the above-described tools except MWSAF. If the WSDL file of the OWL-S description is hooked up to a real running Web Service, both the OWL-S IDE and the OWL-S Editor can be used to execute the Web Service. In this case, the user is typically presented with a window to select values of input parameters based on predefined parameter types. In WSMX, there is a component called the *Communication Manager* that invokes selected Web Services. The communication Manager is responsible for controlling the data transmission between the two parties and, specifically, it performs *lifting* and *lowering* transformations between the semantically described information that is provided by the services and the XML data that is transmitted through the wire.[18] As in the case of the discovery process, the interaction between two services may also involve the use of Data Mediators that transform the incoming data from the ontologies used by the requester to the ontologies used by the provider. IRS-III also supports invocation of a given Web Service, both for debugging a Web Service and for providing the basis for an interaction tool between the user and the Web Service.

[18] Lifting corresponds to translating from XML to WSML, lowering is the opposite transformation from WSML to XML. For more information on ontology mediation, refer to Chapter 10

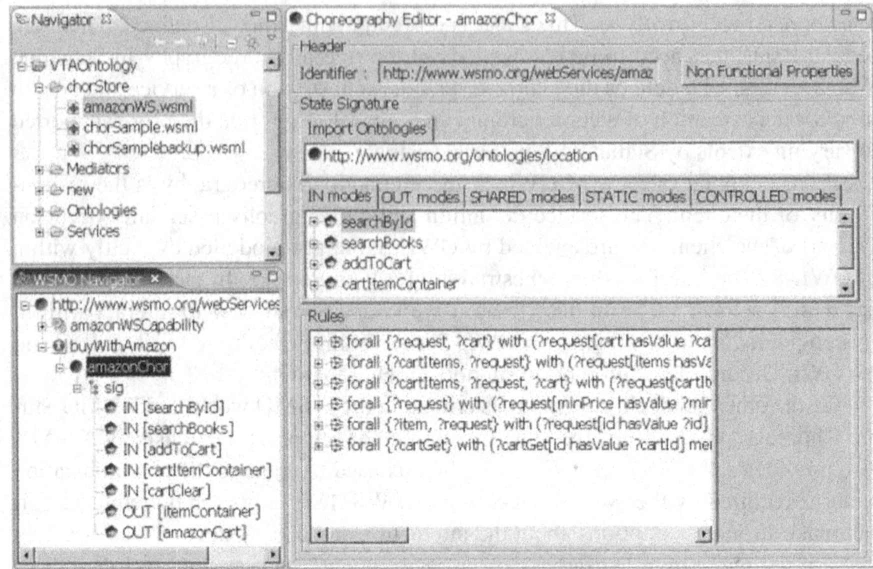

Fig. 11.15. The WSMO Studio Choreography Editor

11.7 Conclusions

In this chapter, we reviewed a number of existing tools to support developers trying to deploy and use Semantic Web Services. The OWL-S IDE builds on the Eclipse software development platform to support all four stages of the Semantic Web Service deployment lifecycle. The OWL-S Editor builds on the Protégé ontology development platform to support three stages of the lifecycle, i.e. service modelling, service definition and service delivery, but not service discovery. The MWSAF tool supports a developer primarily in the service modelling phase. IRS-III and WSMO Studio also support the developers in all four stages of the service deployment lifecycle.

As Semantic Web Service standards stabilise and become part of the software development process, these tools will probably also merge and become more closely tied with existing software development environments and tools. Currently, very few of the tools really support the model-driven approach to developing a Web Service, although this is likely to be a fairly common use case for Web Service developers, in particular if they use models for their standard code development process. Thus, an important area to address in the future is how a model of the Web Service described in OWL-S or UML with additional semantic annotations can be used to directly develop the implementation code, at least partially. In addition, a verification module that can check the correctness of the semantic descriptions would be very useful. For example, the verification module could check the correctness of an OWL-S Process Model, of the mapping between the OWL-S Grounding and the corresponding WSDL file etc. helping a developer detect problems at development and compilation time and thus reducing the likelihood of execution time errors.

References

1. R. Akkiraju, J. Farrell, J. Miller, M. Nagarajan, M.-T. Schmidt, A. Sheth, and K. Verma. Web Service Semantics - WSDL-S. A joint UGA-IBM Technical Note, version 1.0, April 2005.
2. Axis web site. `http://ws.apache.org/axis/`.
3. E. Christensen, F. Curbera, G. Meredith, and S. Weerawarana. Web Service Description Language (WSDL 1.1). `http://www.w3.org/TR/wsdl`.
4. J. Colgrave, R. Akkiraju, and R. Goodwin. External Matching in UDDI. In *Proceedings of the 2nd International Conference on Web Services (ICWS-2004)*, 2004.
5. J. Colgrave and K. Januszewski. Using WSDL in a UDDI Registry, Version 2.0.2 - Technical Note. Technical Report uddi-spec-tc-tn-wsdl-v2, OASIS, 2004.
6. G. Denker, D. Elenius, and D. Martin. The OWL-S Editor. `http://owlseditor.semwebcentral.org/`.
7. J. Domingue, L. Cabral, F. Hakimpour, D. Sell, and E. Motta. IRS-III: A Platform and Infrastructure for Creating WSMO-Based Semantic Web Services. In *Proceedings of the Workshop on WSMO Implementations (WIW 2004)*, Frankfurt, Germany, 2004.
8. Eclipse. `http://www.eclipse.org`.
9. Jena. `http://jena.sourceforge.net/`.
10. N. F. Noy, R. W. Fergerson, and M. A. Musen. The Knowledge Model of Protégé-2000: Combining Interoperability and Flexibility. In *2nd International Conference on Knowledge Engineering and Knowledge Management (EKAW-2000)*, Juan-les-Pins, France, 2000.
11. N. Srinivasan, M. Paolucci, and K. Sycara. CODE: A Development Environment for OWL-S Web Services. *Demo paper in 3rd International Semantic Web Conference*, 2004.
12. N. Srinivasan, M. Paolucci, and K. Sycara. An Efficient Algorithm for OWL-S Based Semantic Search in UDDI. In *Proceedings of the 1st International Workshop on Semantic Web Services and Web Process Composition (SWSWPC-2004)*, San Diego, California, USA, 2004.
13. SWeDE. `http://owl-eclipse.projects.semwebcentral.org/`.
14. UDDI. `http://www.uddi.org`.
15. K. Verma, K. Sivashanmugam, A. Sheth, A. Patil, S. Oundhakar, and J. Miller. METEOR-S WSDI: A Scalable Infrastructure of Registries for Semantic Publication and Discovery of Web Services. *Journal of Information Technology and Management, Special Issue on Universal Global Integration*, 6(1):17–39, 2005.

12

Ontology-Based Change Management in an eGovernment Application Scenario

Ljiljana Stojanović

FZI Research Center for Information Technologies, University of Karlsruhe, Germany
ljiljana.stojanovic@fzi.de

Summary. Permanent changes in the environment (political, economical and ecological) cause frequent changes in the governments' regulations that may affect public administration processes, online services and software systems. To reduce "time-to-market" with regard to new decisions, regulations, and law, it is necessary to equip public administration with tools supporting the agile response to changes. In this chapter we present an ontology-based system for managing changes in the eGovernment domain. The novelty of the approach lies in the formal verification of the service description as well as in the usage of formal methods for achieving consistency when a problem is discovered.

12.1 Introduction

Change management is the timely adaptation of a system to the changes in business requirements, users' needs, etc. as well as the consistent propagation of these changes to dependent artefacts [13]. A modification in one part of the system may generate many inconsistencies in other parts of the same system [14]. This variety of causes and consequences of changes makes the change management a very complex operation that should be considered as both an organisational and a technical process. Existing approaches for change management in eGovernment focus mainly on manual management of a particular, isolated service and on supporting only message-based[1] communication between public administrators. These approaches require a growing number of highly skilled personnel, making the maintenance costly. Moreover, the changes that affect the system are resolved and propagated in an ad hoc manner.

However, the ad hoc management of changes might work only for particular cases. It can scale neither in space nor in time. Therefore, in order to avoid unnecessary complexity and failures in the long run, change management must be treated in a more systematic way. It is especially important for eGovernment applications that are distributed over different systems, like eGovernment portals that enable integration

[1] This means that public administrators can exchange raw data, but not semantically more complex structures, like decisions, since e.g. they are missing common agreed description of problems

of various, physically distributed services differing in the level of formality and in the structure. For example, there are four availability levels of online public services [3] such as (i) showing only information needed to start the procedures to obtain public service (ii) enabling downloadable forms to start services (iii) supporting two-way interaction through online forms and (iv) full electronic case handling by offering the possibility to completely treat the public service via the Web site, including decision and delivery. Moreover, the description of an eGovernment service (e.g. issuing of a driving license) is quite similar for the various service providers (e.g. for different municipalities) due to binding rules and regulations that every public administration has to obey. However, there are no two services that are identical, since public administrations have the liberty of how to act on it.

The changes to be managed lie within and are controlled by the public administration. The most frequent changes are changes of existing processes based on the adaptation of business goals, propagating changes in the organisational structure, or due to possibility to organise processes in a better way. For example, public administrations at the government level or at the federal level work on supporting unification of eGovernment services, on standards for data exchange as well as on providing examples of the process models of public services that are implemented by municipalities.

The internal changes might have been triggered by events originating outside the public administration, i.e. by "the environment". Hence, the change management must take into account the response to changes over which the public administration exercises little or no control (e.g. legislation, social and political upheaval, the actions of competitors, shifting economic tides and currents, etc.). On the other hand, in a dynamically changing political and economical environment, the regulations themselves have to be continually improved, in order to enable the efficient function of a modern society. Taking into account an enormous number of public services and dependencies between them, as well as the complexity of interpreting and implementing changes in government regulations, the process of reconfiguring the existing public services according to changes in the regulations seems to be quite complex. Hence, it is necessary to provide support for propagating changes to all dependent artefacts[2] by ensuring the consistency of the whole system. Otherwise, the reliability, accuracy and effectiveness of the eGovernment system decrease significantly.

Although the importance of change management is demonstrated in practice [6], as known to the authors, the corresponding methods and tools are still missing. However, since the demands for change-aware eGovernment are much higher [18], in this chapter we propose an approach that enables agile response to frequent and huge changes in the environment or in the system itself.

[2] For example, the eGovernment service for birthday certificate can be treated as a separate service or as a composite service in the context of other services such as passport issuance. The addition of a new input in the birthday certificate service may make necessary follow-up changes in the data-flow of many other services that include it (e.g. the passport issuance service) in order to achieve one-step eGovernment

In our previous work [19], we have introduced a change management process that enables consistent propagation of changes within a service and between the services in order to ensure the quality of the decision-making process. Here we focus on the change preservation phase that prevents inconsistencies by computing additional changes which guarantee the transition of the service description into another consistent state. We propose proof-driven verification of the service description.[3] The verification is driven by a set of desirable properties including the standard set of properties (e.g. reachability, liveness, etc.) as well as domain-specific constraints (e.g. all activities are grounded on some law or regulation). Even though it is very desirable to identify errors and problems in an early state of the service modelling, there are no tools that provide means to verify the models.

The novelty of the approach lies not only in the formal verification of service descriptions, but also in the usage of formal methods for achieving consistency when a problem is discovered. While performing the checks, the system generates specific suggestions on how to fix errors based on the type of errors and the situation at hand. Due to our tasks in an ongoing project,[4] we have realised our approach in the eGovernment domain. However, the approach is general enough to be applied in an arbitrary application domain that uses ontology-based description of web services.

12.2 Motivating Example

In order to make the description of the approach more understandable, we define here the basic structure of an eGovernment system and give a motivating example that will be used throughout the chapter. There are four basic roles played by actors in an eGovernment system: (i) politicians who define a law; (ii) public administrators who define processes for realising a law; (iii) programmers who implement these processes and (iv) end-users (applicants) who use eGovernment services.

Public administrators have the key role. They possess a very good knowledge about the eGovernment domain. This knowledge is needed for the design of a public service. It includes the legislation that a service is based on, the respective law, related decrees, directives, prerequisites, etc. Based on the interpretation of a law, a public administrator describes a service as a sequence of activities that have to be done, which represents a business process. For example, the generic schema for the public service for issuing (renewal) a driving licence is realised through the following five activities: (i) application, (ii) verification/qualification, (iii) credential issuance, (iv) record management and (v) revenue collection. This model is shown Fig. 12.1.

In the application activity, all the necessary application data/documents are provided by an applicant. In the next activity, the provided information/documents are verified (e.g. validity and liquidity of a credit card) and are qualified by testing whether the applicant meets the qualification requirements. In the issuance activity, either a permanent or a temporary credential document (i.e. driving licence) is

[3] The approach assumes that ontology-based descriptions of eGovernment services are given (see Sect. 12.3)

[4] OntoGov – `http://www.ontogov.org`

Fig. 12.1. A generic process model of the eGovernment service for issuing a driving licence

issued. The record management activity ensures the ongoing integrity of the driving licensing and control record. Finally, the required fee is charged from the applicant's bank account. Each activity requires some inputs, produces some outputs. It can be executed only when its pre-conditions are fulfilled and it has post-conditions that define the next activity in a conditional manner. In the case of the application activity of the driving licence service, inputs include a birthday certificate, the output is an application form, the pre-condition is that the applicant is older than 16 and the post-condition is that all fields in the application form are filled. Further, each activity can also be decomposed into several sub-activities or can be specialised.

The crucial activity is the verification/qualification, since it reflects the constraints contained in the law. For example, it implements a rule that a person younger than 16 cannot apply for issuing the driving licence, whereas for motor cars (category B) the minimal age is 18. From the business process management point of view, the law can be treated as the business rule required to achieve goals of an organisation (defined by its business policy).

Due to the changes in the political goals of a government, changes in the environment, changes in the needs of the people etc., the politicians might (i) make the revision of a law by accepting an amendment, (ii) enact a new law or (iii) even repeal a law. In the case of a new amendment the public administrator must understand the changes in the law caused by the amendment, locate activities/services in which this law has to be implemented and translate changes into the corresponding reconfiguration of the business process.

Let us continue the example with the driving licence. Recently, the German law that regulates issuing driving licences has been changed, so that foreigners from non-EU countries must have the German driving licence, although they have a domestic licence. Let us analyse which changes in the existing business process for issuing the driving licence will be caused by this change in the law. For each change, we discuss the role that an efficient change management system should play. First of all, the public administrator should locate a business process and the corresponding activities that should be modified due to this change in a law. Taking into account an enormous number of public services as well as the complexity of interpreting and implementing changes in the law, this is a time-consuming action if it is performed in a non-systematic way. Therefore, an efficient change management approach should inform the public administrator on these activities automatically. This means that each business activity must contain a reference to a chapter/paragraph/article/amendment of a law that it implements. For example, the activity verification/qualification of the driving licence service is based on the Chap. 2, Paragraph "Mindestalter" in the Law "Bundesgesetz ueber den Fuehrerschein".

After finding the service that has to be modified, the public administrator has to decide how to do that. She can specialise this service in a new one or she can adapt it to include new requirements. Let us assume that the public administrator made a decision to generate a specific driving-licence service for foreigners. This service should not be generated from scratch. Rather, it should be a specialisation of an already existing driving-licence service. The public administrator has to change the pre-conditions of this new service, since it is only for foreigners from non-EU countries. This automatically causes a change in the pre-conditions of the original service, since the pre-conditions of two different services that provide the same functionality must be disjoint. Only in this way, the run-time system will know which service to execute. It is clear that when the pre-conditions are semantically defined, the judgement about the inclusion relation among them can be done automatically.

Further, the verification/qualification activity of the new service requires checking whether a foreigner already has a domestic licence. Therefore, a new input for that activity is necessary. Since each input has to be supplied, this change is propagated to the previous activity, i.e. the application activity which is responsible for the interaction with an applicant. This means that that activity has to deliver (as its output) the information about the domestic licence, the validity of which should be tested in the verification activity. Consequently, the application activity of the new service needs an additional input compared to the original service.

Obviously, different changes in a law have different consequences in the existing services. We briefly discuss one more example. Recently, the German law that regulates issuing driving licences has been changed, so that teenagers older than 17 can obtain a (temporary) licence for motor cars if they pass the exams and if they drive with a person that is older than 25, has the driving licence for more than five years and has scored less than 20 negative points in the last five years. In that case, the older person must have a licence for co-driving. This change in the law requires changes in the post-conditions of the verification/qualification activity: instead of approval and non-approval of the licence, it can be temporarily approved. Further, the credential issuance activity has to generate an additional output, since the new co-driving licence should be printable, as well.

An efficient change management system should enable the public administrator to perform all these changes efficiently (e.g. to make a minimal set of additional changes) and to ensure the overall consistency of the reconfigured service automatically (e.g. to prohibit that an activity has two contradictory pre-conditions). In the rest of the chapter, we present a change management system that fulfils the above-mentioned requirements.

12.3 Modelling eGovernment Services

Before starting with the description of our approach for change management, we briefly describe the set of ontologies used for modelling eGovernment services. This set is introduced in [17] and represents the OntoGov model. Dependencies between

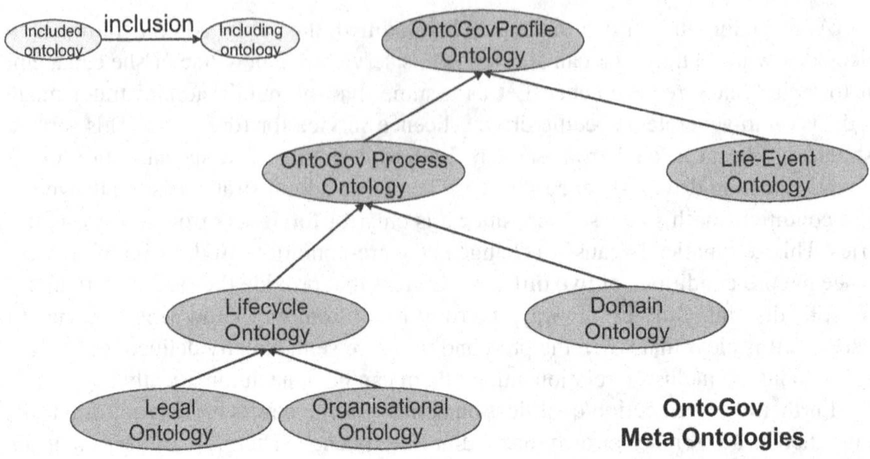

Fig. 12.2. The set of OntoGov ontologies used for modelling eGovernment services

OntoGov ontologies are shown in Fig. 12.2. They are called meta ontologies, since they define the schema, i.e. the language for modelling the eGovernment services.

The OntoGov model consists of two major parts – the *OntoGov Profile ontology* and the *OntoGov Process ontology* which are developed on the basis of OWL-S.[5] However, both of them are extended and adapted in order to take into account unique characteristics of the eGovernment services, as well as some aspects needed for the better management of changes. For example, the OntoGov Profile ontology includes the *Life-Event ontology* which is used for the classification of eGovernment services. It includes concepts such as residential affairs, residential permissions, identification certifications, naturalisation citizenship, moving, education, etc. It has been developed based on the existing standards[6] for modelling life events. It is important to note that it is common for all the users even though they are often geographically distributed and may experience significant problems in the common communication language (e.g. English) and in the style of the communication. More information about this ontology can be found in [2]. Additionally, a typical profile of an eGovernment service contains the usual meta data such as name, short description, version, status, date of creation, creator, etc.

The OntoGov Process ontology models (i) process flow using activities (which can be either atomic or composite) and control constructs (e.g. sequence, split, join, switch, etc.), as well as (ii) data flow through inputs, outputs[7] and equivalence

[5] `http://www.daml.org/services/owl-s/1.0/`

[6] For example, the Swiss Standard eCH-001 (Best Practice Structure Process Inventory – `http://www.ech.ch`) aims to give an overview over all relevant eGovernment services in Switzerland and therefore to provide a consistent and standardised classification of the services. The inventory comprises 1,200 eGovernment services – all services initialised by a citizen or by internal administration processes

[7] Input and output of an activity are represented using entities defined in the Domain Ontology. The Domain Ontology encodes concepts of the public administration domain such as

relationships between them. Moreover, for each activity a set of meta data may be defined that includes name, description, pre-conditions and post-conditions. This standard set of meta data is extended with the legal, organisational and life-cycle aspects defined in the corresponding ontologies. All these ontologies are used for the annotation of the eGovernment services in order to enable better and easier management of them.

For example, while in private organisations the decisions for process definitions are mainly based on time, cost and quality criteria, government processes must be in accordance with the existing law and regulations from different levels (state, region and municipality). Therefore, we have developed the OntoGov Legal ontology[8] that models the structure of the legal documents, which includes paragraphs, sections, amendments, etc. It is very important to document the laws and regulations the process is based upon – not only for the whole process but also for specific activities, since the legislation regulates the accomplishments of the administrative services. By associating legislation to these services, it is possible to trace and propagate the effects that a change in the legislation (or administrative regulations) produces on the models of the administrative services.

The Organisational ontology describes the roles and areas of responsibility and capabilities within an organisation with respect to the activities of a process model. Moreover, it models the structure of an organisation, its resources, know-how, etc. For example, we distinguish two types of resources: (1) human resources who perform an activity and (2) equipment (i.e. hardware, software etc.) that is occupied by the activity. Note that equipment is needed to perform an activity. However, it is released after finishing this activity.

Finally, the OntoGov Process ontology includes the Lifecycle ontology that describes the decision-making process in the public administration. It bridges the gap between decision-making and realisation by providing means for describing these decisions and formally stating reasons that motivate the design decisions. Indeed, it is intended to support the transition from knowledge acquisition to implementation. It provides answers on the following questions: (i) How have the process design (e.g. regarding atomic activities) and flow (e.g. regarding control constructs) been realised? and (ii) Why has a design decision been taken? Since it includes entities for documenting design decisions and the underlying rationale, it gives concrete clues on how the corresponding eGovernment service has to be modified. During ongoing development, it not only helps the public administrators to avoid pursuing unpromising design alternatives repeatedly, but also facilitates maintenance by

the "terminology" used in the eGovernment domain. For example, the Domain Ontology defines the type and structure of documents such as a passport

[8] To develop the Legal ontology we have analysed the structure of legal documents in Switzerland, Greece and Spain, since the goal of the OntoGov project is to pilot the system at our partners coming from these countries. We concluded that the legal documents have a very similar structure independent of the country they are defined for. Even though different countries use different terminology to organise their legal documents, all of them use three levels of abstractions. Therefore, it was possible to extract the general structure of a law and to represent it in a form of the Legal Ontology

improving the understandability of the service design. A description of the design process also supports traceability, since it links parts of the service design to the portions of the specification they were derived from and to the requirements that influenced design decisions. In this way we build automated tools that support not only the specification and design of eGovernment processes, but more important it provides an automated, transparent and user centred support to the entire process life cycle, from analysis to execution, by suggesting solutions that can be adopted, refused or refined by public administrators.

An example of the process part of the eGovernment service *Announcement of moving* modelled by using the OntoGov model is shown in Fig. 12.3. This service is classified as of high potential for European eGovernment improvement, as is typically involving various public and private institutions. Today, the service provided is split into few separated tasks. In case a citizen invokes this service from a web portal, he/she is asked to provide all information needed to perform the complete service (cf. *EnterApplicationForm* in Fig. 12.3). After submitting the requested information, the eligibility is checked (cf. *CheckEligibility*). Based on the result, the service can be either broken (cf. *RejectApplication*) or continued. The next step depends on whether he/she is already registered (cf. *Deregistration*) or not (cf. *Registration*). Deregistration has to be performed in one municipality. In addition, the person has to register himself/herself in the new municipality. In the meantime several private or semi-private entities, like telecommunication companies or the electricity company, have to be notified about the change of address (cf. *GetThirdPatiesAddress* and *NotifyThirdParties*). Finally, the citizen has to be informed about the result of the service. By describing the eGovernment service *Announcement of moving* in this way, the quality of the service is improved, since it is performed by the citizen as one task regardless of what and how much (technical) processes run behind.

Moreover, not only knowledge on how to execute the service is stored, but also why it was designed as it is. Therefore, for every entity in the process model of a service (i.e. either an activity or a control construct), information on the underlying design decisions is recorded. An example of the design decision defined for the activity *CheckEligibility* is shown in Fig. 3. This decision is legally grounded: the information public administrators need to know related to this activity is defined by law (cf. *SR 101 and SR 201 Art. 22A-26A*).

Additionally, a decision may stem from technical reasons or organisational reasons. In the case that a reason changed, this information is used to propagate the change to the affected service(s). Let us consider an example. The change in the organisational ontology could be the split of the organisational unit into two subunits. This "organisational reason" might cause the design decision "Executing an activity in two steps", i.e. two (atomic) activities. For example, the decision to split the activity *CheckEligibility* shown in Fig. 12.3 into two activities can be caused by the fact that two different public authorities are responsible for this action: the residents' registration verifies personal information, and the immigration office verifies the validity of the visa, in case the citizen is a foreigner. More information about this ontology can be found in [2].

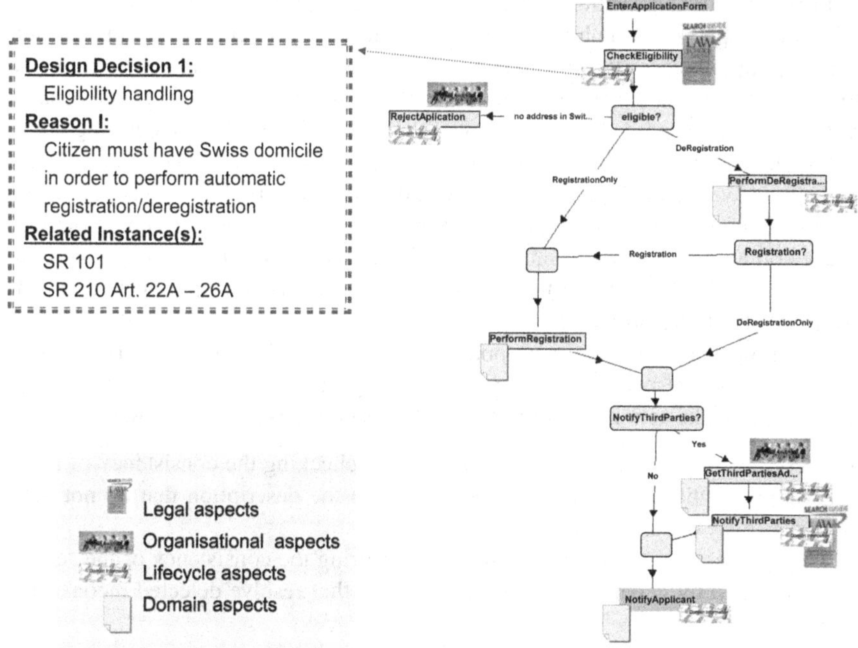

Fig. 12.3. The *announcement of moving* eGovernment service modelled using the OntoGov model

12.4 Consistency Preservation

Changes are forces that drive the evolution. They can be applied to a consistent description of an eGovernment service, and after all the changes are performed, the description must pass into another consistent state. However, when updating a service description, it is not enough just to consider the entities figuring in the request for a change. The other entities in the same description may also be affected by the updates. For example, let us consider the case where a public administrator wants to delete the activity *CheckEligibility* from the service *Announcement of move* shown in Fig. 12.3. This change will generate an inconsistency related to the activity *EnterApplicationForm* because it does not have a next activity anymore and it is not the last activity in the process model. Since it is not sufficient to change only a part of the description that is related to the request for a change while keeping all the other entities intact, we introduce the consistency preservation phase in the change management process [19]. Its task is to enable the resolution of changes in a systematic manner by ensuring the consistency of the whole description of an eGovernment service.

In the rest of this section, we present a novel approach to consistency preservation that supports the public administrators in managing and optimising the service descriptions according to their needs. The underlying system is able to find the "weak places" in the description of the eGovernment services (e.g. unreachable entities, non-expected data, etc.) by considering the semantics on underlying OntoGov model (see Sect. 12.3). It is focused on discovering inconsistencies in a service description. We assume that the update would be only a partially automated process rather than a fully automated process. For example, we do not want to update service description automatically, but rather to notify the public administrators about problems and about all the possibilities to resolve the problems. It is up to them to decide how to resolve those problems.

The proposed approach incorporates mechanisms for verifying the service description with respect to different consistency criteria as well as mechanisms enabling us to take actions to optimise it. It has been realised through two sub-tasks:

1. Inconsistency detection: It is responsible for checking the consistency of a service description. Its goal is to find "parts" in the description that do not meet consistency conditions.
2. Change generation: It is responsible for ensuring the consistency of the service description by generating additional changes that resolve detected inconsistencies.

In the rest of this section, we describe our approach for inconsistency detection. Thereafter, we present our approach for "moving" the inconsistent ontology back into a consistent state, i.e. change generation.

12.4.1 Formal Method for Inconsistency Detection

In this section, we explore the verification of the OntoGov model introduced in Sect. 12.3. Verification in general concerns correctness. Verification of an eGovernment service is checking of the correctness of the service description with respect to the service consistency definition. Moreover, it provides enough information to analyse the sources of conflicts. Its role will be to inform a public administrator about the necessity for updating the description of an eGovernment service, and to allow the application of the service changes, enabling an easy spotting of potential problems. The description of the eGovernment services (or, more generally, the description of the semantic web services) can be arbitrarily complex, containing multiple concurrent threads that may interact in an unexpected way [1]. We propose an approach that is able to verify numerous properties. The set of properties is not pre-defined, which means that it does not include only the standard properties such as safety, liveness, etc. [12], but, more importantly, it can be easily extended by application-specific properties.

Verification of the description of eGovernment services is realised using formal methods. These methods seek to establish a logical proof that a system works correctly. A formal approach provides the following:

1. A modelling language to describe the system.
2. A specification language to describe the correctness requirements.
3. An analysis technique to verify that the system meets its specification.

The model describes the possible behaviours of the system, and the specification describes the desired behaviours of the system. The statement that the model P satisfies the specification is now a logical statement, to be proved or disproved using the analysis technique.

Since the goal of the inconsistency detection is to check whether a service description satisfies the required specification, it can be treated as a formal verification problem in which a modelling language to describe a system is defined through the OntoGov model, a specification language corresponds to the consistency constraints that must be preserved, and an analysis technique can be treated as inference process. The model of the eGovernment services is described in Sect. 12.3. In the rest of this section we focus on the points 2 and 3.

Consistency Definition

To formally prove the correctness of a model, the first decision is about what claims to prove. Typically, two kinds of properties are proven about a given protocol:

1. Safety properties, which guarantee that specified undesired states, such as deadlocking states, are never reached.
2. Liveness properties, which specify that desired states are eventually reached [1].

However, to achieve the completeness, the solution is not to specify in advance the possible checks, but to enable the extension of the claims by allowing the users to specify their needs.

Indeed, for a more complex service model, the number of possible problems increases dramatically. Since the needs of a user cannot be anticipated, it is also impossible to determine exactly which kinds of checking should be built into a system. Thus, for a verification system to be useful, effective and efficient, it has to address the issue of how a user can specify his/her request for a checking. This problem requires a method for expressing a user's need in an exacter, easier and more declarative manner. It is in contrast to all existing approaches, where a user can only select a claim from a pre-defined set, which does not necessarily cover all the users' needs. In the rest of this section, we propose the declarative specification of the consistency constraints of the model.

According to [7], consistency is the degree of uniformity, standardisation, and freedom from contradiction among the parts of a system or component. From the point of view of logic, consistency is an attribute of a (logical) system that is so constituted that none of the facts deducible from the model contradict each other. Therefore, the consistency of an ontology-based description can be considered as an agreement among ontology entities with respect to the semantics of the underlying language used for modelling.

We define the consistency of an eGovernment service description in the following ways.

Definition 1 (eGovernment service consistency). An ontology-based eGovernment service description is consistent

- if it is ontology-consistent and
- if it satisfies a set of consistency constraints defined for the OntoGov model.

Since we use the OWL ontology language (see Chap. 3) for representing the OntoGov ontologies introduced in Sect. 12.3, the set of constraints can be defined on the basis of OWL plus rules as shown in [5]. The second aspect of eGovernment service consistency takes into account specificities of the OntoGov ontologies, since they represent the language for describing services. This set of consistency constraints belongs to the user-defined consistency constraints,[9] since they represent users' requirements that need to be expressed "outside" of the ontology language itself.

Definition 2 (OntoGov consistency constraints). A set of consistency constraints defined for the OntoGov model includes

- generic conditions that are applicable across domains and represent, e.g., best design practice or modelling-quality criteria (e.g. redundancy);
- domain-dependent conditions that take into account the semantics of a particular formalism of the domain.

Whereas the generic conditions are elaborated in [18], the domain-dependent conditions[10] are enumerated in [15]. In order to make the definition of consistency more clearly, we show in Fig. 12.4 a service that satisfies neither generic nor domain-dependent conditions. The generic conditions are not fulfilled since a profile of the eGovernment service is annotated with a class and its subclass, which is considered as redundant. Regarding the domain-dependent conditions, the process model of the service contains an unreachable activity.

Previously mentioned consistency constraints are formally represented as DL-safe rules [13], since inference by KAON2[11] engine is used to perform the model verification. This is described in the next sub-section. The rules for finding unreachable entities in a process model are shown in Fig. 12.5. By assuming that the activity A is set as a first entity in the process flow, and that C and D are last activities, the system will find that the atomic activity B is unreachable.

We do not only test the reachability of an activity, but also verify the reachability with respect to the policies that the service must satisfy. For example, the

[9] An ontology is user-defined consistent if it meets the constraints explicitly defined by the users which cannot be captured by the underlying ontology language itself, but rather given by some application or usage context

[10] The set of domain-dependent consistency constraints covers constraints related to the profile and to the process model of a service description. Regarding the process model we consider (i) the control flow, i.e. the order of execution and dependencies among the various activities and (ii) the data flow, i.e. how the business entities are manipulated by the various activities and the dependencies between entities belonging to different activities

[11] `http://kaon2.semanticweb.org/`

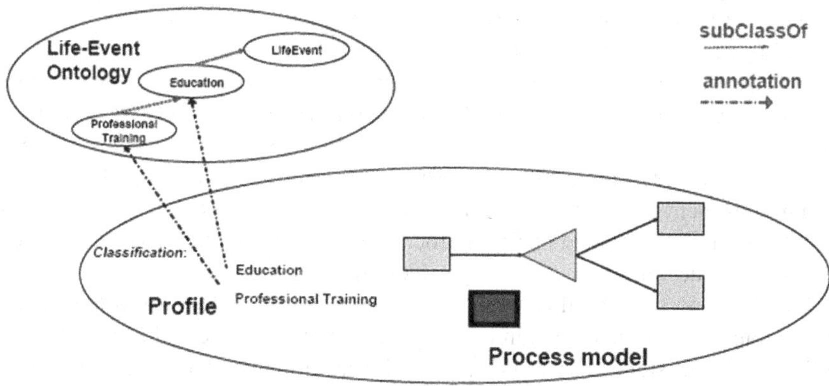

Fig. 12.4. An example of an inconsistent eGovernment service

PerformDeregistration activity cannot be executed before the *PerformRegistration* activity (according to the consistency constraint C13[12]). Let us assume that there is a data-flow link between the output of the *PerformDeregistration* activity and the *RejectApplication* activity in the eGovernment model shown in Fig. 12.3. The underlying ontology is OWL consistent. Moreover, the process model satisfies all consistency constraints related to the process flow. However, there is a problem with the data flow. This is because in the run-time either the *PerformDeregistration* activity or the *RejectApplication* activity will be executed. In the case that the *RejectApplication* activity is executed, its input is not instantiated, since the *PerformDeregistration* activity cannot be executed. All consistency checking rules are organised in the

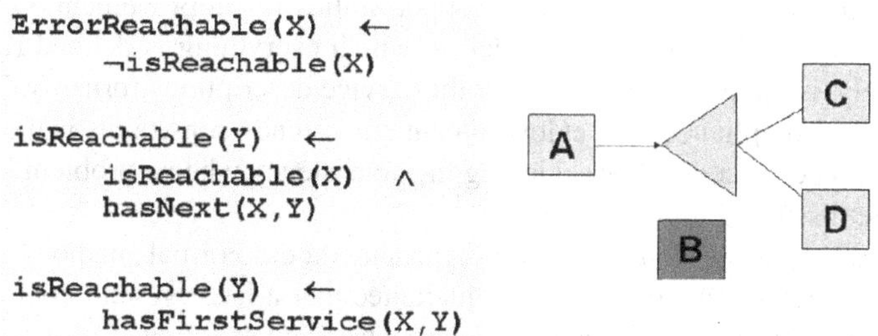

Fig. 12.5. Verification based on the domain-specific constraints. A part of consistency rules is depicted in the left part. The right part shows the process model that does not satisfy the rules (see activity B)

[12] C13: Any specialisation of the activity A1 must always be a predecessor of any specialisation of the activity A2, where A1 and A2 are two activities defined in the OntoGov model and their order is given in advance (i.e. A1 precedes A2)

so-called *Error hierarchy* that is also defined using the rules. This allows checking consistency at different levels of abstractions.

Here we note that the additional consistency constraints defined for the OntoGov model allow us to model not only the business process model[13] of eGovernment services, but more important the business requirement model.[14] The business requirement model provides a higher-level description of the different actors in the business domain with their goals and their mutual dependencies and expectations, and provides the motivations behind business processes [4]. It drives the design of business processes and the verification that they achieve desired goals.

The OntoGov system allows public administrators to capture knowledge about the concrete eGovernment domain in a way that is both intuitive and formal. Indeed, the OntoGov consistency constraints concern the truthfulness of a service description with respect to its problem domain – does the service description represent a piece of reality and the users' requirements correctly? They help finding the "weak places" in the service description regarding the users' needs, ensures that generated recommendations reflect the users' needs and promotes accountability of a public administrator who does not need to be an experienced modeller. In this way, the change management system provides an easy-to-use management system for public administrators, since they are able to use it productively, with minimal training.

However, current approaches do not address the issues of how to model the requirements that semantic web services (e.g. OWL-S processes) are supposed to satisfy and how to manage the evolution of service descriptions and requirements. This work presents the first steps towards this vision, since it provides the ability to capture the specific aspects of eGovernment services.

An Approach for Inconsistency Detection

Creating a proposed description of an eGovernment service is instructive in itself, revealing anomalies, inefficiencies and opportunities for improvement. One of the main advantages of the proposed model, in which everything is defined rigorously and precisely, is the possibility to verify the service descriptions formally. The verification of the compliance with eGovernment consistency constraints is the focus of this section. The procedure for achieving the consistency when a problem is discovered will be discussed in Sect. 12.4.2.

Verification can be done by using formal methods. Formal methods are those that provide a rigourous mathematical guarantee that a large system conforms to a specification. Formal methods can be roughly classified as follows:

- Proof-theoretic: A suitable deductive system is used, and correctness proofs are built using a theorem prover.

[13] This is the traditional model which OWL-S or other languages are using to describe both the flow of activities internal to an organisation and its interactions with external processes and services

[14] The business requirement model describes both the internal requirements, i.e. the business needs of an organisation, and the external requirements, i.e. the expectations over the external services the organisation has to use to realise its own business

- Model-theoretic: A model of the run-time behaviour of the system is built, and this model is checked for the required properties.

In this section, we explore the verification of the OntoGov model using proof-theoretic method. Once we have a service description (see Sect. 12.3) plus the formally defined consistency constraints that correspond to the users' requirements, we can automatically check whether these constrains are satisfied in the service description with the help of the reasoning. The KAON2 inference engine is used, since it implements the proof-theory for DL and DL-safe rules. By performing an efficient exploration of the possible inconsistencies that can be built in the service description, the system is able to verify all the consistency constraints[15] defined for the OntoGov model.

The set of the consistency constraints as well as a description of the concrete service are inputs to the KAON2 inference engine that is used to automatically verify whether the service description satisfies the consistency. Practically, a query is sent, since possible problems are hierarchically organised. A trace of the answer to a query is considered as a model that reflects how different pieces of a service description are put together to generate the answer. If the KAON2 verifies that the consistency constrains are fulfilled (i.e. there is no answer), then the service description is consistent. Otherwise, the KAON2 provides explanation about causes of problems, since it can identify the conditions under which the problem occurs.

The realised verification procedure is depicted in Fig. 12.6. The set of the consistency constraints selected/defined[16] by the public administrator are transformed into a set of DL-safe rules and these rules are included in the temporary version of the OntoGov Profile and OntoGov Process ontology, respectively. Since the description of a concrete service includes both of these ontologies, it will include the rules to be checked. The service description is given to the KAON2 reasoner and the query "about all possible errors" is initiated. The result produced by KAON2 reasoner is then presented to the public administrator in the form that he/she can understand. Even though logic provides an unambiguous formal specification, it is hard to imagine that a public administrator will comprehend it. Therefore, "wrapping" into a more friendly formalisms, i.e. natural language explanation,[17] has been proposed. It means that in the case of any violations of consistency constraints, the reasoner will output a counterexample, which demonstrates the courses of wrong behaviour. An analysis of this counterexample provides information that helps to correct and refine the service description.

For example, a pre-condition of an activity is not achieved because there are some previous activities that undo the pre-condition. Let us consider the driving licence service for foreigners in Germany. The pre-conditions of the Application activity

[15] Since in this work we use the KAON2 inference engine, the consistency constraints must be specified as DL-safe rules

[16] A user can select consistency criteria from the list of available consistency constraints and/or can define a new consistency criterion

[17] We do not use logical notations since public administrators do not have logic background knowledge. For each possible problem, an explanation in natural language is generated

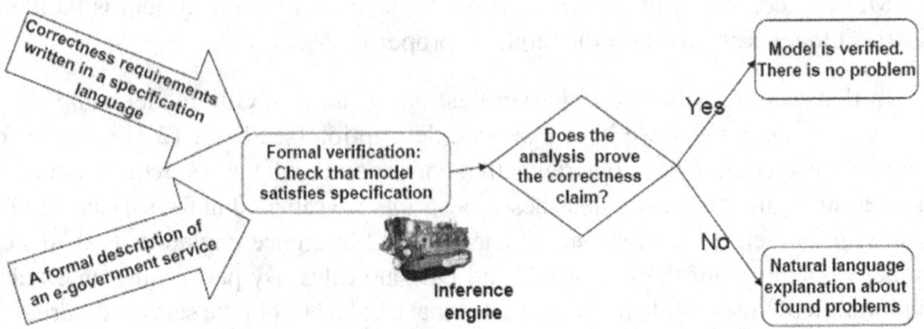

Fig. 12.6. Formal verification: based on the possible behaviours (i.e. a ontology-based service description) and on the desirable behaviours (i.e. formally defined consistency constraints), the system constructs a proof that either proves or disproves the correctness claim

includes that foreigners come from non-EU countries. Since a special verification is required for the countries emerged from the break-up of Yugoslavia, there is an activity in the process model that has a pre-condition that the foreigners must be from Slovenia. However, the Application activity undoes this pre-condition, since Slovenia is a member of EU. It is very difficult for a user to notice that some of the paths in the model are not possible due to at least two reasons: (i) this service description is very complicated with many disjunctive branches, and (ii) the background knowledge (i.e. the fact that Slovenia is in EU) is needed. Our system is able to detect this problem by applying reasoning methods (based on the consistency constraint C8[18]) and to help the user fix problem. It can find activities in the process model that should be executed before the failed activity that have effects that undid the unachieved pre-conditions. Moreover, it suggests modifying the activity whose pre-condition can never be achieved. For the above-mentioned type of failure, our system suggests (i) changing or adding constraints for the Application activity and (ii) deleting or modifying the Verification activity.

Moreover, the system is also able to propose changing ordering constraints among the activities. For example, the user may either forget to specify connections between the activities or may specify wrong connections. These problems may be detected by checking the consistency constraint C13 [15], since it defines the certain ordering constraints already specified for the type of these activities. During the verification, the system checks (among others) the dependencies between activities using the ordering consistency constraint. In the case that some activity does not satisfy the ordering constraint, the system produces the error message containing the fixes such as adding or modifying dependency between activities.

We note that the same problem can be a consequence of different inconsistencies in the model, since one abnormality can lead to another. For example, missing the first activity in a process model causes unreachable activities. To help avoid

[18] C8: If an activity precedes another activity, then its pre-conditions have to subsume the pre-conditions of the next one

confusion, our system can selectively present suggestions for improvement by focusing the user on the actual cause of a problem. For the previous example, the system suggests staring with the resolution of the first activity problem. However, the user can check other problems as well, if he/she wants to do that. For the description of eGovernment services, the proposed solution seems to be an ideal technique, since only consistency constraints defined by the public administrators need to be considered. The probability of running into the undecidable solution is quite low, since the restriction to the DL-subset of SWRL rules has been chosen to make reasoning decidable. Moreover, reasoning in KAON2 is implemented by novel algorithms that allow applying well-known deductive database techniques, such as magic sets or join-order optimisations, to DL reasoning. According to the performance evaluation [10], such algorithms make answering queries in KAON2 one or more orders of magnitude faster than in existing systems.

12.4.2 Change Generation

Changes are applied to a consistent service description, and after all the changes are performed the description must remain consistent. This is done by finding inconsistencies in the description and completing required changes with additional changes, which guarantee the transfer of the initial consistent description into another consistent state. Indeed, the updated service description is not defined directly by applying a requested change. Instead, it is indirectly characterised as a service description that satisfies the user's requirement for a change and it is at the same time a consistent eGovernment service description.

Therefore, there are two major issues involved in the change generation. The first issue is the understanding how an ontology-based service description can be changed since the change management is realised by means of applying changes. To resolve the first issue a possible set of changes is defined in [17]. The second issue involves deciding when and how to modify a service description to keep its consistency, which is elaborated in the rest of this section.

Dependency Graph

The role of a change management system is much more than finding inconsistencies in a service description and alerting a public administrator about them. This is pretty much the kind of support provided by conventional compilers. However, helping public administrators notice the inconsistencies only partially addresses the issue. Ideally, the change management should be able to support public administrators in resolving the problems at least by making suggestions how to do that. In the rest of this section, we discuss our formal approach for suggesting fixes that directly point to the source of the errors.

In order to formally define the way of generating additional changes, the OntoGov changes are modelled in the following ways.

Definition 3 (Change). A change Ch is a 5-tuple

$$\text{Ch} := (\text{name}, \text{args}, \text{preconditions}, \text{postconditions}, \text{rules})^{19}$$

where

- *name* is the identifier of the change. All possible change identifiers can be derived from the OntoGov model.
- *args* is a list of one or more change arguments. For example, to remove the atomic activity *X* from a service description, the only argument of the change *RemoveAtomicActivity* has to be *X*. To remove the input *I* of the activity *X*, the change *RemoveActivityInput(X, I)* has to be applied.
- *pre-conditions* are a set of assertions that must be true to be able to apply a change. For example, preconditions for the removal of the atomic activity *X* is that the atomic activity *X* has been defined.
- *post-conditions* are a set of assertions that must be true after applying a change and it describes the result of a change. For example, post-conditions for the removal of the atomic activity *X* includes assertion that the atomic activity *X* does not exist anymore.
- *rules* are additional changes that have to be generated.

The most critical part of a definition change is rules specify the side effects of a change on the other related entities. To define the rules for each change, we started by finding out the cause–effect relationship between the changes. This kind of dependency between the changes forms the so-called *change dependency graph.*

Definition 4 (Change dependency graph). A change dependency graph is a directed graph defined as

$$CDG := (CH, E)$$

where

- $CH = \{Ch_i\}, 1 \leq i \leq |CH|$, is a set of nodes and each node represents a change Ch_i;
- $E = \{Ek\}, 1 \leq k \leq |E|$, is a set of labelled edges and each edge represents the cause–effect dependency between changes (i.e. nodes). An edge is defined in the following way:

$$Ek = (Ch_i, Condition_j, Ch_l), Ch_i, Ch_l \in CH, 1 \leq i, l \leq |CH|, i \neq l.$$

$Condition_j$ is a prerequisite for the edge existence. It states when a change Ch_i may cause a change Ch_l. It is represented as a logical formula that contains only ontology entities.

[19] In order to simplify the notation of changes, the following simplified syntax is used: *name(args, preconditions, postconditions, rules).* Moreover, to specify the request for a change the notation *name(args)* is used since the pre-conditions, the post-conditions and the rules are general and do not depend on the concrete application of a change

Therefore, $E_k = (Ch_i, Condition_j, Ch_l)$ can be read as

IF Ch_i THEN Ch_l
WHEN $Condition_j$

For example, one has to interpret the edge

$$(RemoveAtomicActivity(x), (hasPrevious(x,y) \wedge Activity(y)), RemoveSequence(y,x))$$

as the change *RemoveAtomicActivity* triggering the change *RemoveSequence*, i.e. the rule

$$\text{IF } RemoveAtomicActivity(x) \text{ THEN } RemoveSequence(y,x)$$

can be applied if the condition $hasPrevious(x,y) \wedge Activity(y)$ is satisfied.

The applicability of a condition depends on the content of a service description. For example, for the request *RemoveAtomicActivity(NotifyThirdParties)* for the model shown in Fig. 12.7, the dependency between the change *RemoveAtomicActivity* and the change *RemoveSequence* would be taken into account, since the activity *NotifyThirdParties* has a previous entity that is an activity *GetThirdPartiesAddress*. However, the request for the removal of the activity *GetThirdPartiesAddress* would not provoke the generation of changes related to sequence since this activity is not

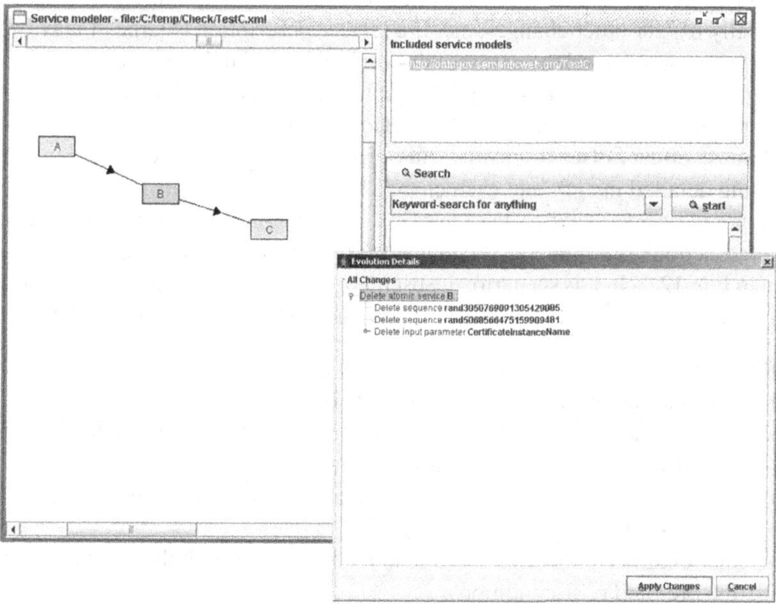

Fig. 12.7. Change generation for the request *RemoveAtomicActivity(B)*: (a) The initial model; (b) the generated changes

related to any sequence, but to the switch control construct. In this way, the change dependency graph can be considered as a schema for generating additional changes.

The change dependency graph is a directed graph. Moreover, it is worth mentioning that the size of the graph is fixed since the number of changes is pre-defined. Nevertheless, the change dependency graph has a very complex, interwoven structure.[20]

The approach is based on a common technique for the maintenance of knowledge-based systems [9] which states that dependencies between knowledge have to be represented explicitly. However, while in these systems the dependency graph consists of knowledge elements (e.g. rules in the expert systems), in our change management system the nodes of this graph are changes – as defined in [17].

Definition 5 (Change generation). The change generation is defined as

$$ChangeGeneration : CH \rightarrow 2^{CH}$$

where each $ChangeGeneration(Ch_k) = \{Ch_{k1}, ..., Ch_{ki}, ..., Ch_{kn}\}$ consists of the *THEN* part of those rules, defined for a particular change Ch_k, that can be applied. We note that the applicability of a rule is determined by the conditions.

Note that each of generated changes can cause new problems in the service description. Resolving these problems is treated as a request for a new change, which can induce new problems that cause new changes etc. Therefore, one change can potentially trigger other changes, etc. If a service description is large, it may be difficult to fully comprehend the extent and meaning of each induced change. The task of "change generation" phase is to enable resolution of induced changes in a systematic manner, ensuring consistency of the service description. To help in better understanding of effects of each change, this phase contributes maximum transparency providing detailed insight into each change being performed.

A sample screen shot of the OntoGov change management system illustrating triggered actions (i.e. generated changes) for the removal of the atomic activity is given in Fig. 12.7. In this scenario, the user requested to remove the *AtomicActivity B*. According to the change dependency graph, this change may cause the following:

- Remove all input links[21] of *AtomicActivity B*.
- Remove all output links of *AtomicActivity B*.
- Remove all meta data defined for *AtomicActivity B* that includes the following:
  - the attributes such as name, description, first and last service
  - the relations to the associated ontologies (i.e. Legal, Organisational and Lifecycle ontology)
  - the relations to the inputs and outputs defined through the Domain ontology
  - the pre- and post-conditions.

[20] The richer the set of changes, the more difficult it becomes to give a precise characterisation of the dependency between changes

[21] A link can be a sequence or a relation to the split, join or switch control construct

Before changes are performed, their impact is reported to the user (the right part of Fig. 12.7). Presentation of changes follows the progressive disclosure principle: related changes are grouped together and organised in a tree-like form. The user initially sees only the general description of changes (cf. "Delete atomic service B" in Fig. 12.7). By opening a node in the tree, the user can see what changes will actually be performed (cf. "Delete input parameter CertificateInstanceName" in Fig. 12.7). Hence, the change information can be viewed at different levels of granularity. If the user is interested in details, he/she can expand the tree and view complete information. The user may cancel the operation before it is actually performed.

Additionally, the role of the change preservation is not only to ensure the preservation of the consistency in the case that a request for a change can be applied. Its role is also to prevent illegal changes, i.e. changes that would cause inconsistencies [4]. Whereas the change-dependency graph is responsible for keeping consistency, the prohibition of illegal changes is settled by checking the pre-conditions of a change, since they are applicability conditions, i.e. to say the conditions under which changes are semantically correct.

Let us consider an example. Suppose that we start to model a new eGovernment service. We annotate the profile of this service with the concept *Education* defined in the Life-Event ontology as shown in Fig. 12.4. This service description is consistent with respect to the consistency definition. Suppose we now want to add the axiom stating that the service is about *Professional Training* as well. Obviously, this change would result in a service description that is inconsistent with respect to compactness generic condition, since there is an alternative path (through the concept *Professional Training*) between the service profile and the concept *Education* (see Fig. 12.4). Our change management system suggests a change that removes the annotation of the service with the most general concept *Education* before applying the required change.

12.5 Implementation

OMS is the ontology management system that has been developed within the OntoGov project. It is a management system for the ontology-based description of the eGovernment services. The set of ontologies needed to model eGovernment services and their life-cycle aspects are described in sect. 12.3. Indeed, OMS is a framework for creating, modifying, querying and storing ontology-based description of eGovernment services. It provides support for the service life-cycle management, which includes service modelling, service reconfiguration, service reuse, service discovery and service analysis.

The simplified conceptual architecture of the OMS system is presented in Fig. 12.8. Roughly, the OMS components can be divided into three layers:

1. Applications and services layer: It realises UI applications and provides interfaces to non-human agents. It includes the following:

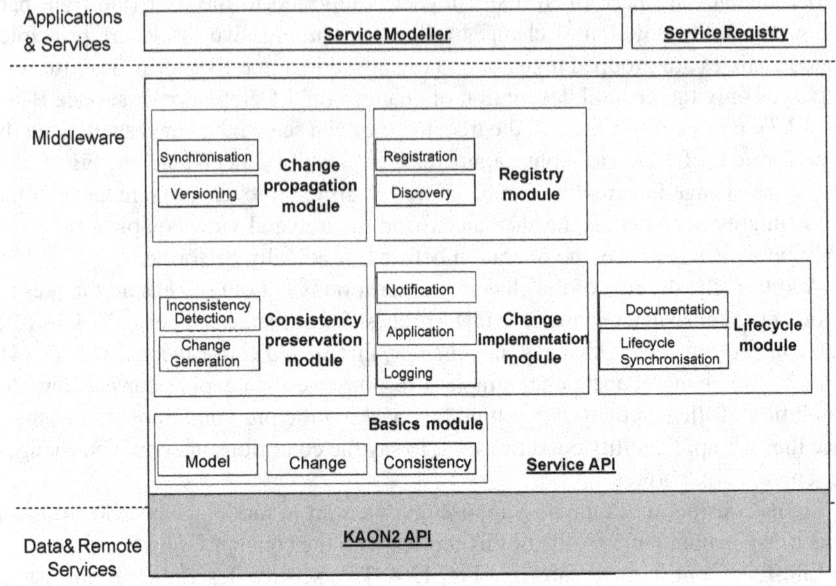

Fig. 12.8. Conceptual architecture of the OMS

- Service modeller: It is an editor for the semantic description of the eGovernment services.[22]:
- Service registry: – it is a registry of the eGovernment services.

2. Middleware layer: The Service API as part of the Middleware Layer is the focal point of the OMS architecture. The bulk of requirements related to the management of eGovernment service description is realised in this layer.
3. Data and remote services layer: It provides data storage facilities. It is based on KAON2 API, which is an API for OWL ontologies.

The middleware layer of the OMS shown in Fig. 12.8 emphasises points of interest related to the change management. The main modules are (i) basics module, (ii) consistency preservation module, (iii) change implementation module, (iv) change propagation module, (v) lifecycle module and (vi) registry module. The functionality as well as the implementation of these modules is described in [16]. Our initial evaluation shows that the OMS is able to find all inconsistencies in the service description

[22] OIModeller is used as an editor for the "standard" ontologies. It is a graphical tool for ontology creation and maintenance. Since it is based on the different ontology model, we have realised a translator of the KAON ontologies (`http://kaon.semanticweb.org/`) into the KAON2 ontologies (`http://kaon2.semanticweb.org/`). We note that each KAON ontology can be transformed into a KAON2 ontology without loss of information

and to suggest useful fixes including the fixes that directly point to the source of the inconsistencies.

12.6 Related Work

OWL-S process models are typically verified using human inspection, simulation and testing. In this chapter we proposed the formal verification, which has two main advantages over traditional techniques such as testing and simulation:

1. Formality: The intuitive correctness claim is made formally.
2. Verification: The goal of the analysis is to prove or disprove the correctness claim.

It is not sufficient to check a representative sample of possible behaviours as in simulation; rather a guarantee is required that all behaviours satisfy the specification. The verification of OWL-S process models is described in [11] and [1]. Whereas the first paper proposes a Petri Net-based operational semantics which models the control-flow of a process model, the second paper additionally models the data flow and applies the SPIN model-checker as an automatic verification tool. We extend these works in several dimensions. First, we not only model the control-flow and data-flow consistency constraints, but allow to the public administrators to specify arbitrary domain-dependent consistency constraints. In this way, we are able to cover all perspectives of the business models, i.e. control flow, data flow, operational issues (e.g. interactions between systems) and resources (e.g. humans, machines, etc.). Second, we do not consider only the process model but also the profile of a service. Finally, we have realised the verification of the eGovernment service descriptions using a rule-based inference process.

Many AI researchers have investigated useful ways of verifying and validating knowledge bases with ontologies and rules. However, it is not easy to directly apply this work to checking process models. In [8] the authors discussed the KANAL system that relates pieces of information in process models among themselves and to the existing knowledge base, analysing how different pieces of input are put together to achieve some effect. It builds interdependency models from this analysis and uses them to find errors and to propose fixes. However, it does not allow the user to specify their specific conditions, event though the pre-defined set of constraints does not cover all the users' needs. Our approach allows the user to define the user-defined conditions. Moreover, it separates the specification of consistency from the realisation of the change preservation procedure. Finally, the inconsistency detection and the change generation procedures are governed by well-defined formal models that are fully automated. Therefore, the approach is accessible by public administrators who are not experts in formal methods.

There are many graphical tools (ADONIS, ARIS, iThink, to name just a few) to lay out a process model and draw connections among steps. Often, these tools lack formal methods for verifying properties of processes. Indeed, they are mostly limited to simple checks on process models, since there is no semantics associated to the individual steps. In contrast, we propose an approach that allows to the users to formally specify consistency constraints. Ontologies and rules are used to represent this kind of background knowledge or users' needs. With this context, our system is much more helpful in checking the process model. Moreover, our system can check the service profile as well, and it proposes suggestions for resolving the problems.

12.7 Outlook

eGovernment systems are subject to a continual change. The importance of better change management is nowadays more important due to the evolution of Europe towards a multi-cultural, more open and international society with changing common values, increasing levels of education, demographic involvement and adoption of new technologies. This is especially true for the new EU countries, since the European integration has paved the way for new legislation, regulations and corresponding changes that affect the way public administrations in the enlarged Europe are organised and operated.

It is clear that ad hoc management of changes in eGovernment might work only for particular cases. To avoid drawbacks in the long-run, the change management must be treated in a more systematic way. In this chapter, we presented an approach for ontology-based change management. The approach enables (i) detection of inconsistencies that may arise in the description of the eGovernment services and (ii) generating specific suggestions to the public administrators about how to fix the problems found in the models. Our approach goes beyond a standard change management process; rather it is a continual improvement process. It allows the public administrators to specify their own continually changing needs through the application-specific consistency constraints. Moreover, it provides enough information to analyse the sources of inconsistencies by pointing out what existing knowledge needs to be modified or what additional knowledge needs to be acquired.

The main contribution of this work is the use of formal methods for modelling and analysis of eGovernment service descriptions. We strongly believe that the use of formal methods such as the ones discussed here can be of significant benefit to public administrators (or business analysts in general). The main advantage of the proposed approach is that it can be used to capture domain knowledge which includes knowledge about the service descriptions, as well knowledge about requirements that these descriptions have to satisfy, in an intuitive and unambiguous way. The approach can also be used to analyse the service description (i.e. to notice the problems and to fix them) in a formal way, what would be impossible if an informal approach is used.

The work presented here is a starting point, and we see many possibilities to extend it. Limitations of the tool include a user-friendly editor for consistency constraints as well as consistency checking between these constraints (e.g. contradiction, generalisation, cycles, etc.). The system could be expanded to accommodate the resolution strategies, i.e. more than one possibility to resolve the problems. However, we believe that the existing tool provides a very good base for future expansions in the field. Finally, the goal of this work has been to build a general framework for change management. As the basis of this framework, the OntoGov model (with its consistency definition and its changes) is used. However, the basic ideas are not strongly bound to this model. The main principles can be more or less easily adapted to other models.

References

1. A. Ankolekar, M. Paolucci, and K. Sycara. Towards a Formal Verification of OWL-S Process Models. In *4th International Semantic Web Conference (ISWC 2005)*, Galway, Ireland, 2005. Springer-Verlag.
2. D. Apostolou, L. Stojanovic, T. Pariente Lobo, and B. Thoenssen. Towards a Semantically-driven Software Engineering Environment for e-Government. In *TCGOV 2005*, volume 3416 of *LNCS*, pages 157–168, 2005. Springer-Verlag.
3. Cap Gamini Ernst and Young. Online availability of public services. `http://europa.eu.int/information_society/eeurope/2005/doc/highlights/whats_new/capgemini4.pdf`.
4. A. Fuxman, L. Liu, J. Mylopoulos, M. Pistore, and M. Roveri. Specifying and Analyzing Early Requirements in Tropos. *Requirements Engineering Journal*, 9(2):132–150, 2004.
5. P. Haase and L. Stojanovic. Consistent Evolution of OWL Ontologies. In *Proceedings of the 2nd European Semantic Web Conference (ESWC 2005)*, volume 3298 of *LNCS*, pages 182–197, Heraklion, Crete, Greece, 2005. Springer-Verlag.
6. C. Hardless, R. Lindgren, U. Nulden, and K. Pessi. The Evolution of Knowledge Management System Need to be Managed. *Journal of Knowledge Management Practice*, 3, 2000.
7. Institute of Electrical IEEE 90 and Electronics Engineers. IEEE Standard Computer Dictionary: A compilation of IEEE Standard Computer Glossaries.
8. J. Kim and Y. Gil. Knowledge analysis on process models. In *Proceedings of the 17th International Joint Conference on Artificial Intelligence (IJCAI 2001)*, pages 935–942, Seattle, Washington, USA, 2001.
9. T. Menzies and J. Debenham. Expert System Maintenance. In *Encyclopaedia of Computer Science and Technology*, volume 47, pages 35–54, 2000.
10. B. Motik and U. Sattler. Practical DL Reasoning over Large ABoxes with KAON2. `http://www.fzi.de/KCMS/kcms_file.php?action=link&id=580/`.
11. S. Narayanan and S. McIlraith. Simulation, Verification and Automated Composition of Web Services. In *Proceedings of the 11th International Conference on World Wide Web (WWW 2002)*, pages 77–88, Honolulu, Hawaii, USA, 2002.
12. G. Naumovich and L. Clarke. Classifying Properties, an Alternative to the Safety-Liveness Classification. *ACM SIGSOFT Software Engineering Notes*, 25(6):159–168, 2000.
13. F. Nickols. Change Management 101: A Primer. `http://home.att.net/~nickols/change.htm`.
14. L. Stojanovic. *Methods and Tools for Ontology Evolution*. PhD thesis, University of Karlsruhe, 2004.
15. L. Stojanovic, A. Abecker, N. Stojanovic, and R. Studer. On Managing Changes in the Ontology-Based E-Government. In *Proceedings of the 3rd International Conference on Ontologies, Databases and Application of Semantics (ODBASE 2004)*, number 3291 in LNCS, pages 1080–1097, Agia Napa, Cyprus, 2004. Springer-Verlag.

16. L. Stojanovic and D. Apostolou. Ontology-based Change Management of e-Government Services. In *Proceedings of Web Intelligence (WI2005) Conference - Semantics and Orchestration of eGovernment Processes Workshop*, France, 2005.
17. L. Stojanovic, G. Kavadias, D. Apostolou, F. Probst, and K. Hinkelmann. E-Gov Lifecycle Ontology. In *Deliverable D2, EU/IST Project OntoGov*, `http://www.ontogov.org`, 2004.
18. L. Stojanovic, N. Stojanovic, and D. Apostolou. Change Management in e-Government: OntoGov Case Study. *Electronic Government: International Journal, Special Issue on Exploiting Knowledge Management for Ubiquitous E-Government in the Semantic Web Era*, 3(1), 2006.
19. N. Stojanovic and L. Stojanovic. A Change-Aware Framework for the Knowledge Management in eGovernment. In *Electronic Government - Workshop and Poster Proceedings of the Fourth International EGOV Conference 2005*, pages 3–10, Copenhagen, Denmark, 2005.

13

An eGovernment Case Study

Integrating Governmental Services Using Semantic Web Technology

Christian Drumm[1] and Liliana Cabral[2]

[1] SAP Research, CEC Karlsruhe, Germany, christian.drumm@sap.com
[2] Knowledge Media Institute, The Open University, Milton Keynes, UK
l.s.cabral@open.ac.uk

Summary. In this section we will describe a prototypical application that shows how Semantic Web Services and current state-of-the-art Enterprise Application Integration software can be used to integrate eGovernment services across different service providers. Starting from a use case scenario and the general requirements that build the basis for our prototype, we will describe the generic integration architecture we have developed focusing mainly on the integration aspects of the Semantic Web Services. Following this we will describe the actual prototype application as well as some implementation details. Finally, we will close by a description of the challenges we faced when developing the prototype and by some general conclusions.

13.1 Introduction

Current eGovernment initiatives across Europe (e.g. eGovernment Interoperability Framework (eGIF) [1], European Interoperability Framework for pan-European eGovernment Services [3]) present governmental organisations with strong requirements regarding the integration of data and services across organisation boundaries. Currently, the ability to aggregate and reuse all the information resources relevant to a given problem and further to make this available as a basis for transparent interaction with community partner organisations and individual citizens is very restricted. Furthermore, the goals of citizens using eGovernment services and of government providers of services are often not conceptually aligned, contributing to misunderstanding, low take up and poor relations between citizens and their governments. We have created a prototype application for the use case on eGovernment within the DIP[1] project for illustrating how Semantic Web Services could be applied to this domain in order to overcome these problems and thereby enable the provision of better eGovernment services.

In this chapter, we will describe a prototypical application which builds on Semantic Web Services and current state-of-the-art Enterprise Application

[1] http://dip.semanticweb.org

Integration software in order to integrate eGovernment services offered by different service providers. We start with an overview of the use case scenario and general requirements. Following this, we describe the generic application architecture and the Semantic Web Service infrastructure used to develop the prototype. Next, we describe some implementation details including examples of the domain ontologies and semantic descriptions of the services used by the application. Finally, we present some of the challenges faced when using Semantic Web Services technology and our conclusions.

13.2 Use Case Overview

The application scenario we used as a basis for our use case is a real-world scenario from Essex County Council (ECC) in the UK named *Change-of-Circumstances*. In the given scenario, a case worker of the Community Care department of ECC helps a citizen to report his/her change of circumstance (e.g. address) to all the agencies that need to know of this change. In that way, the citizen only needs to inform the council once about his/her change, and the government agency automatically notifies all the agencies involved.

An example for a more complex change of circumstance might be when a disabled mother moves into her daughter's home. This changes the circumstances of both, the mother and the daughter. A case worker would in this situation open the case of the mother who is eligible to receive different services and benefits – health, housing, etc. He/she would then set the mother's new address. This would trigger an update of the necessary information at multiple service providing agencies. Furthermore, many different agencies and also private service providers might need to interact in order to provide the required services.

For the first implementation of prototype application for ECC, two governmental agencies were involved:

1. Community care (social services) in Essex County Council. They typically have a coordinating role in relation to a range of services from a number of providers and special responsibility for key services such as support for elderly and disabled people (day centres, transportation). It uses the SWIFT database as its main records management tool.
2. The Housing Department of Chelmsford District Council. They handle housing services and use the ELMS database.

However, the current prototype could easily be extended in order to also involve other agencies.

In order to illustrate the functionality of the prototype and how the different components interact, we will use the following example. A citizen with different impairments including a mobility impairment moves from his/her current house to a new one. This simple change of address requires several actions in the involved systems. First, the citizen address needs to be changed in the SWIFT and the ELMS systems. Secondly, all required services need to be delivered to the new instead of the old address. Finally, the necessary equipment has to be relocated to the new house.

13.3 Prototype Architecture

Developers trying to create applications solving scenarios similar to the one described in the previous section are facing a large number of challenges. Based on these challenges we derived a set of requirements a SWS-based integration architecture needs to fulfill in order to simplify the application development.

Cross-agency scenarios in eGovernment generally present a developer with three main requirements. First, a developer needs to be able to discover services capable of fulfilling the requirements of a given step in a business process. Secondly, by he/she needs to be able to seamlessly invoke services provided by different agencies. With respect to the application scenario described above, a developer would, e.g., need to invoke a service ordering "Meals-on-Wheels" published by a private provider. Thirdly, a developer usually needs to develop transformation between different data formats in order to actually invoke a given service. Therefore, the main requirements for our architecture is to simplify the tasks of service discovery, service invocation and service mediation in an eGovernment setting.

In order to show the applicability of the integration architecture in real eGovernment settings where numerous agencies are involved, the architecture should enable the easy development of new applications in highly heterogeneous system landscapes. Furthermore the integration of systems and services across organisational boundaries should be transparent to the application developer.

Based on these requirements, we developed a high-level architecture for the prototype. This architecture reflects our methodology for integrating eGovernment services through Semantic Web Services, which allows the functionality provided by existing legacy systems from the involved agencies to be exposed as Web Services. These Web Services are then semantically annotated and published using the Semantic Web Service infrastructure. Finally, the front-end application (portal) can be built on the published Semantic Web Services provided by different agencies. As depicted in Fig. 13.1, the architecture consists of four layers: (i) the legacy system layer, (ii) the service abstraction layer, (iii) the Semantic Web Service layer and (iv) the presentation layer.

The *legacy system layer* contains the legacy applications available from each of the agencies involved in the integration project. In a general setting, this layer could contain an arbitrary number of databases and legacy systems from different partner applications.

The *service abstraction layer* sits on top of the legacy system layer. This layer is responsible for providing low-level functionality available from the involved legacy systems to the SWS layer as well as for abstracting from the given implementation details of these systems. This is done by implementing standard Web Services, which execute specific functionalities of the legacy systems. Current Enterprise Application Integration (EAI) software generally enables the easy creation of the necessary Web Services. Note that for the integration of standard databases the necessary functionality of the Web Services can simply be CRUD[2] functions.

---

[2] Create, Read, Update, Delete

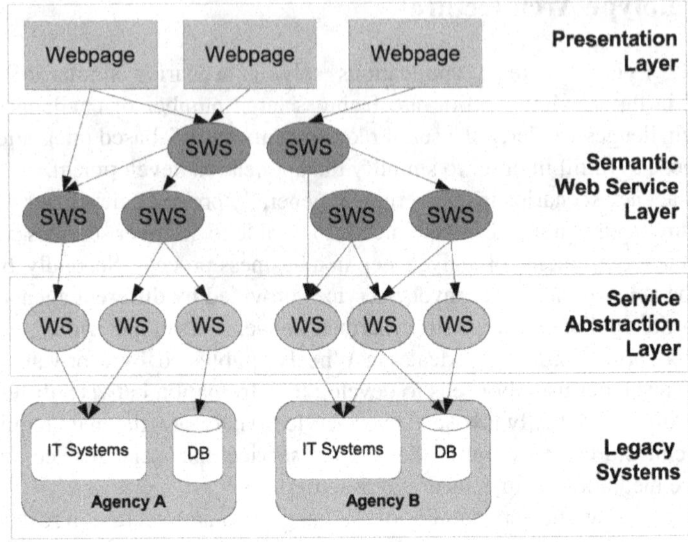

Fig. 13.1. The high-level architecture of the prototype

The *Semantic Web Services layer* is based on the Web Services provided by the service abstraction layer. It consists of two main parts: (i) a set of SWSs and (ii) a set of goal invocation templates. The set of SWSs is created by providing semantic annotations to the deployed Web Services in the abstraction layer. These annotations enable the invocation of Semantic Web Services through goal achievement. This is supported by an infrastructure for describing and invoking Semantic Web Services. This infrastructure also includes an ontology repository and a reasoner. A detailed description of the SWS infrastructure will be given in Sect. 13.4.

Table 13.1. Description of the four architecture layers

abstract layer	functionality
legacy system layer	all IT systems that will be integrated using the presented architecture. Examples could be citizen databases, systems for calculating housing benefits, etc.
service abstraction layer	all standards Web Services encapsulating legacy system functionality. These services are developed using standard EAI solutions.
semantic web service layer	all SWSs developed on the basis of the services in the service abstraction layer. Furthermore, this layer contains the necessary ontologies, goals and mediators.
presentation layer	depending on the requirements of a concrete implementation, this layer contains webpages allowing the users to invoke the available SWSs.

Finally, the *Presentation layer* consists of the user interface, which is built on top of the SWS layer as an Web application accessible using a standard web browser. The goal invocation templates mentioned earlier are filled with the data entered by the user through the user interface and sent to the Semantic Web Service layer where they trigger the invocation of applicable SWSs which in turn after several steps trigger the execution of Web Services in the service abstraction layer. The contents of the different layers is summarised again in Table 13.1.

In conclusion, this architecture enables integration by allowing applications to be composed of Semantic Web Services provided by different partner organisations.

13.4 Semantic Web Service Infrastructure

In order to develop the functionality necessary for the Semantic Web Service Layer, we used the IRS-III platform, which supports application developers and service providers with the creation of Semantic Web Services.

IRS-III [2] is an implemented infrastructure which allows the description, publication and execution of Semantic Web Services according to the WSMO conceptual model. IRS-III provides a powerful execution environment for knowledge models. A WSMO description can be instantiated into the IRS-III operational framework so that Web Services are selected and invoked to achieve a goal. IRS-III is based on a distributed architecture which communicates via SOAP. The server component handles ontology management and the execution of knowledge models for Semantic Web Services. The server also receives SOAP requests (through the API) from client applications for creating and editing WSMO descriptions of Goals, Services and Mediators as well as invocation of goals. The publisher component allows providers of services to attach WSMO descriptions to their deployed Web Services and provides handlers (proxies) to invoke them from specific implementation language/platforms (Lisp, Java, WSDL, HTTP Get requests).

The underlying ontology language and reasoner of IRS-III is OCML [5]. That means the WSMO service ontology is represented internally in IRS-III as a metamodel in OCML.

In the following we explain the activities supported by IRS-III.

Creation of domain ontologies: The concepts involved in the prototype scenario which are used in the description of services are provided in domain ontologies. For example, the concept *Address* represents part of the data about a citizen in the SWIFT database, which is retrieved by a service.

Semantic description of deployed services: Once a domain ontology is created, the concepts available can be used to represent the type of inputs or outputs of services according to a service ontology. For example, at the semantic level the service *Citizen-Address-By-Code* receives as input a citizen code and returns one or more instances of Address as output. By using WSMO as the service ontology, IRS-III can as well represent and reason over many other aspects of the service such as orchestration and choreography.

Resolving conceptual mismatches: Mediator descriptions declare which mediation service or mapping rules will provide conceptual alignment between goals, Web Services and domain ontologies.

Publication of semantically described services: Once a semantic description has been created for a deployed service, it can be registered into IRS-III for goal-based invocation.

Goal-based invocation: We use WSMO for representing the request of a user for a service as a goal. A SWS execution environment based on WSMO such as IRS-III is able to use this goal description for selecting and invoking an applicable published service.

13.5 Application Implementation

In this section, we describe the implementation of the eGovernment application scenario according to the architecture and Semantic Web Service infrastructure presented in the previous sections.

The graphical user interface representing the *Change-of-Circumstance scenario* is depicted in Fig. 13.2. From this interface a case worker from Essex County Council has access to some functionalities such as "query client details", "create client details", "create client assessment" and "list available services". Behind each

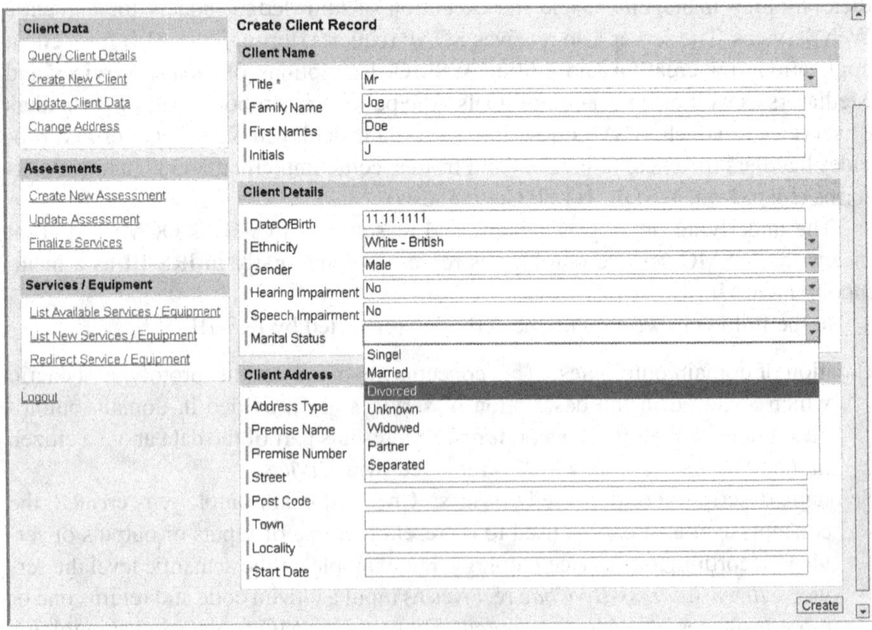

Fig. 13.2. The graphical user interface of the Change-of-Circumstance application

functionality there is one or more associated invocation templates used to invoke the underlying goals such as “update citizen address” or “find equipment”.

A case worker can select a suitable functionality, fill in the required fields and then submit the request to the Web application, which will build the corresponding invocation templates. After the execution of a goal the Web application sends the result back to the case worker and informs him about what data has been changed and which additional actions (e.g. delivery of new services to the client) has been trigged.

At the legacy systems level, in order to show the integration capability of our architecture, we have recreated the content of the existing data sources (SWIFT database of ECC and the ELMS database of the Chelmsford housing department) into two new test databases (see the set-up environment in the next subsection). Furthermore, we have mimicked the real data available in the systems by including duplicate, inconsistent and conflicting dummy records. The Web Services created for the prototype access this data.

At the service level, we developed a set of Web Services which perform basic CRUD operations on top of the two involved databases. These Web services were deployed into the SAP Exchange Infrastructure (SAP XI)[6], which offers standard functionality to easily create the necessary services based on the available databases. These include for instance the following services:

- Create a citizen record : This service accesses the SWIFT database exposing functionality from Essex County Council (ECC).
- Get equipment : This service accesses the ELMS database exposing functionality from Chelmsford District Council (CDC).

At the semantic level, we used IRS-III to provide WSMO descriptions to the deployed Web Services, including mediator descriptions for declaring the mappings between concepts not aligned. We then made the Web Services available as Semantic Web Services by publishing them in IRS-III. First, there are basic Semantic Web Services which simply wrap the Web Services mentioned before. Secondly, there are more complex Semantic Web Services which fulfil more complex goals. These complex services are implemented by composing one or more basic services or other complex ones. Examples of complex Semantic Web Services developed include the following:

- Notify change of address : This service is composed of two basic services. The first changes the address of the citizen within ECC, and the second service change the address related to equipment of this citizen within CDC.
- Provide suitable housing equipment for citizen : This service is composed of basic services which use information from the SWIFT system at ECC (citizen weight and purpose) for searching for suitable equipment in the ELMS system at CDC. This service will be explained in more details in the following illustration for the WSMO descriptions; it will be called *Housing-Dept-Assess-Items-WS*.

For illustration purposes (Fig. 13.3), we describe the structure of the WSMO descriptions associated with one of the complex SWS (Housing-Dept-Assess-Items-WS)

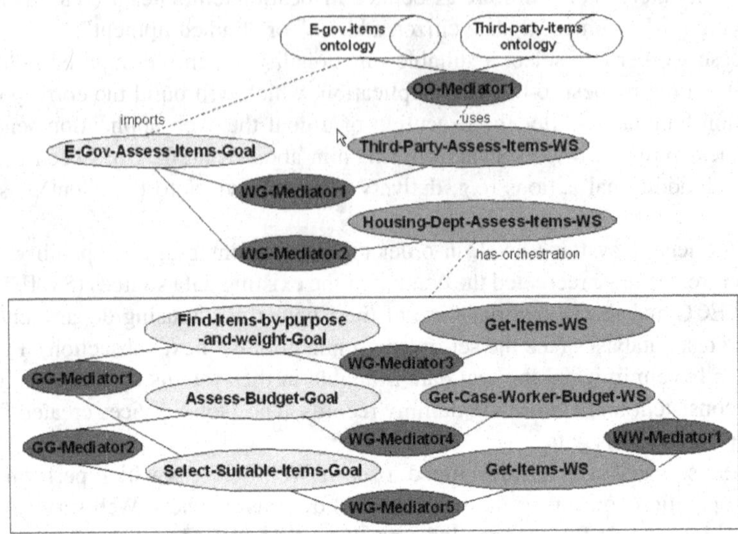

Fig. 13.3. Sample structure of WSMO descriptions for the eGovernment prototype

through a goal (E-Gov-Assess-Items-Goal). This goal describes a request for a service that can assess housing equipments for a citizen who has registered for benefits within Essex County Council. The selected service must find all suitable equipments according to the citizen's purpose (mobility-impairment, visual-impairment, hearing-impairment, baby-care, etc.) and weight, and the budget of the council's case worker. Restrictions on the way the service can solve the goal are given by preconditions and post-conditions. The different types of mediators will provide data alignment between WSMO elements. In particular, a WG-Mediator allows a (target) Web Service to connect to the (source) *Goal* it can solve and inherit its (imported) ontologies.

13.5.1 Prototype Set-Up

After describing the implementation details of the prototype application we will now describe the technical set-up we chose for developing the prototype.

As depicted in Fig. 13.4, we chose a highly distributed set-up for the prototype in order to show the feasibility of operating a SWS-based application across several physically distributed locations. The two databases are running in a database server at the SAP Research Center in Karlsruhe, Germany. These databases have a similar design as the real databases of the agencies involved. They are accessed by the Service Abstraction layer through the JDBC [7] standard.

The Service Abstraction layer runs also at the SAP Research Centre in Karlsruhe. The Semantic Web Service layer, which is running inside the IRS-III server at the

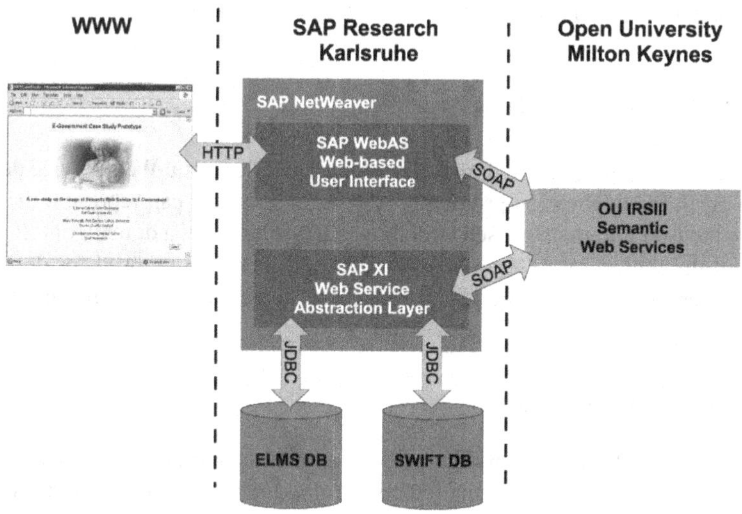

Fig. 13.4. The distributed set-up of the prototype

Open University in Milton Keynes, UK, connects to the Service Abstraction layer using SOAP over HTTP. The same protocol is used to connect the User Interface layer, which again is running in Karlsruhe, to the Semantic Web Service layer.

The user interface is simply a Web application available using a standard web browser. Technically, the User Interface Layer is based on SAP Web Dynpro [4] which provides a comprehensive environment for the model-driven design and development of web-based user interfaces. The user interface uses the standard Java API provided by the IRS-III server to communicate with the Semantic Web Service layer of the prototype.

The rationale behind the presented set-up of the prototype is twofold. First, we wanted to show the feasibility of running a SWS-based solution across several physically distributed locations, thereby enabling agencies to benefit from an integrated solution without the need to change their existing systems. The enabling factor for this feature are the integration capabilities of current state-of-the-art EAI applications. We used the SAP XI, SAP's version of an EAI software, in our prototype. SAP XI is capable of integrating heterogeneous applications by acting as a middleware for the message exchange.

Secondly, we wanted to demonstrate the possibility to non-intrusively integrate SWS frameworks that are currently mainly in the state of research prototypes into current enterprise application software stacks using well-known industry standards like, e.g., SOAP. This integration enables access to the flexibility of SWS-based application inside current solutions without any major changes to the underlying software stack or the programming model. As a result, this integration shows a nice transition path from current technologies to SWS-based solutions.

13.6 Service Descriptions

In this section, we present the domain ontologies and Semantic Web Service descriptions used in the application prototype. A domain ontology can represent the viewpoint of the user and then be used to define goals. Otherwise, a domain ontology can represent the viewpoint of a service provider and therefore be used for describing deployed services; in this case it will reflect the objects used to represent database records.

13.6.1 Domain Ontologies

Each agency involved in the prototype development has to provide a domain ontology which represents the information concerning the application scenario. For this prototype, the domain ontology provided by each agency was developed independently but were based on a common upper-level ontology describing general concepts from the eGovernment domain. The two developed ontologies are as follows:

1. Citizens ontology : Domain ontology created by Essex County Council describing information related to a citizen assessment for social benefits and services. Contains classes defining, for example, address, assessment, health problem, benefit, case worker and others.
2. Items ontology : Domain ontology created by the Housing Department describing information related to ordering housing equipments. Contains classes defining, for example, order, care-item (equipment), supplier, delivery descriptor, etc.

Figure 13.5 shows an excerpt of the items ontology containing two of the main concepts. The class "care-item" represents an equipment and the attributes are self-explanatory. The class "order" represents an order for equipment. Notice that the attribute "ordered-item" is of type "care-item". Instances of these classes can be created with the values of attributes provided through the user interface. Otherwise, they can be lifted from the results of service invocations.

13.6.2 WSMO Descriptions

In this section we provide the WSMO Goal, Web Service and Mediator for the "e-gov-assess-item" service as an illustration.

Figure 13.6 shows the definition of goal "e-gov-assess-item-goal". This instance of a WSMO goal defines two inputs ("has-input-role" slot) and one output ("has-output-role" slot). This goal takes the client weight and purpose and return a list of suitable equipments (items).

Figure 13.7 shows a partial definition of the Web Service "housing-dept-assess-item-ws". This instance of a WSMO Web Service declares a capability and an

```
(def-class care-item (tangible-thing)
  ((code :type string)
   (used-for :type care-descriptor)
   (cost :type number)
   (currency :type string :default-value GBP)
   (max-user-weight :type number)
   (max-user-weight-measure :type string :default-value kilogram)
   (item-width :type number)
   (item-width-measure :type string :default-value meter)
   (item-height :type number)
   (item-height-measure :type string :default-value meter)
   (item-seat-height :type number)
   (item-seat-height-measure :type string :default-value meter)
   (item-depth :type  amount-of-length)
   (item-depth-measure :type string :default-value meter)
   (item-weight :type number)
   (item-weight-measure :type string :default-value kilogram)
   (narrative-detail :type string)
   (to-be-approved-by :type case-worker-category)
   (picture :type string :min-cardinality 0)
   (main-supplier :type supplier :cardinality 1)
   (other-suppliers :type supplier :min-cardinality 0)
   (needs-technician-fit :type boolean))
)


(def-class order (intangible-thing)
  ((reason-of-order :type care-descriptor)
   (ordered-item :type care-item :cardinality 1)
   (case-worker-required-for-approval :type case-worker-category)
   (due-to-equipment-failure :type Boolean)
   (needs-minor-adaptations :type minor-adaptations :cardinality 1)
   (level-of-order :type level-of-delivery-descriptor :cardinality 1)
   (date-ordered :type calendar-date :cardinality 1)
   (time-ordered :type time-point :min-cardinality 0 :max-cardinality 1)
   (date-delivery :type calendar-date :cardinality 1)
   (date-returned :type calendar-date :min-cardinality 0 :max-cardinality
1))
)
```

Fig. 13.5. Excerpt of the items ontology

interface which are described in corresponding classes. The interface declares an orchestration, which is defined in another class. The "problem-solving pattern" slot of the orchestration defines the workflow (sequence) for the composition of three sub-goals. The choreography of one of the sub-goals is defined by another class ("get-items-ws-interface-choreography")which has a grounding and guarded transitions. The grounding includes information about the WSDL associated with the described service, and the guarded transitions are rules defining the communication with the described service.

Figure 13.8 shows the definition of mediator "weight-to-list-intersection-mediator". This is an instance of a WSMO GG-mediator. It declares the source and target component for which the mediation service is going to be used. The mediation service is of type goal and its instance is shown as well.

```
(DEF-CLASS E-GOV-ASSESS-ITEM-GOAL (GOAL) ?GOAL
          ((HAS-INPUT-ROLE
            :VALUE HAS-CLIENT-WEIGHT
            :VALUE HAS-CLIENT-PURPOSE)
           (HAS-INPUT-SOAP-BINDING
            :VALUE (HAS-CLIENT-WEIGHT "float")
            :VALUE (HAS-CLIENT-PURPOSE "sexpr"))
           (HAS-OUTPUT-ROLE :VALUE HAS-SUITABLE-ITEMS-LIST)
           (HAS-OUTPUT-SOAP-BINDING
            :VALUE (HAS-SUITABLE-EQUIPMENT-LIST "sexpr"))
           (HAS-CLIENT-WEIGHT :TYPE NUMBER)
           (HAS-CLIENT-PURPOSE :TYPE IMPAIRMENT-DESCRIPTOR)
           (HAS-SUITABLE-ITEM-LIST :TYPE LIST)
           (HAS-NON-FUNCTIONAL-PROPERTIES
            :VALUE E-GOV-ASSESS-ITEM-GOAL-NON-FUNCTIONAL-PROPERTIES)))
```

Fig. 13.6. E-gov-assess-item-goal- Mainly specifies the types of inputs and output for the goal. Concepts may be defined in the domain ontology

13.7 Conclusions

The conclusions we want to give in this section focus on our experiences when developing the prototype application for the change-of-circumstance scenario based on our generic architecture.

From a technical point of view the presented generic architecture proved capable of developing SWS-based solutions on it. Especially, the layering of the architecture proved very useful when developing the prototype application. The development of the ontologies, Semantic Web Services, goal descriptions and necessary mediators could be decoupled from the implementation of the user interface and the technical integration. Using a state-of-the-art EAI software for coping with integration problems on the technical level (e.g. providing Web Service on top of different database systems) enabled us to focus on development of the semantic descriptions in the SWS layer. Furthermore, the advanced tools for wrapping legacy systems into Web Service simplified this development process. In addition to the simplification of the development process, the usage of current EAI software also allows to achieve the security and data privacy constraints necessary in productive environments and eGovernment in particular. Security is one of the topics not yet solved in the context of SWS but using SAP XI the access to the involved legacy systems can be controlled on a fine granularity.

With respect to usability of the prototypical application the usage of invocation templates in the user interface seems to be a good choice. These templates hide the complexity of the underlying SWS-based application away and also provide the user with a familiar interface.

From an implementation point of view, basing cross-organisational eGovernment applications on SWS technology seem to be a suitable approach. First of all, the usages of an ontology as a central hub for integrating the data available in the different legacy systems enable developers to focus on the functional aspects of the

```
DEF-CLASS HOUSING-DEPT-ASSESS-ITEMS-WS (WEB-SERVICE) ?WEB-SERVICE
            ((HAS-CAPABILITY :VALUE
                        GET-ITEM-WEB-WEB-SERVICE-CAPABILITY)
             (HAS-INTERFACE :VALUE
                        GET-ITEM-WEB -WEB-SERVICE-INTERFACE)
             (HAS-NON-FUNCTIONAL-PROPERTIES :VALUE
                    GET-ITEM-WEB-WEB-SERVICE-NON-FUNCTIONAL-PROPERTIES)))

(DEF-CLASS HOUSING-DEPT-ASSESS-ITEMS-WS-INTERFACE (INTERFACE)
?INTER-FACE
            ((HAS-CHOREOGRAPHY :VALUE
             HOUSING-DEPT-ASSESS-ITEMS-WS -INTERFACE-CHOREOGRAPHY)
             (HAS-ORCHESTRATION
             :VALUE
             HOUSING-DEPT-ASSESS-ITEMS-WS-INTERFACE-ORCHESTRATION)
             (HAS-NON-FUNCTIONAL-PROPERTIES
             :VALUE
             HOUSING-DEPT-ASSESS-ITEMS-WS-INTERFACE-NON-FUNCTIONAL-
PROPERTIES)))


(DEF-CLASS HOUSING-DEPT-ASSESS-ITEMS-WS-INTERFACE-ORCHESTRATION
(OR-CHESTRATION)
            ((HAS-PROBLEM-SOLVING-PATTERN
             :VALUE
             HOUSING-DEPT-ASSESS-ITEMS-WS-INTERFACE-
                                   ORCHESTRATION-PROBLEM-SOLVING-PATTERN
)))


(DEF-CLASS HOUSING-DEPT-ASSESS-ITEMS-WS-INTERFACE-
                                   ORCHESTRATION-PROBLEM-SOLVING-PATTERN
  (PROBLEM-SOLVING-PATTERN)
  ((has-body
    :value (lambda (?ontology ?web-service)
             (run-orchestration
              (sequence ?ontology ?web-service
                        find-items-by-purpose-and-weight-goal
                        get-case-worker-budget-goal
                        select-suitable-items-goal))))))

(DEF-CLASS GET-ITEMS-WS-INTERFACE-CHOREOGRAPHY
            (CHOREOGRAPHY)
            ((HAS-GROUNDING :VALUE
              (GROUNDED-TO-WSDL normal
               ("c:/CatalogueEntryByWeightInterfaceOut.wsdl"
                "CatalogueEntryByWeightInterfaceOut"
                "CatalogueEntryByWeightInterfaceOut"
                "http://sap.com/research/dip/wp9/elmdb"
                "SAP"
                ((has-client-weight "CatalogueEntryByWeightRequest-Type"))
                "CatalogueEntryResponseType")))
          (has-guarded-transitions :value
              ((start
               (init-choreography)
                 then
               (send-message 'normal))
))
```

Fig. 13.7. Housing-dept-assess-items-ws – inherits the inputs and output from the goal above. This service is decomposed in three sub-goals as described by the orchestration. The choreography of one of the sub-goals contains the grounding (mapping of operations to be invoked) and guarded transitions (rules for interaction) of the service

```
(DEF-CLASS WEIGHT-TO-LIST-INTERSECTION-MEDIATOR (MEDIATOR) ?MEDIATOR
          ((HAS-SOURCE-COMPONENT :VALUE
              FIND-ITEMS-MATCHING-IMPAIRMENT-GOAL)
           (HAS-TARGET-COMPONENT :VALUE LIST-INTERSECTION-GOAL)
           (HAS-MEDIATION-SERVICE :VALUE
              WEIGHT-TO-LIST-INTERSECTION-MEDIATION-SERVICE)
           (HAS-NON-FUNCTIONAL-PROPERTIES :VALUE
              WEIGHT-TO-LIST-INTERSECTION-MEDIATOR-NON-FUNCTIONAL-
PROPERTIES)))

(DEF-CLASS WEIGHT-TO-LIST-INTERSECTION-MEDIATION-SERVICE  (GOAL)
?GOAL
          ((HAS-INPUT-ROLE :VALUE HAS-ITEMS-LIST)
           (HAS-INPUT-SOAP-BINDING :VALUE (HAS-ITEMS-LIST "sexpr"))
           (HAS-OUTPUT-ROLE :VALUE HAS-LIST2)
           (HAS-OUTPUT-SOAP-BINDING :VALUE (HAS-LIST2 "sexpr"))
           (HAS-ITEMS-LIST :TYPE LIST)
           (HAS-LIST2 :TYPE LIST)
           (HAS-NON-FUNCTIONAL-PROPERTIES
            :VALUE
            WEIGHT-TO-LIST-INTERSECTION-MEDIATION-SERVICE-NON-FUNCTIONAL-
PROPERTIES)))
```

Fig. 13.8. Weight-to-list-intersection-mediator – this mediator connects two sub-goals described in the orchestration above. The mediation service (goals) declares the inputs to be passed to the next sub-goal

(semantic) services rather than on data interoperability problems. In addition to that is, the ontologies simplified the communication between developers and domain expert as there was an agreed conceptualisation of the domain available.

13.8 Challenges

Besides the positive conclusions we gave in the previous section, there are still a number of challenges that need to be solved prior to running our prototypical application in a productive environment.

Most important, neither of the currently available SWS infrastructures is an industrial strength infrastructure but all of them are research prototypes that are still under heavy development. As a result of that, none of the existing SWS infrastructure is capable of coping with the tough requirements on uptime, performance, etc. usually necessary for productive applications. Therefore, the development of the currently available systems into a stable and robust infrastructure is the major challenge that need to be solved before a SWS-based solution can be deployed into a productive environment.

If we take a closer look at the application we developed on top of our general architecture, one important bit of functionality is still missing. In Section 13.3, we stated the ability to discover suitable services as an important requirement. One of the reasons for that requirement is that the solution built on our architecture should enable the flexible integration of new service providers. This kind of flexible integration requires the capability to enable partners to easily publish new services into the SWS infrastructure. However, in our current prototype application that kind of functionality is not present. In order to enable this flexibility, the prototype application would, e.g., need some kind of UI-enabling partners to publish new services without much knowledge of the underlying SWS infrastructure. The template-based approach already taken in the UI for case workers could be one possible solution to that requirement.

References

1. Cabinet Office. e-Government Interoperability Framework. `http://www.govtalk.gov.uk/schemasstandards/egif.asp`, 2005.
2. J. Domingue, L. Cabral, F. Hakimpour, D. Sell, and E. Motta. IRS-III: A Platform and Infrastructure for Creating WSMO-based Semantic Web Services. In *Workshop on WSMO Implementations (WIW 2004), Frankfurt, Germany*, 2004.
3. European Commision IDABC. European Interoperability Framework for pan-European e-Government services. `http://europa.eu.int/idabc/servlets/Doc?id=19528`, 2004.
4. K. Kessler. Your "Easy Way In" to Web Dynpro Development. `https://www.sdn.sap.com/irj/servlet/prt/portal/prtroot/docs/library/uuid/a422d090-0201-0010-6ebf-b323b0a44de0`, 2003.
5. E. Motta. *Reusable Components for Knowledge Modelling: Case Studies in Parametric Design Problem Solving*. IOS Press, Amsterdam, The Netherlands, The Netherlands, 1999.
6. SAP. SAP Exchange Infrastructure: The Integration Solution for Process-Centric Collaboration. `http://www.sap.com/xi`, 2005.
7. Sun Microsystems. JDBC Technology. `http://java.sun.com/products/jdbc/overview.html`, 1994–2005.

An eHealth Case Study

Applying Semantic Web Service Technology in the Healthcare Environment

Emanuele Della Valle[1], Dario Cerizza[1], Irene Celino[1], Asuman Dogac[2], Gokce B. Laleci[2], Yildiray Kabak[2], Alper Okcan[2], Ozgur Gulderen[2], Tuncay Namli[2] and Veli Bicer[2]

[1] CEFRIEL – Politecnico di Milano, Milano, Italy
{dellavalle,cerizza,celino}@cefriel.it

[2] SRDC-METU, Turkey; OFFIS, Germany; SEBT, UK ; ALTEC, Greece; Tepe Technology, Turkey; It Innovation Center, UK {asuman,gokce,yildiray,alper,ozgur, tuncay,veli}@srdc.metu.edu.tr

Summary. In this chapter we describe two case studies of Semantic Web Services applied in the eHealth domain. Starting from the interoperability problem, which naturally arises in distributed environments such as the healthcare systems, we briefly introduce the state of the art in eHealth standards (e.g. HL7, openEHR, etc.) and the trends towards semantic interoperability. In particular, we claim that eHealth will greatly benefit from the adoption of Semantic Web Service technology and we show how we proof this concept in two case studies: Glue, a WSMO discovery engine, used to automate the discovery of second opinion services for General Practitioners, and Artemis which enables eHealthcare institutes to exchange health care messages in an interoperable manner through semantically enriched Web Services and semantic mediation.

14.1 Introduction

The healthcare organisational structure in all countries is naturally distributed, being a geographical spread of centres at different levels of complexity: from general hospitals down to individual physicians. The ultimate objective of such a structure is to build a network of complementary centres (hospitals, laboratories, ambulatories, coordination centres, etc.) spread over the territory, to meet effectively the social needs in the area. Moreover, healthcare practice has life-and-death implications, and thus the adoption of new processes involving any kind of technology must meet the highest standards of accuracy and effectiveness.

For all these reasons, healthcare practice has used for long ICT-based solutions for administrative tasks within the organisational boundaries, while the whole healthcare field as a naturally networked system has more slowly adopted ICT technology to improve delivery of services. As a result, medical information systems are mainly isolated solutions, grown around an administrative application. For instance, a typical Hospital Information System (HIS) has an *economic/financial management and administrative core with various clinical information services attached* (cf. Fig. 14.1). The administrative core helps in managing accounts, human resources, logistics and controlling; it stores all the data necessary for the billing of the healthcare services. The clinical information services manage the clinical treatment of the patient, offering functionalities for the treatment process documentation, for enabling the staff to follow the best medical practices and for gathering the most completed medical history of a patient in an electronic format. These systems should provide support in the healthcare delivery environment and should be used by both medical and nursing staff.

Moreover, the decentralised structure of a clinical environment promote the development of a wide range of specialist information systems such as Picture Archiving and Communication Systems (PACS) in the radiology department of the hospitals, Laboratory Information Systems (LIS) both inside and outside hospitals, and also a huge number of heterogeneous Electronic Health Records (EHR) in most of the General Practitioners' (GP) and Specialists' surgeries.

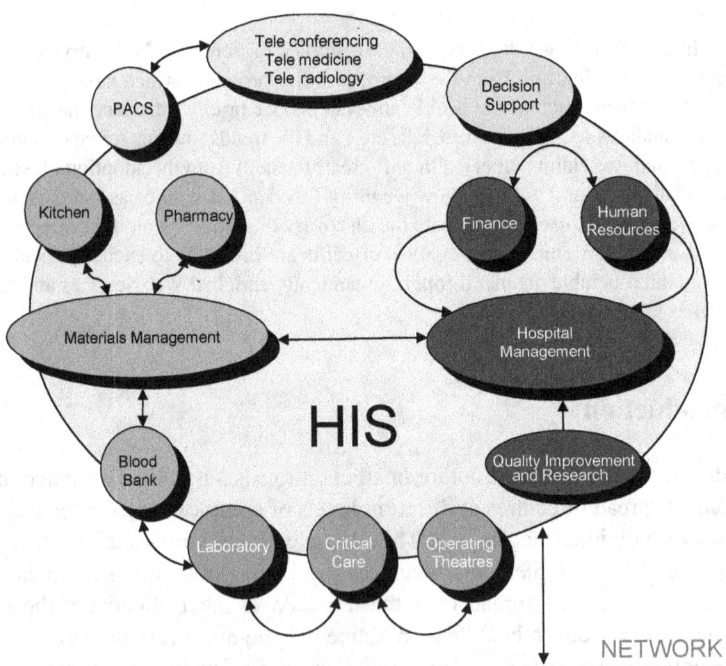

Fig. 14.1. A Hospital Information System (HIS) has an economic/financial management and administrative core with various clinical information services attached and it is interconnected to other hospitals, General Practitioners EHRs, etc.

In this context, the term eHealth was introduces [23] not only referring to health services and information delivered or enhanced through the Internet and related technologies, but also characterising a state-of-mind, a way of thinking, an attitude, and a commitment for networked, global thinking, to improve healthcare locally, regionally and worldwide by using information and communication technology. The main reasons driving the development of eHealth are as follows:

- *Management of continuously growing knowledge*: Healthcare workers manage an increasingly large base of scientific and technological knowledge; however highly specialised they may be, they do not have enough time to acquire all the "state of the art" knowledge related to their specialisations. Therefore, it becomes necessary to make both information on best practices and their evidence easily available.
- *From disease management to wellness management*: Diseases are increasingly becoming more chronic and less acute; therefore, keeping trace of the care-path of patients becomes necessary for a correct process management, avoiding complications and maintaining a high quality of life. In particular, the identification of risk factors and the availability of data about the care-path make it possible to activate prevention processes.
- *Risk management*: Recent analyses show that medical errors and, more generally, inappropriate treatment can lead to serious consequences for patients, causing new or worse disabilities or even resulting in death; the main cause for these events is the lack of communication between the various healthcare workers that, although belonging to different organisations, participate in the care process.

One of the most important enabling factors for eHealth is the availability of tools for collecting, storing, analysing and linking the different types of data daily produced by so many knowledge-driven organisations. The realisation of an effective solution, to help the clinicians in their daily activity and to provide them with a complete array of patient information, is out of scope for the current ICT technologies and calls for a new generation of ICT solutions. The future ICT solutions should serve as a complete Clinical Information System, supporting all medical processes across organisational boundaries. eHealth shall serve as a complete clinical data repository and shall allow a unique access point to all medical information, so that authorised healthcare workers can access all data, signals and images in a patient-centred model with a few mouse clicks.

The next generation of eHealth solutions must be based on a powerful integration technology that allows for immediate access to the databases of specialist tools (e.g. LIS, PACS, etc.) and GPs' EHRs.

14.2 Semantic Interoperability in Healthcare

Comprehensive eHealth solutions (e.g. various HIS interconnected to a large number of GPs' EHRs; pharmacies, laboratories and insurers companies information systems; Ministry of Health services, etc.) are far to appear. The problem underestimated today by most Clinical Information Systems under development (e.g. the CRS-SISS in Lombardy region – Italy[3]) is how to maintain such distributed systems on the long term: they are often implemented using proprietary solutions that exchange information in a number of proprietary formats including XML-based ones.

The relative easiness in creating formats using XML makes thousand of niche groups proposing their own XML structures. However, Internet history teaches us that only by defining an application protocol (e.g. the email) numerous systems can be combined to make a single distributed one. Furthermore, a standard application protocol is much more than the syntax and the transport protocol for messages, because it is a formal and largely shared agreement on the structure and semantics of messages, as well as on the sequencing information for concrete interactions. Additionally, the dynamics of such a protocol must be considered: often the requirements change fast and depend on the needs of a few systems among those involved. An application protocol needs to accommodate all these additional requirements; therefore maintenance is not an easy task.

The way out Internet taught us is thinking in terms of interoperability instead of integration. As defined by [14], *integration* is the combination of diverse application entities into a relationship which functions as a whole, whereas *interoperability* is a state which exists between two application entities when, with regard to a specific task, one application entity can accept data from the other and perform that task in an appropriate and satisfactory manner without the need for extra operator intervention.

14.2.1 Current Interoperability Attempts

Defining an application protocol for the healthcare field that addresses the interoperability problem is *the current major challenge for eHealth.*[4] A number of standardisation initiative are progressing to address this interoperability problem such as the following:

- HL7 (Health Level Seven) [25], a non-profit, ANSI accredited Standards Developing Organisation, founded in 1987, that provides standards for the exchange, management and integration of data to support patient clinical care and the management, delivery and evaluation of healthcare services.
- GEHR/openEHR [36], an initiative that foster EHR interoperability started in 1992 as the "Good European Health Record" EU research project that is currently maintained by the openEHR Foundation.
- CEN/TC 251 [15], the technical committee on Health Informatics of the European Committee for Standardisation, which, since 1998, is standardising CEN EN 13606/EHRcom [12, 13].
- IHE (Integrating the Healthcare Enterprise) [30], a not-for-profit initiative founded in 1998 that does not develop standards as such, but selects and recommends appropriate standards for specific use cases.

[3] `http://www.crs.lombardia.it/`

[4] A summary of the relevant EHR standards and their interoperability support is presented in [34]

Most of those initiatives have been active for more than a decade and, after a first attempt in specifying the format of each of the message that can be exchanged among any pair of systems (e.g. HL7 v2.x [26]), they realised that they need to derive messages and interaction patterns from a common shared conceptual model.

In 1999, CEN/TC 251 was the first to introduce, with CEN ENV 13606 / EHRcom, a list of machine-readable terms to be used for structuring EHR content. The standard defines an *EHR information model* and a modelling approach for deriving concrete interoperable messages to be exchanged between heterogeneous EHRs. However, the single-level modelling approach, the big number of optionality and the high level of abstraction limited market uptake.

GEHR/openEHR in 2002 moved a step forward proposing the *archetype* concept [5] and the respective two-level methodology. The first level specifies a healthcare domain reference model [6, 8] that contains concepts such as *role*, *act*, *entity*, *participation*, *observation*, etc., while the second level specifies healthcare and application specific concepts such as *patient*, *GP*, *lab result*, modelling them as archetypes. Each archetype constrains a set of concepts in the reference model (e.g. "Observation") to a specialise data structure (e.g. "Blood Pressure") and defines the vocabulary, such as SNOMED [37] or LOINC [33], to be used within instances of the archetype. The formal language for expressing archetypes, introduced by the openEHR initiative, is the Archetype Definition Language [7]. A complete example of the "Blood Pressure" Archetype is available in [11].

An alternative approach is offered by HL7 Reference Information Model (RIM) [28] which is the ultimate source from which all HL7 v3 protocol specification standards [29] draw their information-related content. The RIM model is an explicit data semantics model by which the messages can be implemented locally and top-down, emphasising reuse across multiple contexts. Moreover, RIM offers a formalism for vocabulary support that permits to get domain concepts from the best terminologies (SNOMED, LOINC, etc.).

14.2.2 The *Semantic* Interoperability Problem

All these proposals may differ in the progress achieved in the standardisation process, but they are similar in concept and capabilities. They all try to address the interoperability problem by introducing a shared conceptual model (i.e. an ontology). This is very similar to the Semantic Web Services approach in which "semantic interoperability" is achieved by modelling, at a conceptual level, Web Services and the domain they are deployed in. In all eHealth standardisation efforts, data structure and sequencing information are enhanced with semantic information that encodes the definition of each element of data including its relationship with other elements. Differently from Semantic Web Services, all eHealth standardisation efforts are focusing on developing a horizontal ontology to capture the healthcare information reference model, which can be linked to the most appropriate vertical domain ontology specifying domain vocabularies. Furthermore, *eHealth standardisation efforts lack*

- the possibility of *dealing with* systems that commit to *different horizontal* (e.g. one uses HL7's RIM in CDA, the other uses openEHR archetypes based on EN

13606 RIM) *and vertical ontology* (e.g. one uses SNOMED, the other some proprietary coding)
- a comprehensive model for *automating service usage* such as discovery, choreography and mediation, at both data and process levels.

So, even if a clear trend towards a harmonisation can be perceived and many people expect a unification of the reference information models, nevertheless, such result will only be achieved in the long term and many systems, implemented following different version of all these standard protocols, will be online even longer. For all these reasons, we believe that eHealth could greatly benefit from the adoption of Semantic Web Service technology [22].

14.3 Case Studies

In the following two sections, we report two case studies of Semantic Web Services applied to eHealth. The first describes Glue [17], a WSMO compliant discovery engine that was used to automate the discovery of second opinion services for GPs. The application developed over Glue was deployed within the COCOON project[5] [18] as a GP's EHR application and in the Nomadic Media project[6] [35] as a mobile application. The second describes Artemis [2] that enables eHealthcare institutes to exchange healthcare messages in an interoperable manner through semantically enriched Web Services and semantic mediation.

14.3.1 Glue WSMO Discovery Engine

Glue[7] [16, 17] is a WSMO compliant discovery engine that aims at developing an efficient system for the management of semantically described Web Services and their discovery. We put Glue at work in a usage scenario in which a GP intends to arrange a teleconsultation meeting with a colleague available for providing medical advice services or teaching services. The colleagues can work either alone or in Communities of Practice (CoPs) specifically organised in order to provide teleconsultation services.

Application Scenario

Nowadays a GP works in contact with a limited number of colleagues (either other GPs or specialists); therefore, when a GP is seeking for advice, it may happen that he/she does not know the right colleague to contact or the suitable one is unavailable.

[5] COCOON is the sixth Framework EU integrated project (FP6-507126) aimed at setting up a set of regional semantics-based healthcare information infrastructure with the goal of reducing medical errors

[6] Nomadic Media is a Eureka/ITEA project (ITEA 02019), in which CEFRIEL addressed the problem of how to provide mobile access to healthcare services

[7] The application of Glue described in this section can be tried at `http://glue.cefriel.it/glueclient`

In order to cover this need, all over Europe, the healthcare systems are supporting projects with the aim of building up directories of medical doctors willing to provide advice, second opinion and teaching services. For instance, Lombardy region in Italy has been running the SUMMA project [38] since 2003 with the aim of supporting GPs seeking for advice and second opinion. The GPs taking part in the trial can call a healthcare service centre,[8] they can explain to the call-centre operators their problems and the operators arrange for them a teleconsultation meeting with the right CoP.

The call-centre acts as a collection point for all the available CoPs. It continuously updates the list of expertises provided by each of the CoPs and their nominal availability (e.g. Hypertension Foundation has thirty hypertension experts available every day from Monday to Friday and Saturday morning). When a GP asks for advice about a problem, the call-centre operator maps the problem to the needed expertises, checks the nominal availability and, if they both fit, tries to arrange the teleconsultation meeting.

On the contrary, in the usage scenario we envision for Glue, we tried to automate the work of the call- centre by exposing the agenda of each CoP as a Web Service. The Web Service enables a GP to remotely access the agenda of a CoP and to arrange a meeting. However, the agenda Web Services are only gateways to the advice services: while the agenda of a hypertension CoP does not technically differ from the agenda of a Parkinson CoP, their actual services (advice on hypertension vs advice on Parkinson) differ a lot.

Figure 14.2 provides more details about the scenario. On the right side we draw the medical experts (eventually organised in CoPs). Each expert or CoP has an agenda that is exposed as a Web Service. Such Web Service is registered into Glue together with a semantic description of the medical expertises of the CoP and its nominal available times. On the left side we draw the GP that needs some advice. Glue is in the middle: the CoPs register their agenda Web Services in Glue and a GUI interconnected with Glue supports the GPs in discovering the most suitable agenda to interact with. Therefore, without Glue, the GP should have explored the CoP agendas one by one until he/she would finally get to the right CoP. With Glue, on the contrary, the GP starts discovering the most suitable services and he/she has only to look into the smaller set of matched agendas.

Glue is an infrastructural component with no specific interface, which means that Glue can be invoked remotely by any application that provides a GUI to the users. In Fig. 14.3 we show the Mobile interface we developed for Nomadic Media project. The GP starts the discovery process by describing the problem of the patient[9] and his/her preferred date-times to arrange the teleconsultation meeting (cf. Step A). Then, Glue performs the discovery by matching the problem expressed by the GP

[8] In SUMMA, Health Telematic Network (`http://www.e-htn.it/english/homei.htm`) is running the call-centre for both GPs and their patients. For further information, refer to `http://www.e-htn.it/english/teleconsultii.htm`

[9] In Nomadic Media scenario, we provide a mobile application in which the GP inserts a set of keywords, whereas in the COCOON project a richer description of the patient can be directly extracted from the patient EHR the GP is using

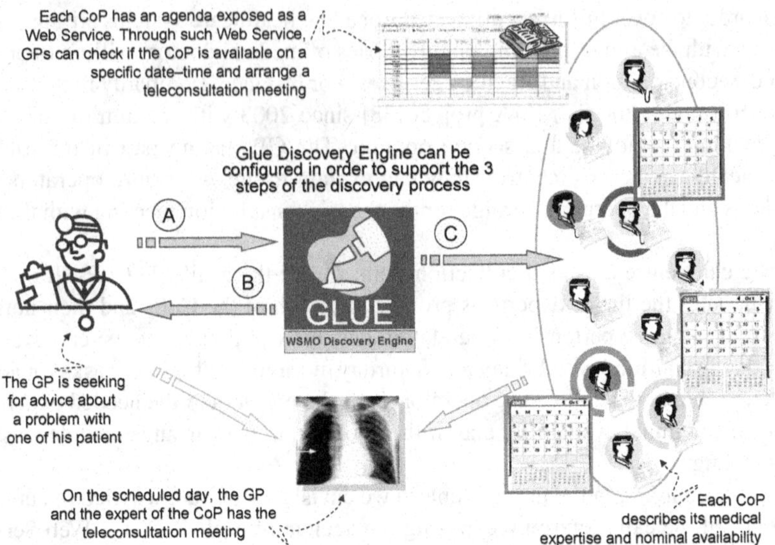

Fig. 14.2. Glue, by automating Web Service Discovery, drastically reduce the effort of a GP that is willing to book an appointment with an expert for a teleconsultation meeting

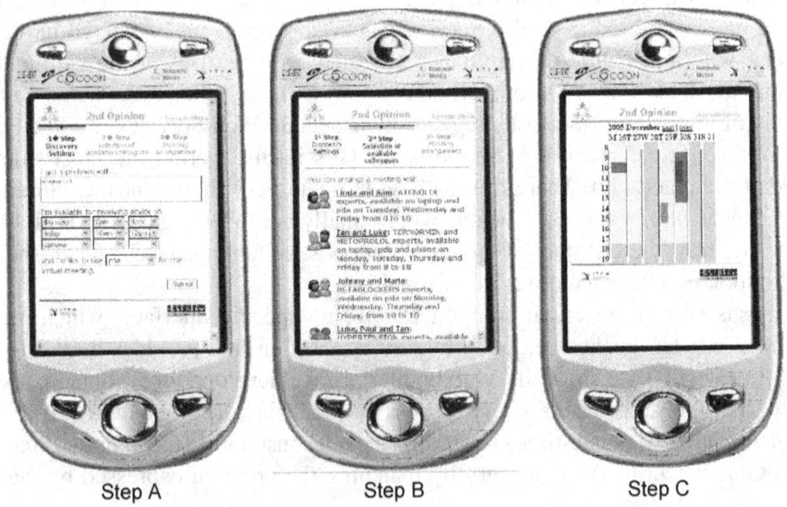

Fig. 14.3. The three steps of GP's interaction: (Step A) the GP inserts the data to arrange a meeting; (Step B) a ranked list is returned to the GP; (Step C) the GP finds an available teaching service and can proceed with the arrangement

against the descriptions of the Web Services offered by each CoP, and it returns to the mobile application a list of references to agenda Web Services, ordered by decreasing relevance (cf. Step B). At this point, the GP interactively selects one of the agendas exposed as Web Service finding a slot available for the teleconsultation meeting (cf. Step C).

Application Implementation

In this usage scenario, we describe an interaction between a GP and an application (latter named GlueClient) that uses Glue WSMO Discovery Engine with the intent of arranging a teleconsultation meeting with a medical *advice* and *teaching* services offered by a CoP (Fig. 14.4). In particular, Glue WSMO Discovery Engine takes the responsibility of gathering all the descriptions of the agenda Web Services and matches them against the GP problem. GlueClient provides a GUI for GPs to express the problems of their patients. It is responsible to invoke Glue and to show the result list and, finally, it offers on demand access to the agendas of the CoPs exposed as Web Services. The actual arrangement of the meeting and the subsequent teleconsultation are supported by external applications.

We distinguish between advice and teaching services. Advice will predictably be the more frequent reason for a GP to start an interaction, as it normally could be

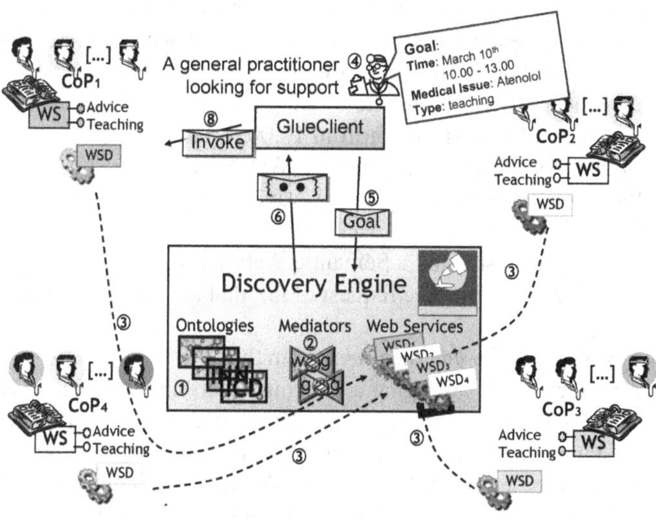

Fig. 14.4. The figure shows Glue WSMO discovery engine surrounded by a set of CoPs *(which are provider entities)* and a GlueClient *(which is the requester entity)*. Each of the CoP exposes its agenda as a Web Service. The same Web Service is used for arranging the two types of meeting *(advice vs. teaching)*

triggered by facts happening during the practice time (e.g. a problem reported by a patient). Teaching, on the other hand, will be predictably less frequent and a request of this kind could take place in the one-hour-a-week that is normally reserved for contacting peers, and it normally could be triggered by GP's reflection on his/her week's practice.

The general criteria for matching a GP goal against the description of the Web Service offered by a CoP are based on the correspondence between the GP's problem and CoP's expertises and on the matching between the GPs' date–time preferences and the nominal availability of each CoP. We distinguish between clinical capabilities (i.e. those used in the daily practice) and research capabilities (i.e. the topics of interest of those medical doctors that are active in research). Most times, the *clinical capabilities* of the CoP may be the ones the GP wishes, but sometimes *research capabilities* may be sought too (e.g. for more difficult and rare patient cases).

The process enabled by Glue, in order to support GP in arranging a meeting with the most suitable CoP, can be broken down in the following tasks.

Set up time:

1. The service provider and requester entities *agree on the ontologies to use* for modelling pathologies (e.g. ICD[10]), drugs (e.g. INN[11]), advice services, date–time, etc..
2. *If they cannot agree* on the use of a specific set of common ontologies, the use of *mediators is required*. In this scenario, for instance, the provider and the requester entities cannot agree on the use of a common date–time ontology. The provider entities prefer to express the nominal availability of each CoP using a *week-based calendar* (e.g. the advice service is available on Thursday afternoon and Friday morning), whereas the requester entity prefer to express users' preferences using a *Gregorian calendar* (e.g. Is the service available on April, 9th from 10.00 to 12.00?).
3. The service provider and a Semantic Web Service expert *define the classes of Web Service descriptions* for the Advice and Teaching services provided by the CoP.
4. The service requester and a Semantic Web Service expert *define the classes of Goals* for describing the request of GP that are using GlueClient.

Publishing time:

5. Each provider entity can then *register* in the Glue WSMO Discovery Engine its Web Service for arranging a meeting describing the clinical capabilities the CoP holds and the date–time intervals the CoP is normally available. For instance, a provider entity may register its CoP as "one that delivers intervention based on alpha and beta blockers with nominal availability on Monday, Tuesday and Friday in the afternoon for advice and teaching".

[10] International Classification of Diseases, see `http://www.who.int/classifications/icd/en/`

[11] International Nonproprietary Names for Pharmaceutical Substances, see `http://www.who.int/medicines/services/inn/en/`

Discovery time:

6. Similarly, a GP can discover the most suitable CoP by using a GUI, provided by the requester entity, in order to *express his/her goal* in terms of the available ontologies. For instance, the GP asks for "a teaching session on the use of Atenolol preferring the meeting to be arranged on June 8th from 10.00 to 13.00 or on June 9th from 13.00 to 16.00" (see step A in Fig. 14.3);
7. The requester entity *submits the GP goal* to the Discovery Engine.
8. The Semantic Discovery engine uses the ontologies and the mediators for *matching* the GP goal against the descriptions of the advice services offered by each CoP; then it returns a list of references to Web Services for arranging a meeting, ordered by decreasing relevance (the exact matchings come first followed by plug-in and subsumed).
9. The requester entity *displays the results list* to the GP (see step B in Fig. 14.3).
10. The GP interactively *selects* one of the CoPs until he/she finds one suitable to arrange a meeting with (see step C in Fig. 14.3).

In Fig. 14.5 we report part of the conceptual model employed in configuring Glue in terms of WSMO elements: ontologies, goals, Web Services and, of course, mediators.

First of all, a *medical ontology* is needed. The one we used for our trials is a demonstrative ontology of hypertension and breast cancer domains derived from ICD-10 and INN. It contains the definition of a hundred concepts (like `disease`,

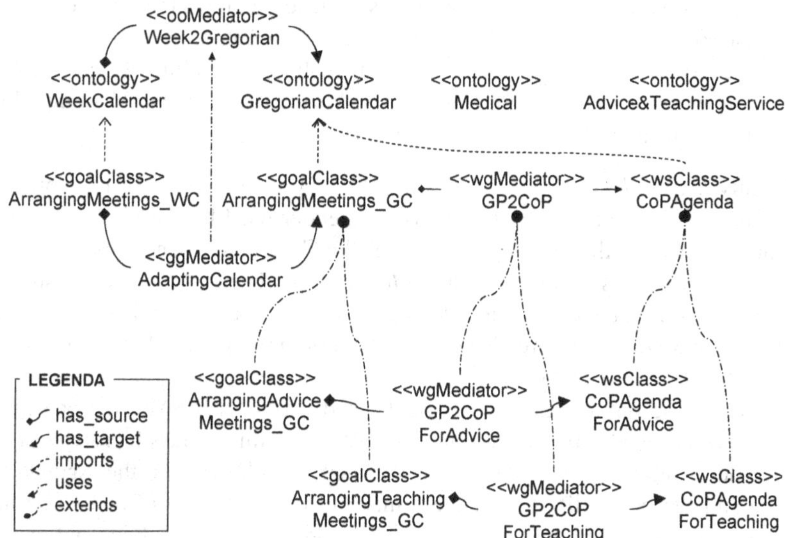

Fig. 14.5. An high-level view of the conceptual model employed in configuring Glue in terms of WSMO elements: ontologies, goals, Web Services and mediators. Only important relationships among the elements are shown

`hypertension`, `breast neoplasm`, etc., `medication`, `beta-blockers`, etc., `part of the body`, `heart`, etc., `specialist`, `cardiologist`, etc.) and the relations among them (like beta blockers `control` hypertension, cardiologists `deal with` heart, hypertension `affects` heart and arteries, etc.).

Moreover, an *advice/teaching service ontology* is needed. It describes the concepts of clinical, research and teaching capabilities of a Community of Practice.

- *Clinical Capabilities* describes the CoP in terms of the following:
  - `hasClinicalSpecialists`: the list of the kind of specialists grouped by the CoP (e.g. Cardiologist, Urologist, Pneumatologist, Dermatologist, etc.).
  - `managesDiseases`: the list of diseases managed by the CoP as ICD codes (e.g. Diabetes – ICD9CM 250.00).
  - `deliversInterventions`: the list of the diagnostic/therapeutic/preventive interventions (including pharmaceuticals) delivered by the CoP .
- *Clinical Research Capabilities* describes the CoP in terms of the following.
  - `hasResearchSpecialists`: the list of the kind of specialists grouped by the CoP (e.g. Statistician, Social worker, Psychologist).
  - `studiesDiseases`: the list of diseases which are actively researched by the CoP (e.g. Gastric ulcer [ICD10–K25] Prevention).
  - `studiesInterventions`: the list of the diagnostic/therapeutic/preventive interventions (including pharmaceuticals) which are actively researched by the CoP.
- *Teaching Capabilities* describes the CoP in terms of the following:
  - `hasTeachingExpertise`: the list of teaching roles that the CoP can satisfy (e.g. Teacher, OnlineTeacher, Tutor, OnlineTutor, etc.).
  - `hasAuthoringExpertise`: the availability of online/offline collaborative working tools (i.e. for teaching) within the CoP (e.g. NetMeeting, Skype, Messenger, etc.).

Finally, two *calendar ontologies* are necessary in our use case to express the date–time intervals: one is the week-based calendar used by the CoPs to describe their nominal availability and the other one is the Gregorian calendar used by GPs in expressing their goals. Therefore, an *ooMediator* has been employed in translating the date–times from the Gregorian calendar to the week-based one. In our implementation, this ooMediator was realised with a Java program exposed as a Web Service used at discovery time by Glue.

Having these ontologies, we were able to describe in WSMO the capabilities of the class of agenda, *Web Services* of a CoP. We define a class hierarchy of Web Service descriptions with a generic class on top, which describe the Agenda Web Service and the possibility to arrange a meeting in a given set of date–time intervals, and two specific classes below (for arranging respectively advice and teaching meetings). The description of the agenda class of Web Service asserts the following:

- The *pre-conditions* are the input which has to be the information about an advice request, the GP has to ask for advice on one of the medical issues treated by the various CoPs; and the booking date has to be after the current date.
- The only *assumption* is that the GP has the right to use the advice service.
- The *post-conditions* describe the possible meetings the CoP is available for: it can offer support that regards its capabilities and it can provide support only during its nominal available times.
- The *effect* is that the agendas of both the GP and the specialists in the CoP are updated with a reference to the scheduled meeting.

In a similar manner, we defined a hierarchy of *classes of goals* that asserts GP's need of finding a CoP that can provide an advice or teaching service about a given medical issue in the date-times intervals the GP prefers. The classes of goals and the class of Web Services differ in the date-time ontology they respectively import (week-based calendar vs Gregorian calendar) and in the way they are described. The class of Web Services describe the expertises of a CoP, whereas the class of goals describes a problem of a GP's patient. The first form of heterogeneity is bypassed with the introduction of a ggMediator[12] for adapting the calendars; the second form is bypassed in the hierarchy of wgMediator responsible for matching goals against Web Services.

Glue adopts a mediator-centric approach in discovering the Web Services [17]. Instead of using a generic approach (e.g. DL matching), we expect a Semantic Web Service expert to define in Glue a set of *wgMediators* that encodes the similarity rules for matching a class of goals against a class of Web Services descriptions. In this use case, the rule that performs an exact match between what the `GP is asking for` and the medical capabilities of a CoP asserts that a goal exactly matches a Web Service when:

- the `GP is asking for` a specialist and
  - the CoP `has that clinical specialist`, or
  - the CoP `manages a disease` that affects a body part dealt by the specialist the GP is asking for, or
  - the CoP `delivers an intervention` that controls one of diseases treated by the specialist the GP is asking for,
- the `GP is asking for` a disease and
  - the CoP `has a clinical specialist` that deals with a body part affected by the disease the GP is asking for, or
  - the CoP `manages the disease` that the GP is asking for, or
  - the CoP `delivers an intervention` that controls the disease the GP is asking for,
- the `GP is asking for` an intervention and
  - the CoP `has a clinical specialist` that deals with a body part affected by a disease controlled by the intervention the GP is asking for, or

[12] This ggMediator, when invoked, simply rewrites the goal, formulated by the GP using Gregorian dates (e.g. June, 8th 2005), into days of the week (e.g. Wednesday) through the ooMediator previously introduced

– the CoP `manages a disease` controlled by the intervention the GP is asking for, or
– the CoP `delivers the intervention` that the GP is asking for.

The rules for subsume and plug-in matching mainly differ from the one presented above in the sense that they broaden the search space to subconcepts and superconcepts respectively, navigating the medical ontology. Besides these rules that match medical capabilities, there are other different rules that matches date–time intervals between goal and Web Services description. An excerpt of the concrete F-logic syntax used inside Glue is showed in Fig. 14.6.

Having opted in Glue for a mediator – centric approach, writing wgMediators becomes the critic task. We foster reuse of wgMediators by modelling the usage scenario with two parallel hierarchies of classes, linked by a hierarchy of wgMediators. The generic one (labelled GP2CoP in Fig. 14.5) links a generic agenda Web Service to a generic goal for arranging a meeting, while the other two link respectively an agenda Web Service for arranging advice meetings to a request for advice and an agenda Web Service for arranging a teaching meeting with a request for teaching support. The two specific one (respectively labelled GP2CoPForAdvice and GP2CoPForTeaching) are defined by extending the generic one, hence reusing its rules.

In conclusion, by using Glue we deal not only with the matching of temporal availability, but also with the reasons for arranging a meeting, i.e. the "meaning" of the GP's request for a teleconsultation meeting. All these functionalities, however, are offered to GPs with a straightforward interface that *brings the power of Semantic Web Services in a* "simple box".

14.3.2 Artemis: A Semantic Web Service–based P2P Infrastructure for the Interoperability of Medical Information Systems

One of the most important problems in healthcare domain is the lack of infrastructures enabling the share of electronic healthcare records of a patient. There are a number of obstacles avoiding physicians to capture a complete medical history of a patient:

- Due to the nature of healthcare domain, a patient's medical history is usually spread out over a number of different institutes.

```
exactMatchMedicationWithCoP(GP,CoP) :-
 GP[askForMedications->M], (
   (CoP[developsMedications->>M]);
   (M[controlsDiseases=>>D], CoP[studiesDiseases->>D]);
   (M[controlsDiseases=>>D], D[affectsBodyPart=>>B],
    CoP[hasSpecialists->>S], S[dealsWithBodyPart=>>B])
  ).
```

Fig. 14.6. An excerpt of the concrete F-logic syntax used in describing a wgMediators.

- There are no mechanisms provided to locate the other healthcare institutes to collaborate with, e.g. to refer a patient to, or to retrieve specific electronic healthcare records of a patient from, in a distributed environment in an automated way. It should be possible to locate the healthcare organisations based on their expertise, or based on the fact that they may have electronic healthcare records of a specific patient. The second problem introduces additional challenges, because in many countries there are no unique patient identifiers used by different healthcare institutes, and when there is there may be unique patient identifiers, it may not be ethical and may not be legal to make a distributed search based on patient demographics. Once the probable healthcare organisations are discovered, the second challenge is to locate the specific application of the organisation providing the requested service or specific piece of electronic healthcare record of a patient.
- When such an organisation is found, the medical information systems used by the institutions may not interoperate with each other. The interoperability problem has two facets: first, the applications may not be "technically interoperable" with each other, i.e. it may not be possible for them to exchange information; secondly, they may not be semantically interoperable, i.e. the information exchanged may not be a meaningful piece of information for the receiving side if the institutes use different healthcare standards to represent the messages exchanged.

IST-002103 Artemis project [2] provides a P2P interoperability platform addressing these problems.

Artemis has a peer-to-peer architecture based on JXTA [32] in order to facilitate the discovery of healthcare organisations, Web Services and patient records. In Artemis, healthcare institutes are represented as peers as presented in Fig. 14.7 [21]. Each peer is connected to a super peer, which we call the mediator, and communicate with the rest of the network through these mediators. Artemis peers provide a number of interfaces to healthcare information systems both as servlets and as Web Services for the following functionalities:

- Each healthcare organisation first registers itself to Artemis P2P network. We have defined an "Expertise Ontology" based on HIPAA product taxonomy [3], and a "Geographic Ontology" based on ISO 3166-2 codes [31]. While organisations registers themselves to the Artemis P2P network, they indicate their expertise such as "EmergencyMedicalServiceProviders" from the Expertise Ontology and its location by selecting a node from the Geographic Ontology. The peer sends these to its mediator, which in turn shares a summary of this information with other mediators in the network, so that the queries searching for these organisations can be semantically routed back to the mediator.
- In Artemis architecture each healthcare organisation exposes its already existing applications as Web Services. Web Services provide functional interoperability through well-accepted standards like SOAP and WSDL. In order to facilitate the discovery of medical Web Services of the healthcare organisations, there is a need to semantically annotate their functionality through ontologies. For example, in the healthcare domain, when a user is looking for a service to admit a patient

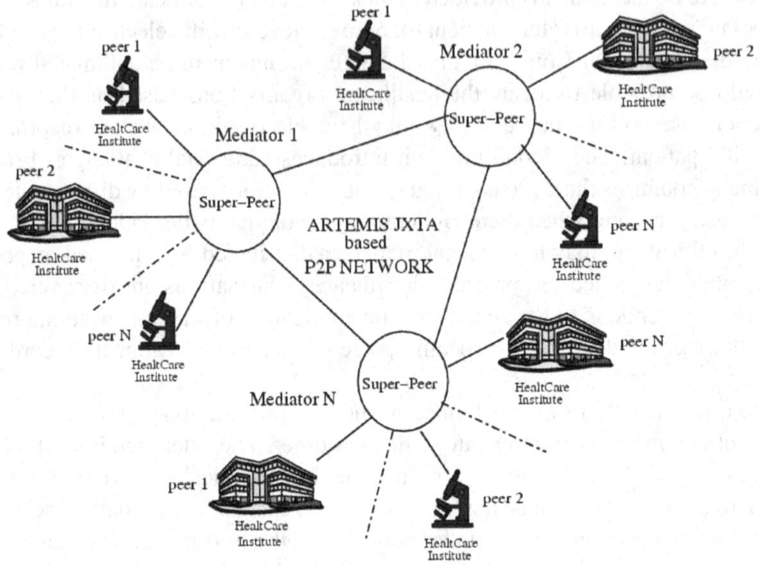

Fig. 14.7. Artemis P2P architecture

to a hospital, he/she should be able to locate such a service through its meaning, independent of what the service is called and in which language. An essential element in defining the semantic of Web Services is the domain knowledge. Medical informatics is one of the few domains to have considerable domain knowledge exposed through standards. These standards offer significant value in terms of expressing the semantic of Web Services in the healthcare domain. In Artemis project, prominent healthcare standards are used to semantically annotate Web services whenever possible. For example, HL7 has categorised the events in healthcare domain by considering service functionality which reflects the business logic in this domain. We use this classification as a basis for defining the service action semantics through a "Service Functionality Ontology" presented in [4]. Artemis peers provide interfaces to annotate the functionality of Web Services with the nodes of functionality ontology as depicted in Fig. 14.8.

- Artemis enables medical institutes to communicate with each other in their own message schemas. While registering to the network, each organisation provides its application message schemas as XSDs through the interfaces provided by the Artemis peer. This means that a medical information system will send and expect messages conforming to its own schema definition. Similarly, when an organisation publishes Web Services to the network, the input and output parameter's schemas are provided as XML schemas. These are normalised to OWL ontologies and sent to the Mediator as the "Local Message Ontologies" of the organisations. When the messages of the Web services are also annotated through

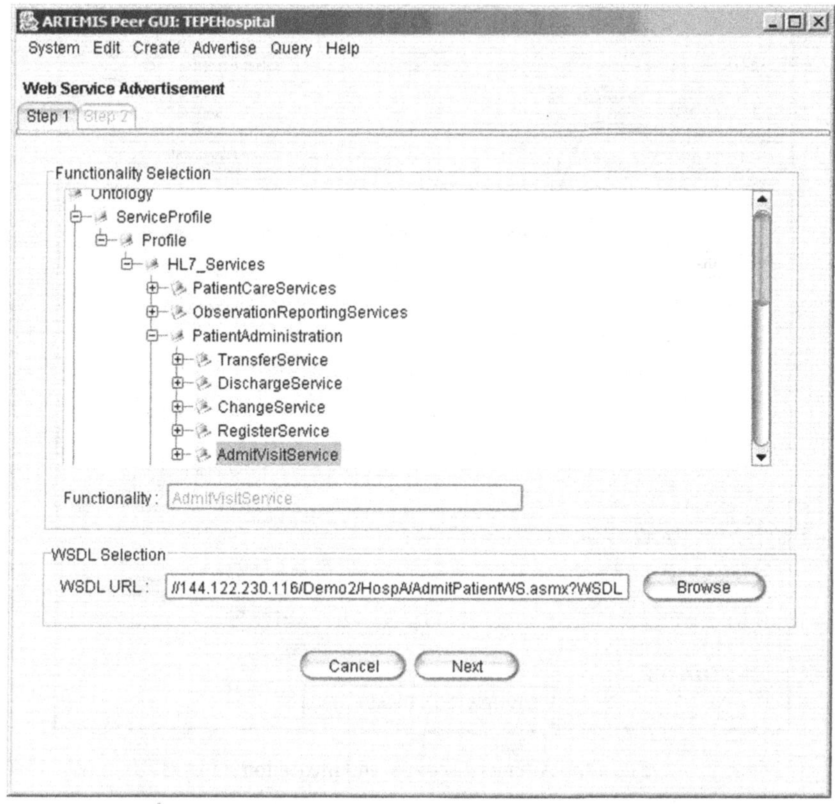

Fig. 14.8. Artemis peer interface: annotating service functionality

"Local message ontologies", the message semantics specified and the functionality semantics provided through the nodes of Functionality ontology are packed in to the OWL-S definition of the service and sent to the Mediator. In the Mediator, services are published to semantically enriched Web Service Registries to facilitate their semantic discovery. Artemis Mediators support both semantically enriched UDDI and ebXML registries. The details of the work presenting how to enrich UDDI and ebXML registries through service semantics are presented in [19] and [20] respectively.

- Artemis peer provides interfaces to the medical information systems discovering other healthcare organisations in the P2P network through their expertise, discovering the medical services provided by healthcare organisations based on their functionalities as presented in Fig. 14.9.
- One crucial aspect in ARTEMIS is to find and retrieve clinical information about a particular patient from different healthcare organisations where concrete sources are unknown. To complicate matters, in most countries, there are no unique person identifiers that would be valid for the lifetime of an individual and used by all parties in healthcare and for all episodes of care. On the

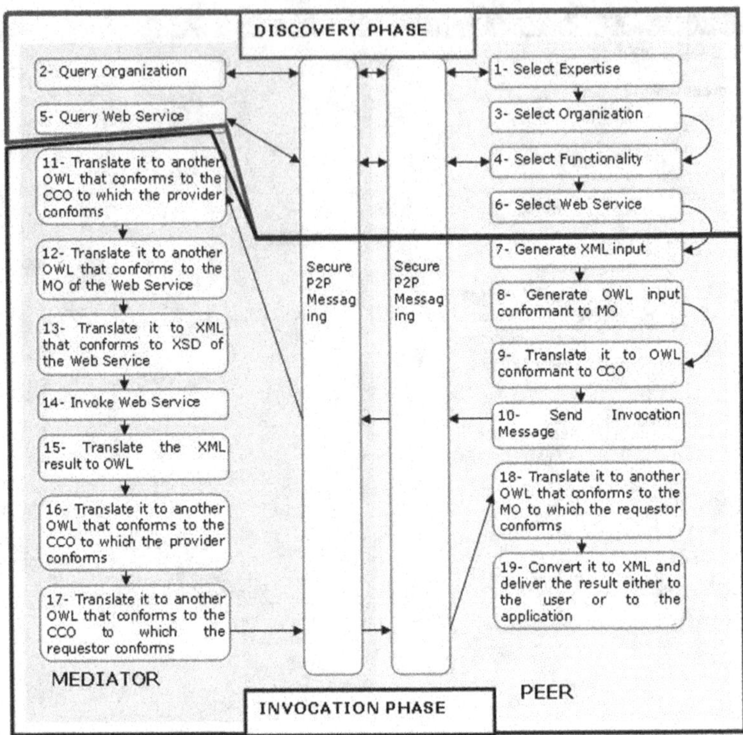

Fig. 14.9. Artemis discovery and invocation steps

contrary, in many cases, several identifiers exist for a patient even within a single organisation. Consequently, a protocol is needed that allows for the identification of patients by means of non-unique patient-related attributes in a P2P network. Within the scope of Artemis project the "Patient Identification Process Protocol (PIP)" is developed as a solution for this problem in the healthcare sector that is likely to become very important with the increasing mobility of the workforce in Europe: locating and accessing prior clinical records of a patient through patient demographics information. Artemis PIP establishes a concept that has not been available in the healthcare sector before: an undirected search for patient records that does not violate data protection requirements [1]. The solution combines techniques from different domains: control numbers, blocking variables and record linkage procedures as used in epidemiological registries, knowledge distribution and Trusted Third Party services from cryptographic communication protocols and semantic annotation and ontology-based mediation, core technologies of the semantic web. Through PIP protocol, Artemis peer provides interfaces through which healthcare organisations may be located based on the possibility that they may have electronic healthcare records of a patient.

As stated, Artemis mediators have another important role in the P2P network, other than facilitating semantic discovery mechanisms: semantic mediation of the messages exchanged between the peers. This is achieved through the "Artemis Message Exchange Framework". The framework involves first providing the mapping of source ontology into target message ontology with the help of a mapping tool which produces a mapping definition. This mapping definition is then used to automatically transform the source ontology message instances into target message instances. Through a prototype implementation, we demonstrate how to mediate between HL7 Version 2 and HL7 Version 3 messages [9]. However, the framework proposed is generic enough to mediate between any incompatible healthcare standards that are currently in use.

The semantic mediation is realised in two phases:

1. Message ontology mapping process: In the first phase, the local message ontologies of two healthcare institutes are mapped one another. Assume that Web Service requester peer is HL7 Version 2 compliant and Web Service provider is HL7 Version 3 compliant. The message ontologies of these institutes are mapped one into other by using an ontology mapping tool. For this purpose, we used an OWL ontology mapping tool, namely OWLmt [9]. With the help of a GUI, OWLmt allows defining semantic mappings between structurally different but semantically overlapping OWL ontologies, and produces a "Mapping Definition". Since message ontologies for HL7 messages do not exist yet, we use the HL7 Version 2 and Version 3 XML Schemas (XSDs) to generate OWL ontologies. This process, called "Conceptual Normalisation" produces a "Normalisation map" describing how a specific message XSD is transformed into the corresponding OWL schema. We have used the "Normalisation Engine" provided by the Harmonise project [24] and adopted it for our needs. The "Mapping Definitions" and the "Normalisation map", produced in the first phase are used during the second phase to automatically transform the message instances one into another. It should be noted that, in addition to direct mappings between two local ontologies, Artemis also supports semantic mediation through mapping to "Clinical Concept Ontologies" (CCO). CCOs can be thought as global ontologies supported by mediators, and can be created based on prominent healthcare standards such as EN 13606 (EHRcom) [13], openEHR [36] and HL7 CDA [27]. When two healthcare institutes provide the mapping definitions of their local ontology to one of the CCOs, Artemis mediator handles the semantic mediation of the exchanged messages between the institutes through a set of mappings between the clinical concept ontologies.
2. Message instance mapping: In the second phase, when a service to be invoked as depicted in Fig. 14.9, first the XML message instances provided by the requester institute as the inputs of the Web Service are transformed into OWL instances by using the "Data Normalisation" engine (Step 8). Then by using the "Mapping definitions", OWL source messages instances (provided by the requester peer) are transformed into the OWL target message instances (expected by the provider peer). This may include a number of additional mappings between the

CCOs conformed by the institutes as presented in Fig. 14.9 in steps 9 and 16. Finally, the OWL messages are converted to XML again by the Mediator and the Web Service is invoked. The output provided by the Web Service is similarly transferred to the requester peer.

It should be noted that healthcare information systems operate within a strict regulatory framework that is enforced to ensure the protection of personal data against processing and outlines conditions and rules in which processing is allowed. Hence, ARTEMIS also provides robust and flexible security and privacy mechanisms as presented in [10].

14.4 Summary

In this chapter we discussed the use of ontology-based approaches in eHealth scenarios; in particular, we highlighted the added- value of these approaches in terms of more powerful interoperability facilities to interconnect different systems.

Glue and Artemis are successfully using medical domain ontologies to describe and discover their services in a more effective way than what was provided by common UDDI or ebXML registries. In fact, semantics can be employed in describing Web Service capabilities and user goals, in defining rules for matching goals with Web Service capabilities and, finally, in enabling semantic data mediation to achieve XML message interoperability.

The main lesson we are learning in applying semantics to the eHealth field is that the clear separation between the ontologies used by each system simplifies and speeds up the gathering of consensus, which is always difficult to reach in large groups. This is mainly due to the adoption of mediators.

References

1. T. Aden, M. Eichelberg, and W. Thoben. A Fault-Tolerant Cryptographic Protocol for Patient Record Requests. In *Proceedings of EuroPACS-MIR 2004 in the Enlarged Europe*, pages 103–106. EuroPACS, 2004.
2. The ARTEMIS Project. `http://www.srdc.metu.edu.tr/webpage/projects/artemis`.
3. Artemis Expertise Ontology. `http://www.srdc.metu.edu.tr/webpage/projects/artemis/ExpertiseOnt.owl`.
4. Artemis Service Functionality Ontology. `http://www.srdc.metu.edu.tr/webpage/projects/artemis/functionalityOntology.owl`.
5. T. Beale. Archetypes: Constraint-based Domain Models for Future-proof Information Systems. In *OOPSLA 2002 Workshop on Behavioural Semantics*, 2002. `http://www.deepthought.com.au/it/archetypes/archetypes_new.pdf`.
6. T. Beale and S. Heard. The openEHR EHR Service Model, Revision 0.2. openEHR Reference Model, the openEHR foundation, 2003.
7. T. Beale and S. Heard. Archetype Definition Language (ADL), Revision 2.0rc1 (Release 1.0 draft). openEHR Specification, the openEHR foundation, 2005.

8. T. Beale, S. Heard, D. Kalra, and D. Lloyd. The openEHR Data Structures Information Model, Revision 1.6rc1 (Release 1.0 draft). openEHR Reference Model, the openEHR foundation, 2005.
9. V. Bicer, G. Laleci, A. Dogac, and Y. Kabak. Artemis Message Exchange Framework: Semantic Interoperability of Exchanged Messages in the Healthcare Domain. *ACM Sigmod Record*, 34(3), September 2005.
10. M. Boniface and P. Wilken. ARTEMIS: Towards a Secure Interoperability Infrastructure for Healthcare Information Systems. In T. Solomonides, R. McClatchey, V. Breton, Y. Legré, and S. Nørager, editors, *Studies in Health Technology and Informatics – From Grid to Healthgrid: Proceedings of Healthgrid 2005*, volume 112, pages 181–189. IOS Press, April 2005.
11. Complete Blood Count Archetype ADL Definition. `http://www.openehr.org/repositories/archetype-dev/adl_1.1/adl/archetypes/openehr/ehr/entry/openehr-ehr-observation.haematology-cbc.draft.adl.html`.
12. CEN ENV 13606. Medical Informatics – Electronic Healthcare Record Communication. European Prestandard ENV 13606, European Committee for Standardization, Brussels, 2000.
13. CEN prEN 13606-1. Health Informatics – Electronic Health Record Communication – Part 1: Reference Model. Draft European Standard for CEN Enquiry prEN 13606-1, European Committee for Standardization, Brussels, Belgium, 2004.
14. CEN/ISSS eHealth Standardization Focus Group. Current and Future Standardization Issues in the e-Health Domain: Achieving Interoperability. Draft European Standard for CEN Enquiry Part One: Main text, page 58, European Committee for Standardization, Brussels, Belgium, 2005.
15. European Committee for Standardization – Technical Committee on Health Informatics. `http://www.centc251.org/`.
16. E. Della Valle and D. Cerizza. Cocoon Glue: A Prototype of WSMO Discovery Engine for the Healthcare Field. In *Proceedings of 2nd WSMO Implementation Workshop WIW'2005*, 2005.
17. E. Della Valle and D. Cerizza. The mediators centric approach to automatic web service discovery of glue. In M. Hepp, A. Polleres, F. van Harmelen, and M.R. Genesereth, editors, *MEDIATE2005*, volume 168 of *CEUR Workshop Proceedings*, pages 35–50. CEUR-WS.org, 2005. online `http://CEUR-WS.org/Vol-168/MEDIATE2005-paper3.pdf`.
18. E. Della Valle, D. Cerizza, I. Celino, L. Gadda, and A. Savoldelli. The COCOON project. In *Demos and Posters of the 2nd European Semantic Web Conference (ESWC-2005), Heraklion, Greece, 29*.
19. A. Dogac, I. Cingil, G. B. Laleci, and Y. Kabak. Improving the Functionality of UDDI Registries through Web Service Semantics. In *3rd VLDB Workshop on Technologies for E-Services (TES-02)*, 2002.
20. A. Dogac, Y. Kabak, G. Laleci, C. Mattocks, F. Najmi, and J. Pollock. Enhancing ebXML Registries to Make them OWL Aware. *Distributed and Parallel Database Journal*, 18(1), 2005.
21. A. Dogac, G. Laleci, S. Kirbas, Y. Kabak, S. Sinir, A. Yildiz, and Y. Gurcan. Artemis: Deploying Semantically Enriched Web Services in the Healthcare Domain. *Information Systems Journal, Special Issue on Semantic Web and Web Services*, 2005.
22. E. Della Valle, D. Cerizza, V. Bicer, Y. Kabak, G. Laleci, and H. Lausen. The Need for Semantic Web Service in the ehealth. *W3C Workshop on Frameworks for Semantics in Web Services*, 2005.

23. G. Eysenbach. What is e-health? *Journal of Medical Internet Research (JMIR)*, 3(2):e20, 2001.
24. Harmonise, IST-20002-9329, Tourism Harmonisation Network, Deliverable 3.2: Semantic Mapping and Reconciliation Engine Subsystems.
25. Health Level 7 (HL7). http://www.hl7.org/.
26. *HL7, Application Protocol for Electronic Data Exchange in Healthcare Environments, Version 2.5, ANSI Standard.* Ann Arbor MI, USA, 2000.
27. The HL7 Version 3 Standard: Clinical Data Architecture, Release 2.0, ANSI Standard, 2005.
28. HL7 Reference Information Model. http://www.hl7.org/library/data-model/RIM/modelpage_non.htm.
29. HL7 Version 3 Message Development Framework. http://www.hl7.org/library/mdf99/mdf99.pdf.
30. Integrating the Healthcare Enterprise. http://www.ihe.net/.
31. ISO 3166-2 Codes for the Representation of Names of Countries and Their Subdivisions, Part 2. http://www.iso.org/iso/en/prods-services/iso3166ma/04background-on-iso-3166/iso3166-2.html.
32. JXTA Technology. http://www.jxta.org/.
33. Logical Observation Identifiers Names and Codes (LOINC). http://www.loinc.org/.
34. Eichelberg M., Aden T., Riesmeier J., Dogac A., and Laleci G. A Survey and Analysis of Electronic Healthcare Record Standards. *ACM Computing Surveys*, 37(4), December 2005.
35. NOMADIC MEDIA (ITEA 02019). http://www.hitech-projects.com/euprojects/nomadic-media/.
36. openEHR Community. http://www.openehr.org/.
37. SNOMED (The Systematized Nomenclature of Medicine) Clinical Terms. http://www.snomed.org/snomedct_txt.html.
38. The SUMMA Project. http://summa.cefriel.it.

Glossary

Composition – Composition of semantically annotated Web Services is the process of combining and coordinating several Web Services, based on machine-interpretable descriptions of their functionality and their choreography. The result of this process is an orchestration including several Web Services.

Choreography – Web Services Choreography concerns the description of how Web Services interact with their users. Such a description of behaviour involves message protocols, interfaces and sequencing of multiple separate interactions. The choreography of a Web Service determines how to consume its functionality in terms of message exchange patterns.

Discovery – Discovery of semantically annotated Web Services is the process of identifying and locating Web Services that are relevant for a given request, based on machine-interpretable descriptions of their functionality. The result of this process is a set of Web Services which potentially meet the needs of the requester party in terms of the capabilities they provide.

Mediation – Mediation between semantically annotated Web Services aims at assuring interoperability of Web Services that are designed according to different approaches. Such differences can be in terms of data structures and messages they exchange, ontologies their semantic annotation is based on, or interaction patterns they adhere to. Differences in data formats and in the conceptual model for message content are addressed by *data mediation* and *ontology mediation*, whereas differences in message exchange patterns and business process models are addressed by *choreography mediation* and *process mediation*.

Ontology – An ontology is a formal explicit specification of a domain conceptualisation shared by the members of a community. It provides applications with a conceptual yet executable model of a domain of interest on which they base their decisions. Ontologies make use of knowledge-representation principles and formalisms, which allows applications to reason about domain knowledge.

Orchestration – Web Services Orchestration concerns the realisation of composite Web Services by means of other Web Services. The orchestration of a Web Service determines the set of operations and interactions that must be followed in order to realise its overall functionality.

Semantic Annotation – Semantic annotation is meta data that captures the meaning of resources by means of a machine-interpretable description. Such descriptions are expressed in terms of an ontological vocabulary provided by an ontology for some domain of interest. In the context of Semantic Web Services, semantic annotation describes the functionality offered through a Web Service.

Semantic Web – The vision of the Semantic Web is to semantically annotate content in the World Wide Web by machine-interpretable meta data, such that computer programs are enabled to reason about the meaning of this content. Ontologies play a key role in this vision, in that they provide the domain vocabulary in terms of which semantic annotation is formulated. This semantic enhancement supports various areas of web-based applications such as document search, web portals, information integration or service-oriented systems.

Semantic Web Services – The Semantic Web Services' vision is to semantically annotate Web Services with machine-interpretable meta data, such that computer programs are enabled to reason about their functionality. In this way, various kinds of services, such as book selling, shipment of goods or provision of stock market information, can be advertised and discovered on the Internet in an automated way, and their functionalities can be combined in composite services at run-time in order to achieve higher-level goals. Semantic Web Services particularly aim at realising smooth information integration through flexible architectures within and across organisation boundaries.

Service – A service is an activity of value that a *provider* party offers to a *requester* party. In the context of Semantic Web Services, a service, such as book selling, is realised through a (set of) Web Service(s), such as Amazon's Web Service interface, which provide(s) technical means to access a service via the Internet.

Service-Oriented Architecture (SOA) – The term Service-Oriented Architecture expresses a software architectural concept that defines the use of services to support the requirements of software users. In a SOA environment, nodes on a network make resources available to other participants in the network as independent services that the participants access in a standardised way. One can implement SOA using any service-based technology.

Web Service – A Web Service is a software system designed to support interoperable machine-to-machine interaction over a network. It has an interface described in a machine-processable format (specifically WSDL). Other systems interact with the Web Service in a manner prescribed by its description using SOAP messages, typically conveyed using the HTTP protocol with an XML serialisation in conjunction with other web-related standards.

Index